Hands-On Data Analysis with Pandas

W0006964

Efficiently perform data collection, wrangling, analysis, and visualization using Python

Stefanie Molin

BIRMINGHAM - MUMBAI

Hands-On Data Analysis with Pandas

Commissioning Editor: Sunith Shetty
Acquisition Editor: Devika Battike
Content Development Editor: Athikho Sapuni Rishana
Senior Editor: Martin Whittemore
Technical Editor: Vibhuti Gawde
Copy Editor: Safis Editing
Project Coordinator: Kirti Pisat
Proofreader: Safis Editing
Indexer: Pratik Shirodkar
Production Designer: Arvindkumar Gupta

First published: July 2019

Production reference: 1250719

Published by Packt Publishing Ltd.
Livery Place
35 Livery Street
Birmingham
B3 2PB, UK.

ISBN 978-1-78961-532-6

www.packtpub.com

When I think back on all I have accomplished, I know that I couldn't have done it without the support and love of my parents. This book is dedicated to both of you: to Mom, for always believing in me and teaching me to believe in myself. I know I can do anything I set my mind to because of you. And to Dad, for never letting me skip school and sharing a countdown with me.

`Packt.com`

Subscribe to our online digital library for full access to over 7,000 books and videos, as well as industry leading tools to help you plan your personal development and advance your career. For more information, please visit our website.

Why subscribe?

- Spend less time learning and more time coding with practical eBooks and Videos from over 4,000 industry professionals

- Improve your learning with Skill Plans built especially for you

- Get a free eBook or video every month

- Fully searchable for easy access to vital information

- Copy and paste, print, and bookmark content

Did you know that Packt offers eBook versions of every book published, with PDF and ePub files available? You can upgrade to the eBook version at `www.packt.com` and as a print book customer, you are entitled to a discount on the eBook copy. Get in touch with us at `customercare@packtpub.com` for more details.

At `www.packt.com`, you can also read a collection of free technical articles, sign up for a range of free newsletters, and receive exclusive discounts and offers on Packt books and eBooks.

Foreword

Recent advancements in computing and artificial intelligence have completely changed the way we understand the world. Our current ability to record and analyze data has already transformed industries and inspired big changes in society.

Stefanie Molin's *Hands-On Data Analysis with Pandas* is much more than an introduction to the subject of data analysis or the pandas Python library; it's a guide to help you become part of this transformation.

Not only will this book teach you the fundamentals of using Python to collect, analyze, and understand data, but it will also expose you to important software engineering, statistical, and machine learning concepts that you will need to be successful.

Using examples based on real data, you will be able to see firsthand how to apply these techniques to extract value from data. In the process, you will learn important software development skills, including writing simulations, creating your own Python packages, and collecting data from APIs.

Stefanie possesses a rare combination of skills that makes her uniquely qualified to guide you through this process. Being both an expert data scientist and a strong software engineer, she can not only talk authoritatively about the intricacies of the data analysis workflow, but also about how to implement it correctly and efficiently in Python.

Whether you are a Python programmer interested in learning more about data analysis, or a data scientist learning how to work in Python, this book will get you up to speed fast, so you can begin to tackle your own data analysis projects right away.

Felipe Moreno
New York, June 10, 2019.

Felipe Moreno has been working in information security for the last two decades. He currently works for Bloomberg LP, where he leads the Security Data Science team within the Chief Information Security Office, and focuses on applying statistics and machine learning to security problems.

Contributors

About the author

Stefanie Molin is a data scientist and software engineer at Bloomberg LP in NYC, tackling tough problems in information security, particularly revolving around anomaly detection, building tools for gathering data, and knowledge sharing. She has extensive experience in data science, designing anomaly detection solutions, and utilizing machine learning in both R and Python in the AdTech and FinTech industries. She holds a B.S. in operations research from Columbia University's Fu Foundation School of Engineering and Applied Science, with minors in economics, and entrepreneurship and innovation. In her free time, she enjoys traveling the world, inventing new recipes, and learning new languages spoken among both people and computers.

Writing this book was a tremendous amount of work, but I have grown a lot through the experience: as a writer, as a technologist, and as a person. This wouldn't have been possible without the help of my friends, family, and colleagues. I'm very grateful to you all. In particular, I want to thank Aliki Mavromoustaki, Felipe Moreno, Suphannee Sivakorn, Lucy Hao, Javon Thompson, Alexander Comerford, and Ryan Molin. (The full version of my acknowledgments can be found on my GitHub; see the preface for the link.)

About the reviewer

Aliki Mavromoustaki is the lead data scientist at Tasman Analytics. She works with direct-to-consumer companies to deliver scalable infrastructure and implement event-driven analytics. Previously, she worked at Criteo, an AdTech company that employs machine learning to help digital commerce companies target valuable customers. Aliki worked on optimizing marketing campaigns and designed statistical experiments comparing Criteo products. Aliki holds a PhD in fluid dynamics from Imperial College London, and was an assistant adjunct professor in applied mathematics at UCLA.

Table of Contents

Preface

Data science is often described as an interdisciplinary field where programming skills, statistical know-how, and domain knowledge intersect. It has quickly become one of the hottest fields of our society, and knowing how to work with data has become essential in today's careers. Regardless of the industry, role, or project, data skills are in high demand, and learning data analysis is the key to making an impact.

Fields in data science cover many different aspects of the spectrum: data analysts focus more on extracting business insights, while data scientists focus more on applying machine learning techniques to the business's problems. Data engineers focus on designing, building, and maintaining data pipelines used by data analysts and scientists. Machine learning engineers share much of the skill set of the data scientist and, like data engineers, are adept software engineers. The data science landscape encompasses many fields, but for all of them, data analysis is a fundamental building block. This book will give you the skills to get started, wherever your journey may take you.

The traditional skill set in data science involves knowing how to collect data from various sources, such as databases and APIs, and process it. Python is a popular language for data science that provides the means to collect and process data, as well as to build production-quality data products. Since it is open source, it is easy to get started with data science by taking advantage of the libraries written by others to solve common data tasks and issues.

Pandas is the powerful and popular library synonymous with data science in Python. This book will give you a hands-on introduction to data analysis using pandas on real-world datasets, such as those dealing with the stock market, simulated hacking attempts, weather trends, earthquakes, wine, and astronomical data. Pandas makes data wrangling and visualization easy by giving us the ability to work efficiently with tabular data.

Once we have learned how to conduct data analysis, we will explore a number of applications. We will build Python packages and try our hand at stock analysis, anomaly detection, regression, clustering, and classification with the help of additional libraries commonly used for data visualization, data wrangling, and machine learning, such as Matplotlib, Seaborn, NumPy, and Scikit-Learn. By the time you finish this book, you will be well-equipped to take on your own data science projects in Python.

Who this book is for

This book is written for people with varying levels of experience who want to learn data science in Python, perhaps to apply it to a project, collaborate with data scientists, and/or progress to working on machine learning production code with software engineers. You will get the most out of this book if your background is similar to one (or both) of the following:

- You have prior data science experience in another language, such as R, SAS, or MATLAB, and want to learn pandas in order to move your workflow to Python.
- You have some Python experience and are looking to learn about data science using Python.

What this book covers

Chapter 1, *Introduction to Data Analysis*, teaches you the fundamentals of data analysis, gives you a foundation in statistics, and guides you through getting your environment set up for working with data in Python and using Jupyter Notebooks.

Chapter 2, *Working with Pandas DataFrames*, introduces you to the pandas library and shows you the basics of working with DataFrames.

Chapter 3, *Data Wrangling with Pandas*, discusses the process of data manipulation, shows you how to explore an API to gather data, and guides you through data cleaning and reshaping with pandas.

Chapter 4, *Aggregating Pandas DataFrames*, teaches you how to query and merge DataFrames, perform complex operations on them, including rolling calculations and aggregations, and how to work effectively with time series data.

Chapter 5, *Visualizing Data with Pandas and Matplotlib*, shows you how to create your own data visualizations in Python, first using the matplotlib library, and then from pandas objects directly.

Chapter 6, *Plotting with Seaborn and Customization Techniques*, continues the discussion on data visualization by teaching you how to use the seaborn library to visualize your long-form data and giving you the tools you need to customize your visualizations, making them presentation-ready.

Chapter 7, *Financial Analysis – Bitcoin and the Stock Market*, walks you through the creation of a Python package for analyzing stocks, building upon everything learned from Chapter 1, *Introduction to Data Analysis*, through Chapter 6, *Plotting with Seaborn and Customization Techniques*, and applying it to a financial application.

Chapter 8, *Rule-Based Anomaly Detection*, covers simulating data and applying everything learned from Chapter 1, *Introduction to Data Analysis*, through Chapter 6, *Plotting with Seaborn and Customization Techniques*, to catch hackers attempting to authenticate to a website, using rule-based strategies for anomaly detection.

Chapter 9, *Getting Started with Machine Learning in Python*, introduces you to machine learning and building models using the scikit-learn library.

Chapter 10, *Making Better Predictions – Optimizing Models*, shows you strategies for tuning and improving the performance of your machine learning models.

Chapter 11, *Machine Learning Anomaly Detection*, revisits anomaly detection on login attempt data, using machine learning techniques, all while giving you a taste of how the workflow looks in practice.

Chapter 12, *The Road Ahead*, contains resources for taking your skills to the next level and further avenues for exploration.

To get the most out of this book

You should be familiar with Python, particularly Python 3 and up. You should also know how to write functions and basic scripts in Python, understand standard programming concepts such as variables, data types, and control flow (if/else, for/while loops), and be able to use Python as a functional programming language. Some basic knowledge of object-oriented programming may be helpful, but is not necessary. If your Python prowess isn't yet at this level, the Python documentation includes a helpful tutorial for quickly getting up to speed: https://docs.python.org/3/tutorial/index.html.

The accompanying code for the book can be found on GitHub at https://github.com/stefmolin/Hands-On-Data-Analysis-with-Pandas. To get the most out of the book, you should follow along in the Jupyter Notebooks as you read through each chapter. We will cover setting up your environment and obtaining these files in Chapter 1, *Introduction to Data Analysis*.

Lastly, be sure to do the exercises at the end of each chapter. Some of them may be quite difficult, but they will make you much stronger with the material. Solutions for each chapter's exercises can be found at `https://github.com/stefmolin/Hands-On-Data-Analysis-with-Pandas/tree/master/solutions` in their respective folders.

Download the color images

We also provide a PDF file that has color images of the screenshots/diagrams used in this book. You can download it here:

`https://static.packt-cdn.com/downloads/9781789615326_ColorImages.pdf`.

Conventions used

There are a number of text conventions used throughout this book.

`CodeInText`: Indicates code words in text, database table names, folder names, filenames, file extensions, pathnames, dummy URLs, and user input. Here is an example: "Use `pip` to install the packages in the `requirements.txt` file."

A block of code is set as follows. The start of the line will be preceded by >>> and continuations of that line will be preceded by . . . :

```
>>> import pandas as pd

>>> df = pd.read_csv(
...     'data/fb_2018.csv', index_col='date', parse_dates=True
... )
>>> df.head()
```

Any code without the preceding >>> or . . . is not something we will run—it is for reference:

```
try:
    del df['ones']
except KeyError:
    # handle the error here
    pass
```

When we wish to draw your attention to a particular part of a code block, the relevant lines or items are set in bold:

```
>>> df.plot(
...       x='date',
...       y='price',
...       kind='line',
...       title='Price over Time',
...       legend=False,
...       ylim=(0, None)
... )
```

Results will be shown without anything preceding the lines:

```
>>> pd.Series(np.random.rand(2), name='random')
0    0.235793
1    0.257935
Name: random, dtype: float64
```

Any command-line input or output is written as follows:

```
# Windows:
C:\path\of\your\choosing> mkdir pandas_exercises

# Linux, Mac, and shorthand:
$ mkdir pandas_exercises
```

Warnings or important notes appear like this.

Tips and tricks appear like this.

Get in touch

Feedback from our readers is always welcome.

General feedback: If you have questions about any aspect of this book, mention the book title in the subject of your message and email us at customercare@packtpub.com.

Errata: Although we have taken every care to ensure the accuracy of our content, mistakes do happen. If you have found a mistake in this book, we would be grateful if you would report this to us. Please visit www.packt.com/submit-errata, selecting your book, clicking on the Errata Submission Form link, and entering the details.

Piracy: If you come across any illegal copies of our works in any form on the Internet, we would be grateful if you would provide us with the location address or website name. Please contact us at copyright@packt.com with a link to the material.

If you are interested in becoming an author: If there is a topic that you have expertise in and you are interested in either writing or contributing to a book, please visit authors.packtpub.com.

Reviews

Please leave a review. Once you have read and used this book, why not leave a review on the site that you purchased it from? Potential readers can then see and use your unbiased opinion to make purchase decisions, we at Packt can understand what you think about our products, and our authors can see your feedback on their book. Thank you!

For more information about Packt, please visit packt.com.

Section 1: Getting Started with Pandas

Our journey begins with an introduction to data analysis and statistics, which will lay a strong foundation for the concepts we will cover throughout the book. Then, we will set up our Python data science environment, which contains everything we will need to work through the examples, and get started with learning the basics of pandas.

The following chapters are included in this section:

- Chapter 1, *Introduction to Data Analysis*
- Chapter 2, *Working with Pandas DataFrames*

Introduction to Data Analysis 1

Before we can begin our hands-on introduction to data analysis with `pandas`, we need to learn about the fundamentals of data analysis. Those who have ever looked at the documentation for a software library know how overwhelming it can be if you have no clue what you are looking for. Therefore, it is essential that we not only master the coding aspect, but also the thought process and workflow required to analyze data, which will prove the most useful in augmenting our skill set in the future.

Much like the scientific method, data science has some common workflows that we can follow when we want to conduct an analysis and present the results. The backbone of this process is **statistics**, which gives us ways to describe our data, make predictions, and also draw conclusions about it. Since prior knowledge of statistics is not a prerequisite, this chapter will give us exposure to the statistical concepts we will use throughout this book, as well as areas for further exploration.

After covering the fundamentals, we will get our Python environment set up for the remainder of this book. Python is a powerful language, and its uses go way beyond data science: building web applications, software, and web scraping, to name a few. In order to work effectively across projects, we need to learn how to make **virtual environments**, which will isolate each project's dependencies. Finally, we will learn how to work with Jupyter Notebooks in order to follow along with the text.

The following topics will be covered in this chapter:

- The core components of conducting data analysis
- Statistical foundations
- How to set up a Python data science environment

Chapter materials

All the files for this book are on GitHub at `https://github.com/stefmolin/Hands-On-Data-Analysis-with-Pandas`. While having a GitHub account isn't necessary to work through this book, it is a good idea to create one, as it will serve as a portfolio for any data/coding projects. In addition, working with Git will provide a version control system and make collaboration easy.

 Check out this article to learn some Git basics: `https://www.freecodecamp.org/news/learn-the-basics-of-git-in-under-10-minutes-da548267cc91/`.

In order to get a local copy of the files, we have a few options (ordered from least useful to most useful):

- Download the ZIP file and extract the files locally
- Clone the repository without forking it
- Fork the repository and then clone it

This book includes exercises for every chapter; therefore, for those who want to keep a copy of their solutions along with the original content on GitHub, it is highly recommended to **fork** the repository and **clone** the forked version. When we fork a repository, GitHub will make a repository under our own profile with the latest version of the original. Then, whenever we make changes to our version, we can push the changes back up. Note that if we simply clone, we don't get this benefit.

The relevant buttons for initiating this process are circled in the following screenshot:

The cloning process will copy the files to the current working directory in a folder called `Hands-On-Data-Analysis-with-Pandas`. To make a folder to put this repository in, we can use `mkdir my_folder && cd my_folder`. This will create a new folder (directory) called `my_folder` and then change the current directory to that folder, after which we can clone the repository. We can chain these two commands (and any number of commands) together by adding `&&` in between them. This can be thought of as *and then* (provided the first command succeeds).

This repository has folders for each chapter. This chapter's materials can be found at `https://github.com/stefmolin/Hands-On-Data-Analysis-with-Pandas/tree/master/ch_01`. While the bulk of this chapter doesn't involve any coding, feel free to follow along in the `introduction_to_data_analysis.ipynb` notebook on the GitHub website until we set up our environment toward the end of the chapter. After we do so, we will use the `check_your_environment.ipynb` notebook to get familiar with Jupyter Notebooks and to run some checks to make sure that everything is set up properly for the rest of this book.

Since the code that's used to generate the content in these notebooks is not the main focus of this chapter, the majority of it has been separated into the `check_environment.py` and `stats_viz.py` files. If you choose to inspect these files, don't be overwhelmed; everything that's relevant to data science will be covered in this book.

Every chapter includes exercises; however, for this chapter only, there is an `exercises.ipynb` notebook, with some code to generate some starting data. Knowledge of basic Python will be necessary to complete these exercises. For those who would like to review the basics, the official Python tutorial is a good place to start: `https://docs.python.org/3/tutorial/index.html`.

Fundamentals of data analysis

Data analysis is a highly iterative process involving collection, preparation (wrangling), **exploratory data analysis (EDA)**, and drawing conclusions. During an analysis, we will frequently revisit each of these steps. The following diagram depicts a generalized workflow:

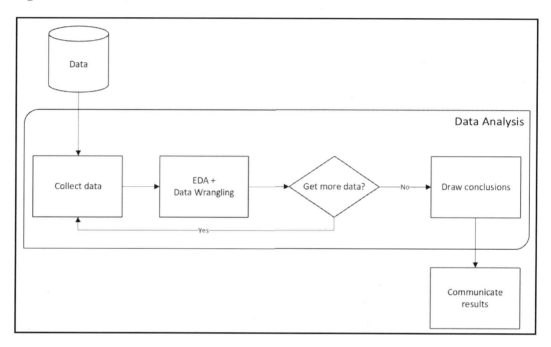

In practice, this process is heavily skewed towards the data preparation side. Surveys have found that, although data scientists enjoy the data preparation side of their job the least, it makes up 80% of their work (https://www.forbes.com/sites/gilpress/ 2016/03/23/data-preparation-most-time-consuming-least-enjoyable-data- science-task-survey-says/#419ce7b36f63). This data preparation step is where pandas really shines.

Data collection

Data collection is the natural first step for any data analysis—we can't analyze data we don't have. In reality, our analysis can begin even before we have the data: when we decide what we want to investigate or analyze, we have to think of what kind of data we can collect that will be useful for our analysis. While data can come from anywhere, we will explore the following sources throughout this book:

- Web scraping to extract data from a website's HTML (often with Python packages such as `selenium`, `requests`, `scrapy`, and `beautifulsoup`)
- **Application Programming Interfaces (APIs)** for web services from which we can collect data with the `requests` package
- Databases (data can be extracted with SQL or another database-querying language)
- Internet resources that provide data for download, such as government websites or Yahoo! Finance
- Log files

Chapter 2, *Working with Pandas DataFrames*, will give us the skills we need to work with the aforementioned data sources. `Chapter 12`, *The Road Ahead*, provides countless resources for finding data sources.

We are surrounded by data, so the possibilities are limitless. It is important, however, to make sure that we are collecting data that will help us draw conclusions. For example, if we are trying to determine if hot chocolate sales are higher when the temperature is lower, we should collect data on the amount of hot chocolate sold and the temperatures each day. While it might be interesting to see how far people traveled to get the hot chocolate, it's not relevant to our analysis.

Don't worry too much about finding the perfect data before beginning an analysis. Odds are, there will always be something we want to add/remove from the initial dataset, reformat, merge with other data, or change in some way. This is where data wrangling comes into play.

Data wrangling

Data wrangling is the process of preparing the data and getting it into a format that can be used for analysis. The unfortunate reality of data is that it is often dirty, meaning that it requires cleaning (preparation) before it can be used. The following are some issues we may encounter with our data:

- **Human errors**: Data is recorded (or even collected) incorrectly, such as putting 100 instead of 1000, or typos. In addition, there may be multiple versions of the same entry recorded, such as New York City, NYC, and nyc

- **Computer error**: Perhaps we weren't recording entries for a while (missing data)

- **Unexpected values**: Maybe whoever was recording the data decided to use ? for a missing value in a numeric column, so now all the entries in the column will be treated as text instead of numeric values

- **Incomplete information**: Think of a survey with optional questions; not everyone will answer them, so we have missing data, but not due to computer or human error

- **Resolution**: The data may have been collected per second, while we need hourly data for our analysis

- **Relevance of the fields**: Often, data is collected or generated as a product of some process rather than explicitly for our analysis. In order to get it to a usable state, we will have to clean it up

- **Format of the data**: The data may be recorded in a format that isn't conducive to analysis, which will require that we reshape it

- **Misconfigurations in data-recording process**: Data coming from sources such as misconfigured trackers and/or webhooks may be missing fields or passing them in the wrong order

Most of these data quality issues can be remedied, but some cannot, such as when the data is collected daily and we need it on an hourly resolution. It is our responsibility to carefully examine our data and to handle any issues, so that our analysis doesn't get distorted. We will cover this process in depth in Chapter 3, *Data Wrangling with Pandas*, and Chapter 4, *Aggregating Pandas DataFrames*.

Exploratory data analysis

During EDA, we use visualizations and summary statistics to get a better understanding of the data. Since the human brain excels at picking out visual patterns, data visualization is essential to any analysis. In fact, some characteristics of the data can only be observed in a plot. Depending on our data, we may create plots to see how a variable of interest has evolved over time, compare how many observations belong to each category, find outliers, look at distributions of continuous and discrete variables, and much more. In Chapter 5, *Visualizing Data with Pandas and Matplotlib*, and Chapter 6, *Plotting with Seaborn and Customization Techniques*, we will learn how to create these plots for both EDA and presentation.

 Data visualizations are very powerful; unfortunately, they can often be misleading. One common issue stems from the scale of the *y*-axis. Most plotting tools will zoom in by default to show the pattern up-close. It would be difficult for software to know what the appropriate axis limits are for every possible plot; therefore, it is our job to properly adjust the axes before presenting our results. You can read about some more ways plots can mislead here: https://venngage.com/blog/misleading-graphs/.

In the workflow diagram we saw earlier, EDA and data wrangling shared a box. This is because they are closely tied:

- Data needs to be prepped before EDA.
- Visualizations that are created during EDA may indicate the need for additional data cleaning.
- Data wrangling uses summary statistics to look for potential data issues, while EDA uses them to understand the data. Improper cleaning will distort the findings when we're conducting EDA. In addition, data wrangling skills will be required to get summary statistics across subsets of the data.

When calculating summary statistics, we must keep the type of data we collected in mind. Data can be **quantitative** (measurable quantities) or **categorical** (descriptions, groupings, or categories). Within these classes of data, we have further subdivisions that let us know what types of operations we can perform on them.

For example, categorical data can be **nominal**, where we assign a numeric value to each level of the category, such as `on = 1`/`off = 0`, but we can't say that one is greater than the other because that distinction is meaningless. The fact that `on` is greater than `off` has no meaning because we arbitrarily chose those numbers to represent the states `on` and `off`. Note that in this case, we can represent the data with a Boolean (`True`/`False` value): `is_on`. Categorical data can also be **ordinal**, meaning that we can rank the levels (for instance, we can have `low < medium < high`).

With quantitative data, we can be on an **interval scale** or a **ratio scale**. The interval scale includes things such as temperature. We can measure temperatures in Celsius and compare the temperatures of two cities, but it doesn't mean anything to say one city is twice as hot as the other. Therefore, interval scale values can be meaningfully compared using addition/subtraction, but not multiplication/division. The ratio scale, then, are those values that can be meaningfully compared with ratios (using multiplication and division). Examples of the ratio scale include prices, sizes, and counts.

Drawing conclusions

After we have collected the data for our analysis, cleaned it up, and performed some thorough EDA, it is time to draw conclusions. This is where we summarize our findings from EDA and decide the next steps:

- Did we notice any patterns or relationships when visualizing the data?
- Does it look like we can make accurate predictions from our data? Does it make sense to move to modeling the data?
- Do we need to collect new data points?
- How is the data distributed?
- Does the data help us answer the questions we have or give insight into the problem we are investigating?
- Do we need to collect new or additional data?

If we decide to model the data, this falls under machine learning and statistics. While not technically data analysis, it is usually the next step, and we will cover it in Chapter 9, *Getting Started with Machine Learning in Python*, and Chapter 10, *Making Better Predictions – Optimizing Models*. In addition, we will see how this entire process will work in practice in Chapter 11, *Machine Learning Anomaly Detection*. As a reference, in the *Machine learning workflow* section in the appendix, there is a workflow diagram depicting the full process from data analysis to machine learning. Chapter 7, *Financial Analysis – Bitcoin and the Stock Market*, and Chapter 8, *Rule-Based Anomaly Detection*, will focus on drawing conclusions from data analysis, rather than building models.

Statistical foundations

When we want to make observations about the data we are analyzing, we are often, if not always, turning to statistics in some fashion. The data we have is referred to as the **sample**, which was observed from (and is a subset of) the **population**. Two broad categories of statistics are descriptive and inferential statistics. With **descriptive statistics**, as the name implies, we are looking to *describe* the sample. **Inferential statistics** involves using the sample statistics to *infer*, or deduce, something about the population, such as the underlying distribution.

 The sample statistics are used as estimators of the population parameters, meaning that we have to quantify their bias and variance. There are a multitude of methods for this; some will make assumptions on the shape of the distribution (parametric) and others won't (non-parametric). This is all well beyond the scope of this book, but it is good to be aware of.

Often, the goal of an analysis is to create a story for the data; unfortunately, it is very easy to misuse statistics. It's the subject of a famous quote:

"There are three kinds of lies: lies, damned lies, and statistics."

— *Benjamin Disraeli*

This is especially true of inferential statistics, which are used in many scientific studies and papers to show significance of their findings. This is a more advanced topic, and, since this isn't a statistics book, we will only briefly touch upon some of the tools and principles behind inferential statistics, which can be pursued further. We will focus on descriptive statistics to help explain the data we are analyzing.

The next few sections will be a review of statistics; those with statistical knowledge can skip to the *Setting up a virtual environment* section.

Sampling

There's an important thing to remember before we attempt any analysis: our sample must be a **random sample** that is representative of the population. This means that the data must be sampled without bias (for example, if we are asking people if they like a certain sports team, we can't only ask fans of the team) and that we should have (ideally) members of all distinct groups from the population in our sample (in the sports team example, we can't just ask men).

There are many methods of sampling. You can read about them, along with their strengths and weaknesses, here: `https://www.khanacademy.org/math/statistics-probability/designing-studies/sampling-methods-stats/a/sampling-methods-review`.

When we discuss machine learning in `Chapter 9`, *Getting Started with Machine Learning in Python*, we will need to sample our data, which will be a sample to begin with. This is called **resampling**. Depending on the data, we will have to pick a different method of sampling. Often, our best bet is a **simple random sample**: we use a random number generator to pick rows at random. When we have distinct groups in the data, we want our sample to be a **stratified random sample**, which will preserve the proportion of the groups in the data. In some cases, we don't have enough data for the aforementioned sampling strategies, so we may turn to random sampling with replacement (**bootstrapping**); this is a **bootstrap sample**. Note that our underlying sample needs to have been a random sample or we risk increasing the bias of the estimator (we could pick certain rows more often because they are in the data more often if it was a convenience sample, while in the true population these rows aren't as prevalent). We will see an example of this in `Chapter 8`, *Rule-Based Anomaly Detection*.

A thorough discussion of the theory behind bootstrapping and its consequences is well beyond the scope of this book, but watch this video for a primer: `https://www.youtube.com/watch?v=gcPIyeqymOU`.

Descriptive statistics

We will begin our discussion of descriptive statistics with **univariate statistics**; univariate simply means that these statistics are calculated from one (**uni**) variable. Everything in this section can be extended to the whole dataset, but the statistics will be calculated per variable we are recording (meaning that if we had 100 observations of speed and distance pairs, we could calculate the averages across the dataset, which would give us the average speed and the average distance statistics).

Descriptive statistics are used to describe and/or summarize the data we are working with. We can start our summarization of the data with a measure of **central tendency**, which describes where most of the data is centered around, and a measure of **spread** or **dispersion**, which indicates how far apart values are.

Measures of central tendency

Measures of central tendency describe the center of our distribution of data. There are three common statistics that are used as measures of center: mean, median, and mode. Each has its own strengths, depending on the data we are working with.

Mean

Perhaps the most common statistic for summarizing data is the average, or **mean**. The population mean is denoted by the Greek symbol *mu* (μ), and the sample mean is written as $\bar{x}$ (pronounced X-bar). The sample mean is calculated by summing all the values and dividing by the count of values; for example, the mean of `[0, 1, 1, 2, 9]` is `2.6` (`(0 + 1 + 1 + 2 + 9)/5`):

$$\bar{x} = \frac{\sum_1^n x_i}{n}$$

We use x_i to represent the ith observation of the variable X. Note how the variable as a whole is represented with a capital letter, while the specific observation is lowercase. Σ (Greek capital letter *sigma*) is used to represent a summation, which, in the equation for the mean, goes from *1* to *n*, which is the number of observations.

One important thing to note about the mean is that it is very sensitive to **outliers** (values created by a different generative process than our distribution). We were dealing with only five values; nevertheless, the 9 is much larger than the other numbers and pulled the mean higher than all but the 9.

Median

In cases where we suspect outliers to be present in our data, we may want to use the **median** as our measure of central tendency. Unlike the mean, the median is robust to outliers. Think of income in the US; the top 1% is much higher than the rest of the population, so this will skew the mean to be higher and distort the perception of the average person's income.

The median represents the 50th percentile of our data; this means that 50% of the values are greater than the median and 50% are less than the median. It is calculated by taking the middle value from an ordered list of values; in cases where we have an even number of values, we take the average of the middle two values. If we take the numbers [0, 1, 1, 2, 9] again, our median is 1.

 The ith percentile is the value at which i% of the observations are less than that value, so the 99th percentile is the value in X, where 99% of the x's are less than it.

Mode

The **mode** is the most common value in the data (if we have [0, 1, 1, 2, 9], then 1 is the mode). In practice, this isn't as useful as it would seem, but we will often hear things like *the distribution is bimodal or multimodal* (as opposed to **unimodal**) in cases where the distribution has two or more most popular values. This doesn't necessarily mean that each of them occurred the same amount of times, but, rather, they are more common than the other values by a significant amount. As shown in the following plots, a unimodal distribution has only one mode (at 0), a bimodal distribution has two (at –2 and 3), and a multimodal distribution has many (at –2, 0.4, and 3):

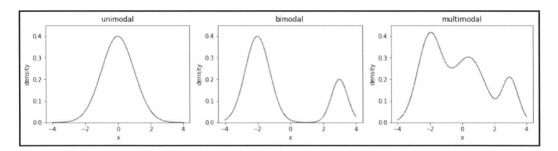

Understanding the concept of the mode comes in handy when describing continuous distributions; however, most of the time when we're describing our data, we will use either the mean or the median as our measure of central tendency.

Measures of spread

Knowing where the center of the distribution is only gets us partially to being able to summarize the distribution of our data—we need to know how values fall around the center and how far apart they are. Measures of spread tell us how the data is dispersed; this will indicate how thin (low dispersion) or wide (very spread out) our distribution is. As with measures of central tendency, we have several ways to describe the spread of a distribution, and which one we choose will depend on the situation and the data.

Range

The **range** is the distance between the smallest value (**minimum**) and the largest value (**maximum**):

$$range = max(X) - min(X)$$

The units of the range will be the same units as our data. Therefore, unless two distributions of data are in the same units and measuring the same thing, we can't compare their ranges and say one is more dispersed than the other.

Variance

Just from the definition of the range, we can see why that wouldn't always be the best way to measure the spread of our data. It gives us upper and lower bounds on what we have in the data, however, if we have any outliers in our data, the range will be rendered useless.

Another problem with the range is that it doesn't tell us how the data is dispersed around its center; it really only tells us how dispersed the entire dataset is. Enter the **variance**, which describes how far apart observations are spread out from their average value (the mean). The population variance is denoted as *sigma-squared* (σ^2), and the sample variance is written as (s^2).

The variance is calculated as the average squared distance from the mean. The distances must be squared so that distances below the mean don't cancel out those above the mean. If we want the sample variance to be an unbiased estimator of the population variance, we divide by *n - 1* instead of *n* to account for using the sample mean instead of the population mean; this is called Bessel's correction (`https://en. wikipedia.org/wiki/Bessel%27s_correction`). Most statistical tools will give us the sample variance by default, since it is *very* rare that we would have data for the entire population:

$$s^2 = \frac{\sum_1^n (x_i - \bar{x})^2}{n - 1}$$

Standard deviation

The variance gives us a statistic with *squared* units. This means that if we started with data on gross domestic product (GDP) in dollars ($), then our variance would be in dollars squared ($\$^2$). This isn't really useful when we're trying to see how this describes the data; we can use the **magnitude** (size) itself to see how spread out something is (large values = large spread), but beyond that, we need a measure of spread with units that are the same as our data.

For this purpose, we use the **standard deviation**, which is simply the square root of the variance. By performing this operation, we get a statistic in units that we can make sense of again ($ for our GDP example):

$$s = \sqrt{\frac{\sum_1^n (x_i - \bar{x})^2}{n - 1}} = \sqrt{s^2}$$

The population standard deviation is represented as σ, and the sample standard deviation is denoted as *s*.

We can use the standard deviation to see how far from the mean data points are *on average*. Small standard deviation means that values are close to the mean; large standard deviation means that values are dispersed more widely. This can be tied to how we would imagine the distribution curve: the smaller the standard deviation, the skinnier the peak of the curve; the larger the standard deviation, the fatter the peak of the curve. The following plot is a comparison of a standard deviation of 0.5 to 2:

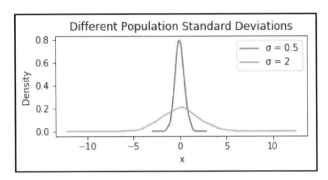

Coefficient of variation

When we moved from variance to standard deviation, we were looking to get to units that made sense; however, if we then want to compare the level of dispersion of one dataset to another, we would need to have the same units once again. One way around this is to calculate the **coefficient of variation** (**CV**), which is the ratio of the standard deviation to the mean. It tells us how big the standard deviation is relative to the mean:

$$CV = \frac{s}{\bar{x}}$$

Interquartile range

So far, other than the range, we have discussed mean-based measures of dispersion; now, we will look at how we can describe the spread with the median as our measure of central tendency. As mentioned earlier, the median is the 50th percentile or the 2nd **quartile** (**Q₂**). Percentiles and quartiles are both **quantiles**—values that divide data into equal groups each containing the same percentage of the total data; percentiles give this in 100 parts, while quartiles give it in four (25%, 50%, 75%, and 100%).

Since quantiles neatly divide up our data, and we know how much of the data goes in each section, they are a perfect candidate for helping us quantify the spread of our data. One common measure for this is the **interquartile range (IQR)**, which is the distance between the 3rd and 1st quartiles:

$$IQR = Q_3 - Q_1$$

The IQR gives us the spread of data around the median *and* quantifies how much dispersion we have in the middle 50% of our distribution. It can also be useful to determine outliers, which we will cover in `Chapter 8`, *Rule-Based Anomaly Detection*.

Quartile coefficient of dispersion

Just like we had the coefficient of variation when using the mean as our measure of central tendency, we have the **quartile coefficient of dispersion** when using the median as our measure of center. This statistic is also unitless, so it can be used to compare datasets. It is calculated by dividing the **semi-quartile range** (half the IQR) by the **midhinge** (midpoint between the first and third quartiles):

$$QCD = \frac{\frac{Q_3 - Q_1}{2}}{\frac{Q_1 + Q_3}{2}} = \frac{Q_3 - Q_1}{Q_3 + Q_1}$$

Summarizing data

We have seen many examples of descriptive statistics that we can use to summarize our data by its center and dispersion; in practice, looking at the **5-number summary** or visualizing the distribution prove to be helpful first steps before diving into some of the other aforementioned metrics. The 5-number summary, as its name indicates, provides five descriptive statistics that summarize our data:

	Quartile	Statistic	Percentile
1.	Q_0	minimum	0th
2.	Q_1	N/A	25th
3.	Q_2	median	50th
4.	Q_3	N/A	75th
5.	Q_4	maximum	100th

Looking at the 5-number summary is a quick and efficient way of getting a sense of our data. At a glance, we have an idea of the distribution of the data and can move on to visualizing it.

The **box plot** (or box and whisker plot) is the visual representation of the 5-number summary. The median is denoted by a thick line in the box. The top of the box is Q_3 and the bottom of the box is Q_1. Lines (whiskers) extend from both sides of the box boundaries toward the minimum and maximum. Based on the convention our plotting tool uses, though, they may only extend to a certain statistic; any values beyond these statistics are marked as outliers (using points). For this book, the lower bound of the whiskers will be $Q_1 - 1.5 * IQR$ and the upper bound will be $Q_3 + 1.5 * IQR$, which is called the Tukey box plot:

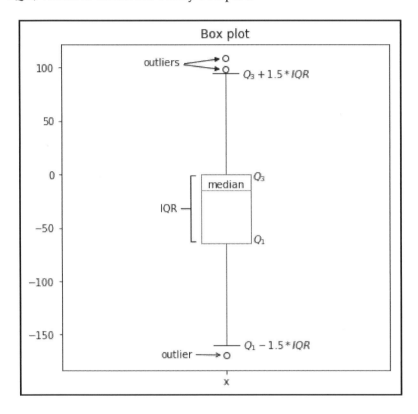

While the box plot is a great tool to get an initial understanding of the distribution, we don't get to see how things are distributed inside each of the quartiles. We know that 25% of the data is in each and the bounds, but we don't know how many of them have which values. For this purpose, we turn to **histograms** for **discrete** variables (for instance, number of people or books) and **kernel density estimates** (**KDEs**) for **continuous** variables (for instance, heights or time). There is nothing stopping us from using KDEs on discrete variables, but it is easy to confuse people that way. Histograms work for both discrete and continuous variables; however, in both cases, we must keep in mind that the number of bins we choose to divide the data into can easily change the shape of the distribution we see.

To make a histogram, a certain number of equal-width bins are created, and then bars with heights for the number of values we have in each bin are added. The following plot is a histogram with 10 bins, showing the three measures of central tendency for the same data that was used to generate the box plot:

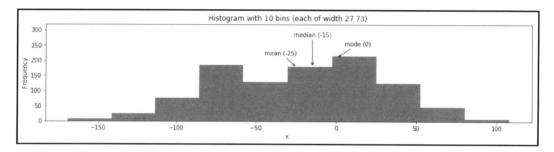

In practice, we need to play with the number of bins to find the best value. However, we have to be careful as this can misrepresent the shape of the distribution.

Kernel density estimates are similar to histograms, except, rather than creating bins for the data, they draw a smoothed curve, which is an estimate of the distribution's **probability density function** (**PDF**). The PDF is for continuous variables, and tells us how probability is distributed over the values. Higher values for the PDF indicate higher likelihoods:

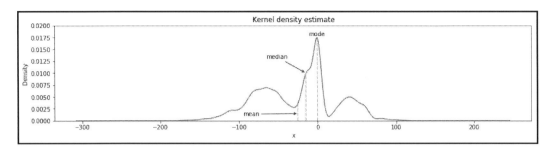

When the distribution starts to get a little lopsided with long tails on one side, the mean measure of center can easily get pulled to that side. Distributions that aren't symmetric have some **skew** to them. A **left (negative) skewed distribution** has a long tail on the left-hand side; a **right (positive) skewed distribution** has a long tail on the right-hand side. In the presence of negative skew, the mean will be smaller than the median, while the reverse happens with a positive skew. When there is no skew, both will be equal:

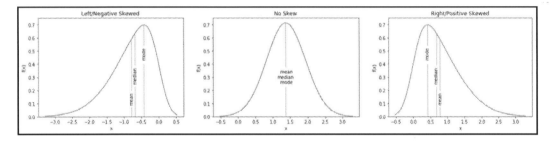

There is also another statistic called **kurtosis**, which compares the density of the center of the distribution with the density at the tails. Both skewness and kurtosis can be calculated with the `scipy` package.

Each column in our data is a **random variable**, because every time we observe it, we get a value according to the underlying distribution—it's not static. When we are interested in the probability of getting a value of *x* or less, we use the **cumulative distribution function (CDF)**, which is the integral (area under the curve) of the PDF:

$$CDF = F(x) = \int_{-\infty}^{x} f(t)dt$$

where $f(t)$ is the PDF and $\int_{-\infty}^{\infty} f(t)dt = 1$

The probability of the random variable X being less than or equal to the specific value of x is denoted as $P(X \leq x)$. With a continuous variable, the probability of getting exactly x is 0. This is because the probability will be the integral of the PDF from x to x (area under a curve with zero width), which is zero:

$$P(X = x) = \int_{x}^{x} f(t)dt = 0$$

In order to visualize this, we can find an estimate of the CDF from the sample, called the **empirical cumulative distribution function** (**ECDF**). Since this is cumulative, at the point where the value on the x-axis is equal to x, the y value is the cumulative probability of $P(X \leq x)$. As an example, let's visualize `P(X ≤ 50)`, `P(X = 50)`, and `P(X > 50)`:

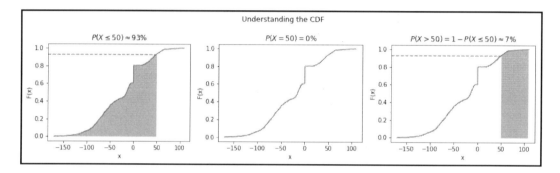

Common distributions

While there are many probability distributions, each with specific use cases, there are some that we will come across often. The **Gaussian**, or **normal**, looks like a bell curve and is parameterized by its mean (μ) and standard deviation (σ). The **standard normal** (Z) has a mean of 0 and a standard deviation of 1. Many things in nature happen to follow the normal distribution, such as heights. Note that testing if our distribution is normal is not trivial. Check the *Further reading* section for more information.

The **Poisson distribution** is a discrete distribution that is often used to model arrivals. The time between arrivals can be modeled with the **exponential distribution**. Both are defined by their mean, lambda (λ). We will use these distributions in `Chapter 8`, *Rule-Based Anomaly Detection*, when we simulate some login attempt data for anomaly detection.

The **uniform distribution** places equal likelihood on each value within its bounds. We often use this for random number generation. When we pick a random number to simulate a single success/failure outcome, it is called a **Bernoulli trial**. This is parameterized by the probability of success (p). When we run the same experiment multiple times (n), the total number of successes is then a **binomial** random variable. Both the Bernoulli and binomial are discrete distributions.

We can visualize both discrete and continuous distributions; however, discrete distributions give us a **probability mass function (PMF)** instead of a PDF:

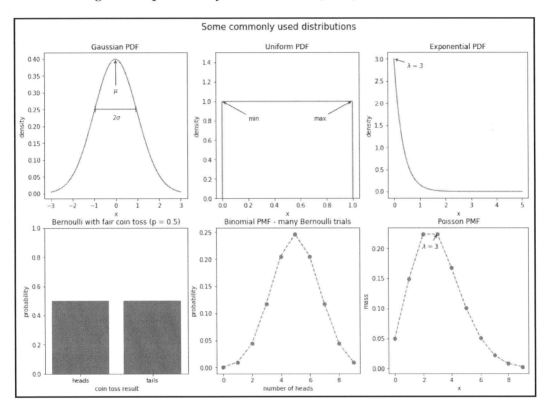

Scaling data

In order to compare variables from different distributions, we would have to **scale** the data, which we could do with the range by using **min-max scaling**. We take *each* data point, subtract the minimum of the dataset, then divide by the range.
This **normalizes** our data (scales it to the range [0, 1]):

$$x_{scaled} = \frac{x - min(X)}{range(X)}$$

This isn't the only way to scale data; we can also use the mean and standard deviation. In this case, we would subtract the mean from each observation and then divide by the standard deviation to **standardize** the data:

$$z_i = \frac{x_i - \bar{x}}{s}$$

This gives us what is known as a **Z-score**. We are left with a normalized distribution with a mean of 0 and a standard deviation (and variance) of 1. The Z-score tells us how many standard deviations from the mean each observation is; the mean has a Z-score of 0 while an observation of 0.5 standard deviations below the mean will have a Z-score of -0.5.

There are, of course, additional ways to scale our data, and the one we end up choosing will be dependent on our data. By keeping the measures of central tendency and measures of dispersion in mind, you will be able to identify how the scaling of data is being done in any other methods you come across.

Quantifying relationships between variables

In the previous sections, we were dealing with univariate statistics and were only able to say something about the variable we were looking at. With multivariate statistics, we can look to quantify relationships between variables. This allows us to look into things such as **correlations** (how one variable changes with respect to another) and attempt to make predictions for future behavior.

The **covariance** is a statistic for quantifying the relationship between variables by showing their joint variance:

$$cov(X, Y) = E[(X - E[X])(Y - E[Y])]$$

E[X] is new notation for us. It is read as *the expected value of X* or *the expectation of X*, and it is calculated by summing all the possible values of *X* multiplied by their probability—it's the long-run average of *X*.

The magnitude of the covariance isn't easy to interpret, but its sign tells us if the variables are positively or negatively correlated. However, we would also like to quantify how *strong* the relationship is between the variables, which brings us to correlation. Correlation tells us how variables change together both in direction (same or opposite) and in magnitude (strength of the relationship). To find the correlation, we calculate the **Pearson correlation coefficient**, symbolized by ρ (the Greek letter rho), by dividing the covariance by the product of the standard deviations of the variables:

$$\rho_{X,Y} = \frac{cov(X,Y)}{s_X s_Y}$$

This normalizes the covariance and results in a statistic bounded between -1 and 1, making it easy to describe both the direction of the correlation (sign) and the strength of it (magnitude). Correlations of 1 are said to be perfect positive (linear) correlations, while those of -1 are perfect negative correlations. Values near 0 aren't correlated. If correlation coefficients are near 1 in absolute value, then the variables are said to be strongly correlated; those closer to 0.5 are said to be weakly correlated.

Let's look at some examples using scatter plots. In the leftmost corner (ρ = 0.11), we see that there is no correlation between the variables: they appear to be random noise with no pattern. The next plot with ρ = -0.52 has weak negative correlation: we can see that the variables appear to move together with the *x* variable increasing, while the *y* variable decreases, but there is still a bit of randomness. In the third plot from the left (ρ = 0.87), there is a strong positive correlation: *x* and *y* are increasing together. The rightmost plot with ρ = -0.99 has near perfect negative correlation: as *x* increases, *y* decreases. We can also see how the points form a line:

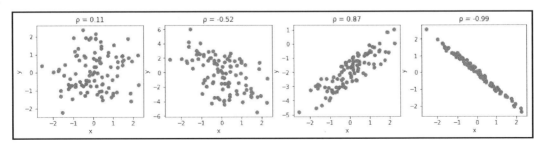

One very important thing to remember is that, while we may find a correlation between X and Y, it doesn't mean that X *causes* Y or that Y *causes* X. There could be some Z that actually causes both; perhaps X causes some intermediary event that causes Y, or perhaps it is actually just a coincidence. Keep in mind that we often don't have enough information to report causation:

"Correlation does not imply causation."

To quickly eyeball the strength and direction of the relationship between two variables (and see if there even seems to be one), we will often use scatter plots rather than calculating the exact correlation coefficient. This is for a couple of reasons:

- It's easier to find patterns in visualizations, but it's more work to arrive at the same conclusion by looking at numbers and tables.
- We might see that the variables seem related, but they may not be *linearly* related. Looking at a visual representation will make it easy to see if our data is actually quadratic, exponential, logarithmic, or some other non-linear function.

Both of the following plots depict data with strong positive correlations, but it's pretty obvious, when looking at the scatter plots, that these are not linear. The one on the left is logarithmic, while the one on the right is exponential:

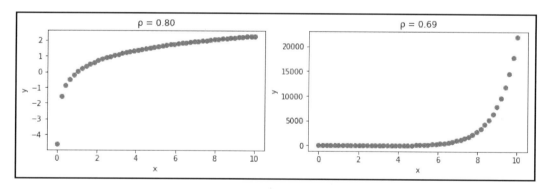

Pitfalls of summary statistics

Not only can correlation coefficients be misleading—so can summary statistics. There is a very interesting dataset illustrating how careful we must be when only using summary statistics and correlation coefficients to describe our data. It also shows us that plotting is not optional.

Anscombe's quartet is a collection of four different datasets that have identical summary statistics and correlation coefficients, but when plotted, it is obvious they are not similar:

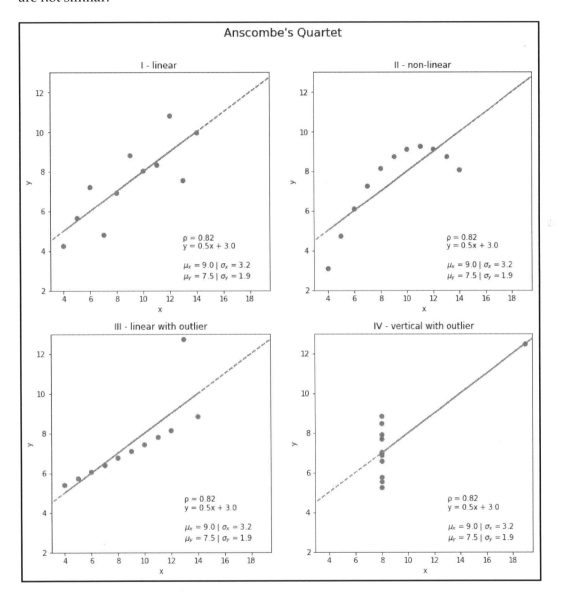

Summary statistics are very helpful when we're getting to know the data, but be wary of relying exclusively on them. Remember, statistics can mislead; be sure to also plot the data before drawing any conclusions or proceeding with the analysis. You can read more about Anscombe's quartet here: `https://en.wikipedia.org/wiki/Anscombe%27s_quartet`.

Prediction and forecasting

Say our favorite ice cream shop has asked us to help predict how many ice creams they can expect to sell on a given day. They are convinced that the temperature outside has a strong influence on their sales, so they collected data on the number of ice creams sold at a given temperature. We agree to help them, and the first thing we do is make a scatter plot of the data they gave us:

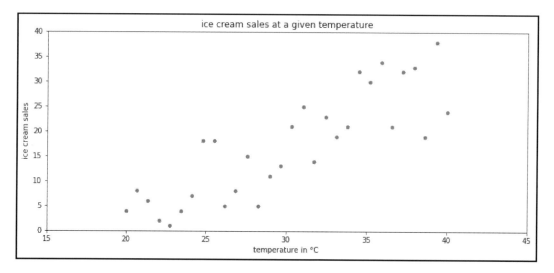

We can observe an upward trend in the scatter plot: more ice creams are sold at higher temperatures. In order to help out the ice cream shop, though, we need to find a way to make predictions from this data. We can use a technique called **regression** to model the relationship between temperature and ice cream sales with an equation. Using this equation, we will be able to **predict** ice cream sales at a given temperature.

In `Chapter 9`, *Getting Started with Machine Learning in Python*, we will go over regression in depth, so this discussion will be a high-level overview. There are many types of regression that will yield a different type of equation, such as linear and logistic. Our first step will be to identify the **dependent variable**, which is the quantity we want to predict (ice cream sales), and the variables we will use to predict it, which are called **independent variables**. While we can have many independent variables, our ice cream sales example only has one: temperature. Therefore, we will use simple linear regression to model the relationship as a line:

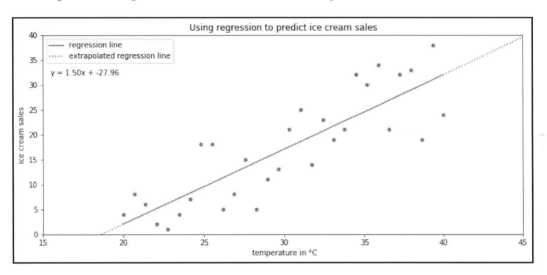

The regression line in the previous scatter plot yields the following equation for the relationship:

$$ice\ cream\ sales = 1.5 \times temperature - 27.96$$

Today the temperature is 35°C, so we plug that in for *temperature* in the equation. The result predicts that the ice cream shop will sell 24.54 ice creams. This prediction is along the red line in the previous plot. Note that the ice cream shop can't actually sell fractions of an ice cream.

 Remember that correlation does not imply causation. People may buy ice cream when it is warmer, but warmer temperatures don't cause people to buy ice cream.

Before leaving the model in the hands of the ice cream shop, it's important to discuss the difference between the dotted and solid portions of the regression line that we obtained. When we make predictions using the solid portion of the line, we are using **interpolation**, meaning that we will be predicting ice cream sales for temperatures the regression was created on. On the other hand, if we try to predict how many ice creams will be sold at 45°C, it is called **extrapolation** (dotted portion of the line), since we didn't have any temperatures this high when we ran the regression. Extrapolation can be very dangerous as many trends don't continue indefinitely. It may be so hot that people decide not to leave their houses. This means that instead of selling the predicted 39.54 ice creams, they would sell zero.

 We can also predict categories. Imagine that the ice cream shop wants to know which flavor of ice cream will sell the most on a given day. This type of prediction will be introduced in `Chapter 9`, *Getting Started with Machine Learning in Python*.

When working with time series, our terminology is a little different: we often look to **forecast** future values based on past values. Forecasting is a type of prediction for time series. Before we try to model the time series, however, we will often use a process called **time series decomposition** to split the time series into components, which can be combined in an additive or multiplicative fashion and may be used as parts of a model.

The **trend** component describes the behavior of the time series in the **long term** without accounting for the seasonal or cyclical effects. Using the trend, we can make broad statements about the time series in the long run, such as *the population of Earth is increasing* or *the value of Facebook stock is stagnating*. **Seasonality** of a time series explains the systematic and calendar-related movements of a time series. For example, the number of ice cream trucks on the streets of New York City is high in the summer and drops to nothing in the winter; this pattern repeats every year, regardless of whether the actual amount each summer is the same. Lastly, the **cyclical** component accounts for anything else unexplained or irregular with the time series; this could be something such as a hurricane driving the number of ice cream trucks down in the **short term** because it isn't safe to be outside. This component is difficult to anticipate with a forecast due to its unexpected nature.

We can use Python to **decompose** the time series into trend, seasonality, and **noise** or **residuals**. The cyclical component is captured in the noise (random, unpredictable data); after we remove the trend and seasonality from the time series, what we are left with is the residual:

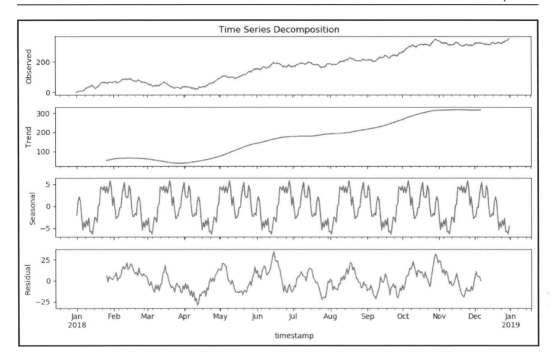

When building models to forecast time series, some common methods include exponential smoothing and ARIMA-family models. **ARIMA** stands for **autoregressive (AR)**, **integrated (I)**, **moving average (MA)**. **Autoregressive** models take advantage of the fact that an observation at time *t* is *correlated* to a previous observation, for example at time *t - 1*. In Chapter 5, *Visualizing Data with Pandas and Matplotlib*, we will look at some techniques for determining whether a time series is autoregressive; note that not all time series are. The **integrated** component concerns the **differenced** data, or the *change* in the data from one time to another. For example, if we were concerned with a **lag** (distance between times) of 1, the differenced data would be the value at time *t* subtracted by the value at time *t - 1*. Lastly, the **moving average** component uses a sliding window to average the last *x* observations, where *x* is the length of the sliding window; if, for example, we have a 3-period moving average, by the time we have all of the data up to time 5, our moving average calculation only uses time periods 3, 4, and 5 to forecast time 6. We will build an ARIMA model in Chapter 7, *Financial Analysis – Bitcoin and the Stock Market*.

The moving average puts equal weight on each time period in the past involved in the calculation. In practice, this isn't always a realistic expectation of our data. Sometimes, *all* past values are important, but they *vary* in their influence on future data points. For these cases, we can use **exponential smoothing**, which allows us to put more weight on more recent values and less weight on values further away from what we are predicting.

Note that we aren't limited to predicting numbers; in fact, depending on the data, our predictions could be categorical in nature—things such as determining what color the next observation will be or if an email is spam or not. We will cover more on regression, time series analysis, and other methods of prediction using machine learning in later chapters.

Inferential statistics

As mentioned earlier, inferential statistics deals with inferring or deducing things from the sample data we have in order to make statements about the population as a whole. When we're looking to state our conclusions, we have to be mindful of whether we conducted an **observational study** or an **experiment**. An **observational study** is where the independent variable is not under the control of the researchers, and so we are *observing* those taking part in our study (think about studies on smoking—we can't force people to smoke). The fact that we can't control the independent variable means that we *cannot* conclude causation.

An **experiment** is where we are able to directly influence the independent variable and randomly assign subjects to the control and test groups, like A/B tests (for anything from website redesigns to ad copy). Note that the control group doesn't receive treatment; they can be given a placebo (depending on what the study is). The ideal setup for this will be **double-blind**, where the researchers administering the treatment don't know which is the placebo and also don't know which subject belongs to which group.

 We can often find reference to Bayesian inference and frequentist inference. These are based on two different ways of approaching probability. Frequentist statistics focuses on the frequency of the event, while Bayesian statistics uses a degree of belief when determining the probability of an event. We will see an example of this in Chapter 11, *Machine Learning Anomaly Detection*. You can read more about how these methods differ here: https://www.probabilisticworld.com/frequentist-bayesian-approaches-inferential-statistics/.

Inferential statistics gives us tools to translate our understanding of the sample data to a statement about the population. Remember that the sample statistics we discussed earlier are estimators for the population parameters. Our estimators need **confidence intervals**, which provide a point estimate and a margin of error around it. This is the range that the true population parameter will be in at a certain **confidence level**. At the 95% confidence level, 95% of the confidence intervals that are calculated from random samples of the population contain the true population parameter. Frequently, 95% is chosen for the confidence level and other purposes in statistics, although 90% and 99% are also common; the higher the confidence level, the wider the interval.

Hypothesis tests allow us to test whether the true population parameter is less than, greater than, or not equal to some value at a certain **significance level** (called **alpha**). The process of performing a hypothesis test involves stating our initial assumption or **null hypothesis**: for example, *the true population mean is 0*. We pick a level of statistical significance, usually 5%, which is the probability of rejecting the null hypothesis when it is true. Then, we calculate the critical value for the test statistic, which will depend on the amount of data we have and the type of statistic (such as the mean of one population or the proportion of votes for a candidate) we are testing. The critical value is compared to the test statistic from our data, and we decide to either reject or fail to reject the null hypothesis. Hypothesis tests are closely related to confidence intervals. The significance level is equivalent to 1 minus the confidence level. This means that a result is statistically significant if the null hypothesis value is not in the confidence interval.

There are many things we have to be aware of when picking the method to calculate a confidence interval or the proper test statistic for a hypothesis test. This is beyond the scope of this book, but check out the link in the *Further reading* section at the end of this chapter for more information. Also be sure to look at some of the mishaps with p-values, such as p-hacking, here: `https://en.wikipedia.org/wiki/Misunderstandings_of_p-values`.

Setting up a virtual environment

This book was written using Python 3.6.4, but the code should work for Python 3.6+, which is available on all major operating systems. In this section, we will go over how to set up the virtual environment in order to follow along with this book. If Python isn't already installed on your computer, read through the following sections on virtual environments first, and then decide whether to install Anaconda, since it will also install Python. To install Python without Anaconda, download it here: `https://www.python.org/downloads/`. Then, continue with the section on `venv`.

 To check if Python is already installed, run `where python3` from the command line on Windows or `which python3` from the command line on Linux/macOS. If this returns nothing, try running it with just `python` (instead of `python3`). If Python is installed, check the version by running `python3 --version`.

Virtual environments

Most of the time, when we want to install software on our computer, we simply download it, but the nature of programming languages where packages are constantly being updated and rely on specific versions of others means this can cause issues. We can be working on a project one day where we need a certain version of a Python package (say 0.9.1), but the next day be working on an analysis where we need the most recent version of that same package (1.1.0). Sounds like there wouldn't be an issue, right? Well, what happens if this update causes a breaking change to the first project or another package in our project that relies on this one? This is a common enough problem that a solution already exists to prevent this from being an issue—virtual environments.

A **virtual environment** allows us to create separate environments for each of our projects. Each of our environments will only have the packages that it needs installed. This makes it easy to share our environment with others, have multiple versions of the same package installed on our machine for different projects without interfering with each other, and avoid unexpected side effects from installing packages that update or have dependencies on others. It's good practice to make a dedicated virtual environment for any projects we work on.

We will discuss two common ways to achieve this setup, and you can decide which fits best. Note that all the code in this section will be executed on the command line.

venv

Python 3 comes with the `venv` module, which will create a virtual environment in the location of our choice. The process of setting up and using a development environment is as follows (after Python is installed):

1. Create a folder for the project
2. Use `venv` to create an environment in this folder
3. Activate the environment
4. Install Python packages in the environment with `pip`
5. Deactivate the environment when finished

In practice, we will create environments for each project we work on, so our first step will be to create a directory for all of our project files. For this, we can use the `mkdir` command. Once this has been created, we will change our current directory to be that one using the `cd` command. Since we already obtained the project files (from the instructions in the *Chapter materials* section), the following is for reference only. To make a new directory and move to that directory, we can use the following command:

```
$ mkdir my_project && cd my_project
```

 `cd <path>` changes the current directory to the path specified in `<path>`, which can be an **absolute** (full) path or **relative** (how to get there from the current directory) path.

Before moving on, use `cd` to navigate to the directory containing this book's repository. Note that the path will depend on where it was cloned/downloaded:

```
$ cd path/to/Hands-On-Data-Analysis-with-Pandas
```

Since there are slight differences in operating systems for the remaining steps, we will go over Windows and Linux/macOS separately. Note that if you have both Python 2 and Python 3, you will need to replace `python` with `python3` in the following commands.

Windows

To create our environment for this book, we will use the `venv` module from the standard library. Note that we must provide a name for our environment:

```
C:\...> python -m venv book_env
```

Now, we have a folder for our virtual environment named book_env inside the repository folder that we cloned/downloaded earlier. In order to use the environment, we need to activate it:

```
C:\...> %cd%\book_env\Scripts\activate.bat
```

Windows replaces %cd% with the path to the current directory. This saves us from having to type the full path up to the book_env part.

Note that, after we activate the virtual environment, we can see (book_env) in front of our prompt on the command line; this lets us know we are in the environment:

```
(book_env) C:\...>
```

When we are finished using the environment, we simply deactivate it:

```
(book_env) C:\...> deactivate
```

Any packages that are installed in the environment don't exist outside the environment. Note that we no longer have (book_env) in front of our prompt on the command line. You can read more about venv in the Python documentation: https:/ /docs.python.org/3/library/venv.html.

Linux/macOS

To create our environment for this book, we will use the venv module from the standard library. Note that we must provide a name for our environment:

```
$ python -m venv book_env
```

Now, we have a folder for our virtual environment named book_env inside of the repository folder we cloned/downloaded earlier. In order to use the environment, we need to activate it:

```
$ source book_env/bin/activate
```

Note that, after we activate the virtual environment, we can see (book_env) in front of our prompt on the command line; this lets us know we are in the environment:

```
(book_env) $
```

When we are finished using the environment, we simply deactivate it:

```
(book_env) $ deactivate
```

Any packages that are installed in the environment don't exist outside the environment. Note that we no longer have `(book_env)` in front of our prompt on the command line. You can read more about `venv` in the Python documentation: `https://docs.python.org/3/library/venv.html`.

Anaconda

Anaconda provides a way to set up a Python environment specifically for data science. It includes some of the packages we will use in this book, along with several others, which may be necessary for tasks that aren't covered in this book (and also deals with dependencies outside of Python that might be tricky to install otherwise). Anaconda uses `conda` as the environment and package manager instead of `pip`, although packages can still be installed with `pip` (as long as the `pip` installed by Anaconda is called). Be warned that this is a very large install (although the Miniconda version is much lighter).

People who use Python for purposes aside from data science may prefer the `venv` method we discussed earlier in order to have more control over what gets installed. Anaconda can also be packaged with the Spyder **integrated development environment** (IDE) and Jupyter Notebooks, which we will discuss later. Note that we can use Jupyter with the `venv` option, as well.

You can read more about Anaconda and how to install it in their official documentation:

- **Windows**: `https://docs.anaconda.com/anaconda/install/windows/`
- **macOS**: `https://docs.anaconda.com/anaconda/install/mac-os/`
- **Linux**: `https://docs.anaconda.com/anaconda/install/linux/`
- **User guide**: `https://docs.anaconda.com/anaconda/user-guide/`

Installing the required Python packages

The `requirements.txt` file in the repository contains all the packages we need to install to work through this book. It will be in our current directory, but it can also be found here: `https://github.com/stefmolin/Hands-On-Data-Analysis-with-Pandas/blob/master/requirements.txt`. This file can be used to install a bunch of packages at once with the `-r` flag in the call to `pip3 install` and has the advantage of being easy to share.

We can generate our own `requirements.txt` files with `pip3 freeze` by running `pip3 freeze > requirements.txt` to send the list of packages we have installed in our environment and their respective versions to the `requirements.txt` file.

Before installing anything, be sure to activate the virtual environment we created with either `venv` or Anaconda. Be advised that if the environment is not activated before running the following command, the packages will be installed outside the environment:

```
$ source book_env/bin/activate
(book_env) $ pip3 install -r requirements.txt
```

We can do a lot with the Python standard library; however, we will often find the need to install and use an outside package to extend functionality. To install a package without using the `requirements.txt` file, run `pip3 install <package_name>`. Optionally, we can provide a specific version to install: `pip3 install pandas==0.23.4`. Without that specification, we will get the most recent stable version.

Why pandas?

When it comes to data science in Python, the `pandas` library is pretty much ubiquitous. It is built on top of the NumPy library, which allows us to perform mathematical operations on arrays of single-type data efficiently. Pandas expands this to **dataframes**, which can be thought of as tables of data. We will get a more formal introduction to dataframes in `Chapter 2`, *Working with Pandas DataFrames*.

Aside from efficient operations, `pandas` also provides **wrappers** around the `matplotlib` plotting library, making it very easy to create a variety of plots without needing to write many lines of `matplotlib` code. We can always tweak our plots using `matplotlib`, but for quickly visualizing our data, we only need one line of code in `pandas`. We will explore this functionality in `Chapter 5`, *Visualizing Data with Pandas and Matplotlib*, and `Chapter 6`, *Plotting with Seaborn and Customization Techniques*.

Wrapper functions wrap around code from another library, obscuring some of its complexity and leaving us with a simpler interface for repeating that functionality. This is a core principle of **object-oriented programming** (**OOP**) called **abstraction**, which reduces complexity and the duplication of code. We will create our own wrapper functions throughout this book.

Jupyter Notebooks

Each chapter of this book includes Jupyter Notebooks for following along. Jupyter Notebooks are omnipresent in Python data science because they make it very easy to write and test code in more of a discovery environment compared to writing a program. We can execute one block of code at a time and have the results printed to the notebook, right beneath the code that generated it. In addition, we can use **Markdown** to add text explanations to our work. Jupyter Notebooks can be easily packaged up and shared: they can be pushed to GitHub (where they display as we saw them on our computer), converted into HTML or PDF, sent to someone else, or presented.

Launching JupyterLab

JupyterLab is an IDE that allows us to create Jupyter Notebooks and Python scripts, interact with the terminal, create text documents, reference documentation, and much more from a clean web interface on our local machine. There are lots of keyboard shortcuts to master before really becoming a power-user, but the interface is pretty intuitive. When we created our environment, we installed everything we needed to run JupyterLab, so let's take a quick tour of the IDE and make sure that our environment is set up properly. First, we activate our environment and then launch JupyterLab:

```
$ source book_env/bin/activate
(book_env) $ jupyter lab
```

This will then launch a window in the default browser with JupyterLab. We will be greeted with the **Launcher**:

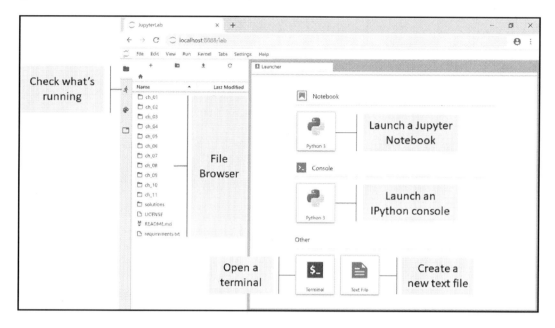

Google also has a cloud-based Jupyter Notebook interface called **Colaboratory**. It requires no setup on our end and has lots of common packages already available. If we need to install another one, we can. Everything will be saved to Google Drive and links to the notebooks can easily be shared with others. This can be a good option for working through this book as we won't have any sensitive data. In practice, we may be working with proprietary data that can't be stored in the cloud and so easily accessed; therefore, it is useful to know how to set up a local Jupyter environment. You can read more on Colaboratory here: `https://colab.research.google.com/notebooks/welcome.ipynb`.

Validating the virtual environment

Now, let's open the `checking_your_setup.ipynb` notebook in the `ch_01` folder, as shown in the following screenshot:

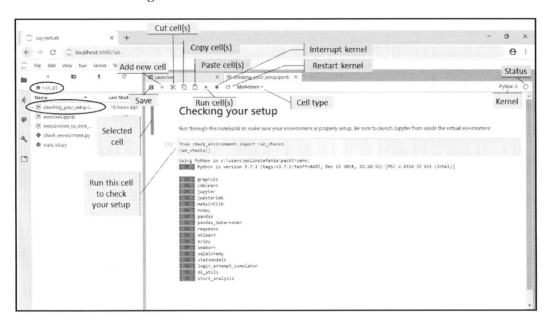

 The **kernel** is the process that runs and introspects our code in a Jupyter Notebook. By default, we will be using the IPython kernel. We will learn a little more about IPython in later chapters.

Click on the code cell indicated in the previous screenshot and run it by clicking the play (▶) button. If everything shows up in green, the environment is all set up. However, if this isn't the case, run the following command from the virtual environment to create a special kernel with `book_env` for use with Jupyter:

```
(book_env) $ ipython kernel install --user --name=book_env
```

There is now an additional option in the **Launcher**, and we can also change our kernel from a Jupyter Notebook as well:

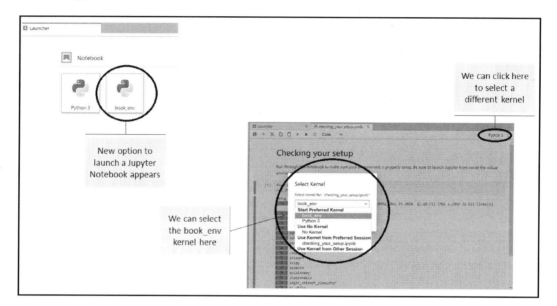

 It's important to note that Jupyter Notebooks will retain the values we assign to variables while the kernel is running, and the results in the **Out[#]** cells will be saved when we save the file.

Closing JupyterLab

Closing the browser with JupyterLab in it doesn't stop JupyterLab or the kernels it is running (we also won't have the command-line interface back). To shut down JupyterLab entirely, we need to hit *Ctrl + C* (which is a keyboard interrupt signal that lets JupyterLab know we want to shut it down) a couple of times in the terminal until we get the prompt back:

```
. . .
[I 17:36:53.166 LabApp] Interrupted...
[I 17:36:53.168 LabApp] Shutting down 1 kernel
[I 17:36:53.770 LabApp] Kernel shutdown: a38e1[...]b44f

(book_env) $
```

Jupyter is a very useful tool, and we aren't limited to running Python—we can run kernels for R, Julia, Scala, and other languages as well. You can read more about Jupyter and work through a tutorial at `http://jupyter.org/` and learn more about JupyterLab at `https://jupyterlab.readthedocs.io/en/stable/`.

Summary

In this chapter, we learned about the main processes in conducting data analysis: data collection, wrangling, EDA, and drawing conclusions. We followed that up with an overview of descriptive statistics and learned how to describe the central tendency and spread of our data; how to summarize it both numerically and visually using the 5-number summary, box plots, histograms, and kernel density estimates; how to scale our data; and how to quantify relationships between variables in our dataset.

We got an introduction to prediction and time series analysis. Then, we had a very brief overview of some core topics in inferential statistics that can be explored after mastering the contents of this book. Note that, while all the examples in this chapter were of one or two variables, real-life data is often high-dimensional. `Chapter 10`, *Making Better Predictions – Optimizing Models*, will touch on some ways to address this. Lastly, we set up our virtual environment for this book and learned how to work with Jupyter Notebooks.

Now that we have built a strong foundation, we will start working with data in Python.

Exercises

Run through the `introduction_to_data_analysis.ipynb` notebook for a review of this chapter's content, and then complete the following exercises to practice working with JupyterLab and calculating summary statistics in Python:

1. Explore the JupyterLab interface and look at some of the shortcuts that are available. Don't worry about memorizing them for now (eventually, they will become second nature and save you a lot of time)—just get comfortable using Jupyter Notebooks.
2. Is all data normally distributed? Explain why or why not.

3. When would it make more sense to use the median instead of the mean for the measure of center?

4. Run the code in the first cell of the `exercises.ipynb` notebook. It will give you a list of 100 values to work with for the rest of the exercises in this chapter.

5. Using the data from exercise #4, calculate the following statistics without importing anything from the `statistics` module in the standard library (https://docs.python.org/3/library/statistics.html) and then confirm your results match up to those that are obtained when using the `statistics` module (where possible):
    * Mean
    * Median
    * Mode (hint: check out the `Counter` in the `collections` module of the standard library at https://docs.python.org/3/library/collections.html#collections.Counter)
    * Sample variance
    * Sample standard deviation

6. Using the data from exercise #4, calculate the following statistics using the functions in the `statistics` module where appropriate:
    * Range
    * Coefficient of variation
    * Interquartile range
    * Quartile coefficient of dispersion

7. Scale the data created in exercise #4 using the following strategies:
    * Min-max scaling (normalizing)
    * Standardizing

8. Using the scaled data from exercise #7, calculate the following:
    * Covariance between the standardized and normalized data
    * Pearson correlation coefficient between the standardized and normalized data (this is actually 1, but due to rounding along the way, the result will be slightly less)

Further reading

The following are some resources that you can use to become more familiar with Jupyter:

- *Jupyter Notebook Basics:* https://nbviewer.jupyter.org/github/jupyter/notebook/blob/master/docs/source/examples/Notebook/Notebook%20Basics.ipynb
- *JupyterLab introduction*: https://blog.jupyter.org/jupyterlab-is-ready-for-users-5a6f039b8906
- *Learning Markdown to make your Jupyter Notebooks presentation-ready*: https://medium.com/ibm-data-science-experience/markdown-for-jupyter-notebooks-cheatsheet-386c05aeebed
- *28 Jupyter Notebook Tips, Tricks, and Shortcuts*: https://www.dataquest.io/blog/jupyter-notebook-tips-tricks-shortcuts/

The following resource shows you how to use conda to manage virtual environments instead of the venv solution that was explained earlier in this chapter:

- *Managing virtual environments with Conda*: https://medium.freecodecamp.org/why-you-need-python-environments-and-how-to-manage-them-with-conda-85f155f4353c

Some books on web scraping in Python and designing data visualizations for readability are as follows:

- *Information Dashboard Design: Displaying Data for At-a-Glance Monitoring, Second Edition by Stephen Few*: https://www.amazon.com/Information-Dashboard-Design-At-Glance/dp/1938377001/
- *Web Scraping with Python: Collecting More Data from the Modern Web, 2nd Edition by Ryan Mitchell*: https://www.amazon.com/Web-Scraping-Python-Collecting-Modern/dp/1491985577

Some resources for learning more advanced concepts of statistics (that we won't cover here) and carefully applying them are as follows:

- *A Gentle Introduction to Normality Tests in Python*: `https:// machinelearningmastery.com/a-gentle-introduction-to-normality- tests-in-python/`
- *How Hypothesis Tests Work: Confidence Intervals and Confidence Levels*: `https://statisticsbyjim.com/hypothesis-testing/hypothesis- tests-confidence-intervals-levels/`
- *Intro to Inferential Statistics (Making Predictions with Data) on Udacity:* `https://www.udacity.com/course/intro-to-inferential- statistics--ud201`
- *Penn State elementary statistics lesson 4 confidence intervals*: `https:// newonlinecourses.science.psu.edu/stat200/lesson/4`
- *Seeing Theory: A visual introduction to probability and statistics*: `https:// seeing-theory.brown.edu/index.html`
- *Statistics Done Wrong: The Woefully Complete Guide by Alex Reinhart*: `https:/ /www.amazon.com/Statistics-Done-Wrong-Woefully-Complete/dp/ 1593276206`
- *Survey Sampling Methods:* `https://stattrek.com/survey-research/ sampling-methods.aspx`

2
Working with Pandas DataFrames

The time has come for us to begin our journey into the pandas universe. We will start this chapter with an introduction to the main **data structures** we will encounter when working with pandas. Data structures provide a format for organizing, managing, and storing data. Knowledge of pandas data structures will prove infinitely helpful when it comes to troubleshooting or looking up how to perform a certain operation on the data. Keep in mind that these data structures are different for a reason: they were created for specific analysis tasks; we must remember that a given method may only work on a certain data structure, so we need to be able to identify the best structure for the problem we are looking to solve.

Next, we will bring our first dataset into Python. We will learn how to get data from an API, create dataframes from other data structures in Python, read in files, and interact with databases. Initially, we may wonder why we would ever need to create dataframes from other Python data structures; however, if we ever want to test something quickly, create our own data, pull data from an API, or repurpose Python code from another project, then we will find this knowledge indispensable. Finally, we will master ways to inspect, describe, filter, and summarize our data.

This chapter will get us comfortable working with some of the basic, yet powerful, operations we will be performing when conducting our data analyses with pandas.

The following topics will be covered in this chapter:

- Learning about the main `pandas` data structures
- Creating dataframes from files, API requests, SQL queries, and other Python objects
- Inspecting dataframes and calculating summary statistics
- Grabbing subsets from dataframes by selection, slicing, indexing, and filtering
- Adding and removing columns and rows

Chapter materials

The files we will be working with for this chapter can be found in the GitHub repository at `https://github.com/stefmolin/Hands-On-Data-Analysis-with-Pandas/tree/master/ch_02`. We will be working with earthquake data from the **US Geological Survey (USGS)** by using the USGS API and CSV files, which can be found in the `data/` directory.

There are four CSV files and a SQLite database file in the `data/` directory, which will be used at different points throughout this chapter. The `earthquakes.csv` file contains data that's been pulled from the USGS API for September 18, 2018 through October 13, 2018. For our discussion of data structures, we will work with the `example_data.csv` file, which contains five rows from `earthquakes.csv` for a few columns. The `tsunamis.csv` file is a subset of this data for all earthquakes that also had tsunamis during the aforementioned date range. The `quakes.db` file contains a SQLite database with a single table for the tsunamis data. We will use this to learn how to read from and write to a database with `pandas`. Lastly, the `parsed.csv` file will be used for the end of chapter exercises, and we will also walk through the creation of it during this chapter.

This chapter has been divided into six Jupyter Notebooks, which are numbered in the order they are to be used. They contain the code snippets we will run throughout the chapter, along with the full output of any command that has to be trimmed for this text. Each time we are to switch notebooks, the text will let us know.

We will start with `1-pandas_data_structures.ipynb` to learn the basic `pandas` data structures. Then, we will move on to `2-creating_dataframes.ipynb` as we discuss the various ways to bring data into `pandas`. Our discussion on this topic will continue in `3-making_dataframes_from_api_requests.ipynb`, where we will explore the USGS API to gather data for use with `pandas`. After learning about how we can collect our data, we will move on to `4-inspecting_dataframes.ipynb` as we begin to learn how to conduct **exploratory data analysis** (**EDA**) with `pandas`. In the following notebook, `5-selection.ipynb`, we will discuss various ways to select and filter data. Finally, we will move to `6-adding_and_removing_data.ipynb`, where we will learn how to add and remove parts of our data.

Pandas data structures

Python has several data structures already, such as tuples, lists, and dictionaries. Pandas provides two main structures to facilitate working with data: `Series` and `DataFrame`. The `Series` and `DataFrame` data structures each contain another `pandas` data structure, which is very important to be aware of: `Index`. However, in order to understand the `pandas` data structures, we need to take a look at NumPy, which provides the n-dimensional arrays that `pandas` builds upon.

 For the remainder of this book, we will refer to `DataFrame` objects as dataframes, `Series` objects as series, and `Index` objects as index, unless we are referring to the class itself.

The aforementioned data structures are created as Python **classes**; when we actually create one, they are referred to as **objects** or **instances**. This is an important distinction, since, as we will see, some actions can be performed using the object itself (a **method**), whereas others will require that we pass our object in as an argument to some **function**.

We use a `pandas` function to read a CSV file into an object of the `DataFrame` class, but we use methods on our `DataFrame` objects to perform actions on them, such as dropping columns or calculating summary statistics. With `pandas`, we will often want to access the **attributes** of the object we are working with. This won't generate action as a method or function would; rather, we will be given information about our `pandas` object, such as dimensions, column names, data types, and whether it is empty.

Class names in Python are traditionally written in CapWords. We can use this to help us distinguish an object from a class. Say we are reading someone's code and see a variable called `dataframe`. We know that `pandas` adheres to the CapWords convention and that the class is `DataFrame`. Therefore, we can assume that the variable is an instance of the `DataFrame` class.

For this section, we will work in the `1-pandas_data_structures.ipynb` notebook. To begin, we will import `numpy` and use it to read in the `example_data.csv` file into a `numpy.array`. The data comes from the **US Geological Survey (USGS)** API for earthquakes (source: `https://earthquake.usgs.gov/fdsnws/event/1/`). Note that this is the only time we will use `numpy` to read in a file, and it is just for illustrative purposes only; the important part is to look at the way the data is represented when using `numpy`:

```
>>> import numpy as np

>>> data = np.genfromtxt(
...     'data/example_data.csv', delimiter=';',
...     names=True, dtype=None, encoding='UTF'
... )

>>> data
array([('2018-10-13 11:10:23.560', '262km NW of Ozernovskiy, Russia',
        'mww', 6.7, 'green', 1),
       ('2018-10-13 04:34:15.580', '25km E of Bitung, Indonesia',
        'mww', 5.2, 'green', 0),
       ('2018-10-13 00:13:46.220', '42km WNW of Sola, Vanuatu',
        'mww', 5.7, 'green', 0),
       ('2018-10-12 21:09:49.240',
        '13km E of Nueva Concepcion, Guatemala', 'mww', 5.7, 'green',
        0),
       ('2018-10-12 02:52:03.620',
        '128km SE of Kimbe, Papua New Guinea', 'mww', 5.6, 'green',
        1)],
      dtype=[('time', '<U23'), ('place', '<U37'), ('magType', '<U3'),
             ('mag', '<f8'), ('alert', '<U5'), ('tsunami', '<i4')])
```

We now have our data in a NumPy array. Using the `shape` and `dtype` attributes, we can get information on the dimensions of the array and the data types it contains, respectively:

```
>>> data.shape
(5,)
>>> data.dtype
dtype([('time', '<U23'), ('place', '<U37'), ('magType', '<U3'),
       ('mag', '<f8'), ('alert', '<U5'), ('tsunami', '<i4')])
```

Each of the entries in the array is a row from the CSV file. NumPy arrays contain a single data type (unlike lists, which allow mixed types); this allows for fast, vectorized operations. When we read in the data, we get an array of `numpy.void` objects, which are created to store flexible types. This is because NumPy has to store several different data types per row: four strings, a float, and an integer. This means that we can't take advantage of the performance improvements NumPy provides for single data type objects.

Say we want to find the maximum magnitude—we can use a **list comprehension** (`https://www.python.org/dev/peps/pep-0202/`) to select the third index of each row, which is represented as a `numpy.void` object. This makes a list, meaning that we can take the maximum using the `max()` function. We can use the `%%timeit` **magic command** from IPython (a special command preceded by `%`) to see how long this implementation takes (times will vary):

```
>>> %%timeit
>>> max([row[3] for row in data])
9.74 µs ± 177 ns per loop
(mean ± std. dev. of 7 runs, 100000 loops each)
```

 IPython (`https://ipython.readthedocs.io/en/stable/index.html`) provides an interactive shell for Python. Jupyter Notebooks are built on top of IPython. While knowledge of IPython is not required for this book, it can be helpful to be familiar with some of the functionality. IPython includes a tutorial in their documentation: `https://ipython.readthedocs.io/en/stable/interactive/`.

If we create a NumPy array for each column instead, this operation is much easier (and more efficient) to perform. To do so, we will make a dictionary where the keys are the column names and the values are NumPy arrays of the data. Again, the important part here is how the data is now represented using NumPy:

```
>>> array_dict = {}
>>> for i, col in enumerate(data.dtype.names):
...     array_dict[col] = np.array([row[i] for row in data])

>>> array_dict
{'time': array(['2018-10-13 11:10:23.560', '2018-10-13 04:34:15.580',
        '2018-10-13 00:13:46.220', '2018-10-12 21:09:49.240',
        '2018-10-12 02:52:03.620'], dtype='<U23'),
 'place': array(['262km NW of Ozernovskiy, Russia',
        '25km E of Bitung, Indonesia',
        '42km WNW of Sola, Vanuatu',
        '13km E of Nueva Concepcion, Guatemala',
        '128km SE of Kimbe, Papua New Guinea'], dtype='<U37'),
 'magType': array(['mww', 'mww', 'mww', 'mww', 'mww'], dtype='<U3'),
 'mag': array([6.7, 5.2, 5.7, 5.7, 5.6]),
 'alert': array(['green', 'green', 'green', 'green', 'green'],
        dtype='<U5'),
 'tsunami': array([1, 0, 0, 0, 1])}
```

We should use a list comprehension whenever we would write a `for` loop with just a single line under it, or want to run an operation against the members of some initial list. This is a rather simple list comprehension, but we can also add `if...else` statements to these. List comprehensions are an extremely powerful tool to have in our arsenal. More information can be found in the Python documentation: https://docs.python.org/3/tutorial/datastructures.html#list-comprehensions.

Grabbing the maximum magnitude is now simply a matter of selecting the `mag` key and calling the `max()` method on the NumPy array. This is nearly twice as fast as the list comprehension implementation, when dealing with just five entries—imagine how much worse the first attempt will perform on large datasets:

```
>>> %%timeit
>>> array_dict['mag'].max()
5.22 µs ± 100 ns per loop
(mean ± std. dev. of 7 runs, 100000 loops each)
```

However, this representation has other issues. Say we wanted to grab all the information for the earthquake with the maximum magnitude; how would we go about that? We need to find the index of the maximum, and then for each of the keys in the dictionary, grab that index. The result is now a NumPy array of strings (our numeric values were converted), and we are now in the format that we saw earlier:

```
>>> np.array([
...     value[array_dict['mag'].argmax()] \
...     for key, value in array_dict.items()
... ])
array(['2018-10-13 11:10:23.560', '262km NW of Ozernovskiy, Russia',
        'mww', '6.7', 'green', '1'], dtype='<U31')
```

Consider how we would go about sorting the data by magnitude from smallest to largest. In the first representation, we would have to sort the rows by examining the third index. With the second representation, we would have to determine the order for the indices from the mag column, and then sort all the other arrays with those same indices. Clearly, working with several NumPy arrays of different data types at once is a bit cumbersome.

Series

The pandas.Series class provides a data structure for arrays of data of a single type, just like the NumPy array. However, it comes with some additional functionality. This one-dimensional representation can be thought of as a column in a spreadsheet. We have a name for our column, and the data we hold in it is of the same type (since we are measuring the same variable):

```
>>> import pandas as pd

>>> place = pd.Series(array_dict['place'], name='place')
>>> place
0           262km NW of Ozernovskiy, Russia
1                 25km E of Bitung, Indonesia
2                  42km WNW of Sola, Vanuatu
3     13km E of Nueva Concepcion, Guatemala
4       128km SE of Kimbe, Papua New Guinea
Name: place, dtype: object
```

Note the numbers on the left of the result; these correspond to the row number in the original dataset (offset by 1 due to starting at 0). These row numbers form the Index object, which we will discuss in the following section. Next to the row numbers, we have the actual value of the row, which, in this example, is a string representing the place the earthquake occurred. Notice that we have dtype: object next to the name of the place Series object; this is telling us that the data type of the Series is object. A string will be classified as object in pandas.

To access attributes of the Series object, we use attribute notation of the form `<Series_object>.<attribute_name>`. The following are some common attributes we will access. Notice that dtype and shape are available just like what we saw with the NumPy array:

Attribute	Returns
name	The name of the Series object
dtype	The data type of the Series object
shape	Dimensions of the Series object in a tuple of the form (number of rows,)
index	The Index object that is part of the Series object
values	The data in the Series object as a NumPy array

The pandas documentation on Series (https://pandas.pydata.org/pandas-docs/stable/generated/pandas.Series.html) contains more information on how to create a Series object, as well as the actions we can perform on it and a link to the source code.

Index

The addition of the Index class makes the Series class significantly more powerful than a NumPy array. The Index class gives us row labels, which enable selection by row; depending on the type of Index, we can provide a row number, a date, or even a string to select our row. It plays a key role in identifying entries in the data and is used for a multitude of operations in pandas, as we will see throughout this book. We access the Index object through the index attribute:

```
>>> place_index = place.index
>>> place_index
RangeIndex(start=0, stop=5, step=1)
```

Note that this is a `RangeIndex` starting at index 0, with the last index at 4. The `step` of 1 indicates that the indices are each 1 apart, meaning that we have all the integers in that range. The default index is the `RangeIndex`; however, we can change the index, which will discuss in `Chapter 3`, *Data Wrangling with Pandas*. Often, we will either work with an `Index` object of row numbers or date(time)s.

The index is built on top of a NumPy array as well:

```
>>> place_index.values
array([0, 1, 2, 3, 4], dtype=int64)
```

Some useful attributes that are available on `Index` objects include the following:

Attribute	Returns
name	The name of the `Index` object
dtype	The data type of the `Index` object
shape	Dimensions of the `Index` object
values	The data in the `Index` object as a NumPy array
is_unique	Check if the `Index` object has all unique values

Both NumPy and `pandas` support arithmetic operations, which will be performed element-wise. NumPy will use the position in the array for this:

```
>>> np.array([1, 1, 1]) + np.array([-1, 0, 1])
array([0, 1, 2])
```

With `pandas`, this element-wise arithmetic is performed on matching values of the index. If we add a `Series` object with a `RangeIndex` from 0 to 4 and another from 1 to 5, we will only get results were the indices align (1 through 4). In `Chapter 3`, *Data Wrangling with Pandas*, we will discuss some ways to change and align the index in order to be able to perform these types of operations without losing data:

```
>>> pd.Series(np.linspace(0, 10, num=5))\
... + pd.Series(
...      np.linspace(0, 10, num=5), index=pd.Index([1, 2, 3, 4, 5])
... )
0     NaN
1     2.5
2     7.5
3    12.5
4    17.5
5     NaN
dtype: float64
```

More information on the `Index` class can be found in the `pandas` documentation at `https://pandas.pydata.org/pandas-docs/stable/generated/pandas.Index.html`.

DataFrame

With the `Series` class, we essentially had columns of a spreadsheet, with the data all being of the same type. The `DataFrame` class builds upon the `Series` class; we can think of it as representing the spreadsheet as a whole. It can have many columns, each with its own data type. We can turn either of the NumPy representations we built of the example data into a `DataFrame` object:

```
>>> df = pd.DataFrame(array_dict)
>>> df
```

This gives us a dataframe of six series. Note the column before the `time` column; this is the `Index` object for the rows. When creating a `DataFrame` object, `pandas` aligns all the series to the same index. In this case, it is just the row number, but we could easily use the `time` column for this, which would enable some additional `pandas` features, as we will see in Chapter 3, *Data Wrangling with Pandas*:

	time	place	magType	mag	alert	tsunami
0	2018-10-13 11:10:23.560	262km NW of Ozernovskiy, Russia	mww	6.7	green	1
1	2018-10-13 04:34:15.580	25km E of Bitung, Indonesia	mww	5.2	green	0
2	2018-10-13 00:13:46.220	42km WNW of Sola, Vanuatu	mww	5.7	green	0
3	2018-10-12 21:09:49.240	13km E of Nueva Concepcion, Guatemala	mww	5.7	green	0
4	2018-10-12 02:52:03.620	128km SE of Kimbe, Papua New Guinea	mww	5.6	green	1

Our columns each have a single data type, but they don't all share the same data type:

```
>>> df.dtypes
time          object
place         object
magType       object
mag          float64
alert         object
tsunami        int32
dtype: object
```

The values of the dataframe look very similar to the initial NumPy representation we had:

```
>>> df.values
array([['2018-10-13 11:10:23.560', '262km NW of Ozernovskiy, Russia',
        'mww', 6.7, 'green', 1],
       ['2018-10-13 04:34:15.580', '25km E of Bitung, Indonesia',
        'mww', 5.2, 'green', 0],
       ['2018-10-13 00:13:46.220', '42km WNW of Sola, Vanuatu', 'mww',
        5.7, 'green', 0],
       ['2018-10-12 21:09:49.240', '13km E of Nueva Concepcion,
        Guatemala', 'mww', 5.7, 'green', 0],
       ['2018-10-12 02:52:03.620','128 km SE of Kimbe,
        Papua New Guinea', 'mww', 5.6, 'green', 1]], dtype=object)
```

The column names are actually an `Index` object as well:

```
>>> df.columns
Index(['time', 'place', 'magType', 'mag', 'alert', 'tsunami'],
      dtype='object')
```

The following are some common attributes we will access:

Attribute	Returns
`dtypes`	The data types of each column
`shape`	Dimensions of the `DataFrame` object in a tuple of the form `(number of rows, number of columns)`
`index`	The `Index` object that is part of the `DataFrame` object
`columns`	The names of the columns (as an `Index` object)
`values`	The values in the `DataFrame` object as a NumPy array

Note that we can also perform arithmetic on dataframes, but the results may seem a little strange, depending on what kind of data we have:

```
>>> df + df
```

Pandas will only perform the operation when both the index and column match. Here, since + with strings means concatenation, `pandas` concatenated the `time`, `place`, `magType`, and `alert` columns across dataframes. The `mag` and `tsunami` columns were summed:

	time	place	magType	mag	alert	tsunami
0	2018-10-13 11:10:23.5602018-10-13 11:10:23.560	262km NW of Ozernovskiy, Russia262km NW of Oze...	mwwmww	13.4	greengreen	2
1	2018-10-13 04:34:15.5802018-10-13 04:34:15.580	25km E of Bitung, Indonesia25km E of ...	mwwmww	10.4	greengreen	0
2	2018-10-13 00:13:46.2202018-10-13 00:13:46.220	42km WNW of Sola, Vanuatu42km WNW of ...	mwwmww	11.4	greengreen	0
3	2018-10-12 21:09:49.2402018-10-12 21:09:49.240	13km E of Nueva Concepcion, Guatemala ...	mwwmww	11.4	greengreen	0
4	2018-10-12 02:52:03.6202018-10-12 02:52:03.620	128km SE of Kimbe, Papua New Guinea ...	mwwmww	11.2	greengreen	2

You can find more information on creating `DataFrame` objects and all the operations that can be performed directly on them in the official documentation at `https://pandas.pydata.org/pandas-docs/stable/generated/pandas.DataFrame.html`.

Bringing data into a pandas DataFrame

Now that we understand the data structures we will be working with, we can focus on different ways we can create them. To do so, let's turn to the next notebook, `2-creating_dataframes.ipynb`, and import the packages we will need for the upcoming examples. We will be using `datetime` from the Python standard library, along with the third-party packages `numpy` and `pandas`. We are only aliasing `numpy` and `pandas`, but feel free to alias `datetime` if you are accustomed to doing so:

```
>>> import datetime
>>> import numpy as np
>>> import pandas as pd
```

 This allows us to use the `pandas` package by referring to it with the alias we assign to be `pd`, which is the common way to import it. In fact, we can only refer to it as `pd`, since that is what we imported into the namespace. Packages need to be imported before we can use them; installation puts the files we need on our computer, but, in the interest of memory, Python won't load every installed package when we start it up—just the ones we tell it to.

Before we dive into the code, it's important to know how to get help right from Python. Should we ever find ourselves unsure of how to use something in Python, we can utilize the built-in `help()` function. We simply run `help()`, passing in the package, module, class, object, method, or function that we want to read the documentation on. We can, of course, look up the documentation online; however, in most cases, **docstrings** (the documentation text written in the code) that's returned with `help()` will be equivalent to this since they are used to generate the documentation.

Assuming we aliased `pandas` as `pd` when we imported it, we can run `help(pd)` to see information on the `pandas` package; `help(pd.DataFrame)` for all the methods and attributes of a dataframe (note we can also pass in an already created `DataFrame` object instead); and `help(pd.read_csv)` to learn more about the `pandas` function for reading CSV files into Python and how to use it. We can also try `dir()` and `<item>.__dict__`, which will give us a list or dictionary of what's available, respectively; these might not be as useful as the `help()` function, though.

Additionally, we can use `?` and `??` to get help thanks to IPython, which is part of what makes Jupyter Notebooks so powerful. Unlike the `help()` function, we can use question marks by putting them after whatever we want to know more about, as if we were asking Python a question; for example, `pd.read_csv?` and `pd.read_csv??`. These three will yield slightly different outputs: `help()` ;will give us the docstring; `?` will give the docstring, plus some additional information depending on what we are inquiring about; and `??` will give us even more information, and if possible, the source code behind it.

From a Python object

Before we cover all the ways we can turn a Python object into a `DataFrame`, we should see how to make a `Series` object. Remember that a `Series` object is essentially a column of our `DataFrame` object, so, once we know this, it should be easy to guess how to create a `DataFrame` object. Say that we wanted to create a `Series` of five random numbers between 0 and 1. We could use `numpy` to generate an array of the random numbers and create the `Series` from that.

To ensure that the result is reproducible, we will set the seed here. The **seed** gives a starting point for the generation of pseudorandom numbers. No algorithms for random number generation are truly random—they are deterministic, and therefore, by setting this starting point, the numbers generated will be the same each time the code is run. This is good for testing things, but not for simulation (where we want randomness), which we will look at in Chapter 8, *Rule-Based Anomaly Detection*:

```
>>> np.random.seed(0) # set a seed for reproducibility
>>> pd.Series(np.random.rand(5), name='random'))
0    0.548814
1    0.715189
2    0.602763
3    0.544883
4    0.423655
Name: random, dtype: float64
```

NumPy makes it very easy to generate these numerical columns. Aside from generating random numbers, we can use it to get evenly-spaced numbers in a certain range with `np.linspace()`; obtain a range of integers with `np.arange()`; sample from the standard normal with `np.random.normal()`; and easily create arrays of all zeros with `np.zeros()` and all ones with `np.ones()`.

We can make a `Series` object with any list-like structure (such as NumPy arrays) by passing it to `pd.Series()`. Making a `DataFrame` object is an extension of making a `Series` object; our dataframe will be composed of one or more series, and each will be distinctly named. This should remind us of dictionary-like structures in Python: the keys are the column names, and the values are the content of the columns.

In the case were we want to turn a single `Series` object into a `DataFrame` object, we can use its `to_frame()` method. Check out the Jupyter Notebook for this section to view an example.

Since `DataFrame` columns can all be different data types, let's get a little fancy with this example. We are going to create a `DataFrame` object of three columns, with five observations each:

- `random`: Five random numbers between 0 and 1 as a NumPy array
- `text`: A list of five strings or `None`
- `truth`: A list of five random Booleans

We will also create a `DatetimeIndex` object with the `pd.date_range()` function. The index will be five dates (`periods`), all one day apart (`freq='1D'`), ending with April 21, 2019 (`end`), and be called `date`.

More information on the values the `pd.date_range()` function accepts for frequencies can be found at `https://pandas.pydata.org/pandas-docs/stable/user_guide/timeseries.html#offset-aliases`.

All we have to do is package the columns in a dictionary using the desired column names as the keys and pass this to `pd.DataFrame()`.

The index gets passed as the `index` argument:

```
>>> np.random.seed(0) # set seed so result reproducible
>>> pd.DataFrame(
...     {
...         'random': np.random.rand(5),
...         'text': ['hot', 'warm', 'cool', 'cold', None],
...         'truth': [np.random.choice([True, False])
...                   for _ in range(5)]
...     },
...     index=pd.date_range(
...         end=datetime.date(2019, 4, 21),
...         freq='1D',
...         periods=5,
...         name='date'
...     )
... )
```

 By convention, we use _ to hold variables in a loop that we don't care about. Here, we use `range()` as a counter, and its values are unimportant. More information on the roles _ plays in Python can be found here: `https://hackernoon.com/understanding-the-underscore-of-python-309d1a029edc`.

Having dates in the index makes it easy to select entries by date (or even in a date range), as we will see in Chapter 3, *Data Wrangling with Pandas*:

	random	text	truth
date			
2019-04-17	0.548814	hot	False
2019-04-18	0.715189	warm	True
2019-04-19	0.602763	cool	True
2019-04-20	0.544883	cold	False
2019-04-21	0.423655	None	True

In cases where the data isn't a dictionary, but rather a list of dictionaries, we can still use pd.DataFrame(). Data in this format is what we would expect from consuming an API. Each entry in the list will be a dictionary, where the keys are the column names and the values are the values for that column at that index:

```
>>> pd.DataFrame([
...     {'mag' : 5.2, 'place' : 'California'},
...     {'mag' : 1.2, 'place' : 'Alaska'},
...     {'mag' : 0.2, 'place' : 'California'},
... ])
```

This gives us a dataframe of three rows (one for each entry in the list), with two columns (one for each key in the dictionaries):

	mag	place
0	5.2	California
1	1.2	Alaska
2	0.2	California

In fact, pd.DataFrame() also works for lists of tuples. Note that we can also pass in the column names as a list through the columns argument, as well:

```
>>> list_of_tuples = [(n, n**2, n**3) for n in range(5)]
>>> list_of_tuples
[(0, 0, 0), (1, 1, 1), (2, 4, 8), (3, 9, 27), (4, 16, 64)]
>>> pd.DataFrame(
...     list_of_tuples, columns=['n', 'n_squared', 'n_cubed']
... )
```

Each tuple is treated like a record and becomes a row in the dataframe:

	n	n_squared	n_cubed
0	0	0	0
1	1	1	1
2	2	4	8
3	3	9	27
4	4	16	64

We also have the option of using `pd.DataFrame()` with NumPy arrays:

```
>>> pd.DataFrame(
...     array([
...         [0, 0, 0],
...         [1, 1, 1],
...         [2, 4, 8],
...         [3, 9, 27],
...         [4, 16, 64]
...     ]), columns=['n', 'n_squared', 'n_cubed']
... )
```

This will have the effect of stacking each entry in the array as rows in a dataframe:

	n	n_squared	n_cubed
0	0	0	0
1	1	1	1
2	2	4	8
3	3	9	27
4	4	16	64

From a file

The data we want to analyze will most often come from outside Python. In many cases, we may have a **data dump** from a database or website and have to bring it into Python to sift through it. A data dump gets its name from containing a large amount of data (possibly at a very granular level) and often not discriminating against any of it initially; for this reason, they can often be unwieldy.

Often, these data dumps will come in the form of a text file (`.txt`) or a CSV file (`.csv`). Pandas provides many methods to read in different types of files, so it is simply a matter of looking up the one that matches our file format. Our earthquake data is a CSV file; therefore, we use the `pd.read_csv()` function to read it in. However, we should always do some initial inspection of the file before attempting to read it in; this will inform us whether we need to pass additional arguments, such as `sep` to specify the delimiter or `names` to provide the column names ourselves in the absence of a header row in the file.

We can perform our due diligence directly in our Jupyter Notebook thanks to IPython, provided we prefix our commands with ! to indicate they are to be run as shell commands. First, we should check how big the file is, both in terms of lines and in terms of bytes. To check the number of lines, we use the wc utility (word count) with the -l flag to count the number of lines:

```
>>> !wc -l data/earthquakes.csv
9333 data/earthquakes.csv
```

We have 9,333 rows in the file. Now, let's check the file size. For this task, we will use ls on the data directory. This will tell us the list of files in that directory. We add the -lh flag to get information about the files in a human-readable format. Finally, we send this output to the grep utility, which will help us isolate the files we want. This tells us that the data/earthquakes.csv file is 3.4 MB:

```
>>> !ls -lh data | grep earthquakes.csv
-rw-r--r-- 1 Stefanie 4096 3.4M Mar  7 13:19 earthquakes.csv
```

Note that IPython also lets us capture the result of the command in a Python variable, so if we aren't comfortable with pipes (|) or grep, we can do the following:

```
>>> files = !ls -lh data
>>> [file for file in files if 'earthquake' in file]
['-rw-r--r-- 1 Stefanie 4096 3.4M Mar  7 13:19 earthquakes.csv']
```

Now, let's take a look at the top few rows to see if the file comes with headers. We will use the head utility and specify the number of rows with the -n flag. This tells us that the first row contains the headers for the data and that the data is delimited with commas (just because the file has the .csv extension doesn't mean it is comma-delimited):

```
>>> !head -n 2 data/earthquakes.csv
alert,cdi,code,detail,dmin,felt,gap,ids,mag,magType,mmi,net,nst,place,
rms,sig,sources,status,time,title,tsunami,type,types,tz,updated,url

,,37389218,https://earthquake.usgs.gov/fdsnws/event/1/query?eventid=ci
37389218&format=geojson,0.008693,,85.0,",ci37389218,",1.35,ml,,ci,26.0
,"9km NE of Aguanga, CA",0.19,28,",ci,",automatic,1539475168010,"M 1.4
- 9km NE of Aguanga, CA",0,earthquake,",geoserve,nearby-
cities,origin,phase-data,",-480.0,1539475395144,
https://earthquake.usgs.gov/earthquakes/eventpage/ci37389218
```

We can check the bottom rows to make sure there is no extraneous data that we will need to ignore by using the `tail` utility. This file is fine, so the result won't be reproduced here; however, the notebook contains the result.

Lastly, we may be interested in seeing the column count in our data. While we could just count the fields in the first row of the result of `head`, we have the option of using the `awk` utility (for pattern scanning and processing) to count our columns. The `-F` flag allows us to specify the delimiter (comma, in this case). Then, we specify what to do for each record in the file. We choose to print `NF`, which is a predefined variable whose value is the number of fields in the current record. Here, we say `exit` immediately after the print so that we print the number of fields in the first row of the file; then, we stop. This will look a little complicated, but by no means is this something we need to memorize:

```
>>> !awk -F',' '{print NF; exit}' data/earthquakes.csv
26
```

Since we know that the first line of the file has headers and that the file is comma-separated, we can also count the columns by using `head` to get the headers, and then parsing them in Python:

```
>>> headers = !head -n 1 data/earthquakes.csv
>>> len(headers[0].split(','))
26
```

The ability to run shell commands directly from our Jupyter Notebook dramatically streamlines our workflow. However, if we don't have past experience with the command line, it may be complicated at first to learn these commands. IPython has some helpful information on running shell commands in their documentation at https://ipython.readthedocs.io/en/stable/interactive/reference.html#system-shell-access.

We have 26 columns and 9,333 rows, with the first one being the header. The file is 3.4 MB and is comma-delimited. This means that we can use `pd.read_csv()` with the defaults:

```
>>> df = pd.read_csv('earthquakes.csv')
```

We aren't limited to reading in data from files on our local machines; file paths can be URLs as well.

Pandas is usually very good at figuring out which options to use based on the input data, so we often won't need to add arguments to this call; however, there are many options available should we need them, some of which include the following:

Parameter	Purpose
sep	Specifies the delimiter
header	Row number where the column names are located; the default option has pandas infer whether they are present
names	List of column names to use as the header
index_col	Column to use as the index
usecols	Specifies which columns to read in
dtype	Specifies data types for the columns
converters	Specifies functions for converting data into certain columns
skiprows	Rows to skip
nrows	Amount of rows to read at a time (combine with skiprows to read a file bit by bit)
parse_dates	Automatically parse columns containing dates into datetime objects
chunksize	For reading the file in chunks
compression	For reading in compressed files without extracting beforehand
encoding	Specifies the file encoding

 We can use the read_excel() function for Excel files, the read_json() function for **JSON (JavaScript Object Notation)** files, and for other delimited files, such as tab (\t), we can use the read_csv() function with the sep argument equal to the delimiter.

It would be remiss if we didn't also learn how to save our dataframe to a file to share with others. Here, we have to be careful; if our dataframe's index is just row numbers, we probably don't want to write that to our file (it will have no meaning to consumers of the data), but it is the default:

```
>>> df.to_csv('output.csv', index=False)
```

As with reading from files, `Series` and `DataFrames` have methods to write data to Excel (`to_excel()`) and JSON files (`to_json()`). Note that, while we use functions from `pandas` to read our data in, we must use methods to write our data; the reading functions create the `pandas` objects that we want to work with, but the writing methods are actions that we take using the `pandas` object.

The preceding file paths to read from and write to were **relative** to our **current directory**. The current directory is where we are running our code from. An **absolute** path will be the full path to the file. For example, if the file we want to work with has an absolute path of `C:\Users\Stefanie\hands_on_pandas\data.csv` and our current directory is `C:\Users\Stefanie\hands_on_pandas`, then we can simply use the relative path of `data.csv` as the file path.

From a database

Pandas provides capabilities to read and write from many other data sources, including databases. Without installing any additional packages, `pandas` can interact with SQLite databases; the SQLAlchemy package needs to be installed in order to interact with other database flavors. This interaction can be achieved by opening a connection to the database using the `sqlite3` module in the Python standard library and then using either the `pd.read_sql()` function to query the database or the `to_sql()` method on a `DataFrame` object to write to the database.

Before we read from a database, let's write to one. We simply call `to_sql()` on our dataframe, telling it which table to write to, which database connection to use, and how to handle if the table already exists. There is already a SQLite database (`data/quakes.db`) in the folder for this chapter in this book's GitHub repository. Let's write the tsunami data from the `data/tsunamis.csv` file to a table in the database called `tsunamis`, replacing the table if it already exists:

```
>>> import sqlite3

>>> with sqlite3.connect('data/quakes.db') as connection:
...     pd.read_csv('data/tsunamis.csv').to_sql(
...         'tsunamis', connection, index=False, if_exists='replace'
...     )
```

To create a new database, we can change `'data/quakes.db'` to the path to save the new database file at.

Querying the database is just as easy as writing to it. Note this will require knowledge of **Structured Query Language** (**SQL**). While it's not required for this book, we will use some simple SQL statements to illustrate certain concepts. See the *Further reading* section for a resource on how `pandas` compares to SQL and `Chapter 4`, *Aggregating Pandas DataFrames*, for some examples of how `pandas` actions relate to SQL statements.

Let's query our database for the full `tsunamis` table. When we write a SQL query, we first state the columns that we want to select, which in our case is all of them, so we write `"SELECT *"`. Next, we state the table to select the data from, which for us is `tsunamis`, so we add `"FROM tsunamis"`. This is our full query now (of course, it can get much more complicated than this).

To actually query the database, we use the `pd.read_sql()` function, passing in our query and the database connection:

```
>>> import sqlite3

>>> with sqlite3.connect('data/quakes.db') as connection:
...     tsunamis = pd.read_sql('SELECT * FROM tsunamis', connection)

>>> tsunamis.head()
```

The `connection` object is an example of a **context manager**, which, when used with the `with` statement, automatically handles cleanup after the code in the block executes (closing the connection in this case). This makes cleanup easy and makes sure we don't leave any loose ends. We will discuss these concepts in more depth in the *Exploring the data* section of `Chapter 11`, *Machine Learning Anomaly Detection*.

We now have the `tsunamis` data in a `DataFrame` object:

	alert	type	title	place	magType	mag	time
0	None	earthquake	M 5.0 - 165km NNW of Flying Fish Cove, Christm...	165km NNW of Flying Fish Cove, Christmas Island	mww	5.0	1539459504090
1	green	earthquake	M 6.7 - 262km NW of Ozernovskiy, Russia	262km NW of Ozernovskiy, Russia	mww	6.7	1539429023560
2	green	earthquake	M 5.6 - 128km SE of Kimbe, Papua New Guinea	128km SE of Kimbe, Papua New Guinea	mww	5.6	1539312723620
3	green	earthquake	M 6.5 - 148km S of Severo-Kuril'sk, Russia	148km S of Severo-Kuril'sk, Russia	mww	6.5	1539213362130
4	green	earthquake	M 6.2 - 94km SW of Kokopo, Papua New Guinea	94km SW of Kokopo, Papua New Guinea	mww	6.2	1539208835130

Check out the following resource on the `pandas` documentation for more ways to read in data: https://pandas.pydata.org/pandas-docs/stable/user_guide/io.html.

From an API

We can now easily create `Series` and `DataFrames` from data we have in Python or from files we are given, but how can we get data from online resources? Each data source is not guaranteed to give us data in the same format, so we have to remain flexible in our approach and be comfortable examining the data source to find the appropriate import method. Let's request some earthquake data from the USGS API and see how we can make a dataframe out of the result.

For this section, we will use `3-making_dataframes_from_api_requests.ipynb`, so we have to import the packages we need once again. As with the previous notebook, we need `pandas` and `datetime`, but we also need the `requests` package to make API requests:

```
>>> import datetime
>>> import pandas as pd
>>> import requests
```

Next, we will make a GET request to the USGS API for a JSON payload (a dictionary-like response containing the data that's sent with a request or response) by specifying the `format` of `geojson`. We will ask for earthquake data for the last 26 days (we can use `datetime.timedelta` to perform arithmetic on `datetime` objects). Note that we are using `yesterday` as the end of our date range, since the API won't have complete information for today yet:

```
>>> yesterday = datetime.date.today() - datetime.timedelta(days=1)
>>> api = 'https://earthquake.usgs.gov/fdsnws/event/1/query'
>>> payload = {
...     'format' : 'geojson',
...     'starttime' : yesterday - datetime.timedelta(days=26),
...     'endtime' : yesterday
... }
>>> response = requests.get(api, params=payload)
```

 GET is an HTTP method. This action tells the server we want to read some data. Different APIs may require that we use different methods to get the data; some will require a POST request, where we authenticate with the server. You can read more about API requests and HTTP methods at https://restfulapi.net/http-methods/.

Before we try to create a dataframe out of this, we should make sure that our request was successful. We can do this by checking the `status_code` of the `response`; a `200` response will indicate that everything is OK:

```
>>> response.status_code
200
```

Check out the following resource for additional response codes and their meanings: `https://en.wikipedia.org/wiki/List_of_HTTP_status_codes`.

Our request was successful, so let's see what the data we got looks like. We asked the API for a JSON payload, which is essentially a dictionary, so we can use dictionary methods on it to get more information about its structure. This is going to be a lot of data; hence, we don't want to print it to the screen just to inspect it.

We need to isolate the JSON payload from the HTTP response (stored in the `response` variable), and then look at the keys to view the main sections of the resulting data:

```
>>> earthquake_json = response.json()
>>> earthquake_json.keys()
dict_keys(['type', 'metadata', 'features', 'bbox'])
```

We can inspect what kind of data we have as values for each of these keys; one of them will be the data we are after. The `metadata` portion tells us some information about our request; while this can certainly be useful, it isn't what we are after right now:

```
>>> earthquake_json['metadata']
{'generated': 1539539358000,
 'url':
'https://earthquake.usgs.gov/fdsnws/event/1/query?format=geojson&start
time=2018-09-17&endtime=2018-10-13',
 'title': 'USGS Earthquakes',
 'status': 200,
 'api': '1.5.8',
 'count': 9332}
```

The `features` key looks promising; if this does indeed contain all our data, we should check what type it is so that we don't end up trying to print everything to the screen:

```
>>> type(earthquake_json['features'])
list
```

This key contains a list; let's take a look at the first entry of the list to see if this is the data we want:

```
>>> earthquake_json['features'][0]
{'type': 'Feature',
 'properties': {'mag': 1.35,
  'place': '9km NE of Aguanga, CA',
  'time': 1539475168010,
  'updated': 1539475395144,
  'tz': -480,
  'url':
'https://earthquake.usgs.gov/earthquakes/eventpage/ci37389218',
  'detail':
'https://earthquake.usgs.gov/fdsnws/event/1/query?eventid=ci37389218&f
ormat=geojson',
  'felt': None,
  'cdi': None,
  'mmi': None,
  'alert': None,
  'status': 'automatic',
  'tsunami': 0,
  'sig': 28,
  'net': 'ci',
  'code': '37389218',
  'ids': ',ci37389218,',
  'sources': ',ci,',
  'types': ',geoserve,nearby-cities,origin,phase-data,',
  'nst': 26,
  'dmin': 0.008693,
  'rms': 0.19,
  'gap': 85,
  'magType': 'ml',
  'type': 'earthquake',
  'title': 'M 1.4 - 9km NE of Aguanga, CA'},
 'geometry': {'type': 'Point',
  'coordinates': [-116.7968369, 33.5041656, 3.46]},
 'id': 'ci37389218'}
```

This is definitely the data we are after, but do we need all of it? Upon closer inspection, we only really care about what is inside the properties dictionary. Now, we have a problem because we have a list of dictionaries where we only want a specific key from inside them. How can we pull this information out so that we can make our dataframe? We can use a list comprehension to isolate the properties section from each of the dictionaries in the features list:

```
>>> data = [quake['properties'] for quake in
...             earthquake_json['features']]
```

Finally, we are ready to create our dataframe. Pandas knows how to handle data in this format already (a list of dictionaries), so all we have to do is call the `DataFrame` **constructor**. In computer science, the constructor is a piece of code that creates instances of a class. The `pd.DataFrame()` function is a constructor for `DataFrame` objects:

```
>>> df = pd.DataFrame(data)
```

Now that we know how to create dataframes from a variety of sources, we can begin to learn how to work with dataframes.

Inspecting a DataFrame object

We just learned a few ways in which we can create dataframes from various sources, but we still don't know what to do with them or how we should start our analysis. The first thing we should do when we read in our data is inspect it; we want to make sure that our dataframe isn't empty and that the rows look as we would expect. Our main goal is to verify that it was read in properly and that all of the data is there; however, this initial inspection will also give us ideas on where to direct our data wrangling efforts. In this section, we will explore ways in which we can inspect our dataframes in the `4-inspecting_dataframes.ipynb` notebook.

Since this is a new notebook, we once again must handle our setup. This time, we need to import `pandas` and `numpy`, as well as read in the CSV file with the earthquake data:

```
>>> import numpy as np
>>> import pandas as pd

>>> df = pd.read_csv('data/earthquakes.csv')
```

Examining the data

First, we want to make sure that we actually have data in our dataframe. We can check the `empty` attribute for this answer:

```
>>> df.empty
False
```

So far, so good; we have data. Next, we should check how much data we read in; we want to know the number of observations (rows) and the number of variables (columns) we have. For this task, we use the `shape` attribute:

```
>>> df.shape
(9332, 26)
```

Our data has 9,332 observations of 26 variables, which matches our inspection of the file before we read it in, but what does our data actually look like? For this task, we can use the `head()` and `tail()` methods to look at the top and bottom rows, respectively. This will default to five rows, but we can change this by passing a different number to the method:

```
>>> df.head()
```

The following are the first five rows we get using `head()`:

	alert	cdi	code	...	mag	...	time	title	...
0	NaN	NaN	37389218	...	1.35	...	1539475168010	M 1.4 - 9km NE of Aguanga, CA	...
1	NaN	NaN	37389202	...	1.29	...	1539475129610	M 1.3 - 9km NE of Aguanga, CA	...
2	NaN	4.4	37389194	...	3.42	...	1539475062610	M 3.4 - 8km NE of Aguanga, CA	...
3	NaN	NaN	37389186	...	0.44	...	1539474978070	M 0.4 - 9km NE of Aguanga, CA	...
4	NaN	NaN	73096941	...	2.16	...	1539474716050	M 2.2 - 10km NW of Avenal, CA	...

Then, to get the last two rows, we use the `tail()` method and pass 2 as the number of rows:

```
>>> df.tail(2)
```

The following is the result:

	alert	cdi	code	...	mag	...	time	title	...
9330	NaN	NaN	38063959	...	1.10	...	1537229545350	M 1.1 - 9km NE of Aguanga, CA	...
9331	NaN	NaN	38063935	...	0.66	...	1537228864470	M 0.7 - 9km NE of Aguanga, CA	...

We know there are 26 columns, but we can't see them all using `head()` or `tail()`. Let's use the `columns` attribute to at least see what columns we have:

```
>>> df.columns
Index(['alert', 'cdi', 'code', 'detail', 'dmin', 'felt', 'gap', 'ids',
       'mag', 'magType', 'mmi', 'net', 'nst', 'place', 'rms', 'sig',
       'sources', 'status', 'time', 'title', 'tsunami', 'type',
       'types', 'tz', 'updated', 'url'],
      dtype='object')
```

 Having a list of columns doesn't necessarily mean that we know what all of them mean. Especially in cases where our data comes from the Internet, be sure to read up on what the columns mean before drawing any conclusions. We can read up on the fields in the `geojson` format on the USGS website (https://earthquake.usgs.gov/earthquakes/feed/v1.0/geojson.php), which tells us what each field in the JSON payload means, along with some example values.

We can use the `dtypes` attribute to at least see the data types of the columns. In this step, we can easily see when columns are being stored as the wrong type. (Remember that strings will say `object`.) Here, the `time` column is stored as an `integer`, which is something we will learn how to fix in Chapter 3, *Data Wrangling with Pandas*:

```
>>> df.dtypes
alert        object
cdi          float64
code         object
detail       object
dmin         float64
felt         float64
gap          float64
ids          object
mag          float64
magType      object
mmi          float64
net          object
nst          float64
place        object
rms          float64
sig          int64
sources      object
status       object
time         int64
title        object
tsunami      int64
```

```
type        object
types       object
tz          float64
updated      int64
url         object
dtype: object
```

Lastly, we can use the `info()` method to see how many **non-null** entries of each column we have and get information on our `Index`. **Null** values are missing values, which, in `pandas`, will typically be represented as `None` for objects and `NaN` (**Not a Number**) for non-numeric values in a `float` or `integer` column:

```
>>> df.info()
<class 'pandas.core.frame.DataFrame'>
RangeIndex: 9332 entries, 0 to 9331
Data columns (total 26 columns):
alert       59 non-null object
cdi         329 non-null float64
code        9332 non-null object
detail      9332 non-null object
dmin        6139 non-null float64
felt        329 non-null float64
gap         6164 non-null float64
ids         9332 non-null object
mag         9331 non-null float64
magType     9331 non-null object
mmi         93 non-null float64
net         9332 non-null object
nst         5364 non-null float64
place       9332 non-null object
rms         9332 non-null float64
sig         9332 non-null int64
sources     9332 non-null object
status      9332 non-null object
time        9332 non-null int64
title       9332 non-null object
tsunami     9332 non-null int64
type        9332 non-null object
types       9332 non-null object
tz          9331 non-null float64
updated     9332 non-null int64
url         9332 non-null object
dtypes: float64(9), int64(4), object(13)
memory usage: 1.4+ MB
```

After this initial inspection, we know a lot about the structure of our data and can now begin to try and make sense of it.

Describing and summarizing the data

So far, we've examined the structure of the `DataFrame` object we created from the earthquake data, but we don't know anything about the data. Pandas provides several methods for easily getting summary statistics and getting to know our data better. Now that we know what our data looks like, the next step is to get summary statistics with the `describe()` method:

```
>>> df.describe()
```

We get the 5-number summary along with the count, mean, and standard deviation of the numeric columns:

	cdi	dmin	felt	gap	mag	...
count	329.000000	6139.000000	329.000000	6164.000000	9331.000000	...
mean	2.754711	0.544925	12.310030	121.506588	1.497345	...
std	1.010637	2.214305	48.954944	72.962363	1.203347	...
min	0.000000	0.000648	0.000000	12.000000	-1.260000	...
25%	2.000000	0.020425	1.000000	66.142500	0.720000	...
50%	2.700000	0.059050	2.000000	105.000000	1.300000	...
75%	3.300000	0.177250	5.000000	159.000000	1.900000	...
max	8.400000	53.737000	580.000000	355.910000	7.500000	...

If we want different percentiles, we can pass them in with the `percentiles` argument. For example, if we wanted only the 5th and 95th percentiles, we would run the following: `df.describe(percentiles=[0.05, 0.95])`. Note we will still get the 50th percentile back because that is the median.

By default, `describe()` won't give us any information on the columns of the `object` type, but we can either provide `include='all'` as an argument or run it separately for the data of type `np.object`:

```
>>> df.describe(include=np.object)
```

When describing non-numeric data, we still get the count of non-null occurrences (count); however, instead of the other summary statistics, we get the number of unique values (unique), the mode (top), and the number of times the mode was observed (freq):

	alert	...	place	...	status	title	type	...
count	59	...	9332	...	9332	9332	9332	...
unique	2	...	5433	...	2	7807	5	...
top	green	...	10km NE of Aguanga, CA	...	reviewed	M 0.4 - 10km NE of Aguanga, CA	earthquake	...
freq	58	...	306	...	7797	55	9081	...

The describe() method also works on Series if we are only interested in a particular column.

The describe() method makes it easy to get a snapshot of our data, but sometimes we just want a particular statistic, either for a specific column or for all the columns. Pandas makes this a cinch as well.

It is important to note that describe() only gives us summary statistics for non-null values. This means that, if we had 100 rows and half of our data was null, then the average would be calculated as the sum of the 50 non-null rows divided by 50. If this is not the result we want, we need to change the null values to 0 before we run describe().

The following table includes methods that will work for both Series and DataFrames:

Method	Description	Data types
count()	The number of non-null observations	Any
nunique()	The number of unique values	Any
sum()	The total of the values	Numerical or Boolean
mean()	The average of the values	Numerical or Boolean
median()	The median of the values	Numerical
min()	The minimum of the values	Numerical
idxmin()	The index where the minimum value occurs	Numerical

Method	Description	Data types
max()	The maximum of the values	Numerical
idxmax()	The index where the maximum value occurs	Numerical
abs()	The absolute value of the values	Numerical
std()	The standard deviation	Numerical
var()	The variance	Numerical
cov()	The covariance between two Series, or a covariance matrix for all column combinations in a DataFrame	Numerical
corr()	The correlation between two Series, or a correlation matrix for all column combinations in a DataFrame	Numerical
quantile()	Gets a specific quantile	Numerical
cumsum()	The cumulative sum	Numerical or Boolean
cummin()	The cumulative minimum	Numerical
cummax()	The cumulative maximum	Numerical

Python makes it easy to count how many times something is True. Under the hood, True evaluates to 1 and False evaluates to 0. Therefore, we can run the sum() method on a column of Booleans and get the count of True outputs.

With Series, we have some additional methods we can use to describe our data:

- unique(): Gets the distinct values of the column
- value_counts(): Gets a frequency table of the number of times each unique value in a given column appears; gets the percentage of times each unique value appears when passed normalize=True
- mode(): Gets the most common value of the column

These Series methods can help us understand what some of these columns might mean. Up until now, we know that the alert column is a string of two unique values, and the most common value is 'green' with many null values. What is the other unique value, though?

```
>>> df.alert.unique()
array([nan, 'green', 'red'], dtype=object)
```

Given that the values are either `'red'` or `'green'`, we may wonder whether that alert has anything to do with the severity of the earthquake. By consulting the USGS API documentation for the `alert` field (`https://earthquake.usgs.gov/data/comcat/data-eventterms.php#alert`), we see that it can be `'green'`, `'yellow'`, `'orange'`, or `'red'` (when populated), and that it is the alert level from the **Prompt Assessment of Global Earthquakes for Response (PAGER)** earthquake impact scale. According to the USGS (`https://earthquake.usgs.gov/data/pager/`), *the PAGER system provides fatality and economic loss impact estimates following significant earthquakes worldwide.*

Now that we understand what this field means and the values we have in our data, we would expect there to be far more `'green'` than `'red'`; we can check this with a frequency table by using `value_counts()`:

```
>>> df.alert.value_counts()
green     58
red        1
Name: alert, dtype: int64
```

 We can also select `Series` objects from a `DataFrame` object using the `get()` method. This has the benefits of not raising an error if that column doesn't exist, and allowing us to provide a backup value—the default is `None`. For example, if we call `df.get('event', 'earthquake')`, it will return `'earthquake'` since we don't have an `'event'` column.

Note that `Index` objects also have several methods to help describe and summarize our data:

Method	Description
`argmax()`/`argmin()`	Find the location of maximum/minimum value in the index
`contains()`	Check whether the index contains a value
`equals()`	Compare the index to another `Index` object for equality
`isin()`	Check if the index values are in a list of values and return an array of Booleans
`max()`/`min()`	Find the maximum/minimum value in the index
`nunique()`	Get the number of unique values in the index
`to_series()`	Create a `Series` object from the index object
`unique()`	Find the unique values of the index
`value_counts()`	Create a frequency table for the unique values in the index

Grabbing subsets of the data

So far, we have learned how to work with and summarize the dataframe as a whole; however, we will often be interested in performing operations and/or analyses on subsets of our data. There are many types of subsets we may look to isolate from our data, such as selecting only specific columns or rows as a whole or when a specific criterion is met. In order to obtain subsets of the data, we need to be familiar with selection, slicing, indexing, and filtering with `pandas`.

For this section, we will work in the `5-selection.ipynb` notebook. Our setup is as follows:

```
>>> import pandas as pd

>>> df = pd.read_csv('data/earthquakes.csv')
```

Selection

With selection, we grab entire columns. Using our earthquake data, let's grab the `mag` column, which contains the magnitudes of the earthquakes:

```
>>> df.mag
0       1.35
1       1.29
2       3.42
3       0.44
4       2.16
        ...
9327    0.62
9328    1.00
9329    2.40
9330    1.10
9331    0.66
Name: mag, Length: 9332, dtype: float64
```

In the preceding example, we selected the `mag` column as an attribute of the dataframe; however, we can also access it with a dictionary-like notation:

```
>>> df['mag']
0        1.35
1        1.29
2        3.42
3        0.44
4        2.16
         ...
9327     0.62
9328     1.00
9329     2.40
9330     1.10
9331     0.66
Name: mag, Length: 9332, dtype: float64
```

We aren't limited to selecting one column at a time. By passing a list to the dictionary lookup, we can select many columns, giving us a `DataFrame` object that is a subset of our original dataframe:

```
>>> df[['mag', 'title']]
```

This gives us the full `mag` and `title` columns from the original dataframe:

	mag	title
0	1.35	M 1.4 - 9km NE of Aguanga, CA
1	1.29	M 1.3 - 9km NE of Aguanga, CA
2	3.42	M 3.4 - 8km NE of Aguanga, CA
3	0.44	M 0.4 - 9km NE of Aguanga, CA
...	...	...
9328	1.00	M 1.0 - 3km W of Julian, CA
9329	2.40	M 2.4 - 35km NNE of Hatillo, Puerto Rico
9330	1.10	M 1.1 - 9km NE of Aguanga, CA
9331	0.66	M 0.7 - 9km NE of Aguanga, CA

Any list of column names will work for this, so we can use some of Python's string methods to help us pick out the columns. For example, if we wanted to select all of the columns that start with `mag`, along with the `title` and `time` columns, we would do the following:

```
>>> df[
...     ['title', 'time']
...     + [col for col in df.columns if col.startswith('mag')]
... ]
```

We get back a dataframe composed of the four columns that matched our criteria:

	title	time	mag	magType
0	M 1.4 - 9km NE of Aguanga, CA	1539475168010	1.35	ml
1	M 1.3 - 9km NE of Aguanga, CA	1539475129610	1.29	ml
2	M 3.4 - 8km NE of Aguanga, CA	1539475062610	3.42	ml
3	M 0.4 - 9km NE of Aguanga, CA	1539474978070	0.44	ml
...	...	...	...	...
9328	M 1.0 - 3km W of Julian, CA	1537230135130	1.00	ml
9329	M 2.4 - 35km NNE of Hatillo, Puerto Rico	1537229908180	2.40	md
9330	M 1.1 - 9km NE of Aguanga, CA	1537229545350	1.10	ml
9331	M 0.7 - 9km NE of Aguanga, CA	1537228864470	0.66	ml

Notice how the columns were returned in the order we requested, which is not the order they originally appeared in. This means that if we want to reorder our columns, all we have to do is select them in the order we want them to appear.

Let's break this last example down. We used a list comprehension to go through each of the columns in the dataframe and only keep the ones whose names started with `mag`:

```
>>> [col for col in df.columns if col.startswith('mag')]
['mag', 'magType']
```

Then, we added this result to the other two columns we wanted to keep (`title` and `time`):

```
>>> ['title', 'time'] \
... + [col for col in df.columns if col.startswith('mag')]
['title', 'time', 'mag', 'magType']
```

Finally, we were able to use this list to run the actual column selection on the dataframe (the result is omitted for brevity):

```
>>> df[
...     ['title', 'time']
...     + [col for col in df.columns if col.startswith('mag')]
... ]
```

 String methods are a very powerful way to select `DataFrame` columns. A complete list of these can be found in the Python 3 documentation at https://docs.python.org/3/library/stdtypes.html#string-methods.

Slicing

When we want to extract certain rows (slices) from our dataframe, we use **slicing**. `DataFrame` slicing works similarly to slicing with other Python objects, such as lists and tuples, with the first index being inclusive and the last being one exclusive:

```
>>> df[100:103]
```

When specifying a slice of `100:103`, we get back rows 100, 101, and 102:

	alert	...	mag	magType	...	time	title	...
100	NaN	...	1.20	ml	...	1539435449480	M 1.2 - 25km NW of Ester, Alaska	...
101	NaN	...	0.59	md	...	1539435391320	M 0.6 - 8km ESE of Mammoth Lakes, CA	...
102	NaN	...	1.33	ml	...	1539435293090	M 1.3 - 8km ENE of Aguanga, CA	...

We can combine our row and column selections in what is known as **chaining**:

```
>>> df[['title', 'time']][100:103]
```

First, we selected the `title` and `time` columns for all rows, and then we pulled out rows with indices 100, 101, and 102:

	title	time
100	M 1.2 - 25km NW of Ester, Alaska	1539435449480
101	M 0.6 - 8km ESE of Mammoth Lakes, CA	1539435391320
102	M 1.3 - 8km ENE of Aguanga, CA	1539435293090

In the preceding example, we selected the columns and then sliced the rows, but the order doesn't matter:

```
>>> df[100:103][['title', 'time']].equals(
...     df[['title', 'time']][100:103]
...     )
True
```

 We can slice on whatever is in our index; however, it would be hard to determine the text or date after the last one we want, so with `pandas`, slicing dates and text is different from integer slicing and is inclusive of both endpoints. When slicing with dates, we can easily select subsets, such as all data from 2018 with `df['2018']`, or everything in October 2018 with `df['2018-10']`, or a specific range in October with `df['20181010':'20181020']`. Date slicing will work as long as the strings we provide can be parsed into a `datetime`. We will see examples of this throughout this book.

Indexing

As we saw in the previous section, we can easily combine column selection and row slicing; however, it got a little messy and rather long. If we decide to use the chained selection methods discussed in the *Selection* and *Slicing* sections to update values in our data, we will find `pandas` complaining that we aren't doing it correctly (even if it works). This is to warn us that setting data with a sequential selection may not give us the result we anticipate. More information can be found at `http://pandas.pydata.org/pandas-docs/stable/indexing.html#indexing-view-versus-copy`.

Let's trigger this warning to understand it better. We will try to update the `title` of a few earthquakes to be in lowercase:

```
>>> df[110:113]['title'] = df[110:113]['title'].str.lower()
c:\users\...\book_env\lib\site-packages\ipykernel_launcher.py:1:
SettingWithCopyWarning:
A value is trying to be set on a copy of a slice from a DataFrame.
Try using .loc[row_indexer,col_indexer] = value instead

See the caveats in the documentation:
http://pandas.pydata.org/pandas-docs/stable/indexing.html#indexing-vie
w-versus-copy
    """Entry point for launching an IPython kernel.
```

As indicated by the warning, to be an effective `pandas` user, it's not enough to know selection and slicing—we must also master **indexing**. Since this is just a warning, our values have been updated, but this may not always be the case:

```
>>> df[110:113]['title']
110                 m 1.1 - 35km s of ester, alaska
111     m 1.9 - 93km wnw of arctic village, alaska
112       m 0.9 - 20km wsw of smith valley, nevada
Name: title, dtype: object
```

Pandas indexing operations provide us with a one-method way to select both the rows and the columns we want. We can use `loc[]` and `iloc[]` to subset our dataframe using label-based or integer-based lookups, respectively. A good way to remember the difference is to think of them as <u>loc</u>ation versus <u>i</u>nteger <u>loc</u>ation. For all indexing methods, we first provide the row indexer and then the column indexer with a comma separating them: `df.loc[row_indexer, column_indexer]`. Note that by using `loc`, as indicated in the warning message, we no longer trigger any warnings from `pandas` for this operation:

```
>>> df.loc[110:112, 'title'] = df.loc[110:112, 'title'].str.lower()
>>> df.loc[110:112, 'title']
110                 m 1.1 - 35km s of ester, alaska
111     m 1.9 - 93km wnw of arctic village, alaska
112       m 0.9 - 20km wsw of smith valley, nevada
Name: title, dtype: object
```

We can select all rows (columns) if we use : as the row (column) indexer, just like with regular Python slicing. Let's grab all the rows of the `title` column with `loc[]`:

```
>>> df.loc[:,'title']
0     M 1.4 - 9km NE of Aguanga, CA
1     M 1.3 - 9km NE of Aguanga, CA
2     M 3.4 - 8km NE of Aguanga, CA
3     M 0.4 - 9km NE of Aguanga, CA
4     M 2.2 - 10km NW of Avenal, CA
      ...
Name: title, dtype: object
```

We can select multiple rows and columns at the same time with `loc[]`:

```
>>> df.loc[10:15, ['title', 'mag']]
```

This leaves us with rows 10 through 15 for the `title` and `mag` columns only:

	title	mag
10	M 0.5 - 10km NE of Aguanga, CA	0.50
11	M 2.8 - 53km SE of Punta Cana, Dominican Republic	2.77
12	M 0.5 - 9km NE of Aguanga, CA	0.50
13	M 4.5 - 120km SSW of Banda Aceh, Indonesia	4.50
14	M 2.1 - 14km NW of Parkfield, CA	2.13
15	M 2.0 - 156km WNW of Haines Junction, Canada	2.00

Notice how, when using `loc[]`, our end index was inclusive. This isn't the case with `iloc[]`:

```
>>> df.iloc[10:15, [19, 8]]
```

Observe how we had to provide a list of integers to select the same columns; these are the column numbers (starting from 0). Using `iloc[]`, we lost the row at index 15; this is because the integer slicing that `iloc[]` employs is exclusive of the end index, as with Python slicing syntax:

	title	mag
10	M 0.5 - 10km NE of Aguanga, CA	0.50
11	M 2.8 - 53km SE of Punta Cana, Dominican Republic	2.77
12	M 0.5 - 9km NE of Aguanga, CA	0.50
13	M 4.5 - 120km SSW of Banda Aceh, Indonesia	4.50
14	M 2.1 - 14km NW of Parkfield, CA	2.13

We aren't limited to using the slicing syntax for the rows though; columns work as well:

```
>>> df.iloc[10:15, 8:10]
```

By using slicing, we can easily grab adjacent rows and columns:

	mag	magType
10	0.50	ml
11	2.77	md
12	0.50	ml
13	4.50	mb
14	2.13	md

When using `loc[]`, this slicing can be done on the column names, as well. This gives us many ways to achieve the same result:

```
>>> df.iloc[10:15, 8:10].equals(df.loc[10:14, 'mag':'magType'])
True
```

> When we want to select the entire row based on position, we can use the `take()` method instead of `iloc`. The notebook contains an example of this.

To look up scalar values, we use the faster `at[]` and `iat[]`. Let's get the magnitude (the `mag` column) of the earthquake recorded in the row at index 10:

```
>>> df.at[10, 'mag']
0.5
```

The magnitude column has a column index of 8; therefore, we can also look up the magnitude with `iat[]`:

```
>>> df.iat[10, 8]
0.5
```

Filtering

We saw how to get subsets of our data using row and column ranges, but how do we only take the data that meets some criteria? Pandas gives us a few options, including **Boolean masks** and some special methods. With Boolean masks, we test our data against some value and get a structure of the same shape back, except it is filled with `True`/`False` values; `pandas` can use this to select the appropriate values for us. For example, we can see which entries in the `mag` column had a magnitude greater than 2:

```
>>> df.mag > 2
0     False
1     False
2      True
3     False
4      True
      ...
Name: mag, dtype: bool
```

While we can run this on the entire dataframe, it wouldn't be too useful with our earthquake data since we have columns of various data types.

However, we can use this strategy to get the subset of the dataframe where the magnitude of the earthquake was greater than or equal to `7.0`:

```
>>> df[df.mag >= 7.0]
```

Our resulting dataframe has just two rows:

	alert	...	mag	magType	...	title	tsunami	type	...
837	green	...	7.0	mww	...	M 7.0 - 117km E of Kimbe, Papua New Guinea	1	earthquake	...
5263	red	...	7.5	mww	...	M 7.5 - 78km N of Palu, Indonesia	1	earthquake	...

We got back a lot of columns we didn't need, though. We could have chained a column selection to the end of the last code snippet; however, `loc[]` can handle this Boolean mask as well:

```
>>> df.loc[
...        df.mag >= 7.0,
...        ['alert', 'mag', 'magType', 'title', 'tsunami', 'type']
... ]
```

The following dataframe has been filtered to only contain relevant columns:

	alert	mag	magType	title	tsunami	type
837	green	7.0	mww	M 7.0 - 117km E of Kimbe, Papua New Guinea	1	earthquake
5263	red	7.5	mww	M 7.5 - 78km N of Palu, Indonesia	1	earthquake

We aren't limited to just one criterion, either. Let's grab the earthquakes with a `red` alert and a `tsunami`. In order to combine masks, we need to surround each of our conditions in parentheses and use the **AND operator** (`&`) to require **both** to be true:

```
>>> df.loc[
...        (df.tsunami == 1) & (df.alert == 'red'),
...        ['alert', 'mag', 'magType', 'title', 'tsunami', 'type']
... ]
```

There was only a single earthquake in the data that met our criteria:

	alert	mag	magType	title	tsunami	type
5263	red	7.5	mww	M 7.5 – 78km N of Palu, Indonesia	1	earthquake

If, instead, we want **at least one** of them to be true, we can use the **OR operator** (|):

```
>>> df.loc[
...     (df.tsunami == 1) | (df.alert == 'red'),
...     ['alert', 'mag', 'magType', 'title', 'tsunami', 'type']
... ]
```

Notice that this filter is much less restrictive since, while both of the conditions can be true, we only require that one of them be:

	alert	mag	magType	title	tsunami	type
36	NaN	5.00	mww	M 5.0 – 165km NNW of Flying Fish Cove, Christm...	1	earthquake
118	green	6.70	mww	M 6.7 – 262km NW of Ozernovskiy, Russia	1	earthquake
...	...	...	...	...	...	...
9175	NaN	5.20	mb	M 5.2 – 126km N of Dili, East Timor	1	earthquake
9304	NaN	5.10	mb	M 5.1 – 34km NW of Finschhafen, Papua New Guinea	1	earthquake

In the previous two examples, our conditions involved equality; however, we are by no means limited to this. Let's select all the earthquakes in Alaska where we have a non-null value for the `alert` column:

```
>>> df.loc[
...     (df.place.str.contains('Alaska')) & (df.alert.notnull()),
...     ['alert', 'mag', 'magType', 'title', 'tsunami', 'type']
... ]
```

All earthquakes in Alaska that have a value for `alert` are `green`, and some have tsunamis with the highest magnitude being `5.1`:

	alert	mag	magType	title	tsunami	type
1015	green	5.0	ml	M 5.0 - 61km SSW of Chignik Lake, Alaska	1	earthquake
1273	green	4.0	ml	M 4.0 - 71km SW of Kaktovik, Alaska	1	earthquake
...	...	...	...	...	...	...
8524	green	3.8	ml	M 3.8 - 69km SSW of Kaktovik, Alaska	0	earthquake
9133	green	5.1	ml	M 5.1 - 64km SSW of Kaktovik, Alaska	1	earthquake

Let's break down how we got this. `Series` objects have some string methods that can be accessed after getting the `str` attribute. Using this, we are able to create a Boolean mask of all the rows where the `place` column contained the word `Alaska`:

```
df.place.str.contains('Alaska')
```

To get all the rows where the `alert` column was not null, we used the `notnull()` method of the `Series` (this works for `DataFrame` objects as well) to create a Boolean mask of all the rows where the `alert` column was not null:

```
df.alert.notnull()
```

> We can use the `pandas` **negation operator** (~), also called **NOT**, to negate all the Boolean values, which makes all `True` values `False` and vice versa. So, instead of writing `df.alert.notnull()`, we could write `~df.alert.isnull()`.

Then, like we did previously, we combine the two conditions with the `&` operator to complete our mask:

```
(df.place.str.contains('Alaska')) & (df.alert.notnull())
```

We aren't limited to checking if each row contains text; we can use regular expressions as well. **Regular expressions (regex**, for short) are very powerful because they allow us to define a search pattern rather than the exact content we want to find. This means that we can do things like find all the words or digits in a string without having to know what all the words or digits are beforehand (or go through one character at a time). To do so, we simply pass in a string preceded by an r outside the quotes; this lets Python know it is a **raw string,** which means that we can include backslash (\) characters in the string without Python thinking we are trying to escape the character immediately following it (such as when we use \n to mean a new line character instead of the letter n). This makes it perfect for use with regular expressions. The re module in the Python standard library (https://docs.python.org/3/library/re.html) handles regular expression operations; however, pandas lets us use regular expressions directly.

Using regex, let's select all the earthquakes in California that have magnitudes of at least 3.8. We need to select entries in the place column that end in CA or California because the data isn't consistent (we will look at how to fix this in the next section). The $ means *end* and 'CA$' gives us entries that end in CA, so we can use 'CA|California$' to get entries that end in either:

```
>>> df.loc[(df.place.str.contains(r'CA|California$')) &
...        (df.mag > 3.8),
...        ['alert', 'mag', 'magType', 'title', 'tsunami', 'type']]
```

There were only two earthquakes in California with magnitudes greater than 3.8 over the time period of the data:

	alert	mag	magType	title	tsunami	type
1465	green	3.83	mw	M 3.8 - 109km WNW of Trinidad, CA	0	earthquake
2414	green	3.83	mw	M 3.8 - 5km SW of Tres Pinos, CA	1	earthquake

Regular expressions (regex) are extremely powerful, but unfortunately, also difficult to get right. It is often helpful to grab some sample lines for parsing and use a website to test them. Note that regular expressions come in many flavors, so be sure to select Python. This website supports Python flavor regex and also provides a nice regex cheat sheet on the side: https://regex101.com/.

What if we want to get all earthquakes with magnitudes between 6.5 and 7.5? We could use two Boolean masks—one to check for magnitudes greater than or equal to 6.5, and another to check for magnitudes less than or equal to 7.5, and then combine them with the & operator. Thankfully, pandas makes this type of mask much easier to create—we can use the between() method:

```
>>> df.loc[
...     df.mag.between(6.5, 7.5),
...     ['alert', 'mag', 'magType', 'title', 'tsunami', 'type']
... ]
```

The result contains all the earthquakes with magnitudes in the range of [6.5, 7.5]—it's inclusive of both ends:

	alert	mag	magType	title	tsunami	type
118	green	6.7	mww	M 6.7 - 262km NW of Ozernovskiy, Russia	1	earthquake
799	green	6.5	mww	M 6.5 - 148km S of Severo-Kuril'sk, Russia	1	earthquake
837	green	7.0	mww	M 7.0 - 117km E of Kimbe, Papua New Guinea	1	earthquake
4363	green	6.7	mww	M 6.7 - 263km NNE of Ndoi Island, Fiji	1	earthquake
5263	red	7.5	mww	M 7.5 - 78km N of Palu, Indonesia	1	earthquake

The between() method will give us an inclusive selection on both ends by default; however, we can pass inclusive=False if we don't want this behavior.

We can use the isin() method to create a Boolean mask for values that match one of a list of values. This means that we don't have to write one mask for each of the values that we could match and use | to join them. The USGS site mentions that the alert column can be green, yellow, orange, or red (when provided); let's grab the data for rows with a red or orange alert:

```
>>> df.loc[
...     df.alert.isin(['orange', 'red']),
...     ['alert', 'mag', 'magType', 'title', 'tsunami', 'type']
... ]
```

We don't have any `orange` alerts, so we only get the one `red` alert:

	alert	mag	magType	title	tsunami	type
5263	red	7.5	mww	M 7.5 - 78km N of Palu, Indonesia	1	earthquake

Sometimes, we aren't only interested in the minimum or maximum value of a column that we were able to isolate with summary statistics, but rather the rows when a particular column is at an interesting value. In this case, instead of looking for the value, we can ask `pandas` to give us the index where this value occurs, and easily filter to grab the full row. We can use `idxmin()` and `idxmax()` for the index of the minimum and maximum, respectively. Let's grab the row numbers for the lowest-magnitude and highest-magnitude earthquakes:

```
>>> [df.mag.idxmin(), df.mag.idxmax()]
[2409, 5263]
```

We can use these indices to grab the rows themselves:

```
>>> df.loc[
...     [df.mag.idxmin(), df.mag.idxmax()],
...     ['alert', 'mag', 'magType', 'title', 'tsunami', 'type']
... ]
```

The minimum magnitude earthquake occurred in Alaska and the highest magnitude earthquake occurred in Indonesia, accompanied by a tsunami. We will discuss the earthquake in Indonesia in `Chapter 5`, *Visualizing Data with Pandas and Matplotlib*, and `Chapter 6`, *Plotting with Seaborn and Customization Techniques*:

	alert	mag	magType	title	tsunami	type
2409	NaN	-1.26	ml	M -1.3 - 41km ENE of Adak, Alaska	0	earthquake
5263	red	7.50	mww	M 7.5 - 78km N of Palu, Indonesia	1	earthquake

There are endless possibilities for creating Boolean masks—all we need is some code that returns one Boolean value for each row.

To subset rows or columns based on their names, check out the `filter()` method. This won't filter all the data; just the columns or rows we are looking at. Examples with `DataFrame` and `Series` objects are in the notebook.

Adding and removing data

Often, we want to add or remove rows and columns from our data. In the previous sections, we frequently selected a subset of the columns, but if columns/rows aren't useful to us, we should just get rid of them. We also frequently selected data based on the value of the magnitude; however, if we had made a new column holding the Boolean values for later selection, we would have only needed to calculate the mask once. Very rarely will we get data where we neither want to add nor remove something.

Before we get started, it's important to understand that while most methods will return a new `DataFrame` object, some will be in-place and change our data. If we write a function where we pass in a dataframe and change it, it will change our original dataframe as well. Should we find ourselves in a situation where we don't want to change the original data, but rather want to return a new copy of the data that has been modified, we must be sure to copy our dataframe before making the changes: `df_to_modify = df.copy()`.

By default, `df.copy()` makes a **deep copy** of the dataframe, which allows us to make changes to either the copy or the original without repercussions. If we pass `deep=False`, we can obtain a **shallow copy**—changes to the shallow copy affect the original and vice versa. Almost always we will want the deep copy, since we can change it without affecting the original. More information can be found in the documentation at `https://pandas.pydata.org/pandas-docs/stable/reference/api/pandas.DataFrame.copy.html`.

Now, let's turn to the final notebook, `6-adding_and_removing_data.ipynb`, and get set up for the remainder of this chapter:

```
>>> import numpy as np
>>> import pandas as pd

>>> df = pd.read_csv(
...     'data/earthquakes.csv',
...     usecols=[
...         'time', 'title', 'place', 'magType',
...         'mag', 'alert', 'tsunami'
...     ]
... )
```

Creating new data

First, we will cover adding new rows and columns, and later we will delete them. Creating new columns can be achieved in the same fashion as variable assignment. For example, we can create a column of `ones` for our data:

```
>>> df['ones'] = 1
>>> df.head()
```

The new column is created to the right of the original columns, with a value of 1 for every row:

	alert	mag	magType	place	time	title	tsunami	ones
0	NaN	1.35	ml	9km NE of Aguanga, CA	1539475168010	M 1.4 - 9km NE of Aguanga, CA	0	1
1	NaN	1.29	ml	9km NE of Aguanga, CA	1539475129610	M 1.3 - 9km NE of Aguanga, CA	0	1
2	NaN	3.42	ml	8km NE of Aguanga, CA	1539475062610	M 3.4 - 8km NE of Aguanga, CA	0	1
3	NaN	0.44	ml	9km NE of Aguanga, CA	1539474978070	M 0.4 - 9km NE of Aguanga, CA	0	1
4	NaN	2.16	md	10km NW of Avenal, CA	1539474716050	M 2.2 - 10km NW of Avenal, CA	0	1

We cannot create the column with the attribute notation (`df.ones`) because the dataframe doesn't have that attribute yet, so we must use the dictionary notation (`df['ones']`).

We aren't limited to broadcasting one value to the entire column; we can have the column hold the result of Boolean logic or a mathematical equation. For example, if we had data on distance and time, we could create a speed column that is the result of dividing the distance column by the time column. With our earthquake data, let's create a column that tells us whether the earthquake's magnitude was negative:

```
>>> df['mag_negative'] = df.mag < 0
>>> df.head()
```

Note that the new column has been added to the right:

	alert	mag	magType	place	time	title	tsunami	ones	mag_negative
0	NaN	1.35	ml	9km NE of Aguanga, CA	1539475168010	M 1.4 - 9km NE of Aguanga, CA	0	1	False
1	NaN	1.29	ml	9km NE of Aguanga, CA	1539475129610	M 1.3 - 9km NE of Aguanga, CA	0	1	False
2	NaN	3.42	ml	8km NE of Aguanga, CA	1539475062610	M 3.4 - 8km NE of Aguanga, CA	0	1	False
3	NaN	0.44	ml	9km NE of Aguanga, CA	1539474978070	M 0.4 - 9km NE of Aguanga, CA	0	1	False
4	NaN	2.16	md	10km NW of Avenal, CA	1539474716050	M 2.2 - 10km NW of Avenal, CA	0	1	False

In the previous section, we saw that the place column has some data consistency issues—we have multiple names for the same entity. In some cases, earthquakes occurring in California are marked as CA and as California in others. Needless to say, this is confusing and can easily cause issues for us if we don't carefully inspect our data beforehand. For example, by just selecting 'CA', we miss out on 124 earthquakes marked as 'California'. This isn't the only place with an issue, either (Nevada and NV are also both present).

By using a regular expression to extract everything in the `place` column after the comma, we can see some of the issues firsthand:

```
>>> df.place.str.extract(r', (.*$)')[0].sort_values().unique()
array(['Afghanistan', 'Alaska', 'Argentina', 'Arizona', 'Arkansas',
       'Australia', 'Azerbaijan', 'B.C., MX', 'Barbuda', 'Bolivia',
       'Bonaire, Saint Eustatius and Saba ', 'British Virgin Islands',
       'Burma', 'CA', 'California', 'Canada', 'Chile', 'China',
       ...,
       'East Timor', 'Ecuador', 'Ecuador region',
       ...,
       'Mexico', 'Missouri', 'Montana', 'NV', 'Nevada',
       ...,
       'Yemen', nan], dtype=object)
```

If we want to treat countries and anything near them as a single entity, we have some additional work to do (see `Ecuador` and `Ecuador region`). In addition, our naive attempt at parsing the place by looking at the information after the comma appears to have failed; this is because, in some cases, we don't have a comma. We will need to change our approach to parsing.

This is an **entity recognition problem**, and it's not trivial to solve. With a relatively small list of unique values (which we can view with `df.place.unique()`), we can simply look through and infer how to properly match up these names. We can use the `replace()` method to replace patterns in the `place` name as we see fit:

```
>>> df['parsed_place'] = df.place.str.replace(
...     r'.* of ', '' # remove <something> of <something>
... ).str.replace(
...     r'the ', '' # remove things starting with "the"
... ).str.replace(
...     r'CA$', 'California' # fix California
... ).str.replace(
...     r'NV$', 'Nevada' # fix Nevada
... ).str.replace(
...     r'MX$', 'Mexico' # fix Mexico
... ).str.replace(
...     r' region$', '' # chop off endings with "region"
... ).str.replace(
...     r'northern ', '' # remove "northern"
... ).str.replace(
...     r'Fiji Islands', 'Fiji' # line up the Fiji places
... ).str.replace(
...     r'^.*, ', '' # remove anything else extraneous from beginning
... ).str.strip() # remove any extra spaces
```

Now, we can check the parsed places we are left with:

```
>>> df.parsed_place.sort_values().unique()
array(['Afghanistan', 'Alaska', 'Argentina', 'Arizona', 'Arkansas',
       'Ascension Island', 'Australia', 'Azerbaijan', ...,
       'Barbuda', 'Bolivia', 'British Virgin Islands', 'Burma',
       'California', 'Canada', 'Carlsberg Ridge', ...,
       'Dominican Republic', 'East Timor', 'Ecuador', 'El Salvador',
       'Fiji', 'Greece', 'Greenland', 'Guam', 'Guatemala', 'Haiti',
       ..., 'Mauritius', 'Mayotte', 'Mexico', 'Mid-Indian Ridge',
       'Missouri', 'Montana', 'Nevada', 'New Caledonia', ..,
       'Yemen'], dtype=object)
```

In practice, entity recognition can be an extremely difficult problem, where we may look to employ **natural language processing** (**NLP**) algorithms to help us. While this is well beyond the scope of this book, more information can be found at https://medium.com/ explore-artificial-intelligence/introduction-to-named-entity-recognition-eda8c97c2db1.

Pandas also provides us with a way to make many new columns at once in one method call. With the `assign()` method, the arguments are the names of the columns we want to create (or overwrite), and the values are the data for the columns. Let's create two new columns; one will tell us if the earthquake happened in California, and the other will tell us if it happened in Alaska:

```
>>> df.assign(
...     in_ca=df.parsed_place.str.endswith('California'),
...     in_alaska=df.parsed_place.str.endswith('Alaska')
... ).head()
```

Once again, our new columns are added to the right of the original columns:

	alert	mag	magType	place	time	title	tsunami	ones	mag_negative	parsed_place	in_ca	in_alaska
0	NaN	1.35	ml	9km NE of ...	1539475168010	M 1.4 - 9km NE...	0	1	False	California	True	False
1	NaN	1.29	ml	9km NE of ...	1539475129610	M 1.3 - 9km NE...	0	1	False	California	True	False
2	NaN	3.42	ml	8km NE of ...	1539475062610	M 3.4 - 8km NE...	0	1	False	California	True	False
3	NaN	0.44	ml	9km NE of ...	1539474978070	M 0.4 - 9km NE...	0	1	False	California	True	False
4	NaN	2.16	md	10km NW of ...	1539474716050	M 2.2 - 10km NW...	0	1	False	California	True	False

Notice that `assign()` doesn't change our original dataframe; instead, it returns a new `DataFrame` object with these columns added. If we want to replace our original dataframe with this, we just use variable assignment to store the result of `assign()` in `df` (for example, `df = df.assign(...)`).

The `assign()` method accepts **lambda functions** (anonymous functions usually defined in one line and for single use), so if our dataframe has a long name (or we just don't feel like typing the whole thing), we can write something like the following: `df.assign(abs_mag=lambda x: x.mag.abs())`. This will pass the dataframe into the `lambda` function as `x`, and we can work from there.

Say we were working with two separate dataframes, one with earthquakes accompanied by tsunamis and the other with earthquakes without tsunamis:

```
>>> tsunami = df[df.tsunami == 1]
>>> no_tsunami = df[df.tsunami == 0]

>>> tsunami.shape, no_tsunami.shape
((61, 10), (9271, 10)
```

If we wanted to look at earthquakes as a whole, we would want to concatenate the dataframes into a single one. To append rows to the bottom of our dataframe, we can either use `pd.concat()` or the `append()` method of the dataframe itself. The `concat()` function allows us to specify the axis along which the operation will be performed—0 for appending rows to the bottom of the dataframe, and 1 for appending to the right of the last column with respect to the leftmost `pandas` object in the concatenation list. Let's use `pd.concat()` with the default `axis` of 0 for rows:

```
>>> pd.concat([tsunami, no_tsunami]).shape
(9332, 10) # 61 rows + 9271 rows
```

Note that the previous result is equivalent to running the `append()` method on the dataframe. This still returns a new `DataFrame` object, but it saves us from having to remember which axis is which, since `append()` is really a wrapper around the `concat()` function:

```
>>> tsunami.append(no_tsunami).shape
(9332, 10) # 61 rows + 9271 rows
```

Both `Index` and `Series` objects have `append()` methods.

We have been working with a subset of the columns from the CSV file, but now we want to get some of the columns we ignored when we read in the data. Since we have added new columns in this notebook, we won't want to read in the file again and perform those operations again. Instead, we will concatenate along the columns (`axis=1`) to add back what we are missing:

```
>>> additional_columns = pd.read_csv(
...         'data/earthquakes.csv', usecols=['tz', 'felt', 'ids']
... )
>>> pd.concat([df.head(2), additional_columns.head(2)], axis=1)
```

Since the index of our dataframe and the additional columns we read in match up, the columns are placed to the right of our original columns:

	alert	mag	magType	place	time	title	tsunami	ones	mag_negative	parsed_place	felt	ids	tz
0	NaN	1.35	ml	9km NE of Aguanga, CA	1539475168010	M 1.4 - 9km NE of Aguanga, CA	0	1	False	California	NaN	,ci37389218,	-480.0
1	NaN	1.29	ml	9km NE of Aguanga, CA	1539475129610	M 1.3 - 9km NE of Aguanga, CA	0	1	False	California	NaN	ci37389202,	-480.0

The `concat()` function uses the index to determine how to concatenate the values. If they don't align, this will generate additional rows because `pandas` won't know how to align them. Say we forgot that our original dataframe had the row numbers as the index, and we read in the additional columns by setting the `time` column as the index:

```
>>> additional_columns = pd.read_csv(
...     'data/earthquakes.csv', usecols=['tz', 'felt', 'ids', 'time'],
...     index_col='time'
... )
>>> pd.concat([df.head(2), additional_columns.head(2)], axis=1)
```

Despite the additional columns containing data for the first two rows, `pandas` creates a new row for them because their index doesn't match. In `Chapter 3`, *Data Wrangling with Pandas*, we will see how to reset the index and set the index; both of which could resolve this issue:

	alert	mag	magType	place	time	title	tsunami	ones	mag_negative	parsed_place	felt	ids	tz
0	NaN	1.35	ml	9km NE of Aguanga, CA	1.539475e+12	M 1.4 – 9km NE of Aguanga, CA	0.0	1.0	False	California	NaN	NaN	NaN
1	NaN	1.29	ml	9km NE of Aguanga, CA	1.539475e+12	M 1.3 – 9km NE of Aguanga, CA	0.0	1.0	False	California	NaN	NaN	NaN
1539475129610	NaN	NaN	NaN	NaN	NaN	NaN	NaN	NaN	NaN	NaN	NaN	,ci37389202,	−480.0
1539475168010	NaN	NaN	NaN	NaN	NaN	NaN	NaN	NaN	NaN	NaN	NaN	,ci37389218,	−480.0

In `Chapter 4`, *Aggregating Pandas DataFrames*, we will discuss merging, which will also handle some of these issues when we're augmenting the columns in the dataframe. Often, we will use `concat()` or `append()` to add rows, but `merge()` or `join()` to add columns.

Say we want to concatenate the `tsunami` and `no_tsunami` dataframes, but the `no_tsunami` dataframe has an additional column. The `join` parameter specifies how to handle any overlap in column names (when appending to the bottom) or in row names (when concatenating to the left/right). By default, this is `outer`, so we keep everything; however, if we use `inner`, we will only keep what they have in common:

```
>>> pd.concat(
...     [
...         tsunami.head(2),
...         no_tsunami.head(2).assign(type='earthquake')
...     ],
...     join='inner'
... )
```

Notice that the `type` column from the `no_tsunami` dataframe doesn't show up because it wasn't present in the `tsunami` dataframe. Take a look at the index, though; these were the row numbers from the original dataframe before we divided it up into `tsunami` and `no_tsunami`:

	alert	mag	magType	place	time	title	tsunami	ones	mag_negative	parsed_place
36	NaN	5.00	mww	165km NNW of Flying Fish Cove, Christmas Island	1539459504090	M 5.0 – 165km NNW of Flying Fish Cove, Christm...	1	1	False	Christmas Island
118	green	6.70	mww	262km NW of Ozernovskiy, Russia	1539429023560	M 6.7 – 262km NW of Ozernovskiy, Russia	1	1	False	Russia
0	NaN	1.35	ml	9km NE of Aguanga, CA	1539475168010	M 1.4 – 9km NE of Aguanga, CA	0	1	False	California
1	NaN	1.29	ml	9km NE of Aguanga, CA	1539475129610	M 1.3 – 9km NE of Aguanga, CA	0	1	False	California

If the index is not meaningful, we can also pass in `ignore_index` to get sequential values in the index:

```
>>> pd.concat(
...         [
...             tsunami.head(2),
...             no_tsunami.head(2).assign(type='earthquake')
...         ],
...         join='inner', ignore_index=True
... )
```

The index is now sequential and the row numbers no longer match the original dataframe:

	alert	mag	magType	place	time	title	tsunami	ones	mag_negative	parsed_place
0	NaN	5.00	mww	165km NNW of Flying Fish Cove, Christmas Island	1539459504090	M 5.0 – 165km NNW of Flying Fish Cove, Christm...	1	1	False	Christmas Island
1	green	6.70	mww	262km NW of Ozernovskiy, Russia	1539429023560	M 6.7 – 262km NW of Ozernovskiy, Russia	1	1	False	Russia
2	NaN	1.35	ml	9km NE of Aguanga, CA	1539475168010	M 1.4 – 9km NE of Aguanga, CA	0	1	False	California
3	NaN	1.29	ml	9km NE of Aguanga, CA	1539475129610	M 1.3 – 9km NE of Aguanga, CA	0	1	False	California

Be sure to consult the `pandas` documentation for more information on the `concat()` function and other operations for combining data, which we will discuss in Chapter 4, *Aggregating Pandas DataFrames*: http://pandas.pydata.org/pandas-docs/stable/ user_guide/merging.html#concatenating-objects.

Deleting unwanted data

After adding that data to our dataframe in the previous section, we can see the need to delete unwanted data. We need a way to undo our mistakes and get rid of data that we aren't going to use. Like adding data, we can use dictionary syntax to delete unwanted columns, just as we would when removing keys from a dictionary. Both `del df['<column_name>']` and `df.pop('<column_name>')` will work, provided that there is indeed a column with that name; otherwise, we will get a `KeyError`. The difference here is that while `del` removes it right away, `pop()` will return the column that we are removing. Remember that both of these operations will change our original dataframe, so use them with care.

Let's use dictionary notation to delete the `ones` column:

```
>>> del df['ones']
>>> df.columns
Index(['alert', 'mag', 'magType', 'place', 'time', 'title', 'tsunami',
        'mag_negative', 'parsed_place'],
    dtype='object')
```

If we aren't sure whether the column exists, we should use a `try...except` block:

```
try:
    del df['ones']
except KeyError:
    # handle the error here
    pass
```

Earlier, we created the `mag_negative` column for filtering our dataframe; however, we don't want this column as part of our dataframe. We can use `pop()` to grab the series for the `mag_negative` column, which we can use as a Boolean mask later without having it in our dataframe. Notice that the `'mag_negative'` column no longer appears in the result of `df.columns`:

```
>>> mag_negative = df.pop('mag_negative')

>>> df.columns
Index(['alert', 'mag', 'magType', 'place', 'time', 'title', 'tsunami',
       'parsed_place'],
      dtype='object')
```

We now have a Boolean mask in the `mag_negative` variable that used to be a column in `df`:

```
>>> mag_negative.value_counts()
False    8841
True      491
Name: mag_negative, dtype: int64
```

This can be used to filter `df` without needing to be a column:

```
>>> df[mag_negative].head()
```

We are able to filter our dataframe without needing to store the column in the dataframe itself:

	alert	mag	magType	place	time	title	tsunami	parsed_place
39	NaN	−0.10	ml	6km NW of Lemmon...	1539458844506	M −0.1 − 6km NW of Lemmon...	0	Nevada
49	NaN	−0.10	ml	6km NW of Lemmon...	1539455017464	M −0.1 − 6km NW of Lemmon...	0	Nevada
135	NaN	−0.40	ml	10km SSE of Beatty...	1539422175717	M −0.4 − 10km SSE of Beatty...	0	Nevada
161	NaN	−0.02	md	20km SSE of Ronan, Montana	1539412475360	M −0.0 − 20km SSE of Ronan...	0	Montana
198	NaN	−0.20	ml	60km N of Pahrump...	1539398340822	M −0.2 − 60km N of Pahrump...	0	Nevada

`DataFrame` objects have a `drop()` method for removing multiple rows or columns either in-place (overwriting the original dataframe without having to reassign it) or returning a new `DataFrame` object. To remove rows, we pass the list of the indices. Let's remove the first two rows:

```
>>> df.drop([0, 1]).head(2)
```

Notice that the index starts at 2 because we dropped 0 and 1:

	alert	mag	magType	place	time	title	tsunami	parsed_place
2	NaN	3.42	ml	8km NE of Aguanga, CA	1539475062610	M 3.4 – 8km NE of Aguanga, CA	0	California
3	NaN	0.44	ml	9km NE of Aguanga, CA	1539474978070	M 0.4 – 9km NE of Aguanga, CA	0	California

By default, `drop()` assumes that we want to delete rows (`axis=0`). If we want to drop columns, we can either pass `axis=1` or simply pass our list of columns as the `columns` argument. Let's delete some more columns:

```
>>> df.drop(
...     columns=[col for col in df.columns \
...              if col not in \
...              ['alert', 'mag', 'title', 'time', 'tsunami']]
... ).head()
```

This drops all the columns that aren't in the list we wanted to keep:

	alert	mag	time	title	tsunami
0	NaN	1.35	1539475168010	M 1.4 – 9km NE of Aguanga, CA	0
1	NaN	1.29	1539475129610	M 1.3 – 9km NE of Aguanga, CA	0
2	NaN	3.42	1539475062610	M 3.4 – 8km NE of Aguanga, CA	0
3	NaN	0.44	1539474978070	M 0.4 – 9km NE of Aguanga, CA	0
4	NaN	2.16	1539474716050	M 2.2 – 10km NW of Avenal, CA	0

Whether we decide to pass `axis=1` to `drop()` or use the `columns` argument, our result will be equivalent:

```
>>> df.drop(
...     columns=[col for col in df.columns \
...             if col not in \
...             ['alert', 'mag', 'title', 'time', 'tsunami']]
... ).equals(
...     df.drop(
...         [col for col in df.columns \
...          if col not in ['alert', 'mag', 'title', \
...                     'time', 'tsunami']],
...         axis=1
...     )
... )
True
```

By default, `drop()` will return a new `DataFrame` object; however, if we really want to remove the data from our original dataframe, we can pass in `inplace=True`, which will save us from having to reassign the result back into our dataframe:

```
>>> df.drop(
...     columns=[col for col in df.columns \
...             if col not in \
...             ['alert', 'mag', 'title', 'time', 'tsunami']],
...     inplace=True
... )
>>> df.head()
```

We are left with only the columns we excluded in the `if` statement of the list comprehension:

	alert	mag	time	title	tsunami
0	NaN	1.35	1539475168010	M 1.4 - 9km NE of Aguanga, CA	0
1	NaN	1.29	1539475129610	M 1.3 - 9km NE of Aguanga, CA	0
2	NaN	3.42	1539475062610	M 3.4 - 8km NE of Aguanga, CA	0
3	NaN	0.44	1539474978070	M 0.4 - 9km NE of Aguanga, CA	0
4	NaN	2.16	1539474716050	M 2.2 - 10km NW of Avenal, CA	0

Summary

In this chapter, we learned how to use `pandas` for the data collection process of data analysis, and to describe our data with statistics, which will be helpful when we get to the drawing conclusions phase. We learned the main data structures of the `pandas` library, along with some of the operations we can perform on them. Next, we learned how to create `DataFrame` objects from a variety of sources, including flat files and API requests. Using earthquake data, we discussed how to summarize our data and calculate statistics from it. Subsequently, we addressed how to take subsets of data through selection, slicing, indexing, and filtering. Finally, we practiced adding and removing both columns and rows from our dataframe.

These tasks also form the backbone of our `pandas` workflow and the foundation for the new topics we will cover in the next few chapters on data wrangling, aggregation, and data visualization.

Exercises

Using the `data/parsed.csv` file and the material from this chapter, complete the following exercises to practice your `pandas` skills:

1. Find the 95th percentile of earthquake magnitude in Japan using the `magType` of `'mb'`.
2. Find the percentage of earthquakes in Indonesia that were coupled with tsunamis.
3. Get summary statistics for earthquakes in Nevada.
4. Add a column to the dataframe indicating whether or not the earthquake happened in a country or US state that is on the Ring of Fire. Use Bolivia, Chile, Ecuador, Peru, Costa Rica, Guatemala, Mexico (be careful not to select New Mexico), Japan, Philippines, Indonesia, New Zealand, Antarctica (look for Antarctic), Canada, Fiji, Alaska, Washington, California, Russia, Taiwan, Tonga, and Kermadec Islands.
5. Calculate the number of earthquakes in the Ring of Fire locations and the number outside them.
6. Find the tsunami count along the Ring of Fire.

Further reading

The following are some interesting links from the pandas documentation:

- *Styling DataFrames*: https://pandas.pydata.org/pandas-docs/stable/style.html
- *The pandas ecosystem*: https://pandas.pydata.org/pandas-docs/stable/ecosystem.html

Those with an R and/or SQL background may find it helpful to see how the pandas syntax compares:

- *Comparison with R / R Libraries*: https://pandas.pydata.org/pandas-docs/stable/comparison_with_r.html
- *Comparison with SQL*: https://pandas.pydata.org/pandas-docs/stable/comparison_with_sql.html
- *SQL Queries*: https://pandas.pydata.org/pandas-docs/stable/user_guide/io.html#sql-queries

Some resources for learning more about regular expressions are as follows:

- *Mastering Python Regular Expressions by Félix López, Víctor Romero*: https://www.packtpub.com/application-development/mastering-python-regular-expressions
- *Regular Expression Tutorial — Learn How to Use Regular Expressions*: https://www.regular-expressions.info/tutorial.html

Section 2: Using Pandas for Data Analysis

2

Now that we have some exposure to the pandas library, understand what comprises data analysis, and know various ways to collect data, we will focus on the skills we need to perform data wrangling and exploratory data analysis. This section will give us the tools we need to manipulate, reshape, summarize, aggregate, and visualize data in Python.

The following chapters are included in this section:

- Chapter 3, *Data Wrangling with Pandas*
- Chapter 4, *Aggregating Pandas DataFrames*
- Chapter 5, *Visualizing Data with Pandas and Matplotlib*
- Chapter 6, *Plotting with Seaborn and Customization Techniques*

Data Wrangling with Pandas

3

In the previous chapter, we learned about the `pandas` data structures, how to bring our collected data into `DataFrame` objects, and various ways to inspect, summarize, filter, select, and work with `DataFrame` objects. Now that we are well-versed in the initial data collection and inspection stage, we can begin our foray into the world of data wrangling.

As mentioned in `Chapter 1`, *Introduction to Data Analysis*, preparing data for analysis is often the largest portion of the job time-wise for those working with data, and often the least enjoyable. On the bright side, `pandas` is well-equipped to help with these tasks, and, by mastering the skills presented in this book, we will be able to get to the more interesting parts sooner.

It should be noted that data wrangling isn't something we do merely once in our analysis; it is highly likely that we will do some data wrangling and move on to another analysis task, such as data visualization, only to find that we need to do more data wrangling. The more familiar we are with the data, the better we will be able to prepare the data for our analysis. It's crucial to form an intuition of what types our data should be, what format we need our data to be in for the visualization that would best convey what we are looking to show, and the data points we should collect for our analysis. This comes with experience, so we must practice the skills that are covered in this chapter on our own data every chance we get.

Being a very large topic, our coverage of data wrangling will be split between this chapter and `Chapter 4`, *Aggregating Pandas DataFrames*. In this chapter, we will get an overview of data wrangling before walking through the process of collecting temperature data from the **National Centers for Environmental Information (NCEI)** API. Then, we will cover data wrangling tasks that deal with preparing data for some initial analyses and visualizations (which we will learn about in `Chapter 5`, *Visualizing Data with Pandas and Matplotlib*, and `Chapter 6`, *Plotting with Seaborn and Customization Techniques*). We will address some more advanced aspects of data wrangling that relate to aggregations and combining datasets in `Chapter 4`, *Aggregating Pandas DataFrames*.

In this chapter, we will cover the following topics:

- Understanding data wrangling
- Exploring an API to find and collect temperature data
- Cleaning data
- Reshaping data for the analysis at hand
- Handling data that is missing or doesn't make sense

Chapter materials

The materials for this chapter can be found on GitHub at `https://github.com/stefmolin/Hands-On-Data-Analysis-with-Pandas/tree/master/ch_03`. There are five notebooks that we will work through, each numbered according to when they will be used. We will begin with a discussion about wide versus long format data in `1-wide_vs_long.ipynb`. Then, we will collect daily temperature data from the NCEI API, which can be found at `https://www.ncdc.noaa.gov/cdo-web/webservices/v2`, in the `2-using_the_weather_api.ipynb` notebook. The documentation for the **Global Historical Climatology Network - Daily (GHCND)** dataset we will be using can be found here: `https://www1.ncdc.noaa.gov/pub/data/cdo/documentation/GHCND_documentation.pdf`.

 The NCEI is part of the **National Oceanic and Atmospheric Administration (NOAA)**. As indicated by the URL for the API, this resource was created when the NCEI was called the NCDC. Should the URL for this resource change in the future, search for the NCEI weather API to find the updated one.

In `3-cleaning_data.ipynb`, we will learn how to perform an initial round of cleaning on the temperature data and some financial data, which was collected using the `stock_analysis` package that we will build in Chapter 7, *Financial Analysis – Bitcoin and the Stock Market*. We will walk through ways to reshape our data in `4-reshaping_data.ipynb`. Finally, in `5-handling_data_issues.ipynb`, we will learn about some strategies for dealing with duplicate, missing, or invalid data using some dirty data that can be found in `data/dirty_data.csv`. The text will prompt when to switch between notebooks.

There are also two directories:

- data/: This directory contains all of the CSV files we will use in the aforementioned notebooks.
- exercises/: This directory contains the CSV files that are required to complete the end-of-chapter exercises.

The following files are in the data/ directory:

File	Description	Source
bitcoin.csv	Daily opening, high, low, and closing price of bitcoin, along with volume traded and market capitalization for 2017 through 2018.	The *stock_analysis* package (see Chapter 7, *Financial Analysis – Bitcoin and the Stock Market*).
dirty_data.csv	2018 weather data for New York City, manipulated to introduce data issues.	Modified version of the data from the NCEI API's GHCND dataset.
long_data.csv	Long format temperature data for New York City in October 2018 from the Boonton 1 station, containing daily temperature at time of observation, minimum temperature, and maximum temperature.	The NCEI API's GHCND dataset.
nyc_temperatures.csv	Temperature data for New York City in October 2018 measured from LaGuardia airport, containing daily minimum, maximum, and average temperature.	The NCEI API's GHCND dataset.
sp500.csv	Daily opening, high, low, and closing price of the S&P 500 stock index, along with volume traded and adjusted close for 2017 through 2018.	The *stock_analysis* package (see Chapter 7, *Financial Analysis – Bitcoin and the Stock Market*).
wide_data.csv	Wide format temperature data for New York City in October 2018 from the Boonton 1 station, containing daily temperature at time of observation, minimum temperature, and maximum temperature.	The NCEI API's GHCND dataset.

What is data wrangling?

Like any professional field, data analysis is filled with buzzwords, and it can often be difficult for newcomers to understand the lingo—the topic of this chapter is no exception. When we perform **data wrangling**, we are taking our input data from its original state to a format where we can perform meaningful analysis on it. **Data manipulation** is another way to refer to this process. There is no set list or order of operations; the only goal is that the data post-wrangling is more useful to us than when we started.

In practice, there are three common tasks involved in the data wrangling process:

- Data cleaning
- Data transformation
- Data enrichment

It should be noted that there is no inherent order to these tasks, and it is highly probable that we will perform each many times throughout our data wrangling. This idea brings up an interesting conundrum: if we need to wrangle our data to prepare it for our analysis, isn't it possible to wrangle it in such a way that we tell the data what to say instead of us learning what it's saying?

> *"If you torture the data long enough, it will confess to anything."*
> —*Ronald Coase, winner of a Nobel Prize in Economics*

Those working with data will find it is very easy to distort the truth by manipulating the data. However, it is our duty to do our best to avoid deceit by keeping the effect our actions have on the data's integrity in mind, and by explaining the process we took to draw our conclusions to the people who consume our analyses, so that they too may make their own judgments.

Data cleaning

Once we have collected our data, brought it into a `DataFrame` object, and used the skills we discussed in `Chapter 2`, *Working with Pandas DataFrames*, to familiarize ourselves with the data, we will need to perform some data cleaning. An initial round of data cleaning on our dataframe will often give us the bare minimum we need to start exploring our data. Some essential data cleaning tasks to master include the following:

- Renaming
- Sorting and reordering
- Data type conversions
- Deduplicating data
- Addressing missing or invalid data
- Filtering to the desired subset of data

Data cleaning is the best starting point for data wrangling since having the data stored as the correct data types and easy-to-reference names will open up many avenues for exploration and wrangling opportunities, such as summary statistics, sorting, and filtering. Since we covered filtering in `Chapter 2`, *Working with Pandas DataFrames*, we will focus on the other topics from the preceding list in this chapter.

Data transformation

Frequently, we will reach the data transformation stage after some initial data cleaning, but it is entirely possible that our dataset is unusable in its current shape, and we must restructure it before attempting to do any data cleaning. In **data transformation**, we focus on changing our data's structure to facilitate our downstream analyses; this usually involves changing which data goes along the rows and which goes down the columns.

Most data we will find is either in a **wide format** or a **long format**; each of these formats has its merits, and it's important to know which one we will need for our analysis. Often, people will record and present data in the wide format, but there are certain visualizations that require the data to be in the long format:

The wide format is preferred for analysis and database design, while the long format is considered poor design because each column should be its own data type and have a singular meaning. However, in cases where new fields will be added (or old ones removed) from a table in a relational database, rather than have to alter all the tables each time, the database's maintainers may decide to use the long format. This allows them to provide a fixed schema for users of the database, while being able to update the data it contains as needed. When building an API, the long format may be chosen if flexibility is required. Perhaps the API will provide a generic response format (date, field name, and field value) that can support various tables from a database. This may also have to do with making the response easier to form, depending on how the data is stored in the database the API uses. Since we will find data in both of these formats, it's important we understand how to work with both of them and go from one to the other.

Now, let's navigate to the `1-wide_vs_long.ipynb` notebook to see some examples. First, we will import `pandas` and `matplotlib` (to help illustrate the strengths and weaknesses of each format when it comes to visualizations, which we will discuss in `Chapter 5`, *Visualizing Data with Pandas and Matplotlib*, and `Chapter 6`, *Plotting with Seaborn and Customization Techniques*), and read in the CSV files containing wide and long format data:

```
>>> import matplotlib.pyplot as plt
>>> import pandas as pd

>>> wide_df = pd.read_csv('data/wide_data.csv', parse_dates=['date'])
>>> long_df = pd.read_csv(
...     'data/long_data.csv',
...     usecols=['date', 'datatype', 'value'],
...     parse_dates=['date']
... )[['date', 'datatype', 'value']] # sort columns
```

The wide data format

With wide format data, we represent measurements of variables with their own columns, and each row represents an observation of those variables. This makes it easy for us to compare variables across observations, get summary statistics, perform operations, and present our data; however, some visualizations don't work with this data format because they may rely on the long format to split, size, and/or color the plot content.

Let's look at the top six observations from the wide format data in `wide_df`:

```
>>> wide_df.head(6)
```

Each column contains the top six observations of a specific class of temperature data in degrees Celsius—maximum temperature (TMAX), minimum temperature (TMIN), and temperature at time of observation (TOBS)—at a daily frequency:

	date	TMAX	TMIN	TOBS
0	2018-10-01	21.1	8.9	13.9
1	2018-10-02	23.9	13.9	17.2
2	2018-10-03	25.0	15.6	16.1
3	2018-10-04	22.8	11.7	11.7
4	2018-10-05	23.3	11.7	18.9
5	2018-10-06	20.0	13.3	16.1

When working with wide format data, we can easily grab summary statistics on this data (saved as the wide_df variable) by using the describe() method:

```
>>> wide_df.describe(include='all')
```

With hardly any effort on our part, we get summary statistics for the dates, maximum temperature, minimum temperature, and temperature at time of observation:

	date	TMAX	TMIN	TOBS
count	31	31.000000	31.000000	31.000000
unique	31	NaN	NaN	NaN
top	2018-10-01 00:00:00	NaN	NaN	NaN
freq	1	NaN	NaN	NaN
first	2018-10-01 00:00:00	NaN	NaN	NaN
last	2018-10-31 00:00:00	NaN	NaN	NaN
mean	NaN	16.829032	7.561290	10.022581
std	NaN	5.714962	6.513252	6.596550
min	NaN	7.800000	-1.100000	-1.100000
25%	NaN	12.750000	2.500000	5.550000
50%	NaN	16.100000	6.700000	8.300000
75%	NaN	21.950000	13.600000	16.100000
max	NaN	26.700000	17.800000	21.700000

As we discussed previously, the summary data in the preceding table is easy to obtain and is informative. This format can easily be plotted with `pandas` as well, provided we tell it exactly what we want to plot:

```
>>> wide_df.plot(
...     kind='line', y=['TMAX', 'TMIN', 'TOBS'], x='date',
...     title='Temperature in NYC in October 2018',
...     figsize=(15, 5)
... ).set_ylabel('Temperature in Celsius')
>>> plt.show()
```

Pandas plots the daily maximum temperature, minimum temperature, and temperature at time of observation as their own lines on a single line plot:

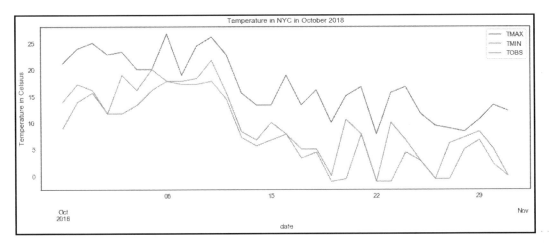

 Don't worry about understanding the visualization code right now; it's here just to illustrate how each of these data formats can make certain tasks easier or harder. We will cover visualizations with `pandas` and `matplotlib` in *Chapter 5*, *Visualizing Data with Pandas and Matplotlib*.

The long data format

We can look at the top six rows of the long format data in `long_df` to see the differences between wide format and long format data:

```
>>> long_df.head(6)
```

Long format data will have a row for each observation of a variable; this means that, if we have three variables being measured daily, we have three rows for each day we record observations. The long format setup can be achieved by turning the variable column names into a column where the data is the variable name and putting their values in a separate values column:

	date	datatype	value
0	2018-10-01	TMAX	21.1
1	2018-10-01	TMIN	8.9
2	2018-10-01	TOBS	13.9
3	2018-10-02	TMAX	23.9
4	2018-10-02	TMIN	13.9
5	2018-10-02	TOBS	17.2

Notice how in the preceding table we now have three entries for each date, and the datatype column tells us what the data in the value column is for that row. If we try to get summary statistics, like we did with the wide format (on long_df, the long format data), we don't get useful information back—it's not helpful to know the average of all the minimum, maximum, and other temperature observations:

```
>>> long_df.describe(include='all')
```

The value column shows us summary statistics, but this is summarizing the daily maximum temperatures, minimum temperatures, and temperatures at time of observation. The maximum will be the maximum of the daily maximum temperatures and the minimum will be the minimum of the daily minimum temperatures. This means that this summary data is useless:

	date	datatype	value
count	93	93	93.000000
unique	31	3	NaN
top	2018-10-01 00:00:00	TMIN	NaN
freq	3	31	NaN
first	2018-10-01 00:00:00	NaN	NaN
last	2018-10-31 00:00:00	NaN	NaN
mean	NaN	NaN	11.470968
std	NaN	NaN	7.362354
min	NaN	NaN	-1.100000
25%	NaN	NaN	6.700000

	date	datatype	value
50%	NaN	NaN	11.700000
75%	NaN	NaN	17.200000
max	NaN	NaN	26.700000

This format is not very easy to digest and certainly shouldn't be how we present data; however, it makes it easy to create visualizations where our plotting library can color lines by the name of the variable, size the dots by the values of a certain variable, and perform splits for faceting.

Pandas expects its data for plotting to be in the wide format, so, in order to easily make the same plot that we did with the wide format data, we must use another plotting library, called `seaborn`, which we will cover in Chapter 6, *Plotting with Seaborn and Customization Techniques*:

```
>>> import seaborn as sns
>>> sns.set(rc={'figure.figsize':(15, 5)}, style='white')
>>> ax = sns.lineplot(
...     data=long_df, hue='datatype', y='value', x='date'
... )
>>> ax.set_ylabel('Temperature in Celsius')
>>> ax.set_title('Temperature in NYC in October 2018')
>>> plt.show()
```

Seaborn is able to subset based on the `datatype` column to give us individual lines for the daily maximum temperature, minimum temperature, and temperature at time of observation:

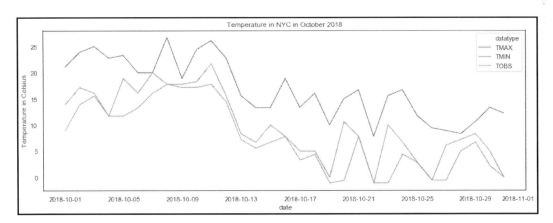

Seaborn lets us specify the column to use for `hue`, which colored the lines by the temperature type. We aren't limited to this, though; with the long data, we can easily facet our plots:

```
>>> sns.set(
...      rc={'figure.figsize':(20, 10)}, style='white', font_scale=2
... )
>>> g = sns.FacetGrid(long_df, col="datatype", height=10)
>>> g = g.map(plt.plot, "date", "value")
>>> g.set_titles(size=25)
>>> g.set_xticklabels(rotation=45)
>>> plt.show()
```

Seaborn is able to use the long format data to create subplots for each distinct `datatype`:

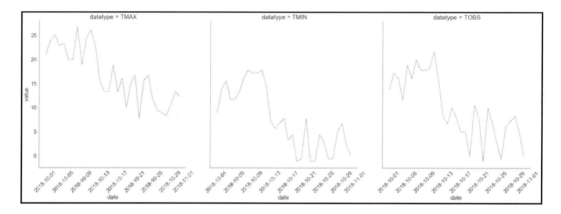

While it is possible to create a similar plot to the preceding one with `pandas` and `matplotlib` using subplots, more complicated combinations of facets will make using `seaborn` infinitely easier. We will cover `seaborn` in `Chapter 6`, *Plotting with Seaborn and Customization Techniques*.

In this chapter, we will cover how to transform our data from wide to long format by melting, and from long to wide format by pivoting. Additionally, we will introduce how to transpose data, which flips the columns and the rows.

Data enrichment

Once we have our cleaned data in the format we need for our analysis, we may find the need to enrich the data a bit. **Data enrichment** (which will be covered in `Chapter 4`, *Aggregating Pandas DataFrames*) improves the quality of the data by adding to it in one way or another. This process becomes very important in modeling and in machine learning, where it forms part of the **feature engineering** process (which we will touch on in `Chapter 10`, *Making Better Predictions – Optimizing Models*).

When we're looking to enrich the data, we can either **merge** new data with the original data (by appending new rows or columns) or use the original data to create new data. The following are ways to enhance our data using the original data:

- **Adding new columns**: Using functions on the data from existing columns to create new values
- **Binning**: Turning continuous data or discrete data with many distinct values into range buckets, which makes the column discrete while letting us control the number of possible values in the column
- **Aggregating**: Rolling up the data and summarizing it
- **Resampling**: Aggregating time series data at specific intervals

Now that we understand what data wrangling is, let's collect some data to wrangle.

Collecting temperature data

In `Chapter 2`, *Working with Pandas DataFrames*, we worked on data collection and how to perform an initial inspection and filtering of the data; this usually gives us ideas of things that need to be addressed before we move further in our analysis. Since this chapter builds on those skills, we will get to practice some of them here as well. To begin, we will start by exploring the weather API that's provided by the NCEI. We will learn about data wrangling with temperature data that's obtained from the API.

 To use the API, you will have to request a token by filling out the form with your email address here: `https://www.ncdc.noaa.gov/cdo-web/token`. If you don't want to do this, you can read through the API code and then read in the CSV file from the GitHub folder and follow along from there.

For this section, we will be working in the `2-using_the_weather_api.ipynb` notebook to request temperature data from the NCEI API. As we learned in `Chapter 2`, *Working with Pandas DataFrames*, we can use the `requests` library to interact with APIs. In the following code block, we import the `requests` library and create a convenience function for making the requests to a specific endpoint, sending our token along. In order to use this function, we need to provide a token, as indicated in bold:

```
>>> import requests

>>> def make_request(endpoint, payload=None):
...     """
...     Make a request to a specific endpoint on the weather API
...     passing headers and optional payload.
...
...     Parameters:
...         - endpoint: The endpoint of the API you want to
...                     make a GET request to.
...         - payload: A dictionary of data to pass along
...                    with the request.
...
...     Returns: Response object.
...     """
...     return requests.get(
...         f'https://www.ncdc.noaa.gov/cdo-web/api/v2/{endpoint}',
...         headers={
...             'token': 'PASTE_YOUR_TOKEN_HERE'
...         },
...         params=payload
...     )
```

This function is making use of **f-strings**, which were introduced in Python 3.6. Those running an older version of Python can use the `format()` method on the string instead:

```
'https://www.ncdc.noaa.gov/cdo-web/api/v2/{}'.format(
    endpoint
)
```

In order to use the `make_request()` function, we need to learn how to form our request. The NCEI has a helpful getting started page (https://www.ncdc.noaa.gov/cdo-web/webservices/v2#gettingStarted) that shows us how to form requests; we can progress through the tabs on the page to figure out all the filters we want on our query. The `requests` library takes care of turning our payload dictionaries into a query string of the parameters that get appended to the end URL (for example, if we pass `2018-08-28` for `start` and `2019-04-15` for `end`, we will get `?start=2018-08-28&end=2019-04-15`), just like the examples on the website. This API provides many different endpoints for exploring what is offered and building up our ultimate request for the actual dataset. We will start by figuring out the ID of the dataset we want to query for (`datasetid`) using the `datasets` endpoint:

```
>>> response = make_request('datasets')
>>> response.status_code
200
```

Remember that we check for the `status_code` of our request to make sure it was successful. Alternatively, we can use `response.ok` to get a Boolean indicator if everything went as expected.

Once we have our response, we can use the `json()` method to get the payload. Then, we can use dictionary methods to determine which part we want to look at:

```
>>> response.json().keys()
dict_keys(['metadata', 'results'])
```

The `metadata` portion of the JSON payload tells us information about the result, and the `results` section contains the actual results. Let's see how much data we got back, so that we know whether we can print the results or whether we should try to limit the output:

```
>>> response.json()['metadata']
{'resultset': {'offset': 1, 'count': 59, 'limit': 100}}
```

We got back 59 rows, which will be a lot to print, so let's see what fields are in the `results` portion of the JSON payload. The `results` key contains a list of dictionaries. If we select the first one, we can look at the keys to see what fields the data contains. We can then reduce the output to the fields we care about:

```
>>> response.json()['results'][0].keys()
dict_keys(['uid', 'mindate', 'maxdate', 'name', 'datacoverage', 'id'])
```

For our purposes, we want to take a look at the IDs and names of the datasets, so let's use a list comprehension to look at those only:

```
>>> [(data['id'], data['name']) \
...   for data in response.json()['results']]
[('GHCND', 'Daily Summaries'),
 ('GSOM', 'Global Summary of the Month'),
 ('GSOY', 'Global Summary of the Year'),
 ('NEXRAD2', 'Weather Radar (Level II)'),
 ('NEXRAD3', 'Weather Radar (Level III)'),
 ('NORMAL_ANN', 'Normals Annual/Seasonal'),
 ('NORMAL_DLY', 'Normals Daily'),
 ('NORMAL_HLY', 'Normals Hourly'),
 ('NORMAL_MLY', 'Normals Monthly'),
 ('PRECIP_15', 'Precipitation 15 Minute'),
 ('PRECIP_HLY', 'Precipitation Hourly')]
```

The first entry in the result is what we are looking for. Now that we have the `datasetid` (GHCND), we proceed to identify the `datacategoryid`, which we need to request temperature data. We do this using the `datacategories` endpoint. We can print the JSON payload here since it isn't that large (only nine entries):

```
>>> response = make_request(
...     'datacategories', payload={'datasetid' : 'GHCND'}
... )
>>> response.status_code
200
>>> response.json()
{'metadata': {'resultset': {'offset': 1, 'count': 9, 'limit': 25}},
 'results': [{'name': 'Evaporation', 'id': 'EVAP'},
  {'name': 'Land', 'id': 'LAND'},
  {'name': 'Precipitation', 'id': 'PRCP'},
  {'name': 'Sky cover & clouds', 'id': 'SKY'},
  {'name': 'Sunshine', 'id': 'Sun'},
  {'name': 'Air Temperature', 'id': 'TEMP'},
  {'name': 'Water', 'id': 'WATER'},
  {'name': 'Wind', 'id': 'WIND'},
  {'name': 'Weather Type', 'id': 'WXTYPE'}]}
```

Based on the previous result, we know that we want the `datacategoryid` of TEMP. Next, we use this to identify the data types we want by using the `datatypes` endpoint. We have to use a list comprehension once again to only print the names and IDs; this is still a rather large list, so the output is abbreviated for brevity:

```
>>> response = make_request(
...     'datatypes', payload={'datacategoryid' : 'TEMP', 'limit' : 100}
... )
```

```
>>> response.status_code
200
>>> [
...     (data['id'], data['name']) \
...     for data in response.json()['results']
... ]
[('CDSD', 'Cooling Degree Days Season to Date'),
 ...,
 ('TAVG', 'Average Temperature.'),
 ('TMAX', 'Maximum temperature'),
 ('TMIN', 'Minimum temperature'),
 ('TOBS', 'Temperature at the time of observation')]
```

The last three data types are what we are looking for (TMAX, TMIN, and TOBS). Now that we have everything we need to request temperature data for all locations, we need to narrow it down to a specific location. In order to do so, we need to use the `locationcategories` endpoint in order to determine the `locationcategoryid`:

```
>>> response = make_request(
...     'locationcategories',
...     {'datasetid': 'GHCND'}
... )
>>> response.status_code
200
```

We can use `pprint` from the Python standard library (https://docs.python.org/3/library/pprint.html) to print our JSON payload in an easier-to-read format:

```
>>> import pprint
>>> pprint.pprint(response.json())
{'metadata': {'resultset': {'count': 12, 'limit': 25, 'offset': 1}},
 'results': [{'id': 'CITY', 'name': 'City'},
             {'id': 'CLIM_DIV', 'name': 'Climate Division'},
             {'id': 'CLIM_REG', 'name': 'Climate Region'},
             {'id': 'CNTRY', 'name': 'Country'},
             {'id': 'CNTY', 'name': 'County'},
             {'id': 'HYD_ACC', 'name': 'Hydrologic Accounting Unit'},
             {'id': 'HYD_CAT', 'name': 'Hydrologic Cataloging Unit'},
             {'id': 'HYD_REG', 'name': 'Hydrologic Region'},
             {'id': 'HYD_SUB', 'name': 'Hydrologic Subregion'},
             {'id': 'ST', 'name': 'State'},
             {'id': 'US_TERR', 'name': 'US Territory'},
             {'id': 'ZIP', 'name': 'Zip Code'}]}
```

We want to look at New York City, so CITY is the proper locationcategoryid. The notebook we are working in has a function to search for a field by name using **binary search** on the API; binary search is a more efficient way of searching through an ordered list. Since we know that the fields can be sorted alphabetically, and the API gives us metadata about the request, we know how many items the API has for a given field and can tell whether we have passed the one we are looking for.

With each request, we grab the middle entry and compare its location in the alphabet with our target; if the result comes before our target, we look at the half of the data that's greater than what we just got; otherwise, we look at the smaller half. Each time, we are slicing the data in half, so when we grab the middle entry to test, we move closer to the value we seek:

```
>>> def get_item(name, what, endpoint, start=1, end=None):
...     """
...     Grab the JSON payload for a given item using binary search.
...
...     Parameters:
...         - name: The item to look for.
...         - what: Dictionary specifying what the item in `name` is.
...         - endpoint: Where to look for the item.
...         - start: The position to start at. We don't need to touch
...           this, but the function will manipulate this
...           with recursion.
...         - end: The last position of the cities. Used to find the
...           midpoint, but like `start` this is not something we need
...           to worry about.
...
...     Returns: Dictionary of the information for the item if found
...              otherwise an empty dictionary.
...     """
...     # find the midpoint which we use to cut the
...     # data in half each time
...     mid = (start + (end if end else 1)) // 2
...
...     # lowercase the name so this is not case-sensitive
...     name = name.lower()
...
...     # define the payload we will send with each request
...     payload = {
...         'datasetid' : 'GHCND', 'sortfield' : 'name',
...         'offset' : mid, # we will change the offset each time
...         'limit' : 1 # we only want one value back
...     }
...
```

```
...        # make request adding additional filter parameters from `what`
...        response = make_request(endpoint, {**payload, **what})
...
...        if response.ok:
...            # if response ok, grab the end index from the response
...            # metadata the first time through
...            end = end if end \
...                else response.json()['metadata']['resultset']['count']
...
...            # grab the lowercase version of the current name
...            current_name = response.json()[
...                'results'
...            ][0]['name'].lower()
...
...            # if what we are searching for is in the current name,
...            # we have found our item
...            if name in current_name:
...                # return the found item
...                return response.json()['results'][0]
...            else:
...                if start >= end:
...                    # if our start index is greater than or equal to our
...                    # end index, we couldn't find it
...                    return {}
...                elif name < current_name:
...                    # our name comes before the current name in the
...                    # alphabet, so we search further to the left
...                    return get_item(name, what, endpoint, start, mid-1)
...                elif name > current_name:
...                    # our name comes after the current name in the
...                    # alphabet, so we search further to the right
...                    return get_item(name, what, endpoint, mid + 1, end)
...        else:
...            # response wasn't ok, use code to determine why
...            print(f'Response not OK, status: {response.status_code}')
```

This is a **recursive** implementation of the algorithm, meaning that we call the function itself from inside; we have to be very careful when doing this to define a **base condition** so that it will eventually stop and not enter an infinite loop. It is possible to implement this iteratively. See the *Further reading* section at the end of this chapter for additional reading on binary search and **recursion**.

In a traditional implementation of binary search, it is trivial to find the length of the list that we are searching. With the API, we have to make one request to get the count; therefore, we must ask for the first entry (offset of 1) to orient ourselves. This means that we have to make an extra request here compared to what we would have needed if we knew how many locations were in the list before starting.

By using binary search here, we find **New York** in **8** requests, despite it being close to the middle of 1,983 entries! For comparison, using linear search, we would have looked at 1,254 entries before finding **New York**. In the following diagram, we can see how binary search eliminates sections of the list of locations systematically, which is represented by black on the number line (white means it is still possible that the desired value is in that section):

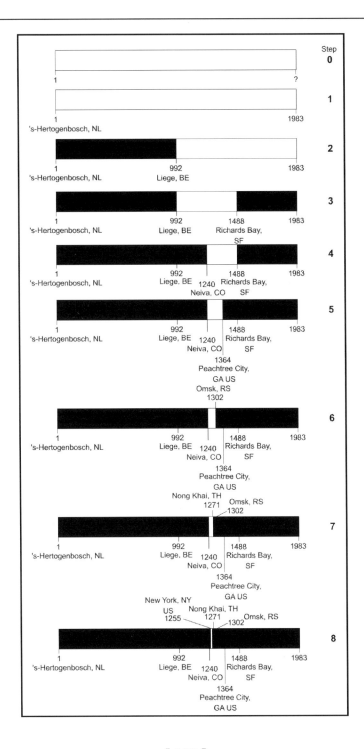

Some APIs restrict the number of requests we can make within certain periods of time, so it's important to be smart about our requests. When searching a very long ordered list, think of binary search. The `get_item()` function we discussed allows us to specify the endpoint and any additional criterion to filter on. Therefore, we can make a convenience function to look up locations and use `get_item()` for the binary search logic:

```
>>> def get_location(name):
...     """
...     Grab the JSON payload for a given location using
...     binary search.
...
...     Parameters:
...         - name: The city to look for.
...
...     Returns: Dictionary of the information for the city if found
...              otherwise an empty dictionary.
...     """
...     return get_item(
...         name, {'locationcategoryid' : 'CITY'}, 'locations'
...     )
```

Let's use the binary search implementation to find the `locationid` for New York City:

```
>>> nyc = get_location('New York')
>>> nyc
{'mindate': '1869-01-01',
 'maxdate': '2019-05-02',
 'name': 'New York, NY US',
 'datacoverage': 1,
 'id': 'CITY:US360019'}
```

Optionally, we can drill down to the `stationid` of the station that is collecting the data. This is the most granular level. Using binary search again, we can grab the station ID for the Central Park station:

```
>>> central_park = get_item(
...     'NY City Central Park', {'locationid' : nyc['id']}, 'stations'
... )
```

```
>>> central_park
{'elevation': 42.7,
 'mindate': '1869-01-01',
 'maxdate': '2019-05-01',
 'latitude': 40.77898,
 'name': 'NY CITY CENTRAL PARK, NY US',
 'datacoverage': 1,
 'id': 'GHCND:USW00094728',
 'elevationUnit': 'METERS',
 'longitude': -73.96925}
```

Now, let's request NYC's temperature data in Celsius for October 2018, recorded from Central Park:

```
>>> response = make_request(
...     'data',
...     {
...         'datasetid' : 'GHCND',
...         'stationid' : central_park['id'],
...         'locationid' : nyc['id'],
...         'startdate' : '2018-10-01',
...         'enddate' : '2018-10-31',
...         'datatypeid' : ['TOBS', 'TMIN', 'TMAX'],
...         'units' : 'metric',
...         'limit' : 100
...     }
... )
>>> response.status_code
200
```

Lastly, we bring our data into a `DataFrame` object; since the `results` portion of the JSON payload is a list of dictionaries, we can pass it directly to `pd.DataFrame()`:

```
>>> import pandas as pd
>>> df = pd.DataFrame(response.json()['results'])
>>> df.head()
```

We get back data in the long format. The `datatype` column is the temperature variable being measured, and the `value` column contains the measured temperature:

	attributes	datatype	date	station	value
0	,,W,2400	TMAX	2018-10-01T00:00:00	GHCND:USW00094728	24.4
1	,,W,2400	TMIN	2018-10-01T00:00:00	GHCND:USW00094728	17.2
2	,,W,2400	TMAX	2018-10-02T00:00:00	GHCND:USW00094728	25.0
3	,,W,2400	TMIN	2018-10-02T00:00:00	GHCND:USW00094728	18.3
4	,,W,2400	TMAX	2018-10-03T00:00:00	GHCND:USW00094728	23.3

We can use the previous code to turn any of the JSON responses we worked with in this section into a `DataFrame` object if we find that easier to work with. However, it should be stressed that JSON payloads are pretty much ubiquitous when it comes to APIs (and, as Python users, we should be familiar with dictionary-like objects), so it won't hurt to get comfortable with them.

We asked for `TOBS`, `TMAX`, and `TMIN`, but notice that we didn't get `TOBS`. This is because the Central Park station isn't recording temperature at the time of observation, despite being listed in the API as offering it—real-world data is dirty:

```
>>> df.datatype.unique()
array(['TMAX', 'TMIN'], dtype=object)

>>> if get_item(
...     'NY City Central Park',
...     {'locationid' : nyc['id'], 'datatypeid': 'TOBS'},
...     'stations'
... ):
...     print('Found!')
Found!
```

Time for plan B: let's use LaGuardia airport as the station instead of Central Park for the remainder of this chapter. The process is the same, but in the interest of brevity, we will read in the data for LaGuardia in the next notebook. Note that the bottom cells of the current notebook contain the code that's used to grab this data.

We could have grabbed data for all the stations that cover New York City; however, since this would give us multiple entries per day for some of the temperature measurements, we won't do so here—we would need skills that are covered in `Chapter 4`, *Aggregating Pandas DataFrames*, to work with that data.

Cleaning up the data

Let's move on to the `3-cleaning_data.ipynb` notebook for our discussion on data cleaning. We will begin by importing `pandas` and reading in the `data/nyc_temperatures.csv` file, which contains the maximum daily temperature (`TMAX`), minimum daily temperature (`TMIN`), and the average daily temperature (`TAVG`) from the LaGuardia airport station in New York City for October 2018:

```
>>> import pandas as pd

>>> df = pd.read_csv('data/nyc_temperatures.csv')
>>> df.head()
```

The data we retrieved from the API is in the long format; for our analysis, we want it in the wide format, but we will address that in the *Pivoting DataFrames* section later this chapter:

	attributes	datatype	date	station	value
0	H,,S,	TAVG	2018-10-01T00:00:00	GHCND:USW00014732	21.2
1	,,W,2400	TMAX	2018-10-01T00:00:00	GHCND:USW00014732	25.6
2	,,W,2400	TMIN	2018-10-01T00:00:00	GHCND:USW00014732	18.3
3	H,,S,	TAVG	2018-10-02T00:00:00	GHCND:USW00014732	22.7
4	,,W,2400	TMAX	2018-10-02T00:00:00	GHCND:USW00014732	26.1

For now, we will focus on little tweaks to the data that will make it easier for us to use: renaming columns, converting each column into the most appropriate data type, sorting columns and values, and reindexing. Often, this will be the time to filter the data down, but we did that when we worked on requesting data from the API; for a review of filtering, refer to `Chapter 2`, *Working with Pandas DataFrames*.

Renaming columns

Since the API endpoint we used could return data of any units and category, it had to call that column `value`. We only pulled temperature data in Celsius, so all of our observations have the same units. This means that we can rename the `value` column so that it's clear what data we are working with:

```
>>> df.columns
Index(['attributes', 'datatype', 'date', 'station', 'value'],
      dtype='object')
```

The `DataFrame` class has a `rename()` method that takes a dictionary that maps the old column name to the new column name. We will also rename the `attributes` column to `flags` since the API documentation mentions that that column contains flags for information about data collection:

```
>>> df.rename(
...     columns={
...         'value' : 'temp_C',
...         'attributes' : 'flags'
...     }, inplace=True
... )
```

Most of the time, `pandas` will return a new `DataFrame` object; however, since we passed in `inplace=True`, our original dataframe was updated instead. Always be careful with in-place operations, as they might be difficult or impossible to undo. Our columns now have their new names:

```
>>> df.columns
Index(['flags', 'datatype', 'date', 'station', 'temp_C'],
      dtype='object')
```

Both `Series` and `Index` objects can also be renamed using their `rename()` methods. Simply pass it the new name. For example, if we have a `Series` called `temperature` and we want to rename it `temp_C`, we run `temperature.rename('temp_C')`. The variable will still be called `temperature`, but the name of the data in the series itself will be `temp_C`.

We can also do transformations on the column names with `rename()`. For instance, we can put all the column names in uppercase:

```
>>> df.rename(str.upper, axis='columns').columns
Index(['FLAGS', 'DATATYPE', 'DATE', 'STATION', 'TEMP_C'],
      dtype='object')
```

This method even lets us rename the values of the `Index`, although this is something we don't have use for until we learn about `groupby()` operations in Chapter 4, *Aggregating Pandas DataFrames*, because our index is just numbers right now. For reference, we would simply change `axis='columns'` in the preceding code to `axis='rows'`.

Type conversion

Now that the column names are indicative of the data they contain, we can check what types of data they hold. We should have formed an intuition as to what the data types should be after looking at the first few rows when we inspected the dataframe with the `head()` method previously. With type conversion, we aim to reconcile what the current data types are with what we believe they should be; we will be changing how our data is represented.

Note that, sometimes, we may have data that we believe should be a certain type, such as a date, but it is stored as a string; this could be for a very valid reason—data could be missing. In the case of missing data encoded as text (for example, `?`), `pandas` will store it as a string when reading it in in order to allow for this data. It will be marked as `object` when we use the `dtypes` attribute on our dataframe. If we try to convert (or cast) these columns, we will either get an error or our result won't be what we expected. For example, if we have strings of decimal numbers, but try to convert the column into integers, we will get an error since Python knows they aren't integers; however, if we try to convert decimal numbers into integers, we will lose any information after the decimal point.

That being said, let's examine the data types in our temperature data. Note that the `date` column isn't actually being stored as a datetime:

```
>>> df.dtypes
flags        object
datatype     object
date         object
station      object
temp_C       float64
dtype: object
```

We can have `pandas` cast it to a datetime for us with a handy convenience function, `pd.to_datetime()`:

```
>>> df.loc[:,'date'] = pd.to_datetime(df.date)
>>> df.dtypes
flags               object
datatype            object
date         datetime64[ns]
station             object
temp_C              float64
dtype: object
```

This is much better. Now, we can get useful information when we summarize the `date` column:

```
>>> df.date.describe()
count                        93
unique                       31
top         2018-10-01 00:00:00
freq                          3
first       2018-10-01 00:00:00
last        2018-10-31 00:00:00
Name: date, dtype: object
```

Dealing with dates can be tricky since they come in many different formats and time zones; fortunately, `pandas` has more methods we can use for dealing with the conversion of datetime objects. For example, when working with a `DatetimeIndex` or `PeriodIndex`, if we need to keep track of time zones, we can use the `tz_localize()` method to tie our datetimes to a time zone:

```
>>> pd.date_range(start='2018-10-25', periods=2, freq='D')\
...     .tz_localize('EST')
DatetimeIndex(['2018-10-25 00:00:00-05:00',
               '2018-10-26 00:00:00-05:00'],
              dtype='datetime64[ns, EST]', freq='D')
```

This also works with `Series` and `DataFrame` objects that have one of the aforementioned (`DatetimeIndex` or `PeriodIndex`) as their `Index`. We can read in the CSV file again and, this time, specify that the `date` column will be our index and that we should parse any dates in the CSV file into datetimes:

```
>>> eastern = pd.read_csv(
...     'data/nyc_temperatures.csv',
...     index_col='date',
...     parse_dates=True
... ).tz_localize('EST')
>>> eastern.head()
```

We have to read the file in again for this example because we haven't learned how to change the index of our data yet, which we will cover in the *Reordering, reindexing, and sorting data* section later this chapter. Note that we have added the Eastern standard time zone offset (-05:00 from UTC) to the datetimes in the index:

date	attributes	datatype	station	value
2018-10-01 00:00:00-05:00	H,,S,	TAVG	GHCND:USW00014732	21.2
2018-10-01 00:00:00-05:00	,,W,2400	TMAX	GHCND:USW00014732	25.6
2018-10-01 00:00:00-05:00	,,W,2400	TMIN	GHCND:USW00014732	18.3
2018-10-02 00:00:00-05:00	H,,S,	TAVG	GHCND:USW00014732	22.7
2018-10-02 00:00:00-05:00	,,W,2400	TMAX	GHCND:USW00014732	26.1

We can use tz_convert() to change the time zone into a different one. Let's change our Eastern standard time data into UTC:

```
>>> eastern.tz_convert('UTC').head()
```

Now, the offset is UTC (+00:00), but note that the time portion of the date is now 5 AM; this conversion took into account the fact that Eastern standard times have an offset of -05:00:

date	attributes	datatype	station	value
2018-10-01 05:00:00+00:00	H,,S,	TAVG	GHCND:USW00014732	21.2
2018-10-01 05:00:00+00:00	,,W,2400	TMAX	GHCND:USW00014732	25.6
2018-10-01 05:00:00+00:00	,,W,2400	TMIN	GHCND:USW00014732	18.3
2018-10-02 05:00:00+00:00	H,,S,	TAVG	GHCND:USW00014732	22.7
2018-10-02 05:00:00+00:00	,,W,2400	TMAX	GHCND:USW00014732	26.1

We can also truncate datetimes with `to_period()`, which comes in handy if we don't care about the full date. For example, if we wanted to aggregate our data by month, we could truncate our index to just the month and year and then perform the aggregation. Since we will cover aggregation in `Chapter 4`, *Aggregating Pandas DataFrames*, we will just do the truncation here:

```
>>> eastern.to_period('M').index
PeriodIndex(['2018-10', '2018-10', '2018-10', '2018-10', '2018-10',
             ...,
             '2018-10', '2018-10', '2018-10', '2018-10', '2018-10'],
            dtype='period[M]', name='date', freq='M')
```

Note how, when we truncated the datetimes, the object we got back was a `PeriodIndex` instead of a `DatetimeIndex`. We can use `to_timestamp()` to undo this; however, the datetimes all start at the first of the month now:

```
>>> eastern.to_period('M').to_timestamp().index
DatetimeIndex(['2018-10-01', '2018-10-01', '2018-10-01', '2018-10-01',
               ...,
               '2018-10-01', '2018-10-01', '2018-10-01'],
              dtype='datetime64[ns]', name='date', freq=None)
```

Alternatively, we could have used the `assign()` method to handle this conversion by passing the column names as named parameters and their new values as the value for that argument to the method call. In practice, this will be more beneficial since we can perform many tasks in one call and use columns we create in that call to calculate additional columns. For example, let's use the original dataframe we created that doesn't have any time zone awareness (`df`) and cast the `date` column to a datetime and add a `temp_F` column for the temperature in Fahrenheit. The `assign()` method returns a new `DataFrame` object, so we must remember to assign it to a variable if we want to keep it. Here, we will create a new dataframe. Note that our original conversion of the datetime modified the column, so, in order to illustrate that we can use `assign()`, we need to read our data in once more:

```
>>> df = pd.read_csv('data/nyc_temperatures.csv').rename(
...     columns={'value' : 'temp_C', 'attributes' : 'flags'}
... )

>>> new_df = df.assign(
...     date=pd.to_datetime(df.date),
...     temp_F=(df.temp_C * 9/5) + 32
... )

>>> new_df.dtypes
flags                 object
datatype              object
date           datetime64[ns]
station               object
temp_C               float64
temp_F               float64
dtype: object

>>> new_df.head()
```

We now have datetimes in the `date` column and a new column, `temp_F`:

	flags	datatype	date	station	temp_C	temp_F
0	H,,S,	TAVG	2018-10-01	GHCND:USW00014732	21.2	70.16
1	,,W,2400	TMAX	2018-10-01	GHCND:USW00014732	25.6	78.08
2	,,W,2400	TMIN	2018-10-01	GHCND:USW00014732	18.3	64.94
3	H,,S,	TAVG	2018-10-02	GHCND:USW00014732	22.7	72.86
4	,,W,2400	TMAX	2018-10-02	GHCND:USW00014732	26.1	78.98

TIP

It is very common (and useful) to use **lambda functions** with `assign()`. In the preceding example, the calculation of the temperature in Fahrenheit could be rewritten as follows: `temp_F=lambda x: (x.temp_C * 9/5) + 32`. This comes in handy when our dataframe has a long name, say `temperature_in_nyc_oct_2018`. We can also use lambda functions to access columns being created in this call to `assign()` to calculate other columns.

Additionally, we can use the `astype()` method to convert one column at a time. As an example, let's say we only cared about the temperatures at every whole number, but we don't want to round. In this case, we simply want to chop off the information after the decimal. To accomplish this, we can cast the floats as integers:

```
>>> df = df.assign(
...     date=pd.to_datetime(df.date),
...     temp_C_whole=df.temp_C.astype('int'),
...     temp_F=(df.temp_C * 9/5) + 32,
...     temp_F_whole=lambda x: x.temp_F.astype('int')
... )
>>> df.head()
```

Note that we can refer to columns we just created if we use a lambda function. It's also important to mention that we don't have to know whether to convert the column into a float or integer; we can use `pd.to_numeric()`, which will convert the data into floats if it sees decimals. If all the numbers are whole, they will be integers (obviously, we will still get errors if the data isn't numeric at all):

	flags	datatype	date	station	temp_C	temp_F	temp_C_whole	temp_F_whole
0	H,,S,	TAVG	2018-10-01	GHCND:USW00014732	21.2	70.16	21	70
1	,,W,2400	TMAX	2018-10-01	GHCND:USW00014732	25.6	78.08	25	78
2	,,W,2400	TMIN	2018-10-01	GHCND:USW00014732	18.3	64.94	18	64
3	H,,S,	TAVG	2018-10-02	GHCND:USW00014732	22.7	72.86	22	72
4	,,W,2400	TMAX	2018-10-02	GHCND:USW00014732	26.1	78.98	26	78

Lastly, we have two columns with data currently being stored as strings that can be represented in a better way for this dataset. The station and datatype columns only have one and three distinct values, respectively, meaning that we aren't being efficient with our memory use since we are storing them as strings. We could potentially have issues with analyses further down the line. Pandas has the ability to define columns as **categorical**; certain statistical operations both within pandas and other packages will be able to handle this data, provide meaningful statistics on them, and use them properly. Categorical variables can take on one of a few values; for example, blood type would be a categorical variable—people can only have one of A, B, AB, or O.

Going back to the temperature data, we only have one value for the station column and only three distinct values for the datatype (TMIN, TMAX, TAVG). We can use the astype() method to cast these to categories and look at the summary statistics for categories:

```
>>> df_with_categories = df.assign(
...        station=df.station.astype('category'),
...        datatype=df.datatype.astype('category')
... )

>>> df_with_categories.dtypes
flags                  object
datatype               category
date           datetime64[ns]
station                category
temp_C                 float64
temp_F                 float64
dtype: object

>>> df_with_categories.describe(include='category')
```

The summary statistics for categories are just like those for strings and datetimes. We can see the amount of non-null entries (count), the number of unique values (unique), the mode (top), and the number of occurrences of the mode (freq):

	datatype	station
count	93	93
unique	3	1
top	TMIN	GHCND:USW00014732
freq	31	93

The categories we just made don't have any order to them, but `pandas` does support this:

```
>>> pd.Categorical(
...     ['med', 'med', 'low', 'high'],
...     categories=['low', 'med', 'high'],
...     ordered=True
... )
[med, med, low, high]
Categories (3, object): [low < med < high]
```

Reordering, reindexing, and sorting data

We will often find the need to sort our data by the values of one or many columns. Say we wanted to find the hottest days in New York City during October 2018; we could sort our values by the `temp_C` (or `temp_F`) column in descending order and use `head()` to select the number of days we wanted to see. To accomplish this, we can use the `sort_values()` method. Let's look at the top 10 days:

```
>>> df.sort_values(by='temp_C', ascending=False).head(10)
```

This shows us that October 7th was the warmest day during the month in October 2018, according to the LaGuardia station. Notice that we have ties between October 2nd and 4th and October 1st and 9th:

	flags	datatype	date	station	temp_C	temp_C_whole	temp_F	temp_F_whole
19	,,W,2400	TMAX	2018-10-07	GHCND:USW00014732	27.8	27	82.04	82
28	,,W,2400	TMAX	2018-10-10	GHCND:USW00014732	27.8	27	82.04	82
31	,,W,2400	TMAX	2018-10-11	GHCND:USW00014732	26.7	26	80.06	80
4	,,W,2400	TMAX	2018-10-02	GHCND:USW00014732	26.1	26	78.98	78
10	,,W,2400	TMAX	2018-10-04	GHCND:USW00014732	26.1	26	78.98	78
25	,,W,2400	TMAX	2018-10-09	GHCND:USW00014732	25.6	25	78.08	78
1	,,W,2400	TMAX	2018-10-01	GHCND:USW00014732	25.6	25	78.08	78
7	,,W,2400	TMAX	2018-10-03	GHCND:USW00014732	25.0	25	77.00	77
27	H,,S,	TAVG	2018-10-10	GHCND:USW00014732	23.8	23	74.84	74
30	H,,S,	TAVG	2018-10-11	GHCND:USW00014732	23.4	23	74.12	74

By default, `sort_values()` will put any NaN values last. We can change this behavior by passing `na_position='first'`. This can be helpful when we're checking our data for null values.

The `sort_values()` method can be used with a list of column names to break ties. The order in which the columns are provided will determine the order in which they are sorted on, with each subsequent column being used to break ties. As an example, we can break ties with the `date` column:

```
>>> df.sort_values(by=['temp_C', 'date'], ascending=False).head(10)
```

Since we are sorting in descending order, in the case of a tie, the date that comes later in the year will be above the earlier one. Notice how October 4th is now above October 2nd, despite both having the same temperature reading:

	flags	datatype	date	station	temp_C	temp_C_whole	temp_F	temp_F_whole
28	,,W,2400	TMAX	2018-10-10	GHCND:USW00014732	27.8	27	82.04	82
19	,,W,2400	TMAX	2018-10-07	GHCND:USW00014732	27.8	27	82.04	82
31	,,W,2400	TMAX	2018-10-11	GHCND:USW00014732	26.7	26	80.06	80
10	,,W,2400	TMAX	2018-10-04	GHCND:USW00014732	26.1	26	78.98	78
4	,,W,2400	TMAX	2018-10-02	GHCND:USW00014732	26.1	26	78.98	78
25	,,W,2400	TMAX	2018-10-09	GHCND:USW00014732	25.6	25	78.08	78
1	,,W,2400	TMAX	2018-10-01	GHCND:USW00014732	25.6	25	78.08	78
7	,,W,2400	TMAX	2018-10-03	GHCND:USW00014732	25.0	25	77.00	77
27	H,,S,	TAVG	2018-10-10	GHCND:USW00014732	23.8	23	74.84	74
30	H,,S,	TAVG	2018-10-11	GHCND:USW00014732	23.4	23	74.12	74

Pandas also provides an additional way to look at a subset of the sorted values, like we did in the previous example when we called `head()` after sorting; we can use `nlargest()` to grab the n rows with the largest values according to a specific criteria and `nsmallest()` to grab the n smallest rows, without the need to sort the data beforehand. Both accept a list of column names or a string for a single column. Let's just grab the top five this time:

```
>>> df.nlargest(n=5, columns='temp_C')
```

Just like for the preceding output, we get the warmest days in October:

	flags	datatype	date	station	temp_C	temp_C_whole	temp_F	temp_F_whole
19	,,W,2400	TMAX	2018-10-07	GHCND:USW00014732	27.8	27	82.04	82
28	,,W,2400	TMAX	2018-10-10	GHCND:USW00014732	27.8	27	82.04	82
31	,,W,2400	TMAX	2018-10-11	GHCND:USW00014732	26.7	26	80.06	80
4	,,W,2400	TMAX	2018-10-02	GHCND:USW00014732	26.1	26	78.98	78
10	,,W,2400	TMAX	2018-10-04	GHCND:USW00014732	26.1	26	78.98	78

We aren't limited to sorting values; if we wish, we can even order the columns alphabetically and sort the rows by their index values. For these tasks, we use the `sort_index()` method. By default, `sort_index()` will target the rows so that we can do things like order the index after an operation that shuffles it. The `sample()` method will give us randomly selected rows, which will lead to a jumbled index, so we can use `sort_index()` to order them afterwards:

```
>>> df.sample(5, random_state=0).index
Int64Index([2, 30, 55, 16, 13], dtype='int64')

>>> df.sample(5, random_state=0).sort_index().index
Int64Index([2, 13, 16, 30, 55], dtype='int64')
```

If we need the result of `sample()` to be reproducible, we can also pass in a **random state** set to the number of our choosing (also called a **seed**); for example, `df.sample(5, random_state=26)`. The seed initializes a pseudorandom number generator so, provided that the same seed is used, the results will be the same.

When we want to target columns, we must pass `axis=1`; rows will be the default (`axis=0`). Note that this argument is present in many `pandas` methods and functions (including `sample()`), so it's important to understand what this means. Let's use this knowledge to sort the columns of our dataframe alphabetically:

```
>>> df.sort_index(axis=1).head()
```

Having our columns in alphabetical order can come in handy with `loc` because we can specify a range of columns with similar names; for example, we could use `df.loc[:, 'temp_C':'temp_F_whole']` to easily grab all of our temperature columns:

	datatype	date	flags	station	temp_C	temp_C_whole	temp_F	temp_F_whole
0	TAVG	2018-10-01	H,,S,	GHCND:USW00014732	21.2	21	70.16	70
1	TMAX	2018-10-01	,,W,2400	GHCND:USW00014732	25.6	25	78.08	78
2	TMIN	2018-10-01	,,W,2400	GHCND:USW00014732	18.3	18	64.94	64
3	TAVG	2018-10-02	H,,S,	GHCND:USW00014732	22.7	22	72.86	72
4	TMAX	2018-10-02	,,W,2400	GHCND:USW00014732	26.1	26	78.98	78

Both `sort_index()` and `sort_values()` return new `DataFrame` objects. We must pass in `inplace=True` to update the dataframe we are working with.

The `sort_index()` method can also help us get an accurate answer when we're testing two dataframes for equality. Pandas will check that, in addition to having the same data, both have the same values for the index when it compares the rows. If we sort our dataframe by temperature in Celsius and check whether it is equal to the original dataframe, `pandas` tells us they aren't. We must sort the index to see that they are the same:

```
>>> df.equals(df.sort_values(by='temp_C'))
False
>>> df.equals(df.sort_values(by='temp_C').sort_index())
True
```

In `pandas`, the index is tied to the row of data—when we drop rows, filter, or do anything that returns only some of the rows, our index will have some holes in it. Should we want to go back to an index without missing entries, we can reset it with the `reset_index()` method. This will move our original index into a column (keeping its name if it had one) and give us a `RangeIndex`:

```
>>> df[df.datatype == 'TAVG'].head().reset_index()
```

Our index is now a `RangeIndex` starting at 0, and our original index is now a column called `index`. This is especially useful if we have data that we don't want to lose on the index, such as the date, but need to perform an operation as if the date weren't the index:

	index	flags	datatype	date	station	temp_C	temp_C_whole	temp_F	temp_F_whole
0	0	H,,S,	TAVG	2018-10-01	GHCND:USW00014732	21.2	21	70.16	70
1	3	H,,S,	TAVG	2018-10-02	GHCND:USW00014732	22.7	22	72.86	72
2	6	H,,S,	TAVG	2018-10-03	GHCND:USW00014732	21.8	21	71.24	71
3	9	H,,S,	TAVG	2018-10-04	GHCND:USW00014732	21.3	21	70.34	70
4	12	H,,S,	TAVG	2018-10-05	GHCND:USW00014732	20.3	20	68.54	68

Sometimes, we don't care too much about the numeric index like we have in the previous examples, but we would like to use one (or more) of the other columns as the index. In this case, we can use the `set_index()` method. Let's set the `date` column as our index:

```
>>> df.set_index('date', inplace=True)
>>> df.head()
```

Our result looks like it is stacked differently than we are used to seeing, and our index column has a name now: `date`.

Notice that the date column has moved to the far left where the index goes, and we no longer have the numeric index:

date	flags	datatype	station	temp_C	temp_C_whole	temp_F	temp_F_whole
2018-10-01	H,,S,	TAVG	GHCND:USW00014732	21.2	21	70.16	70
2018-10-01	,,W,2400	TMAX	GHCND:USW00014732	25.6	25	78.08	78
2018-10-01	,,W,2400	TMIN	GHCND:USW00014732	18.3	18	64.94	64
2018-10-02	H,,S,	TAVG	GHCND:USW00014732	22.7	22	72.86	72
2018-10-02	,,W,2400	TMAX	GHCND:USW00014732	26.1	26	78.98	78

We can also provide a list of columns to use as the index. This will create a MultiIndex, where the first element in the list is the outermost level and the last is the innermost. We will discuss this further in the *Pivoting DataFrames* section.

Setting the index to a datetime lets us take advantage of the datetime slicing we discussed in Chapter 2, *Working with Pandas DataFrames*. For example, we can select dates from October 11, 2018 through October 12, 2018 (inclusive of both endpoints) by executing the following command:

```
>>> df['2018-10-11':'2018-10-12']
```

As long as we provide a date format that pandas understands, we can grab the data. To select all of 2018, we simply use df['2018']; for the third quarter of 2018, we can use ['2018-Q3']; and grabbing October is as simple as using df['2018-10']. These can also be combined to build ranges, as in this case:

date	flags	datatype	station	temp_C	temp_C_whole	temp_F	temp_F_whole
2018-10-11	H,,S,	TAVG	GHCND:USW00014732	23.4	23	74.12	74
2018-10-11	,,W,2400	TMAX	GHCND:USW00014732	26.7	26	80.06	80
2018-10-11	,,W,2400	TMIN	GHCND:USW00014732	21.7	21	71.06	71
2018-10-12	H,,S,	TAVG	GHCND:USW00014732	18.3	18	64.94	64
2018-10-12	,,W,2400	TMAX	GHCND:USW00014732	22.2	22	71.96	71
2018-10-12	,,W,2400	TMIN	GHCND:USW00014732	12.2	12	53.96	53

In some cases, we may have an index we want to continue to use, but we need to align it to certain values. For this purpose, we have the reindex() method. We provide it with an index to align our data to, and it adjusts the index accordingly. Note that this new index isn't necessarily part of the data—we simply have an index and want to match the current data up to it.

As an example, we will turn to the S&P 500 stock data in the `data/sp500.csv` file. It contains the opening, high, low, and closing (also called **OHLC**) price daily for the S&P 500 from 2017 through the end of 2018, along with volume traded and the adjusted close (which we won't use). Let's read it in by setting the `date` column as the index and parsing dates:

```
>>> sp = pd.read_csv(
...     'data/sp500.csv', index_col='date', parse_dates=True
... ).drop(columns=['adj_close']) # not using this column
```

Let's see what our data looks like and mark the day of the week for each row in order to understand what the index contains. We can easily isolate the date part from the index when it is a datetime. When isolating date parts, `pandas` will give us the numeric representation of what we are looking for; if we are looking for the string version, we should look to see whether there is a method for that before writing our own conversion function. In this case, it's `day_name()`:

```
>>> sp.head(10).assign(day_of_week=lambda x: x.index.day_name())
```

> We can also do this with a series, but first we need to access the `dt` attribute. For example, if we had a `date` column in the `sp` dataframe, we could use `sp.date.dt.month` to grab the month out. You can find the full list of what can be accessed here: `https://pandas.pydata.org/pandas-docs/stable/api.html#datetimelike-properties`.

Since the stock market is closed on the weekend (and holidays), we only have data for weekdays:

date	high	low	open	close	volume	day_of_week
2017-01-03	2263.879883	2245.129883	2251.570068	2257.830078	3770530000	Tuesday
2017-01-04	2272.820068	2261.600098	2261.600098	2270.750000	3764890000	Wednesday
2017-01-05	2271.500000	2260.449951	2268.179932	2269.000000	3761820000	Thursday
2017-01-06	2282.100098	2264.060059	2271.139893	2276.979980	3339890000	Friday
2017-01-09	2275.489990	2268.899902	2273.590088	2268.899902	3217610000	Monday
2017-01-10	2279.270020	2265.270020	2269.719971	2268.899902	3638790000	Tuesday
2017-01-11	2275.320068	2260.830078	2268.600098	2275.320068	3620410000	Wednesday
2017-01-12	2271.780029	2254.250000	2271.139893	2270.439941	3462130000	Thursday
2017-01-13	2278.679932	2271.510010	2272.739990	2274.639893	3081270000	Friday
2017-01-17	2272.080078	2262.810059	2269.139893	2267.889893	3584990000	Tuesday

If we were analyzing the performance of a group of assets in a portfolio that included the S&P 500 and something that trades on the weekend, like bitcoin, we would need to have values for every day of the year for the S&P 500. Otherwise, when we wanted to see how much our portfolio was worth every day, we would see huge drops every day the market was closed. To illustrate this, let's read in the bitcoin data from the `data/bitcoin.csv` file and concatenate the S&P 500 and bitcoin data into a portfolio. The bitcoin data also contains OHLC data and volume traded, but it comes with a column called `market_cap` that we don't need, so we have to drop it first:

```
>>> bitcoin = pd.read_csv(
...     'data/bitcoin.csv', index_col='date', parse_dates=True
... ).drop(columns=['market_cap'])
```

We will need to aggregate the data by day for the portfolio; this is a topic for Chapter 4, *Aggregating Pandas DataFrames*, so, for now, don't worry too much about how this aggregation is being performed—just know that we are summing up the data by day. For example, each day's closing price will be the sum of the closing price of the S&P 500 and the closing price of bitcoin:

```
# every day's closing price = S&P 500 close + Bitcoin close
# (same for other metrics)
>>> portfolio = pd.concat(
...     [sp, bitcoin], sort=False
... ).groupby(pd.Grouper(freq='D')).sum()

>>> portfolio.head(10).assign(
...     day_of_week=lambda x: x.index.day_name()
... )
```

Now, if we examine our portfolio, we will see that we have values for every day of the week; so far, so good:

date	high	low	open	close	volume	day_of_week
2017-01-01	1003.080000	958.700000	963.660000	998.330000	147775008	Sunday
2017-01-02	1031.390000	996.700000	998.620000	1021.750000	222184992	Monday
2017-01-03	3307.959883	3266.729883	3273.170068	3301.670078	3955698000	Tuesday
2017-01-04	3432.240068	3306.000098	3306.000098	3425.480000	4109835984	Wednesday
2017-01-05	3462.600000	3170.869951	3424.909932	3282.380000	4272019008	Thursday
2017-01-06	3328.910098	3148.000059	3285.379893	3179.179980	3691766000	Friday
2017-01-07	908.590000	823.560000	903.490000	908.590000	279550016	Saturday
2017-01-08	942.720000	887.250000	908.170000	911.200000	158715008	Sunday
2017-01-09	3189.179990	3148.709902	3186.830088	3171.729902	3359486992	Monday
2017-01-10	3194.140020	3166.330020	3172.159971	3176.579902	3754598000	Tuesday

However, there is a problem with this approach, which is much easier to see with a visualization. Plotting will be covered in depth in `Chapter 5`, *Visualizing Data with Pandas and Matplotlib*, and `Chapter 6`, *Plotting with Seaborn and Customization Techniques*, so don't worry about the details for now:

```
>>> import matplotlib.pyplot as plt # we use this module for plotting

>>> portfolio['2017-Q4':'2018-Q2'].plot(
...     y='close', figsize=(15, 5), legend=False,
...     title='Bitcoin + S&P 500 value without accounting '\
...         'for different indices'
... ) # plot the closing price from Q4 2017 through Q2 2018
>>> plt.ylabel('price ($)') # label the y-axis
>>> plt.show() # show the plot
```

Notice how there is a cyclical pattern here? It is dropping every day the market is closed because the aggregation only had bitcoin data to sum for those days:

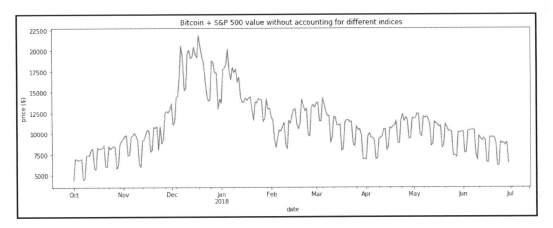

Clearly, this is a problem; an asset's value doesn't drop to zero just because the market is closed. If we want `pandas` to fill the missing data in for us, we can reindex the S&P 500 data using bitcoin's index with the `reindex()` method and pass one of the following strategies to the `method` parameter:

- `'ffill'`: This method brings values forward. In the previous example, this fills the days the market was closed with the data for the last time the market was open before those days.
- `'bfill'`: This method back propagates the values, which will result in carrying future results to past dates, meaning that this isn't the right option here.
- `'nearest'`: This method fills according to the rows closest to the missing ones, which in this case will result in Sundays getting the data for the following Mondays, and Saturdays getting the data from the previous Fridays.

Forward-filling seems to be the best option, but, since we aren't sure, we will see how this works on a few rows of the data first:

```
>>> sp.reindex(
...     bitcoin.index, method='ffill'
... ).head(10).assign(
...     day_of_week=lambda x: x.index.day_name()
... )
```

Notice any issues with this? Well, the volume traded (`volume`) column makes it seem that the days we used forward-filling for are actually days when the market is open:

	high	low	open	close	volume	day_of_week
2017-01-01	NaN	NaN	NaN	NaN	NaN	Sunday
2017-01-02	NaN	NaN	NaN	NaN	NaN	Monday
2017-01-03	2263.879883	2245.129883	2251.570068	2257.830078	3.770530e+09	Tuesday
2017-01-04	2272.820068	2261.600098	2261.600098	2270.750000	3.764890e+09	Wednesday
2017-01-05	2271.500000	2260.449951	2268.179932	2269.000000	3.761820e+09	Thursday
2017-01-06	2282.100098	2264.060059	2271.139893	2276.979980	3.339890e+09	Friday
2017-01-07	2282.100098	2264.060059	2271.139893	2276.979980	3.339890e+09	Saturday
2017-01-08	2282.100098	2264.060059	2271.139893	2276.979980	3.339890e+09	Sunday
2017-01-09	2275.489990	2268.899902	2273.590088	2268.899902	3.217610e+09	Monday
2017-01-10	2279.270020	2265.270020	2269.719971	2268.899902	3.638790e+09	Tuesday

Ideally, we only want to maintain the value of the stock when the stock market is closed; however, the volume traded should be zero. In order to handle the NaN data in a different manner for each column, we will turn to the `assign()` method. To fill any NaN data in the `volume` column with 0, we will use the `fillna()` method, which we will see more of in the *Handling duplicate, missing, or invalid data* section later this chapter. The `fillna()` method also allows us to pass in a method instead of a value, so we can forward-fill the `close` column, which was the only column that made sense from our previous attempt. Lastly, we can use the `np.where()` function for the remaining columns, which allows us to build a vectorized `if...else`.

The `np.where()` function takes the following form:
```
np.where(
    boolean condition, value if True, value if False
)
```

Vectorized operations are performed on all elements in the array at once; since each element has the same data type, these calculations can be run rather quickly. As a general rule of thumb with `pandas`, we should avoid writing loops in favor of vectorized operations for better performance. NumPy functions are designed to work on arrays, so they are perfect candidates for high-performance `pandas` code. This will make it easy for us to set any NaN values in the `open`, `high`, or `low` columns to the value in the `close` column for the same day. Since these come after the `close` column gets worked on, we will have the forward-filled value for `close` to use for the other columns where necessary:

```
>>> import numpy as np


>>> sp_reindexed = sp.reindex(
...     bitcoin.index
... ).assign(
...     # put 0 when market is closed
...     volume=lambda x: x.volume.fillna(0),
...     close=lambda x: x.close.fillna(method='ffill'), # carry
...     # take the closing price if these aren't available
...     open=lambda x: np.where(x.open.isnull(), x.close, x.open),
...     high=lambda x: np.where(x.high.isnull(), x.close, x.high),
...     low=lambda x: np.where(x.low.isnull(), x.close, x.low)
... )

>>> sp_reindexed.head(10).assign(
...     day_of_week=lambda x: x.index.day_name()
... )
```

On Saturday January 7th and Sunday January 8th, we have volume traded at zero. The opening, closing, high, and low prices are all equal to the closing price on Friday January 6th:

date	high	low	open	close	volume	day_of_week
2017-01-01	NaN	NaN	NaN	NaN	0.000000e+00	Sunday
2017-01-02	NaN	NaN	NaN	NaN	0.000000e+00	Monday
2017-01-03	2263.879883	2245.129883	2251.570068	2257.830078	3.770530e+09	Tuesday
2017-01-04	2272.820068	2261.600098	2261.600098	2270.750000	3.764890e+09	Wednesday
2017-01-05	2271.500000	2260.449951	2268.179932	2269.000000	3.761820e+09	Thursday
2017-01-06	2282.100098	2264.060059	2271.139893	2276.979980	3.339890e+09	Friday
2017-01-07	2276.979980	2276.979980	2276.979980	2276.979980	0.000000e+00	Saturday
2017-01-08	2276.979980	2276.979980	2276.979980	2276.979980	0.000000e+00	Sunday
2017-01-09	2275.489990	2268.899902	2273.590088	2268.899902	3.217610e+09	Monday
2017-01-10	2279.270020	2265.270020	2269.719971	2268.899902	3.638790e+09	Tuesday

Now let's recreate the portfolio with the reindexed S&P 500 data and use a visualization to compare it with the previous attempt (again, don't worry about the aggregation or plotting code, which will be covered in Chapter 4, *Aggregating Pandas DataFrames*, Chapter 5, *Visualizing Data with Pandas and Matplotlib*, and Chapter 6, *Plotting with Seaborn and Customization Techniques*, respectively):

```
# every day's closing price = S&P 500 close adjusted for market
# closure + Bitcoin close (same for other metrics)
>>> fixed_portfolio = pd.concat(
...     [sp_reindexed, bitcoin], sort=False
... ).groupby(pd.Grouper(freq='D')).sum()

>>> ax = fixed_portfolio['2017-Q4':'2018-Q2'].plot(
...     y='close', label='reindexed portfolio of S&P 500 + Bitcoin',
...     figsize=(15, 5), linewidth=2,
...     title='Reindexed portfolio vs.' \
...         'portfolio with mismatches indices'
... ) # plot reindexed portfolio's close (Q4 2017 through Q2 2018)

# add line for original portfolio for comparison and label y-axis
>>> portfolio['2017-Q4':'2018-Q2'].plot(
...     y='close', ax=ax, linestyle='--',
...     label='portfolio of S&P 500 + Bitcoin w/o reindexing'
... ).set_ylabel('price ($)')

>>> plt.show() # display the plot
```

The orange dotted line is our original attempt at studying the portfolio (without reindexing), and the blue solid line is the portfolio we just built with reindexing and different filling strategies per column. Keep this strategy in mind for the exercises in `Chapter 7`, *Financial Analysis – Bitcoin and the Stock Market*:

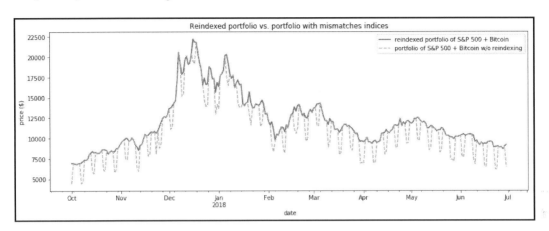

 We can also use `reindex()` to reorder the rows. For example, `df[df.datatype == 'TAVG'].reindex([32, 20, 11])` will return a `DataFrame` object with the `TAVG` data with three rows: 32, 20, and 11 (in that order). Note that we can also reindex along the columns with `axis=1` (the default is `axis=0` for rows).

Restructuring the data

Data isn't always given to us in the format that's most convenient for our analysis. Therefore, we need to be able to restructure data into both wide and long formats, depending on the analysis we want to perform. For many analyses, we will want wide format data so that we can look at the summary statistics easily and share our results in that format.

However, this isn't always as black and white as going from long format to wide format or vice versa. Consider the following data from the *Exercises* section:

	ticker	date	open	high	low	close	volume
0	AAPL	2018-01-02	166.9271	169.0264	166.0442	168.9872	25555934
0	AMZN	2018-01-02	1172.0000	1190.0000	1170.5100	1189.0100	2694494
0	FB	2018-01-02	177.6800	181.5800	177.5500	181.4200	18151903
0	GOOG	2018-01-02	1048.3400	1066.9400	1045.2300	1065.0000	1237564
0	NFLX	2018-01-02	196.1000	201.6500	195.4200	201.0700	10966889

It's possible to have data where some of the columns are in wide format (open, high, low, close, volume), but others are in long format (ticker, date). Summary statistics using describe() on this data aren't helpful unless we first filter on ticker. This format makes it easy to compare the stocks; however, as we briefly discussed when we learned about wide and long formats, we wouldn't be able to easily plot the closing price for each stock using pandas—we would need seaborn. Alternatively, we could restructure the data for that visualization.

Now that we understand the motivation for restructuring data; let's move to the 4-reshaping_data.ipynb notebook. We will begin by importing pandas and reading in the data/long_data.csv file, adding the temperature in Fahrenheit column (temp_F), and performing some of the data cleaning we just learned about:

```
>>> import pandas as pd

>>> long_df = pd.read_csv(
...        'data/long_data.csv', usecols=['date', 'datatype', 'value']
... ).rename(
...        columns={'value' : 'temp_C'}
... ).assign(
...        date=lambda x: pd.to_datetime(x.date),
...        temp_F=lambda x: (x.temp_C * 9/5) + 32
... )
```

Our long format data looks like this:

	datatype	date	temp_C	temp_F
0	TMAX	2018-10-01	21.1	69.98
1	TMIN	2018-10-01	8.9	48.02
2	TOBS	2018-10-01	13.9	57.02
3	TMAX	2018-10-02	23.9	75.02
4	TMIN	2018-10-02	13.9	57.02

While we will be pretty much only working with wide or long formats, `pandas` provides ways to restructure our data as we see fit, including taking the **transpose** (flipping the rows with the columns), which we may find useful to make better use of our display area when we're printing parts of our dataframe:

```
>>> long_df.head().T
```

Notice that the index is now in the columns, and the column names are in the index. It may not be immediately apparent how useful this can be, but we will see this a few times throughout this book; for example, to make content easier to display in `Chapter 7`, *Financial Analysis – Bitcoin and the Stock Market*, and to build a particular visualization for machine learning in `Chapter 9`, *Getting Started with Machine Learning in Python*:

	0	1	2	3	4
datatype	TMAX	TMIN	TOBS	TMAX	TMIN
date	2018-10-01 00:00:00	2018-10-01 00:00:00	2018-10-01 00:00:00	2018-10-02 00:00:00	2018-10-02 00:00:00
temp_C	21.1	8.9	13.9	23.9	13.9
temp_F	69.98	48.02	57.02	75.02	57.02

After reshaping the data, we will often revisit the data cleaning tasks as things may have changed, or we may need to change things we couldn't access easily before. For example, we will want to perform some type conversion if the values were all turned into strings in the long format, but in the wide format some columns should be numeric and others are clearly strings.

Pivoting DataFrames

We **pivot** our data to go from long format to wide format. The `pivot()` method performs the restructuring of our `DataFrame` object. In order to pivot, we need to tell `pandas` which column currently holds the values (with the `values` argument) and the column that contains what will become the column names in the wide format (the `columns` argument). Optionally, we can provide a new index (the `index` argument). Let's pivot into a wide format where we have a column for each of the `datatypes` that contain the temperature in Celsius and use the dates as the index:

```
>>> pivoted_df = long_df.pivot(
...     index='date', columns='datatype', values='temp_C'
... )
>>> pivoted_df.head()
```

In our starting dataframe, there was a `datatype` column that contained only TMAX, TMIN, or TOBS as strings. Now, these are column names because we passed in `columns='datatype'`. By passing `index='date'`, our index became the date, without running `set_index()`. Lastly, since we passed in `values='temp_C'`, the values for each `date`-`datatype` combination are the corresponding temperatures in Celsius:

datatype	TMAX	TMIN	TOBS
date			
2018-10-01	21.1	8.9	13.9
2018-10-02	23.9	13.9	17.2
2018-10-03	25.0	15.6	16.1
2018-10-04	22.8	11.7	11.7
2018-10-05	23.3	11.7	18.9

 The same output can be achieved using the `pd.pivot()` function. An example is provided in the notebook.

As we discussed at the beginning of this chapter, with the data in wide format, we can easily get meaningful summary statistics with the `describe()` method:

```
>>> pivoted_df.describe()
```

We can see that we have 31 observations of all three `datatypes` and that this month has a wide range of temperatures (highest daily maximum of 26.7°C and lowest daily minimum of -1.1°C):

datatype	TMAX	TMIN	TOBS
count	31.000000	31.000000	31.000000
mean	16.829032	7.561290	10.022581
std	5.714962	6.513252	6.596550
min	7.800000	−1.100000	−1.100000
25%	12.750000	2.500000	5.550000
50%	16.100000	6.700000	8.300000
75%	21.950000	13.600000	16.100000
max	26.700000	17.800000	21.700000

We lost the temperature in Fahrenheit, though. If we want to keep it, we can provide multiple columns to use as the `values`:

```
>>> pivoted_df = long_df.pivot(
...     index='date', columns='datatype', values=['temp_C', 'temp_F']
... )
>>> pivoted_df.head()
```

However, we now get an extra level above our `datatype` names. This is called a **hierarchical index**:

	temp_C			temp_F		
datatype	TMAX	TMIN	TOBS	TMAX	TMIN	TOBS
date						
2018-10-01	21.1	8.9	13.9	69.98	48.02	57.02
2018-10-02	23.9	13.9	17.2	75.02	57.02	62.96
2018-10-03	25	15.6	16.1	77	60.08	60.98
2018-10-04	22.8	11.7	11.7	73.04	53.06	53.06
2018-10-05	23.3	11.7	18.9	73.94	53.06	66.02

With this hierarchical index, if we want to select TMIN in Fahrenheit, we will first need to select `temp_F` and then TMIN:

```
>>> pivoted_df['temp_F']['TMIN'].head()
date
2018-10-01    48.02
2018-10-02    57.02
2018-10-03    60.08
2018-10-04    53.06
2018-10-05    53.06
Name: TMIN, dtype: float64
```

 In cases where we need to perform an aggregation as we pivot (due to duplicate values in the index), we can use the `pivot_table()` method, which we will discuss in `Chapter 4`, *Aggregating Pandas DataFrames*.

We have been working with a single index throughout this chapter; however, we can create an index from any number of columns with `set_index()`. This gives us a `MultiIndex`, where the outermost level corresponds to the first element in the list provided to `set_index()`:

```
>>> multi_index_df = long_df.set_index(['date', 'datatype'])
>>> multi_index_df.index
MultiIndex(levels=[[2018-10-01 00:00:00, 2018-10-02 00:00:00,
                    2018-10-03 00:00:00, 2018-10-04 00:00:00,
                    ...,
                    2018-10-30 00:00:00, 2018-10-31 00:00:00],
                   ['TMAX', 'TMIN', 'TOBS']],
           labels=[[0, 0, 0, 1, 1, 1, 2, 2, 2, 3, 3, 3,
                    ..., 28, 28, 28, 29, 29, 29, 30, 30, 30],
                   [0, 1, 2, 0, 1, 2, 0, 1, 2, 0, 1, 2,
                    ..., 0, 1, 2, 0, 1, 2, 0, 1, 2]],
           names=['date', 'datatype'])

>>> multi_index_df.head()
```

Notice that we now have two levels in the index; the `date` is the outermost level and the `datatype` is the innermost:

date	datatype	temp_C	temp_F
	TMAX	21.1	69.98
2018-10-01	TMIN	8.9	48.02
	TOBS	13.9	57.02
2018-10-02	TMAX	23.9	75.02
	TMIN	13.9	57.02

The `pivot()` method expects the data to only have one column to set as the index; if we have a multi-level index, we should use `unstack()` instead. We can use `unstack()` on `multi_index_df` and get a similar result to what we had before. Order matters here because, by default, `unstack()` will move the innermost level of the index to the columns; in this case, that means we will keep the `dates` in the index and move the `datatypes` to the column names:

```
>>> unstacked_df = multi_index_df.unstack()
>>> unstacked_df.head()
```

With `multi_index_df`, we had `datatype` as the innermost index, so, after using `unstack()`, it is along the columns. Note that we once again have a hierarchical index in the columns. In Chapter 4, *Aggregating Pandas DataFrames*, we will discuss a way to squash this back into a single level of columns:

datatype	temp_C			temp_F		
date	TMAX	TMIN	TOBS	TMAX	TMIN	TOBS
2018-10-01T00:00:00	21.1	8.9	13.9	69.98	48.02	57.02
2018-10-02T00:00:00	23.9	13.9	17.2	75.02	57.02	62.96
2018-10-03T00:00:00	25	15.6	16.1	77	60.08	60.98
2018-10-04T00:00:00	22.8	11.7	11.7	73.04	53.06	53.06
2018-10-05T00:00:00	23.3	11.7	18.9	73.94	53.06	66.02

The `unstack()` method has the added benefit of allowing us to specify how to fill in missing values that come into existence upon reshaping the data. To do so, we use the `fill_value` parameter. Consider the case where we have been given the data for TAVG for October 1, 2018 only. We could append this to `long_df` and set our index to the `date` and `datatype` columns, like we did previously:

```
>>> extra_data = long_df.append([{
...        'datatype' : 'TAVG',
...        'date': '2018-10-01',
...        'temp_C': 10,
...        'temp_F': 50
... }]).set_index(['date', 'datatype']).sort_index()

>>> extra_data.head(8)
```

We now have four `datatypes` for October 1, 2018, but only three for the remaining days:

date	datatype	temp_C	temp_F
2018-10-01	TAVG	10	50
	TMAX	21.1	69.98
	TMIN	8.9	48.02
	TOBS	13.9	57.02
2018-10-02	TMAX	23.9	75.02
	TMIN	13.9	57.02
	TOBS	17.2	62.96
2018-10-03	TMAX	25	77

Using `unstack()`, like we did previously, will result in NaN values for most of the TAVG data:

```
>>> extra_data.unstack().head()
```

Take a look at the `TAVG` average columns after we unstack:

datatype	temp_C				temp_F			
	TAVG	TMAX	TMIN	TOBS	TAVG	TMAX	TMIN	TOBS
date								
2018-10-01	10.0	21.1	8.9	13.9	50.0	69.98	48.02	57.02
2018-10-02	NaN	23.9	13.9	17.2	NaN	75.02	57.02	62.96
2018-10-03	NaN	25.0	15.6	16.1	NaN	77.00	60.08	60.98
2018-10-04	NaN	22.8	11.7	11.7	NaN	73.04	53.06	53.06
2018-10-05	NaN	23.3	11.7	18.9	NaN	73.94	53.06	66.02

To address this, we can pass in an appropriate `fill_value`. However, we are restricted to passing in a value for this, not a strategy (as we saw when we discussed reindexing), so while there is no good value for this case, we can use `-40` to illustrate how this works:

```
>>> extra_data.unstack(fill_value=-40).head()
```

The `NaN` values have now been replaced with `-40.0`. However, note that both `temp_C` and `temp_F` now have the same temperature reading. Actually, this is the reason we picked `-40` for our `fill_value`; it is the temperature at which both Fahrenheit and Celsius are equal, so we won't confuse people with them both being the same number, for example 0 (since 0°C = 32°F and 0°F = -17.78°C). Since this is data for New York City, this temperature is also way colder than temperatures measured there, and it is below `TMIN` for all the data we have, so it is more likely to be deemed a data entry error or a signal that data is missing compared to if we had used 0. Note that, in practice, it is better to be explicit about the missing data if we are sharing this with others and leave the `NaN` values:

datatype	temp_C				temp_F			
	TAVG	TMAX	TMIN	TOBS	TAVG	TMAX	TMIN	TOBS
date								
2018-10-01	10.0	21.1	8.9	13.9	50.0	69.98	48.02	57.02
2018-10-02	-40.0	23.9	13.9	17.2	-40.0	75.02	57.02	62.96
2018-10-03	-40.0	25.0	15.6	16.1	-40.0	77.00	60.08	60.98
2018-10-04	-40.0	22.8	11.7	11.7	-40.0	73.04	53.06	53.06
2018-10-05	-40.0	23.3	11.7	18.9	-40.0	73.94	53.06	66.02

To summarize, the `unstack()` method should be our method of choice when we have a multi-level index and would like to move one or more of the levels to the columns; however, if we are simply using a single index, the `pivot()` syntax is likely to be easier to specify correctly since it's more apparent which data will end up where.

Melting DataFrames

In order to go from wide format to long format, we need to **melt** the data. Melting undoes a pivot. `DataFrame` objects have a `melt()` method for flexible reshaping. There is also a wrapper function called `pd.wide_to_long()` that uses the `melt()` method, but is less flexible.

For this example, we need to read in the wide format of this data from the `data/wide_data.csv` file:

```
>>> wide_df = pd.read_csv('data/wide_data.csv')
>>> wide_df.head()
```

Our wide data contains a column for the date and a column for each temperature measurement we have been working with:

	date	TMAX	TMIN	TOBS
0	2018-10-01	21.1	8.9	13.9
1	2018-10-02	23.9	13.9	17.2
2	2018-10-03	25.0	15.6	16.1
3	2018-10-04	22.8	11.7	11.7
4	2018-10-05	23.3	11.7	18.9

We can use `melt()` to turn this back into a long format, similar to what we got from the API. Melting our dataframe requires that we specify the following:

- Which column(s) uniquely identify a row in the wide format data with the `id_vars` argument
- Which column(s) contain(s) the variable(s) with the `value_vars` argument

Optionally, we can also specify how to name the column containing the variable names in the long format data (`var_name`) and the name for the column containing their values (`value_name`). By default, these will be `variable` and `value`, respectively.

Now, let's use the `melt()` method to turn the wide format data into long format:

```
>>> melted_df = wide_df.melt(
...     id_vars='date',
...     value_vars=['TMAX', 'TMIN', 'TOBS'],
...     value_name='temp_C',
...     var_name='measurement'
... )
>>> melted_df.head()
```

The `date` column was the identifier for our rows, so we provided that as `id_vars`. We turned the values in the `TMAX`, `TMIN`, and `TOBS` columns into a single column with the temperatures (`value_vars`) and used their column names as the values for a measurement column (`var_name='measurement'`). Lastly, we passed `value_name='temp_C'` to name the values column. We now have just three columns; the `date`, the temperature reading in Celsius (`temp_C`), and a column indicating which temperature measurement is in that row's `temp_C` cell (`measurement`):

	date	measurement	temp_C
0	2018-10-01	TMAX	21.1
1	2018-10-02	TMAX	23.9
2	2018-10-03	TMAX	25.0
3	2018-10-04	TMAX	22.8
4	2018-10-05	TMAX	23.3

 There is also a `pd.melt()` function, which yields the same outcome, but requires that we pass in a `DataFrame` object as the first argument. The notebook provides an example of this.

Just as we had an alternative way of pivoting our data with the `unstack()` method, we also have another way of melting the data with the `stack()` method. This method will pivot the columns into the innermost level of the index (resulting in a `MultiIndex`), so we need to double-check our index before calling it. It also lets us drop row/column combinations that result in no data, if we choose. We can do the following to get a similar output to the `melt()` method:

```
>>> wide_df.set_index('date', inplace=True) # use date for index
>>> stacked_series = wide_df.stack() # move datatypes into index
>>> stacked_series.head()
```

```
date
2018-10-01   TMAX     21.1
             TMIN      8.9
             TOBS     13.9
2018-10-02   TMAX     23.9
             TMIN     13.9
dtype: float64
```

Notice that the result came back as a `Series` object, so we will need to create the `DataFrame` object once more. We can use the `to_frame()` method and pass in a name to use for the column once it is a dataframe:

```
>>> stacked_df = stacked_series.to_frame('values')
>>> stacked_df.head()
```

Now, we have a dataframe with a multi-level index, containing `date` and `datatype`, with `values` as the only column. Notice, however, that only the `date` portion of our index has a name:

date		values
	TMAX	21.1
2018-10-01	TMIN	8.9
	TOBS	13.9
2018-10-02	TMAX	23.9
	TMIN	13.9

Initially, we used `set_index()` to set the index to the `date` column because we didn't want to melt that; this formed the first level of the multi-level index. Then, the `stack()` method moved the TMAX, TMIN, and TOBS columns into the second level of the index. However, this level never got named, so it shows up as `None`, but we know that is the `datatype`:

```
>>> stacked_df.index
MultiIndex(levels=[['2018-10-01', '2018-10-02', ...,
                    '2018-10-30', '2018-10-31'],
                   ['TMAX', 'TMIN', 'TOBS']],
           labels=[[0, 0, 0, 1, 1, 1, 2, 2, 2, ..., 30, 30, 30],
                   [0, 1, 2, 0, 1, 2, 0, 1, 2, ..., 0, 1, 2]],
           names=['date', None])
```

As we learned previously in this chapter, we can use the `rename()` method to address this:

```
>>> stacked_df.index.rename(['date', 'datatype'], inplace=True)
>>> stacked_df.index.names
FrozenList(['date', 'datatype'])
```

Handling duplicate, missing, or invalid data

In the section on data cleaning, we discussed things we could change with the way the data was represented with zero ramifications. However, we didn't discuss a very important part of data cleaning: how to deal with data that appears to be duplicated, invalid, or missing. This is separated from the rest of the data cleaning because it is an example where we will do some initial data cleaning, then reshape our data, and finally look to handle these potential issues; it is also a rather hefty topic.

For this section, we will be working in the `5-handling_data_issues.ipynb` notebook using the `data/dirty_data.csv` file. This file contains wide format data from the weather API that has been altered to introduce many common data issues that we will encounter in the wild. It contains the following fields:

- `PRCP`: Precipitation in millimeters
- `SNOW`: Snowfall in millimeters
- `SNWD`: Snow depth in millimeters
- `TMAX`: Maximum daily temperature in Celsius
- `TMIN`: Minimum daily temperature in Celsius
- `TOBS`: Temperature at time of observation in Celsius
- `WESF`: Water equivalent of snow in millimeters

Let's import `pandas` and read in our data:

```
>>> import pandas as pd
>>> df = pd.read_csv('data/dirty_data.csv')
```

Finding the problematic data

Now that we have our data, let's see how to identify and fix data issues. In `Chapter 1`, *Introduction to Data Analysis*, we learned the importance of examining our data when we get it; it's not a coincidence that many of the ways to inspect the data will help us find the issues. Examining the `head()` and `tail()` of the data is always a good first step:

```
>>> df.head()
```

In practice, `head()` and `tail()` aren't as robust as the rest of what we will discuss here, but we can still get some useful information by starting here. Our data is in the wide format, and at a quick glance we can see that we have some potential issues. Sometimes, the `station` field is recorded with a `?`, while other times it has a station ID. We have values of negative infinity (`-inf`) for snow depth (`SNWD`), along with very hot temperatures for `TMAX`. Lastly, we can observe many `NaN` values in several columns, including the `inclement_weather` column, which appears to also contain Boolean values:

	date	station	PRCP	SNOW	SNWD	TMAX	TMIN	TOBS	WESF	inclement_weather
0	2018-01-01T00:00:00	?	0.0	0.0	-inf	5505.0	-40.0	NaN	NaN	NaN
1	2018-01-01T00:00:00	?	0.0	0.0	-inf	5505.0	-40.0	NaN	NaN	NaN
2	2018-01-01T00:00:00	?	0.0	0.0	-inf	5505.0	-40.0	NaN	NaN	NaN
3	2018-01-02T00:00:00	GHCND:USC00280907	0.0	0.0	inf	-8.3	-16.1	-12.2	NaN	False
4	2018-01-03T00:00:00	GHCND:USC00280907	0.0	0.0	-inf	-4.4	-13.9	-13.3	NaN	False

Using `describe()`, we can see if we have any missing data and look at the 5-number summary to spot potential issues:

```
>>> df.describe()
```

The SNWD column appears to be useless, and the TMAX column seems unreliable. For perspective, the temperature of the Sun's photosphere is around 5,505°C, so we certainly wouldn't expect to observe those air temperatures in New York City (or anywhere on Earth, for that matter). This likely means that the TMAX column was set to a nonsensical, large number when it wasn't available. The fact that it is so large is actually what helps identify it using the summary statistics we get from describe(). If unknowns were encoded with another value, say 40°C, we couldn't be sure it wasn't actual data:

	PRCP	SNOW	SNWD	TMAX	TMIN	TOBS	WESF
count	765.000000	577.000000	577.000000	765.000000	765.000000	398.000000	11.000000
mean	5.360392	4.202773	NaN	2649.175294	-15.914379	8.632161	16.290909
std	10.002138	25.086077	NaN	2744.156281	24.242849	9.815054	9.489832
min	0.000000	0.000000	-inf	-11.700000	-40.000000	-16.100000	1.800000
25%	0.000000	0.000000	NaN	13.300000	-40.000000	0.150000	8.600000
50%	0.000000	0.000000	NaN	32.800000	-11.100000	8.300000	19.300000
75%	5.800000	0.000000	NaN	5505.000000	6.700000	18.300000	24.900000
max	61.700000	229.000000	inf	5505.000000	23.900000	26.100000	28.700000

We can use the info() method to see if we have any missing values and that our columns have the expected data types. In doing so, we immediately see two issues: we have 765 rows, but for five of the columns, we have many fewer non-null entries. This output also shows us that the inclement_weather column is not a Boolean, though we may have thought it was one from the name. Notice that the ? we saw for the station column when we used head() doesn't show up here—it's important to inspect our data from many different angles:

```
>>> df.info()
<class 'pandas.core.frame.DataFrame'>
RangeIndex: 765 entries, 0 to 764
Data columns (total 10 columns):
date                 765 non-null object
station              765 non-null object
PRCP                 765 non-null float64
SNOW                 577 non-null float64
SNWD                 577 non-null float64
TMAX                 765 non-null float64
TMIN                 765 non-null float64
TOBS                 398 non-null float64
WESF                 11 non-null float64
inclement_weather    408 non-null object
dtypes: float64(7), object(3)
memory usage: 50.8+ KB
```

Now, let's track down those null values. We have many options for this task; we can use any of the following to find out where the null values are:

- The `pd.isnull()` function
- The `pd.isna()` function
- The `isnull()` method of a `Series` or `DataFrame` object
- The `isna()` method of a `Series` or `DataFrame` object

Note that, if we use the method on the `DataFrame` object, the result will tell us which rows have all null values, which isn't what we want in this case. Here, we want to examine the rows that have null values in the `SNOW`, `SNWD`, `TOBS`, `WESF`, or `inclement_weather` columns. This means that we will need to combine checks for each of the columns with the `|` (OR) operator:

```
>>> contain_nulls = df[
...     df.SNOW.isnull() | df.SNWD.isna() \
...     | pd.isnull(df.TOBS) | pd.isna(df.WESF) \
...     | df.inclement_weather.isna()
... ]

>>> contain_nulls.shape[0]
765
>>> contain_nulls.head(10)
```

If we look at the `shape` attribute of our `contain_nulls` dataframe, we will see that every single row has some null data. Looking at the top 10 rows, we can see some NaN values in each of these rows:

	date	station	PRCP	SNOW	SNWD	TMAX	TMIN	TOBS	WESF	inclement_weather
0	2018-01-01T00:00:00	?	0.0	0.0	-inf	5505.0	-40.0	NaN	NaN	NaN
1	2018-01-01T00:00:00	?	0.0	0.0	-inf	5505.0	-40.0	NaN	NaN	NaN
2	2018-01-01T00:00:00	?	0.0	0.0	-inf	5505.0	-40.0	NaN	NaN	NaN
3	2018-01-02T00:00:00	GHCND:USC00280907	0.0	0.0	-inf	-8.3	-16.1	-12.2	NaN	False
4	2018-01-03T00:00:00	GHCND:USC00280907	0.0	0.0	-inf	-4.4	-13.9	-13.3	NaN	False
5	2018-01-03T00:00:00	GHCND:USC00280907	0.0	0.0	-inf	-4.4	-13.9	-13.3	NaN	False
6	2018-01-03T00:00:00	GHCND:USC00280907	0.0	0.0	-inf	-4.4	-13.9	-13.3	NaN	False
7	2018-01-04T00:00:00	?	20.6	229.0	inf	5505.0	-40.0	NaN	19.3	True
8	2018-01-04T00:00:00	?	20.6	229.0	inf	5505.0	-40.0	NaN	19.3	True
9	2018-01-05T00:00:00	?	0.3	NaN	NaN	5505.0	-40.0	NaN	NaN	NaN

Note that we can't check whether the value of the column is equal to NaN because np.nan is not equal to anything:

```
>>> import numpy as np
>>> df[df.inclement_weather == 'NaN'].shape[0] # doesn't work
0
>>> df[df.inclement_weather == np.nan].shape[0] # doesn't work
0
```

We must use the aforementioned options (isna()/isnull()):

```
>>> df[df.inclement_weather.isna()].shape[0] # works
357
```

Note that inf and -inf are actually np.inf and -np.inf. Therefore, we can find the number of rows with inf or -inf values by doing the following:

```
>>> df[df.SNWD.isin([-np.inf, np.inf])].shape[0]
577
```

This only tells us a single column, though, so we could write a function that will use a **dictionary comprehension** (https://www.python.org/dev/peps/pep-0274/) to return the number of infinite values per column in our dataframe. We saw list comprehensions in Chapter 2, *Working with Pandas DataFrames*; the only difference here is that we are creating a key-value mapping, instead of a list:

```
>>> import numpy as np

>>> def get_inf_count(df):
...     """
...     Find the number of inf/-inf values per column
...     in dataframe
...     """
...     return {
...         col : df[
...             df[col].isin([np.inf, -np.inf])
...         ].shape[0] for col in df.columns
...     }
```

Using our function, we find that the `SNWD` column is the only column with infinite values, but the majority of the values in the column are infinite:

```
>>> get_inf_count(df)
{'date': 0,
 'station': 0,
 'PRCP': 0,
 'SNOW': 0,
 'SNWD': 577,
 'TMAX': 0,
 'TMIN': 0,
 'TOBS': 0,
 'WESF': 0,
 'inclement_weather': 0}
```

Before we can decide how to handle the infinite values of snow depth, we should look at the summary statistics for snowfall (`SNOW`), which forms a big part in determining the snow depth (`SNWD`). To do so, we can make a dataframe with two series, where one is the summary statistics for the snow column when the snow depth is `np.inf`, and the other when it is `-np.inf`. In addition, we will use the `T` attribute to transpose the data for easier viewing:

```
>>> pd.DataFrame({
...     'np.inf Snow Depth': df[df.SNWD == np.inf].SNOW.describe(),
...     '-np.inf Snow Depth': df[df.SNWD == -np.inf].SNOW.describe()
... }).T
```

The snow depth is being recorded as negative infinity when there was no snowfall; however, we can't be sure this isn't just a coincidence going forward. If we are just going to be working with this fixed date range, we can treat that as having a depth of 0 or NaN because it didn't snow. Unfortunately, we can't really make any assumptions with the positive infinity entries. They most certainly aren't that, but we can't decide what they should be, so it's probably best to leave them alone or not look at this column:

	count	mean	std	min	25%	50%	75%	max
np.inf Snow Depth	24.0	101.041667	74.498018	13.0	25.0	120.5	152.0	229.0
-np.inf Snow Depth	553.0	0.000000	0.000000	0.0	0.0	0.0	0.0	0.0

We are working with a year of data, but somehow we have 765 rows, so we should check why. The only columns we have yet to inspect are the `date` and `station` columns. We can use the `describe()` method to see summary statistics for them:

```
>>> df.describe(include='object')
```

In 765 rows of data, the `date` column only has 324 unique values (meaning that some dates are missing), with some dates being present as many as eight times (`freq`). The `station` column indicates that there are only two unique values, with the most frequent being the `station` with a station ID of GHCND:USC00280907. Since we saw a ? when we used `head()` earlier, we know that is the other value; however, we can use `unique()` to see all the unique values if we hadn't. We also know that ? occurs 367 times (765 - 398) without the need to use `value_counts()`:

	date	station	inclement_weather
count	765	765	408
unique	324	2	2
top	2018-07-05T00:00:00	GHCND:USC00280907	False
freq	8	398	384

In practice, we may not know why the station is sometimes recorded as ?—it could be intentional to show that they don't have the station, an error in the recording software, or an accidental omission that got encoded as ?. How we deal with this would be a judgment call, as we will discuss in the next section.

Upon seeing that we had 765 rows of data and two distinct values for `station`, we might have assumed that each day had two entries—one per station. However, this would only account for 730 rows, and we also now know that we are missing some dates. Let's see whether we can find any duplicate data that could account for this. We can use the result of the `duplicated()` method as a Boolean mask to find the rows with duplicates:

```
>>> df[df.duplicated()].shape[0]
284
```

Depending on what we are trying to achieve, we may handle duplicates differently. The rows that are returned can be modified with the `keep` argument. By default, it is `'first'`, and, for each row that is present more than once, we will get only the additional rows (besides the first). However, if we pass in `keep=False`, we get all the rows that are present more than once, not just each additional appearance they make:

```
>>> df[df.duplicated(keep=False)].shape[0]
482
```

There is also a `subset` argument (first positional argument), which allows us to focus just on duplicates of certain columns. Using this, we can see that when the `date` and `station` columns are duplicated, so is the rest of the data because we get the same result as before. However, we don't know if this is actually a problem:

```
>>> df[df.duplicated(['date', 'station'])].shape[0]
284
```

Now, let's examine a few of the duplicated rows:

```
>>> df[df.duplicated()].head()
```

Just looking at the first five rows shows us that some rows are repeated at least three times. The first four entries are only two unique entries, but remember the default behavior of `duplicated()` is to not show the first occurrence, which means these both have another matching value in the data:

	date	station	PRCP	SNOW	SNWD	TMAX	TMIN	TOBS	WESF	inclement_weather
1	2018-01-01T00:00:00	?	0.0	0.0	-inf	5505.0	-40.0	NaN	NaN	NaN
2	2018-01-01T00:00:00	?	0.0	0.0	-inf	5505.0	-40.0	NaN	NaN	NaN
5	2018-01-03T00:00:00	GHCND:USC00280907	0.0	0.0	-inf	-4.4	-13.9	-13.3	NaN	False
6	2018-01-03T00:00:00	GHCND:USC00280907	0.0	0.0	-inf	-4.4	-13.9	-13.3	NaN	False
8	2018-01-04T00:00:00	?	20.6	229.0	inf	5505.0	-40.0	NaN	19.3	True

Now that we know how to find problems in our data, let's learn about some ways we can try to address them. Note that there is no panacea here, and it will often come down to knowing the data we are working with and making judgment calls.

Mitigating the issues

We are in an unsatisfactory state with our data, and while we can work to make it better, the best plan of action isn't always evident. Perhaps the easiest thing we can do when faced with this class of data issues is to remove the duplicate rows. However, it is crucial that we evaluate the ramifications such a decision may have on our analysis. Even in cases where it appears that the data we are working with was collected from a larger dataset that had additional columns, thus making all our data distinct, we can't be sure that the removal of these columns is the reason the remaining data was duplicated—we would need to consult the source of the data and any available documentation.

Since we know that both of the stations will be for New York City, we may have decided to drop the `station` column—they may have just been collecting different data. If we decide to remove duplicate rows using the `date` column and keep the data for the station that wasn't `?` in the case of duplicates, we will lose all data we have for the `WESF` column. We can look at unique values for the `station` column when `WESF` is not `NaN` using the `notna()` method:

```
>>> df[df.WESF.notna()].station.unique()
array(['?'], dtype=object)
```

One satisfactory solution in this case may be to perform the following actions:

1. Save the `WESF` column as a series
2. Sort the dataframe by `station` in descending order to put the `?` last
3. Remove rows that are duplicated based on the date, keeping the first occurrence, which will be ones where `station` is not `?` (if they have measurements)
4. Drop the `station` and `WESF` columns
5. Sort the data by the `date` column
6. Create a column for the `WESF` series using `assign()`, which will be properly matched to the appropriate date because we have retained the index we started with in both the dataframe and in the series (we have not called `reset_index()` or `set_index()`)

This may sound a little complicated, but that's largely because we haven't learned about aggregation yet. In Chapter 4, *Aggregating Pandas DataFrames*, we will look at another way to go about this. For now, let's move forward with this implementation:

```
# 1. save this information for later
>>> station_qm_wesf = df[df.station == '?'].WESF

# 2. sort ? to the bottom
>>> df.sort_values('station', ascending=False, inplace=True)

# 3. drop duplicates based on the date column keeping the first
#    occurrence which will be the valid station if it has data
>>> df_deduped = df.drop_duplicates('date').drop(
...     # 4. remove the station column because we are done with it
...     #    and WESF because we need to replace it later
...     columns=['station', 'WESF']
... ).sort_values('date').assign( # 5. sort by the date
...     # 6. add back WESF, which will be properly
...     #    matched due to index
...     WESF=station_qm_wesf
... )

>>> df_deduped.shape
(324, 9)
>>> df_deduped.head()
```

 Note that drop_duplicates() can be done in-place, but, as we saw from this example, if what we are trying to do is complicated, it's best not to start out with the in-place operation.

We are now left with 324 rows—one for each unique date in our data—and we were able to save the WESF column by putting it alongside the data from the other station:

	date	PRCP	SNOW	SNWD	TMAX	TMIN	TOBS	inclement_weather	WESF
0	2018-01-01T00:00:00	0.0	0.0	-inf	5505.0	-40.0	NaN	NaN	NaN
3	2018-01-02T00:00:00	0.0	0.0	-inf	-8.3	-16.1	-12.2	False	NaN
6	2018-01-03T00:00:00	0.0	0.0	-inf	-4.4	-13.9	-13.3	False	NaN
8	2018-01-04T00:00:00	20.6	229.0	inf	5505.0	-40.0	NaN	True	19.3
11	2018-01-05T00:00:00	14.2	127.0	inf	-4.4	-13.9	-13.9	True	NaN

We also could have specified to keep the last instead of the first or drop all duplicates with the `keep` argument, just like when we checked for duplicates with `duplicated()`. Keep this in mind as the `duplicated()` method can be useful in giving the results of a dry run on a deduplication task.

Now, let's deal with the null data. We can choose to drop it, replace it with some arbitrary value, or impute it using surrounding data. Each of these options has its ramifications. If we drop the data, we are going about our analysis with only part of the data; if we end up dropping half the rows, this is going to have a large effect on our outcome. When changing values for the data, we may be affecting the outcome of our analysis.

To drop all the rows with any null data (this doesn't have to be true for all the columns of the row, so be careful), use the `dropna()` method; in our case, this leaves us with no data:

```
>>> df_deduped.dropna().shape
(0, 9)
```

We can change the default behavior to only drop a row if all the columns are null with the `how` argument, except this doesn't get rid of anything:

```
>>> df_deduped.dropna(how='all').shape # default is 'any'
(324, 9)
```

We can use a subset of columns to determine what to drop. Say we wanted to look at snow data; we would most likely want to make sure that our data had values for `SNOW`, `SNWD`, and `inclement_weather`. This can be achieved with the `subset` argument:

```
>>> df_deduped.dropna(
...     how='all', subset=['inclement_weather', 'SNOW', 'SNWD']
... ).shape
(293, 9)
```

Note that this operation can also be performed along the columns and that we can provide a threshold for the number of null values that must be observed, before we drop the data with the `thresh` argument. For example, if we say that 75% of the rows must be null to drop the column, we will drop the `WESF` column:

```
>>> df_deduped.dropna(
...     axis='columns',
...     thresh=df_deduped.shape[0]*.75 # 75% of rows
... ).columns
```

```
Index(['date', 'PRCP', 'SNOW', 'SNWD', 'TMAX', 'TMIN', 'TOBS',
       'inclement_weather'],
      dtype='object')
```

Since we have a lot of null values, we will likely be more interested in keeping these values, and perhaps finding a better way to represent them. If we replace the null data, we must use care when deciding what to fill in instead; filling all values we don't have with some other value may yield strange results later on, so we must think about how we will use this data first.

To fill null values in with other data, we use the `fillna()` method, which gives us the option of specifying a value or a strategy of how to perform the filling. Let's discuss filling with a single value first. The WESF column is mostly null values, but since it is a measurement in milliliters that takes on the value of NaN when there is no water equivalent of snowfall, we can fill the nulls with zeroes. Note that this can be done in-place (again, as a general rule of thumb, we should use caution with in-place operations):

```
>>> df_deduped.loc[:,'WESF'].fillna(0, inplace=True)
>>> df_deduped.head()
```

Our WESF column no longer has NaN values:

	date	PRCP	SNOW	SNWD	TMAX	TMIN	TOBS	inclement_weather	WESF
1	2018-01-01T00:00:00	0.0	0.0	-inf	5505.0	-40.0	NaN	NaN	0.0
3	2018-01-02T00:00:00	0.0	0.0	-inf	-8.3	-16.1	-12.2	False	0.0
6	2018-01-03T00:00:00	0.0	0.0	-inf	-4.4	-13.9	-13.3	False	0.0
8	2018-01-04T00:00:00	20.6	229.0	inf	5505.0	-40.0	NaN	True	19.3
11	2018-01-05T00:00:00	14.2	127.0	inf	-4.4	-13.9	-13.9	True	0.0

At this point, we have done everything we can without distorting the data. We know that we are missing dates, but if we reindex, we don't know how to fill in the NaN data. With the weather data, we can't assume that because it snowed one day that it will snow the next or that the temperature will be the same. For this reason, note that the following few examples are just for illustrative purposes only—just because we can do something doesn't mean we should. The right solution will most likely depend on the domain and the problem we are looking to solve.

That being said, let's try to address some of the remaining issues with the temperature data. We know that when TMAX is the temperature of the Sun, it must be because there was no measured value, so let's replace it with NaN and then make an assumption that the temperature won't change drastically day-to-day. Note that this is actually a big assumption, but it will allow us to understand how fillna() works when we provide a strategy through the method parameter. We will also do this for TMIN, which currently uses -40°C for its placeholder, despite the coldest temperature ever recorded in NYC being -15°F (-26.1°C) on February 9, 1934 (https://www. weather.gov/media/okx/Climate/CentralPark/extremes.pdf).

The fillna() method gives us two options for the method parameter: 'ffill' to forward-fill and 'bfill' to back-fill. Notice we don't have the 'nearest' option, like we did when we were reindexing, which would have been the best option; so, to illustrate how this works, let's use 'ffill':

```
>>> df_deduped.assign(
...     TMAX=lambda x: x.TMAX.replace(5505, np.nan)\
...         .fillna(method='ffill'),
...     TMIN=lambda x: x.TMIN.replace(-40, np.nan)\
...         .fillna(method='ffill')
... ).head()
```

Take a look at the TMAX and TMIN columns on January 1st and 4th. Both are NaN on the 1st because we don't have data before then to bring forward, but the 4th now has the same values as the 3rd:

	date	PRCP	SNOW	SNWD	TMAX	TMIN	TOBS	inclement_weather	WESF
1	2018-01-01T00:00:00	0.0	0.0	-inf	NaN	NaN	NaN	NaN	0.0
3	2018-01-02T00:00:00	0.0	0.0	-inf	-8.3	-16.1	-12.2	False	0.0
6	2018-01-03T00:00:00	0.0	0.0	-inf	-4.4	-13.9	-13.3	False	0.0
8	2018-01-04T00:00:00	20.6	229.0	inf	-4.4	-13.9	NaN	True	19.3
11	2018-01-05T00:00:00	14.2	127.0	inf	-4.4	-13.9	-13.9	True	0.0

If we want to handle the inf cases in the SNWD column, we could have used the np.nan_to_num() function; this turns NaN into 0 and inf/-inf into very large positive/negative finite numbers:

```
>>> df_deduped.assign(
...     SNWD=lambda x: np.nan_to_num(x.SNWD)
... ).head()
```

Again, this doesn't make sense for our data. In cases of `-np.inf`, we may choose to set `SNWD` to 0 since we saw there was no snowfall those days. However, we don't know what to do with `np.inf`, and the large positive numbers, arguably, make this more confusing to interpret:

	date	PRCP	SNOW	SNWD	TMAX	TMIN	TOBS	inclement_weather	WESF
1	2018-01-01T00:00:00	0.0	0.0	-1.797693e+308	5505.0	-40.0	NaN	NaN	0.0
3	2018-01-02T00:00:00	0.0	0.0	-1.797693e+308	-8.3	-16.1	-12.2	False	0.0
6	2018-01-03T00:00:00	0.0	0.0	-1.797693e+308	-4.4	-13.9	-13.3	False	0.0
8	2018-01-04T00:00:00	20.6	229.0	1.797693e+308	5505.0	-40.0	NaN	True	19.3
11	2018-01-05T00:00:00	14.2	127.0	1.797693e+308	-4.4	-13.9	-13.9	True	0.0

Our last strategy is imputation. When we replace a missing value with a new value derived from the data, using summary statistics or data from other observations, it is called **imputation**. For example, we can impute with the rolling mean to replace temperature values. Unfortunately, if we are only missing values for the end of the month of October, and we replace them with the mean of the values from the rest of the month, this is likely to be skewed toward the extreme values, which are the warmer temperatures at the beginning of October, in this case. Like everything else that was discussed in this section, we must use caution and think about any potential consequences or side effects of our actions.

We can combine imputation with the `fillna()` method. As an example, let's fill in the NaN data for `TMAX` and `TMIN` with their medians and `TOBS` with the average of `TMIN` and `TMAX` (after imputing them):

```
>>> df_deduped.assign(
...     TMAX=lambda x: x.TMAX.replace(5505, np.nan)\
...         .fillna(x.TMIN.median()),
...     TMIN=lambda x: x.TMIN.replace(-40, np.nan)\
...         .fillna(x.TMIN.median()),
...     # average of TMAX and TMIN
...     TOBS=lambda x: x.TOBS.fillna((x.TMAX + x.TMIN) / 2)
... ).head()
```

Notice from the changes to the data for January 1st and 4th that the median maximum and minimum temperatures were 0°C. This means that when we impute TOBS and also don't have TMAX and TMIN in the data, we get 0°C:

	date	PRCP	SNOW	SNWD	TMAX	TMIN	TOBS	inclement_weather	WESF
0	2018-01-01T00:00:00	0.0	0.0	-inf	0.0	0.0	0.0	NaN	0.0
3	2018-01-02T00:00:00	0.0	0.0	-inf	-8.3	-16.1	-12.2	False	0.0
6	2018-01-03T00:00:00	0.0	0.0	-inf	-4.4	-13.9	-13.3	False	0.0
8	2018-01-04T00:00:00	20.6	229.0	inf	0.0	0.0	0.0	True	19.3
11	2018-01-05T00:00:00	14.2	127.0	inf	-4.4	-13.9	-13.9	True	0.0

We can also use the `apply()` method to run the same calculation across columns. For example, let's fill in all the missing values with the rolling 7-day median of their values, setting the number of periods required for the calculation to 0 to ensure that we don't introduce extra NaN values. We will cover rolling calculations in Chapter 4, *Aggregating Pandas DataFrames*, so this is just a preview. We need to set the date column as the index so that `apply()` doesn't try to take the rolling 7-day median of the date:

```
>>> df_deduped.assign(
...     # make TMAX and TMIN NaN where appropriate
...     TMAX=lambda x: x.TMAX.replace(5505, np.nan),
...     TMIN=lambda x: x.TMIN.replace(-40, np.nan)
... ).set_index('date').apply(
...     # rolling calculations will be covered in chapter 4,
...     # this is a rolling 7 day median
...     # we set min_periods (# of periods required for calculation)
...     # to 0 so we always get a result
...     lambda x: x.fillna(x.rolling(7, min_periods=0).median())
... ).head(10)
```

 This could have been done with `assign()`, but we would have had to write the rolling calculation for every column, creating a lot of redundancy.

It's kind of hard to tell where our imputed values are here—temperatures can fluctuate quite a bit day-to-day. We know that the 4th had missing data from our previous attempt; our imputed temperatures are colder that day than those around it with this strategy. In reality, it was slightly warmer that day (around -3°C):

	PRCP	SNOW	SNWD	TMAX	TMIN	TOBS	inclement_weather	WESF
date								
2018-01-01T00:00:00	0.0	0.0	-inf	NaN	NaN	NaN	NaN	0.0
2018-01-02T00:00:00	0.0	0.0	-inf	-8.30	-16.1	-12.20	False	0.0
2018-01-03T00:00:00	0.0	0.0	-inf	-4.40	-13.9	-13.30	False	0.0
2018-01-04T00:00:00	20.6	229.0	inf	-6.35	-15.0	-12.75	True	19.3
2018-01-05T00:00:00	14.2	127.0	inf	-4.40	-13.9	-13.90	True	0.0
2018-01-06T00:00:00	0.0	0.0	-inf	-10.00	-15.6	-15.00	False	0.0
2018-01-07T00:00:00	0.0	0.0	-inf	-11.70	-17.2	-16.10	False	0.0
2018-01-08T00:00:00	0.0	0.0	-inf	-7.80	-16.7	-8.30	False	0.0
2018-01-10T00:00:00	0.0	0.0	-inf	5.00	-7.8	-7.80	False	0.0
2018-01-11T00:00:00	0.0	0.0	-inf	4.40	-7.8	1.10	False	0.0

It's important to exercise caution when imputing. If we pick the wrong strategy for the data, we can make a real mess of it.

Another way of imputing missing data is to have `pandas` calculate what the values should be with **interpolation**. Interpolation should be used with care since we are going to impute a value based on the values seen. Say that we were missing all of the data for the winter months. If we try to interpolate using values from the remaining months to fill these in, we are going to have much higher temperatures than we should.

This is because our data doesn't describe winter, and interpolation will only be able to use the non-winter temperature data. We are actually performing **extrapolation** in this case because we are making a big assumption that the winter months are like the remaining months of the year. This assumption simply isn't true. This distinction between interpolation and extrapolation is why some models can make very poor predictions, despite having good scores; they are good at making predictions within the range of values they have been trained or fit on, but not always outside that range (they don't generalize well).

To interpolate `NaN` values, we use the `interpolate()` method. By default, the `interpolate()` method will perform linear interpolation, assuming that all the rows are evenly spaced. Our data is daily, although some days are missing, so it is just a matter of reindexing first. Let's combine this with `apply()` to interpolate all of our columns at once:

```
>>> df_deduped.assign(
...     # make TMAX and TMIN NaN where appropriate
...     TMAX=lambda x: x.TMAX.replace(5505, np.nan),
...     TMIN=lambda x: x.TMIN.replace(-40, np.nan),
...     date=lambda x: pd.to_datetime(x.date)
... ).set_index('date').reindex(
...     pd.date_range('2018-01-01', '2018-12-31', freq='D')
... ).apply(
...     lambda x: x.interpolate()
... ).head(10)
```

Check out January 9th, which we didn't have previously—the values for TMAX, TMIN, and TOBS are the average of values for the day prior (January 8th) and the day after (January 10th):

	PRCP	SNOW	SNWD	TMAX	TMIN	TOBS	inclement_weather	WESF
2018-01-01	0.0	0.0	-inf	NaN	NaN	NaN	NaN	0.0
2018-01-02	0.0	0.0	-inf	-8.3	-16.10	-12.20	False	0.0
2018-01-03	0.0	0.0	-inf	-4.4	-13.90	-13.30	False	0.0
2018-01-04	20.6	229.0	inf	-4.4	-13.90	-13.60	True	19.3
2018-01-05	14.2	127.0	inf	-4.4	-13.90	-13.90	True	0.0
2018-01-06	0.0	0.0	-inf	-10.0	-15.60	-15.00	False	0.0
2018-01-07	0.0	0.0	-inf	-11.7	-17.20	-16.10	False	0.0
2018-01-08	0.0	0.0	-inf	-7.8	-16.70	-8.30	False	0.0
2018-01-09	0.0	0.0	NaN	-1.4	-12.25	-8.05	NaN	0.0
2018-01-10	0.0	0.0	-inf	5.0	-7.80	-7.80	False	0.0

The `interpolate()` method allows us to specify how pandas goes about this through the `method` argument; we are simply using the default, which assumes evenly-spaced observations (`method='linear'`). See the `interpolate()` method documentation for more, or run `help()` to view the available options.

Summary

Congratulations on making it through this chapter! Data wrangling isn't the most exciting part of the analytics workflow, but we will spend a lot of time on it, so it's best to be well-versed in what `pandas` has to offer. In this chapter, we learned more about what data wrangling is (aside from a data science buzzword) and got some firsthand experience with data cleaning and reshaping our data. Utilizing the `requests` library, we once again practiced working with APIs to extract data of interest; then, we used `pandas` to begin our data wrangling, which we will continue in the next chapter. Finally, we learned how to deal with duplicate, missing, and invalid data points in various ways and discussed the ramifications of those decisions.

In the next chapter, we will learn how to aggregate dataframes.

Exercises

Solve the following exercises using what we have learned so far in this book and the stock data in the `exercises/` directory:

1. We want to look at data for the **Facebook, Apple, Amazon, Netflix, and Google (FAANG)** stocks, but we were given each as a separate CSV file (obtained using the `stock_analysis` package we will build in *Chapter 7, Financial Analysis – Bitcoin and the Stock Market*). Combine them into a single file and store the dataframe of the FAANG data as `faang` for the rest of the exercises:
    1. Read each file in.
    2. Add a column to each dataframe, called `ticker`, indicating the ticker symbol it is for (Apple's is AAPL, for example). This is how you look up a stock. Each file's name is also the ticker symbol, so be sure to capitalize it.
    3. Append them together into a single dataframe.
    4. Save the result in a CSV file called `faang.csv`.

2. With `faang`, use type conversion to change the `date` column into a datetime and the `volume` column into integers. Then, sort by `date` and `ticker`.

3. Find the seven rows with the highest value for `volume`.

4. Right now, the data is somewhere between long and wide format. Use `melt()` to make it completely long format. Hint: `date` and `ticker` are our ID variables (they uniquely identify each row). We need to melt the rest so that we don't have separate columns for `open`, `high`, `low`, `close`, and `volume`.

5. Suppose we found out there was a glitch in how the data was recorded on July 26, 2018. How should we handle this? Note that there is no coding required for this exercise.

Further reading

Check out the following resources for more information on the topics that were covered in this chapter:

- *A Quick-Start Tutorial on Relational Database Design*: `https://www.ntu.edu.sg/home/ehchua/programming/sql/relational_database_design.html`
- *Binary search*: `https://www.khanacademy.org/computing/computer-science/algorithms/binary-search/a/binary-search`
- *How Recursion Works—explained with flowcharts and a video*: `https://medium.freecodecamp.org/how-recursion-works-explained-with-flowcharts-and-a-video-de61f40cb7f9`
- *Python f-strings*: `https://realpython.com/python-f-strings/`
- *Tidy Data (article by Hadley Wickham)*: `https://www.jstatsoft.org/article/view/v059i10`
- *5 Golden Rules for Great Web API Design*: `https://www.toptal.com/api-developers/5-golden-rules-for-designing-a-great-web-api`

4
Aggregating Pandas DataFrames

In this chapter, we will continue our discussion of data wrangling from `Chapter 3`, *Data Wrangling with Pandas*, by addressing the enrichment and aggregation of data. This includes essential skills, such as merging dataframes, performing window calculations and aggregations, creating new columns, and changing the possible values of the columns. Calculating aggregations and summaries will help us draw conclusions about our data.

We will also take a look at the additional functionality `pandas` has for working with time series data beyond the time series slicing we introduced in previous chapters, including how we can roll up the data with aggregation and select it based on the time part of our datetimes. Much of the data we will encounter is time series data, hence being able to effectively work with time series is paramount. Of course, performing these operations efficiently is important, so we will also review how to write efficient `pandas` code.

This chapter will get us comfortable with performing analyses using `DataFrame` objects. Consequently, these topics are more advanced compared to the prior content and may require a few rereads, so be sure to follow along with the notebooks, which contain additional examples.

The following topics will be covered in this chapter:

- Querying and merging dataframes
- Performing advanced calculations on dataframes
- Aggregating dataframes with `pandas` and `numpy`
- Working with time series data

Chapter materials

The materials for this chapter can be found on GitHub at `https://github.com/stefmolin/Hands-On-Data-Analysis-with-Pandas/tree/master/ch_04`. There are four notebooks that we will work through, each numbered according to when they will be used. The text will prompt when to switch. We will begin with the `1-querying_and_merging.ipynb` notebook to learn about querying and merging dataframes. Next, we will move on to the `2-dataframe_operations.ipynb` notebook to discuss data enrichment through operations such as binning, window functions, and pipes. For this section, we will use the function in the `window_calc.py` Python file.

> The `understanding_window_calculations.ipynb` notebook contains some interactive visualizations for understanding window functions. This may require some additional setup, but the instructions are in the notebook.

Then, we will discuss aggregations with `groupby()`, pivot tables, and crosstabs in the `3-aggregations.ipynb` notebook. Finally, we will focus on additional capabilities `pandas` provides when working with time series data in the `4-time_series.ipynb` notebook.

We will not go over the `0-weather_data_collection.ipynb` notebook; however, for those interested, it contains the code that was used to collect the data from the **National Centers for Environmental Information (NCEI)** API, which can be found at `https://www.ncdc.noaa.gov/cdo-web/webservices/v2`.

There are also two directories: `data/`, which contains all of the CSV and SQLite database files we will use in the aforementioned notebooks, and `exercises/`, which contains the CSV files that are required to complete the end-of-chapter exercises. The following files are in the `data/` directory:

File	Contents	Source
`dirty_data.csv`	Dirty weather data from the *Handling duplicate, missing, or invalid data* section in `Chapter 3`, *Data Wrangling with Pandas*.	Adapted from the NCEI API's GHCND dataset.
`fb_2018.csv`	Facebook stock's opening, high, low, and closing price daily, along with volume traded for 2018.	`stock_analysis` package (see `Chapter 7`, *Financial Analysis – Bitcoin and the Stock Market*).
`fb_week_of_may_20_per_minute.csv`	Facebook stock's opening, high, low, and closing price per minute, along with volume traded for May 20, 2019 through May 24, 2019.	Adapted from `https://www.nasdaq.com/symbol/fb/interactive-chart`

File	Contents	Source
`melted_stock_data.csv`	`fb_week_of_may_20_per_minute.csv` melted into a single column for the price and another for the timestamp.	Adapted from `https://www.nasdaq.com/symbol/fb/interactive-chart.`
`nyc_weather_2018.csv`	Long format weather data for New York City across various stations.	The NCEI API's GHCND dataset.
`stocks.db`	The `fb_prices` and `aapl_prices` tables contain the stock prices for Facebook and Apple, respectively, for May 20, 2019 through May 24, 2019. Facebook is at a minute granularity, whereas Apple has timestamps, including seconds.	Facebook data: `https://www.nasdaq.com/symbol/fb/interactive-chart.` Apple data, adapted from: `https://www.nasdaq.com/symbol/aapl/interactive-chart.`
`weather_by_station.csv`	Long format weather data for New York City across various stations, along with station information.	The NCEI API's GHCND dataset and the `stations` endpoint.
`weather_stations.csv`	Information on all of the stations providing weather data for New York City.	The NCEI API's `stations` endpoint.
`weather.db`	The `weather` table contains New York City weather data, while the `stations` table contains information on the stations.	The NCEI API's GHCND dataset and the `stations` endpoint.

Database-style operations on DataFrames

`DataFrame` objects are analogous to tables in a database: each has a name we refer to it by, is composed of rows, and contains columns of specific data types. Consequently, `pandas` provides the ability to carry out database-style operations on them. Traditionally, databases support a minimum of four operations, called **CRUD**:

- Create
- Read
- Update
- Delete

A database query language—most commonly **SQL** (pronounced *sequel* or *S-Q-L*), which stands for **Structured Query Language**—is used to ask the database to perform these operations. Knowledge of SQL is not required for this book; however, we will look at the SQL equivalent for the `pandas` operations that are discussed in this section since it may aid the understanding of those familiar with SQL. Many data professionals have some familiarity with basic SQL, so consult the *Further reading* section for resources that provide a more formal introduction.

In Chapter 2, *Working with Pandas DataFrames*, we covered how to create dataframes; this was the pandas equivalent of a "CREATE TABLE ..." SQL statement. When we discussed selection and filtering in Chapter 2, *Working with Pandas DataFrames*, and Chapter 3, *Data Wrangling with Pandas*, we were focusing on reading from dataframes, which equated to the SELECT (picking columns) and WHERE (filtering by Boolean criteria) SQL clauses. We carried out update (UPDATE in SQL) and delete (DELETE FROM in SQL) operations when we discussed working with missing data in Chapter 3, *Data Wrangling with Pandas*.

In addition to those basic CRUD operations, the concept of a **join** or **merge** of tables exists. We will discuss the pandas implementation in this section, along with the idea of querying the dataframe.

For this section, we will be working in the 1-querying_and_merging.ipynb notebook. We will begin with our imports and read in the NYC weather data CSV file:

```
>>> import pandas as pd
>>> weather = pd.read_csv('data/nyc_weather_2018.csv')
>>> weather.head()
```

Our data is in the long format—we have several different datatypes per day for various stations covering NYC in 2018:

	attributes	datatype	date	station	value
0	,,N,	PRCP	2018-01-01T00:00:00	GHCND:US1CTFR0039	0.0
1	,,N,	PRCP	2018-01-01T00:00:00	GHCND:US1NJBG0015	0.0
2	,,N,	SNOW	2018-01-01T00:00:00	GHCND:US1NJBG0015	0.0
3	,,N,	PRCP	2018-01-01T00:00:00	GHCND:US1NJBG0017	0.0
4	,,N,	SNOW	2018-01-01T00:00:00	GHCND:US1NJBG0017	0.0

Querying DataFrames

Pandas provides a query() method so that we can easily write complicated filters instead of using a mask. The syntax is similar to the WHERE clause in a SQL statement. To illustrate this, let's query the weather data for all rows where the value of SNOW was greater than zero:

```
>>> snow_data = weather.query('datatype == "SNOW" and value > 0')
>>> snow_data.head()
```

Each row is a snow observation for a given combination of date and station. Notice that the values vary quite a bit for January 4th—some stations received more snow than others:

	attributes	datatype	date	station	value
126	,,N,	SNOW	2018-01-01T00:00:00	GHCND:US1NYWC0019	25.0
722	,,N,	SNOW	2018-01-04T00:00:00	GHCND:US1NJBG0015	229.0
725	,,N,	SNOW	2018-01-04T00:00:00	GHCND:US1NJBG0017	10.0
729	,,N,	SNOW	2018-01-04T00:00:00	GHCND:US1NJBG0018	46.0
736	,,N,	SNOW	2018-01-04T00:00:00	GHCND:US1NJES0018	10.0

When using AND/OR logic with `query()`, we have the option of using `&` or `and` for AND, and `|` or `or` for OR. For example, we could use `weather.query('datatype == "SNOW" & value > 0')` and get the same result. Note that when using `and`/`or`, it will only work in lowercase.

This query is equivalent to the following in SQL:

```
SELECT *
FROM weather
WHERE datatype == 'SNOW' AND value > 0;
```

`SELECT *` selects all the columns in the table (our dataframe, in this case).

In Chapter 2, *Working with Pandas DataFrames*, we learned how to use a Boolean mask to get the same result:

```
>>> weather[
...     (weather.datatype == 'SNOW') & (weather.value > 0)
... ].equals(snow_data)
True
```

For the most part, which one we use is a matter of preference; however, if we have a long name for our dataframe, we will probably prefer the `query()` method. In the previous example, we had to type the dataframe name twice more in order to use the mask.

Merging DataFrames

Merging dataframes deals with how to line them up by row. When we discussed stacking dataframes one on top of the other with `pd.concat()` and the `append()` method in `Chapter 2`, *Working with Pandas DataFrames*, we were performing the equivalent of the SQL `UNION ALL` statement (or just `UNION` if we also removed the duplicates as we saw in the previous chapter).

When referring to databases, merging is traditionally called a **join**. There are four types of joins: full (outer), left, right, and inner. These join types let us know how the result will be affected by values that are only present on one side of the join. This is a concept that's much more easily understood visually, so let's look at some Venn diagrams and then do some sample joins on the weather data:

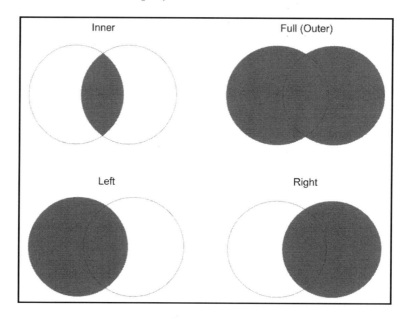

We have been working with data from numerous weather stations, but we don't know anything about them besides their IDs. It would be helpful to know exactly where each of the stations is located to better understand discrepancies between weather readings for the same day in NYC. When we queried for the snow data, we saw quite a bit of variation in the readings for January 4th. This is most likely due to the location of the station. Stations at higher elevations or further north may record more snow. Depending on how far they actually are from NYC, they may have been experiencing a snowstorm that was heavier somewhere else, such as Connecticut or Northern New Jersey.

The NCEI API's `stations` endpoint gives us all the information we need for the stations. This is in the `data/weather_stations.csv` file, as well as the `stations` table in the SQLite database. Let's read this data into a dataframe:

```
>>> station_info = pd.read_csv('data/weather_stations.csv')
>>> station_info.head()
```

For reference, Central Park in NYC is at 40.7829° N, 73.9654° W (latitude 40.7829 and longitude -73.9654), and NYC has an elevation of 10 meters. The first five stations that record NYC data are not in New York. The ones in New Jersey are southwest of NYC and the ones in Connecticut are northeast of NYC:

	id	name	latitude	longitude	elevation
0	GHCND:US1CTFR0022	STAMFORD 2.6 SSW, CT US	41.0641	-73.5770	36.6
1	GHCND:US1CTFR0039	STAMFORD 4.2 S, CT US	41.0378	-73.5682	6.4
2	GHCND:US1NJBG0001	BERGENFIELD 0.3 SW, NJ US	40.9213	-74.0020	20.1
3	GHCND:US1NJBG0002	SADDLE BROOK TWP 0.6 E, NJ US	40.9027	-74.0834	16.8
4	GHCND:US1NJBG0003	TENAFLY 1.3 W, NJ US	40.9147	-73.9775	21.6

Joins require us to specify how to match the data up. The only data the `weather` dataframe has in common with the `station_info` dataframe is the station ID. However, the columns containing this information are not named the same: in the `weather` dataframe, this column is called `station` and, in the `station_info` dataframe, it is called `id`. Before we join the data, let's get some information on how many distinct stations we have and how many entries are in each dataframe:

```
>>> station_info.id.describe()
count                      262
unique                     262
top          GHCND:US1NJBG0008
freq                         1
Name: id, dtype: object

>>> weather.station.describe()
count                    80256
unique                     109
top          GHCND:USW00094789
freq                      4270
Name: station, dtype: object
```

The difference in the number of unique stations across the dataframes tells us they don't contain all the same stations. Depending on the type of join we pick, we may lose some data. Therefore, it's important to look at the row count before and after the join. We can see this is the `count` entry from the output of `describe()`, but we don't need to run that just to get the row count. Instead, we can use the `shape` attribute, which gives us a tuple of the form `(number of rows, number of columns)`. To select the rows, we just grab the value at index 0 (1 for columns):

```
>>> station_info.shape[0], weather.shape[0] # 0 = rows, 1 = columns
(262, 80256)
```

Since we will be checking the row count often, it makes more sense to write a function that will give us the row count for any number of dataframes. The `*dfs` argument collects all the input to this function in a tuple, which we can iterate over in a list comprehension to get the row count:

```
>>> def get_row_count(*dfs):
...     return [df.shape[0] for df in dfs]
>>> get_row_count(station_info, weather)
[262, 80256]
```

For a faster, more efficient strategy, we can use the `map()` function, which lets us run a function on each member of a list (a list of dataframes, in this case). We could generalize this into a function by allowing the caller to specify the dataframes, along with the name of the attribute to grab. The attribute name gets passed to the `getattr()` function, which lets us access an attribute of an object without having to use the dot notation, keeping our function flexible:

```
>>> def get_info(attr, *dfs):
...     return list(map(lambda x: getattr(x, attr), dfs))
>>> get_info('shape', station_info, weather)
[(262, 5), (80256, 5)]
```

The last strategy is obviously the most flexible because we can access any attribute. The `get_row_count()` function is a close second since we can also run it on many dataframes at once. The lesson here is that we will often find that there are many ways to perform the same action; what we choose will ultimately depend on what other uses we see for that code and how reusable we want it to be. Now that we know that we have 80,256 rows of weather data and 262 rows of station information data and five columns for each, we can begin looking at the types of joins.

First, let's discuss the inner join, which will result in the least amount of rows (unless the two dataframes have all the same values for the column being joined on, in which case all the joins will be equivalent). The **inner join** will return the columns from both dataframes where they have a match on the specified key column. Since we will be joining on the `weather.station` column and the `station_info.id` column, we will only get weather data for stations in `station_info`. We will use the `merge()` method to perform the join (which is an inner join by default) by providing the left and right dataframes, along with specifying which columns to join on. Since the station column is named differently across dataframes, we have to specify the names with `left_on` and `right_on`. The left dataframe is the one we call `merge()` on, while the right one is the dataframe that gets passed in as an argument:

```
>>> inner_join = weather.merge(
...     station_info, left_on='station', right_on='id'
... )
>>> inner_join.sample(5, random_state=0)
```

Notice that we have five additional columns, which have been added to the right. These came from the `station_info` dataframe. This operation also kept both the `station` and `id` columns, which are identical:

	attributes	datatype	date	station	value	id	name	latitude	longitude	elevation
27422	,,N,	PRCP	2018-01-23T00:00:00	GHCND:US1NYSF0061	2.3	GHCND:US1NYSF0061	CENTERPORT 0.9 SW, NY US	40.8917	-73.3831	53.6
19317	T,,N,	PRCP	2018-08-10T00:00:00	GHCND:US1NJUN0014	0.0	GHCND:US1NJUN0014	WESTFIELD 0.6 NE, NJ US	40.6588	-74.3358	36.3
13778	,,N,	WESF	2018-02-18T00:00:00	GHCND:US1NJMS0089	19.6	GHCND:US1NJMS0089	PARSIPPANY TROY HILLS TWP 1.3, NJ US	40.8716	-74.4055	103.6
39633	,,7,0700	PRCP	2018-04-06T00:00:00	GHCND:USC00301309	0.0	GHCND:USC00301309	CENTERPORT, NY US	40.8838	-73.3722	9.1
51025	,,W,2400	SNWD	2018-12-14T00:00:00	GHCND:USW00014734	0.0	GHCND:USW00014734	NEWARK LIBERTY INTERNATIONAL AIRPORT, NJ US	40.6825	-74.1694	2.1

In order to remove the duplication of information with the `station` and `id` columns, we can rename one of them before the join. Consequently, we will only have to supply the `on` argument because the columns will share the same name:

```
>>> weather.merge(
...     station_info.rename(dict(id='station'), axis=1),
...     on='station'
... ).sample(5, random_state=0)
```

Since the columns shared the name, we only get one back after joining on them:

	attributes	datatype	date	station	value	name	latitude	longitude	elevation
27422	,,N,	PRCP	2018-01-23T00:00:00	GHCND:US1NYSF0061	2.3	CENTERPORT 0.9 SW, NY US	40.8917	-73.3831	53.6
19317	T,,N,	PRCP	2018-08-10T00:00:00	GHCND:US1NJUN0014	0.0	WESTFIELD 0.6 NE, NJ US	40.6588	-74.3358	36.3
13778	,,N,	WESF	2018-02-18T00:00:00	GHCND:US1NJMS0089	19.6	PARSIPPANY TROY HILLS TWP 1.3, NJ US	40.8716	-74.4055	103.6
39633	,,7,0700	PRCP	2018-04-06T00:00:00	GHCND:USC00301309	0.0	CENTERPORT, NY US	40.8838	-73.3722	9.1
51025	,,W,2400	SNWD	2018-12-14T00:00:00	GHCND:USW00014734	0.0	NEWARK LIBERTY INTERNATIONAL AIRPORT, NJ US	40.6825	-74.1694	2.1

We can join on multiple columns by passing the list of column names to the `on` parameter or to the `left_on` and `right_on` parameters.

Remember that we had 262 unique stations in the `station_info` dataframe, but only 109 unique stations for the weather data. When we performed the inner join, we lost all the stations that didn't have weather observations associated with them. If we don't want to lose rows on a particular side of the join, we can perform a left or right join instead. A **left join** requires us to list the dataframe with the rows that we want to keep (even if they don't exist in the other dataframe) on the left and the other dataframe on the other; a **right join** is the inverse:

```
>>> left_join = station_info.merge(
...     weather, left_on='id', right_on='station', how='left'
... )
>>> right_join = weather.merge(
...     station_info, left_on='station', right_on='id', how='right'
... )
>>> right_join.tail()
```

Wherever the other dataframe has no data, we will get NaN. We may want to investigate why we don't have any weather data associated with these stations. Alternatively, our analysis may involve determining the availability of data per station, so getting null values isn't necessarily an issue:

	attributes	datatype	date	station	value	id	name	latitude	longitude	elevation
80404	NaN	NaN	NaN	NaN	NaN	GHCND:USC00309400	WHITE PLAINS MAPLE M, NY US	41.01667	-73.733330	45.7
80405	NaN	NaN	NaN	NaN	NaN	GHCND:USC00309466	WILLETS POINT	40.80000	-73.766667	16.8
80406	NaN	NaN	NaN	NaN	NaN	GHCND:USC00309576	WOODLANDS ARDSLEY, NY US	41.01667	-73.850000	42.7
80407	NaN	NaN	NaN	NaN	NaN	GHCND:USW00014708	HEMPSTEAD MITCHELL FIELD AFB, NY US	40.73333	-73.600000	38.1
80408	NaN	NaN	NaN	NaN	NaN	GHCND:USW00014786	NEW YORK FLOYD BENNETT FIELD, NY US	40.58333	-73.883330	4.9

Since the station_info dataframe is on the left for the left join and on the right for the right join, the results here are equivalent. In both cases, we chose to keep all the stations present in the station_info dataframe, accepting NaN for the weather observations. To prove they are equivalent, we need to put the columns in the same order, reset the index, and sort the data:

```
>>> left_join.sort_index(axis=1).sort_values(
...     ['date', 'station']).reset_index().drop(
...         columns='index'
... ).equals(
...     right_join.sort_index(axis=1).sort_values(
...         ['date', 'station']
...     ).reset_index().drop(columns='index')
... )
True
```

Note that we have additional rows in the left and right joins because we kept all the stations that didn't have weather observations:

```
>>> get_info('shape', inner_join, left_join, right_join)
[(80256, 10), (80409, 10), (80409, 10)]
```

The final type of join is a **full outer join**, which will keep all the values, regardless of whether or not they exist in both dataframes. For instance, say we queried for stations that had `"NY"` in their names because we believed that stations measuring NYC weather would have to be located in New York. This means that an inner join would result in losing observations from the stations in Connecticut and New Jersey, while a left/right join would result in either lost station information or lost weather data. The outer join will preserve all the data. We will also pass in `indicator=True` to add an additional column to the resulting dataframe, which will indicate which dataframe each row came from:

```
>>> outer_join = weather.merge(
...        station_info[station_info.name.str.contains('NY')],
...        left_on='station', right_on='id', how='outer', indicator=True
... )
# view effect of outer join
>>> outer_join.sample(4, random_state=0)\
...        .append(outer_join[outer_join.station.isna()].head(2))
```

Indices `17259`, `76178`, and `74822` are for stations that don't have `NY` in their name, causing nulls for the station information columns. Index `73410` comes from a station that has `NY` in its name, and the match gives us information about the station. The bottom two rows are stations with `NY` in their name that aren't providing weather observations; note these are actually in New Jersey, but they have `NY` in the city name. This join keeps all the data and will often introduce `NaN` values, unlike inner joins, which won't:

	attributes	datatype	date	station	value	id	name	latitude	longitude	elevation	_merge
17259	,,N,	PRCP	2018-05-15T00:00:00	GHCND:US1NJPS0022	0.3	NaN	NaN	NaN	NaN	NaN	left_only
76178	,,N,	PRCP	2018-05-19T00:00:00	GHCND:US1NJPS0015	8.1	NaN	NaN	NaN	NaN	NaN	left_only
73410	,,N,	MDPR	2018-08-05T00:00:00	GHCND:US1NYNS0018	12.2	GHCND:US1NYNS0018	HICKSVILLE 1.3 ENE, NY US	40.7687	-73.5017	45.7	both
74822	,,N,	SNOW	2018-04-02T00:00:00	GHCND:US1NJMS0016	178.0	NaN	NaN	NaN	NaN	NaN	left_only
80256	NaN	NaN	NaN	NaN	NaN	GHCND:US1NJMS0036	PARSIPPANY TROY HILLS TWP 2.1, NJ US	40.8656	-74.3851	64.3	right_only
80257	NaN	NaN	NaN	NaN	NaN	GHCND:US1NJMS0039	PARSIPPANY TROY HILLS TWP 1.3, NJ US	40.8533	-74.4470	94.2	right_only

The aforementioned joins are equivalent to SQL statements of the following form, where we simply change `<JOIN_TYPE>` to `(INNER) JOIN`, `LEFT JOIN`, `RIGHT JOIN`, or `FULL OUTER JOIN` for the appropriate join:

```
SELECT *
FROM left_table
<JOIN_TYPE> right_table ON left_table.<col> == right_table.<col>;
```

Joining dataframes makes working with the dirty data in Chapter 3, *Data Wrangling with Pandas*, easier. Remember, we had data from two distinct stations; one had a valid station ID and the other was ?. The ? station was the only one recording WESF data. Now that we know about joining dataframes, we can join the data from the valid station ID to the data from the ? station that we are missing by the date. First, we will need to read in the CSV file, setting the date column as the index. We will drop the duplicates and the SNWD column, which we found to be uninformative:

```
>>> dirty_data = pd.read_csv(
...     'data/dirty_data.csv', index_col='date'
... ).drop_duplicates().drop(columns='SNWD')
```

Our starting data looks like this:

	station	PRCP	SNOW	TMAX	TMIN	TOBS	WESF	inclement_weather
date								
2018-01-01T00:00:00	?	0.0	0.0	5505.0	-40.0	NaN	NaN	NaN
2018-01-02T00:00:00	GHCND:USC00280907	0.0	0.0	-8.3	-16.1	-12.2	NaN	False
2018-01-03T00:00:00	GHCND:USC00280907	0.0	0.0	-4.4	-13.9	-13.3	NaN	False
2018-01-04T00:00:00	?	20.6	229.0	5505.0	-40.0	NaN	19.3	True
2018-01-05T00:00:00	?	0.3	NaN	5505.0	-40.0	NaN	NaN	NaN

Now, we need to create a dataframe for each station. To reduce output, we will drop some additional columns:

```
>>> valid_station = dirty_data.query(
...     'station != "?"'
... ).copy().drop(columns=['WESF', 'station'])
>>> station_with_wesf = dirty_data.query(
...     'station == "?"'
... ).copy().drop(columns=['station', 'TOBS', 'TMIN', 'TMAX'])
```

This time, the column we want to join on (the date) is actually the index, so we will pass in left_index to indicate that the column to use from the left dataframe is the index and right_index to indicate the same for the right dataframe:

```
>>> valid_station.merge(
...     station_with_wesf, left_index=True, right_index=True
... ).query('WESF > 0').head()
```

For all the columns that the dataframes had in common, but weren't part of the join, we have two versions now. The versions coming from the left dataframe have the _x suffix appended to the column names, and those coming from the right dataframe have _y as the suffix:

date	PRCP_x	SNOW_x	TMAX	TMIN	TOBS	inclement_weather_x	PRCP_y	SNOW_y	WESF	inclement_weather_y
2018-01-30T00:00:00	0.0	0.0	6.7	-1.7	-0.6	False	1.5	13.0	1.8	True
2018-03-08T00:00:00	48.8	NaN	1.1	-0.6	1.1	False	28.4	NaN	28.7	NaN
2018-03-13T00:00:00	4.1	51.0	5.6	-3.9	0.0	True	3.0	13.0	3.0	True
2018-03-21T00:00:00	0.0	0.0	2.8	-2.8	0.6	False	6.6	114.0	8.6	True
2018-04-02T00:00:00	9.1	127.0	12.8	-1.1	-1.1	True	14.0	152.0	15.2	True

We can provide our own suffixes with the `suffixes` parameter. Let's use a suffix for the ? station:

```
>>> valid_station.merge(
...        station_with_wesf, left_index=True, right_index=True,
...        suffixes=('', '_?')
... ).query('WESF > 0').head()
```

Since we specified an empty string for the left suffix, the columns coming from the left dataframe have their original names. However, the right suffix of _? was added to the names of the columns that came from the right dataframe:

date	PRCP	SNOW	TMAX	TMIN	TOBS	inclement_weather	PRCP_?	SNOW_?	WESF	inclement_weather_?
2018-01-30T00:00:00	0.0	0.0	6.7	-1.7	-0.6	False	1.5	13.0	1.8	True
2018-03-08T00:00:00	48.8	NaN	1.1	-0.6	1.1	False	28.4	NaN	28.7	NaN
2018-03-13T00:00:00	4.1	51.0	5.6	-3.9	0.0	True	3.0	13.0	3.0	True
2018-03-21T00:00:00	0.0	0.0	2.8	-2.8	0.6	False	6.6	114.0	8.6	True
2018-04-02T00:00:00	9.1	127.0	12.8	-1.1	-1.1	True	14.0	152.0	15.2	True

Since we are joining on the index, an easier way is to use the `join()` method instead of `merge()`. It also defaults to an inner join, but this behavior can be changed with the `how` parameter, just like with `merge()`. Note that suffixes are now specified using `lsuffix` for the left dataframe's suffix and `rsuffix` for the right one:

```
>>> valid_station.join(
...        station_with_wesf, rsuffix='_?'
... ).query('WESF > 0').head()
```

 The `join()` method will always use the index of the left dataframe to join, but it can use a column in the right dataframe if its name is passed to the `on` parameter.

One important thing to keep in mind is that joins can be rather resource-intensive, so it is often beneficial to figure out what will happen to the rows before going through with it. If we don't already know what type of join we want, this can help give us an idea. We can use **set operations** on the index we plan to join on to figure this out.

Remember that the mathematical definition of a **set** is a collection of distinct objects. By definition, the index is a set. Set operations are often explained with Venn diagrams:

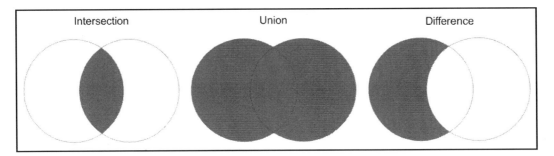

> `Set` is also a Python type that's available in the standard library. A common use of sets is to remove duplicates from a list. More information on sets in Python can be found in the documentation at `https://docs.python.org/3/library/stdtypes.html#set-types-set-frozenset`.

Let's use the `weather` and `station_info` dataframes to illustrate set operations. First, we must set the index to the column(s) that will be used for the join operation:

```
>>> weather.set_index('station', inplace=True)
>>> station_info.set_index('id', inplace=True)
```

To see what will remain with an inner join, we can take the **intersection** of the indices, which shows us the overlap:

```
>>> weather.index.intersection(station_info.index)
Index(['GHCND:US1CTFR0039', ..., 'GHCND:USW00094789'],
      dtype='object', length=80256)
```

As we saw when we ran the inner join, we only got station information for the stations with weather observations. This doesn't tell us what we lost, though; for this, we need to find the **set difference**, which will subtract the sets and give us the values of the first index that aren't in the second. With the set difference, we can easily see that, when performing an inner join, we don't lose any rows from the weather data, but we lose 153 stations that don't have weather observations:

```
>>> weather.index.difference(station_info.index)
Index([], dtype='object')

>>> station_info.index.difference(weather.index)
Index(['GHCND:US1CTFR0022', ..., 'GHCND:USW00014786'],
      dtype='object', length=153)
```

Note that this output also tells us how the left and right joins will turn out. To avoid losing rows, we want to put the station_info dataframe on the same side as the join (on the left for a left join and on the right for a right join).

> We can use the symmetric_difference() method on the index to get back what will be lost both from that index and the other one: index_1.symmetric_difference(index_2). The result will be the values that are only in one of the indices. An example is in the notebook.

Lastly, we can use the **union** to view all the values we will get if we run a full outer join. Since sets by definition contain unique values, in order to union the values, we have to make sure that we pass in only the unique values in order to avoid an error. Remember, the weather dataframe has the stations repeated throughout because they provide daily measurements:

```
>>> weather.index.unique().union(station_info.index)
Index(['GHCND:US1CTFR0022', ..., 'GHCND:USW00094789'],
      dtype='object', length=262)
```

> The *Further reading* section at the end of this chapter contains some resources on set operations and how pandas compares to SQL.

DataFrame operations

Now that we've discussed how to query and merge `DataFrame` objects, let's learn how to perform complex operations on our dataframes to create and modify columns and rows. We will begin with a review of operations that summarize entire rows and columns before moving on to binning, imposing threshold limits on the data, applying functions across rows and columns, and window calculations, which summarize data along a certain number of observations at a time (like moving averages).

For this section, we will be working in the `2-dataframe_operations.ipynb` notebook and using weather data, along with Facebook stock's volume traded and opening, high, low, and closing prices daily for 2018. Let's import what we will need and read in the data:

```
>>> import numpy as np
>>> import pandas as pd

>>> weather = pd.read_csv(
...     'data/nyc_weather_2018.csv', parse_dates=['date']
... )
>>> fb = pd.read_csv(
...     'data/fb_2018.csv', index_col='date', parse_dates=True
... )
```

Arithmetic and statistics

In the *Describing and summarizing the data* section of `Chapter 2`, *Working with Pandas DataFrames*, there was a table showing some operations that we could run on `Series` and `DataFrame` objects. Here, we are going to use some of those to create new columns and modify our data to see how we can use new data to draw some initial conclusions.

First, let's create a column with the Z-score for the volume traded in Facebook stock and use it to find the days where the Z-score is greater than 3 in absolute value. These values are more than three standard deviations from the mean, which may be abnormal (depending on the data). Remember from our discussion of Z-scores in `Chapter 1`, *Introduction to Data Analysis*, that we calculate them by subtracting the mean from all the values and dividing by the standard deviation.

Rather than using mathematical operators for subtraction and division, we will use the `sub()` and `div()` methods, respectively:

```
>>> fb.assign(
...     abs_z_score_volume=lambda x: x.volume.sub(
...         x.volume.mean()
...     ).div(x.volume.std()).abs()
... ).query('abs_z_score_volume > 3')
```

Five days in 2018 had Z-scores for volume traded greater than three in absolute value. These dates in particular will come up often in the rest of this chapter as they mark some trouble points for Facebook's stock price:

date	open	high	low	close	volume	abs_z_score_volume
2018-03-19	177.01	177.17	170.06	172.56	88140060	3.145078
2018-03-20	167.47	170.20	161.95	168.15	129851768	5.315169
2018-03-21	164.80	173.40	163.30	169.39	106598834	4.105413
2018-03-26	160.82	161.10	149.02	160.06	126116634	5.120845
2018-07-26	174.89	180.13	173.75	176.26	169803668	7.393705

Pandas has several of these methods for mathematical operations, including comparisons, floor division, and the modulo operation, which can be found here: `https://pandas.pydata.org/pandas-docs/stable/reference/series.html#binary-operator-functions`. These methods give us more flexibility in how we define the calculation by allowing us to specify the axis to perform the calculation on (when performing it on a `DataFrame` object). The default will be to perform the calculation along the columns (`axis=1` or `axis='columns'`), which generally contain observations of a single variable of single data type. However, we can pass in `axis=0` or `axis='index'` to perform the calculation along the rows instead.

Two other very useful methods are `rank()` and `pct_change()`, which let us rank the values of a column (and store them in a new column) and calculate the percentage change between periods. By combining these, we can see which five days had the largest percentage change of the volume traded in Facebook stock from the day prior:

```
>>> fb.assign(
...     volume_pct_change=fb.volume.pct_change(),
...     pct_change_rank=lambda x: x.volume_pct_change.abs().rank(
...         ascending=False
...     )
... ).nsmallest(5, 'pct_change_rank')
```

The day with the largest percentage change in volume traded was January 12, 2018, which happens to be one of the many Facebook scandals that shook the stock in 2018 (`https://www.cnbc.com/2018/11/20/facebooks-scandals-in-2018-effect-on-stock.html`). This was when they announced changes to the news feed to prioritize content from a users' friends over brands they follow. Given that a large component of Facebook's revenue comes from advertising (nearly 89% in 2017, *source*: `https://www.investopedia.com/ask/answers/120114/how-does-facebook-fb-make-money.asp`), this caused panic as many sold the stock, driving up the volume that was traded drastically, thus dropping the stock price:

date	open	high	low	close	volume	volume_pct_change	pct_change_rank
2018-01-12	178.06	181.48	177.40	179.37	77551299	7.087876	1.0
2018-03-19	177.01	177.17	170.06	172.56	88140060	2.611789	2.0
2018-07-26	174.89	180.13	173.75	176.26	169803668	1.628841	3.0
2018-09-21	166.64	167.25	162.81	162.93	45994800	1.428956	4.0
2018-03-26	160.82	161.10	149.02	160.06	126116634	1.352496	5.0

We can use slicing on the `DatetimeIndex` to look at the change this announcement caused:

```
>>> fb['2018-01-11':'2018-01-12']
```

Notice how we are able to combine everything we learned in the last few chapters to get interesting insights from our data. We were able to sift through a year's worth of stock data and find some days that had large effects on Facebook stock (good or bad):

date	open	high	low	close	volume
2018-01-11	188.40	188.40	187.38	187.77	9588587
2018-01-12	178.06	181.48	177.40	179.37	77551299

Lastly, we can inspect the dataframe with aggregated Boolean operations. For example, we can check whether all the columns in the Facebook dataframe have at least one value above 215 with `any()`:

```
>>> (fb > 215).any()
open         True
high         True
low          False
close        True
volume       True
dtype: bool
```

We can see that the Facebook stock never had a value for `low` greater than 215 in 2018. If we want to see if all the rows in a column meet the criteria, we can use `all()`. This tells us that Facebook has at least one row for `open`, `high`, `low`, and `close` with a value less than or equal to 215:

```
>>> (fb > 215).all()
open         False
high         False
low          False
close        False
volume       True
dtype: bool
```

Binning and thresholds

Sometimes, it's more convenient to work with categories rather than the specific values. A common example is working with ages—most likely, we don't want to look at the data for each age, such as 25 compared to 26; however, we may very well be interested in how the group of 25-34 year-olds compares to the group of 35-44 year-olds. This is called **binning** or **discretizing** (going from continuous to discrete); we take our data and place the observations into bins (or buckets) matching the range they fall into. By doing so, we can drastically reduce the number of distinct values our data can take on and make it easier to analyze.

One interesting thing we could do with the volume traded would be to see which days had high trade volume and look for news about Facebook on those days or large swings in price. Unfortunately, it is highly unlikely that the volume will be the same any two days; in fact, we can confirm that, in the data, no two days have the same volume traded:

```
>>> (fb.volume.value_counts() > 1).sum()
0
```

Remember that `value_counts()` gives us the number of occurrences for each unique value for `volume`. We can then create a mask for whether the count is greater than 1 and sum up the Boolean mask (`True` evaluates to 1 and `False` evaluates to 0). Alternatively, we can use `any()` instead of `sum()`, which, rather than telling us the number of unique values of volume that had more than one occurrence, would give us `True` if at least one volume amount occurred more than once and `False` otherwise.

Clearly, we will need to create some ranges for the volume traded in order to look at the days of high trading volume, but how do we decide which range is a good range? Pandas provides the `pd.cut()` function for binning based on value. First, we should decide how many bins we want to create—three seems like a good split, since we can label the bins low, medium, and high. Next, we need to determine what size we want each bin to be; `pandas` tries to make this process as painless as possible, so if we want equally-sized bins, all we have to do is specify the number of bins we want:

```
>>> volume_binned = pd.cut(
...     fb.volume, bins=3, labels=['low', 'med', 'high']
... )
>>> volume_binned.value_counts()
low      240
med        8
high       3
Name: volume, dtype: int64
```

Note that we provided labels for each bin here; if we don't do this, each bin will be labeled by the interval of values it includes, which may or may not be helpful for us, depending on our application. If we want to both label the values and see the bins afterwards, we can pass `retbins=True` to the call to `pd.cut()` and access the binned data as the first element of the tuple that is returned and the bin ranges themselves as the second element.

It looks like an overwhelming majority of the trading days were in the low-volume bin; keep in mind that this is all relative because we evenly divided the space between the minimum and maximum trading volumes. Let's look at the data for the three days of high volume:

```
>>> fb[volume_binned == 'high'].sort_values('volume', ascending=False)
```

Even among the high-volume days, we can see that July 26, 2018 had a much higher volume compared to the other two dates in March (nearly 40 million additional shares were traded). In fact, querying a search engine for `Facebook stock price July 26, 2018` reveals that Facebook had announced their earnings and disappointing user growth after market close on July 25th, which was followed by lots of after-hours selling. When the market opened the next morning, the stock had dropped from $217.50 at close on the 25th to $174.89 at market open on the 26th:

date	open	high	low	close	volume
2018-07-26	174.89	180.13	173.75	176.26	169803668
2018-03-20	167.47	170.20	161.95	168.15	129851768
2018-03-26	160.82	161.10	149.02	160.06	126116634

Using datetime slicing on the index, we can pull out this data:

```
>>> fb['2018-07-25':'2018-07-26']
```

Not only was there a huge drop in stock price, but the volume traded also skyrocketed, increasing by more than 100 million! All of this resulted in a loss of about $120 billion in Facebook's market capitalization (https://www.marketwatch.com/story/facebook-stock-crushed-after-revenue-user-growth-miss-2018-07-25):

date	open	high	low	close	volume
2018-07-25	215.715	218.62	214.27	217.50	64592585
2018-07-26	174.890	180.13	173.75	176.26	169803668

If we look at the other two days marked as high-volume trading days, we will find a plethora of information as to why. Both of these days were marked by scandal for Facebook. The Cambridge Analytica political data privacy scandal broke on March 17, 2018, which was a Saturday, so trading with this information didn't commence until Monday the 19th (https://www.nytimes.com/2018/03/19/technology/facebook-cambridge-analytica-explained.html):

```
>>> fb['2018-03-16':'2018-03-20']
```

Things only got worse once more information was revealed in the following days with regards to the severity of the incident:

date	open	high	low	close	volume
2018-03-16	184.49	185.33	183.41	185.09	24403438
2018-03-19	177.01	177.17	170.06	172.56	88140060
2018-03-20	167.47	170.20	161.95	168.15	129851768

As for the third day of high trading volume, the FTC launched an investigation into the Cambridge Analytica scandal, so Facebook's woes continued (`https://www.cnbc.com/2018/03/26/ftc-confirms-facebook-data-breach-investigation.html`).

If we look at some of the dates within the medium trading volume group, we can see that many are part of the three trading events we just discussed. This forces us to reexamine how we created the bins in the first place. Perhaps equal-width bins wasn't the answer? Most days were pretty close in volume traded; however, a few days caused the bin width to be rather large, which left us with a large imbalance of days per bin:

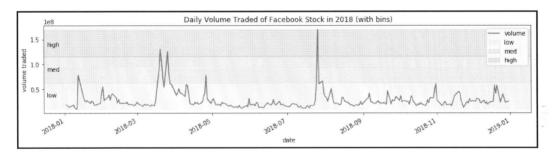

 While binning our data can make certain parts of the analysis easier, keep in mind that it will reduce the information in that field since the granularity is reduced.

If we want each bin to have an equal number of observations, we can split the bins based on evenly-spaced quantiles using `pd.qcut()`. We can bin the volumes into quartiles to evenly bucket the observations into bins of varying width, giving us the `63` highest trading volume days in the `q4` bin:

```
>>> volume_qbinned = pd.qcut(
...     fb.volume, q=4, labels=['q1', 'q2', 'q3', 'q4']
... )
>>> volume_qbinned.value_counts()
q4    63
q2    63
q1    63
q3    62
Name: volume, dtype: int64
```

Notice that the bins don't cover the same range of volume traded anymore:

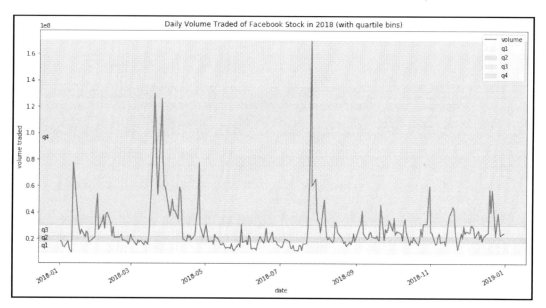

In both of these examples, we let `pandas` calculate the bin ranges; however, both functions allow us to specify the right bounds for each bin as a list if we want.

Sometimes, we aren't interested in the exact values beyond certain limits because they are spaced far apart; usually, in these cases, we would want to represent all the values beyond these thresholds with a value for the bucket. Say we only care about whether snow was recorded in Central Park. One way of dealing with bucketing in this case, while keeping the data the same type (float), would be to mark any value of SNOW above zero as one. First, we need to select the Central Park station and then pivot our data, as we learned in Chapter 3, *Data Wrangling with Pandas*:

```
>>> central_park_weather = weather.query(
...     'station == "GHCND:USW00094728"'
... ).pivot(index='date', columns='datatype', values='value')
```

Then, we can use the clip() method and provide thresholds for clipping. The first will be the lower bound, while the second will be the upper bound. Alternatively, we can use the upper and/or lower keyword arguments for the clipping:

```
>>> central_park_weather.SNOW.clip(0, 1).value_counts()
0.0    354
1.0     11
Name: SNOW, dtype: int64
```

This tells us that the Central Park station recorded snowfall on 11 days in 2018. Since our column is still numeric, we will have saved ourselves some extra work if we decide to build a model with this data, which we will see in the *Encoding* section in Chapter 9, *Getting Started with Machine Learning in Python*. Note that the clip() method can also be called on the dataframe itself.

Applying functions

So far, most of the actions we have taken on our data have been column-specific. When we want to run the same code on all the columns in our dataframe, we don't have to repeat ourselves—we can use the apply() method. Note that this will not be done in-place.

Let's calculate the Z-scores of the `TMIN` (minimum temperature), `TMAX` (maximum temperature), and `PRCP` (precipitation) observations in Central Park in October 2018. It's important that we don't try to take the Z-scores across the full year. NYC has four seasons, and what is considered normal weather will depend on which season we are in. By isolating our calculation to October, we can see if October had any days with very different weather:

```
>>> oct_weather_z_scores = central_park_weather.loc[
...     '2018-10', ['TMIN', 'TMAX', 'PRCP']
... ].apply(lambda x: x.sub(x.mean()).div(x.std()))
>>> oct_weather_z_scores.describe().T
```

`TMIN` and `TMAX` don't appear to have any values that differ much from the rest of October, but `PRCP` does:

datatype	count	mean	std	min	25%	50%	75%	max
TMIN	31.0	-1.790682e-16	1.0	-1.339112	-0.751019	-0.474269	1.065152	1.843511
TMAX	31.0	1.951844e-16	1.0	-1.305582	-0.870013	-0.138258	1.011643	1.604016
PRCP	31.0	4.655774e-17	1.0	-0.394438	-0.394438	-0.394438	-0.240253	3.936167

We can use `query()` to extract the value for this date:

```
>>> oct_weather_z_scores.query('PRCP > 3')
datatype          TMIN       TMAX       PRCP
date
2018-10-27   -0.751019  -1.201045   3.936167
```

If we look at the summary statistics for precipitation in October, we can see that this day had much more precipitation than the rest:

```
>>> central_park_weather.loc['2018-10', 'PRCP'].describe()
count    31.000000
mean      2.941935
std       7.458542
min       0.000000
25%       0.000000
50%       0.000000
75%       1.150000
max      32.300000
Name: PRCP, dtype: float64
```

The `apply()` method lets us run vectorized operations on entire columns or rows at once. We can apply pretty much any function we can think of as long as those operations are valid on all the columns (or rows) in our data. For example, we can use the `cut()` and `qcut()` binning functions we discussed in the previous section to divide each column into bins (provided we want the same number of bins or value ranges). Note that there is also an `applymap()` method if the function we want to apply isn't vectorized. Alternatively, we can use `np.vectorize()` to vectorize our functions for use with `apply()`. Consult the notebook for an example.

Pandas does provide some functionality for iterating over the dataframe, including the `iteritems()`, `itertuples()`, and `iterrows()` methods; however, we should avoid using these unless we absolutely can't find another solution. Pandas and NumPy are designed for vectorized operations, which are much faster because they are written in efficient C code; by writing a loop to iterate one element at a time, we are making it more computationally intensive due to the way Python implements integers and floats. For instance, look at how the time to complete the simple operation of adding the number 10 to each value in a series grows linearly with the number of rows when using `iteritems()`, but stays near zero, regardless of size, when using a vectorized operation:

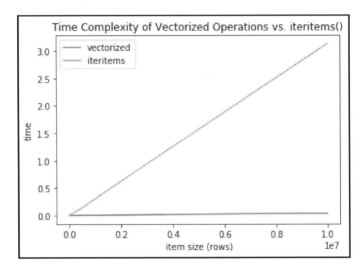

Window calculations

All the functions and methods we have used so far have involved the full row or column; however, sometimes, we are more interested in the values over a certain window or range of rows/columns. When we have a `DatetimeIndex`, we can specify the windows in day parts (such as `2H` for two hours or `3D` for three days), otherwise we can specify the number of periods as an integer. Say we are interested in the amount of rain that has fallen in a rolling three-day window; it would be quite tedious (and probably inefficient) to implement this with what we have learned so far. Fortunately, we can use the `rolling()` method on dataframes to get this information easily:

```
>>> central_park_weather['2018-10'].assign(
...     rolling_PRCP=lambda x: x.PRCP.rolling('3D').sum()
... )[['PRCP', 'rolling_PRCP']].head(7).T
```

After performing the rolling three-day sum, each date will show the sum of that day's and the previous two days' precipitation:

date	2018-10-01 00:00:00	2018-10-02 00:00:00	2018-10-03 00:00:00	2018-10-04 00:00:00	2018-10-05 00:00:00	2018-10-06 00:00:00	2018-10-07 00:00:00
datatype							
PRCP	0.0	17.5	0.0	1.0	0.0	0.0	0.0
rolling_PRCP	0.0	17.5	17.5	18.5	1.0	1.0	0.0

We provided a window of `'3D'` for three days; however, this will also work with an integer index. In that case, we provide the integer 3 as the window.

To change the aggregation, all we have to do is call a different method on the result of `rolling()`; for example, `mean()` for the average and `max()` for the maximum. The rolling calculation can also be applied to all of the columns of the dataframe at once:

```
>>> central_park_weather['2018-10']\
...     .rolling('3D').mean().head(7).iloc[:,:6]
```

This gives us the three-day rolling average for all the weather observations from Central Park:

datatype	AWND	PRCP	SNOW	SNWD	TMAX	TMIN
date						
2018-10-01	0.900000	0.000000	0.0	0.0	24.400000	17.200000
2018-10-02	0.900000	8.750000	0.0	0.0	24.700000	17.750000
2018-10-03	0.966667	5.833333	0.0	0.0	24.233333	17.566667
2018-10-04	0.800000	6.166667	0.0	0.0	24.233333	17.200000
2018-10-05	1.033333	0.333333	0.0	0.0	23.133333	16.300000
2018-10-06	0.833333	0.333333	0.0	0.0	22.033333	16.300000
2018-10-07	1.066667	0.000000	0.0	0.0	22.600000	17.400000

To apply different aggregations across columns, we can use the agg() method instead. It allows us to specify the aggregations to perform per column. This can be a predefined function or a custom function. We simply pass in a dictionary mapping the columns to the aggregation to perform on them. Let's find the rolling three-day maximum temperature (TMAX), minimum temperature (TMIN), average wind speed (AWND), and total precipitation (PRCP). Then, we will join it to the original data so that we can compare the outcome:

```
>>> central_park_weather['2018-10-01':'2018-10-07'].rolling('3D').agg(
...     {'TMAX': 'max', 'TMIN': 'min', 'AWND': 'mean', 'PRCP': 'sum'}
... ).join( # join with original data for comparison
...     central_park_weather[['TMAX', 'TMIN', 'AWND', 'PRCP']],
...     lsuffix='_rolling'
... ).sort_index(axis=1) # sort rolling calcs next to originals
```

Using agg(), we were able to calculate different rolling aggregations for each column:

	AWND	AWND_rolling	PRCP	PRCP_rolling	TMAX	TMAX_rolling	TMIN	TMIN_rolling
date								
2018-10-01	0.9	0.900000	0.0	0.0	24.4	24.4	17.2	17.2
2018-10-02	0.9	0.900000	17.5	17.5	25.0	25.0	18.3	17.2
2018-10-03	1.1	0.966667	0.0	17.5	23.3	25.0	17.2	17.2
2018-10-04	0.4	0.800000	1.0	18.5	24.4	25.0	16.1	16.1
2018-10-05	1.6	1.033333	0.0	1.0	21.7	24.4	15.6	15.6
2018-10-06	0.5	0.833333	0.0	1.0	20.0	24.4	17.2	15.6
2018-10-07	1.1	1.066667	0.0	0.0	26.1	26.1	19.4	15.6

With rolling calculations, we had a sliding window on which we calculated our functions; however, in some cases, we are more interested in the output of a function on all the data up to that point, in which case we use the `expanding()` method instead of `rolling()`. Expanding calculations will give us the cumulative value of our aggregation function. We can use `expanding()` to calculate the cumulative sum of precipitation:

```
>>> precip.expanding().sum().equals(precip.cumsum())
True
```

 While this was the same as `cumsum()` here, `expanding()` gives us additional flexibility. We can specify the minimum number of periods before the calculation starts with the `min_periods` parameter, which defaults to 1.

Like we did with `rolling()`, we can provide column-specific aggregations with the `agg()` method to our expanding window calculations. Let's find the expanding maximum temperature, minimum temperature, average wind speed, and total precipitation. Note that we can also pass in NumPy functions to `agg()`:

```
>>> central_park_weather['2018-10-01':'2018-10-07'].expanding().agg({
...     'TMAX': np.max,
...     'TMIN': np.min,
...     'AWND': np.mean,
...     'PRCP': np.sum
... }).join(
...     central_park_weather[['TMAX', 'TMIN', 'AWND', 'PRCP']],
...     lsuffix='_expanding'
... ).sort_index(axis=1)
```

Once again, we joined the window calculations with the original data for comparison:

date	AWND	AWND_expanding	PRCP	PRCP_expanding	TMAX	TMAX_expanding	TMIN	TMIN_expanding
2018-10-01	0.9	0.900000	0.0	0.0	24.4	24.4	17.2	17.2
2018-10-02	0.9	0.900000	17.5	17.5	25.0	25.0	18.3	17.2
2018-10-03	1.1	0.966667	0.0	17.5	23.3	25.0	17.2	17.2
2018-10-04	0.4	0.825000	1.0	18.5	24.4	25.0	16.1	16.1
2018-10-05	1.6	0.980000	0.0	18.5	21.7	25.0	15.6	15.6
2018-10-06	0.5	0.900000	0.0	18.5	20.0	25.0	17.2	15.6
2018-10-07	1.1	0.928571	0.0	18.5	26.1	26.1	19.4	15.6

Lastly, `pandas` also provides the `ewm()` method for exponentially weighted moving functions. We can use this to calculate a 5-period exponentially weighted moving average of the closing price of Facebook stock:

```
>>> fb.assign(
...     close_ewma=lambda x: x.close.ewm(span=5).mean()
... ).tail(10)[['close', 'close_ewma']]
              close   close_ewma
date
2018-12-17   140.19   142.235433
2018-12-18   143.66   142.710289
2018-12-19   133.24   139.553526
2018-12-20   133.40   137.502350
2018-12-21   124.95   133.318234
2018-12-24   124.06   130.232156
2018-12-26   134.18   131.548104
2018-12-27   134.52   132.538736
2018-12-28   133.20   132.759157
2018-12-31   131.09   132.202772
```

 Check out `understanding_window_calculations.ipynb`, which contains some interactive visualizations for understanding window functions. This may require some additional setup, but the instructions are in the notebook.

Pipes

Pipes facilitate chaining together operations that expect `pandas` data structures as their first argument. By using pipes, we can build up complex workflows without needing to write highly nested and hard to read code. In general, pipes let us turn something like `f(g(h(df), 20), x=True))` into the following, making it much easier to read:

```
df.pipe(h)\ # first call h(df)
  .pipe(g, 20)\ # call g on the result with positional arg 20
  .pipe(f, x=True) # call f on the result with keyword arg x=True
```

Say we wanted to print the dimensions of a subset of the Facebook dataframe with some formatting, but after calculating the Z-scores for all the columns. We could define this function as follows:

```
>>> def get_info(df):
...     return '%d rows, %d columns and max closing z-score was %d' \
...            % (*df.shape, df.close.max())
```

To call the function, we could do the following:

```
>>> get_info(fb['2018-Q1'].apply(lambda x: (x - x.mean())/x.std()))
```

Alternatively, we could pipe the dataframe after calculating the Z-scores to this function:

```
>>> fb['2018-Q1'].apply(lambda x: (x - x.mean())/x.std())\
...      .pipe(get_info)
```

Pipes can also make it easier to write reusable code. In several of the code snippets in this book, we have seen the idea of passing a function into another function, such as when we pass a NumPy function to `apply()` and it gets executed on each column. We can use pipes to extend that functionality to methods of `pandas` data structures:

```
>>> fb.pipe(pd.DataFrame.rolling, '20D').mean().equals(
...      fb.rolling('20D').mean()
... ) # the pipe is calling pd.DataFrame.rolling(fb, '20D')
True
```

To illustrate how this can benefit us, let's look at a function that will give us the result of a window calculation of our choice. The function is in the `window_calc.py` file. We will import the function and use `??` from IPython to view the function definition:

```
>>> from window_calc import window_calc
>>> window_calc??
Signature: window_calc(df, func, agg_dict, *args, **kwargs)
Source:
def window_calc(df, func, agg_dict, *args, **kwargs):
    """
    Run a window calculation of your choice on a DataFrame.
    Parameters:
        - df: The DataFrame to run the calculation on.
        - func: The window calculation method that takes df
                as the first argument.
        - agg_dict: Information to pass to `agg()`, could be a
                dictionary mapping the columns to the aggregation
                function to use, a string name for the function,
                or the function itself.
        - args: Positional arguments to pass to `func`.
        - kwargs: Keyword arguments to pass to `func`.
    Returns:
        - A new DataFrame object.
    """
    return df.pipe(func, *args, **kwargs).agg(agg_dict)
File:      c:\...\ch_04\window_calc.py
Type:      function
```

Our `window_calc()` function takes the dataframe, the function to execute (as long as it takes a dataframe as its first argument), and information on how to aggregate the result, along with any optional parameters, and gives us back a new dataframe with the window calculations. Let's use this function to find the expanding median of the Facebook stock data:

```
>>> window_calc(fb, pd.DataFrame.expanding, np.median).head()
```

Take note that the `expanding()` method doesn't require us to specify any parameters, so all we had to do was pass `pd.DataFrame.expanding` (no parentheses) along with the aggregation to perform as the window calculation on the dataframe:

	open	high	low	close	volume
date					
2018-01-02	177.68	181.580	177.5500	181.420	18151903.0
2018-01-03	179.78	183.180	179.4400	183.045	17519233.0
2018-01-04	181.88	184.780	181.3300	184.330	16886563.0
2018-01-05	183.39	185.495	182.7148	184.500	15383729.5
2018-01-08	184.90	186.210	184.0996	184.670	16886563.0

The function also takes `*args` and `**kwargs`; these are optional parameters that, if supplied, will be collected by Python into `kwargs` when they are passed by name (such as `span=20`) and into `args` if not (passed by position). These can then be **unpacked** and passed to another function or method call by using `*` for `args` and `**` for `kwargs`. We need this behavior in order to use the `ewm()` method for the exponentially weighted moving average of the closing price of Facebook stock:

```
>>> window_calc(fb, pd.DataFrame.ewm, 'mean', span=3).head()
```

In the previous example, we had to use `**kwargs` because the `span` argument is not the first argument that `ewm()` receives, and we didn't want to pass the ones before it:

	open	high	low	close	volume
date					
2018-01-02	177.680000	181.580000	177.550000	181.420000	1.815190e+07
2018-01-03	180.480000	183.713333	180.070000	183.586667	1.730834e+07
2018-01-04	183.005714	185.140000	182.372629	184.011429	1.534980e+07
2018-01-05	184.384000	186.078667	183.736560	185.525333	1.440299e+07
2018-01-08	185.837419	187.534839	185.075110	186.947097	1.625679e+07

To calculate the rolling three-day weather aggregations for Central Park, we take advantage of `*args` since we know that the window is the first argument to `rolling()`:

```
>>> window_calc(
...     central_park_weather['2018-10'],
...     pd.DataFrame.rolling,
...     {'TMAX': 'max', 'TMIN': 'min', 'AWND': 'mean', 'PRCP': 'sum'},
...     '3D'
... ).head()
```

We were able to aggregate each of the columns differently since we passed in a dictionary instead of a single value:

	TMAX	TMIN	AWND	PRCP
date				
2018-10-01	24.4	17.2	0.900000	0.0
2018-10-02	25.0	17.2	0.900000	17.5
2018-10-03	25.0	17.2	0.966667	17.5
2018-10-04	25.0	16.1	0.800000	18.5
2018-10-05	24.4	15.6	1.033333	1.0

Notice how were able to create a consistent API for the window calculations without the caller needing to figure out the aggregation method to call after the window function. This hides some of the implementation details, while making it easier to use. We will be using this function as the base for some of the functionality in the `StockVisualizer` class we will build in Chapter 7, *Financial Analysis – Bitcoin and the Stock Market*.

Aggregations with pandas and numpy

We already got a sneak peek at aggregation when we discussed window calculations and pipes in the previous section. Here, we will focus on summarizing the dataframe through aggregation, which will change the shape of our dataframe (often through row reduction). We also saw how easy it is to take advantage of vectorized NumPy functions on `pandas` data structures, especially to perform aggregations. This is what NumPy does best: computationally-efficient mathematical operations on numeric arrays.

NumPy pairs well with aggregating dataframes since it gives us an easy way to summarize data with different pre-written functions; often, when aggregating, we just need the NumPy function, since most of what we would want to write ourselves has already been built. We have seen some common NumPy functions to use with aggregations, such as `np.sum()`, `np.mean()`, `np.min()`, and `np.max()`; however, we aren't limited to numeric operations—we can use things such as `np.unique()` on strings. Always check whether NumPy already has a function before implementing one yourself.

For this section, we will be working in the `3-aggregations.ipynb` notebook. Let's import `pandas` and NumPy and read in the data we will be working with:

```
>>> import numpy as np
>>> import pandas as pd

>>> weather = pd.read_csv(
...     'data/weather_by_station.csv',
...     index_col='date',
...     parse_dates=True
... )
>>> fb = pd.read_csv(
...     'data/fb_2018.csv', index_col='date', parse_dates=True
... ).assign(
...     trading_volume=lambda x: pd.cut(
...         x.volume, bins=3, labels=['low', 'med', 'high']
...     )
... )
```

Our weather data has been merged with some of the station data for this section:

	datatype	station	value	station_name
date				
2018-01-01	PRCP	GHCND:US1CTFR0039	0.000000	STAMFORD ...
2018-01-01	PRCP	GHCND:US1NJBG0015	0.000000	NORTH ARLINGTON ...
2018-01-01	SNOW	GHCND:US1NJBG0015	0.000000	NORTH ARLINGTON ...
2018-01-01	PRCP	GHCND:US1NJBG0017	0.000000	GLEN ROCK ...
2018-01-01	SNOW	GHCND:US1NJBG0017	0.000000	GLEN ROCK ...

Before we dive into any calculations, let's make sure that our data won't be displayed in scientific notation. We will modify how floats are formatted for displaying. The format we will apply is `.2f`, which will provide the float with two digits after the decimal point:

```
>> pd.set_option('display.float_format', lambda x: '%.2f' % x)
```

Summarizing DataFrames

When we discussed window calculations, we saw that we could run the `agg()` method on the result of `rolling()`, `expanding()`, or `ewm()`; however, we can also call it directly on the dataframe in the same fashion. The only difference is that the aggregations done this way will be performed on all the data, meaning that we will only get a series back that contains the overall result. Let's aggregate the Facebook stock data the same way we did with the window calculations. Note that we won't get anything back for the `trading_volume` column, which contains the volume traded bins from `pd.cut()`; this is because we aren't specifying an aggregation to run on that column:

```
>>> fb.agg({
...     'open': np.mean, 'high': np.max, 'low': np.min,
...     'close': np.mean, 'volume': np.sum
... })
open              171.45
high              218.62
low               123.02
close             171.51
volume    6949682394.00
dtype: float64
```

We can use aggregations to easily find the total snowfall and precipitation for 2018 in Central Park. In this case, since we will be performing the sum on both, we can either use `agg('sum')` or call `sum()` directly:

```
>>> weather.query(
...     'station == "GHCND:USW00094728"'
... ).pivot(
...     columns='datatype', values='value'
... )[['SNOW', 'PRCP']].sum()
datatype
SNOW    1007.00
PRCP    1665.30
dtype: float64
```

Additionally, we can provide multiple functions to run on each of the columns we want to aggregate. As we have already seen, we get a `Series` object when each column has a single aggregation. In order to be able to distinguish between the aggregations in the case of multiple ones per column, `pandas` will return a `DataFrame` object instead. The index of this dataframe will tell us which metric is being calculated for which column:

```
>>> fb.agg({
...     'open': 'mean', 'high': ['min', 'max'],
...     'low': ['min', 'max'], 'close': 'mean'
... })
```

This results in a dataframe where the rows indicate the aggregation function being applied to the data columns. Note that we get NaN for any combination of aggregation and column that we didn't explicitly ask for:

	open	high	low	close
max	NaN	218.62	214.27	NaN
mean	171.45	NaN	NaN	171.51
min	NaN	129.74	123.02	NaN

Using groupby

So far, we have learned how to aggregate over specific windows and over the entire dataframe; however, the real power comes with the ability to aggregate by group membership. This lets us calculate things such as the total precipitation per month per station and average OHLC stock prices for each volume bin we've created.

OHLC is a common abbreviation with stock pricing data; it stands for the prices at **open**, **high**, **low**, and **close** during a given trading day.

In order to calculate the aggregations per group, we must first call the `groupby()` method on the dataframe and provide the column(s) we want to be used to determine distinct groups. Let's look at the average of our stock data points for each of the volume traded bins we created with `pd.cut()`; remember, these are the three equal-width bins:

```
>>> fb.groupby('trading_volume').mean()
```

The average prices for OHLC are smaller for larger trading volumes, which was to be expected given that the three dates in the high-volume traded bin were selloffs:

	open	high	low	close	volume
trading_volume					
low	171.36	173.46	169.31	171.43	24547207.71
med	175.82	179.42	172.11	175.14	79072559.12
high	167.73	170.48	161.57	168.16	141924023.33

After running `groupby()`, we can select specific columns for aggregation:

```
>>> fb.groupby('trading_volume')['close'].agg(['min', 'max', 'mean'])
```

This gives us the aggregations for the closing price for each value of `trading_volume`:

	min	max	mean
trading_volume			
low	124.06	214.67	171.43
med	152.22	217.50	175.14
high	160.06	176.26	168.16

If we need more fine-tuned control over how each column gets aggregated, we use the agg() method again with a dictionary that maps the columns to their aggregation function. As we did previously, we can provide lists of functions per column; the result, however, will look a little different:

```
>>> fb_agg = fb.groupby('trading_volume').agg({
...         'open': 'mean',
...         'high': ['min', 'max'],
...         'low': ['min', 'max'],
...         'close': 'mean'
... })
>>> fb_agg
```

We now have a hierarchical index in the columns. Remember, this means that if we want to select the minimum low for the medium volume traded bucket, we need to use fb_agg.loc['med', 'low']['min']:

	open		high		low	close
	mean	min	max	min	max	mean
trading_volume						
low	171.36	129.74	216.2	123.02	212.6	171.43
med	175.82	162.85	218.62	150.75	214.27	175.14
high	167.73	161.1	180.13	149.02	173.75	168.16

The columns are stored in a MultiIndex object:

```
>>> fb_agg.columns
MultiIndex(levels=[['open', 'high', 'low', 'close'],
                   ['max', 'mean', 'min']],
           labels=[[0, 1, 1, 2, 2, 3], [1, 2, 0, 2, 0, 1]])
```

We can use a list comprehension to remove this hierarchy and instead have our column names in the form of <column>_<agg>. At each iteration, we will get a tuple of the levels from the MultiIndex object, which we can combine into a single string to remove the hierarchy:

```
>>> fb_agg.columns = ['_'.join(col_agg) for col_agg in fb_agg.columns]
>>> fb_agg.head()
```

This replaces the hierarchy in the columns with a single level:

trading_volume	open_mean	high_min	high_max	low_min	low_max	close_mean
low	171.36	129.74	216.20	123.02	212.60	171.43
med	175.82	162.85	218.62	150.75	214.27	175.14
high	167.73	161.10	180.13	149.02	173.75	168.16

Say we want to see the average observed precipitation across all the stations per day. We would need to group by the date, but it is in the index. In this case, we have three options:

- Resampling, which we will cover in the *Time series* section later this chapter
- Resetting the index and using the date column that gets created from the index
- Using a `Grouper` object

Here, we will use a `Grouper` object. To group by day, we will create a `Grouper` with a daily frequency and pass that to `groupby()`:

```
>>> weather['2018-10'].query('datatype == "PRCP"').groupby(
...         pd.Grouper(freq='D')
... ).mean().head()
```

This gives us the average precipitation observations across the stations, which may give us a better idea of the weather than simply picking a station to look at:

date	value
2018-10-01	0.01
2018-10-02	2.23
2018-10-03	19.69
2018-10-04	0.32
2018-10-05	0.96

We can also group by many categories at once. Let's find the quarterly total recorded precipitation per station. This will create a multi-level index, so we will use `unstack()` to put the inner-level (the quarter) on the columns:

```
>>> weather.query('datatype == "PRCP"').groupby(
...     ['station_name', pd.Grouper(freq='Q')]
... ).sum().unstack().sample(5, random_state=1)
```

There are many possible follow-ups for this result. We could look at which stations receive the most/least precipitation. We could go back to the location and elevation information we had for each station to see if that affects precipitation. We could also see which quarter has the most/least precipitation across the stations:

	value			
date	2018-03-31	2018-06-30	2018-09-30	2018-12-31
station_name				
WANTAGH 1.1 NNE, NY US	279.9	216.8	472.5	277.2
STATEN ISLAND 1.4 SE, NY US	379.4	295.3	438.8	409.9
SYOSSET 2.0 SSW, NY US	323.5	263.3	355.5	459.9
STAMFORD 4.2 S, CT US	338	272.1	424.7	390
WAYNE TWP 0.8 SSW, NJ US	246.2	295.3	620.9	422

The `DataFrameGroupBy` objects returned by the `groupby()` method have a `filter()` method, which allows us to filter groups. We can use this to prevent them from being part of any aggregations. Simply pass a function that returns a Boolean for each group's subset of the dataframe. An example is in the notebook.

Let's see which months have the most precipitation. First, we need to group by day and average the precipitation across the stations. Then, we can group by month and sum the resulting precipitation. We use `nlargest()` to get the five months with the most precipitation:

```
>>> weather.query('datatype == "PRCP"') \
...     .groupby(pd.Grouper(freq='D')).mean() \
...     .groupby(pd.Grouper(freq='M')).sum().value.nlargest()
```

```
date
2018-11-30    210.59
2018-09-30    193.09
2018-08-31    192.45
2018-07-31    160.98
2018-02-28    158.11
Name: value, dtype: float64
```

Perhaps the previous result was surprising. The saying goes *April showers bring May flowers*; however, April wasn't in the top five (neither was May, for that matter). Snow will count toward precipitation, but that doesn't explain why summer months are higher than April. Let's look for days that accounted for a large percentage of the precipitation in a given month to see if April shows up there.

In order to do so, we need to calculate the average daily precipitation across stations and then find the total per month; this will be the denominator. However, in order to divide the daily values by the total for their month, we will need a `Series` of equal dimensions. This means that we will need to use the `transform()` method, which will perform the specified calculation on the data while always returning an object of equal dimensions to what we started with. Therefore, we can call it on a `Series` object and always get a `Series` object back, regardless of what the aggregation function itself would return:

```
>>> weather.query('datatype == "PRCP"').rename(
...     dict(value='prcp'), axis=1
... ).groupby(pd.Grouper(freq='D')).mean().groupby(
...     pd.Grouper(freq='M')
... ).transform(np.sum)['2018-01-28':'2018-02-03']
```

Rather than getting a single sum for January and another for February, notice that we have the same value being repeated for the January entries and a different one for the February ones. The value for February is the value we found in the previous result:

	prcp
date	
2018-01-28	69.31
2018-01-29	69.31
2018-01-30	69.31
2018-01-31	69.31
2018-02-01	158.11
2018-02-02	158.11
2018-02-03	158.11

We can make this a column in our dataframe in order to easily calculate the percentage of the monthly precipitation that occurred each day. Then, we can use `nlargest()` to pull out the largest values:

```
>>> weather\
...     .query('datatype == "PRCP"')\
...     .rename(dict(value='prcp'), axis=1)\
...     .groupby(pd.Grouper(freq='D')).mean()\
...     .assign(
...         total_prcp_in_month=lambda x: x.groupby(
...             pd.Grouper(freq='M')
...         ).transform(np.sum),
...         pct_monthly_prcp=lambda x: x.prcp.div(
...             x.total_prcp_in_month
...         )
...     ).nlargest(5, 'pct_monthly_prcp')
```

The 4th and 5th place days in terms of the amount of monthly precipitation they accounted for make up more than 50% of the rain in April. They were also consecutive days:

date	prcp	total_prcp_in_month	pct_monthly_prcp
2018-10-12	34.77	105.63	0.33
2018-01-13	21.66	69.31	0.31
2018-03-02	38.77	137.46	0.28
2018-04-16	39.34	140.57	0.28
2018-04-17	37.30	140.57	0.27

The `transform()` method also works on `DataFrame` objects. In this case, it will return a `DataFrame` object. We can use it to easily standardize all the columns at once. An example is in the notebook.

Pivot tables and crosstabs

To wrap up this section, we will discuss some `pandas` functions that will aggregate our data into some common formats. The dataframe methods we discussed previously will give us the highest level of customization; however, `pandas` provides some functions to quickly generate a pivot table and a crosstab in a common format.

In order to generate a pivot table, we must specify what to group on and, optionally, which subset of columns we want to aggregate and/or how to aggregate (average, by default). Let's create a pivot table of averaged OHLC data for Facebook by the volume traded bins:

```
>>> fb.pivot_table(columns='trading_volume')
```

Since we passed in the `trading_volume` column to the `columns` argument, the distinct values for the trading volumes were placed along the columns. The columns from the original dataframe then went to the index. Notice that the index for the columns has a name, which is `trading_volume`:

trading_volume	low	med	high
close	171.43	175.14	168.16
high	173.46	179.42	170.48
low	169.31	172.11	161.57
open	171.36	175.82	167.73
volume	24547207.71	79072559.12	141924023.33

We can also use the `pd.pivot_table()` function by providing the dataframe as the first argument.

If we pass `trading_volume` to the `index` argument instead, we will get the exact same output that we got when we used `groupby()`:

```
>>> fb.pivot_table(index='trading_volume')
```

Switching the arguments that are passed to `columns` and `index` results in the transpose:

	close	high	low	open	volume
trading_volume					
low	171.43	173.46	169.31	171.36	24547207.71
med	175.14	179.42	172.11	175.82	79072559.12
high	168.16	170.48	161.57	167.73	141924023.33

 We aren't limited to passing the name of a column to `index` or `columns`; we can pass a `Series` object directly as long as it is the same length as the dataframe.

With `pivot()`, we weren't able to handle multi-level indices or indices with repeated values. For this reason, we haven't been able to put the weather data in the wide format. The `pivot_table()` method solves this issue. To do so, we need to put the `date` and `station` information on the index and the `datatype` along the columns. The values will come from the `value` column. We will use the median to aggregate any overlapping combinations (if any):

```
>>> weather.reset_index().pivot_table(
...     index=['date', 'station', 'station_name'],
...     columns='datatype',
...     values='value',
...     aggfunc='median'
... ).reset_index().tail()
```

After resetting the index, we have our data in the wide format. One final step would be to rename the index:

datatype	date	station	station_name	AWND	...	PRCP	SNOW	SNWD	...
28740	2018-12-31	GHCND:USW00054787	FARMINGDALE REPUBLIC AIRPORT, NY US	5.00	...	28.70	NaN	NaN	...
28741	2018-12-31	GHCND:USW00094728	NY CITY CENTRAL PARK, NY US	NaN	...	25.90	0.00	0.00	...
28742	2018-12-31	GHCND:USW00094741	TETERBORO AIRPORT, NJ US	1.70	...	29.20	NaN	NaN	...
28743	2018-12-31	GHCND:USW00094745	WESTCHESTER CO AIRPORT, NY US	2.70	...	24.40	NaN	NaN	...
28744	2018-12-31	GHCND:USW00094789	JFK INTERNATIONAL AIRPORT, NY US	4.10	...	31.20	0.00	0.00	...

We can use the `pd.crosstab()` function to create a frequency table. For example, if we want to see how many low-, medium-, and high-volume trading days Facebook stock had each month, we can use a crosstab. The syntax is pretty straightforward; we pass to `index` what we want to label the rows as and to `columns` what to label the columns as. By default, the values in the cells will be the count:

```
>>> pd.crosstab(
...     index=fb.trading_volume,
...     columns=fb.index.month,
...     colnames=['month'] # name the columns index
... )
```

This makes it easy to see the months when high volumes of Facebook stock were traded:

month	1	2	3	4	5	6	7	8	9	10	11	12
trading_volume												
low	20	19	15	20	22	21	18	23	19	23	21	19
med	1	0	4	1	0	0	2	0	0	0	0	0
high	0	0	2	0	0	0	1	0	0	0	0	0

We can normalize the output to percentages of the row/column totals by passing in `normalize='rows'`/`normalize='columns'`. An example is in the notebook.

To change the aggregation function, we can provide an argument to `values` and then specify `aggfunc`. To illustrate this, let's show the average closing price for that trading volume and month instead of the count in the previous example (anywhere that has a 0 will be replaced with `NaN`):

```
>>> pd.crosstab(
...        index=fb.trading_volume,
...        columns=fb.index.month,
...        colnames=['month'],
...        values=fb.close,
...        aggfunc=np.mean
... )
```

We now get the average closing price per month per volume traded bin with `NaN` values when that combination wasn't present in the data:

month	1	2	3	4	5	6	7	8	9	10	11	12
trading_volume												
low	185.24	180.27	177.07	163.29	182.93	195.27	201.92	177.49	164.38	154.19	141.64	137.16
med	179.37	NaN	164.76	174.16	NaN	NaN	194.28	NaN	NaN	NaN	NaN	NaN
high	NaN	NaN	164.11	NaN	NaN	NaN	176.26	NaN	NaN	NaN	NaN	NaN

We can also get row and column subtotals with the `margins` parameter. Let's count the number of times each station recorded snow per month and include the subtotals:

```
>>> snow_data = weather.query('datatype == "SNOW"')
>>> pd.crosstab(
...        index=snow_data.station_name,
...        columns=snow_data.index.month,
...        colnames=['month'],
...        values=snow_data.value,
...        aggfunc=lambda x: (x > 0).sum(),
...        margins=True, # show row and column subtotals
...        margins_name='total observations of snow' # name the subtotals
... )
```

Just by looking at a few stations, we can see that, despite all of them supplying weather information for NYC, they don't share every facet of the weather. Depending on which stations we choose to look at, we could be adding/subtracting snow from what really happened in NYC:

month	1	2	3	4	5	6	7	8	9	10	11	12	total observations of snow
station_name													
ALBERTSON 0.2 SSE, NY US	3.00	1.00	3.00	1.00	0.00	0.00	0.00	0.00	0.00	0.00	1.00	0.00	9.00
...	...	...	...	...	...	...	...	...	...	...	...	...	...
STATEN ISLAND 1.4 SE, NY US	4.00	2.00	5.00	2.00	0.00	0.00	0.00	0.00	0.00	0.00	1.00	0.00	14.00
...	...	...	...	...	...	...	...	...	...	...	...	...	...
WAYNE TWP 0.8 SSW, NJ US	NaN	1.00	2.00	1.00	NaN	NaN	NaN	NaN	NaN	NaN	1.00	NaN	5.00
WEST CALDWELL TWP 1.3 NE, NJ US	0.00	3.00	4.00	2.00	0.00	0.00	0.00	0.00	0.00	0.00	1.00	0.00	10.00
WEST NYACK 1.3 WSW, NY US	3.00	1.00	5.00	1.00	NaN	NaN	NaN	NaN	NaN	NaN	1.00	NaN	11.00
WESTFIELD 0.6 NE, NJ US	3.00	0.00	4.00	1.00	0.00	NaN	0.00	0.00	0.00	NaN	1.00	NaN	9.00
WOODBRIDGE TWP 1.1 ESE, NJ US	4.00	1.00	3.00	2.00	0.00	0.00	0.00	0.00	0.00	0.00	1.00	0.00	11.00
...	...	...	...	...	...	...	...	...	...	...	...	...	...
total observations of snow	190.00	97.00	237.00	81.00	0.00	0.00	0.00	0.00	0.00	0.00	49.00	13.00	667.00

Time series

With time series, we have some additional operations we can use, for anything from selection and data wrangling to aggregation. When we have time series data, we should set the index to our date (or datetime) column, which will allow us to take advantage of what we will discuss in this section. Some operations may work without doing this, but for a smooth process throughout our analysis, using a `DatetimeIndex` is recommended.

For this section, we will be working in the `4-time_series.ipynb` notebook. We will start off by working with the Facebook data from previous sections:

```
>>> import numpy as np
>>> import pandas as pd

>>> fb = pd.read_csv(
...     'data/fb_2018.csv', index_col='date', parse_dates=True
... ).assign(
...     trading_volume=lambda x: pd.cut(
...         x.volume, bins=3, labels=['low', 'med', 'high']
...     )
... )
```

Time-based selection and filtering

Let's do a quick recap of datetime slicing as we discuss some of the additional functionality that the `pandas` time series have. We can easily isolate data for the year by indexing on it: `fb['2018']`. In the case of our stock data, the full dataframe would be returned because we only have 2018 data; however, we can filter to a month (`fb['2018-10']`) or to a range of dates:

```
>>> fb['2018-10-11':'2018-10-15']
```

We only get three days back because the stock market is closed on the weekends:

date	open	high	low	close	volume	trading_volume
2018-10-11	150.13	154.81	149.1600	153.35	35338901	low
2018-10-12	156.73	156.89	151.2998	153.74	25293492	low
2018-10-15	153.32	155.57	152.5500	153.52	15433521	low

Keep in mind that the date range can also be supplied using other slicing options, such as month or the quarter of the year:

```
>>> fb['2018-q1'].equals(fb['2018-01':'2018-03'])
True
```

When we're dealing with the beginning or end of our date range, pandas has some additional methods to select the first or last rows within a specified date range. We can select the first week of stock prices in 2018 using the `first()` method and an offset of `1W`:

```
>>> fb.first('1W')
```

January 1, 2018 was a holiday, meaning that the market was closed. It was also a Monday, so the week here is only four days long:

	open	high	low	close	volume	trading_volume
date						
2018-01-02	177.68	181.58	177.5500	181.42	18151903	low
2018-01-03	181.88	184.78	181.3300	184.67	16886563	low
2018-01-04	184.90	186.21	184.0996	184.33	13880896	low
2018-01-05	185.59	186.90	184.9300	186.85	13574535	low

We can perform a similar operation for the most recent dates as well. Selecting the last week in the data is as simple as switching the `first()` method with the `last()` method:

```
>>> fb.last('1W')
```

Since December 31, 2018 was on a Monday, the last week of the year is only one day:

	open	high	low	close	volume	trading_volume
date						
2018-12-31	134.45	134.64	129.95	131.09	24625308	low

For the next few examples, we will need time information in addition to the date. The datasets we have been working with lack a time component, so we will switch to the per minute stock data for Facebook from May 20, 2019 through May 24, 2019 from Nasdaq.com (`https://www.nasdaq.com/symbol/fb/interactive-chart`). In order to properly parse the datetimes, we need to pass in a `date_parser` to `pd.read_csv()` since they are not in a standard format:

```
>>> stock_data_per_minute = pd.read_csv(
...     'data/fb_week_of_may_20_per_minute.csv',
...     index_col='date',
...     parse_dates=True,
...     date_parser=lambda x: pd.to_datetime(
...         x, format='%Y-%m-%d %H-%M'
...     )
... )
```

For instance, May 20, 2019 at 9:30 AM is represented as `2019-05-20 09-30`. In order to properly parse this, we need to specify the format it is in. Consult the Python documentation for a reference on the available codes: `https://docs.python.org/3/library/datetime.html#strftime-and-strptime-behavior`.

We have the OHLC data per minute, along with the volume traded per minute:

date	open	high	low	close	volume
2019-05-20 09:30:00	181.6200	181.6200	181.6200	181.6200	159049.0
2019-05-20 09:31:00	182.6100	182.6100	182.6100	182.6100	468017.0
2019-05-20 09:32:00	182.7458	182.7458	182.7458	182.7458	97258.0
2019-05-20 09:33:00	182.9500	182.9500	182.9500	182.9500	43961.0
2019-05-20 09:34:00	183.0600	183.0600	183.0600	183.0600	79562.0

We can use `first()` and `last()` with `agg()` to bring this data to a daily granularity. To get the true open value, we need to take the first datetime per day; conversely, for the true closing value, we need to take the last datetime per day. The high and low will be the maximum and minimum of their respective columns per day. Volume traded will be the daily sum:

```
>>> stock_data_per_minute.groupby(pd.Grouper(freq='1D')).agg({
...     'open': 'first', 'high': 'max', 'low': 'min',
...     'close': 'last', 'volume': 'sum'
... })
```

This rolls the data up to a daily frequency:

	open	high	low	close	volume
date					
2019-05-20	181.62	184.1800	181.6200	182.72	10044838.0
2019-05-21	184.53	185.5800	183.9700	184.82	7198405.0
2019-05-22	184.81	186.5603	184.0120	185.32	8412433.0
2019-05-23	182.50	183.7300	179.7559	180.87	12479171.0
2019-05-24	182.33	183.5227	181.0400	181.06	7686030.0

The next two methods we will discuss help us slice based on the time part of the datetime. The `at_time()` method allows us to isolate rows where the time part of the `DatetimeIndex` is the time we specify. By running `at_time('9:30')`, we can grab all the market open prices (the stock market opens at 9:30 AM):

```
>>> stock_data_per_minute.at_time('9:30')
```

This tells us what the stock data looked like at the opening bell each day:

	open	high	low	close	volume
date					
2019-05-20 09:30:00	181.62	181.62	181.62	181.62	159049.0
2019-05-21 09:30:00	184.53	184.53	184.53	184.53	58171.0
2019-05-22 09:30:00	184.81	184.81	184.81	184.81	41585.0
2019-05-23 09:30:00	182.50	182.50	182.50	182.50	121930.0
2019-05-24 09:30:00	182.33	182.33	182.33	182.33	52681.0

We can use the `between_time()` method to grab all the rows where the time portion of the `DatetimeIndex` is between two times (inclusive of the endpoints by default). This method can be very useful if we want to look at data within a certain time range day-over-day. Let's grab all the rows within the last two minutes of trading each day (`15:59 - 16:00`):

```
>>> stock_data_per_minute.between_time('15:59', '16:00')
```

It looks like the last minute (`16:00`) has significantly more volume traded each day compared to the previous minute (`15:59`). Perhaps people rush to make trades before close:

date	open	high	low	close	volume
2019-05-20 15:59:00	182.915	182.915	182.915	182.915	134569.0
2019-05-20 16:00:00	182.720	182.720	182.720	182.720	1113672.0
2019-05-21 15:59:00	184.840	184.840	184.840	184.840	61606.0
2019-05-21 16:00:00	184.820	184.820	184.820	184.820	801080.0
2019-05-22 15:59:00	185.290	185.290	185.290	185.290	96099.0
2019-05-22 16:00:00	185.320	185.320	185.320	185.320	1220993.0
2019-05-23 15:59:00	180.720	180.720	180.720	180.720	109648.0
2019-05-23 16:00:00	180.870	180.870	180.870	180.870	1329217.0
2019-05-24 15:59:00	181.070	181.070	181.070	181.070	52994.0
2019-05-24 16:00:00	181.060	181.060	181.060	181.060	764906.0

We may wonder if this also happens in the first two minutes. Do people put their trades in the night before, and it executes when the market opens? It is trivial to change the previous code to answer that question. Instead, let's see if, on average, more shares are traded within the first 30 minutes of trading or in the last 30 minutes. We can combine `between_time()` with `Groupers` to answer this question. In addition, we need to use `filter()` to exclude groups from the aggregation. The excluded groups are times that aren't in the time range we want:

```
>>> shares_traded_in_first_30_min = stock_data_per_minute\
...     .between_time('9:30', '10:00')\
...     .groupby(pd.Grouper(freq='1D'))\
...     .filter(lambda x: (x.volume > 0).all())\
...     .volume.mean()
```

```
>>> shares_traded_in_last_30_min = stock_data_per_minute\
...      .between_time('15:30', '16:00')\
...      .groupby(pd.Grouper(freq='1D'))\
...      .filter(lambda x: (x.volume > 0).all())\
...      .volume.mean()
```

For the week in question, there are more trades on average around opening time than closing time:

```
>>> shares_traded_in_first_30_min - shares_traded_in_last_30_min
18592.967741935485
```

> We can use `normalize()` on the `DatetimeIndex` or through the `dt` attribute of a `Series` to normalize all the datetimes to midnight. This is helpful when the time isn't adding value to our data. There are examples of this in the notebook.

Shifting for lagged data

We can use `shift()` to create lagged data. By default, the shift will be by one period, but this can be any integer (positive or negative). Let's use `shift()` to create a new column that indicates the previous day's closing price for the daily Facebook stock data. From this new column, we can calculate the price change due to after-hours trading (after the market close one day right up to the market open the following day):

```
>>> fb.assign(
...      prior_close=lambda x: x.close.shift(),
...      after_hours_change_in_price=lambda x: x.open - x.prior_close,
...      abs_change=lambda x: x.after_hours_change_in_price.abs()
... ).nlargest(5, 'abs_change')
```

This gives us the days that were most affected by after-hours trading:

date	open	high	low	close	volume	trading_volume	prior_close	after_hours_change_in_price	abs_change
2018-07-26	174.89	180.13	173.75	176.26	169803668	high	217.50	-42.61	42.61
2018-04-26	173.22	176.27	170.80	174.16	77556934	med	159.69	13.53	13.53
2018-01-12	178.06	181.48	177.40	179.37	77551299	med	187.77	-9.71	9.71
2018-10-31	155.00	156.40	148.96	151.79	60101251	low	146.22	8.78	8.78
2018-03-19	177.01	177.17	170.06	172.56	88140060	med	185.09	-8.08	8.08

> We can use `tshift()` to move the `DatetimeIndex` instead of the data itself. However, if the goal is to add/subtract time from the datetimes, consider using `pandas.Timedelta` objects instead. There is an example of this in the notebook.

When working with daily stock data, we only have data for the dates the stock market was open. We can use `first_valid_index()` to give us the index of the first non-null entry in our data, which will be the first day of trading in the data. The `last_valid_index()` method will give us the last day of trading. For September 2018, the first day of trading was September 4th and the last was September 28th:

```
>>> fb['2018-09'].first_valid_index()
Timestamp('2018-09-04 00:00:00')
>>> fb['2018-09'].last_valid_index()
Timestamp('2018-09-28 00:00:00')
```

If we wanted to know what Facebook's stock price looked like as of September 30th, our initial idea may be to use slicing to retrieve it. However, if we try `fb['2018-09-30']`, we will get a `KeyError` since that date doesn't exist in the index. If we use the `asof()` method instead, it will give us the closest data to the datetime we ask for, which in this case is September 28th. Say we wanted to see how Facebook performed on the last day in each month; by using `asof()`, we don't have to first check if the market was open that day and can still access the data:

```
>>> fb.index.contains('2018-09-30')
False
>>> fb.asof('2018-09-30')
open                     168.33
high                     168.79
low                      162.56
close                    164.46
volume              3.42656e+07
trading_volume               low
Name: 2018-09-30 00:00:00, dtype: object
```

Differenced data

We've already discussed creating lagged data with the `shift()` method. However, often, we are interested in how the values change from one day to the next. For this, `pandas` has the `diff()` method. By default, this will calculate the change from period *t* to period *t+1*; however, we can pass an alternate value to `diff()` when we call it:

$$diff = x_{t+1} - x_t$$

Note that this is equivalent to subtracting the result of `shift()` from the original data:

```
>>> (
...        fb.drop(columns='trading_volume')
...        - fb.drop(columns='trading_volume').shift()
... ).equals(
...        fb.drop(columns='trading_volume').diff()
... )
True
```

We can use `diff()` to easily calculate the day-over-day change in Facebook stock:

```
>>> fb.drop(columns='trading_volume').diff().head()
```

For the first few trading days of the year, we can see that the stock price increased and that the volume traded decreased daily:

	open	high	low	close	volume
date					
2018-01-02	NaN	NaN	NaN	NaN	NaN
2018-01-03	4.20	3.20	3.7800	3.25	-1265340.0
2018-01-04	3.02	1.43	2.7696	-0.34	-3005667.0
2018-01-05	0.69	0.69	0.8304	2.52	-306361.0
2018-01-08	1.61	2.00	1.4000	1.43	4420191.0

To specify the number of periods that are used for the difference, simply pass in an integer to `diff()`. Note that this number can be negative. An example of this is in the notebook.

Resampling

Sometimes, the data is at a granularity that isn't conducive to our analysis. Consider the case where we have data per minute for the full year of 2018. The level of granularity and nature of the data may render plotting useless. Therefore, we will need to aggregate the data to a less granular frequency:

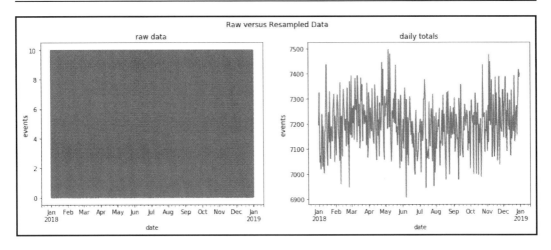

Consider the minute-by-minute stock data we were working with previously. If we had a full year of data by the minute, it's possible that this level of granularity is beyond what is useful for us:

	open	high	low	close	volume
date					
2019-05-20 09:30:00	181.6200	181.6200	181.6200	181.6200	159049.0
2019-05-20 09:31:00	182.6100	182.6100	182.6100	182.6100	468017.0
2019-05-20 09:32:00	182.7458	182.7458	182.7458	182.7458	97258.0
2019-05-20 09:33:00	182.9500	182.9500	182.9500	182.9500	43961.0
2019-05-20 09:34:00	183.0600	183.0600	183.0600	183.0600	79562.0

We can use the `resample()` method to aggregate our time series data to a different granularity. To use `resample()`, all we have to do is say how we want to roll up the data and tack on an optional call to an aggregation method. For example, we can resample this minute-by-minute data to a daily frequency and specify how to aggregate each column:

```
>>> stock_data_per_minute.resample('1D').agg({
...     'open': 'first', 'high': 'max', 'low': 'min',
...     'close': 'last', 'volume': 'sum'
... })
```

This is equivalent to the result we got when we used the `Grouper` object back in the *Time-based selection and filtering* section:

	open	high	low	close	volume
date					
2019-05-20	181.62	184.1800	181.6200	182.72	10044838.0
2019-05-21	184.53	185.5800	183.9700	184.82	7198405.0
2019-05-22	184.81	186.5603	184.0120	185.32	8412433.0
2019-05-23	182.50	183.7300	179.7559	180.87	12479171.0
2019-05-24	182.33	183.5227	181.0400	181.06	7686030.0

We can resample to any frequency supported by `pandas` (more information can be found in the documentation at `http://pandas.pydata.org/pandas-docs/stable/user_guide/timeseries.html`). Let's resample the daily Facebook stock data to the quarterly average:

```
>>> fb.resample('Q').mean()
```

This gives us the average quarterly performance of the stock. The fourth quarter of 2018 was clearly troublesome:

	open	high	low	close	volume
date					
2018-03-31	179.472295	181.794659	177.040428	179.551148	3.292640e+07
2018-06-30	180.373770	182.277689	178.595964	180.704687	2.405532e+07
2018-09-30	180.812130	182.890886	178.955229	181.028492	2.701982e+07
2018-12-31	145.272460	147.620121	142.718943	144.868730	2.697433e+07

Rather than looking at the average performance over the quarters, we can use the `apply()` method to look at the difference between how the quarter began and how it ended. We will also need the `first()` and `last()` methods from the *Time-based selection and filtering* section:

```
>>> fb.drop(columns='trading_volume').resample('Q').apply(
...     lambda x: x.last('1D').values - x.first('1D').values
... )
```

Facebook's stock price declined in all but the second quarter:

	open	high	low	close	volume
date					
2018-03-31	-22.53	-20.1600	-23.410	-21.63	41282390
2018-06-30	39.51	38.3997	39.844	38.93	-20984389
2018-09-30	-25.04	-28.6600	-29.660	-32.90	20304060
2018-12-31	-28.58	-31.2400	-31.310	-31.35	-1782369

Consider the melted minute-by-minute stock data in `melted_stock_data.csv`:

```
>>> melted_stock_data = pd.read_csv(
...     'data/melted_stock_data.csv',
...     index_col='date',
...     parse_dates=True
... )
>>> melted_stock_data.head()
```

The OHLC format makes it easy to analyze the stock data, but a single column is trickier:

	price
date	
2019-05-20 09:30:00	181.6200
2019-05-20 09:31:00	182.6100
2019-05-20 09:32:00	182.7458
2019-05-20 09:33:00	182.9500
2019-05-20 09:34:00	183.0600

The `Resampler` object we get back after calling `resample()` has a `ohlc()` method, which we can use to retrieve the OHLC data we are used to seeing:

```
>>> ohlc_data = melted_stock_data.resample('1D').ohlc()['price']
```

Since the column in the original data was called `price`, we select it after calling `ohlc()`, which is pivoting our data. Otherwise, we will have a hierarchical index in the columns:

date	open	high	low	close
2019-05-20	181.62	184.1800	181.6200	182.72
2019-05-21	184.53	185.5800	183.9700	184.82
2019-05-22	184.81	186.5603	184.0120	185.32
2019-05-23	182.50	183.7300	179.7559	180.87
2019-05-24	182.33	183.5227	181.0400	181.06

In the previous examples, we **downsampled** to reduce the granularity of the data; however, we can also **upsample** to increase the granularity of the data. We can even call `asfreq()` after to not aggregate the result:

```
>>> fb.resample('6H').asfreq().head()
```

Note that when we resample at a granularity that's finer than the data we have, it will introduce NaN values:

date	open	high	low	close	volume	trading_volume
2018-01-02 00:00:00	177.68	181.58	177.55	181.42	18151903.0	low
2018-01-02 06:00:00	NaN	NaN	NaN	NaN	NaN	NaN
2018-01-02 12:00:00	NaN	NaN	NaN	NaN	NaN	NaN
2018-01-02 18:00:00	NaN	NaN	NaN	NaN	NaN	NaN
2018-01-03 00:00:00	181.88	184.78	181.33	184.67	16886563.0	low

The following are a few ways we can handle the NaN values. In the interest of brevity, examples of these are in the notebook:

- Use `pad()` after `resample()` to forward-fill
- Call `fillna()` after `resample()`, as we saw in Chapter 3, *Data Wrangling with Pandas* when we handled missing values
- Use `asfreq()` followed by `assign()` to handle each column individually

Merging

Time series often go down to the second or even more granular, meaning that it can be difficult to merge if the entries don't have the same datetime. Pandas solves this problem with two additional merging functions. When we want to pair up observations that are close in time, we can use `pd.merge_asof()` to match on nearby keys rather than on equal keys, like we did with joins. On the other hand, if we want to match up the equal keys and order the keys without matches, we can use `pd.merge_ordered()`.

To illustrate how these work, we are going to use the `fb_prices` and `aapl_prices` tables in the `data/stocks.db` SQLite database. These contain the price of Facebook and Apple stock, respectively, along with a timestamp of when the price was recorded. Let's read these from the database:

```
>>> import sqlite3

>>> with sqlite3.connect('data/stocks.db') as connection:
...     fb_prices = pd.read_sql(
...         'SELECT * FROM fb_prices', connection,
...         index_col='date', parse_dates=['date']
...     )
...     aapl_prices = pd.read_sql(
...         'SELECT * FROM aapl_prices', connection,
...         index_col='date', parse_dates=['date']
...     )
```

The Facebook data is at the minute granularity; however, we have seconds for the Apple data:

```
>>> fb_prices.index.second.unique()
Int64Index([0], dtype='int64', name='date')
>>> aapl_prices.index.second.unique()
Int64Index([ 0, 52, 36, 34, 55, 35,  7, 12, 59, 17,  5, 20, 26,
            23, 54, 49, 19, 53, 11, 22, 13, 21, 10, 46, 42, 38,
            33, 18, 16,  9, 56, 39,  2, 50, 31, 58, 48, 24, 29,
             6, 47, 51, 40,  3, 15, 14, 25,  4, 43,  8, 32, 27,
            30, 45,  1, 44, 57, 41, 37, 28],
           dtype='int64', name='date')
```

If we use `merge()` or `join()`, we will only have values for both Apple and Facebook when the Apple price was at the top of the minute. Instead, to try and line these up, we can perform an `asof` merge. In order to handle the mismatch, we will specify to fill in with the `direction` of `nearest` and a `tolerance` of 30 seconds. This will place the Apple data with the minute that it is closest to, so `9:31:52` will go with `9:32` and `9:37:07` will go with `9:37`. Since the times are on the index, we pass `left_index` and `right_index`, just like we did with merges:

```
>>> pd.merge_asof(
...     fb_prices, aapl_prices,
...     left_index=True, right_index=True, # datetimes on index
...     # merge with nearest minute
...     direction='nearest', tolerance=pd.Timedelta(30, unit='s')
... ).head()
```

This is similar to a left join; however, we are more lenient on the matching of the keys. We get an NaN value for `9:31` because the entry for Apple at `9:31` was `9:31:52`, which gets placed at `9:32` when using `nearest`:

date	FB	AAPL
2019-05-20 09:30:00	181.6200	183.5200
2019-05-20 09:31:00	182.6100	NaN
2019-05-20 09:32:00	182.7458	182.8710
2019-05-20 09:33:00	182.9500	182.5000
2019-05-20 09:34:00	183.0600	182.1067

If we don't want the behavior of a left join, we can use the `pd.merge_ordered()` function instead. This will allow us to specify our join type, which will be `'outer'` by default. We will have to reset our index to be able to join on the datetimes, however:

```
>>> pd.merge_ordered(
...        fb_prices.reset_index(), aapl_prices.reset_index()
... ).set_index('date').head()
```

This strategy will give us NaN values anytime the times don't match exactly, but it will at least sort them for us:

	FB	AAPL
date		
2019-05-20 09:30:00	181.6200	183.520
2019-05-20 09:31:00	182.6100	NaN
2019-05-20 09:31:52	NaN	182.871
2019-05-20 09:32:00	182.7458	NaN
2019-05-20 09:32:36	NaN	182.500

We can pass `fill_method='ffill'` to `pd.merge_ordered()` to front-fill the first NaN after a value, but it stops there; alternatively, we can chain a call to `fillna()`. There is an example of this in the notebook.

Summary

In this chapter, we discussed how to join dataframes, how to determine the data we will lose for each type of join using set operations, and how to query dataframes as we would a database. We then went over some more involved transformations on our columns, such as binning and clipping based on thresholds, and how to do so efficiently with the `apply()` method. We also learned the importance of vectorized operations in writing efficient `pandas` code. Then, we explored window calculations and using pipes for cleaner code. Our discussion on window calculations served as a primer for aggregating across whole dataframes and by groups. We also went over how to generate pivot tables and crosstabs. Finally, we looked at some time series-specific functionality in `pandas` for everything from selection and aggregation to merging.

In the next chapter, we will cover visualization, which `pandas` implements by providing a wrapper around `matplotlib`. Data wrangling will play a key role in prepping our data for visualization, so be sure to complete the exercises that are provided in the following section before moving on.

Exercises

Using the CSV files in the `exercises/` folder and what we have learned so far in this book, complete the following exercises:

1. With the `earthquakes.csv` file, select all the earthquakes in Japan with a `magType` of `mb` and a magnitude of 4.9 or greater.

2. Create bins for each full number of magnitude (for example, the first bin is 0-1, the second is 1-2, and so on) with a `magType` of `ml` and count how many are in each bin.

3. Using the `faang.csv` file, group by the ticker and resample to monthly frequency. Make the following aggregations:
   - Mean of the opening price
   - Maximum of the high price
   - Minimum of the low price
   - Mean of the closing price
   - Sum of the volume traded

4. Build a crosstab with the earthquake data between the `tsunami` column and the `magType` column. Rather than showing the frequency count, show the maximum magnitude that was observed for each combination. Put the `magType` along the columns.

5. Calculate the rolling 60-day aggregations of OHLC data by ticker for the FAANG data. Use the same aggregations as exercise #3.

6. Create a pivot table of the FAANG data that compares the stocks. Put the ticker in the rows and show the averages of the OHLC and volume traded data.

7. Calculate the Z-scores for each numeric column of Netflix's data (`ticker` is NFLX) using `apply()`.

8. Add event descriptions:
    1. Create a dataframe with the following three columns: `ticker`, `date`, and `event`. The columns should have the following values:
        - `ticker: 'FB'`
        - `date: ['2018-07-25', '2018-03-19', '2018-03-20']`
        - `event: ['Disappointing user growth announced after close.', 'Cambridge Analytica story', 'FTC investigation']`
    2. Set the index to `['date', 'ticker']`
    3. Merge this data with the FAANG data using an outer join
9. Use the `transform()` method on the FAANG data to represent all the values in terms of the first date in the data. To do so, divide all the values for each ticker by the values for the first date in the data for that ticker. This is referred to as an index, and the data for the first date is the base (`https://ec.europa.eu/eurostat/statistics-explained/index.php/Beginners:Statistical_concept_-_Index_and_base_year`). When data is in this format, we can easily see growth over time. Hint: `transform()` can take a function name.

Further reading

Check out the following resources for more information on the topics that were covered in this chapter:

- *Intro to SQL: Querying and managing data*: `https://www.khanacademy.org/computing/computer-programming/sql`
- *Map, Filter and Reduce*: `http://book.pythontips.com/en/latest/map_filter.html`
- *(Pandas) Comparison with SQL*: `https://pandas.pydata.org/pandas-docs/stable/comparison_with_sql.html`
- *Set Operations*: `https://www.probabilitycourse.com/chapter1/1_2_2_set_operations.php`
- **args and **kwargs in Python explained*: `https://pythontips.com/2013/08/04/args-and-kwargs-in-python-explained/`

5
Visualizing Data with Pandas and Matplotlib

So far, we have been working with data strictly in a tabular format. However, the human brain excels at picking out visual patterns; hence, our natural next step is learning how to visualize our data. Visualizations make it much easier to spot aberrations in our data and explain our findings to others. However, we should not reserve data visualizations exclusively for those we present our conclusions to, as visualizations will be crucial in helping us understand our data quicker and more completely in our exploratory data analysis.

There are numerous types of visualizations that go way beyond what we may have seen in the past. In this chapter, we will cover the most common plot types, such as line plots, histograms, scatter plots, and bar plots, along with several other plot types that build upon these. We won't be covering pie charts—they are notorious for being difficult to read properly, and there are better ways to get our point across.

Python has many libraries for creating visualizations, but the main one for data analysis (and other purposes) is `matplotlib`. The `matplotlib` library can be a little tricky to learn at first, but, thankfully, `pandas` has its own wrappers around some of the `matplotlib` functionality, allowing us to create many different types of visualizations without needing to write a single line with `matplotlib` (or, at least, very few). For more complicated plot types that aren't built into `pandas` or `matplotlib`, we have the `seaborn` library, which we will discuss next chapter. With these three at our disposal, we should be able to create most (if not all) of the visualizations we desire. Animations and interactive plots are beyond the scope of this book, but check out the *Further reading* section for more information.

In this chapter, we will cover the following topics:

- An introduction to `matplotlib`
- Creating data visualizations with `pandas`
- Utilizing select functions from the `pandas.plotting` subpackage

Chapter materials

The materials for this chapter can be found on GitHub at `https://github.com/stefmolin/Hands-On-Data-Analysis-with-Pandas/tree/master/ch_05`. We will be working with two datasets, both of which can be found in the `data/` directory. In the `data/fb_stock_prices_2018.csv` file, we have the daily opening, high, low, and closing prices of Facebook stock from January through December 2018, along with the volume traded. This was obtained using the `stock_analysis` package we will build in Chapter 7, *Financial Analysis – Bitcoin and the Stock Market*. The stock market is closed on the weekends, so we only have data for the trading days.

The `data/earthquakes.csv` file contains earthquake data pulled from the USGS API (`https://earthquake.usgs.gov/fdsnws/event/1/`) for September 18, 2018 through October 13, 2018. For each earthquake, we have the value of the magnitude (the `mag` column), the scale it was measured on (the `magType` column), when (the `time` column) and where (the `place` column) it occurred, and the `parsed_place` column for the state or country where the earthquake occurred (we added this column back in Chapter 2, *Working with Pandas DataFrames*). Other unnecessary columns have been removed.

Throughout the chapter, we will be working through three notebooks. These are numbered in the order they will be used—one for each of the main sections of this chapter. We will begin our discussion of plotting in Python with an introduction to `matplotlib` in `1-introducing_matplotlib.ipynb`. Next, we will learn how to plot using `pandas` in `2-plotting_with_pandas.ipynb`. Finally, we will explore some additional plotting options that `pandas` provides in a subpackage in `3-pandas_plotting_subpackage.ipynb`. The text will prompt us when it is time to switch between the notebooks.

An introduction to matplotlib

The plotting capabilities in `pandas` and `seaborn` are powered by `matplotlib`; both of these packages provide wrappers around the lower-level functionality in `matplotlib`. Consequently, we have many visualization options at our fingertips with minimal code to write; however, this comes at a price: reduced flexibility in what we can create.

We may find that the `pandas` or `seaborn` implementation isn't quite meeting our needs, and, indeed, it may be impossible to override a particular setting after creating the plot with them, meaning we will have to do some of the legwork with `matplotlib`. Therefore, it would greatly benefit us to have some understanding of how `matplotlib` works. Additionally, many of the tweaks to the final appearance of the visualization will be handled with `matplotlib` commands, which we will discuss in the next chapter.

The basics

The `matplotlib` package is rather large, since it encompasses quite a lot of functionality. Fortunately for us, for most of our plotting tasks, all we need is the `pyplot` module, which provides a MATLAB-like plotting framework. Occasionally, we will need to import additional modules for other tasks, such as animations, changing the style, or altering the default parameters. The following code block is how `pyplot` is traditionally imported in Python, using the alias `plt`:

```
import matplotlib.pyplot as plt
```

 Notice that, rather than importing the whole package, we only import the module using the dot notation; this reduces the amount of typing we need to do in order to access what we need, and we don't take up more space in memory with code we won't use.

Before we look at our first plots, let's cover how to actually see them. Matplotlib will create our visualizations with the plot commands; however, we won't see the visualization until we request to see it. It is done in this fashion so that we can continually tweak the visualization with additional code, until we are ready to finalize it. Unless we save a reference to our plot, once it is displayed, we will have to recreate it to change something, since the reference to the last plot will have been destroyed to free up resources in memory.

Matplotlib uses the `plt.show()` function to display the visualization. We will need to call this after each visualization we create, and, if using the Python shell, this will also prevent the execution of additional code, until the window is closed. This is because `plt.show()` is a blocking function. In Jupyter Notebooks, we can simply use the `%matplotlib inline` **magic command** (a special IPython command preceded by a `%` sign) once, and our visualizations will be automatically displayed when the cell with our visualization code is executed. Magic commands (or magics for short) are run as regular code within a Jupyter Notebook cell. If, up to this point in the book, you haven't been keen on using Jupyter Notebooks and would like to get that set up now, you can refer to `Chapter 1`, *Introduction to Data Analysis* (I'll wait).

Let's create our first plot in the `1-introducing_matplotlib.ipynb` notebook, using the Facebook stock prices data from the `data/fb_stock_prices_2018.csv` file in the repository for this chapter. First, we need to import `pyplot` and `pandas` (in this example, we will use `plt.show()`, so we don't need to run the magic here):

```
>>> import matplotlib.pyplot as plt
>>> import pandas as pd
```

Next, we read in the CSV file and specify the index as the `date` column, since we know what the data looks like already (this just saves us from having to do so with `pandas` after the import):

```
>>> fb = pd.read_csv(
...     'data/fb_stock_prices_2018.csv',
...     index_col='date',
...     parse_dates=True
... )
```

In order to understand how Facebook stock evolved over time, we could create a line plot of the daily opening price. For this task, we use the `plt.plot()` function and provide the data to use on the *x*-axis and *y*-axis, respectively; we then follow up with a call to `plt.show()` to display it:

```
>>> plt.plot(fb.index, fb.open)
>>> plt.show()
```

The result is the following plot:

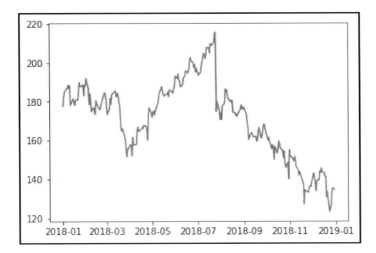

We have to go back and add our axis labels, plot title, legend (if applicable), and possibly fix the y-axis range if we want to present this visualization; this will be covered in the next chapter when we discuss formatting and customizing the appearance of our plots. Pandas and `seaborn` will take care of some of this for us, at least.

For the remainder of the book, we will be using the `%matplotlib inline` magic command (remember, this needs to be used in a Jupyter Notebook to work), so we won't be calling `plt.show()` after our plotting code. The following code gives the same output as the preceding one:

```
>>> %matplotlib inline
>>> import matplotlib.pyplot as plt
>>> import pandas as pd

>>> fb = pd.read_csv(
...     'data/fb_stock_prices_2018.csv',
...     index_col='date',
...     parse_dates=True
... )
>>> plt.plot(fb.index, fb.open)
```

 Be sure to run the `%matplotlib inline` magic command now if you are using a Jupyter Notebook, so that the code in the rest of the chapter shows the output automatically.

We can also use the `plt.plot()` function to generate scatter plots, provided that we specify a format string for the plot as the third argument. A format string is of the form `'[color][marker][linestyle]'`; for example, `'k--'` for a black dashed line. Since we don't want a line for the scatter plot, we omit the `linestyle` component. We can make a scatter plot of red dots with the format string of `'ro'`; here, `r` is for the color red and `o` is for dots. The following code generates a scatter plot of high price versus low price. Notice that we are able to pass our dataframe in the `data` argument, and then use the string names for the columns, instead of passing the series as `x` and `y`:

```
>>> plt.plot('high', 'low', 'ro', data=fb.head(20))
```

Barring days of large fluctuations, we would expect the points to be in the form of a line, since the high and low prices won't be far from each other. This is true for the most part, but be careful of the scale that was generated automatically—the *x*-axis and the *y*-axis don't perfectly line up:

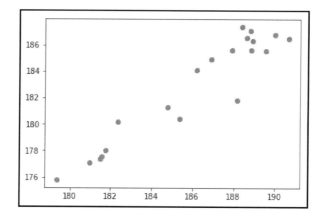

The following table shows some of the format string options that we can use; the complete list can be found in the **Notes** section in the documentation (https://matplotlib.org/api/_as_gen/matplotlib.pyplot.plot.html):

Format string component	Result
b	blue
k	black
r	red
g	green
m	magenta
c	cyan

Format string component	Result
–	solid line
– –	dashed line
.	points
–o	solid line with points
:	dotted line
–.	dot-dashed line

The format string is a handy way of specifying many options at once, and the good news is that it works with the plot() method in pandas as well. If we would rather specify each option separately, we can use the color, linestyle, and marker arguments; check out the values we can pass as keyword arguments to plt.plot() in the documentation—pandas will also pass these down to matplotlib for us.

Consider trying out cycler from the matplotlib team to set what combinations matplotlib should cycle between as a default or on a specific Axes object (https://matplotlib.org/gallery/color/color_cycler.html#sphx-glr-gallery-color-color-cycler-py).

To create histograms with matplotlib, we use the hist() function instead. Let's make a histogram of the earthquake magnitudes in the data/earthquakes.csv file, using those measured with the magType of ml:

```
>>> quakes = pd.read_csv('data/earthquakes.csv')
>>> plt.hist(quakes.query('magType == "ml"').mag)
```

The resulting histogram gives us an idea of the range of earthquake magnitudes we can expect using the ml measurement technique:

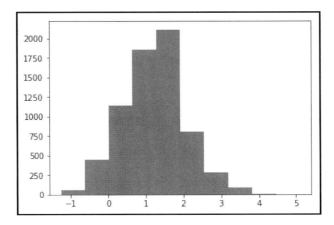

As we could have guessed, the magnitudes tend to be small, and the distribution appears to be somewhat normal, but a word of caution regarding histograms—bin size matters! There are cases where we can change the number of bins the data is divided into and change what the histogram indicates the distribution to be. For example, if we make two histograms for this data using different numbers of bins, the distributions look different:

```
>>> x = quakes.query('magType == "ml"').mag
>>> fig, axes = plt.subplots(1, 2, figsize=(10, 3))
>>> for ax, bins in zip(axes, [7, 35]):
...     ax.hist(x, bins=bins)
...     ax.set_title(f'bins param: {bins}')
```

Notice how the distribution seems unimodal in the left subplot, but seems bimodal in the right subplot:

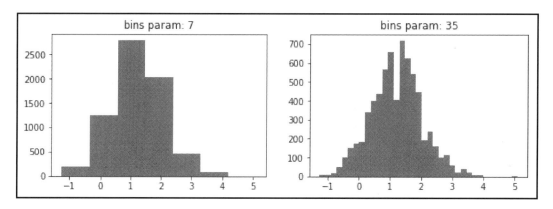

A couple of additional things to note from the last example, which we will address in the next section on plot components:

- We can make subplots.
- Plotting functions in `pyplot` can also be used as methods of `matplotlib` objects, such as `Figure` and `Axes` objects.

In some cases, a bee swarm plot can be easier to interpret than a histogram. This can be created with `seaborn`, as we will see in `Chapter 6`, *Plotting with Seaborn and Customization Techniques*.

One last thing regarding basic usage that we will find handy is saving plots as images—we shouldn't be limited to showing the figures in Python only. We can save the last figure with the `plt.savefig()` function by passing in the path to save the image at; for example, `plt.savefig('my_plot.png')`.

> Note that, if using `plt.show()`, the file will be empty, since the reference to the last plot will be gone after the call to `plt.show()` (`matplotlib` closes the `Figure` object to free up the resource in memory). With the `%matplotlib inline` magic command, we can both see and save our image in the same cell.

Plot components

In the prior examples using `plt.plot()`, we didn't have to create a `Figure` object—`matplotlib` took care of creating it for us in the background. However, as we saw with the example showing how bin size affects our output, anything beyond a basic plot will require a little more legwork, including creating a `Figure` object ourselves. The `Figure` is the top-level object for `matplotlib` visualizations. It contains the `Axes` objects, which themselves contain additional plot objects, such as the lines and ticks. In the case of subplots, the `Figure` object contains `Axes` objects with additional functionality.

We use the `plt.figure()` function to create `Figure` objects; these will have zero `Axes` objects until a plot is added:

```
>>> fig = plt.figure()
<Figure size 432x288 with 0 Axes>
```

The `plt.subplots(<nrows>, <ncols>)` function creates a `Figure` object with `Axes` objects for subplots in the arrangement specified; this returns a tuple of the form `(Figure, Axes)`, which we unpack:

```
>>> fig, axes = plt.subplots(1, 2)
```

When using the `%matplotlib inline` magic command, we will see the figure that was created:

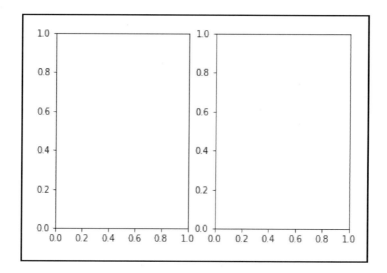

If we ask `plt.subplots()` for one row and one column, we will get back a `Figure` object with one `Axes` object, which can be useful when writing functions that generate subplot layouts based on the input, since we don't need to worry about needing a special case to handle for a single subplot.

The alternative to using `plt.subplots()` would be to use the `add_axes()` method on the `Figure` object that we get after running `plt.figure()`. The `add_axes()` method takes a list in the form of `[left, bottom, width, height]` as proportions of the figure dimensions, representing the position in the figure this subplot should take up:

```
>>> fig = plt.figure(figsize=(3, 3))
>>> outside = fig.add_axes([0.1, 0.1, 0.9, 0.9])
>>> inside = fig.add_axes([0.7, 0.7, 0.25, 0.25])
```

This enables the creation of plots inside plots:

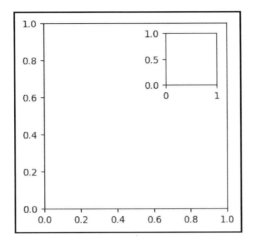

If our goal is having all plots separate, but not all equally sized, we can use the add_gridspec() method on the figure to create the grid for the subplots and then run add_subplot() on the figure by passing in the area(s) from the grid that the given subplot should occupy:

```
>>> fig = plt.figure(figsize=(8, 8))
>>> gs = fig.add_gridspec(3, 3)
>>> top_left = fig.add_subplot(gs[0, 0])
>>> mid_left = fig.add_subplot(gs[1, 0])
>>> top_right = fig.add_subplot(gs[:2, 1:])
>>> bottom = fig.add_subplot(gs[2,:])
```

This results in the following layout:

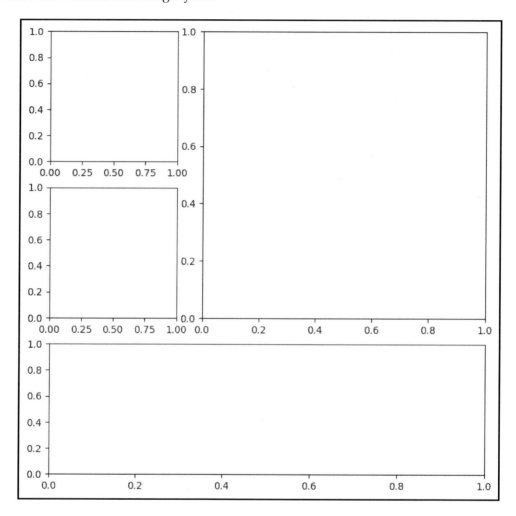

In the previous section, we discussed how we can save our figures using the `plt.savefig()` function, but we also can use the `savefig()` method on the `Figure` object itself:

```
>>> fig.savefig('empty.png')
```

This is very useful to remember, since with `plt.<func>()` we only have access to the last figure object; however, if we save the references to our figures, we can work with any of them, regardless of when they were created. Additionally, this foreshadows an important concept that you will notice throughout this chapter: the `Figure` and `Axes` objects have methods with similar or identical names to their `pyplot` function counterparts.

While it's convenient to have references to all of the figures we create, we must be sure to close them when we are done with them so as not to waste resources. This can be accomplished using the `plt.close()` function. If we don't pass in anything, it will close the last figure; however, we can pass in a specific figure to close only that one or `'all'` to close all of the figures we have open:

```
>>> plt.close('all')
```

Additional options

A few of our visualizations looked a little squished. To remedy this, we can pass the `figsize` argument to `plt.figure()` or `plt.subplots()` with a tuple in the form of `(width, height)` in inches:

```
>>> fig = plt.figure(figsize=(10, 4))
<Figure size 720x288 with 0 Axes>
>>> fig, axes = plt.subplots(1, 2, figsize=(10, 4))
```

This results in the following subplots:

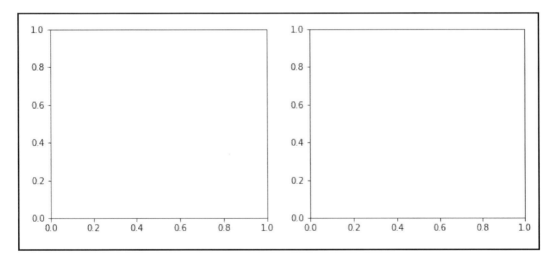

The `plot()` method we will see with `pandas` also accepts the `figsize` parameter, so bear this in mind.

It's not so bad specifying the `figsize` parameter for our plots one-by-one. However, if we find that we are resizing everything to the same size, there's a better alternative. Matplotlib houses its defaults in `rcParams`, which acts like a dictionary, meaning we can easily overwrite what we wish for our session and get the defaults back when we restart Python. Since there are many options in this dictionary (nearly 300 at the time of writing), let's randomly select a few of them to get an idea of what is available:

```
>>> import random
>>> import matplotlib as mpl
>>> rcparams_list = list(mpl.rcParams.keys())
>>> random.seed(20) # make this repeatable
>>> random.shuffle(rcparams_list)
>>> sorted(rcparams_list[:20])
['axes.axisbelow',
 'axes.labelweight',
 'boxplot.capprops.linestyle',
 'boxplot.meanline',
 'boxplot.whiskers',
 'datapath',
 'date.autoformatter.microsecond',
 'figure.constrained_layout.hspace',
 'font.sans-serif',
 'font.variant',
 'interactive',
 'keymap.forward',
 'lines.dash_capstyle',
 'lines.solid_capstyle',
 'pgf.texsystem',
 'ps.distiller.res',
 'xtick.bottom',
 'xtick.major.width',
 'ytick.major.left',
 'ytick.major.right']
```

The default number of bins used for a histogram can be found using `mpl.rcParams['hist.bins']`.

As you can see, there are many options we can tinker with here. Let's check what the current default value for `figsize` is:

```
>>> mpl.rcParams['figure.figsize']
[6.0, 4.0]
```

To change this for our current session, simply set it equal to a new value:

```
>>> mpl.rcParams['figure.figsize'] = (300, 10)
>>> mpl.rcParams['figure.figsize']
[300.0, 10.0]
```

> If we find ourselves changing this every time we start Python for various settings, we should look into reading our configuration in rather than overwriting this each time. Consult the `mpl.rc_file()` function for more information.

Before we move on, let's restore the default settings by using the `mpl.rcdefaults()` function:

```
>>> mpl.rcdefaults()
>>> mpl.rcParams['figure.figsize']
[6.8, 4.8]
```

Note that we can also use the `plt.rc()` function to update a particular setting if we know its group (`figure`, in this case) and the parameter name (`figsize`). As before, we can use `plt.rcdefaults()` to reset to the defaults:

```
# change figsize default to (20, 20)
>>> plt.rc('figure', figsize=(20, 20))
>>> plt.rcdefaults() # reset the default
```

Plotting with pandas

Both `Series` and `DataFrame` objects have a `plot()` method that allows us to create several different plots and control some aspects of their formatting, such as subplot layout, figure size, titles, and whether to share an axis across subplots. This makes plotting our data much more convenient, as the bulk of the work to create presentable plots is achieved with a single method call. Under the hood, `pandas` is making several calls to `matplotlib` to produce our plot.

Some of the frequently used arguments to the `plot()` method include:

Parameter	Purpose	Type
`kind`	Determines the plot type	String
`x/y`	Column(s) to plot on the *x*-axis and the *y*-axis	String or list
`ax`	Draws the plot on the `Axes` object provided	`Axes`
`subplots`	Determines whether to make subplots	Boolean
`layout`	Specifies how to arrange the subplots	Tuple of `(rows, columns)`
`figsize`	Size to make the `Figure` object	Tuple of `(width, height)`
`title`	The title of the plot or subplots	String for the plot title or a list of strings for subplot titles
`legend`	Determines whether to show the legend	Boolean
`label`	What to call an item in the legend	String if a single column is being plotted; otherwise, a list of strings
`style`	`matplotlib` style strings for each item being plotted	String if a single column is being plotted; otherwise, a list of strings
`color`	The color to plot the item in	String if a single column is being plotted; otherwise, a list of strings
`colormap`	The colormap to use	String or `matplotlib` colormap object
`logx/logy/loglog`	Determines whether to use a logarithmic scale for the *x*-axis, *y*-axis, or both	Boolean
`xticks/yticks`	Determines where to draw the ticks on the *x*-axis/*y*-axis	List of values
`xlim/ylim`	The axis limits for the *x*-axis/*y*-axis	Tuple of the form `(min, max)`
`rot`	The angle to write the tick labels at	Integer
`sharex/sharey`	Determines whether to have subplots share the *x*-axis or the *y*-axis	Boolean
`fontsize`	Controls the size of the tick labels	Integer
`grid`	Turns on or off, the grid lines	Boolean

Rather than have separate functions for each plot type, like we saw during our discussion of `matplotlib`, the `plot()` method from `pandas` has a `kind` argument where we can specify the type of plot we want. The choice of plot will determine which other arguments are required. We can use the `Axes` object returned by the `plot()` method to further modify our plot.

Let's explore this functionality in the `2-plotting_with_pandas.ipynb` notebook. Before we begin, we need to handle our imports for this section and read in the data:

```
>>> %matplotlib inline
>>> import matplotlib.pyplot as plt
>>> import numpy as np
>>> import pandas as pd

>>> fb = pd.read_csv(
...     'data/fb_stock_prices_2018.csv',
...     index_col='date',
...     parse_dates=True
... )
>>> quakes = pd.read_csv('data/earthquakes.csv')
```

Evolution over time

When working with time series (such as the Facebook stock data), we often want to show how data has changed over time. To do this, we use line plots and, in some cases, bar plots (covered in the *Counts and frequencies* section). In the case of a line plot, we simply provide `kind='line'` to `plot()`, indicating which columns will be x and y. We don't need to provide a column for x because `pandas` will use the index (this also makes it possible to generate the line plot of a `Series` object). Additionally, notice that we can provide a format string to the `style` argument just as we did with the `matplotlib` plots:

```
>>> fb.plot(
...     kind='line',
...     y='open',
...     figsize=(10, 5),
...     style='b-',
...     legend=False,
...     title='Evolution of Facebook Open Price'
... )
```

This gives us a plot similar to what we achieved with `matplotlib`; however, in this single method call, we specified the figure size for this plot only, turned off the legend, and gave it a title:

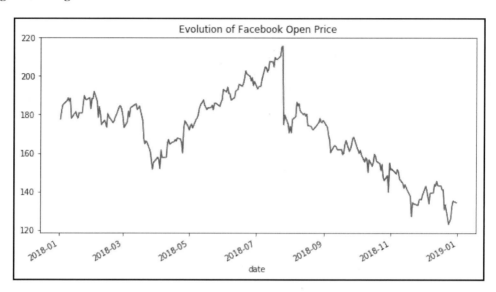

As with `matplotlib`, we don't have to use the style format strings—instead, we can pass each component separately with its associated keyword. For example, the following code gives us the same result as the previous one:

```
fb.plot(
    kind='line',
    y='open',
    figsize=(10, 5),
    color='blue',
    linestyle='solid',
    legend=False,
    title='Evolution of Facebook Open Price'
)
```

We aren't limited to plotting one line at time with the `plot()` method; we can pass a list of columns to plot and style them individually. Note that we actually don't need to specify `kind='line'` because that is the default:

```
>>> fb.iloc[:5,].plot(
...     y=['open', 'high', 'low', 'close'],
...     style=['b-o', 'r--', 'k:', 'g-.'],
...     title='Facebook OHLC Prices during 1st Week of Trading 2018'
... )
```

This results in the following plot, where each line is styled differently than the `matplotlib` default blue line:

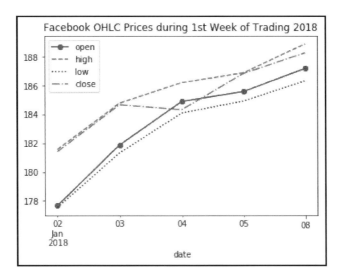

Additionally, we can easily have `pandas` plot all of our columns in that same call. The x and y arguments can take a single column name or a list of them; if we provide nothing, `pandas` will use all of them. Note that the columns must be passed as the y argument when `kind='line'`; however, other plot types support passing lists of columns to x, as well. In this case, it may be helpful to ask for subplots instead of having all the lines on the same plot. Let's visualize all the columns in the Facebook data as line plots:

```
>>> fb.plot(
...     kind='line',
...     subplots=True,
...     layout=(3,2),
...     figsize=(15,10),
...     title='Facebook Stock 2018'
... )
```

Using the `layout` argument, we told `pandas` how to arrange our subplots (three rows and two columns):

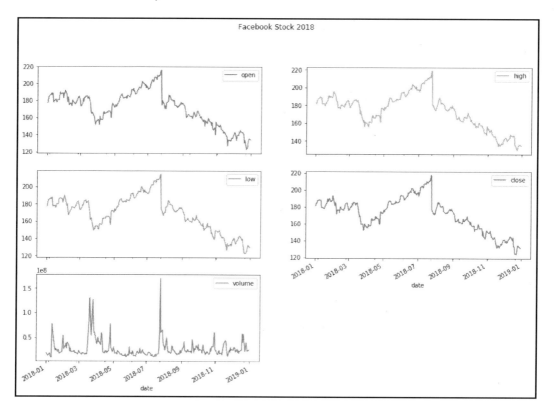

Notice that the subplots automatically share the *x*-axis, since they share a `DatetimeIndex`. The *y*-axis is not shared because the `volume` time series is on a different scale. We can alter this behavior in some plot types by passing the `sharex` or `sharey` argument with a Boolean to `plot()`. The legend will be rendered by default, so, for each subplot, we have a legend of one series indicating which data it contains. We didn't provide a list of subplot titles to the `title` argument in this case, since the legend served that purpose; however, we passed a single string for the title of the plot as a whole. To sum up, when working with subplots, we have two options when it comes to the title:

- Passing a single string for the title of the figure as a whole
- Passing a list of strings to use as the title for each subplot

Relationships between variables

When we want to visualize the relationship between variables, we often begin with scatter plots, which show us the value of the y variable at different values of the x variable. This makes it very easy to spot correlations and possible non-linear relationships. In the previous chapter, when we looked at the Facebook stock data, we saw that the days of large volume traded appeared to be correlated with large drops in stock price. We can use a scatter plot to visualize this relationship:

```
>>> fb.assign(
...     max_abs_change=fb.high - fb.low
... ).plot(
...     kind='scatter', x='volume', y='max_abs_change',
...     title='Facebook Daily High - Low vs. Volume Traded'
... )
```

There seems to be a relationship, but it does not seem linear:

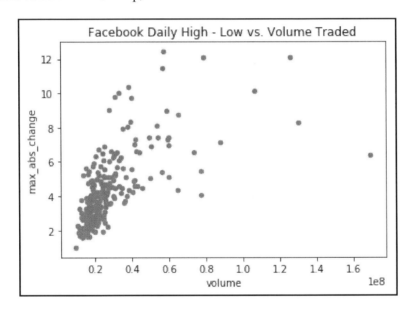

Let's try taking the log of the volume. To do so, we have a few options:

- Create a new column that is the log of the volume using np.log()
- Use a log scale for the *x*-axis by passing in logx=True to the plot() method
- Call plt.xscale('log')

In this case, it makes the most sense to simply change how we display our data, since we aren't going to use the new column:

```
>>> fb.assign(
...      max_abs_change=fb.high - fb.low
... ).plot(
...      kind='scatter', x='volume', y='max_abs_change',
...      title='Facebook Daily High - Low vs. log(Volume Traded)',
...      logx=True
... )
```

After modifying the *x*-axis scale, we get the following scatter plot:

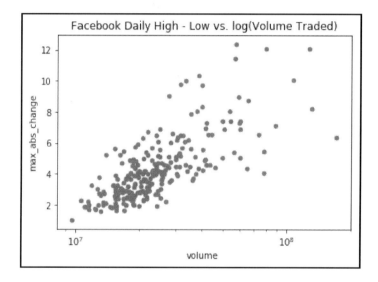

The `plot()` method from `pandas` has three arguments for log scales: `logx`/`logy` for single axis adjustments and `loglog` for setting both to the log scale.

One problem with scatter plots is that it can be very difficult to discern the concentration of points in a given area, since they are simply plotted one of top of the other. We can use the `alpha` argument to control the transparency of the points; this argument takes values from 0 to 1, where 0 is entirely transparent and 1 is completely opaque. By default, they are opaque (value of 1); however, if we make them more transparent, we should be able to see some of the overlap:

```
>>> fb.assign(
...     max_abs_change=fb.high - fb.low
... ).plot(
...     kind='scatter',
...     x='volume',
...     y='max_abs_change',
...     title='Facebook Daily High - Low vs. log(Volume Traded)',
...     logx=True,
...     alpha=0.25
... )
```

We can now begin to make out the density of points in the lower-left region of the plot, but it's still relatively difficult:

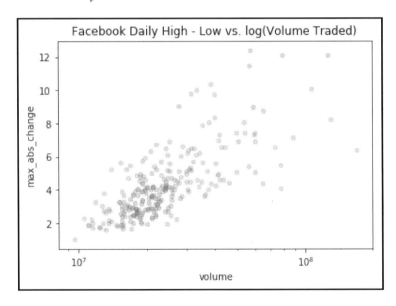

Thankfully, we have another plot type at our disposal: `hexbin`. **Hexbins** form a two-dimensional histogram by dividing the plot up into a grid of hexagons and shading them based on the concentration of points in each bin. Let's view this data as hexbins:

```
>>> fb.assign(
...     volume=np.log(fb.volume),
...     max_abs_change=fb.high - fb.low
... ).plot(
...     kind='hexbin',
...     x='volume',
...     y='max_abs_change',
...     title='Facebook Daily High - Low vs. log(Volume Traded)',
...     colormap='gray_r',
...     gridsize=20,
...     sharex=False # this is a bug fix to keep the x-axis label
... )
```

The color bar on the side indicates the relationship between color and the number of points in that bin. The colormap we chose (`gray_r`) shades the bins darker (toward black) for high density, and lighter (toward white) for low density. By choosing a `gridsize` of 20, we are using 20 hexagons across the *x*-axis, and `pandas` determines how many to use along the *y*-axis, so that they are approximately regular in shape; we can, however, pass a tuple to choose the number in both directions. A larger value for `gridsize` will make the bins harder to see, and a smaller one will result in fuller bins that take up more space on the plot—so, we must strike a balance:

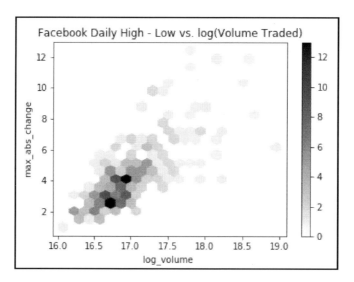

Finally, if we simply want to visualize the correlation between variables, we can plot a correlation matrix. A **correlation matrix** depicts the magnitude and direction (positive or negative) of the correlation. To do so, we can use a combination of `pandas` and either the `plt.matshow()` or `plt.imshow()` function from `matplotlib`. Let's take a look at the correlation matrix for the Facebook data we have been working with:

```
>>> fig, ax = plt.subplots(figsize=(20, 10))

>>> fb_corr = fb.assign(
...     log_volume=np.log(fb.volume),
...     max_abs_change=fb.high - fb.low
... ).corr()

>>> im = ax.matshow(fb_corr, cmap='seismic')

>>> fig.colorbar(im).set_clim(-1, 1)

>>> labels = [col.lower() for col in fb_corr.columns]
>>> ax.set_xticklabels([''] + labels, rotation=45)
>>> ax.set_yticklabels([''] + labels)
```

A **heatmap** lets us easily visualize the correlation coefficients, provided we choose a diverging colormap. We will discuss the different types of colormaps when we discuss customizing plots in `Chapter 6`, *Plotting with Seaborn and Customization Techniques*. Essentially, for this plot, we want red for correlation coefficients greater than zero and blue for those below; correlation coefficients near zero will be devoid of color, and stronger correlations will be darker shades of their respective colors.

We can easily see strong positive correlations among the OHLC time series, and among the volume traded and maximum absolute value of change, we used in the previous plots. However, there are weak negative correlations between these groups. Furthermore, we see that taking the logarithm of the volume does indeed increase the coefficient of correlation with `max_abs_change` from `0.642027` to `0.731542`. When we discuss `seaborn` in the next chapter, we will learn an easier way to generate a heatmap:

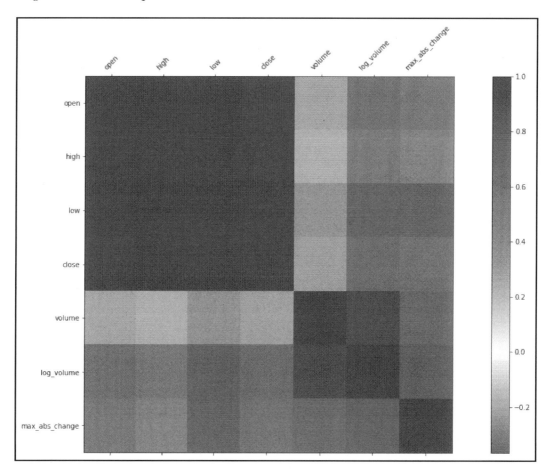

Distributions

Often, we want to visualize the distribution of our data to see what values it takes on. Depending on the type of data we have, we may choose to use histograms, **kernel density estimates (KDEs)**, box plots, or **empirical cumulative distribution functions (ECDFs)**. When working with discrete data, histograms are a good place to start.

Let's take a look at the histogram of daily volume traded in Facebook stock:

```
>>> fb.volume.plot(
...     kind='hist',
...     title='Histogram of Daily Volume Traded in Facebook Stock'
... )
>>> plt.xlabel('Volume traded') # label the x-axis (discussed in ch 6)
```

This is a great example of real-world data that is, most definitely, not normally distributed. The volume traded is right skewed, with a long tail to the right. Remember, in Chapter 4, *Aggregating Pandas DataFrames*, when we discussed binning and looked at low, medium, and high volume traded that almost all of the data fell in the low bucket, which agrees with what we see in this histogram:

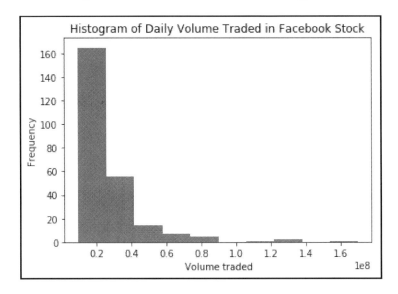

 As with the `plt.hist()` function from `matplotlib`, we can provide a custom value for the number of bins with the `bins` argument. However, we must be careful that we aren't misrepresenting the distribution.

We can also create multiple histograms on the same plot in order to compare distributions by using the `ax` parameter to specify the same `Axes` object for each plot. In this case, we must use the `alpha` parameter to see any overlaps. Given that we have many different measurement techniques for earthquakes (the `magType` column), we may be interested in comparing the different ranges of magnitudes they yield:

```
>>> fig, axes = plt.subplots(figsize=(8, 5))
>>> for magtype in quakes.magType.unique():
...     data = quakes.query(f'magType == "{magtype}"').mag
...     if not data.empty:
...         data.plot(
...             kind='hist', ax=axes, alpha=0.4,
...             label=magtype, legend=True,
...             title='Comparing histograms '\
...                   'of earthquake magnitude by magType'
...         )
>>> plt.xlabel('magnitude') # label the x-axis
```

This shows us that `ml` is the most common `magType` followed by `md`, and that they yield similar ranges of magnitudes; however, `mb`, which is the third most common, yields higher magnitudes:

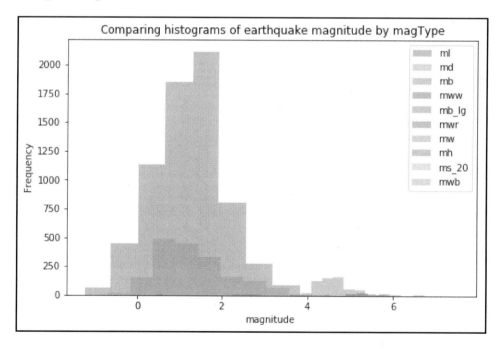

When working with continuous data (such as stock prices), we can use kernel density estimates. Let's take a look at the kernel density estimate of Facebook stock's daily high price:

```
>>> fb.high.plot(
...     kind='kde',
...     title='KDE of Daily High Price for Facebook Stock'
... )
>>> plt.xlabel('Price ($)') # label the x-axis (discussed in ch 6)
```

The resulting density curve has some left skew:

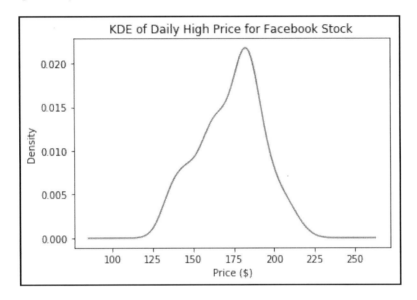

We may also want to visualize the KDE superimposed on top of the histogram. Pandas allows us to pass the `Axes` object we want to plot on, and also returns one after creating the visualization, which makes this a cinch:

```
>>> ax = fb.high.plot(kind='hist', density=True, alpha=0.5)
>>> fb.high.plot(
...     ax=ax, kind='kde', color='blue',
...     title='Distribution of Facebook Stock\'s '\
...         'Daily High Price in 2018'
... )
>>> plt.xlabel('Price ($)') # label the x-axis (discussed in ch 6)
```

Notice that we had to pass `density=True` when we generated the histogram to make sure that the *y*-axis for the histogram and KDE were on the same scale. Otherwise, the KDE would have been too small to see. The histogram then gets plotted with density on the *y*-axis, so that we can better understand how the KDE got its shape. We also increased the transparency of the histogram, so that we could see the KDE line on top. Note that if we remove the `color='blue'` part of the KDE call, we don't need to change the value for `alpha` on the histogram call, since the KDE and histogram will be different colors; we are plotting them both in blue, since they represent the same data:

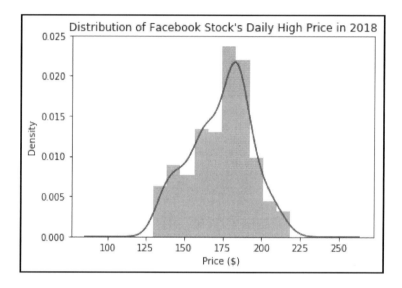

The `plot()` method from `pandas` allows us to pass `kind='kde'` or `kind='density'` to plot the kernel density estimate.

The KDE shows us an estimated **probability density function** (**PDF**), which tells us how probability is distributed over the values of the data. However, in some cases, we are more interested in the probability of getting less than or equal to (or greater than or equal to) some value, which we can see with the **cumulative distribution function** (**CDF**).

With a CDF, the values for the *x* variable go along the *x*-axis and the cumulative probability of getting, at most, a given *x* goes along the *y*-axis. This cumulative probability is between 0 and 1 and is written as $P(X \leq x)$, where the lowercase (*x*) is the value for comparison and the uppercase (*X*) is the random variable *X*. More information can be found at `https://www.itl.nist.gov/div898/handbook/eda/section3/eda362.htm`.

Using the `statsmodels` package, we can estimate the CDF giving us the **empirical cumulative distribution function** (**ECDF**). Let's use this to understand the distribution of magnitudes for earthquakes measured with the `magType` of `ml`:

```
>>> from statsmodels.distributions.empirical_distribution import ECDF
>>> ecdf = ECDF(quakes.query('magType == "ml"').mag)
>>> plt.plot(ecdf.x, ecdf.y)

# axis labels (we will cover this in chapter 6)
>>> plt.xlabel('mag') # add x-axis label
>>> plt.ylabel('cumulative probability') # add y-axis label

# add title (we will cover this in chapter 6)
>>> plt.title('ECDF of earthquake magnitude with magType ml')
```

This yields the following empirical cumulative distribution function:

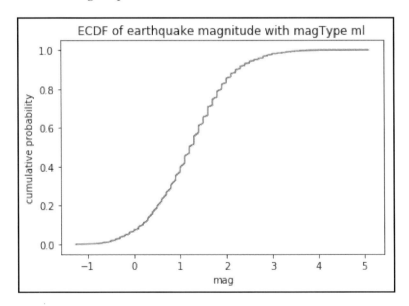

This can be very useful in gaining a better understanding of our data when we conduct our EDA. However, we must be careful how we interpret this and how we explain it to others, if we choose to do so. Here, we can see that, if this distribution is indeed representative of the population, the probability of the `ml` magnitude of the earthquake being less than or equal to 3, is 98% for earthquakes measured with that `magType`:

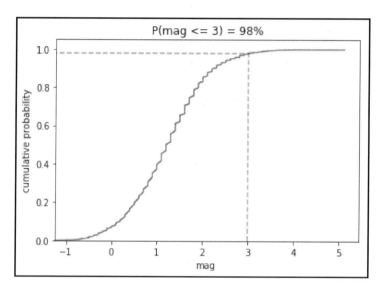

Finally, we can use box plots to visualize potential outliers and the distribution using quartiles. As an example, let's visualize the OHLC prices for Facebook stock across the whole dataset:

```
>>> fb.iloc[:,:4].plot(
...     kind='box',
...     title='Facebook OHLC Prices Boxplot'
... )
>>> plt.ylabel('price ($)') # label the x-axis (discussed in ch 6)
```

Notice that we do lose some information we had in the other plots. We no longer have an idea of the density of points throughout the distribution; with the box plot, we focus on the 5-number summary instead:

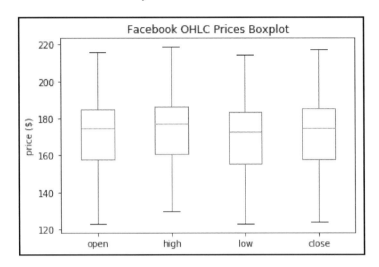

We can also call the `boxplot()` method after calling `groupby()` on the dataframe. Let's examine how the box plots change when we calculate them based on the volume traded:

```
>>> fb.assign(
...     volume_bin=pd.cut(fb.volume, 3, labels=['low', 'med', 'high'])
... ).groupby('volume_bin').boxplot(
...     column=['open', 'high', 'low', 'close'],
...     layout=(1, 3),
...     figsize=(12, 3)
... )
>>> plt.suptitle('Facebook OHLC Boxplots by Volume Traded', y=1.1)
```

Remember from Chapter 4, *Aggregating Pandas DataFrames,* that most of the days fell in the low volume traded bucket, so we would expect to see more variation there because of what the stock data looked like over time:

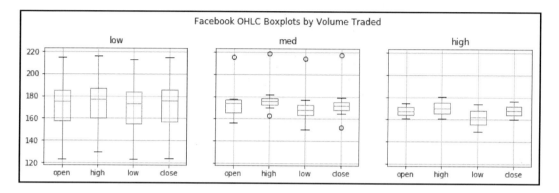

We can call plot() after groupby() to generate subplots per group for various plot types, not just box plots.

We can also use this technique to see the distribution of earthquake magnitudes based on which magType was used and compare it to the expected ranges on the USGS website (https://earthquake.usgs.gov/learn/topics/mag-intensity/magnitude-types.php):

```
>>> quakes[['mag', 'magType']].groupby('magType').boxplot(
...     figsize=(15, 8), subplots=False
... )

# formatting (covered in chapter 6)
>>> plt.title('Earthquake Magnitude Boxplots by magType')
>>> plt.ylabel('magnitude')
```

The USGS website mentions situations in which certain measurement techniques can't be used and what range of magnitudes each measurement technique is authoritative for (when outside that range, other techniques are used). We can see that, together, the techniques cover a wide spectrum of magnitudes, while none of them covers everything:

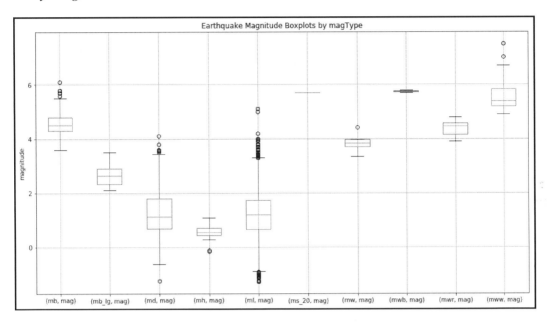

Counts and frequencies

We can use bar plots for displaying counts of our discrete data. For example, we can do the following to plot the total volume traded of Facebook stock per month from February 2018 through August 2018. Rather than passing `kind` to `plot()`, we can append a call to the specific plot type if we know the name, which is `bar()` here:

```
>>> fb['2018-02':'2018-08'].assign(
...     month=lambda x: x.index.month
... ).groupby('month').sum().volume.plot.bar(
...     color='green', rot=0, title='Volume Traded'
... )
>>> plt.ylabel('volume') # label the y-axis (discussed in ch 6)
```

Note that this is also an evolution over time, but we don't use a line plot to avoid interpolating the points:

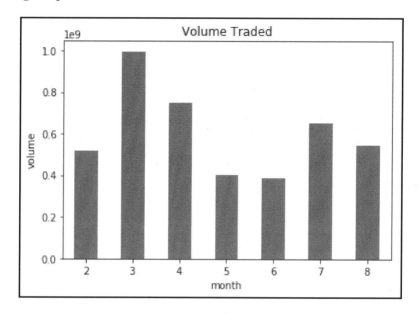

When working with categorical data, we are limited in terms of the types of plots we can use; we often look to display frequencies of certain values of the categories. For these, we will use bar plots on the pandas side, and we will cover some additional alternatives in the *Utilizing seaborn for advanced plotting* section in the next chapter. We will not be using pie charts; however, if you really want to, you can pass kind='pie' to the plot() method from pandas—just make sure that you don't have too many sections (so your eye can discern the colors) and that the sizes of each slice are distinguishable.

Horizontal bar plots make it easy to compare the size of each category while allowing sufficient space on the margin for long category names (without the need to rotate them). We can use this to see which places in our earthquakes data have had the most earthquakes.

First, we use the `value_counts()` method on the `parsed_place` series and take the top 15 places for earthquakes. Next, we reverse the order, so that the smallest ones in this list are on top, which will sort the highest to the top of the bar plot that we will make. Note that we could reverse the sort order as an argument to `value_counts()`, but, since we would still have to grab the top 15, we are doing both in a single `iloc` call:

```
>>> quakes.parsed_place.value_counts().iloc[14::-1,].plot(
...     kind='barh', figsize=(10, 5),
...     title='Top 15 Places for Earthquakes '\
...         '(September 18, 2018 - October 13, 2018)'
... )
>>> plt.xlabel('earthquakes') # label the x-axis (discussed in ch 6)
```

By passing `kind='barh'`, we get a horizontal bar plot that shows that most of the earthquakes in this data occur in Alaska. Perhaps it is surprising to see the number of earthquakes over such a short time period, but many of these earthquakes are so small in magnitude that people don't even feel them:

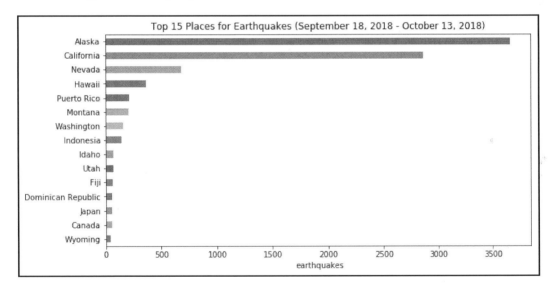

Remember, slicing notation is of the form `[start:stop:step]`, and, in this case, since the `step` is negative, the order is reversed; we start at index `14` (the 15th entry) and get closer to index `0` each time.

Our data also has information about whether the earthquake was accompanied by a tsunami. Let's apply the same technique to see the top 10 places with tsunamis during the time period we have in our data:

```
>>> quakes.groupby(
...     'parsed_place'
... ).tsunami.sum().sort_values().iloc[-10::,].plot(
...     kind='barh', figsize=(10, 5),
...     title='Top 10 Places for Tsunamis '\
...         '(September 18, 2018 - October 13, 2018)'
... )
>>> plt.xlabel('tsunamis') # label the x-axis (discussed in chapter 6)
```

We can see that Indonesia has many more tsunamis than the other places during this time period:

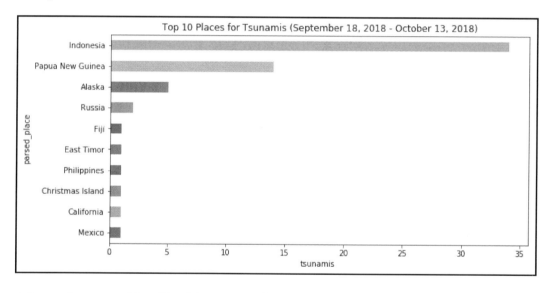

After seeing something like this, we may be prompted to look further into the number of tsunamis in Indonesia each day. We can visualize this evolution over time as a line plot or with a bar plot. Here, we will use bars, and since we have many bars to plot, we will plot with vertical bars by using `kind='bar'`:

```
>>> indonesia_quakes = quakes.query(
...     'parsed_place == "Indonesia"'
... ).assign(
...     time=lambda x: pd.to_datetime(x.time, unit='ms'), earthquake=1
... ).set_index('time').resample('1D').sum()
```

```
>>> indonesia_quakes.index = indonesia_quakes.index.strftime('%b\n%d')

>>> indonesia_quakes.plot(
...     y=['earthquake', 'tsunami'], kind='bar', figsize=(15, 3),
...     rot=0, label=['earthquakes', 'tsunamis'],
...     title='Earthquakes and Tsunamis in Indonesia '\
...         '(September 18, 2018 - October 13, 2018)'
... )

# label the axes (discussed in chapter 6)
>>> plt.xlabel('date')
>>> plt.ylabel('count')
```

Here, we see a spike in both earthquakes and tsunamis in Indonesia on September 28, 2018, which is when a 7.5 magnitude earthquake occurred causing a devastating tsunami:

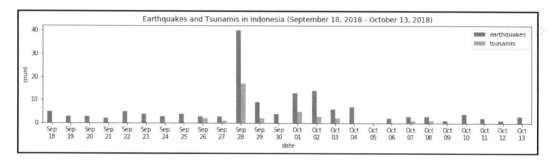

Sometimes, we will choose to make horizontal bars if our categories have long names (as with the top places for earthquakes and tsunamis plots), which can be difficult to read if they are rotated by 90 degrees. When we have many categories, it may be easier to display with vertical bars as we did in the previous plot. Let's now use vertical bars to see which methods of measuring earthquake magnitude are most prevalent by using `kind='bar'`:

```
>>> quakes.magType.value_counts().plot(
...     kind='bar', title='Earthquakes Recorded per magType', rot=0
... )

# label the axes (discussed in ch 6)
>>> plt.xlabel('magType')
>>> plt.ylabel('earthquakes')
```

It appears that `ml` is, by far, the most common method for measuring earthquake magnitudes, which makes sense, since it is the *original magnitude relationship* defined by Richter and Gutenberg in 1935 for local earthquakes according to the USGS page explaining the `magType` field in the dataset we are using (`https://earthquake.usgs.gov/learn/topics/mag-intensity/magnitude-types.php`):

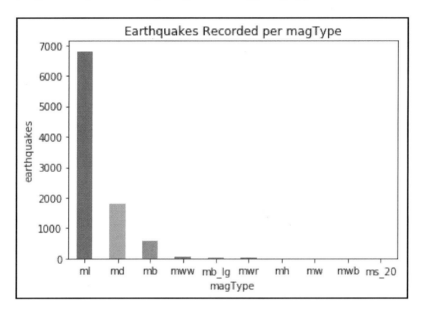

Let's discover what they are using in the top four places with earthquakes using `groupby()`, so that we can see multiple bars per category:

```
>>> quakes[
...     quakes.parsed_place.isin([
...         'California', 'Alaska', 'Nevada', 'Hawaii'
...     ])
... ].groupby(
...     ['parsed_place', 'magType']
... ).mag.count().unstack().plot.bar(
...     title='magTypes used in top 4 places with earthquakes'
... )
>>> plt.ylabel('earthquakes') # label the axes (discussed in ch 6)
```

While `ml` is definitely predominant, it appears that California and Hawaii have an affinity for using `md` as well:

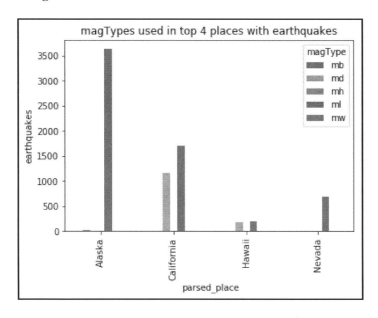

 If we run `plt.savefig()` to save the preceding plots, we may notice that long category names, such as `Dominican Republic`, get cut off; in that case, we can run `plt.tight_layout()` before saving, and that should fix it.

Say we want to see how many earthquakes of a given magnitude there were, and to distinguish them by `magType`. This shows us a few things in a single plot:

- Which magnitudes occur most often across `magType`
- The relative ranges of magnitudes that each `magType` yields
- The most common values for `magType`

To do so, we can make a stacked bar plot. First, we will round all magnitudes down to the nearest integer. This means that all earthquakes will be marked as the part of the magnitude before the decimal point (for example, 5.5 gets marked as 5 just like 5.7, 5.2, and 5.0). Next, we will need to create a pivot table with the magnitude in the index and the `magType` along the columns; we will count up the number of earthquakes for the values:

```
>>> pivot = quakes.assign(
...     mag_bin=lambda x: np.floor(x.mag)
... ).pivot_table(
...     index='mag_bin', columns='magType',
...     values='mag', aggfunc='count'
... )
```

Once we have the pivot table, we can create the stacked bar plot by passing in `stacked=True` when plotting:

```
>>> pivot.plot.bar(
...     stacked=True, rot=0,
...     title='Earthquakes by integer magnitude and magType'
... )
>>> plt.ylabel('earthquakes') # label the axes (discussed in ch 6)
```

This results in the following plot, showing that most of the earthquakes have a `magType` of `ml` and have magnitudes below four:

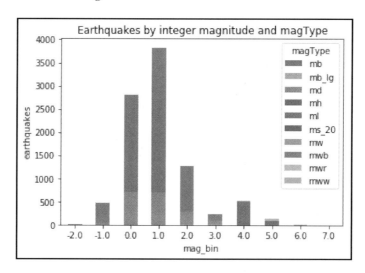

The other `magType` bars are dwarfed in comparison to `ml`, which makes it difficult for us to see which `magTypes` assign higher magnitudes to earthquakes. To address this, we can make a normalized stacked bar plot—rather than showing the count of earthquakes for each combination of magnitude and `magType`, we will show what percentage of earthquakes of a given magnitude used each `magType`. We can handle this using the `apply()` method, as we learned in `Chapter 4`, *Aggregating Pandas DataFrames*, along `axis=1` (to apply row by row):

```
>>> normalized_pivot = pivot.fillna(0).apply(
...     lambda x: x/x.sum(), axis=1
... )
>>> ax = normalized_pivot.plot.bar(
...     stacked=True, rot=0, figsize=(10, 5),
...     title='Percentage of earthquakes by integer magnitude '\
...         'for each magType'
... )
>>> ax.legend(bbox_to_anchor=(1, 0.8)) # move legend to right of plot
>>> plt.ylabel('percentage') # label the axes (discussed in chapter 6)
```

Now we can easily see that `mww` yields higher magnitudes and `ml` appears to be spread across the lower end of the spectrum:

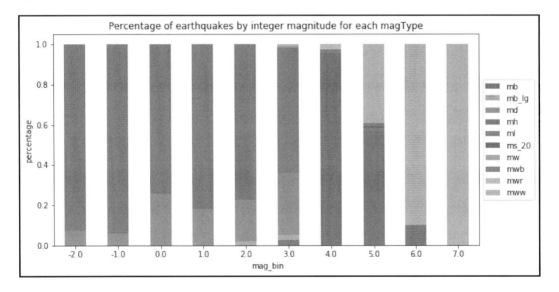

The pandas.plotting subpackage

The preceding `pandas` plotting sections covered standard plots that `pandas` has given an easier implementation. However, `pandas` also has a subpackage (which is appropriately named `plotting`) with special plots that we can use on our data. The customization options of these may be more limited because of how they are composed and returned to us.

For this section, we will be working in `3-pandas_plotting_subpackage.ipynb`. As usual, we begin with our imports and reading in the data:

```
>>> %matplotlib inline
>>> import matplotlib.pyplot as plt
>>> import numpy as np
>>> import pandas as pd

>>> fb = pd.read_csv(
...     'data/fb_stock_prices_2018.csv',
...     index_col='date',
...     parse_dates=True
... )
```

Scatter matrices

Earlier in this chapter, we discussed using scatter plots to show relationships among variables. Often, we want to see these for each combination of variables in the data, which can be tedious to execute. The `pandas.plotting` subpackage contains a `scatter_matrix()` function that makes this much easier.

Let's use `scatter_matrix()` to view the scatter plots for each combination of columns in our Facebook stock prices data:

```
>>> from pandas.plotting import scatter_matrix
>>> scatter_matrix(fb, figsize=(10, 10))
```

This results in the following plot matrix, which is often used in machine learning to see which variables could be useful in building a model:

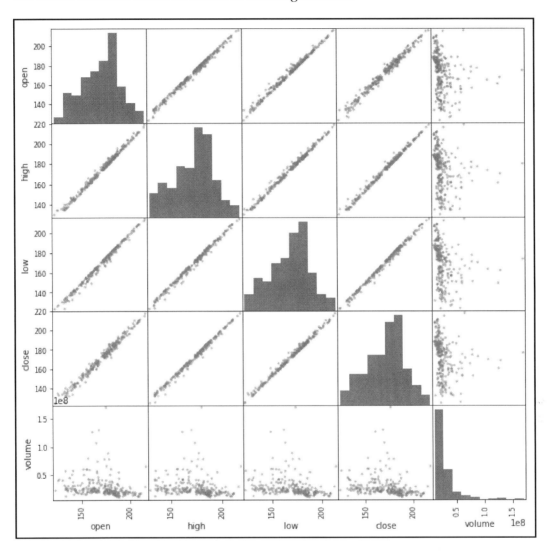

Here, we can also easily see that we have strong positive correlations between `open`, `high`, `low`, and `close`. By default, on the diagonal, where the column is paired with itself, we get its histogram. If we would prefer, we can ask for the KDE by passing `diagonal='kde'`:

```
>>> scatter_matrix(fb, figsize=(10, 10), diagonal='kde')
```

This results in a scatter matrix with KDEs along the diagonal instead of histograms:

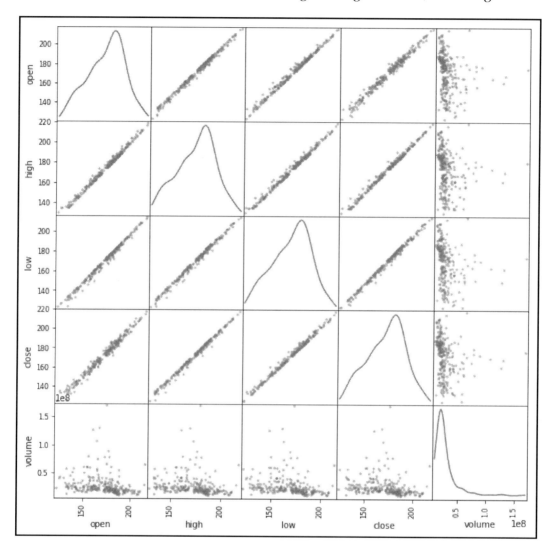

Lag plots

We can use a **lag plot** to check for relationships among values at a given time to those a certain number of periods before that time; that is, we create a scatter plot of `data[:-1]` (all but the last entry) and `data[1:]` (from the second entry to the last one).

If our data is random, this plot will have no pattern. Let's test this with some random data generated with NumPy:

```
>>> from pandas.plotting import lag_plot
>>> np.random.seed(0) # make this repeatable
>>> lag_plot(pd.Series(np.random.random(size=200)))
```

The random data points don't indicate any pattern, just random noise:

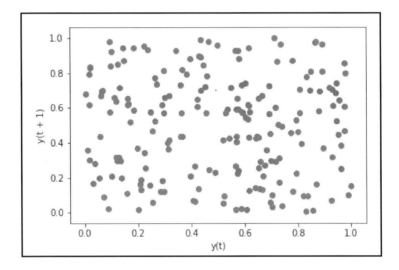

With our stock data, we know that prices on a given day are determined by what happened the day before; therefore, we would expect to see a pattern in the lag plot. Let's use the Facebook closing price data to test whether our intuition is correct:

```
>>> lag_plot(fb.close)
```

This results in a linear pattern, as expected:

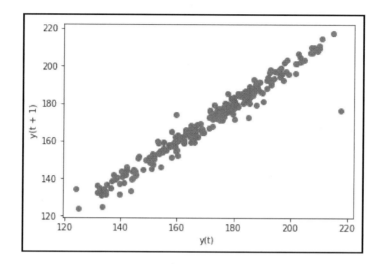

We can also specify the number of periods to use for the lag. The default lag is one, but we can change this with the `lag` parameter. For example, we can compare each value to the value of the week before with a `lag` of 5 (remember that the stock data only has data for weekdays since the market is closed on the weekends):

```
>>> lag_plot(fb.close, lag=5)
```

This still yields a strong correlation, but it definitely looks weaker than before:

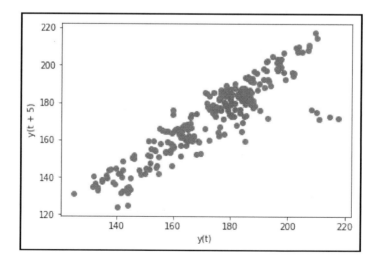

Autocorrelation plots

The lag plots in the preceding section are also a way to visualize **autocorrelation**. Autocorrelation means that the time series is correlated with a lagged version of itself. Pandas provides an additional way to look for this with `autocorrelation_plot()`, which shows the autocorrelation by the number of lags. Random data will be near an autocorrelation of 0 and within the confidence bands (99% is dashed; 95% is solid).

Let's examine what this looks like for random data generated with NumPy:

```
>>> from pandas.plotting import autocorrelation_plot
>>> np.random.seed(0) # make this repeatable
>>> autocorrelation_plot(pd.Series(np.random.random(size=200)))
```

Indeed, the autocorrelation is near zero, and the line is within the confidence bands:

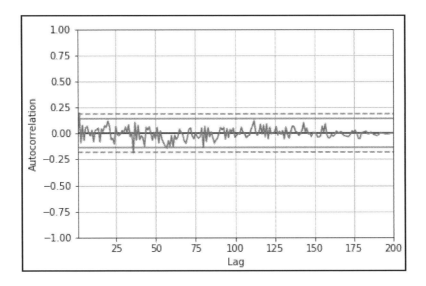

Let's explore what the autocorrelation plot looks like for Facebook stock's closing price, because the lag plots indicated several periods of autocorrelation:

```
>>> autocorrelation_plot(fb.close)
```

Here, we can see that there is autocorrelation for many lag periods before it becomes noise:

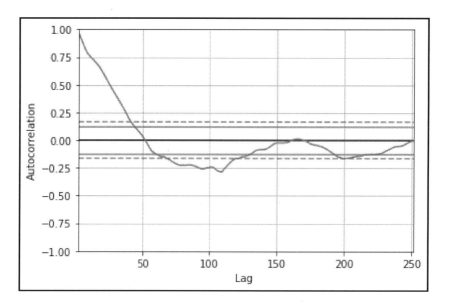

Bootstrap plots

Pandas also provides a plotting function to assess the uncertainty of common summary statistics using **bootstrapping**. The function will take the specified number of random samples of a given size (with replacement) from the variable in question (the `samples` and `size` parameters, respectively) and calculate the summary statistics. Then, it will return a plot with the results.

Let's see what the uncertainty for the summary statistics of the volume traded data looks like:

```
>>> from pandas.plotting import bootstrap_plot
>>> bootstrap_plot(fb.volume, fig=plt.figure(figsize=(10, 6)))
```

This results in the following plot:

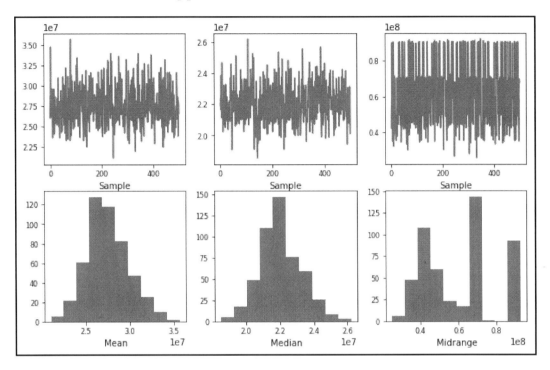

Summary

Now we are well-equipped to quickly create a variety of visualizations in Python using `pandas` and `matplotlib`. We understand the basics of how `matplotlib` works and the main components of a plot. Additionally, we discussed various plot types and the situations in which to use them—a crucial component of data visualization is choosing the appropriate plot. Be sure to check out the *Choosing the appropriate visualization* section in the appendix for future reference.

Note that the best practices for visualization don't just apply to the plot type, but also to the formatting of the plot, which we will discuss in the next chapter. In addition to this, we will build upon the foundation we laid here to discuss additional plots using `seaborn` and how to customize our plots using `matplotlib`.

Exercises

Create the following visualizations using what you have learned up to this point in this book. Use the data from this chapter's data/ directory:

1. Plot the rolling 20-day minimum of the Facebook closing price with the pandas plot() method.
2. Create a histogram and KDE of the change from open to close in the price of Facebook stock.
3. Using the earthquake data, create box plots for the magnitudes of each magType used in Indonesia.
4. Make a line plot of the difference between the weekly maximum high price and the weekly minimum low price for Facebook. This should be a single line.
5. Using matplotlib and pandas, create two subplots side-by-side showing the effect that after-hours trading has had on Facebook's stock price:
    1. The first subplot will contain a line plot of the daily difference between that day's opening price and the prior day's closing price (be sure to review the *Time series* section of Chapter 4, *Aggregating Pandas DataFrames* for an easy way to do this).
    2. The second subplot will be a bar plot showing the net effect this had monthly, using resample().
    3. Bonus #1: Color the bars according to whether they are gains in the stock price (green) or drops in the stock price (red).
    4. Bonus #2: Modify the x-axis of the bar plot to show the three-letter abbreviation for the month.

Further reading

Take a look at the following resources for additional information on the concepts covered in this chapter:

- *Bootstrapping (statistics)*: `https://en.wikipedia.org/wiki/Bootstrapping_%28statistics%2`
- *Data Visualization—Best Practices and Foundations*: `https://www.toptal.com/designers/data-visualization/data-visualization-best-practices`
- *How to Create Animated Graphs in Python (with matplotlib)*: `https://towardsdatascience.com/how-to-create-animated-graphs-in-python-bb619cc2dec1`
- *Interactive plots with JavaScript (D3.js)*: `https://d3js.org/`
- *Intro to Animations in Python (with plotly)*: `https://plot.ly/python/animations/`
- *IPython: Built-in magic commands*: `https://ipython.readthedocs.io/en/stable/interactive/magics.html`
- *The Importance of Integrity: How Plot Parameters Influence Interpretation*: `https://www.t4g.com/insights/plot-parameters-influence-interpretation/`
- *5 Python Libraries for Creating Interactive Plots*: `https://blog.modeanalytics.com/python-interactive-plot-libraries/`

6
Plotting with Seaborn and Customization Techniques

In the previous chapter, we learned how to create many different visualizations using `matplotlib` and `pandas` on wide format data; in this chapter, we will see how we can make visualizations from long format data, using `seaborn`, and how to customize our plots to improve their interpretability. Remember that the human brain excels at finding patterns in visual representations; by making clear and meaningful data visualizations, we can help others (not to mention ourselves) understand what the data is trying to say.

Seaborn is capable of making many of the same plots we created in the previous chapter; however, it also makes quick work of long format data, allowing us to use subsets of our data for encoding additional information into our visualizations, such as facets and/or colors for different categories. We will walk through some implementations of what we did in the previous chapter that are easier (or just more aesthetically pleasing) using `seaborn`, such as heatmaps and pair plots (the `seaborn` version of the scatter plot matrix). In addition, we will explore some new plot types that `seaborn` provides to address issues that other plot types may be susceptible to.

Afterward, we will change gears and begin our discussion on customizing the appearance of our data visualizations. We will walk through the process of creating annotations, adding reference lines, properly labeling our plots, controlling the color palette used, and tailoring the axes to meet our needs. This is the final piece we need to make our visualizations ready to present to others.

In this chapter, we will cover the following topics:

- Utilizing `seaborn` for more advanced plot types
- Formatting our figures with `matplotlib`
- Using `matplotlib` to customize the appearance of our visualizations

Chapter materials

The materials for this chapter can be found on GitHub at `https://github.com/stefmolin/Hands-On-Data-Analysis-with-Pandas/tree/master/ch_06`. We will be working with two datasets once again, both of which can be found in the `data/` directory. In the `fb_stock_prices_2018.csv` file, we have Facebook's stock price for all trading days in 2018. This data is the OHLC data (opening, high, low, and closing price), along with the volume traded. It was gathered using the `stock_analysis` package that we will build in `Chapter 7`, *Financial Analysis – Bitcoin and the Stock Market*.

The `data/earthquakes.csv` file contains earthquake data pulled from the USGS API (`https://earthquake.usgs.gov/fdsnws/event/1/`) for September 18, 2018, through October 13, 2018. For each earthquake, we have the magnitude (the `mag` column), the scale it was measured on (the `magType` column), when (the `time` column) and where (the `place` column) it occurred; we also have the `parsed_place` column, which indicates the state or country in which the earthquake occurred (we added this column back in `Chapter 2`, *Working with Pandas DataFrames*). Other unnecessary columns have been removed.

Throughout the chapter, we will be working through three Jupyter Notebooks. These are all numbered according to their order of use. We will begin exploring the capabilities of `seaborn` with `1-introduction_to_seaborn.ipynb`. Next, we will move to `2-formatting_plots.ipynb` as we discuss formatting and labeling our plots. Finally, we will work with `3-customizing_visualizations.ipynb` to learn how to add reference lines, shade regions, include annotations, and customize our visualizations. The text will prompt us when to switch notebooks.

In addition, we have three Python (`.py`) files that contain functions we will use throughout the chapter: `reg_resid_plot.py`, `std_from_mean_kde.py`, and `color_utils.py`.

Utilizing seaborn for advanced plotting

As we saw in the previous chapter, `pandas` provides implementations for most visualizations we would want to create; however, there is another library, `seaborn`, which provides additional functionality for more involved visualizations and makes creating visualizations with long format data much easier than `pandas`. These also tend to look much nicer than standard visualizations generated by `matplotlib`. While `seaborn` offers alternatives to many of the plot types we covered in the previous chapter, for the most part, we will only cover new types that `seaborn` makes possible and leave learning about the rest as an exercise. Additional available functions using the `seaborn` API can be found at `https://seaborn.pydata.org/api.html`.

For this section, we will be working with the `1-introduction_to_seaborn.ipynb` notebook. First, we must import `seaborn`, which is traditionally aliased as `sns`:

```
>>> import seaborn as sns
```

Let's also import `numpy`, `matplotlib.pyplot`, and `pandas`, and then read in our CSV files:

```
>>> %matplotlib inline
>>> import pandas as pd
>>> import numpy as np
>>> import matplotlib.pyplot as plt

>>> fb = pd.read_csv(
...     'data/fb_stock_prices_2018.csv', index_col='date',
...      parse_dates=True
... )
>>> quakes = pd.read_csv('data/earthquakes.csv')
```

Categorical data

There was a devastating tsunami in Indonesia on September 28, 2018; it came after a 7.5 magnitude earthquake occurred near Palu, Indonesia (`https://www.livescience.com/63721-tsunami-earthquake-indonesia.html`). Let's create a visualization to understand which `magTypes` are used in Indonesia, the range of magnitudes recorded, and how many of the earthquakes were accompanied by a tsunami. To do this, we need a way to plot relationships in which one of the variables is categorical (`magType`) and the other is numeric (`mag`).

When we discussed scatter plots in `Chapter 5`, *Visualizing Data with Pandas and Matplotlib*, we were limited to both variables being numeric; however, with `seaborn`, we have two additional plot types at our disposal that allow us to have one categorical and one numeric variable. The first is the `stripplot()` function, which plots the points in strips that denote each category. The second is the `swarmplot()` function, which we will see later.

Let's create this visualization with `stripplot()`. We pass the subset of earthquakes occurring in Indonesia to the `data` parameter, and specify that we want to put `magType` on the *x*-axis (x), magnitudes on the *y*-axis (y), and color the points by whether the earthquake was accompanied by a tsunami (hue):

```
>>> sns.stripplot(
...        x='magType',
...        y='mag',
...        hue='tsunami',
...        data=quakes.query('parsed_place == "Indonesia"')
... )
```

Using the resulting plot, we can see that the earthquake in question is the highest orange point in the `mww` column (don't forget to call `plt.show()` if not using the Jupyter Notebook provided):

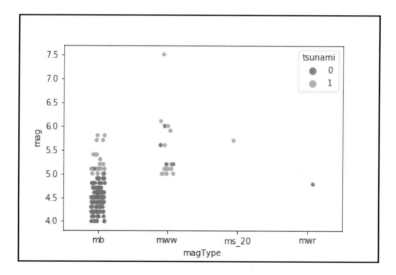

 Information on the different `magTypes` can be found at `https://earthquake.usgs.gov/learn/topics/mag-intensity/magnitude-types.php`.

As we can see, for the most part, the tsunamis occurred with higher magnitude earthquakes, as we would expect; however, due to the high concentration of points at lower magnitudes, we can't really see all the points. We could try to adjust the `jitter` argument, which controls how much random noise to add to the point in an attempt to reduce overlaps, or the `alpha` argument for transparency, as we did previously; fortunately, there is another function, `swarmplot()`, that will reduce the overlap as much as possible, so we will use that instead:

```
>>> sns.swarmplot(
...     x='magType',
...     y='mag',
...     hue='tsunami',
...     data=quakes.query('parsed_place == "Indonesia"')
... )
```

The swarm plot (or bee swarm plot) also has the bonus of giving us a glimpse of what the distribution might be. We can now see many more earthquakes in the lower section of the `mb` column:

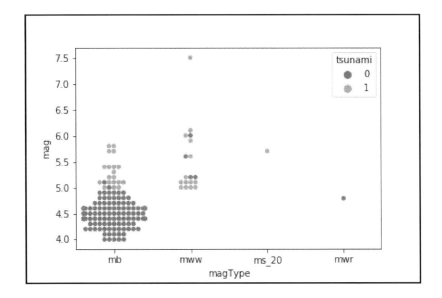

Check out the `countplot()` and `barplot()` functions for variations on the bar plots we did with `pandas` in the previous chapter.

Correlations and heatmaps

As promised, let's learn an easier way to generate heatmaps compared to what we had to do in Chapter 5, *Visualizing Data with Pandas and Matplotlib*. Once again, we will make a heatmap of the correlations between the OHLC stock prices, the log of volume traded, and the daily difference between the highest and lowest prices (max_abs_change); however, this time, we will use seaborn, which gives us the heatmap() function for an easier way to produce this visualization:

```
>>> sns.heatmap(
...     fb.sort_index().assign(
...         volume=np.log(fb.volume),
...         max_abs_change=fb.high - fb.low
...     ).corr(),
...     annot=True, center=0
... )
```

We also pass center=0 so that seaborn puts values of 0 (no correlation) at the center of the colormap it uses. Notice that we also passed in annot=True to write the correlation coefficients in each box—we get the benefit of the numerical data and the visual data all in one plot with a single function call:

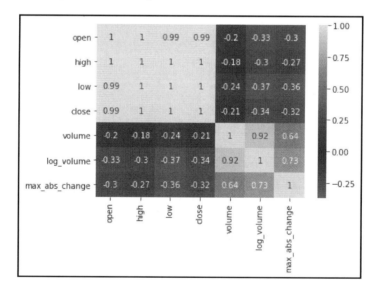

When using seaborn, we can still use functions from matplotlib, such as plt.savefig() and plt.tight_layout(). If there are issues with plt.tight_layout(), pass bbox_inches='tight' to plt.savefig() instead.

Seaborn also provides us with an alternative to the `scatter_matrix()` function provided by `pandas`, called `pairplot()`. We can use this to see the correlations between the columns in the Facebook data as scatter plots instead of the heatmap:

```
>>> sns.pairplot(fb)
```

This result makes it easy to understand the near-perfect positive correlation between the OHLC columns shown in the heatmap, while also showing us histograms for each column along the diagonal:

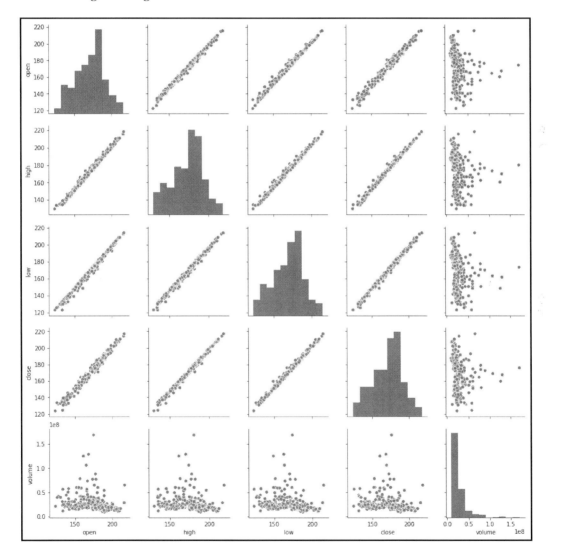

Facebook's performance in the latter half of 2018 was markedly worse than in the first half, so we may be interested to see how the distribution of the data changed each quarter of the year. As with the `pandas.plotting.scatter_matrix()` function, we can specify what to do along the diagonal with the `diag_kind` argument; however, unlike `pandas`, we can easily color everything based on other data with the `hue` argument. To do so, we just add the `quarter` column and then provide it to the `hue` argument:

```
>>> sns.pairplot(
...         fb.assign(quarter=lambda x: x.index.quarter),
...         diag_kind='kde',
...         hue='quarter'
... )
```

We can now see how the distributions of the OHLC columns had lower standard deviations (and, subsequently, lower variances) in the first quarter and how the stock price lost a lot of ground in the fourth quarter (the distribution shifts to the left):

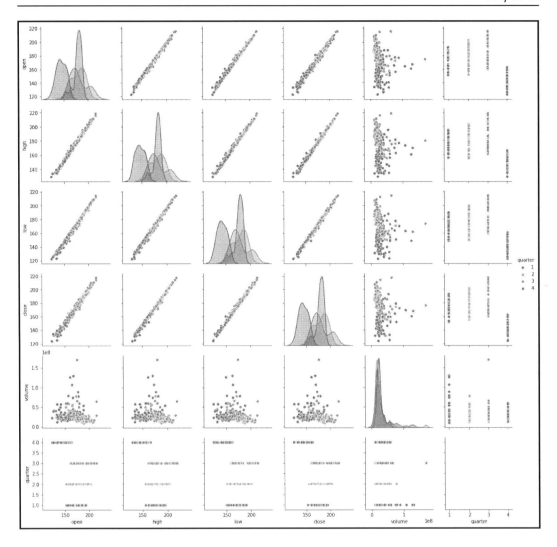

 We can also pass `kind='reg'` to `pairplot()` to show regression lines.

If we only want to compare two variables, we can use `jointplot()`, which will give us a scatter plot along with the distribution of each variable along the side. Let's look once again at how the log of volume traded correlates with the difference between the daily high and low prices in Facebook stock as we did in Chapter 5, *Visualizing Data with Pandas and Matplotlib*:

```
>>> sns.jointplot(
...     x='volume',
...     y='max_abs_change',
...     data=fb.assign(
...         volume=np.log(fb.volume),
...         max_abs_change=fb.high - fb.low
...     )
... )
```

Using the default value for the `kind` argument, we get histograms for the distributions and a plain scatter plot in the center:

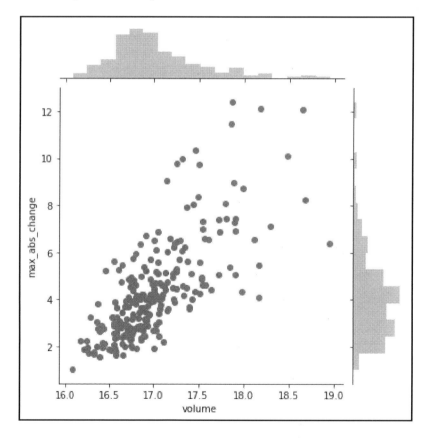

Seaborn gives us plenty of alternatives for the `kind` argument. For example, we can use hexbins because there is a significant overlap when we use the scatter plot:

```
>>> sns.jointplot(
...     x='volume',
...     y='max_abs_change',
...     kind='hex',
...     data=fb.assign(
...         volume=np.log(fb.volume),
...         max_abs_change=fb.high - fb.low
...     )
... )
```

We can now see the large concentration of points in the lower-left corner:

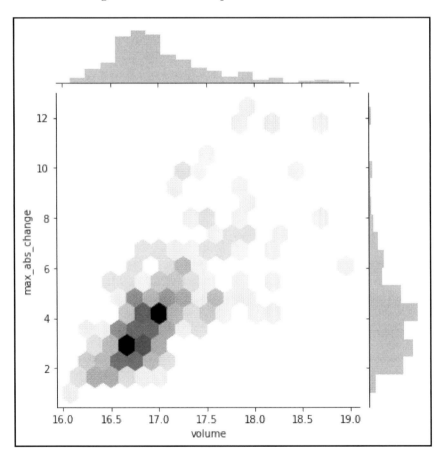

Additionally, we can plot a regression in the center and get kernel density estimates in addition to histograms along the sides:

```
>>> sns.jointplot(
...     x='volume',
...     y='max_abs_change',
...     kind='reg',
...     data=fb.assign(
...         volume=np.log(fb.volume),
...         max_abs_change=fb.high - fb.low
...     )
... )
```

This results in a linear regression line being drawn through the scatter plot, along with a confidence band surrounding the line in a lighter color:

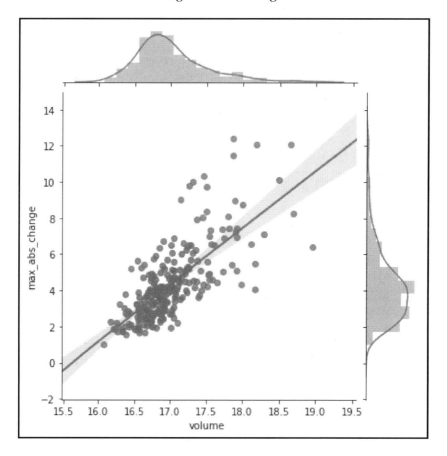

The relationship appears to be linear, but we should look at the **residuals** to check. Residuals are the observed values minus the values predicted using the regression line. We can look directly at the residuals that would result from the previous regression with `kind='resid'`:

```
>>> sns.jointplot(
...     x='volume',
...     y='max_abs_change',
...     kind='resid',
...     data=fb.assign(
...         volume=np.log(fb.volume),
...         max_abs_change=fb.high - fb.low
...     )
... )
```

Notice that the residuals appear to be getting further away from zero at higher quantities of volume traded, which means this probably isn't the right way to model this relationship:

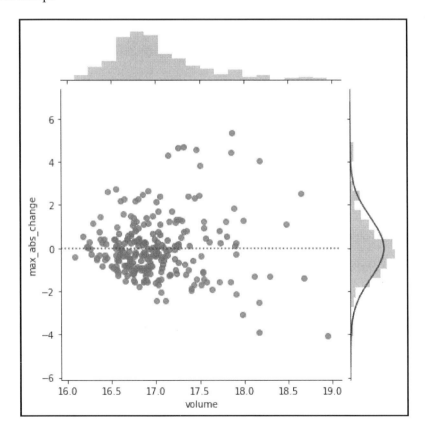

Finally, if we select `kind='kde'`, we get a contour plot to represent the joint density estimate:

```
>>> sns.jointplot(
...     x='volume',
...     y='max_abs_change',
...     kind='kde',
...     data=fb.assign(
...         volume=np.log(fb.volume),
...         max_abs_change=fb.high - fb.low
...     )
... )
```

The following plot is the result:

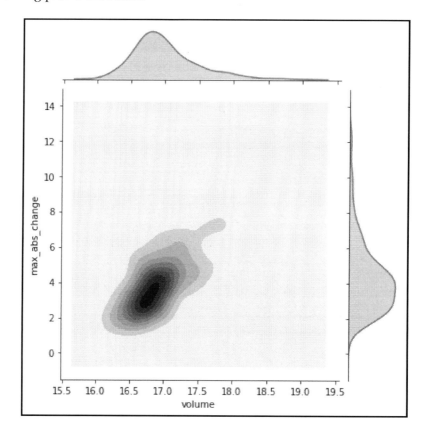

Regression plots

We saw that we could use `jointplot()` to get a regression plot or a residuals plot; naturally, `seaborn` exposes functions to make these directly without the overhead of creating the entire joint plot. The `regplot()` function will calculate a regression line and plot it, while `residplot()` will calculate the regression and plot only the residuals. We can write a function to combine these for us, but first, some setup.

Our function will plot all permutations of any two columns (as opposed to combinations; order matters with permutations, for example, `open and close` is not the same as `close and open`). This allows us to see each column as the regressor and as the dependent variable; since we don't know which direction the relationship is, we let the viewer decide after calling the function. This generates many subplots, so we will create a new dataframe with just a few columns from our Facebook data.

We'll be looking at the logarithm of the volume traded (`volume`) and the daily difference between the highest and lowest price of Facebook stock (`max_abs_change`). Let's use `assign()` to create these new columns and save them in a new dataframe called `fb_reg_data`:

```
>>> fb_reg_data = fb.assign(
...     volume=np.log(fb.volume),
...     max_abs_change=fb.high - fb.low
... ).iloc[:,-2:]
```

Next, we need to import `itertools`, which is part of the Python standard library (`https://docs.python.org/3/library/itertools.html`). When writing plotting functions, `itertools` can be extremely helpful; it makes it very easy to create efficient iterators for things such as permutations, combinations, and infinite cycles or repeats:

```
>>> import itertools
```

Iterables are objects that can be iterated over. When we start a loop, an **iterator** is created from the iterable. At each iteration, the iterator provides its next value, until it is exhausted; this means that once we complete a single iteration through all its items, there is nothing left, and it can't be reused. Iterators are iterables, but not all iterables are iterators. Iterables that aren't iterators can be used repeatedly. The iterators we get back when using `itertools` can only be used once through:

```
>>> iterator = itertools.repeat("I'm an iterator", 1)

>>> for i in iterator:
...     print(f'-->{i}')
>>> print('This printed once because the iterator has been exhausted')
>>> for i in iterator:
...     print(f'-->{i}')
-->I'm an iterator
This printed once because the iterator has been exhausted
```

A list, on the other hand, is an iterable; we can write something that loops over all the elements in the list, and we will still have a list for later reuse:

```
>>> iterable = list(itertools.repeat("I'm an iterable", 1))

>>> for i in iterable:
...     print(f'-->{i}')
>>> print('This prints again because it\'s an iterable:')
>>> for i in iterable:
...     print(f'-->{i}')
-->I'm an iterable
This prints again because it's an iterable:
-->I'm an iterable
```

Now that we have some background on `itertools` and iterators, let's write the function for our regression and residuals permutation plots:

```
def reg_resid_plots(data):
    """
    Using seaborn, plot the regression and residuals plots
    side-by-side for every permutation of 2 columns in the data.

    Parameters:
        - data: A pandas DataFrame

    Returns: A matplotlib Figure object.
    """
    num_cols = data.shape[1]
    permutation_count = num_cols * (num_cols - 1)

    fig, ax = plt.subplots(permutation_count, 2, figsize=(15, 8))

    for (x, y), axes, color in zip(
        itertools.permutations(data.columns, 2),
        ax,
        itertools.cycle(['royalblue', 'darkorange'])
    ):
        for subplot, func in zip(axes, (sns.regplot, sns.residplot)):
            func(x=x, y=y, data=data, ax=subplot, color=color)
    plt.close()
    return fig
```

In this function, we can see that all the material covered so far in this chapter and from the previous chapter is coming together; we calculate how many subplots we need, and since we will have two plots for each permutation, we just need the number of permutations to determine the row count. We take advantage of the `zip()` function, which gives us values from multiple iterables at once in tuples, and tuple unpacking to easily iterate over the permutation tuples and the n-dimensional NumPy array of `Axes` objects. Take some time to make sure you understand what is going on here; there are also resources on `zip()` and tuple unpacking in the *Further reading* section at the end of this chapter.

 If we provide different length iterables to `zip()`, we will only get a number of tuples equal to the smallest length. For this reason, we can use infinite iterators, such as those we get when using `itertools.repeat()`, which repeats the same value infinitely (when we don't specify the number of times to repeat the value), and `itertools.cycle()`, which cycles between all the values provided infinitely.

Calling our function is effortless, with only a single parameter:

```
>>> from reg_resid_plot import reg_resid_plots
>>> reg_resid_plots(fb_reg_data)
```

The first row of subsets is what we saw earlier with the joint plots, and the second row is the regression when flipping the x and the y variables:

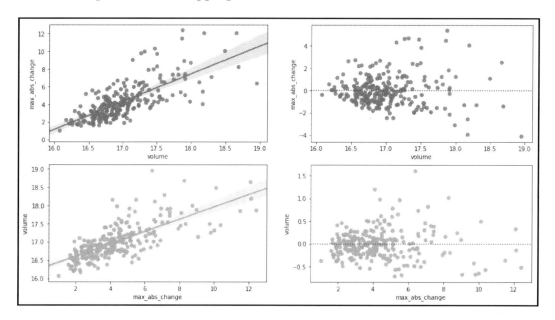

The regplot() function supports polynomial and logistic regression through the order and logistic parameters, respectively.

Seaborn also makes it easy to plot regressions across different subsets of our data with lmplot(). We can split our regression plots with hue, col, and row, which will color by values in a given column, make a new column for each value, and make a new row for each value, respectively.

We saw that Facebook's performance was different across each quarter of the year, so let's calculate a regression per quarter with the Facebook stock data, using the volume traded and the daily difference between the highest and lowest price, to see whether this relationship also changes:

```
>>> sns.lmplot(
...     x='volume',
...     y='max_abs_change',
...     data=fb.assign(
...         volume=np.log(fb.volume),
...         max_abs_change=fb.high - fb.low,
...         quarter=lambda x: x.index.quarter
...     ),
...     col='quarter'
... )
```

Notice that the regression line in the fourth quarter has a much steeper slope than previous quarters:

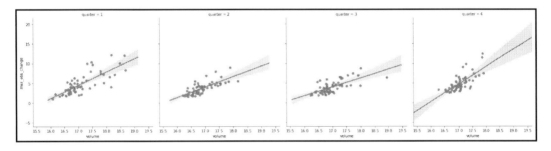

Distributions

In the *Plotting with pandas* section in the previous chapter, when we discussed how to visualize distributions, we discussed the box plot; `seaborn` provides a twist on the standard box plot, called the boxen plot, which shows additional quantiles. Let's use the boxen plot to compare earthquake magnitudes across different values for `magType`, as we did in `Chapter 5`, *Visualizing Data with Pandas and Matplotlib*:

```
>>> sns.boxenplot(
...     x='magType', y='mag', data=quakes[['magType', 'mag']]
... )
>>> plt.suptitle('Comparing earthquake magnitude by magType')
```

This results in the following plot:

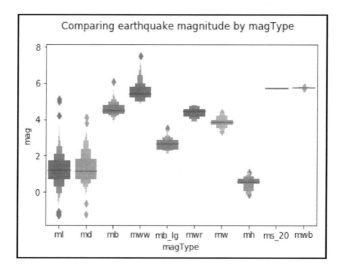

Box plots are great for visualizing the quantiles, but we lose information about the distribution. To get around this, we can use violin plots, which combine kernel density estimates (estimations of the underlying distribution) and box plots:

```
>>> fig, axes = plt.subplots(figsize=(10, 5))
>>> sns.violinplot(
...     x='magType', y='mag', data=quakes[['magType', 'mag']],
...     ax=axes, scale='width' # all violins have same width
... )
>>> plt.suptitle('Comparing earthquake magnitude by magType')
```

The box plot portion runs through the center of each violin plot; the **kernel density estimate (KDE)** is then drawn on both sides using the box plot as its *x*-axis. We can read the KDE from either side of the box plot since it is symmetrical:

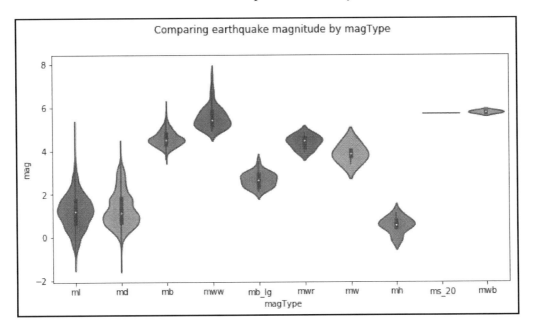

 Be sure to take a look at the distplot() function, which combines a histogram and a KDE. We will use this in Chapter 10, *Making Better Predictions – Optimizing Models*.

Faceting

Faceting allows us to plot subsets (facets) of our data across subplots. We already saw a few as a result of some seaborn functions; however, we can easily make them for ourselves with any function. Let's create a facet grid that will allow us to compare the distributions of earthquake magnitudes across the magTypes of ml and md in California, Alaska, and Hawaii.

First, we create the `FacetGrid` object with the data we will be using and define how it will be subset with the `row` and `col` arguments:

```
>>> g = sns.FacetGrid(
...     quakes[
...         (quakes.parsed_place.isin([
...             'California', 'Alaska', 'Hawaii'
...         ]))\
...         & (quakes.magType.isin(['ml', 'md']))
...     ],
...     row='magType',
...     col='parsed_place'
... )
```

Then, we use the `FacetGrid.map()` method to run a plotting function on each of the subsets, passing along any necessary arguments. We will make histograms for the state and `magType` data subsets:

```
>>> g = g.map(plt.hist, 'mag')
```

We can see that `ml` was used more than `md` and that Alaska had many more earthquakes than California and Hawaii:

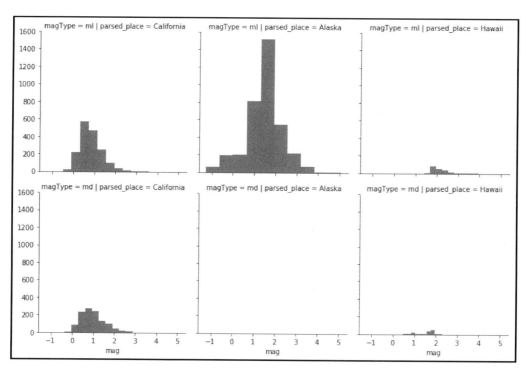

This concludes our discussion of the plotting capabilities of `seaborn`; however, I encourage you to check out their API to see additional functionality: `https://seaborn.pydata.org/api.html`. Also, be sure to consult the *Choosing the appropriate visualization* section in the appendix as a reference when looking to plot some data.

Formatting

A big part of making our visualizations presentable is choosing the right plot type and having them well labeled so they are easy to interpret. By carefully tuning the final appearance of our visualizations, we make them easier to read and understand. Note that everything in this section needs to be called before running `plt.show()` or within the same Jupyter Notebook cell if using the `%matplotlib inline` magic command.

Let's now move to the `2-formatting_plots.ipynb` notebook, run the setup code to import the packages we need, and read in the Facebook stock data:

```
>>> %matplotlib inline
>>> import matplotlib.pyplot as plt
>>> import numpy as np
>>> import pandas as pd
>>> import seaborn as sns

>>> fb = pd.read_csv(
...     'data/fb_stock_prices_2018.csv',
...     index_col='date',
...     parse_dates=True
... )
```

Titles and labels

Some of the visualizations we have created thus far didn't have titles or axis labels. We know what is going on in the figure, but if we were to present them to others, there could be some confusion. It's good practice to be explicit with our labels and titles.

We saw that, when plotting with `pandas`, we could add a title by passing the `title` argument to the `plot()` method, but we can also do this with `matplotlib` using `plt.suptitle()`. Labeling our axes is just as easy; we can use `plt.xlabel()` and `plt.ylabel()`. Let's plot the Facebook closing price and label everything using `matplotlib`:

```
>>> fb.close.plot()
>>> plt.suptitle('FB Closing Price')
>>> plt.xlabel('date')
>>> plt.ylabel('price ($)')
```

This results in the following plot:

 Note that we can pass x/y values to `plt.suptitle()` to control the placement of our text. We can also change the font and its size.

This example used `plt.<function>` for the labeling; however, the `Figure` object also has a `suptitle()` method. In addition, the `Axes` object supports both axis labeling and titles (for subplots), but the method names are different, such as `set_xlabel()`, `set_ylabel()`, and `set_title()`.

Be advised there is also a `plt.title()` function. In the previous example, the result would have been the same. However, when using subplots, `plt.title()` won't yield the expected result. Let's make subplots of Facebook stock's OHLC data and use `plt.title()` to give the entire plot a title:

```
>>> fb.iloc[:,:4].plot(subplots=True, layout=(2, 2), figsize=(12, 5))
>>> plt.title('Facebook 2018 Stock Data')
>>> plt.xlabel('date')
>>> plt.ylabel('price ($)')
```

Using `plt.title()` puts the title on the last subplot, instead of being the title for the plots as a whole, as we intended:

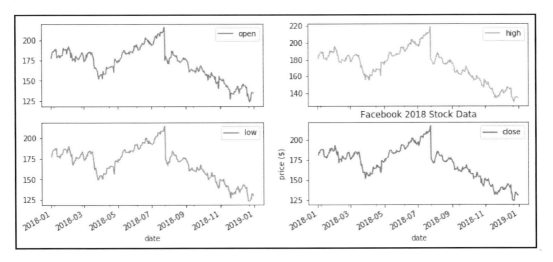

Now, let's use `plt.suptitle()` instead:

```
>>> fb.iloc[:,:4].plot(subplots=True, layout=(2, 2), figsize=(12, 5))
>>> plt.suptitle('Facebook 2018 Stock Data')
>>> plt.xlabel('date')
>>> plt.ylabel('price ($)')
```

This results in a title for the plot as a whole:

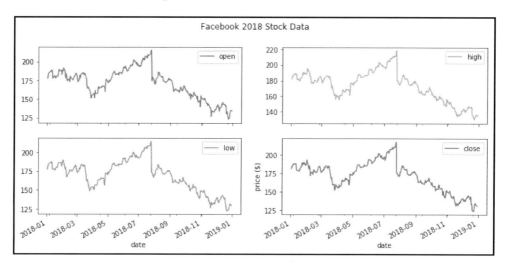

Legends

We have seen that when we have multiple columns plotted on the same plot, `pandas` automatically provides us with a legend by default. If we don't like the location of the legend, we can use `plt.legend()` to move it to a better location; when working with `Axes` objects, we also have the `legend()` method, which will work on the subplot. This can also be used to show a legend when the figure doesn't have one initially, but after the addition of reference lines, one is required for clarity.

The legend will use the label of each object that was plotted. If we don't want something to show up, we can make its label an empty string. However, if we simply want to alter how something shows up, we can pass its display name through the `label` argument. Let's plot Facebook stock's closing price and the 20-day moving average, using the `label` argument to provide a descriptive name for the legend:

```
>>> fb.assign(
...     ma=lambda x: x.close.rolling(20).mean()
... ).plot(
...     y=['close', 'ma'],
...     title='FB closing price in 2018',
...     label=['closing price', '20D moving average']
... )
>>> plt.legend(loc='lower left')
>>> plt.ylabel('price ($)')
```

This results in placing the legend in the lower-left corner of the plot with the text we provided in the `label` argument to `plot()`:

There are even more customization options here. For example, we can also format how the legend looks, including customizing the fonts, colors, and much more. Don't get overwhelmed trying to memorize everything. It is easier if we don't try to learn every possible customization, but rather look up the functionality that matches what we have in mind for our plot when needed.

Notice that we passed a string to the `loc` argument to specify the legend location we wanted; we also have the option of passing the code as an integer or a tuple for the `(x, y)` coordinates to draw the lower-left corner of the legend box. The following table contains the possible locations:

Location	Code
`'best'`	0
`'upper right'`	1
`'upper left'`	2
`'lower left'`	3
`'lower right'`	4
`'right'`	5
`'center left'`	6
`'center right'`	7
`'lower center'`	8

Location	Code
`'upper center'`	9
`'center'`	10

Formatting axes

Back in `Chapter 1`, *Introduction to Data Analysis*, we discussed how our axis limits can make for misleading plots if we aren't careful. With `matplotlib`, we can adjust the limits of each axis with `plt.xlim()` and `plt.ylim()`. We pass values for the minimum and maximum, separately; if we want to keep what was automatically generated, we can pass `None`. Let's plot Facebook stock's closing price and start the *y*-axis at zero:

```
>>> fb.open.plot(figsize=(10, 3), title='FB opening price 2018')
>>> plt.ylim(0, None)
>>> plt.ylabel('price ($)')
```

Notice that the *y*-axis now begins at zero:

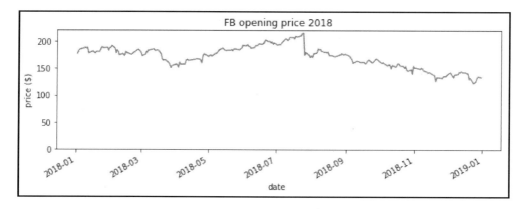

We also have the option of passing this as a tuple to the `xlim`/`ylim` arguments to the `plot()` method from `pandas` or calling the `set_xlim()`/`set_ylim()` method on an `Axes` object.

If we instead want to change the scale of the axis, we can use `plt.xscale()` and `plt.yscale()` and pass the type of scale we want. So, `plt.yscale('log')`, for example, will make the *y*-axis use the log scale; we saw how to do this with `pandas` in the previous chapter.

We can also control which tick marks show up and what they are labeled as. First, we plot our figure and then use `plt.xticks()` or `plt.yticks()` to obtain the tick locations and labels. Using these, we can modify them before passing them back to the same function. For example, let's move the tick mark of the Facebook open price plot to the 15th of each month and then label each month with its name. As a final twist, we will only show every other month:

```
>>> import calendar

>>> fb.open.plot(
...      figsize=(10, 3),
...      rot=0,
...      title='FB opening price 2018'
... )
>>> locs, labels = plt.xticks()
>>> plt.xticks(locs + 15, calendar.month_name[1::2])
>>> plt.ylabel('price ($)')
```

Note that the `calendar` module has January as the month name at index 1 (not at 0). This is for easy lookup when working with months as integers. We now have month names on the *x*-axis in the resulting plot:

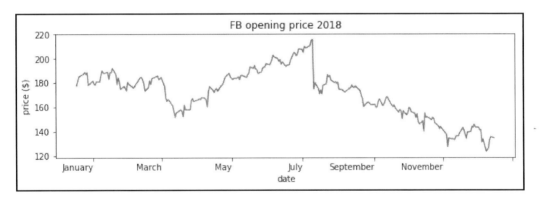

When dealing with numeric values on our axes, we may want ways to format percentages or make sure that only integers are shown. This, and much more, is possible with the `ticker` module:

```
>>> import matplotlib.ticker as ticker
```

Let's say we wanted to plot the Facebook closing price each day as a percentage of the highest price it had throughout the data. The shape of the curve will be the same, but the values on the *y*-axis will need to be represented as percentages. We can use the PercentFormatter from ticker and provide the highest value to xmax for it to calculate and display the percentages for us:

```
>>> ax = fb.close.plot(
...     figsize=(10, 4),
...     title='Facebook Closing Price as Percentage of '\
...         'Highest Price in Time Range'
... )
>>> ax.yaxis.set_major_formatter(
...     ticker.PercentFormatter(xmax=fb.high.max())
... )
>>> ax.set_yticks([
...     fb.high.max()*pct for pct in np.linspace(0.6, 1, num=5)
... ]) # show round percentages only (60%, 80%, etc.)
>>> ax.set_ylabel(f'percent of highest price (${fb.high.max()})')
```

This results in percentages along the *y*-axis:

Also, notice the method we used on the Axes object, after selecting the *y*-axis, to do this: set_major_formatter(). The major ticks are larger than the minor ones, which may not even be present. We will often only label the major ones, but we can do both if we wish.

We can also change how the *x*-axis is formatted. Say that we have the following plot:

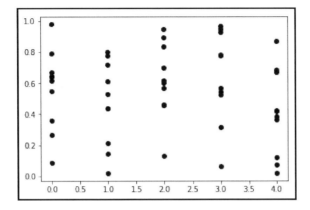

It seems pretty obvious that the x value can only be an integer, yet we have floats for the labels. Let's fix that so it doesn't confuse anyone by using the `MultipleLocator` to hide the ticks at non-integer locations:

```
>>> fig, ax = plt.subplots(1, 1)
>>> np.random.seed(0) # make repeatable
>>> ax.plot(np.tile(np.arange(0, 5), 10), np.random.rand(50), 'ko')
>>> ax.get_xaxis().set_major_locator(ticker.MultipleLocator(base=1))
```

Here, we aren't formatting the axis labels, but rather controlling which ones are shown; for this reason, we have to call `set_major_locator()` instead of `set_major_formatter()`. Finally, notice that we have the option of specifying a base number to determine the multiples, so if we only wanted to show even numbers, we can set that to 2. Since we passed in `base=1`, our *x*-axis now contains integers in increments of one:

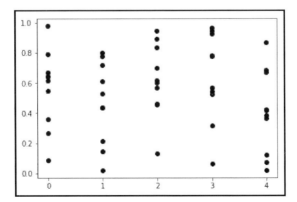

Note that we have the option of accessing the axis to format through an attribute on the `Axes` object (`xaxis`/`yaxis`) or using a method call (`get_xaxis()`/`get_yaxis()`).

These were only two of the features provided with `ticker`, so I highly recommend you check out the documentation for more information. There is also a link in the *Further reading* section at the end of this chapter.

Customizing visualizations

So far, all of the code we've learned for creating data visualizations has been for making the visualization itself, and we didn't deal with customizations such as reference lines, colors, and annotations. That all changes now.

Let's handle our imports and read in the data we will be working with for this section in the `3-customizing_visualizations.ipynb` notebook:

```
>>> %matplotlib inline
>>> import matplotlib.pyplot as plt
>>> import pandas as pd

>>> fb = pd.read_csv(
...     'data/fb_stock_prices_2018.csv',
...     index_col='date',
...     parse_dates=True
... )

>>> quakes = pd.read_csv('data/earthquakes.csv')
```

Before we jump into some specific customization tasks, let's discuss how to change the style in which the plots are created. This is an easy way to change their look and feel without setting each aspect separately. To set the style for `seaborn`, use `sns.set_style()`. With `matplotlib`, we can use `plt.style.use()` to specify the stylesheet(s) we want to use. These will be used for all visualizations created in that session. If, instead, we only want it for a single plot, we can use `sns.set_context()` or `plt.style.context()`. Available styles for `seaborn` can be found in the documentation of the aforementioned functions and in `matplotlib` by taking a look at the values in `plt.style.available`.

Adding reference lines

Quite often, we want to draw attention to a specific value on our plot, perhaps as a boundary or turning point. We may be interested in whether the line gets crossed or serves as a partition. In finance, horizontal reference lines may be drawn on top of the line plot of a stock's price, marking the support and the resistance.

The **support** is a price level at which a downward trend is expected to reverse because the stock is now at a price level at which buyers are more enticed to purchase, driving the price up and away from this point. On the flip side, the **resistance** is the price level at which an upward trend is expected to reverse since the price is an attractive selling point; thus the price falls down and away from this point. Of course, this is not to say these levels don't get surpassed. Since we have Facebook stock data, let's add the support and resistance reference lines to our line plot of the closing price.

Going over how support and resistance are calculated is beyond the scope of this chapter, but Chapter 7, *Financial Analysis – Bitcoin and the Stock Market*, will include some code for calculating these using pivot points. Also, be sure to check out the *Further reading* section for a more in-depth introduction to support and resistance.

Our two horizontal reference lines will be at the support of $124.46 and the resistance of $138.53. Both these numbers were derived using the stock_analysis package that we will build in Chapter 7, *Financial Analysis – Bitcoin and the Stock Market*. We simply need to create an instance of the StockAnalyzer class to calculate these metrics:

```
>>> from stock_analysis import StockAnalyzer

>>> fb_analyzer = StockAnalyzer(fb)
>>> support, resistance = (
...     getattr(fb_analyzer, stat)(level=3) for stat in [
...         'support', 'resistance'
...     ]
... )
>>> support, resistance
(124.4566666666667, 138.5266666666667)
```

We will use `plt.axhline()` for this task, but note that this will also work on the `Axes` object. The text we provide to the `label` arguments will be populated in the legend:

```
>>> fb.close['2018-12'].plot(title='FB Closing Price December 2018')
>>> plt.axhline(
...         y=resistance, color='r', linestyle='--',
...         label=f'resistance (${resistance:,.2f})'
... )
>>> plt.axhline(
...         y=support, color='g', linestyle='--',
...         label=f'support (${support:,.2f})'
... )
>>> plt.ylabel('price ($)')
>>> plt.legend()
```

We should already be familiar with the f-string format from earlier chapters, but notice the additional text after the variable name here (`:,.2f`). The support and resistance are stored as floats in the `support` and `resistance` variables, respectively. The `:` precedes the `format_spec`, which tells Python how to format that variable; in this case, we are formatting it as a decimal (`f`) with a comma as the thousands separator (`,`) and two digits of precision after the decimal (`.2`). This will also work with `format()`, so, for an older version of Python, it would look like `'{:,.2f}'.format(resistance)`. This formatting makes for an informative legend in our plot:

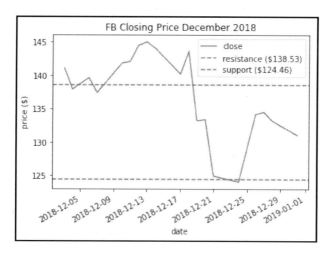

Those with personal investment accounts will likely find some literature there on support and resistance when looking to place limit orders or stop losses based on the stock hitting a certain price point since these can help inform the feasibility of the target price. In addition, these reference lines may be used by traders to analyze the stock's momentum and decide whether it is time to buy/sell the stock.

Let's use `plt.axvline()` to draw vertical reference lines for the number of standard deviations from the mean on the distribution of earthquake magnitudes in Indonesia with the `magType` of `mb`. The `std_from_mean_kde()` function located in the `std_from_mean_kde.py` module in the GitHub repository uses `itertools` to easily make the combinations of the colors and values we need to plot:

```python
import itertools

def std_from_mean_kde(data):
    """
    Plot the KDE of the pandas series along with vertical
    reference lines for each standard deviation from the mean.

    Parameters:
        - data: pandas Series with numeric data

    Returns: Matplotlib Axes object.
    """
    mean_mag, std_mean = data.mean(), data.std()

    ax = data.plot(kind='kde')
    ax.axvline(mean_mag, color='b', alpha=0.2, label='mean')

    colors = ['green', 'orange', 'red']
    multipliers = [1, 2, 3]
    signs = ['-', '+']
```

```
        for sign, (color, multiplier) in itertools.product(
            signs, zip(colors, multipliers)
        ):
            adjustment = multiplier * std_mean
            if sign == '-':
                value = mean_mag - adjustment
                label = '{} {}{}{}'.format(
                    r'$\mu$', r'$\pm$', multiplier, r'$\sigma$'
                )
            else:
                value = mean_mag + adjustment
                label = None # label each color only once

            ax.axvline(value, color=color, label=label, alpha=0.5)

    ax.legend()
    return ax
```

The `product()` function from `itertools` will give us all combinations of items from any number of iterables. Here, we have zipped the colors and multipliers since we always want `green` to be a multiplier of 1, `orange` to be 2, and `red` to be 3; when `product()` uses these tuples, we get positive- and negative-signed combinations for everything. To keep our legend from getting too crowded, we only label each color once using the ± sign. Since we have combinations between a string and a tuple at each iteration, we unpack the tuple in our `for` statement for easier use.

We can use LaTeX math symbols (`https://www.latex-project.org/`) to label our plots if we follow a certain pattern. First, we must mark the string as `raw` by preceding it with the `r` character. Then, we must surround the LaTeX with `$`. For example, we used `r'$\mu$'` for the Greek letter μ in the preceding code.

Let's use the `std_from_mean_kde()` function to see which parts of the estimated distribution of earthquake magnitudes in Indonesia are within one, two, or three standard deviations from the mean:

```
>>> from std_from_mean_kde import std_from_mean_kde
>>> ax = std_from_mean_kde(
...     quakes.query(
...         'magType == "mb" and parsed_place == "Indonesia"'
...     ).mag
... )
>>> ax.set_title('mb magnitude distribution in Indonesia')
>>> ax.set_xlabel('mb earthquake magnitude')
```

Notice the KDE is right skewed—it has a longer tail on the right side, and the mean is to the right of the mode:

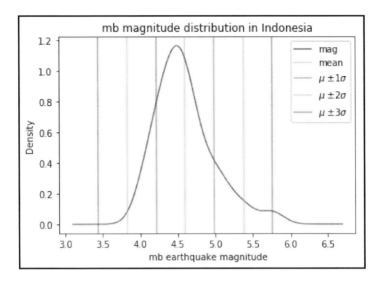

Now, we know how to make horizontal and vertical reference lines; however, we may want to make a line with an arbitrary slope as a reference. With Python, we just run `plot()` again with the same `Axes` object and all the `(x, y)` values for the line. For a straight line, we simply need to specify the endpoints of the line as two `x` values (`[0, 2]`) and two `y` values (`[2, 0]`):

```
>>> plt.plot([0, 2], [2, 0]) # or ax.plot() with Axes object in ax
>>> plt.suptitle('straight line')
>>> plt.xlabel('x')
>>> plt.ylabel('y')
```

This will result in the following diagonal line:

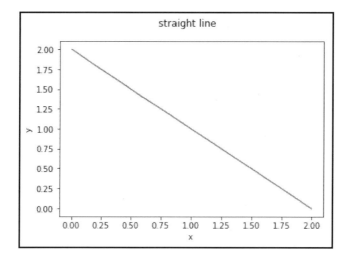

For lines that aren't straight, `np.linspace()` can be used to create a range of evenly-spaced points on `[start, stop)`, which can be used for the x values. These can be used to calculate the y values. As a reminder, when specifying a range, `[]` mean inclusive of both endpoints and `()` are exclusive, so `[0, 1)` goes from 0 to as close to 1 as possible without being 1. We see these when using `pd.cut()` and `pd.qcut()` if we don't name the buckets.

Shading regions

In some cases, the reference line itself isn't so interesting, but the area between two of them is; for this purpose, we have `axvspan()` and `axhspan()`. Let's revisit the resistance and support of the Facebook stock. We can use `axhspan()` to shade the area that falls between the two:

```
>>> ax = fb.close.plot(title='FB Closing Price')
>>> ax.axhspan(support, resistance, alpha=0.2)
>>> plt.ylabel('Price ($)')
```

This results in the following plot:

 The color of the rectangle is determined by the `facecolor` argument.

When we are interested in shading the area between two curves, we can use `plt.fill_between()` and `plt.fill_betweenx()`. Let's shade the area between Facebook's high price and low price each day of the fourth quarter using `plt.fill_between()`:

```
>>> fb_q4 = fb['2018-Q4']
>>> plt.fill_between(fb_q4.index, fb_q4.high, fb_q4.low)
>>> ticks = ['2018-10-01', '2018-11-01', '2018-12-01', '2019-01-01']
>>> plt.xticks(ticks, ticks)
>>> plt.xlabel('date')
>>> plt.ylabel('price ($)')
>>> plt.suptitle('FB differential between high and low price Q4 2018')
```

This gives us a better idea of the variation in price on a given day; the taller the vertical distance, the higher the fluctuation:

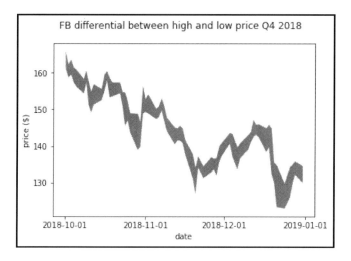

By providing a Boolean mask to the where argument, we can specify when to fill the area between the curves. Let's fill in only December from the previous example. We will add dashed lines for the high price curve and the low price curve throughout the time period to see what is happening:

```
>>> fb_q4 = fb['2018-Q4']
>>> plt.fill_between(
...     fb_q4.index,
...     fb_q4.high,
...     fb_q4.low,
...     where=fb_q4.index.month == 12,
...     color='khaki',
...     label='December differential'
... )
>>> plt.plot(fb_q4.index, fb_q4.high, 'g--', label='daily high')
>>> plt.plot(fb_q4.index, fb_q4.low, 'r--', label='daily low')
>>> ticks = ['2018-10-01', '2018-11-01', '2018-12-01', '2019-01-01']
>>> plt.xticks(ticks, ticks)
>>> plt.xlabel('date')
>>> plt.ylabel('price ($)')
>>> plt.legend()
>>> plt.suptitle('FB differential between high and low price Q4 2018')
```

This results in the following plot:

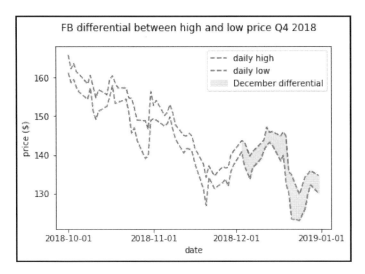

 The `plt.fill_between()` function accepts one set of x values and two sets of y values; we can use `plt.fill_betweenx()` if we require the opposite.

Annotations

We will often find the need to annotate specific points in our visualizations either to point out events, such as the days on which Facebook's stock price dropped due to certain news stories breaking or labeling values that are important for comparisons. For example, let's use the `plt.annotate()` function to label the support and resistance:

```
>>> ax = fb.close.plot(title='FB Closing Price 2018', figsize=(15, 3))
>>> ax.axhspan(support, resistance, alpha=0.2)
>>> plt.annotate(
...     f'support\n(${support:,.2f})',
...     xy=('2018-12-31', support),
...     xytext=('2019-01-21', support),
...     arrowprops={'arrowstyle' : '->'}
... )
```

```
>>> plt.annotate(
...     f'resistance\n(${resistance:,.2f})',
...     xy=('2018-12-23', resistance)
... )
>>> plt.ylabel('price ($)')
```

Notice the annotations are different; when we annotated the resistance, we only provided the text for the annotation and the coordinates of the point being annotated with the xy argument. However, when we annotated the support, we also provided values for the xytext and arrowprops arguments; this allowed us to put the text somewhere other than where the value occurred and add an arrow that points to where it occurred. By doing so, we avoid obscuring the last few days of data with our label:

The arrowprops argument gives us quite a bit of customization over the type of arrow we want, although it might be difficult to get it perfect. As an example, let's annotate the big decline in the price of Facebook in July with the percentage drop:

```
>>> close_price = fb.loc['2018-07-25', 'close']
>>> open_price = fb.loc['2018-07-26', 'open']
>>> pct_drop = (open_price - close_price)/close_price
>>> fb.close.plot(title='FB Closing Price 2018', alpha=0.5)
>>> plt.annotate(
...     f'{pct_drop:.2%}',
...     xy=('2018-07-27', (open_price + close_price)/2),
...     xytext=('2018-08-20', (open_price + close_price)/2 - 1.5),
...     arrowprops=dict(arrowstyle='-[,widthB=4.0,lengthB=0.2')
... )
>>> plt.ylabel('price ($)')
```

Notice that we were able to format the `pct_drop` variable as a percentage with two digits of precision by using `.2%` in the `format_spec` of the f-string:

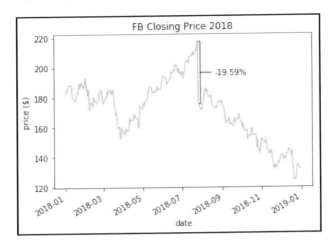

We can also customize colors and fonts used in the annotations. To change colors, simply pass the desired color in the `color` argument. We can also control font size, weight, family, and style through the `fontsize`, `fontweight`, `fontfamily`, and `fontstyle` arguments, respectively. We can pass any option that the `Text` class in `matplotlib` supports (`https://matplotlib.org/api/text_api.html#matplotlib.text.Text`). There is also an example in the notebook for this section.

Colors

For the sake of consistency, the visualizations we produce should stick to a color scheme. Companies and academic institutions alike often have custom color palettes for presentations. We can easily adopt the same color palette in our visualizations too.

So far, we have either been providing colors to the `color` argument with their single character names, such as `'b'` for blue and `'k'` for black, or their names (`'blue'` or `'black'`), but can we use different colors, such as seafoam green or crimson? Well, `matplotlib` has many colors that can be specified by name; these can be found in the documentation at `https://matplotlib.org/examples/color/named_colors.html`.

Remember that if we are providing a color with the `style` argument, we are limited to the colors that have a single-character abbreviation.

If we take a look at the named colors, we will notice that it contains only a small subset of colors that we can create, so how can `matplotlib` support all the possible colors? Well, we can also provide a hex code for the color we want; those who have worked with HTML or CSS in the past will no doubt be familiar with these as a way to specify the exact color (regardless of what different places call it). For those unfamiliar with a hex color code, it specifies the amount of red, green, and blue used to make the color in question in the #RRGGBB format. Black is #000000 and white is #FFFFFF (case-insensitive). This may be confusing because F is most definitely not a number; however, these are hexadecimal numbers (base 16, not the base 10 we traditionally use), where 0-9 represents 0-9, but A-F represents 10-15. Matplotlib accepts hex codes as a string to the `color` argument.

To illustrate this, let's plot Facebook's opening price in #8000FF:

```
>>> fb.plot(
...     kind='line',
...     y='open',
...     figsize=(5, 3),
...     color='#8000FF',
...     legend=False,
...     title='Evolution of FB Opening Price in 2018'
... )
>>> plt.ylabel('price ($)')
```

This results in a purple line plot:

Finally, we may be given the values in RGB or **red, green, blue, alpha (RGBA)** values, in which case we can pass them to the `color` argument as a tuple. If we don't provide the `alpha`, it will default to 1 for opaque. One thing to note here is that, while we will find these numbers presented on the range [0, 255], `matplotlib` requires them to be on the range [0, 1], so we must divide each by 255. The following code is equivalent to the preceding example, except we use the RGB tuple instead of the hex code:

```
fb.plot(
    kind='line',
    y='open',
    figsize=(5, 3),
    color=(128/255, 0, 1),
    legend=False,
    title='Evolution of FB Opening Price in 2018'
)
```

 Browse colors by name, hex, and RGB values at `https://www.color-hex.com/`.

In the previous chapter, we saw several examples in which we needed many different colors for the varying data we were plotting, but where do these colors come from? Well, `matplotlib` has numerous colormaps that are used for this purpose. Rather than having to specify all the colors we want to use up front, `matplotlib` can take a colormap and cycle through the colors there. When we discussed heatmaps in the previous chapter, we considered the importance of using the proper class of colormap for the given task. There are three types of colormaps, each with their own purpose as shown in the following table:

Class	Purpose
Qualitative	No ordering or relationship between colors; just used to distinguish between groups
Sequential	For information with ordering, such as temperature
Diverging	There is a middle value between two extremes that has meaning; for example, correlation coefficients are bounded in the range [-1, 1], and 0 has meaning (no correlation)

Find the color spectrum for the colormaps at `https://matplotlib.org/gallery/color/colormap_reference.html`.

In Python, we can obtain a list of all the available colormaps by running the following code:

```
>>> from matplotlib import cm
>>> cm.datad.keys()
dict_keys(['Blues', 'BrBG', 'BuGn', 'BuPu', 'CMRmap', 'GnBu',
           'Greens', 'Greys', 'OrRd', 'Oranges', 'PRGn', 'PiYG',
           'PuBu', 'PuBuGn', 'PuOr', 'PuRd', 'Purples', 'RdBu',
           'RdGy', 'RdPu', 'RdYlBu', 'RdYlGn', 'Reds', ...,
           'Blues_r', 'BrBG_r', 'BuGn_r', ...])
```

Notice that some of the colormaps are present twice where one is in the reverse order, signified by the _r suffix on the name. This is very helpful since we don't have to invert our data to map the values to the colors we want. Pandas accepts these colormaps as strings or `matplotlib` colormaps with the `colormap` argument of the `plot()` method.

Let's use the `coolwarm_r` colormap to show how Facebook stock's closing price oscillates between the 20-day rolling minimum and maximum prices:

```
>>> ax = fb.assign(
...     rolling_min=lambda x: x.low.rolling(20).min(),
...     rolling_max=lambda x: x.high.rolling(20).max(),
... ).plot(
...     y=['rolling_max', 'rolling_min'],
...     colormap=cm.coolwarm_r,
...     label=['20D rolling max', '20D rolling min'],
...     figsize=(12, 3),
...     title='FB closing price in 2018 oscillating between '\
...         '20-day rolling minimum and maximum price'
... )
>>> ax.plot(fb.close, 'purple', alpha=0.25, label='closing price')
>>> plt.legend()
>>> plt.ylabel('price ($)')
```

This results in the following plot with the `coolwarm_r` colormap:

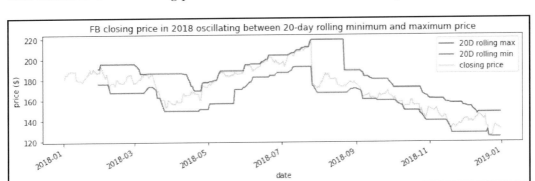

Notice how easy it was to get red to represent hot performance (rolling maximum) and blue for cold (rolling minimum), by using the reversed colormap, rather than trying to make sure `pandas` plotted the rolling minimum first.

We could have passed `colormap=cm.get_cmap('coolwarm_r')` or `colormap='coolwarm_r'` instead and gotten the same result.

The `colormap` object is a callable, meaning we can pass it values in [0, 1] and it will tell us the RGBA value for that point in the colormap, which we can use for the `color` argument. This gives us more fine-tuned control over the colors that we use from the colormap. We can use this technique to control how we spread the colormap across our data. For example, we can ask for the midpoint of the `ocean` colormap to use for the `color` argument:

```
>>> cm.get_cmap('ocean')(.5)
(0.0, 0.2529411764705882, 0.5019607843137255, 1.0)
>>> fb.close.plot(
...      color=cm.get_cmap('ocean')(.5),
...      title='FB closing price 2018'
... )
>>> plt.ylabel('price ($)')
```

This gives us the following plot with a dark blue line instead of a green one, which we would have gotten if we hadn't picked a specific point in the colormap:

Despite the wealth of colormaps available, we may find the need to create our own. Perhaps we have a color palette we like to work with or have some requirement that we use a specific color scheme. We can make our own colormaps with `matplotlib`. Let's make a two-color sequential colormap that goes from a pastel blue (#B2E4DF) to a pastel purple (#C2C1E1). All the functions we need for this are in `color_utils.py` in the GitHub repository for this chapter. We can import the functions like this if we are running Python from the same directory as the file:

```
>>> import color_utils
```

Remember, running `help(color_utils)` will show information about the module and what's in it.

First, we need to translate these hex colors to their RGB equivalents, which is what the hex_to_rgb_color_list() function will do:

```python
import re

def hex_to_rgb_color_list(colors):
    """
    Take color or list of hex code colors and convert them
    to RGB colors in the range [0,1].

    Parameters:
        - colors: Color or list of color strings as hex codes

    Returns: The color or list of colors in RGB representation.
    """
    if isinstance(colors, str):
        colors = [colors]

    for i, color in enumerate(
        [color.replace('#', '') for color in colors]
    ):
        hex_length = len(color)

        if hex_length not in [3, 6]:
            raise ValueError(
                'Your colors must be of the form #FFFFFF or #FFF'
            )
        regex = '.' * (hex_length // 3)
        colors[i] = [
            int(val * (6 // hex_length), 16)/255 \
            for val in re.findall(regex, color)
        ]
    return colors[0] if len(colors) == 1 else colors
```

Notice how easy it is for Python to give us the base 10 representation of hexadecimal numbers with the int() function by specifying the base. This function will also be able to handle the shorthand hex codes of three digits when the RGB values use the same hexadecimal digit for both of the digits (#F1D is the shorthand equivalent of #FF11DD). Also, take a look at the enumerate() function; this lets us grab the index and the value at that index when we iterate, rather than look up the value in the loop.

 Remember that // is integer division. We have to do this since int() expects an integer and not a float.

The next function we need is one to take those RGB colors and create the values for the colormap; this is what the `two_color_sequential_cmap()` function does:

```
from matplotlib.colors import ListedColormap
import numpy as np

def two_color_sequential_cmap(rgb_color_list):
    """
    Created a sequential colormap blending from one color to
    the other.

    Parameters:
        - rgb_color_list: A list of colors represented as [R, G, B]
                          values in the range [0, 1], like
                          [[0, 0, 0], [1, 1, 1]], for black
                          and white, respectively.

    Returns:
        A matplotlib ListedColormap object with your colormap.
    """
    if not isinstance(rgb_color_list, list):
        raise ValueError('Colors must be passed as a list!')
    elif len(rgb_color_list) != 2:
        raise ValueError(
            'Can only specify two colors; '
            'one for each end of the spectrum.'
        )
    elif (
        not isinstance(rgb_color_list[0], list) \
        or not isinstance(rgb_color_list[1], list)
    ) or (
        len(rgb_color_list[0]) != 3 or len(rgb_color_list[1]) != 3
    ):
        raise ValueError(
            'Each color should be represented as a list of size 3.'
        )

    N = 256
    entries = 4 # red, green, blue, alpha
    rgbas = np.ones((N, entries))
    for i in range(entries - 1): # we don't alter alphas
        rgbas[:, i] = np.linspace(
            start=rgb_color_list[0][i],
            stop=rgb_color_list[1][i],
            num=N
        )

    return ListedColormap(rgbas)
```

First, it creates a 4D `numpy` array with 256 slots for color definitions. We don't want to change the transparency so we leave the last dimension (alpha) alone. Then, for each dimension in red, green, and blue, we use the `linspace()` function from NumPy to create 256 evenly-spaced values starting at the value our first color has for the given RGB component and ending at the value for the other color at the same RGB component. This function then returns a `ListedColormap` object that we can use in plotting.

We can use the `draw_cmap()` function to draw a colorbar, which allows us to visualize our colormap:

```
import matplotlib.pyplot as plt

def draw_cmap(cmap):
    """
    Draw a colorbar for visualizing a colormap.

    Parameters:
        - cmap: A matplotlib colormap

    Returns:
        A matplotlib colorbar, which you can save with:
        `plt.savefig(<file_name>, bbox_inches='tight')`
    """
    img = plt.imshow(np.array([[0,1]]), cmap=cmap)
    cbar = plt.colorbar(orientation='horizontal', cmap=cmap)
    img.axes.remove()
    return cbar
```

Now, let's use these functions to create and visualize our colormap. We will be using them by importing the module (which we did earlier):

```
>>> my_edge_colors = ['#B2E4DF', '#C2C1E1']
>>> rgbs = color_utils.hex_to_rgb_color_list(my_edge_colors)
>>> my_cmap = color_utils.two_color_sequential_cmap(rgbs)
>>> color_utils.draw_cmap(my_cmap)
```

This results in the following colorbar showing our colormap:

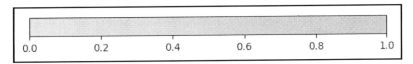

It was pretty easy to create a colormap with just two colors, but if we want to add more, we will have to decide when to transition between them and adjust our calls to `np.linspace()`. For example, if we want three colors, we will have to adjust the number of values we generate to half the full value so that we transition from color one to color two for the first half and from color two to color three in the second half. This would require altering the content of the `for` loop in our function. The `color_utils.py` module also contains the `blended_cmap()` function, which will accept two or more colors and create an evenly-blended colormap:

```python
def blended_cmap(rgb_color_list):
    """
    Create a colormap blending from one color to the other.

    Parameters:
        - rgb_color_list: A list of colors represented as [R, G, B]
                          values in the range [0, 1], like
                          [[0, 0, 0], [1, 1, 1]], for black and white,
                          respectively.

    Returns: A matplotlib ListedColormap object with your colormap.
    """
    if not isinstance(rgb_color_list, list):
        raise ValueError('Colors must be passed as a list!')
    elif len(rgb_color_list) < 2:
        raise ValueError('Must specify at least 2 colors.')
    elif (
        not isinstance(rgb_color_list[0], list) \
        or not isinstance(rgb_color_list[1], list)
    ) or (len(rgb_color_list[0]) != 3 or len(rgb_color_list[1]) != 3):
        raise ValueError(
            'Each color should be represented as a list of size 3.'
        )

    N, entries = 256, 4 # red, green, blue, alpha
    rgbas = np.ones((N, entries))

    segment_count = len(rgb_color_list) - 1
    segment_size = N // segment_count
    remainder = N % segment_count # need to add this back later

    for i in range(entries - 1): # we don't alter alphas
        updates = []
        for seg in range(1, segment_count + 1):
            # handle uneven splits due to remainder
            offset = 0 if not remainder or seg > 1 else remainder
```

```
        updates.append(np.linspace(
            start=rgb_color_list[seg-1][i],
            stop=rgb_color_list[seg][i],
            num=segment_size + offset
        ))
    rgbas[:,i] = np.concatenate(updates)

    return ListedColormap(rgbas)
```

We can use this just like the other function:

```
>>> my_colors = [
...     '#00F', '#B2E4DF', '#C2C1E1', 'C0C0C0', 'EEE', '000000'
... ]
>>> rgbs = color_utils.hex_to_rgb_color_list(my_colors)
>>> my_cmap = color_utils.blended_cmap(rgbs)
>>> color_utils.draw_cmap(my_cmap)
```

Notice how we can use colors with or without the # symbol, in shorthand, or in the full form, to create the following colorbar:

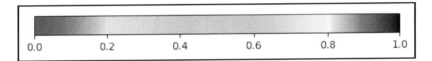

> Seaborn also provides additional color palettes, along with handy utilities for picking colormaps, and making custom ones for use with matplotlib interactively in a Jupyter Notebook. See this tutorial for more information: https://seaborn.pydata.org/tutorial/color_palettes.html. There is also a short example in the notebook for this section.

As we have seen in the colorbars we created, these colormaps had the ability to show different gradients of the colors to capture values on a continuum. If we merely want each line in our line plot to be a different color, we most likely want to cycle between different colors. For that, we can use itertools.cycle() with a list of colors; they won't be blended, but we can cycle through them endlessly because it will be an infinite iterator. We used this technique earlier in the chapter to define our own colors for the regression residuals plots:

```
>>> import itertools
>>> colors = itertools.cycle(['#ffffff', '#f0f0f0', '#000000'])
```

```
>>> colors
<itertools.cycle at 0x1fe4f300>
>>> next(colors)
'#ffffff'
```

The `matplotlib` alternative to this would be to make a `ListedColormap` and define a large value for N so that it repeats for long enough (if we don't provide it, it will only go through the colors once):

```
>>> from matplotlib.colors import ListedColormap
>>> red_black = ListedColormap(['red', 'black'], N=2000)
>>> [red_black(i) for i in range(3)]
[(1.0, 0.0, 0.0, 1.0), (0.0, 0.0, 0.0, 1.0), (1.0, 0.0, 0.0, 1.0)]
```

What happens if we only want to use a color when certain conditions are met? In this case, we could write a **generator**, which will determine which color we need and only calculate it when it is asked for. We don't want to make a list of colors the same length as the number of things we want to plot if it is large. By using generators, we are being efficient with memory without crowding our plotting code with the color logic. Let's say we wanted to assign colors to years from 1992 to 200018 (no, that's not a typo) based on whether they were leap years, and distinguish why they weren't leap years (we want a special color for the case that happens every 100 years); we certainly don't want to keep a list this size in memory, so we create a generator by doing the following:

```
def color_generator():
    for year in range(1992, 200019): # integers in [1992, 200019)
        if year % 100 == 0 and year % 400 != 0:
            # special case (divisible by 100 but not 400)
            color = '#f0f0f0'
        elif year % 4 == 0:
            # leap year (divisible by 4)
            color = '#000000'
        else:
            color = '#ffffff'
        yield color
```

The **modulo operator** (`%`) returns the remainder of a division operation. For example, `4 % 2` equals 0 because 4 is divisible by 2. However, since 4 is not divisible by 3, `4 % 3` is non-zero; it is 1 because we can fit 3 into 4 once and will have 1 leftover (4 − 3). The modulo operator can be used to check for divisibility of one number by another and is often used to check if a number is odd or even. Here, we are using it to see if the conditions for being a leap year (which depend on divisibility) are met.

Notice that a generator is defined as a function, but instead of using `return`, it uses `yield`. This means that Python will remember where we were in this function and resume when `next()` is called:

```
>>> year_colors = color_generator()
>>> year_colors
<generator object color_generator at 0x207B5750>
>>> next(year_colors)
'#000000'
```

Simpler generators can be written with **generator expressions**. For example, if we don't care about the special case anymore, we can run the following commands:

```
>>> year_colors = (
...     '#ffffff' \
...     if (not year % 100 and year % 400) or year % 4 \
...     else '#000000' for year in range(1992, 200019)
... )
>>> year_colors
<generator object <genexpr> at 0x1FEA4150>
>>> next(year_colors)
'#000000'
```

Those not coming from Python might find it strange that our Boolean conditions in the previous code snippet are actually numbers (`year % 400` results in an integer). This is taking advantage of Python's `truthy`/`falsey` values; values that have zero value (such as the number 0) or are empty (such as `[]` or `' '`) are `falsey`. Therefore, while in the first generator, we wrote `year % 400 != 0` to show exactly what was going on; the more **Pythonic** way is `year % 400`, since if there is no remainder (evaluates to 0), the statement will be evaluated as `False`, and vice versa. Obviously, we will have times where we must choose between readability and being Pythonic, but it's good to be aware of how to write Pythonic code, as it will often be more efficient.

Run `import this` in Python to see **the Zen of Python**, which gives some ideas of what it means to be Pythonic.

Even simpler would be the case where we have a list of colors somewhere, but rather than putting that in our plotting code and storing another copy in memory, we can write a simple generator function that just yields from that master list. The following snippet shows a mock-up for this scenario, which is similar to the `itertools` solution; however, it is not infinite:

```
from my_plotting_module import master_color_list

def color_generator():
    yield from master_color_list
```

This just goes to show that we can find many ways to do something in Python; we have to find the implementation that best meets our needs.

Summary

Whew, that was a lot! We learned how to create impressive and customized visualizations using `matplotlib`, `pandas`, and `seaborn`. We discussed how we can use `seaborn` for additional plotting types and cleaner versions of some familiar ones. Now we can easily make our own colormaps, annotate our plots, add reference lines and shaded regions, finesse the axes/legends/titles, and control most aspects of how our visualizations will appear. We also got a taste of working with `itertools` and creating our own generators.

Take some time to practice what we've discussed with the following exercises. In the next chapter, we will apply all that we have learned to finance, as we build our own Python package and compare bitcoin to the stock market.

Exercises

Create the following visualizations using what we have learned so far in this book and the data from this chapter. Be sure to add titles, axis labels, and legends (where needed) to the plots:

1. Using `seaborn`, create a heatmap to visualize the correlation coefficients between earthquake magnitude and whether there was a tsunami with the `magType` of mb.

2. Create a box plot of Facebook volume traded and closing prices, and draw reference lines for the bounds of a Tukey fence with a multiplier of 1.5. The bounds will be at `Q1 - 1.5 * IQR` and `Q3 + 1.5 * IQR`. Be sure to use the `quantile()` method on the data to make this easier. (Pick whichever orientation you prefer for the plot, but make sure to use subplots.)

3. Fill in the area between the bounds in the plot from exercise #2.

4. Use `axvspan()` to shade a rectangle from `'2018-07-25'` to `'2018-07-31'`, which marks the large decline in Facebook price on a line plot of the closing price.

5. Using the Facebook stock price data, annotate the following three events on a line plot of the closing price:
   - **Disappointing user growth announced after close** on July 25, 2018
   - **Cambridge Analytica story breaks** on March 19, 2018 (when it affected the market)
   - **FTC launches investigation** on March 20, 2018

6. Modify the `reg_resid_plots()` function to use a `matplotlib` colormap instead of cycling between two colors. Remember, for this use case, we should pick a qualitative colormap or make our own.

Further reading

Check out the following resources for more information on the topics covered in this chapter:

- *Choosing Colormaps*: `https://matplotlib.org/users/colormaps.html`
- *Controlling figure aesthetics (seaborn)*: `https://seaborn.pydata.org/tutorial/aesthetics.html`
- *Customizing Matplotlib with style sheets and rcParams*: `https://matplotlib.org/tutorials/introductory/customizing.html`
- *Format String Syntax*: `https://docs.python.org/3/library/string.html#format-string-syntax`
- *Generator Expressions (PEP 289)*: `https://www.python.org/dev/peps/pep-0289/`
- *Matplotlib Named Colors*: `https://matplotlib.org/examples/color/named_colors.html`

- *Multiple assignment and tuple unpacking improve Python code readability*: https://treyhunner.com/2018/03/tuple-unpacking-improves-python-code-readability/
- *Python: range is not an iterator!*: https://treyhunner.com/2018/02/python-range-is-not-an-iterator/
- *Python zip() function*: https://www.journaldev.com/15891/python-zip-function
- *Seaborn API reference*: https://seaborn.pydata.org/api.html
- *Show Me the Numbers: Designing Tables and Graphs to Enlighten by Stephen Few*: https://www.amazon.com/gp/product/0970601972/ref=as_li_tf_tl
- *Style sheets reference (Matplotlib)*: https://matplotlib.org/gallery/style_sheets/style_sheets_reference.html
- *Support and Resistance Basics*: https://www.investopedia.com/trading/support-and-resistance-basics/
- *The Iterator Protocol: How "For Loops" Work in Python*: https://treyhunner.com/2016/12/python-iterator-protocol-how-for-loops-work/
- *The Visual Display of Quantitative Information by Edward R. Tufte*: https://www.amazon.com/Visual-Display-Quantitative-Information/dp/1930824130
- *Tick formatters*: https://matplotlib.org/gallery/ticks_and_spines/tick-formatters.html
- *What does pythonic mean?*: https://stackoverflow.com/questions/25011078/what-does-pythonic-mean

Section 3: Applications - Real-World Analyses Using Pandas

It's time to see how to bring together everything we have learned so far. In this section, we will take some real-world datasets and run through analyses from start to finish, combining all the concepts covered in the previous chapters and introducing some new material along the way.

The following chapters are included in this section:

- Chapter 7, *Financial Analysis – Bitcoin and the Stock Market*
- Chapter 8, *Rule-Based Anomaly Detection*

7
Financial Analysis - Bitcoin and the Stock Market

It's time to switch gears and work on an application. In this chapter, we will explore a financial application by performing an analysis of bitcoin and the stock market. This chapter builds upon everything we have learned so far—we will extract data from the Internet with `pandas`; perform some exploratory data analysis; create visualizations with `pandas`, `seaborn`, and `matplotlib`; calculate important metrics for analyzing the performance of financial instruments using `pandas`; and get a taste of building some models. Note that we are not trying to learn financial analysis here, but rather walk through an introduction of how the skills we have learned in this book can be applied to financial analysis.

This chapter is also a departure from the standard workflow in this book. Up until this point, we have been working with Python as more of a functional programming language. However, Python also supports **object-oriented programming** (**OOP**). This means that we can build classes that will carry out the major tasks we need to perform, which in this chapter are collecting data from various websites (with the `StockReader` class), visualizing financial assets (with the `Visualizer` classes), calculating financial metrics (with the `StockAnalyzer` class), and modeling financial data (with the `StockModeler` class). Since we will need a lot of code to make the analysis process clean and easy to reproduce, we will build a Python package to house these classes. The code will be reproduced in the text and explained as usual; however, we don't need to type/run it on our own—be sure to read the *Chapter materials* section for this chapter to get set up properly.

This chapter will be challenging and may require a few rereads; however, it will teach best practices, and the skills acquired here will dramatically improve your coding skills, which will quickly pay off. One main takeaway should be that OOP can be very helpful in packaging up analysis tasks. Each class should have a single purpose and be well-documented. If we have many classes, we should spread them across separate files and make a package. This makes it very easy for others to install/use them and for us to standardize the way certain tasks are performed across a project. As an example, we shouldn't have our collaborators on a project writing their own functions to connect to a database. Standardized, well-documented code will save lots of headaches down the road.

The following topics will be covered in this chapter:

- Building a Python package
- Collecting finance data with `pandas`
- Conducting exploratory data analysis
- Performing a technical analysis on financial instruments
- Modeling performance using historical data

Chapter materials

For this chapter, we will be creating our own package for stock analysis. This makes it extremely easy for us to distribute our code and for others to use our code. The final product of this package is on GitHub at `https://github.com/stefmolin/stock-analysis/tree/pandas_book`. Python's package manager, `pip`, is capable of installing packages from GitHub and also building them locally; this leaves us with either of the following choices of how we want to proceed:

- Install from GitHub if we don't plan on editing the source code for our own use
- Clone the repository and install it on our machine in order to modify the code

If we wish to install from GitHub directly, we don't need to do anything here since this was installed when we set up our environment back in `Chapter 1`, *Introduction to Data Analysis*; however, for reference, we would do the following to install packages from GitHub:

```
(book_env)
$ pip3 install \
    git+https://github.com/stefmolin/stock-analysis.git@pandas_book
```

The `@pandas_book` portion of the URL tells `pip` to install the version that was tagged `pandas_book`. To install the version of the code on a particular branch instead, replace this with `@<branch_name>`. For example, to specify the `master` branch, which typically has the production version of the code, use `@master` (although this will be the default, it helps to be explicit in case something changes); if we want the code being developed on a branch called `dev`, we use `@dev`. Be sure to check that the branch exists first, of course. We can also use the commit hash in the same fashion to grab a specific commit. More information is at `https://pip.pypa.io/en/latest/reference/pip_install/#git`.

To install locally in editable mode, meaning that any changes will automatically be reflected locally without having to reinstall, we use the `-e` flag. Run the following from the command line in the virtual environment we created in `Chapter 1, Introduction to Data Analysis`, to do so. Note that this will clone the latest version of the package, which may be different from the version in the text (the version with the `pandas_book` tag):

```
(book_env) $ git clone git@github.com:stefmolin/stock-analysis.git
(book_env) $ pip3 install -r stock-analysis/requirements.txt
(book_env) $ pip3 install -e stock-analysis
```

This example uses `git clone` over SSH; if SSH keys are not set up already, clone over HTTPS instead by using a variation of the URL: `https://github.com/stefmolin/stock-analysis.git`. Alternatively, follow the instructions on GitHub for generating SSH keys first. Consult this Stack Overflow post if you're interested in just cloning the version with the `pandas_book` tag: `https://stackoverflow.com/questions/20280726/how-to-git-clone-a-specific-tag`.

We will be using this package throughout this chapter. The repository for this chapter has the notebook we will use for our actual analysis (`financial_analysis.ipynb`) and a function in `random_walk.py`, which we will discuss when we do some modeling; both can be found at `https://github.com/stefmolin/Hands-On-Data-Analysis-with-Pandas/tree/master/ch_07`. The `data/` folder contains backup files in case the data sources have changed since publication; simply read in the CSV files rather than using the `StockReader` and follow along with the rest of this chapter should this happen.

If we change a file in a package installed in editable mode when working with Jupyter Notebooks, we will need to restart our kernel or open a new Python shell and reimport the package. This is because Python will cache it after import. Another option is to use `importlib.reload()`.

Building a Python package

Building packages is considered good coding practice since it allows for writing modular code and reuse. **Modular code** is code that is written in many smaller pieces for more pervasive use, without needing to know the underlying implementation details of everything involved in a task. For example, when we use `matplotlib` to plot something, we don't need to know what the code inside the functions we call is doing exactly—it suffices to simply know what the input and output will be to build on top of it.

Package structure

A **module** is a single file of Python code that can be imported; `window_calc.py` from Chapter 4, *Aggregating Pandas DataFrames*, and `color_utils.py` from Chapter 6, *Plotting with Seaborn and Customization Techniques*, were both modules. A **package** is a collection of modules organized into directories. Packages can also be imported, but when we import a package, we have access to certain modules inside, so we don't have to import each one individually. This also allows us to build modules that import from each other without the need to maintain a single very large module.

So, how do we turn our modules into a package? We follow these steps:

1. Create a directory for the name of the package (`stock_analysis` for this chapter)
2. Place the modules in the aforementioned directory
3. Add an `__init__.py` file containing any Python code to run upon importing the package (this can be, and often is, empty)
4. Make a `setup.py` file at the same level as the package's top-level directory (`stock_analysis` here), which will give `pip` instructions on how to install the package. See the *Further reading* section for information on creating this

Once the aforementioned steps are complete, the package can be installed with `pip`. Note that, while our package only contains a single directory, we can build a package with as many subpackages as we desire. These subpackages are created just as if we were creating a package, with the exception that they don't need a `setup.py` file:

1. Create a directory for the subpackage inside the main package directory (or inside some other subpackage)
2. Place the subpackage's modules in this directory
3. Add the `__init__.py` file, with code that should be run when the subpackage is imported (which can be empty)

The directory hierarchy for a package with a single subpackage would look something like this:

```
repo_folder
|-- <package_name>
|   |-- __init__.py
|   |-- some_module.py
|   `-- <subpackage_name>
|       |-- __init__.py
|       |-- another_module.py
|       `-- last_module.py
`-- setup.py
```

Some other things to be aware of when building a package include the following:

- Writing a **README** file for the repository (see https://www.makeareadme.com/) so that others know what it contains
- **Linting** the code in order to conform to coding standards and analyze the code for possible errors (check out the `pylint` package at https://www.pylint.org/)
- Adding tests that will make sure that changes to the code don't break anything and that the code does what it is meant to do (take a look at the `pytest` package at https://docs.pytest.org/en/latest/)

Overview of the stock_analysis package

In this chapter, we will be creating a Python package called `stock_analysis` using the various Python packages we have discussed so far, along with the Python standard library. This package is located in the `stock-analysis` repository (`https://github.com/stefmolin/stock-analysis`), which is arranged like this:

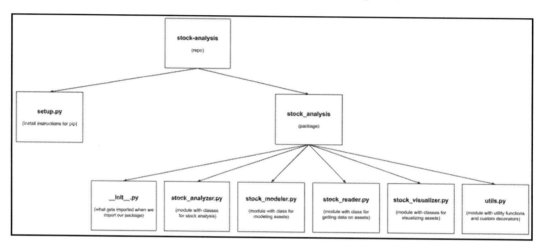

The modules in our package will contain custom classes for conducting the technical analysis of an asset. **Classes** should be designed for a single purpose; this makes it easier to build, use, and debug, if issues arise. Therefore, we will be building several classes in order to cover the various facets of our financial analysis. We will need a class for each of the following purposes:

Purpose	Class(es)	Module
Collecting the data from various sources	StockReader	stock_reader.py
Visualizing the data	Visualizer, StockVisualizer, AssetGroupVisualizer	stock_visualizer.py
Calculating financial metrics	StockAnalyzer, AssetGroupAnalyzer	stock_analyzer.py
Modeling the data	StockModeler	stock_modeler.py

It can be helpful to visualize the interaction between modules in a package and the functionality each class provides. For this purpose, we can build **Unified Modeling Language (UML)** diagrams.

UML diagrams show information about which attributes and methods classes have and how classes are related to others. We can see that all the modules rely on `utils.py` for utility functions:

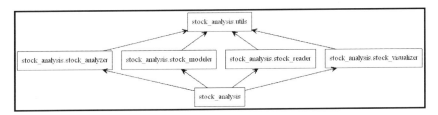

The `pylint` package that was referenced in the previous section also comes with `pyreverse`, which makes UML diagrams. If `graphviz` is installed (`http://www.graphviz.org/download/`), running the following from the command line generates a PNG file for the relationship between modules and a UML diagram for the classes (provided the repository was cloned and `pylint` is installed): `pyreverse -o png stock_analysis`

The UML diagram for the classes in the `stock_analysis` package looks like this:

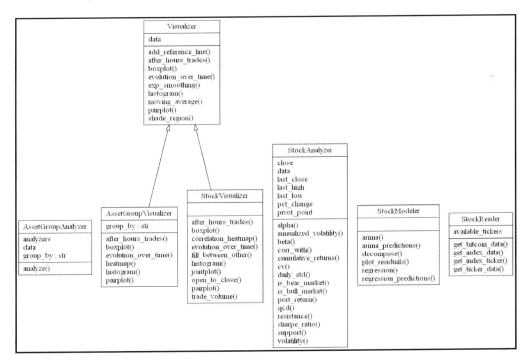

The top section in each box is the class name. The middle section contains the attributes of that class. The bottom section contains any methods defined in that class. Notice the arrows pointing from the `AssetGroupVisualizer` and `StockVisualizer` classes to the `Visualizer` class. This means that both are a type of `Visualizer`. The methods shown for the `AssetGroupVisualizer` and `StockVisualizer` classes are defined differently in those classes compared to the `Visualizer` class. We will explain this more in depth in the *Exploratory data analysis* section. Throughout the remaining sections of this chapter, we will be going over each of these classes in more detail and using their functionality to perform technical analysis of financial assets.

Data extraction with pandas

Back in `Chapter 2`, *Working with Pandas DataFrames*, we discussed various ways to create dataframes from collected data; however, we didn't delve into some of the ways `pandas` can collect data. The `StockReader` class in the `stock_analysis` package uses a `pandas` derivative package called `pandas_datareader` to collect stock data and the `pd.read_html()` function to read data from tables in HTML to extract bitcoin data.

 In case anything has changed with the data sources that are used in this chapter, the CSV files in the `data/` folder can be read in as a replacement so that you can follow along with the text.

The StockReader class

Since our data is coming from different sources, it makes sense to create a class that hides all these implementation details. For this purpose, we will build the `StockReader` class, which will make it easier to collect data for bitcoin, stocks, and indices on the stock market. We can simply create an instance of the `StockReader` class by providing the date range we want for our analysis, and then use the methods it provides to get whichever data we please.

We can use the UML diagram of the `StockReader` to get a high-level overview of its implementation:

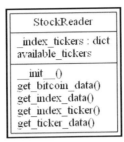

This tells us that the `StockReader` will allow us to perform the following actions:

- Pull bitcoin data with the `get_bitcoin_data()` method
- Pull data for an index on the stock market (like the S&P 500) with the `get_index_data()` method
- Lookup the ticker symbol (stock market symbol) for a specific index (like ^GSPC for the S&P 500 ticker on Yahoo! Finance) with the `get_index_ticker()` method
- Pull data for a ticker symbol on the stock market (like NFLX for Netflix) with the `get_ticker_data()` method

The UML diagram also tells us that the `StockReader` keeps a dictionary of index tickers (`_index_tickers`) and provides an attribute for the available ones (`available_tickers`).

Now that we understand why we need this class and a high-level overview of its structure, we can proceed to looking at the code. Since there is a lot of code in the `stock_analysis/stock_reader.py` module to review, we will break down the file piece by piece. Note that this may change the indentation level, so please consult the file itself for the full version.

The first line of the module is the **docstring** for the module. If we run `help()` on the module itself, that will appear near the top. This describes the purpose of our module. This is immediately followed by any imports we will need:

```
"""Gathering select stock data."""

import datetime
import re

import pandas as pd
import pandas_datareader.data as web

from .utils import label_sanitizer
```

Notice that the import statements are in three groups, following **PEP 8** (Python style guidelines, which are available at `https://www.python.org/dev/peps/pep-0008/`):

1. Standard library imports (`datetime` and `re`)
2. Third-party libraries (`pandas` and `pandas_datareader`)
3. Relative import from another module in the `stock_analysis` package (`.utils`)

After our imports, we define the `StockReader` class. First, we define a dictionary mapping tickers for indices to an easy to remember index name in `_index_tickers`. Notice that our class also has a docstring, which defines its purpose:

```
class StockReader:
    """Class for reading financial data from websites."""

    _index_tickers = {
        'SP500': '^GSPC', 'DOW': '^DJI', 'NASDAQ': '^IXIC'
    }
```

When building a class, there are many **dunder (double underscore) methods** that we can provide to customize the behavior of the class when it's used with language operators:

- Initialize an object (`__init__()`)
- Make an object comparable for sorting (`__eq__()`, `__lt__()`, `__gt__()`, and more)
- Perform arithmetic on the object (`__add__()`, `__sub__()`, `__mul__()`, and so on)
- Be able to use built-in Python functions like `len()` on it (`__len__()`)
- Get a string representation of the object for use with `print()` (`__repr__()` and `__str__()`)
- Support iteration and indexing (`__getitem__()`, `__iter__()`, and `__next__()`)

Thankfully, we don't have to write all this functionality every time we make a class. In most cases, we just need the `__init__()` method, which is run when we create an object. More information on dunder methods can be found at `https://dbader.org/blog/python-dunder-methods` and `https://docs.python.org/3/reference/datamodel.html#special-method-names`.

Chapter 7

Objects of the `StockReader` class hold on to the start and end date that data will be gathered for, so we put this in the `__init__()` method. We parse the dates that are passed in by the caller to allow for the use of any date separator; for example, we will be able to handle inputs of Python `datetime` objects, strings in the form of `'YYYYMMDD'`, or strings representing dates using any separator that matches the non-digit character (`\D`) regular expression like `'YYYY|MM|DD'` or `'YYYY/MM/DD'`. The separator, if there is one, gets replaced with an empty space so that we can build our datetimes using the `'YYYYMMDD'` format in our method. In addition, we raise a `ValueError` if the caller gives us a start date equal to or after the end date:

```python
def __init__(self, start, end=None):
    """
    Create a StockReader object for reading across a given date
    range.

    Parameters:
        - start: The first date to include, as a datetime object
          or a string in the format 'YYYYMMDD'.
        - end: The last date to include, as a datetime object or
          string in the format 'YYYYMMDD'. Defaults to today if
          not provided.
    """
    self.start, self.end = map(
        lambda x: x.strftime('%Y%m%d') if isinstance(
            x, datetime.date
        ) else re.sub(r'\D', '', x),
        [start, end or datetime.date.today()]
    )
    if self.start >= self.end:
        raise ValueError('`start` must be before `end`')
```

The `_index_tickers` class attribute is private (signified by a preceding `_`) in the sense that unless a user of this class knows the name of it, they won't find it easily; note that methods can also be private. This is done with the intention of protecting it (although it isn't guaranteed) and also because the user doesn't need it directly. Instead, we provide a **property**, which we can access as an attribute, and a class method for getting the value for a given key in that dictionary. We don't define this in the `__init__()` method, which is called upon creation of this object, because we only need one copy of this for all the objects that are created from this class.

[385]

Class methods are methods that can be used on the class itself, without having to create an instance of the class beforehand. This contrasts with the instance methods we have seen so far. **Instance methods** are used with instances of a class for actions specific to that instance. We often don't need class methods, but if we have data that is shared across all the instances of a class, it makes more sense to create a class method rather than an instance method.

Since `_index_tickers` is private, we want to provide an easy way for users of our class to see what is available. We do this by creating a property for the keys of `_index_tickers`. To do so, we use the `@property` decorator. **Decorators** are functions that wrap around other functions, allowing for the execution of extra code before and/or after the inner function executes. This class makes heavy use of decorators. We will use some already written decorators (`@property` and `@classmethod`) for this class; in addition, we will be writing our own (`@label_sanitizer`) to clean up results with the methods that gather the data. To use a decorator, we place it above the function or method definition:

```
@property
def available_tickers(self):
    """
    Access the names of the indices whose tickers are supported.
    """
    return list(self._index_tickers.keys())
```

In addition, we also provide a way of getting the ticker using a class method because our tickers are stored in a class variable. Class methods, by convention, receive `cls`, while instance methods receive `self`:

```
@classmethod
def get_index_ticker(cls, index):
    """
    Get the ticker of the specified index, if known.

    Parameters:
        - index: The name of the index; check `available_tickers`
                 property for full list which includes:
                     - 'SP500' for S&P 500,
                     - 'DOW' for Dow Jones Industrial Average,
                     - 'NASDAQ' for NASDAQ Composite Index

    Returns: The ticker as a string if known, otherwise None.
    """
```

```
try:
    index = index.upper()
except AttributeError:
    raise ValueError('`index` must be a string')
return cls._index_tickers.get(index, None)
```

If we want to prohibit certain actions within our code, we can check for them and `raise` errors as we see fit; this allows us to provide more informative error messages or simply accompany specific errors with some additional actions before reraising them (by using `raise` without an expression). If, instead, we wish to run certain code when something goes wrong, we use a `try...except` block: we surround the possibly troublesome code with `try` and put what to do if trouble occurs in `except`.

The remaining method code is replaced with `pass`, which tells Python to do nothing (and reminds us to update it later) so that the code can function as it was reproduced. We will write these methods in the next few sections:

```
@label_sanitizer
def get_ticker_data(self, ticker):
    pass

@label_sanitizer
def get_bitcoin_data(self):
    pass

@label_sanitizer
def get_index_data(self, index='SP500'):
    pass
```

Before creating an instance of the `StockReader` class, let's make sure that we understand decorators. The `@label_sanitizer` decorator aligns the data we receive from various sources to the same column names so that we don't have to clean them later. It is defined in the `stock_analysis/utils.py` module. Like we did previously, let's look at the docstring and imports of the `utils` module:

```
"""Utility functions for stock analysis."""

from functools import wraps
import re

import pandas as pd
```

Next, we have the `_sanitize_label()` function, which will clean up a single label. Note that we prefix the function name with an underscore because we don't intend for the users of our package to use this directly—it is for our decorator to use:

```
def _sanitize_label(label):
    """
    Clean up a label by removing non-letter, non-space characters and
    putting in all lowercase with underscores replacing spaces.

    Parameters:
        - label: The text you want to fix.

    Returns: The sanitized label.
    """
    return re.sub(r'[^\w\s]', '', label).lower().replace(' ', '_')
```

Finally, we define the `@label_sanitizer` decorator—note that it is a function:

```
def label_sanitizer(method):
    """
    Decorator around a method that returns a dataframe to
    clean up all labels in said dataframe (column names and index
    name) by removing non-letter, non-space characters and
    putting in all lowercase with underscores replacing spaces.

    Parameters:
        - method: The method to wrap.

    Returns: A decorated method or function.
    """
    @wraps(method) # keep the docstring of the data method for help()
    def method_wrapper(self, *args, **kwargs):
        df = method(self, *args, **kwargs)

        # fix the column names
        df.columns = [_sanitize_label(col) for col in df.columns]

        # fix the index name
        df.index.rename(_sanitize_label(df.index.name), inplace=True)

        return df
    return method_wrapper
```

In this case, the `label_sanitizer` decorator is cleaning up the column and index names in the dataframes we get from the Internet. This means that if we didn't have the decorator, when we asked for bitcoin data, our column names could have had unexpected characters like * or spaces in them, making them unwieldy. By using the decorator, the methods will always return a dataframe with the names cleaned, saving us a step.

 Using the `@label_sanitizer` syntax is **syntactic sugar**, meaning that it makes it easier to express, compared to defining the method and then writing `method = label_sanitizer(method)`. However, both are valid.

Note that there is also a decorator inside the definition of the `label_sanitizer` function. The `@wraps` decorator from the `functools` module in the standard library gives the decorated function/method the same docstring it had beforehand; this is necessary because decoration actually creates a new function/method, thus rendering `help()` pretty useless unless we intervene.

Let's get started in the `financial_analysis.ipynb` notebook and import the `stock_analysis` package that will be used in the rest of this chapter:

```
>>> import stock_analysis
```

Another thing to note is the contents of the `stock_analysis/__init__.py` file, which Python runs upon importing the package:

```
"""Classes for making technical stock analysis easier."""

from .stock_analyzer import StockAnalyzer, AssetGroupAnalyzer
from .stock_modeler import StockModeler
from .stock_reader import StockReader
from .stock_visualizer import StockVisualizer, AssetGroupVisualizer
```

The package is making it easier for us to access the `StockReader` class. Rather than having to run `stock_analysis.stock_reader.StockReader()` to create the object, we only have to run `stock_analysis.StockReader()`. We create an instance of the `StockReader` class by providing the start and (optionally) end dates for the data to provide:

```
>>> reader = stock_analysis.StockReader('2017-01-01', '2018-12-31')
```

When we call `stock_analysis.StockReader()`, Python is calling the `__init__()` method of the `StockReader` class.

Bitcoin historical data from HTML

The `StockReader` class provides the `get_bitcoin_data()` method for the extraction of bitcoin data. This method uses the `read_html()` function from `pandas` to pull out any data in HTML table elements from a given web page. The page on the CoinMarketCap site where the data is coming from only contains a single table with the data we want, so we select the first element in the list of dataframes returned by `pd.read_html()`:

```
@label_sanitizer
def get_bitcoin_data(self):
    """
    Get bitcoin historical OHLC data from coinmarketcap.com
    for given date range.

    Returns: A pandas dataframe with the bitcoin data.
    """
    return pd.read_html(
        'https://coinmarketcap.com/'
        'currencies/bitcoin/historical-data/?'
        'start={}&end={}'.format(self.start, self.end),
        parse_dates=[0], index_col=[0]
    )[0].sort_index()
```

In case the format of this website has changed since the publication of this book, you can use the `data/bitcoin.csv` file in the folder for this chapter in the GitHub repository.

Since `reader` has the start and end dates for the analysis, the `get_bitcoin_data()` method doesn't require us to pass any arguments:

```
>>> bitcoin = reader.get_bitcoin_data()
```

S&P 500 historical data from Yahoo! Finance

To collect data from a stock market index, we can use the `get_index_data()` method of the `StockReader` class. This method uses the `pandas_datareader` package to grab the data from Yahoo! Finance:

```
@label_sanitizer
def get_index_data(self, index='SP500'):
    """
    Get historical OHLC data from Yahoo! Finance for the chosen index
    for given date range.

    Parameter:
        - index: String representing the index you want data for,
                supported indices include:
                    - 'SP500' for S&P 500,
                    - 'DOW' for Dow Jones Industrial Average,
                    - 'NASDAQ' for NASDAQ Composite Index
                Check the `available_tickers` property for more.

    Returns: A pandas dataframe with the index data.
    """
    if index not in self.available_tickers:
        raise ValueError(
            'Index not supported. Available tickers'
            f"are: {', '.join(self.available_tickers)}"
        )
    return web.get_data_yahoo(
        self.get_index_ticker(index), self.start, self.end
    )
```

 Running `reader.available_tickers` shows us the available indices.

Let's grab the S&P 500 data; note that while this method takes the `index` as a parameter, the default is S&P 500, so we don't have to provide it:

```
>>> sp = reader.get_index_data()
```

FAANG historical data from IEX

Collecting data for individual stocks is just as easy with the `get_ticker_data()` method of the `StockReader`; this time, it will use data from **Investors Exchange (IEX)**. In the following method, we `try` to get the data from IEX, but if there is an issue doing so, we get it from Yahoo! Finance (`except`):

```
@label_sanitizer
def get_ticker_data(self, ticker):
    """
    Get historical OHLC data for given date range and ticker.

    Parameter:
        - ticker: The stock symbol to lookup as a string.

    Returns: A pandas dataframe with the stock data.
    """
    try:
        data = web.DataReader(ticker, 'iex', self.start, self.end)
        data.index = pd.to_datetime(data.index)
    except:
        # get it from Yahoo! Finance if it doesn't work
        data = web.get_data_yahoo(ticker, self.start, self.end)
    return data
```

 We are checking IEX for the data first because there have been issues with the Yahoo! Finance API and `pandas_datareader` in the past, causing the `pandas_datareader` developers to deprecate support for it (`https://pandas-datareader.readthedocs.io/en/latest/whatsnew.html#v0-6-0-january-24-2018`). This means that Yahoo! Finance data can't be accessed using `web.DataReader()` like the other sources can; instead, we have to use their workaround: `web.get_data_yahoo()`.

Let's use a generator expression and tuple unpacking to get dataframes for each FAANG stock with its data:

```
>>> fb, aapl, amzn, nflx, goog = (
...     reader.get_ticker_data(ticker) \
...     for ticker in ['FB', 'AAPL', 'AMZN', 'NFLX', 'GOOG']
... )
```

Be sure to run `help(stock_analysis.StockReader)` or `help(reader)` to see all the methods and properties that are defined. The output clearly denotes which methods are class methods in a different section, and the properties will be listed at the bottom in the `data descriptors` section. This is an important step to take in order to get familiar with new code.

Exploratory data analysis

Now that we have our data, we want to get familiar with it. For this, we have the `Visualizer` classes in `stock_analysis/stock_visualizer.py`. There are three classes in this file:

- `Visualizer`: This is the base class for defining the functionality of a `Visualizer` object. Most of the methods are **abstract**, meaning that the subclasses (children) that inherit from this superclass (parent) will need to override them and implement the code; these define what an object should do without getting into the specifics.
- `StockVisualizer`: This is the subclass we will use to visualize a single asset.
- `AssetGroupVisualizer`: This is the subclass we will use to visualize a dataframe with multiple assets using group by operations.

Before we discuss the code for these classes, let's go over some additional functions in the `stock_analysis/utils.py` file, which will help create these asset groups and describe them for EDA purposes. For these functions, we need to import `pandas`:

```
import pandas as pd
```

The `group_stocks()` function takes in a dictionary that maps the name of the asset to the dataframe for that asset (which we got with the `StockReader` class) and outputs a new dataframe with all the data from those dataframes stacked one on top of the other with a new column, denoting which asset the data belongs to:

```
def group_stocks(mapping):
    """
    Create a new dataframe with many assets and a new column
    indicating the asset that row's data belongs to.

    Parameters:
        - mapping: A key-value mapping of the form
                   {asset_name: asset_df}
```

```
    Returns: A new pandas DataFrame
    """
    group_df = pd.DataFrame()

    for stock, stock_data in mapping.items():
        df = stock_data.copy(deep=True)
        df['name'] = stock
        group_df = group_df.append(df, sort=True)

    group_df.index = pd.to_datetime(group_df.index)

    return group_df
```

Since we will have many methods and functions throughout the package that will expect their dataframes in a specific format, we will build a new decorator: @validate_df. This decorator checks that the input to a given method or function is an object of class DataFrame and that it has at least the columns specified with the columns argument of the decorator. We will provide the columns as a set in Python. This allows us to check the set difference between the columns we must have and the columns in the dataframe passed as input. If the dataframe has the columns we request (at a minimum), the set difference will be empty, which means that the dataframe passes the test. This decorator will raise a ValueError if either of these conditions is violated.

Let's take a look at how this is defined in the stock_analysis/utils.py file:

```
def validate_df(columns, instance_method=True):
    """
    Decorator that raises a ValueError if input isn't a pandas
    DataFrame or doesn't contain the proper columns. Note the
    DataFrame must be the first positional argument passed to
    this method.
    """
    def method_wrapper(method):
        @wraps(method)
        def validate_wrapper(self, *args, **kwargs):
            # functions and static methods don't pass self
            # so self is the first positional argument in that case
            df = (self, *args)[0 if not instance_method else 1]

            if not isinstance(df, pd.DataFrame):
                raise ValueError('Must pass in a pandas DataFrame')
```

```
        if columns.difference(df.columns):
            raise ValueError(
                'Dataframe must contain the following columns: '
                f'{columns}'
            )
        return method(self, *args, **kwargs)
    return validate_wrapper
return method_wrapper
```

Groups made with the `group_stocks()` function can be described in a single output using the `describe_group()` function. The `group_stocks()` function adds a `name` column that `describe_group()` looks for, so we use the `@validate_df` decorator to make sure that the format is correct before trying to run the function:

```
@validate_df(columns={'name'}, instance_method=False)
def describe_group(data):
    """
    Run `describe()` on the asset group created with `group_stocks()`.

    Parameters:
        - data: The group data resulting from `group_stocks()`

    Returns: The transpose of the grouped description statistics.
    """
    return data.groupby('name').describe().T
```

Let's make some asset groups for analysis:

```
>>> from stock_analysis.utils import group_stocks, describe_group
>>> faang = group_stocks({
...     'Facebook' : fb, 'Apple' : aapl, 'Amazon' : amzn,
...     'Netflix' : nflx, 'Google' : goog
... })
>>> faang_sp = group_stocks({
...     'Facebook' : fb, 'Apple' : aapl, 'Amazon' : amzn,
...     'Netflix' : nflx, 'Google' : goog, 'S&P 500' : sp
... })
>>> bit_sp = group_stocks({'Bitcoin' : bitcoin, 'S&P 500' : sp})
>>> all_assets = group_stocks({
...     'Bitcoin' : bitcoin, 'S&P 500' : sp, 'Facebook' : fb,
...     'Apple' : aapl, 'Amazon' : amzn, 'Netflix' : nflx,
...     'Google' : goog
... })
```

Using these groups, the output of `describe()` can be much more informative for comparison purposes compared to running it on each dataframe separately. The `describe_group()` function handles running `describe()` with `groupby()`. This makes it easier to look at the summary for the closing price across assets:

```
>>> describe_group(all_assets).loc['close',]
```

This results in the following output:

name	Amazon	Apple	Bitcoin	Facebook	Google	Netflix	S&P 500
count	502.000000	502.000000	730.000000	502.000000	502.000000	502.000000	502.000000
mean	1304.946594	167.560223	5789.166247	164.043556	1017.503267	242.332281	2597.645281
std	372.471604	27.188378	3794.382038	20.142949	120.077681	85.760208	181.994087
min	753.670000	112.494800	777.760000	116.860000	786.140000	127.490000	2257.830078
25%	967.992500	149.181600	2589.457500	148.500000	929.700000	162.570000	2434.777527
50%	1194.715000	166.577400	6252.710000	167.545000	1028.990000	201.875000	2629.420044
75%	1623.527500	184.964975	7672.175000	178.762500	1103.907500	321.265000	2742.534912
max	2039.510000	231.263100	19497.400000	217.500000	1268.330000	418.970000	2930.750000

If we don't want to look at the assets individually, we can use `make_portfolio()` from `stock_analysis/utils.py` to combine assets into a single asset. It groups the data by date and sums all the columns, giving us the total stock price and volume traded of our portfolio:

```
@validate_df(columns=set(), instance_method=False)
def make_portfolio(data, date_column='date'):
    """
    Make a portfolio of assets by grouping by date and summing all
    columns.

    Note: the caller is responsible for making sure the dates line up
    across assets and handling when they don't.
    """
    return data.reset_index().groupby('date').sum()
```

This function assumes that the assets are traded on the same frequency. Bitcoin trades every day of the week, while the stock market doesn't. For this reason, we would have to decide how to handle this difference before using this function if our portfolio was a mix of bitcoin and the stock market; consult our discussion of reindexing in Chapter 3, *Data Wrangling with Pandas*, for a possible strategy. We will use this function in the exercises at the end of this chapter to build a portfolio of the FAANG stocks, which all trade on the same frequency, and for a portfolio of the S&P 500 and bitcoin, which don't.

The Visualizer class family

At a glance, we can see that we have more data for bitcoin than the rest. This is because the prices change daily, whereas for stocks, we only see the data for trading days. Another thing we can glean from this scale; bitcoin is not only much more volatile, but is much higher than everything else. However, as we learned from previous chapters, visualization will make our analysis much easier, so let's begin our discussion of the `Visualizer` classes in `stock_analysis/stock_visualizer.py`.

First, we will define our base class—the `Visualizer`. The UML diagram tells us this is our base class because it has arrows pointing to it. These arrows originate from the subclasses (`AssetGroupVisualizer` and `StockVisualizer`):

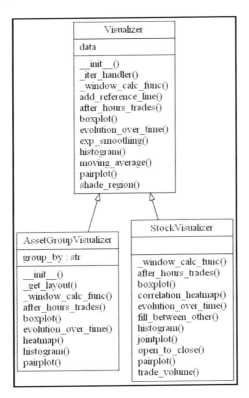

The UML diagram also tells us the methods we will be defining for each of the classes in this section. This includes methods for visualizing the effect of after-hours trading (`after_hours_trades()`) and the evolution over time of a stock price (`evolution_over_time()`), which we will use to compare assets visually.

We start the `stock_analysis/stock_visualizer.py` module with our docstring and imports. For our visualizations, we will need `matplotlib`, `numpy`, `pandas`, and `seaborn`:

```
"""Visualize financial instruments."""

import math

import matplotlib.pyplot as plt
import numpy as np
import pandas as pd
import seaborn as sns

from .utils import validate_df
```

Next, we begin by defining the `Visualizer` class. This class will hold the dataframe it will be used to visualize, so we put this in the `__init__()` method:

```
class Visualizer:
    """Base visualizer class not intended for direct use."""

    @validate_df(columns={'open', 'high', 'low', 'close'})
    def __init__(self, df):
        """Visualizer has a pandas dataframe as an attribute."""
        self.data = df
```

This base class will provide us with **static methods** for adding reference lines to plots and also adding shaded regions without needing to remember which `matplotlib` function we need to call for the orientation; static methods don't depend on the class for data. We define the `add_reference_line()` method for adding horizontal or vertical lines (and anything in between), using the `@staticmethod` decorator (notice we don't pass `self` or `cls`):

```
@staticmethod
def add_reference_line(ax, x=None, y=None, **kwargs):
    """
    Static method for adding reference lines to plots.

    Parameters:
        - ax: Matplotlib Axes object to add the reference line to.
        - x, y: The x, y value to draw the line at as a
                single value or numpy array-like structure.
                    - For horizontal: pass only `y`
                    - For vertical: pass only `x`
                    - For AB line: pass both `x` and `y`
        - kwargs: Additional keyword arguments to pass down.
```

```
Returns: The Axes object passed in.
"""

try:
    # numpy array-like structures are passed -> AB line
    if x.shape and y.shape:
        ax.plot(x, y, **kwargs)
except:
    # error triggers if x or y isn't array-like structure
    try:
        if not x and not y:
            raise ValueError(
                'You must provide an `x` or a `y`'
            )
        elif x and not y:
            ax.axvline(x, **kwargs) # vertical line
        elif not x and y:
            ax.axhline(y, **kwargs) # horizontal line
    except:
        raise ValueError(
            'If providing only `x` or `y`, '
            'it must be a single value'
        )
ax.legend()
return ax
```

See the *Further reading* section for more information on class methods, static methods, and abstract methods.

The `shade_region()` static method for adding shaded regions to a plot is similar to the `add_reference_line()` static method:

```python
@staticmethod
def shade_region(ax, x=tuple(), y=tuple(), **kwargs):
    """
    Static method for shading a region on a plot.

    Parameters:
        - ax: Matplotlib Axes object to add the shaded region to.
        - x: Tuple with the `xmin` and `xmax` bounds for the
             rectangle drawn vertically.
        - y: Tuple with the `ymin` and `ymax` bounds for the
             rectangle drawn vertically.
        - kwargs: Additional keyword arguments to pass to the
                  plotting function.

    Returns: The Axes object passed in.
    """
    if not x and not y:
        raise ValueError(
            'You must provide an x or a y min/max tuple'
        )
    elif x and y:
        raise ValueError('You can only provide `x` or `y`.')
    elif x and not y:
        ax.axvspan(*x, **kwargs) # vertical region
    elif not x and y:
        ax.axhspan(*y, **kwargs) # horizontal region
    return ax
```

Since we want our plotting capabilities to be flexible, we are going to define a static method that will make it easy for us to plot one or many items without needing to check the amount of items beforehand. This will be utilized in the classes we build using the `Visualizer` class as our base:

```python
@staticmethod
def _iter_handler(items):
    """
    Static method for making a list out of a item if it isn't a
    list or tuple already.

    Parameters:
        - items: The variable to make sure it is a list.

    Returns: The input as a list or tuple.
    """
```

```
    if not isinstance(items, (list, tuple)):
        items = [items]
    return items
```

We want to support window functions for single assets and groups of them; however, the implementation of this will vary, so we will define an **abstract method** (a method without implementation) in the superclass, and the subclasses will override it to provide the implementation:

```
def _window_calc_func(self, column, periods, name, func,
                      named_arg, **kwargs):
    """
    To be implemented by subclasses. Defines how to add lines
    resulting from window calculations.
    """
    raise NotImplementedError('To be implemented by subclasses!')
```

This allows us to define functionality that depends on `_window_calc_func()`, but doesn't need to know the exact implementation, just the result. We define the `moving_average()` method that will use `_window_calc_func()` to add moving average lines to the plot:

```
def moving_average(self, column, periods, **kwargs):
    """
    Add line(s) for the moving average of a column.

    Parameters:
        - column: The name of the column to plot.
        - periods: The rule or list of rules for resampling,
                   like '20D' for 20-day periods.
        - kwargs: Additional arguments to pass down to the
                  plotting function.

    Returns: A matplotlib Axes object.
    """
    return self._window_calc_func(
        column, periods, name='MA',
        func=pd.DataFrame.resample, named_arg='rule', **kwargs
    )
```

In a similar fashion, we define the `exp_smoothing()` method, which will use `_window_calc_func()` to add exponentially smoothed moving average lines to the plot:

```
def exp_smoothing(self, column, periods, **kwargs):
    """
    Add line(s) for the exponentially smoothed moving average
    of a column.

    Parameters:
        - column: The name of the column to plot.
        - periods: The span or list of spans for smoothing,
            like 20 for 20-day periods.
        - kwargs: Additional arguments to pass down to the
            plotting function.
    Returns: A matplotlib Axes object.
    """
    return self._window_calc_func(
        column, periods, name='EWMA',
        func=pd.DataFrame.ewm, named_arg='span', **kwargs
    )
```

Note that while we have methods for adding the moving average and the exponentially smoothed moving average to a plot of a column, they both call `_window_calc_func()`, which isn't defined here. This is because each of the subclasses will have its own implementation of `_window_calc_func()`, while they will inherit the top-level method without the need to override `moving_average()` or `exp_smoothing()`.

Remember that methods preceded with a single _ are Python's version of **private methods**—they can still be accessed outside this class, but they don't show up when we run `help()` on objects of that class.

Finally, we add placeholders for the methods all subclasses will have. These are abstract methods that will be defined by each subclass individually after overriding the following methods:

```
def evolution_over_time(self, column, **kwargs):
    """To be implemented by subclasses to create line plots."""
    raise NotImplementedError('To be implemented by subclasses!')

def boxplot(self, **kwargs):
    """To be implemented by subclasses for generating boxplots."""
    raise NotImplementedError('To be implemented by subclasses!')
```

```
    def histogram(self, column, **kwargs):
        """To be implemented by subclasses"""
        raise NotImplementedError('To be implemented by subclasses!')

    def after_hours_trades(self):
        """To be implemented by subclasses."""
        raise NotImplementedError('To be implemented by subclasses!')

    def pairplot(self, **kwargs):
        """To be implemented by subclasses"""
        raise NotImplementedError('To be implemented by subclasses!')
```

There are many abstract methods in the Visualizer class. These will be defined in the subclasses. The subclasses will also define any methods that are unique to them and/or override the implementation of the Visualizer class, if necessary. Anything they don't override, they will inherit. By using **inheritance**, we can define a broad class like the Visualizer by what all Visualizers should do and then have more specific versions, like the StockVisualizer, which handles single assets only.

Let's start the StockVisualizer class by inheriting from the Visualizer; we will choose not to override the __init__() method because the StockVisualizer will only have a dataframe as an attribute. Instead, we will provide implementations for the methods that needed to be overridden or added, which are unique to this class.

First up is evolution_over_time(), which will create a line plot of a column over time:

```
class StockVisualizer(Visualizer):
    """Visualizer for a single stock."""

    def evolution_over_time(self, column, **kwargs):
        """
        Visualize the evolution over time of a column.

        Parameters:
            - column: The name of the column to visualize.
            - kwargs: Additional keyword arguments to pass down
                      to the plotting function.

        Returns:  A matplotlib Axes object.
        """
        return self.data.plot.line(y=column, **kwargs)
```

The `boxplot()` method looks similar, generating box plots for all columns:

```
def boxplot(self, **kwargs):
    """
    Generate box plots for all columns.

    Parameters:
        - kwargs: Additional keyword arguments to pass down
                  to the plotting function.

    Returns: A matplotlib Axes object.
    """
    return self.data.plot(kind='box', **kwargs)
```

The `histogram()` method will create a histogram for a given column:

```
def histogram(self, column, **kwargs):
    """
    Generate the histogram of a given column.

    Parameters:
        - column: The name of the column to visualize.
        - kwargs: Additional keyword arguments to pass down
                  to the plotting function.

    Returns: A matplotlib Axes object.
    """
    return self.data.plot.hist(y=column, **kwargs)
```

Next, we write the `trade_volume()` method, which will generate two subplots, stacked one on top of the other. The top one will show the closing price over time as a line plot, and the bottom one will show the trading volume per month as bars:

```
def trade_volume(self, tight=False, **kwargs):
    """
    Visualize the trade volume and closing price.

    Parameters:
        - tight: Whether or not to attempt to match up the
                 resampled bar plot on the bottom to the line plot
                 on the top.
        - kwargs: Additional keyword arguments to pass down
                  to the plotting function.

    Returns: A matplotlib Axes object.
    """
```

```
fig, axes = plt.subplots(2, 1, figsize=(15, 15))
self.data.close.plot(
    ax=axes[0], title='Closing Price'
).set_ylabel('price')
monthly = self.data.volume.resample('1M').sum()
monthly.index = monthly.index.strftime('%b\n%Y')
monthly.plot(
    kind='bar', ax=axes[1], color='blue',
    rot=0, title='Volume Traded'
).set_ylabel('volume traded')
if tight:
    axes[0].set_xlim(
        self.data.index.min(), self.data.index.max()
    )
    axes[1].set_xlim(-0.25, axes[1].get_xlim()[1] - 0.25)
return axes
```

Now, we add the `after_hours_trades()` method, which helps us visualize the effect after-hours trading had on an individual asset, with bars colored red for losses and green for gains:

```
def after_hours_trades(self):
    """
    Visualize the effect of after-hours trading on this asset.
    Returns: A matplotlib Axes object.
    """
    after_hours = (self.data.open - self.data.close.shift())

    monthly_effect = after_hours.resample('1M').sum()
    fig, axes = plt.subplots(1, 2, figsize=(15, 3))

    after_hours.plot(
        ax=axes[0],
        title='After hours trading\n'\
            '(Open Price - Prior Day\'s Close)'
    ).set_ylabel('price')

    monthly_effect.index = monthly_effect.index.strftime('%b')
    monthly_effect.plot(
        ax=axes[1], kind='bar', rot=90,
        title='After hours trading monthly effect',
        color=np.where(monthly_effect >= 0, 'g', 'r')
    ).axhline(0, color='black', linewidth=1)
    axes[1].set_ylabel('price')
    return axes
```

The `open_to_close()` method will help us visualize the daily differential between opening and closing price via the `plt.fill_between()` function. We will color the area green if the closing price is higher than the opening price and red if the opposite is true:

```python
def open_to_close(self, figsize=(10, 4)):
    """
    Visualize the daily change from open to close price.

    Parameters:
        - figsize: A tuple of (width, height) for the plot
                   dimensions.

    Returns: A matplotlib Figure object.
    """
    is_higher = self.data.close - self.data.open > 0

    fig = plt.figure(figsize=figsize)

    for exclude_mask, color, label in zip(
        (is_higher, np.invert(is_higher)),
        ('g', 'r'),
        ('price rose', 'price fell')
    ):
        plt.fill_between(
            self.data.index, self.data.open, self.data.close,
            figure=fig, where=exclude_mask, color=color,
            label=label
        )
    plt.suptitle('Daily price change (open to close)')
    plt.legend()
    plt.xlabel('date')
    plt.ylabel('price')
    plt.close()
    return fig
```

In addition to seeing the differential between the opening and closing price of an individual asset, we will want to compare prices between assets. The `fill_between_other()` method will help us visualize the differential between the asset we created the visualizer for and another asset, using `plt.fill_between()` again.

We will color the differential green when the visualizer's asset is higher than the other asset and red for when it is lower:

```
def fill_between_other(self, other_df, figsize=(10, 4)):
    """
    Visualize the difference in closing price between assets.

    Parameters:
        - other_df: The dataframe with the other asset's data.
        - figsize: A tuple of (width, height) for the plot
                   dimensions.

    Returns: A matplotlib Figure object.
    """
    is_higher = self.data.close - other_df.close > 0

    fig = plt.figure(figsize=figsize)

    for exclude_mask, color, label in zip(
        (is_higher, np.invert(is_higher)),
        ('g', 'r'),
        ('asset is higher', 'asset is lower')
    ):
        plt.fill_between(
            self.data.index, self.data.close, other_df.close,
            figure=fig, where=exclude_mask, color=color,
            label=label
        )
    plt.suptitle(
        'Differential between asset closing price (this - other)'
    )
    plt.legend()
    plt.close()
    return fig
```

The time has come to override the _window_calc_func() method, which defines how to add reference lines based on window calculations for a single asset. Note how we are able to use pipe() (introduced in Chapter 4, *Aggregating Pandas DataFrames*) to make our window calculation plots work with different functions, and _iter_handler() to make our loop work without having to check if we have more than one reference line to plot:

```
def _window_calc_func(self, column, periods, name, func,
                      named_arg, **kwargs):
    """
    Helper method for plotting a series and adding reference lines
    using a window calculation.
```

```
Parameters:
    - column: The name of the column to plot.
    - periods: The rule/span or list of them to pass to the
      resampling/smoothing function, like '20D' for 20-day
      periods (resampling) or 20 for a 20-day span (smoothing)
    - name: The name of the window calculation (to show in
      the legend).
    - func: The window calculation function.
    - named_arg: The name of the argument `periods` is being
      passed as.
    - kwargs: Additional arguments to pass down to the
      plotting function.

Returns: A matplotlib Axes object.
"""
ax = self.data.plot(y=column, **kwargs)
for period in self._iter_handler(periods):
    self.data[column].pipe(
        func, **{named_arg: period}
    ).mean().plot(
        ax=ax, linestyle='--',
        label=f"""{period if isinstance(
            period, str
        ) else str(period) + 'D'} {name}"""
    )
plt.legend()
return ax
```

For our final three methods, we will need seaborn. We will add the pairplot() method for easier use with our visualizers, rather than having to explicitly pass the data to the seaborn function:

```
def pairplot(self, **kwargs):
    """
    Generate a seaborn pairplot for this asset.

    Parameters:
        - kwargs: Keyword arguments to pass down to
                  `sns.pairplot()`

    Returns: A seaborn pairplot
    """
    return sns.pairplot(self.data, **kwargs)
```

Aside from visualizing the relationship between the OHLC data for individual assets, we want to be able to visualize the relationship between assets. For this, we can build a wrapper around the `jointplot()` function from `seaborn`:

```
def jointplot(self, other, column, **kwargs):
    """
    Generate a seaborn jointplot for given column in asset
    compared to another asset.

    Parameters:
        - other: The other asset's dataframe
        - column: The column name to use for the comparison.
        - kwargs: Keyword arguments to pass down to
                    `sns.pairplot()`

    Returns: A seaborn jointplot
    """
    return sns.jointplot(
        x=self.data[column], y=other[column], **kwargs
    )
```

Pandas `DataFrames` have a `corrwith()` method, which will calculate the correlation coefficient between each column and the same column (by name) in another dataframe. This doesn't fill the matrix that's needed for a heatmap, as we saw in previous chapters; rather, it is the diagonal. The `correlation_heatmap()` method creates a matrix for the `sns.heatmap()` function and fills in the diagonal with the correlation coefficients; then, it makes sure that only the diagonal is filled in using a mask:

```
def correlation_heatmap(self, other):
    """
    Plot the correlations between the same column between this
    asset and another one with a heatmap.

    Parameters:
        - other: The other dataframe.

    Returns: A seaborn heatmap
    """
    corrs = self.data.corrwith(other)
    corrs = corrs[~pd.isnull(corrs)]
    size = len(corrs)
    matrix = np.zeros((size, size), float)
    for i, corr in zip(range(size), corrs):
        matrix[i][i] = corr
```

```
# create mask to only show diagonal
mask = np.ones_like(matrix)
np.fill_diagonal(mask, 0)

return sns.heatmap(
    matrix, annot=True, center=0, mask=mask,
    xticklabels=self.data.columns,
    yticklabels=self.data.columns
)
```

Visualizing a stock

Let's use the `StockVisualizer` to look at Netflix stock:

```
>>> %matplotlib inline
>>> import matplotlib.pyplot as plt
>>> netflix_viz = stock_analysis.StockVisualizer(nflx)
```

Once we initialize the `StockVisualizer` with the Netflix dataframe, we can generate many different plot types. We won't go over examples of everything this object lets us do; I will leave that up to you to experiment with. Let's take a look at the closing price over time and indicate where the maximum value occurred by adding a reference line:

```
>>> ax = netflix_viz.evolution_over_time(
...     'close', figsize=(10, 4), legend=False,
...     title='Netflix closing price over time'
... )
>>> netflix_viz.add_reference_line(
...     ax, x=nflx.high.idxmax(), color='k', linestyle=':', alpha=0.5,
...     label=f'highest value ({nflx.high.idxmax():%b %d})'
... )
>>> ax.set_ylabel('price ($)')
```

We can see that Netflix peaked on June 21, 2018:

Netflix, like Facebook, had a rough time around July 2018. Those who completed the exercises in `Chapter 5`, *Visualizing Data with Pandas and Matplotlib*, wrote code for generating a visualization that represented the effect that after-hours trading had on Facebook; the `StockVisualizer` also has this functionality. Let's use the `after_hours_trades()` method to see how Netflix fared:

```
>>> netflix_viz.after_hours_trades()
```

July was indeed rough for Netflix in terms of after-hours trades:

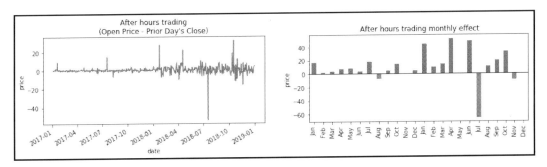

However, Facebook had a tougher time after hours over the same time period:

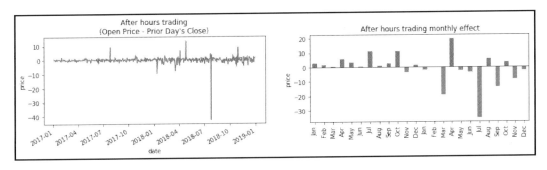

It may be surprising that Facebook has been affected more on a monthly scale since the daily level appears to be much more volatile for Netflix. There must have been a lot of counter-movements canceling each other out. Let's see how volume traded changed with the closing price for Netflix by using the `trade_volume()` method:

```
>>> netflix_viz.trade_volume(True)
```

By passing `True`, the `StockVisualizer` will remove excess space on either side of the *x*-axis to attempt to line up the plots:

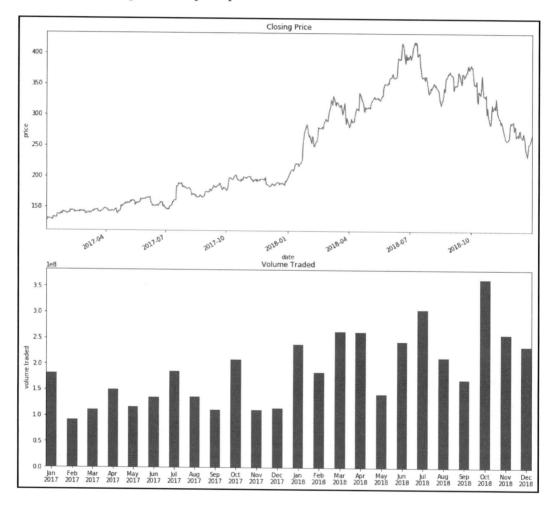

Volume traded grew every month as the stock rose, which is to be expected, as more people likely wanted in. What is interesting is that the highest month is not the sell-off that happened in late June/early July after disappointing subscriber growth, but October after another earnings call, which revealed strong subscriber growth due to many popular Netflix originals. The stock briefly recovered before losing more ground after this, as those who saw this as a way to get out before it got worse sold and those who thought they would continue to thrive bought in.

We can study Netflix's downward trend using window functions. For example, let's plot the 60-day and 200-day moving average and draw attention to July 2018:

```
>>> ax = netflix_viz.moving_average('close', ['60D', '200D'])
>>> netflix_viz.shade_region(
...     ax, x=('2018-07-01', '2018-07-31'), color='blue', alpha=0.2
... )
>>> plt.suptitle('Netflix Closing Price')
>>> plt.ylabel('price ($)')
```

These moving averages give us a smoothed version of the stock price curve. Notice that the fall Netflix took in July pushed the moving averages below the stock price while they had been above the price most of the time in the past:

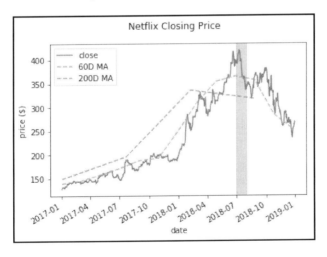

Traders experiment with different period moving averages depending on the task at hand, like anticipating upside moves (increases in stock price) and making planned exits before downside moves (decreases in stock price). Other uses include calculating automatic **support** and **resistance** levels (which we first saw in Chapter 6, *Plotting with Seaborn and Customization Techniques*) by finding the portion of the moving average line that props up the data from beneath or the one that acts as a ceiling for the data, respectively. When a stock price approaches the support, the price tends to be attractive enough that people buy, thus increasing the price (moving up from the support toward resistance). However, when the stock reaches the resistance, it tends to encourage people to sell, bringing the stock price down (moving away from the resistance and toward the support).

The following plot shows an example of how support (green) and resistance (red) act as lower and upper bounds, respectively, for the stock price; once the price hits either of these bounds, it tends to bounce back in the opposite direction due to buyers/sellers of the stock taking action:

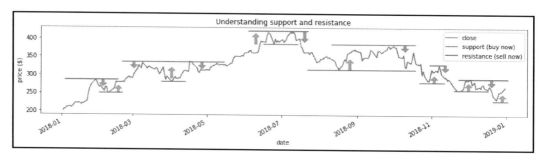

Often, the **exponentially weighted moving average (EWMA)** can provide a better trend since we can put additional emphasis on more recent values. Note that Netflix jumped quite a bit in the first half of 2018, but the moving averages took a while to adjust and were far off from the actual values during this spike. Let's use exponential smoothing instead and also check when the stock fell below the top quartile of the closing price:

```
>>> ax = netflix_viz.exp_smoothing('close', [60, 200])
>>> q_3, q_4 = nflx.close.quantile([0.75, 1])
>>> netflix_viz.shade_region(
...     ax, y=(q_3, q_4), color='grey', alpha=0.2
... )
>>> plt.suptitle('Netflix Closing Price')
>>> plt.ylabel('price ($)')
```

The 200-day EWMA isn't too informative, but the 60-day EWMA does a pretty good job. Notice how it props the closing price line up from below and, once in the gray area, switches over to act as an upper bound. It is acting like support below the gray area and as resistance toward the end of the gray area:

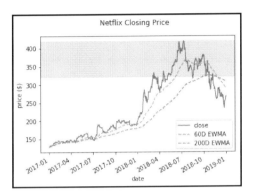

The notebook for this chapter contains a cell for interactive visualization of the moving average and the exponentially smoothed moving average. We can use these types of visualizations to determine the best window for the calculations. Note that using this cell will require some additional setup, but it is all noted right above the cell in the notebook.

Since the 60-period EWMA appears to fit the series the best, let's stick with it and draw attention to the decline with some reference lines:

```
>>> import numpy as np
>>> ax = netflix_viz.exp_smoothing('close', 60)
>>> netflix_viz.add_reference_line(
...     ax, y=nflx.high.max(), color='red', linestyle='-', label='max'
... )
>>> nflx_decline = nflx[nflx.high.idxmax():]
>>> netflix_viz.add_reference_line(
...     ax, x=nflx_decline.index,
...     y=np.linspace(
...         nflx_decline.high.max(), nflx_decline.low.min(),
...         num=nflx_decline.shape[0]
...     ),
...     color='r', linestyle=':', label='decline'
... )
>>> plt.suptitle('Netflix Closing Price')
>>> plt.ylabel('price ($)')
```

Once Netflix hits its maximum closing price, it trends down. This movement can be captured by the dotted red line. Interestingly enough, this line appears to act as support for the stock once the 60-day EWMA becomes the resistance:

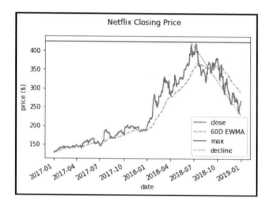

We have already taken a look at a stock in isolation (Facebook) in prior chapters, so let's take this in a different direction and compare Netflix to others. Let's use the `jointplot()` method to see how Netflix compares to the S&P 500:

```
>>> netflix_viz.jointplot(sp, 'close')
```

If we take a look at the plot, they appear to be weakly positively correlated. With financial analysis, we can calculate a metric called **beta** that indicates an asset's correlation to an index, like the S&P 500. We will calculate beta in the *Technical analysis of financial instruments* section later in this chapter:

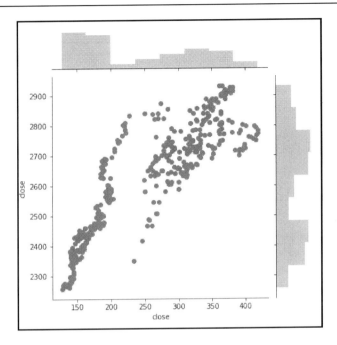

Next, let's see how Facebook's OHLC data correlates with Netflix's, since they both had declines around July 2018:

```
>>> netflix_viz.correlation_heatmap(fb)
```

Netflix and Facebook are also weakly positively correlated, but only on the OHLC data:

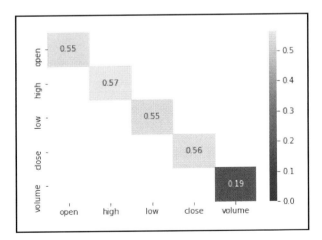

Lastly, we can use the `fill_between_other()` method to see how another asset grew (or fell) in price compared to Netflix. Since both Netflix and Facebook struggled around the same time, let's see how their closing prices compared over time:

```
>>> netflix_viz.fill_between_other(fb)
```

This results in the following plot, showing how Netflix pulled away from Facebook in 2018, despite taking a tumble in July (the green shaded region grows dramatically in vertical distance in 2018):

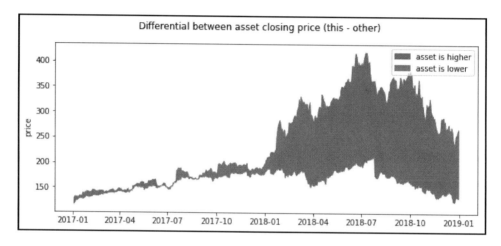

Visualizing multiple assets

Up until this point, we have discussed visualizing a single asset—in this case, Netflix—so let's move on to the `AssetGroupVisualizer` to perform some EDA across asset groups. First, let's look at the code for this class.

As we did previously, we will start by inheriting from the `Visualizer` and defining our docstring. Note that the `AssetGroupVisualizer` also keeps track of the column to use for group by operations, so we override the `__init__()` method; since this change was meant to be in addition to what was already there, we call the `__init__()` method of the superclass, as well:

```
class AssetGroupVisualizer(Visualizer):
    """
    Class for visualizing groups of assets in a single dataframe.
    """
```

```
# override for group visuals
def __init__(self, df, group_by='name'):
    """This object keeps track of which column to group by."""
    super().__init__(df)
    self.group_by = group_by
```

Next, we define the `evolution_over_time()` method to plot the same column for all the assets in the group in a single plot for comparison purposes. Since our data is of a different shape, we will use `seaborn` this time:

```
def evolution_over_time(self, column, **kwargs):
    """
    Visualize the evolution over time of a column for all assets.

    Parameters:
        - column: The name of the column to visualize.
        - kwargs: Additional keyword arguments to pass down
                  to the plotting function.

    Returns: A matplotlib Axes object.
    """
    if 'ax' not in kwargs:
        fig, ax = plt.subplots(1, 1, figsize=(10, 4))
    else:
        ax = kwargs.pop('ax')
    return sns.lineplot(
        x=self.data.index, y=column, hue=self.group_by,
        data=self.data, ax=ax, **kwargs
    )
```

Once again, we will use `seaborn` to rework our `boxplot()` method to work with asset groups:

```
def boxplot(self, column, **kwargs):
    """
    Generate boxplots for a given column in all assets.

    Parameters:
        - column: The name of the column to visualize.
        - kwargs: Additional keyword arguments to pass down
                  to the plotting function.

    Returns: A matplotlib Axes object.
    """
    return sns.boxplot(
        x=self.group_by, y=column, data=self.data, **kwargs
    )
```

When using `seaborn` or only plotting a single asset, we didn't have to worry about the layout of our subplots; however, for some of the other asset group visualizations, we want a way to automatically determine a reasonable subplot layout. For this, we will add the `_get_layout()` method; this method will generate the `Figure` and `Axes` objects we need for a given number of subplots (determined by unique assets in the group):

```
def _get_layout(self):
    """
    Helper method for getting an autolayout of subplots.

    Returns: The matplotlib Figure and Axes objects to plot with.
    """
    subplots_needed = self.data[self.group_by].nunique()
    rows = math.ceil(subplots_needed / 2)
    fig, axes = plt.subplots(rows, 2, figsize=(15, 5*rows))
    if rows > 1:
        axes = axes.flatten()
    if subplots_needed < len(axes):
        # remove excess axes from autolayout
        for i in range(subplots_needed, len(axes)):
            # can't use comprehension here
            fig.delaxes(axes[i])
    return fig, axes
```

Our `histogram()` method will use the `distplot()` function from `seaborn` to plot histograms for a given column for all the assets in the group:

```
def histogram(self, column, **kwargs):
    """
    Generate the histogram of a given column for all assets.

    Parameters:
        - column: The name of the column to visualize.
        - kwargs: Additional keyword arguments to pass down
                  to the plotting function.

    Returns: A matplotlib Axes object.
    """
    fig, axes = self._get_layout()
    for ax, (name, data) in zip(
        axes, self.data.groupby(self.group_by)
    ):
        sns.distplot(
            data[column], ax=ax, axlabel=f'{name} - {column}'
        )
    return axes
```

Now, we need to define how `_window_calc_func()` will work with groups. We will need to use our `_get_layout()` method to build subplots for each of the assets in the group:

```python
def _window_calc_func(self, column, periods, name, func,
                      named_arg,**kwargs):
    """
    Helper method for plotting a series and adding reference lines
    using a window calculation.

    Parameters:
        - column: The name of the column to plot.
        - periods: The rule/span or list of them to pass to the
          resampling/smoothing function, like '20D' for 20-day
          periods (resampling) or 20 for a 20-day span (smoothing)
        - name: The name of the window calculation (to show in
          the legend).
        - func: The window calculation function.
        - named_arg: The name of the argument `periods` is being
          passed as.
        - kwargs: Additional arguments to pass down to the
          plotting function.

    Returns: A matplotlib Axes object.
    """
    fig, axes = self._get_layout()
    for ax, asset_name in zip(
        axes, self.data[self.group_by].unique()
    ):
        subset = self.data[self.data[self.group_by] == asset_name]
        ax = subset.plot(
            y=column, ax=ax, label=asset_name, **kwargs
        )
        for period in self._iter_handler(periods):
            subset[column].pipe(
                func, **{named_arg: period}
            ).mean().plot(
                ax=ax, linestyle='--',
                label=f"""{period if isinstance(
                    period, str
                ) else str(period) + 'D'} {name}"""
            )
        ax.legend()
    return ax
```

We can override `after_hours_trades()` to extend our visualization of the effect of after-hours trading on an individual asset to a group of assets using subplots and iterating over the assets in the group:

```python
def after_hours_trades(self):
    """
    Visualize the effect of after hours trading on this asset.
    Returns: A matplotlib Axes object.
    """
    num_categories = self.data[self.group_by].nunique()
    fig, axes = plt.subplots(
        num_categories, 2, figsize=(15, 8*num_categories)
    )
    for ax, (name, data) in zip(
        axes, self.data.groupby(self.group_by)
    ):
        after_hours = (data.open - data.close.shift())
        monthly_effect = after_hours.resample('1M').sum()

        after_hours.plot(
            ax=ax[0],
            title=f'{name} Open Price - Prior Day\'s Close'
        )
        ax[0].set_ylabel('price')

        monthly_effect.index = monthly_effect.index.strftime('%b')
        monthly_effect.plot(
            ax=ax[1], kind='bar', rot=90,
            title=f'{name} after hours trading monthly effect',
            color=np.where(monthly_effect >= 0, 'g', 'r')
        ).axhline(0, color='black', linewidth=1)
        ax[1].set_ylabel('price')
    return axes
```

With the `StockVisualizer`, we were able to generate a joint plot between two assets' closing prices, but here we can override `pairplot()` to allow us to see the relationships between the closing price across assets in the group:

```python
def pairplot(self, **kwargs):
    """
    Generate a seaborn pairplot for this asset group.

    Parameters:
        - kwargs: Keyword arguments to pass down to
                  `sns.pairplot()`
    Returns: A seaborn pairplot
    """
```

```
    return sns.pairplot(
        self.data.pivot_table(
            values='close', index=self.data.index, columns='name'
        ), diag_kind='kde', **kwargs
    )
```

Finally, we override the `heatmap()` method, which generates a heatmap of the correlations between the closing prices of all the assets in the group:

```
def heatmap(self, pct_change=False, **kwargs):
    """
    Generate a seaborn heatmap for correlations between assets.

    Parameters:
        - pct_change: Whether or not to show the correlations of
                      the daily percent change in price or just
                      use the closing price.
        - kwargs: Keyword arguments to pass down to
                  `sns.heatmap()`

    Returns: A seaborn heatmap
    """
    pivot = self.data.pivot_table(
        values='close', index=self.data.index, columns='name'
    )
    if pct_change:
        pivot = pivot.pct_change()
    return sns.heatmap(
        pivot.corr(), annot=True, center=0, **kwargs
    )
```

We can use the `heatmap()` method to see how the daily percentage change across assets compares. This will handle for the difference in scale between the assets (Google and Amazon have much higher stock prices than Facebook or Apple, meaning that gains of a few dollars mean more to Facebook and Apple):

```
>>> faang_viz = stock_analysis.AssetGroupVisualizer(faang)
>>> faang_viz.heatmap(True)
```

Google-Amazon and Google-S&P 500 have the strongest correlations, with bitcoin having no correlation with anything:

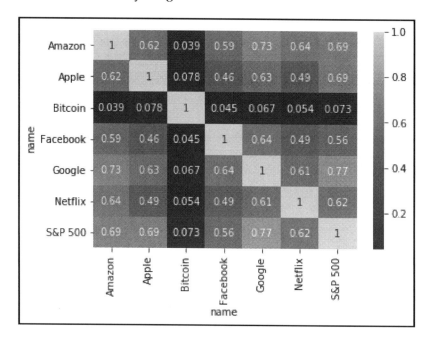

In the interest of brevity, rather than show all the methods for the group, which will result in large plots, I will leave that to you to view and try in the notebook. However, let's illustrate how we can combine these Visualizers to view all of our assets together to see how they all evolved over time:

```
>>> faang_sp_viz = stock_analysis.AssetGroupVisualizer(faang_sp)
>>> bitcoin_viz = stock_analysis.StockVisualizer(bitcoin)
>>> fig, axes = plt.subplots(1, 2, figsize=(15, 5))
>>> faang_sp_viz.evolution_over_time('close', ax=axes[0])
>>> bitcoin_viz.evolution_over_time(
...     'close', ax=axes[1], label='Bitcoin'
... )
```

Note that 2018 was rough for bitcoin (check out the scale on the *y*-axis). All the assets seem to have had a difficult fourth quarter in 2018:

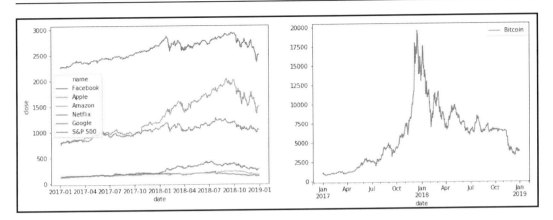

Feel free to try out all the methods in the `Visualizer` classes using the notebook for this chapter; the exercises will also offer an additional occasion to use them.

Now that we have a good feel for our data, let's look at some metrics.

Technical analysis of financial instruments

As with the previous two sections in this chapter, we will be writing a module with classes that will help carry out the main tasks. With technical analysis of assets, metrics (such as cumulative returns and volatility) are calculated to compare various assets to each other. We will need the `StockAnalyzer` class for technical analysis of a single asset and the `AssetGroupAnalyzer` for technical analysis of a group of assets. These classes are in the `stock_analysis/stock_analyzer.py` file.

As with the other modules, we will start with our docstring and imports:

```
"""Classes for technical analysis of assets."""

import math

from .utils import import validate_df
```

The StockAnalyzer class

For analyzing individual assets, we will build the `StockAnalyzer` class, which calculates metrics for a given asset. We can use the UML diagram to see all the metrics that are available:

```
StockAnalyzer
─────────────────
_max_periods
close
data
last_close
last_high
last_low
pct_change
pivot_point
─────────────────
__init__()
alpha()
annualized_volatility()
beta()
corr_with()
cumulative_returns()
cv()
daily_std()
is_bear_market()
is_bull_market()
port_return()
qcd()
resistance()
sharpe_ratio()
support()
volatility()
```

The `StockAnalyzer` will be initialized with the data for the asset we want to perform a technical analysis on. This means that our `__init__()` method will need to accept the data as a parameter:

```python
class StockAnalyzer:
    """
    Class for providing metrics for technical analysis of a stock.
    """

    @validate_df(columns={'open', 'high', 'low', 'close'})
    def __init__(self, df):
        self.data = df
```

Most of the calculations for our technical analysis will rely on the closing price of the stock, so rather than needing to write `self.data.close` in all of our methods, we will create a property so that we can access it with `self.close` instead. This makes our code cleaner and easier to follow:

```
@property
def close(self):
    """Get the close column of the data."""
    return self.data.close
```

A few calculations will also need the percent change of the `close` column, so we will make a property for easier access to that, as well:

```
@property
def pct_change(self):
    """Get the percent change of the close column."""
    return self.close.pct_change()
```

Since we will be calculating support and resistance levels using the **pivot point**, which is the average of the high, low, and close on the last day in the data, we will make a property for it:

```
@property
def pivot_point(self):
    """Calculate the pivot point for support/resistance levels."""
    return (self.last_close + self.last_high + self.last_low) / 3
```

Note that we are also using other properties—`self.last_close`, `self.last_high`, and `self.last_low`—which we define using the `last()` method on the data, before selecting the column in question, and using `iat` to get just the price:

```
@property
def last_close(self):
    """Get the value of the last close in the data."""
    return self.data.last('1D').close.iat[0]

@property
def last_high(self):
    """Get the value of the last high in the data."""
    return self.data.last('1D').high.iat[0]

@property
def last_low(self):
    """Get the value of the last low in the data."""
    return self.data.last('1D').low.iat[0]
```

Now, we have everything we need to calculate support and resistance. We will be calculating them at three different levels, where the first level is the closest to the closing price and the third level is the furthest. The first level will therefore be the most restrictive level, and the third will be the least. We define the `resistance()` method as follows, allowing the caller to specify the level to calculate:

```
def resistance(self, level=1):
    """
    Calculate the resistance at the given level.

    Parameters:
        - level: The resistance level (1, 2, or 3)

    Returns: The resistance value.
    """
    if level == 1:
        res = (2 * self.pivot_point) - self.last_low
    elif level == 2:
        res = self.pivot_point + (self.last_high - self.last_low)
    elif level == 3:
        res = self.last_high \
            + 2*(self.pivot_point - self.last_low)
    else:
        raise ValueError('Not a valid level. Must be 1, 2, or 3')
    return res
```

The `support()` method is defined in a similar fashion:

```
def support(self, level=1):
    """
    Calculate the support at the given level.

    Parameters:
        - level: The support level (1, 2, or 3)

    Returns: The support value.
    """
    if level == 1:
        sup = (2 * self.pivot_point) - self.last_high
    elif level == 2:
        sup = self.pivot_point - (self.last_high - self.last_low)
    elif level == 3:
        sup = self.last_low \
            - 2*(self.last_high - self.pivot_point)
    else:
        raise ValueError('Not a valid level. Must be 1, 2, or 3')
    return sup
```

Next, we work on creating methods for analyzing asset volatility. First, we will calculate the daily standard deviation of the percent change in the closing price. This metric needs to be provided with a number of trading periods to use for the calculation. In order to make sure that we can't use more trading periods than we have in the data, we will define a property with the maximum value we can use for this argument:

```
@property
def _max_periods(self):
    """Get the number of trading periods in the data."""
    return self.data.shape[0]
```

Now that we have our maximum, we can define the `daily_std()` method, which calculates the daily standard deviation of percent change:

```
def daily_std(self, periods=252):
    """
    Calculate the daily standard deviation of percent change.

    Parameters:
        - periods: The number of periods to use for the
          calculation; default is 252 for the trading days
          in a year. Note if you provide a number greater
          than the number of trading periods in the data,
          self._max_periods will be used instead.

    Returns: The standard deviation
    """
    return self.pct_change[
        min(periods, self._max_periods) * -1:
    ].std()
```

While `daily_std()` is useful on its own, we can take this a step further and calculate annualized volatility by multiplying the daily standard deviation by the square root of the number of trading periods in the year, which we assume to be 252:

```
def annualized_volatility(self):
    """Calculate the annualized volatility."""
    return self.daily_std() * math.sqrt(252)
```

In addition, we can look at rolling volatility by using the `rolling()` method from pandas:

```
def volatility(self, periods=252):
    """
    Calculate the rolling volatility.

    Parameters:
        - periods: The number of periods to use for the
          calculation; default is 252 for the trading
          days in a year. Note if you provide a number
          greater than the number of trading periods in
          the data, self._max_periods will be used instead.
    Returns: A pandas series.
    """
    periods = min(periods, self._max_periods)
    return self.close.rolling(periods).std() / math.sqrt(periods)
```

We often want to compare assets, so we provide the `corr_with()` method to calculate the correlations between assets per column in their data:

```
def corr_with(self, other):
    """
    Calculate the correlations between this dataframe and another.

    Parameters:
        - other: The other dataframe.
    Returns: A pandas series
    """
    return self.data.corrwith(other)
```

Next, we define some metrics for comparing the level of dispersion of assets. In Chapter 1, *Introduction to Data Analysis*, we discussed the coefficient of variation (`cv()` method) and the quantile coefficient of dispersion (`qcd()` method), which we can use to achieve this, both of which we will add here:

```
def cv(self):
    """
    Calculate the coefficient of variation for the asset. Note
    that the lower this is, the better the risk/return tradeoff.
    """
    return self.close.std() / self.close.mean()

def qcd(self):
    """Calculate the quantile coefficient of dispersion."""
    q1, q3 = self.close.quantile([0.25, 0.75])
    return (q3 - q1) / (q3 + q1)
```

In addition, we want a way to quantify the volatility of an asset compared to an index, like the S&P 500, for which we calculate **beta**—the ratio of the covariance of the asset's return and the index's return to the variance of the asset's return. We add a `beta()` method, which allows the user to specify the index to use as the benchmark:

```
def beta(self, index):
    """
    Calculate the beta of the asset.

    Parameters:
        - index: The dataframe for the index to compare to.

    Returns: Beta, a float.
    """
    index_change = index.close.pct_change()
    beta = self.pct_change.cov(index_change) / index_change.var()
    return beta
```

Next, we define a method for calculating the cumulative returns of an asset as a series. This is defined as the cumulative product of one plus the percent change in closing price:

```
def cumulative_returns(self):
    """Calculate the series of cumulative returns for plotting."""
    return (1 + self.pct_change).cumprod()
```

The next few metrics we want to support require calculating the return of the portfolio. To make things simpler, we will assume that there is no distribution per share so that the return of the portfolio is the percent change from the starting price to the ending price over the time period covered by the data. We will define this as a static method since we will need to calculate this for an index, and not just the data stored in `self.data`:

```
@staticmethod
def port_return(df):
    """
    Calculate the return assuming no distribution per share.

    Parameters:
        - df: The asset's dataframe.

    Returns: The return, as a float.
    """
    start, end = df.close[0], df.close[-1]
    return (end - start) / start
```

While beta allows us to compare an asset's volatility to an index, **alpha** allows us to compare the returns of the asset to an index. To do so, we also need the risk-free rate of return, which is the rate of return of an investment that has no risk of financial loss; in practice, we use treasury bills for this. At the time of writing, this was a 2.46% return, so we will use that for our calculations later. Calculating alpha requires calculating the portfolio return of the index and the asset, along with beta:

```
def alpha(self, index, r_f):
    """
    Calculates the asset's alpha.

    Parameters:
        - index: The index to compare to.
        - r_f: The risk-free rate of return.

    Returns: Alpha, as a float.
    """
    r_f /= 100
    r_m = self.port_return(index)
    beta = self.beta(index)
    r = self.port_return(self.data)
    alpha = r - r_f - beta * (r_m - r_f)
    return alpha
```

r_f /= 100 in the previous code snippet takes r_f and divides it by 100 before storing the result back in r_f. It's shorthand for r_f = r_f/100. Python has these operators for other arithmetic functions, like +=, -=, *=, and %=.

We also want to add methods that will tell us whether the asset is in a **bear market** or a **bull market**, meaning that they had a decline or increase in stock price of 20% or more in the last two months, respectively:

```
def is_bear_market(self):
    """
    Determine if a stock is in a bear market, meaning its
    return in the last 2 months is a decline of 20% or more.
    """
    return self.port_return(self.data.last('2M')) <= -.2

def is_bull_market(self):
    """
    Determine if a stock is in a bull market, meaning its
    return in the last 2 months is a increase of 20% or more.
    """
    return self.port_return(self.data.last('2M')) >= .2
```

Lastly, we add a method for calculating the **Sharpe ratio**, which tells us the return we receive in excess of the risk-free rate of return for the volatility we take on with the investment:

```
def sharpe_ratio(self, r_f):
    """
    Calculates the asset's sharpe ratio.

    Parameters:
        - r_f: The risk-free rate of return.

    Returns: The sharpe ratio, as a float.
    """
    return (
        self.cumulative_returns().last('1D').iat[0] - r_f
    ) / self.cumulative_returns().std()
```

Take some time to digest the code in this module as we are continuing to build upon what we have discussed. We won't be using all of the metrics in the next section, but I encourage you to try them out in the notebook for this chapter.

The AssetGroupAnalyzer class

All the calculations we will work with in this section are defined on the `StockAnalyzer` class; however, rather than having to run these for each of the assets we want to compare, we will also create the `AssetGroupAnalyzer` class (in the same module) that's capable of providing these metrics for a group of assets.

The `StockAnalyzer` and `AssetGroupAnalyzer` classes will share much of their functionality, which makes a strong argument for designing them with inheritance; however, sometimes, as in this case, composition can make more sense. When objects contain instances of other classes, it is referred to as **composition**. This design decision leaves us with a very simple UML diagram for the `AssetGroupAnalyzer` class:

AssetGroupAnalyzer
analyzers data group_by : str
__init__() _composition_handler() analyze()

Upon creating an `AssetGroupAnalyzer` object by providing the dataframe for the assets and the group by column (if not `'name'`), the `AssetGroupAnalyzer` calls its `_composition_handler()` method to create a dictionary of `StockAnalyzer` objects (one for each asset):

```python
class AssetGroupAnalyzer:
    """Analyzes many assets in a dataframe."""

    @validate_df(columns={'open', 'high', 'low', 'close'})
    def __init__(self, df, group_by='name'):
        self.data = df
        self.group_by = group_by

        if group_by not in self.data.columns:
            raise ValueError(
                f'`group_by` column "{group_by}" not in dataframe.'
            )
        self.analyzers = self._composition_handler()

    def _composition_handler(self):
        """
        Create a dictionary mapping each group to its analyzer,
        taking advantage of composition instead of inheritance.
        """
        return {
            group : StockAnalyzer(data) \
            for group, data in self.data.groupby(self.group_by)
        }
```

The `AssetGroupAnalyzer` class has only one public method, `analyze()`—all the actual calculations are delegated to the `StockAnalyzer` class:

```
def analyze(self, func_name, **kwargs):
    """
    Run a StockAnalyzer method on all assets in the group.

    Parameters:
        - func_name: The name of the method to run.
        - kwargs: Additional keyword arguments to pass to the
                  function.

    Returns: A dictionary mapping each asset to the result of the
             calculation of that function.
    """
    if not hasattr(StockAnalyzer, func_name):
        raise ValueError(
            f'StockAnalyzer has no "{func_name}" method.'
        )
    if not kwargs:
        kwargs = {}
    return {
        group : getattr(StockAnalyzer, func_name)(
            analyzer, **kwargs
        ) \
        for group, analyzer in self.analyzers.items()
    }
```

With inheritance, in this case, all the methods would have to be overridden because they can't handle the group by. Conversely, with composition, all that's necessary is to create `StockAnalyzer` objects for each asset and use dictionary comprehensions for the calculations. Another neat thing is that by using `getattr()`, there is no need to mirror the methods in the `AssetGroupAnalyzer` because `analyze()` can grab the method by name using the `StockAnalyzer` objects!

Comparing assets

Let's use the `AssetGroupAnalyzer` to compare all the assets we have collected data for. As with prior sections, we won't use all the methods in the `StockAnalyzer` class here, so be sure to try them out on your own:

```
>>> all_assets_analyzer = stock_analysis.AssetGroupAnalyzer(
...     all_assets
... )
```

Remember from Chapter 1, *Introduction to Data Analysis*, that the coefficient of variation (CV) is the ratio of the standard deviation to the mean; this helps us compare the variation of asset closing prices, even though their means are of different magnitudes (like Amazon and Apple). CV can also be used to compare the volatility to the expected return of an investment and quantify the risk-return trade-off. Let's use the CV to see which asset's closing price is the most widely dispersed:

```
>>> all_assets_analyzer.analyze('cv')
{'Amazon': 0.2854305350462308,
 'Apple': 0.16226034216914967,
 'Bitcoin': 0.6554280661890078,
 'Facebook': 0.12279024871316224,
 'Google': 0.1180120840412368,
 'Netflix': 0.3538951052577031,
 'S&P 500': 0.07006117737058823}
```

We can also use the qcd() method to calculate this spread with the quantile coefficient of dispersion. The result will be similar to the CV.

It's probably not a surprise that bitcoin has the widest spread. Rather than use the closing price, percent change daily can be used to calculate the annualized volatility. This involves calculating the standard deviations of percent change over the last year and multiplying it by the square root of the number of trading days in the year (the code assumes 252). By using percent change, large changes in price (relative to the asset's price) will be penalized more severely. Using annualized volatility, Facebook looks much more volatile compared to when we used CV (although still not the most volatile):

```
>>> all_assets_analyzer.analyze('annualized_volatility')
{'Amazon': 0.3606494699321407,
 'Apple': 0.28704998389950653,
 'Bitcoin': 0.5395395749357711,
 'Facebook': 0.37984232350933056,
 'Google': 0.2807968929806305,
 'Netflix': 0.46338066251205556,
 'S&P 500': 0.17024852961093584}
```

Given that all the assets have fallen in value toward the end of our dataset, let's check if any of them have entered a **bear market**, meaning that the asset's return in the last two months is a 20% or greater decline:

```
>>> all_assets_analyzer.analyze('is_bear_market')
{'Amazon': False,
 'Apple': True,
 'Bitcoin': True,
 'Facebook': False,
 'Google': False,
 'Netflix': False,
 'S&P 500': False}
```

It looks like Apple and bitcoin had quite a rough November and December in 2018. The other assets appear to have fared better; however, none are in a bull market (we can confirm this by passing `'is_bull_market'` to `analyze()`). Yet another way to analyze volatility is to compare the assets to an index by calculating **beta**. Positive values greater than one indicate volatility higher than the index, while negative values less than negative one indicate inverse relationships to the index:

```
>>> all_assets_analyzer.analyze('beta', index=sp)
{'Amazon': 1.5811322027668804,
 'Apple': 1.2781328940225514,
 'Bitcoin': 0.5036241127304713,
 'Facebook': 1.2773905798855243,
 'Google': 1.3547609746190785,
 'Netflix': 1.832923248791993,
 'S&P 500': 1.0}
```

Using the betas from the previous result, we can see that Netflix is the most volatile compared to the S&P 500, meaning that if this was our portfolio (leaving out bitcoin for the moment), adding Netflix would have increased the portfolio risk. However, we know that bitcoin is not correlated to the S&P 500 (review the heatmap from the previous section), so this low beta is misleading.

The last metric we will take a look at is **alpha**, which is used to compare the return of an investment to the market. Calculating alpha requires that we pass in the risk-free rate of return (r_f); we typically use the return of a US Treasury Bill for this number. At the time of writing, this rate was 2.46%.

Let's compare the alpha for the assets to the S&P 500:

```
>>> all_assets_analyzer.analyze('alpha', index=sp, r_f=2.46)
{'Amazon': 0.8327848879155585,
 'Apple': 0.2665039547528644,
 'Bitcoin': 2.6812043353655053,
 'Facebook': -0.012292189123313632,
 'Google': 0.17664350251938093,
 'Netflix': 0.9177924683678698,
 'S&P 500': 0.0}
```

With the exception of Facebook, everything beat the S&P 500, which essentially being a portfolio of 500 stocks has lower risk and lower returns due to **diversification**. Netflix beat the S&P 500 by 0.92%, despite taking a tumble in the second half of the year. This brings us to cumulative returns, which shows the return for each dollar we invested:

```
>>> fig, axes = plt.subplots(1, 2, figsize=(15, 5))
>>> cumulative_returns = all_assets_analyzer \
...       .analyze('cumulative_returns')
>>> for name, data in cumulative_returns.items():
...       data.plot(
...           ax=axes[0] if name == 'Bitcoin' else axes[1],
...           label=name, legend=True
...       )
>>> plt.suptitle('Cumulative Returns 2017-2018')
```

Bitcoin was certainly a roller coaster, but the stock market was much more tame, despite the struggles late in the year that essentially wiped out the gains in 2018. Notice that the bitcoin subplot's *y*-axis goes from 0 to 20 (left subplot), while the stock market subplot (right) has a much smaller range on the *y*-axis:

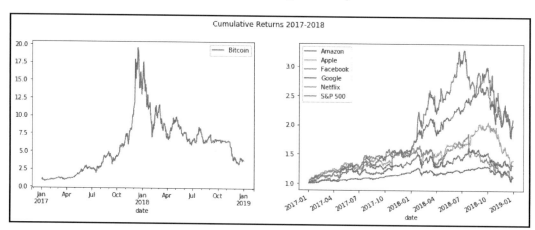

Modeling performance

The goal of this section is to give you a taste of how to build some models; as such, the following examples are not meant to be the best possible model, but rather a simple and relatively quick implementation for learning purposes. Once again, the stock_analysis package has a class for this section's task: StockModeler.

Note that to fully understand the statistical elements of this section and modeling in general, we need a solid understanding of statistics; however, the purpose of this discussion is to show how modeling techniques can be applied to financial data without dwelling on the underlying mathematics.

The StockModeler class

The StockModeler class will make it easier for us to build and evaluate some simple financial models without needing to interact directly with the statsmodels package. In addition, we will reduce the number of steps that are needed to generate a model with the methods we create. The UML diagram for this class shows a rather simple class. Notice that we have no attributes:

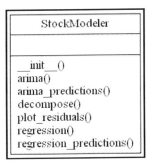

This is because the StockModeler is a **static class** (meaning that we don't instantiate it) and has methods for both building models and doing some preliminary analysis of their performance. The class is in stock_analysis/stock_modeler.py. As usual, we start the module with our docstring and imports:

```
"""Simple time series modeling for stocks."""

import matplotlib.pyplot as plt
import pandas as pd
from statsmodels.tsa.arima_model import ARIMA
```

```
from statsmodels.tsa.seasonal import seasonal_decompose
import statsmodels.api as sm

from .utils import validate_df
```

Next, we will start the `StockModeler` class and raise an error if someone tries to instantiate it:

```
class StockModeler:
    """Static methods for modeling stocks."""

    def __init__(self):
        raise NotImplementedError(
            "This class is to be used statically,"
            "don't instantiate it!"
        )
```

One of the tasks we want this class to support is time series decomposition, which we discussed back in Chapter 1, *Introduction to Data Analysis*. We imported the `seasonal_decompose()` function from `statsmodels`, so we just have to call it on the closing price of our stock data in our `decompose()` method:

```
@staticmethod
@validate_df(columns={'close'}, instance_method=False)
def decompose(df, freq, model='additive'):
    """
    Decompose the closing price of the stock into trend, seasonal,
    and remainder components.

    Parameters:
        - df: The dataframe containing the stock closing price as
          `close` and with a time index.
        - freq: The number of periods in the frequency.
        - model: How to compute the decomposition
          ('additive' or 'multiplicative')

    Returns: A statsmodels decomposition object.
    """
    return seasonal_decompose(df.close, model=model, freq=freq)
```

Notice that we have two decorators for the `decompose()` method. The top-most decorator is applied on the result of the ones below it. In this example, we have the following:

```
staticmethod(
    validate_df(decompose, columns={'close'}, instance_method=False)
)
```

In addition, we also want to support creating ARIMA models, which we also discussed in `Chapter 1`, *Introduction to Data Analysis*. ARIMA models use the `ARIMA(p, d, q)` notation, where *p* is the number of time lags (or order) of the AR model, *d* is the number of past values that were subtracted from the data (the I model), and *q* is the number of periods used in the MA model. So, an `ARIMA(1, 1, 1)` is a model with 1 time lag for the autoregressive portion, data differenced once, and a 1-period moving average. If we have any 0s for the orders, we can eliminate those. For example, `ARIMA(1, 0, 1)` is equivalent to `ARMA(1, 1)`, and `ARIMA(0, 0, 3)` is equivalent to `MA(3)`. A seasonal ARIMA model is written as `ARIMA(p,d,q)(P, D, Q)`$_m$, where *m* is the number of periods in the seasonal model and *P*, *D*, and *Q* are the orders for the seasonal ARIMA model. Our method will take these as parameters, but to avoid confusion, we will name them after the ARIMA feature they represent—for example, `ar` for autoregressive. Once again, we will use `statsmodels`. In addition, we are going to have our static method provide the option of fitting the model before returning it:

```python
@staticmethod
@validate_df(columns={'close'}, instance_method=False)
def arima(df, *, ar, i, ma, fit=True):
    """
    Create an ARIMA object for modeling time series.

    Parameters:
        - df: The dataframe containing the stock closing price as
            `close` and with a time index.
        - ar: The autoregressive order (p).
        - i: The differenced order (q).
        - ma: The moving average order (d).
        - fit: Whether or not to return the fitted model,
            defaults to True.

    Returns: A statsmodels ARIMA object which you can use to fit
        and predict.
    """
    arima_model = ARIMA(
        df.close.asfreq('B').fillna(method='ffill'),
        order=(ar, i, ma)
    )
    return arima_model.fit() if fit else arima_model
```

Note that the method signature (`df, *, ar, i, ma, fit=True`) has a `*` in it. This forces the parameters listed after it to be supplied as keyword arguments when calling the method. It's a nice way to make sure that whoever uses this is explicit about what they want.

To go along with this, we want a way to evaluate the ARIMA model's predictions, so we will add the `arima_predictions()` static method. The predictions from the ARIMA model will be the predicted changes, meaning that we will have to transform them into predicted closing prices in order to use them. We will also provide the option of getting back the predictions as a `pandas.Series` object or as a plot:

```
@staticmethod
@validate_df(columns={'close'}, instance_method=False)
def arima_predictions(df, arima_model_fitted, start, end,
                      plot=True, **kwargs):
    """
    Get ARIMA predictions as pandas Series or plot.

    Parameters:
        - df: The dataframe for the stock.
        - arima_model_fitted: The fitted ARIMA model.
        - start: The start date for the predictions.
        - end: The end date for the predictions.
        - plot: Whether or not to plot the result, default is
                True meaning the plot is returned instead of the
                pandas Series containing the predictions.
        - kwargs: Additional keyword arguments to pass to the
                pandas `plot()` method.

    Returns: A matplotlib Axes object or predictions as a Series
            depending on the value of the `plot` argument.
    """
    predicted_changes = arima_model_fitted.predict(
        start=start, end=end
    )

    predictions = pd.Series(
        predicted_changes, name='close'
    ).cumsum() + df.last('1D').close.iat[0]

    if plot:
        ax = df.close.plot(**kwargs)
        predictions.plot(
            ax=ax, style='r:', label='arima predictions'
        )
        ax.legend()

    return ax if plot else predictions
```

Similar to what we built for ARIMA models, we will also provide the `regression()` method for building a linear regression of the closing price with a lag of one. For this, we will once again use `statsmodels` (in Chapter 9, *Getting Started with Machine Learning in Python*, we will use `scikit-learn` for linear regression instead):

```
@staticmethod
@validate_df(columns={'close'}, instance_method=False)
def regression(df):
    """
    Create linear regression of time series data with a lag of 1.

    Parameters:
        - df: The dataframe with the stock data.

    Returns: X, Y, and the fitted statsmodels linear regression
    """
    X = df.close.shift().dropna()
    Y = df.close[1:]
    return X, Y, sm.OLS(Y, X).fit()
```

As with the `arima_predictions()` method, we want to provide a way to review the predictions from the model, either as a `pandas.Series` object or a plot. Unlike the ARIMA model, the predictions will be the closing price; however, it will only predict one value at a time. Therefore, we will start our predictions at the day after the last closing price and iteratively use the previous prediction to predict the next one. To handle all this, we will write the `regression_predictions()` method:

```
@staticmethod
@validate_df(columns={'close'}, instance_method=False)
def regression_predictions(df, model, start, end,
                           plot=True, **kwargs):
    """
    Get linear regression predictions as pandas Series or plot.

    Parameters:
        - df: The dataframe for the stock.
        - model: The fitted linear regression model.
        - start: The start date for the predictions.
        - end: The end date for the predictions.
        - plot: Whether or not to plot the result, default is
                True meaning the plot is returned instead of the
                pandas Series containing the predictions.
        - kwargs: Additional keyword arguments to pass down.
```

```
Returns: A matplotlib Axes object or predictions as a Series
        depending on the value of the `plot` argument.
"""
predictions = pd.Series(
    index=pd.date_range(start, end), name='close'
)
last = df.last('1D').close
for i, date in enumerate(predictions.index):
    if i == 0:
        pred = model.predict(last)
    else:
        pred = model.predict(predictions.iloc[i-1])
    predictions.loc[date] = pred[0]

if plot:
    ax = df.close.plot(**kwargs)
    predictions.plot(
        ax=ax, style='r:', label='regression predictions'
    )
    ax.legend()

return ax if plot else predictions
```

Lastly, for both the ARIMA and linear regression models, we want to visualize the errors in the predictions, or **residuals**. The fitted models both have a `resid` attribute, which will give us the residuals; we simply need to plot them as a scatter plot to check their variance and a KDE to check their mean. For this, we will add the `plot_residuals()` method:

```
@staticmethod
def plot_residuals(model_fitted):
    """
    Visualize the residuals from the model.

    Parameters:
        - model_fitted: The fitted model

    Returns: A matplotlib Axes object.
    """
    fig, axes = plt.subplots(1, 2, figsize=(15, 5))

    residuals = pd.Series(model_fitted.resid, name='residuals')
    residuals.plot(style='bo', ax=axes[0], title='Residuals')
```

```
axes[0].set_xlabel('Date')
axes[0].set_ylabel('Residual')

residuals.plot(kind='kde', ax=axes[1], title='Residuals KDE')
axes[1].set_xlabel('Residual')
return axes
```

Time series decomposition

As mentioned in `Chapter 1`, *Introduction to Data Analysis*, time series can be decomposed into trend, seasonal, and remainder components utilizing a specified frequency. This can be achieved with the `statsmodels` package, which `StockModeler.decompose()` is using:

```
>>> from stock_analysis import StockModeler
>>> decomposition = StockModeler.decompose(nflx, 20)
>>> fig = decomposition.plot()
>>> fig.suptitle('Netflix Stock Price Time Series Decomposition', y=1)
```

This returns the decomposition plot for Netflix with a frequency of 20 trading days:

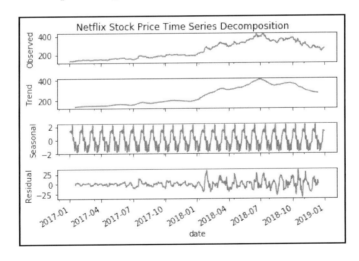

For more complicated models, we could decompose and then build our model around the components. That is beyond the scope of this chapter, however, so let's move on to ARIMA models.

ARIMA

As we discussed in `Chapter 1`, *Introduction to Data Analysis*, ARIMA models have autoregressive, difference, and moving average components. This can also be achieved using the `statsmodels` package. The `StockModeler.arima()` method returns a fitted ARIMA model for the stock according to the specifications provided:

```
>>> arima_model = StockModeler.arima(nflx, ar=10, i=1, ma=5)
```

 We're picking these values because they run in a reasonable amount of time. In practice, we can use the `autocorrelation_plot()` function from `pandas.plotting` that was introduced in `Chapter 5`, *Visualizing Data with Pandas and Matplotlib*, to help find a good value for `ar`.

Once the model is fitted, information on it can be obtained with the model's `summary()` method:

```
>>> arima_model.summary()
```

The summary is quite extensive, and we should read the documentation when looking to interpret it. Be advised that this will require a solid understanding of statistics:

```
                        ARIMA Model Results
=================================================================
Dep. Variable:              D.close   No. Observations:          519
Model:              ARIMA(10, 1, 5)   Log Likelihood        -1703.642
Method:                     css-mle   S.D. of innovations       6.440
Date:               Tue, 30 Apr 2019  AIC                    3441.285
Time:                      21:53:37   BIC                    3513.567
Sample:                  01-04-2017   HQIC                   3469.603
                       - 12-31-2018
=================================================================
                  coef    std err        z      P>|z|     [0.025     0.975]
-----------------------------------------------------------------
const           0.2695      0.310     0.868     0.386     -0.339      0.878
ar.L1.D.close   0.1877      0.254     0.740     0.459     -0.309      0.685
ar.L2.D.close   1.1564      0.128     9.038     0.000      0.906      1.407
ar.L3.D.close  -0.2650      0.335    -0.791     0.430     -0.922      0.392
ar.L4.D.close  -0.5686      0.138    -4.135     0.000     -0.838     -0.299
ar.L5.D.close   0.1855      0.213     0.872     0.384     -0.231      0.602
ar.L6.D.close  -0.0529      0.087    -0.609     0.543     -0.223      0.117
ar.L7.D.close   0.1635      0.087     1.884     0.060     -0.007      0.334
ar.L8.D.close  -0.1371      0.086    -1.600     0.110     -0.305      0.031
ar.L9.D.close  -0.0340      0.055    -0.620     0.536     -0.142      0.074
ar.L10.D.close  0.1584      0.053     3.014     0.003      0.055      0.261
ma.L1.D.close  -0.1690      0.255    -0.664     0.507     -0.668      0.330
ma.L2.D.close  -1.1946      0.126    -9.506     0.000     -1.441     -0.948
ma.L3.D.close   0.3317      0.343     0.968     0.333     -0.340      1.003
ma.L4.D.close   0.6641      0.115     5.791     0.000      0.439      0.889
ma.L5.D.close  -0.4049      0.223    -1.814     0.070     -0.843      0.033
                              Roots
=================================================================
                 Real        Imaginary        Modulus         Frequency
-----------------------------------------------------------------
AR.1          -0.9296         -0.3803j          1.0044          -0.4382
AR.2          -0.9296         +0.3803j          1.0044           0.4382
AR.3          -1.4264         -0.0000j          1.4264          -0.5000
AR.4          -0.4786         -1.2416j          1.3307          -0.3086
AR.5          -0.4786         +1.2416j          1.3307           0.3086
AR.6           1.1073         -0.0000j          1.1073          -0.0000
AR.7           0.9937         -0.4864j          1.1063          -0.0724
AR.8           0.9937         +0.4864j          1.1063           0.0724
AR.9           0.6815         -1.1678j          1.3521          -0.1659
AR.10          0.6815         +1.1678j          1.3521           0.1659
MA.1          -0.9404         -0.3832j          1.0155          -0.4384
MA.2          -0.9404         +0.3832j          1.0155           0.4384
MA.3           1.2160         -0.0000j          1.2160          -0.0000
MA.4           1.1524         -0.8007j          1.4033          -0.0966
MA.5           1.1524         +0.8007j          1.4033           0.0966
-----------------------------------------------------------------
```

For our purposes, a simpler way of analyzing the model is to look at the **residuals**, or the discrepancy between the observed values and predictions made by the model. The residuals should have a mean of zero and have equal variance throughout, meaning that they should not depend on the independent variable (which is the date, in this case). The latter requirement is referred to as **homoskedasticity**; when this assumption is not met, the estimates given by the model are not optimal. The `StockModeler.plot_residuals()` method helps check for this visually:

```
>>> StockModeler.plot_residuals(arima_model)
```

While the residuals are centered at zero, they are **heteroskedastic**—note how their variance increases over time:

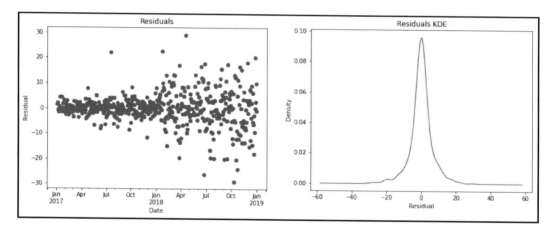

Linear regression with statsmodels

Rather than ARIMA, we could build a linear regression of the prior day's closing price to model closing price using `statsmodels`. This is taken care of by the `StockModeler.regression()` method:

```
>>> X, Y, lm = StockModeler.regression(nflx)
```

Once again, the `summary()` method can be called to look at statistics on the model's fit:

```
>>> lm.summary()
```

This results in the following summary:

```
                            OLS Regression Results
==============================================================================
Dep. Variable:                  close   R-squared:                       0.999
Model:                            OLS   Adj. R-squared:                  0.999
Method:                 Least Squares   F-statistic:                 7.156e+05
Date:                Tue, 30 Apr 2019   Prob (F-statistic):               0.00
Time:                        21:54:07   Log-Likelihood:                -1671.0
No. Observations:                 501   AIC:                             3344.
Df Residuals:                     500   BIC:                             3348.
Df Model:                           1
Covariance Type:            nonrobust
==============================================================================
                 coef    std err          t      P>|t|      [0.025      0.975]
------------------------------------------------------------------------------
close          1.0005      0.001    845.943      0.000       0.998       1.003
==============================================================================
Omnibus:                       56.185   Durbin-Watson:                   2.004
Prob(Omnibus):                  0.000   Jarque-Bera (JB):              282.611
Skew:                          -0.313   Prob(JB):                     4.28e-62
Kurtosis:                       6.626   Cond. No.                         1.00
==============================================================================

Warnings:
[1] Standard Errors assume that the covariance matrix of the errors is correctly specified.
```

The adjusted R^2 makes this model look very good since it is near one; however, we know that this is simply because stock data is highly autocorrelated, so let's look at the residuals again:

```
>>> StockModeler.plot_residuals(lm)
```

This model also suffers from heteroskedasticity:

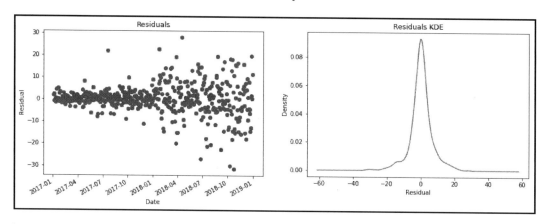

Comparing models

Let's see whether the ARIMA model or the linear regression model performed better at predicting Netflix closing prices in January 2019 by gathering new data and using the prediction methods in the `StockModeler` class:

```
>>> import datetime
>>> start = datetime.date(2019, 1, 1)
>>> end = datetime.date(2019, 1, 31)

>>> jan_2019 = stock_analysis.StockReader(
...     start, end
... ).get_ticker_data('NFLX')

>>> fig, axes = plt.subplots(1, 2, figsize=(15, 5))

>>> arima_ax = StockModeler.arima_predictions(
...     nflx, arima_model, start=start, end=end,
...     ax=axes[0], title='ARIMA'
... )
>>> jan_2019.close.plot(
...     ax=arima_ax, style='b:', label='actual close'
... )
>>> arima_ax.legend()
>>> arima_ax.set_ylabel('price ($)')
```

```
>>> linear_reg = StockModeler.regression_predictions(
...     nflx, lm, start=start, end=end,
...     ax=axes[1], title='Linear Regression'
... )
>>> jan_2019.close.plot(
...     ax=linear_reg, style='b:', label='actual close'
... )
>>> linear_reg.legend()
>>> linear_reg.set_ylabel('price ($)')
```

The ARIMA model's predictions look more in-line with the pattern we would expect, but given the unpredictable nature of the stock market, both models are far off from what actually happened in January 2019; Netflix recovered quite a bit of lost ground at the start of the year:

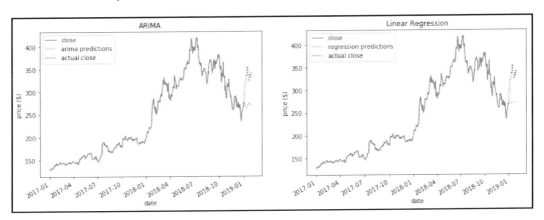

As we can see, predicting stocks is not easy, even for a few days. There is a lot of data that is not being captured by these models, like news stories, regulations, and changes in management, to name a few. No matter how good the model appears to fit, be weary of trusting predictions as these will be extrapolations, and there is a lot of randomness not being accounted for.

To further illustrate this, let's look at the following set of plots that have been generated using random walks and stock data. Only one is real data, but which one? The answer follows the plots, so take a guess before looking:

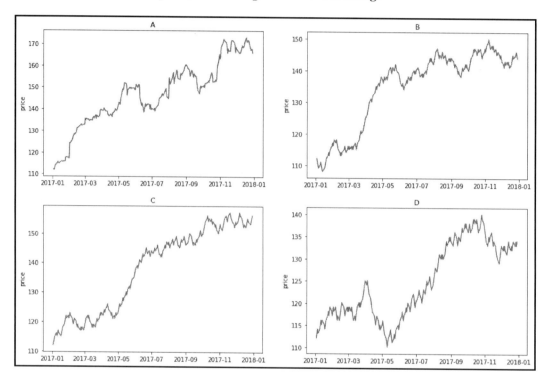

The `random_walk_stock_comparison()` function in the `random_walk.py` file generates the previous subplots and randomly places the actual data in one of the boxes while generating the others randomly. We can specify the steps (direction and value) that are possible at each day and the probability that each will happen.

The top-left (A) is Apple in 2017; the other three are all random walks from the first closing price in the Apple dataframe. Hard (or impossible) to tell, right?

Summary

In this chapter, we saw how building Python packages for our analysis applications can make it very easy for others to carry out their own analyses and reproduce ours. The `stock_analysis` package we created in this chapter contained classes for gathering stock data from the Internet (`StockReader`); visualizing individual assets or groups of them (`Visualizer` family); calculating metrics for single assets or groups of them for comparisons (`StockAnalyzer` and `AssetGroupAnalyzer`, respectively); and time series modeling with decomposition, ARIMA, and linear regression (`StockModeler`). We also got our first look at using the `statsmodels` package in the `StockModeler` class. This chapter showed us how the `pandas`, `matplotlib`, `seaborn`, and `numpy` functionality that we've covered so far in this book have come together and how these libraries can work harmoniously with other packages for custom applications. I strongly encourage you to reread the code in the `stock_analysis` package and test out some of the methods we didn't cover in this chapter to make sure you have the concepts down.

In the next chapter, we will work on another application as we learn how to build a simulator for login attempts and try our hand at rule-based anomaly detection.

Exercises

Use the `stock_analysis` package to complete the following exercises. Unless otherwise noted, use data from 2017 through to the end of 2018:

1. Using the `StockAnalyzer`, calculate and plot three levels of support and resistance for Netflix's closing price from 2017-2018.
2. With the `StockVisualizer`, look at the effect of after-hours trading on the FAANG stocks:
    *   As individual stocks
    *   As a portfolio using the `make_portfolio()` function from `stock_analysis.utils`
3. Using the `StockVisualizer.open_to_close()` method, create a plot that fills the area between the FAANG stocks' opening price (as a portfolio) and its closing price each day in red if the price declined and in green if the price increased. As a bonus, do the same for a portfolio of bitcoin and the S&P 500.

4. Mutual funds and **exchange-traded funds (ETFs)** are funds that are composed of many assets. They are built to mitigate risk, so volatility for the fund will be lower than that of the assets that compose it. Information on how they differ can be found at `https://www.investopedia.com/articles/exchangetradedfunds/08/etf-mutual-fund-difference.asp`. Compare a mutual fund or ETF of your choice to three of its largest stocks (by composition) using annualized volatility and the `AssetGroupAnalyzer`.

5. Write a function that returns a dataframe of one row with columns for `alpha`, `beta`, `annualized_volatility`, `is_bear_market`, and `is_bull_market`, which each contain the results of running the respective methods on a given stock using the `StockAnalyzer`. Dictionary comprehensions and the `getattr()` function, as used in the `AssetGroupAnalyzer.analyze()` method, will be useful.

Further reading

Check out the following resources for more information on the material covered in this chapter:

- *A guide to Python's function decorators*: `https://www.thecodeship.com/patterns/guide-to-python-function-decorators/`
- *Alpha*: `https://www.investopedia.com/terms/a/alpha.asp`
- *An Introduction to Classes and Inheritance (in Python)*: `http://www.jesshamrick.com/2011/05/18/an-introduction-to-classes-and-inheritance-in-python/`
- *Beta*: `https://www.investopedia.com/terms/b/beta.asp`
- *Coefficient of Variation (CV)*: `https://www.investopedia.com/terms/c/coefficientofvariation.asp`
- *Classes (Python Documentation)*: `https://docs.python.org/3/tutorial/classes.html`
- *How to Create a Python Package*: `https://www.pythoncentral.io/how-to-create-a-python-package/`
- *How to Create an ARIMA Model for Time Series Forecasting in Python*: `https://machinelearningmastery.com/arima-for-time-series-forecasting-with-python/`

- *Object-Oriented Programming in Python*: https://python.swaroopch.com/oop.html
- *Random walk*: https://en.wikipedia.org/wiki/Random_walk
- *Stock Analysis*: https://www.investopedia.com/terms/s/stock-analysis.asp
- *Support and Resistance Basics*: https://www.investopedia.com/trading/support-and-resistance-basics/
- *The definitive guide on how to use static, class or abstract methods in Python*: https://julien.danjou.info/guide-python-static-class-abstract-methods/
- *Understand How After-Hours Trading Affects Stock Prices*: https://www.investopedia.com/ask/answers/05/saleafterhours.asp
- *Use statsmodels to Perform Linear Regression in Python*: https://datatofish.com/statsmodels-linear-regression/
- *Writing the Setup Script*: https://docs.python.org/3/distutils/setupscript.html

8
Rule-Based Anomaly Detection

It's time to catch some hackers trying to gain access to a website using a **brute-force attack**—trying to log in with a bunch of username-password combinations until they gain access. This type of attack is very noisy, so it gives us plenty of data points for **anomaly detection**, which is the process of looking for data generated from a process other than the one we deem to be typical activity. The hackers will be simulated and won't be as crafty as they can be in real life, but it will give us great exposure to anomaly detection.

We will be creating a package that will handle the simulation of the login attempts in order to generate the data for this chapter. Knowing how to simulate is an essential skill to have in our toolbox. Sometimes, it's difficult to solve a problem with an exact mathematical solution; however, it might be easy to define how small components of the system work. In these cases, we can model the small components and simulate the behavior of the system as a whole. The result of the simulation gives us an approximation of the solution that may be sufficient for our purposes.

We will utilize rule-based anomaly detection to identify the suspicious activity in the simulated data. By the end of this chapter, we will have an understanding of how to simulate data using random numbers generated from various probability distributions, get more exposure to the Python standard library, gain additional experience building Python packages, practice performing exploratory data analysis, and get an introduction to anomaly detection.

The following topics will be covered in this chapter:

- Simulating login attempts to create our dataset for the chapter
- Performing exploratory data analysis to understand the simulated data
- Using rules and baselines for anomaly detection

Chapter materials

We will be building a simulation package to generate the data for this chapter; it is on GitHub at `https://github.com/stefmolin/login-attempt-simulator/tree/pandas_book`. This package was installed from GitHub when we set up our environment back in `Chapter 1`, *Introduction to Data Analysis*; however, if we want, we can follow the instructions in `Chapter 7`, *Financial Analysis – Bitcoin and the Stock Market*, to install a version of the package that we can edit.

The repository for this chapter, which can be found at `https://github.com/stefmolin/Hands-On-Data-Analysis-with-Pandas/tree/master/ch_08`, has the notebook we will use for our actual analysis (`anomaly_detection.ipynb`), the data files we will be working with in the `logs/` folder, the data used for the simulation in the `user_data/` folder, and the `simulate.py` file, which contains a Python script that we can run on the command line to simulate the data for the chapter.

Simulating login attempts

Since we can't easily find this type of data (it's not typically shared due its sensitive nature), we will be simulating it. Simulation requires a strong understanding of statistical modeling, estimating probabilities of certain events, and identifying appropriate assumptions to simplify where necessary. In order to run the simulation, we will build a Python package (`login_attempt_simulator`) to simulate a login process requiring a correct username and password (without any extra authentication measures, such as two-factor authentication) and a script (`simulate.py`) that can be run on the command line, both of which we will discuss in this section.

Assumptions

Before we jump into the code that handles the simulation, we need to understand the assumptions. It is impossible to control for every possible variable when we make a simulation, so we must identify some simplifying assumptions to get started.

The simulator makes the following assumptions about valid users of the website:

- Valid users come according to a **Poisson process** at an hourly rate that depends on the day of the week and the time of day. A Poisson process models arrivals per unit of time (our simulation will use an hour) as a Poisson distribution with mean λ (lambda). The interarrival times are exponentially distributed with mean $1/\lambda$.
- Valid users connect from 1-3 IP addresses (a unique identifier for each device using the Internet), which are made of 4 random integers in the range of [0, 255] separated by periods. It is possible, although highly unlikely, that two valid users share an IP address.
- Valid users are unlikely to make many mistakes entering their credentials.

The interarrival times have the **memoryless** property, meaning that the time between two consecutive arrivals has no bearing on when the subsequent arrival will happen.

The simulator makes the following assumptions about the hackers:

- The hackers try to avoid an account lockout by only testing a few username-password combinations, rather than a full-blown **dictionary attack** (for every user, trying every password the hacker has in a dictionary of possible passwords that they maintain). However, they don't add delays between their attempts.
- Since the hackers don't want to cause a denial of service, they limit the volume of their attacks and only make one attempt at a time.
- The hackers know the number of accounts that exist in the system and have a good idea of the format the usernames are in, but are guessing the exact usernames. They will choose to try to guess all 133 usernames, or some subset of them.
- Each attack is standalone—meaning there is a single hacker acting for each attack, and a hacker never attacks more than once.
- The hackers don't share information about which username-password combinations are correct.
- The attacks come at random times.

- Each hacker will use a single IP address, which is generated in the same way the valid user ones are. However, our simulator is capable of varying this IP address—a feature that we will look at in Chapter 11, *Machine Learning Anomaly Detection*, to make this scenario more challenging.
- Although highly unlikely, it is possible the hacker has the same IP address as a valid user. The hacker may even be a valid user.

We are abstracting away some of the complexity of password-guessing as well; instead, we are using random numbers to determine whether or not the password is guessed correctly—this means we aren't considering how the website stores passwords, perhaps as plaintext (hopefully not), hashes (the irreversible transformation of the plaintext password that allows verification without storing the actual password), or salted hashes (see the *Further reading* section for an article on this). In practice, a hacker could gain access to the stored passwords and figure out what they are offline (see the article on rainbow tables in the *Further reading* section at the end of this chapter), in which case the techniques discussed in this chapter wouldn't be as helpful, since the logs wouldn't have a record of their attempts. Keep in mind that the hackers in this simulation are very conspicuous.

The login_attempt_simulator package

This package is much more lightweight than the stock_analysis package from the previous chapter; we only have three files:

```
login_attempt_simulator
|-- __init__.py
|-- login_attempt_simulator.py
`-- utils.py
```

Helper functions

Let's start our discussion with the utils.py functions, which are helpers for our simulator class. First, we create our docstring for the module and handle our imports:

```
"""Utility functions for the login attempt simulator."""

import ipaddress
import itertools
import json
import random
import string
```

Next, we define the `make_userbase()` function, which makes the user base for our web application. It creates a file of usernames by combining one lowercase letter from the English alphabet with each last name in the list inside the function, and adds a few administrative accounts, as well; this results in a user base of 133 accounts. By writing to the file, we ensure we don't have to generate this every time we run our simulation and can simply read from it to simulate in the future:

```
def make_userbase(out_file):
    """Generate a userbase and save it to a file."""
    with open(out_file, 'w') as user_base:
        for first, last in itertools.product(
            string.ascii_lowercase,
            ['smith', 'jones', 'kim', 'lopez', 'brown']
        ): # makes 130 accounts
            user_base.write(first + last + '\n')
        # adds 3 more accounts
        for account in ['admin', 'master', 'dba']:
            user_base.write(account + '\n')
```

Since we will need to use this user base in our simulator, we also write a function to read the file into a list. The `get_valid_users()` function reads the file written by `make_userbase()` back into a Python list:

```
def get_valid_users(user_base_file):
    """Read in users from the userbase file."""
    with open(user_base_file, 'r') as file:
        return [user.strip() for user in file.readlines()]
```

The `random_ip_generator()` function creates IP addresses from random numbers of the form xxx.xxx.xxx.xxx, where x is an integer in the range of [0, 255]. We are using `ipaddress` from the Python standard library (https://docs.python.org/3/library/ipaddress.html) to avoid assigning private IP addresses:

```
def random_ip_generator():
    """Randomly generate a fake IP address."""
    try:
        ip_address = ipaddress.IPv4Address('%d.%d.%d.%d' % tuple(
            random.randint(0, 255) for i in range(4)
        ))
    except ipaddress.AddressValueError:
        ip_address = random_ip_generator()
    return str(ip_address) if ip_address.is_global \
        else random_ip_generator()
```

Each of our users will have a few IP addresses from which they attempt to log in.
The `assign_ip_addresses()` function maps 1-3 random IP addresses to each user,
creating a dictionary:

```
def assign_ip_addresses(user_list):
    """Assign users 1-3 fake IP addresses, returning a dictionary."""
    return {
        user : [
            random_ip_generator() for i in range(random.randint(1, 3))
        ] for user in user_list
    }
```

The `save_user_ips()` and `read_user_ips()` functions save the user-IP address
mapping to a JSON file and read it back into the dictionary file, respectively:

```
def save_user_ips(user_ip_dict, file):
    """Save the mapping of users and their IP addresses to JSON
file."""
    with open(file, 'w') as file:
        json.dump(user_ip_dict, file)

def read_user_ips(file):
    """Read in the JSON file of the user-IP address mapping."""
    with open(file, 'r') as file:
        return json.loads(file.read())
```

The Python standard library has lots of helpful modules that we
might not find many occasions to use, but are definitely worth
knowing about. Here, we use the `json` module to save dictionaries
to JSON files and read them back later. We are using the `ipaddress`
module to work with IP addresses, and the `string` module to get
all the characters in the alphabet, among other things, without
having to type them all out.

The LoginAttemptSimulator class

The `LoginAttemptSimulator` class in the `login_attempt_simulator.py` file
handles the heavy-lifting of carrying out the simulation with all the random number
generation logic (parts of the docstrings have been removed for brevity; check the file
itself for the full documentation).

As usual, we start with our module docstring and imports:

```
"""Simulator of login attempts from valid users and hackers."""

import calendar
import datetime as dt
from functools import partial
import math
import random
import string

import numpy as np
import pandas as pd

from .utils import random_ip_generator, read_user_ips
```

Next, we begin defining the `LoginAttemptSimulator` class with its docstring, along with some class variables for storing constants. We do this to avoid magic numbers (numbers in the code that don't seem to have meaning) and spelling errors with strings we will use in multiple spots. Note that these messages are only for our logs; the web application doesn't show the end users why the authentication attempt failed (nor should it):

```
class LoginAttemptSimulator:
    """Simulates login attempts from valid and nefarious users."""

    ATTEMPTS_BEFORE_LOCKOUT = 3
    ACCOUNT_LOCKED = 'error_account_locked'
    WRONG_USERNAME = 'error_wrong_username'
    WRONG_PASSWORD = 'error_wrong_password'
```

 Take note how we used class variables to store constants, such as error messages, so that we don't risk typos in the code; this means that every time we use these error messages, the text will be identical, which will keep the data clean. In Python, constants are typically written in all caps.

The `__init__()` method will handle the setup for the simulator, such as reading in the user base from the file indicated, initializing the logs, storing success probabilities, and determining the start and end dates for the simulation, as needed:

```
def __init__(self, userbase_json_file, start, end=None, *,
             hacker_success_likelihoods=[.25, .45],
             valid_user_success_likelihoods=[.99, .99, .95],
             seed=None
             ):
```

```
# user, ip address dictionary
self.userbase = read_user_ips(userbase_json_file)
self.users = [user for user in self.userbase.keys()]

self.start = start
self.end = end if end else self.start + dt.timedelta(
    days=random.uniform(1, 50)
)

self.hacker_success_likelihoods = hacker_success_likelihoods
self.valid_user_success_likelihoods = \
    valid_user_success_likelihoods

self.log = pd.DataFrame(columns=[
    'datetime', 'source_ip', 'username',
    'success', 'failure_reason'
])
self.hack_log = pd.DataFrame(
    columns=['start', 'end', 'source_ip']
)

self.locked_accounts = []

# set seeds for random numbers from random and numpy:
random.seed(seed)
np.random.seed(seed)
```

The `_record()` method appends the result of each attempt to the log, noting the IP address it came from, which username, at what time, whether it succeeded, and the reason for failure, if there was one:

```
def _record(self, when, source_ip, username, success,
            failure_reason):
    """
    Record the outcome of a login attempt.

    Parameters:
        - when: The datetime of the event.
        - source_ip: The IP address where the attempt came from.
        - username: The username used in the attempt.
        - success: Whether or not the attempt succeeded (boolean).
        - failure_reason: The reason for the failure, if failed.

    Returns: None, the `log` attribute is updated.
    """
```

```
self.log = self.log.append({
    'datetime' : when, 'source_ip' : source_ip,
    'username' : username, 'success' : success,
    'failure_reason' : failure_reason
}, ignore_index=True)
```

The `_attempt_login()` method handles the logic of determining whether the login attempt succeeds:

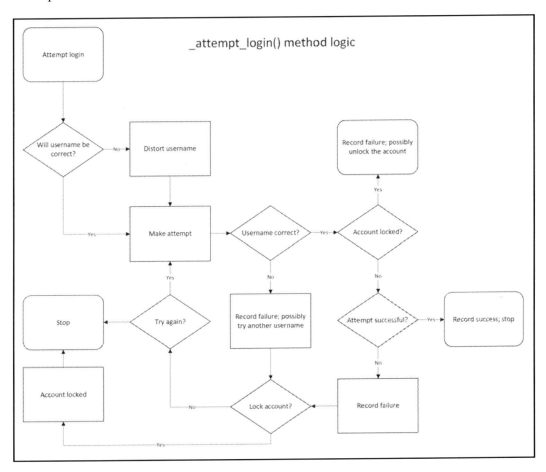

We provide the probability of entering a correct username (`user_name_accuracy`) and the probabilities of successfully entering the password for each attempt (`success_likelihoods`). The number of attempts is the minimum of the number of attempts allowed before an account lockout and the length of the list of success probabilities (`success_likelihoods`). The outcome of each attempt is passed to `_record()` using **partials** (from `functools`), which allow us to create functions that fix certain parameters to a specific value (so we don't have to pass the same value continuously):

```python
def _attempt_login(self, when, source_ip, username,
                   user_name_accuracy, success_likelihoods):
    """Simulates a login attempt, allowing for account lockouts,
    and recording the results.

    Parameters:
        - when: The datetime to start trying.
        - source_ip: The IP address where the attempt is coming
          from.
        - username: The username being used in the attempt.
        - user_name_accuracy: The probability the username is
          correct.
        - success_likelihoods: A list of the probabilities of the
          password being correct. The length is the number of
          attempts.

    Returns: The datetime after trying.
    """
    current = when
    recorder = partial(self._record, source_ip=source_ip)

    if random.random() > user_name_accuracy:
        correct_username = username
        username = self._distort_username(username)

    if username not in self.locked_accounts:
        tries = len(success_likelihoods)
        for i in range(min(tries, self.ATTEMPTS_BEFORE_LOCKOUT)):
            current += dt.timedelta(seconds=1)

            if username not in self.users:
                recorder(
                    when=current, username=username,
                    success=False,
                    failure_reason=self.WRONG_USERNAME
                )
```

```
                if random.random() <= user_name_accuracy:
                    username = correct_username
                continue

            if random.random() <= success_likelihoods[i]:
                recorder(
                    when=current, username=username,
                    success=True, failure_reason=None
                )
                break
            else:
                recorder(
                    when=current, username=username,
                    success=False,
                    failure_reason=self.WRONG_PASSWORD
                )
        else:
            if tries >= self.ATTEMPTS_BEFORE_LOCKOUT \
            and username in self.users:
                self.locked_accounts.append(username)
    else:
        recorder(
            when=current, username=username, success=False,
            failure_reason=self.ACCOUNT_LOCKED
        )
        if random.random() >= .5: # unlock the account randomly
            self.locked_accounts.remove(username)
    return current
```

The `_valid_user_attempts_login()` and `_hacker_attempts_login()` methods are wrappers around `_attempt_login()` that handle the adjustment in probabilities for valid users and hackers, respectively. Notice that while both use a Gaussian (normal) distribution to determine how accurate the username will be, the valid user's distribution has a higher mean and lower standard deviation, meaning they are more likely to provide the correct username when trying to log in. This is because, while valid users may make typos (infrequently), the hackers are guessing:

```
def _hacker_attempts_login(self, when, source_ip, username):
    """Simulates a login attempt from an attacker."""
    return self._attempt_login(
        when=when, source_ip=source_ip, username=username,
        user_name_accuracy=random.gauss(mu=0.35, sigma=0.5),
        success_likelihoods=self.hacker_success_likelihoods
    )
```

```
def _valid_user_attempts_login(self, when, username):
    """Simulates a login attempt from a valid user."""
    return self._attempt_login(
        when=when, username=username,
        source_ip=random.choice(self.userbase[username]),
        user_name_accuracy=random.gauss(mu=1.01, sigma=0.01),
        success_likelihoods=self.valid_user_success_likelihoods
    )
```

When the simulator determines that the username will not be provided correctly, it calls the `_distort_username()` method. It randomly decides to omit a letter from the valid username or to replace one of the letters with another one. While hackers enter incorrect usernames because they are guessing (not due to typos), we abstract away this detail in order to use a single function for introducing username errors for both valid users and hackers:

```
@staticmethod
def _distort_username(username):
    """
    Alters the username to allow for wrong username login
    failures. Randomly removes a letter or replaces a letter
    in a valid username.
    """

    username = list(username)
    change_index = random.randint(0, len(username) - 1)
    if random.random() < .5: # remove random letter
        username.pop(change_index)
    else: # randomly replace a single letter
        username[change_index] = random.choice(
            string.ascii_lowercase
        )
    return ''.join(username)
```

We use the `_valid_user_arrivals()` method to generate the number of users that will arrive in a given hour and the interarrival times using Poisson and exponential distributions, respectively:

```
@staticmethod
def _valid_user_arrivals(when):
    """
    Static method for simulating the Poisson process of arrivals
    (users wanting to log in to the website). Lambda for the
    Poisson varies depending upon the day and time of week.
    """
    is_weekday = when.weekday() not in (
        calendar.SATURDAY, calendar.SUNDAY
    )
    late_night = when.hour < 5 or when.hour >= 11
    work_time = is_weekday and (when.hour >= 9 or when.hour <= 17)

    if work_time:
        # hours 9-5 on work days get higher lambda
        poisson_lambda = random.triangular(1.5, 2.75, 5)
    elif late_night:
        # hours in middle of night get lower lambda
        poisson_lambda = random.uniform(0.0, 1.0)
    else:
        poisson_lambda = random.uniform(1.5, 2.25)

    hourly_arrivals = np.random.poisson(poisson_lambda)
    interarrival_times = np.random.exponential(
        1/poisson_lambda, size=hourly_arrivals
    )

    return hourly_arrivals, interarrival_times
```

We are using numpy for the random number generation from the exponential distribution, instead of random, because we can ask for multiple values at once (one for each of the hourly arrivals determined by the Poisson process). Also, note that random doesn't provide a Poisson distribution, so we need numpy.

Our simulation uses many different distributions, so it can be helpful to see what they look like. The following subplots show examples for each of the distributions we are using. Notice the Poisson distribution is drawn differently. This is because the Poisson distribution is discrete. For this reason, we often use it to model arrivals—here, we use it for modeling the arrivals of users attempting to log in. Discrete distributions have a **probability mass function (PMF)** instead of a **probability density function (PDF)**:

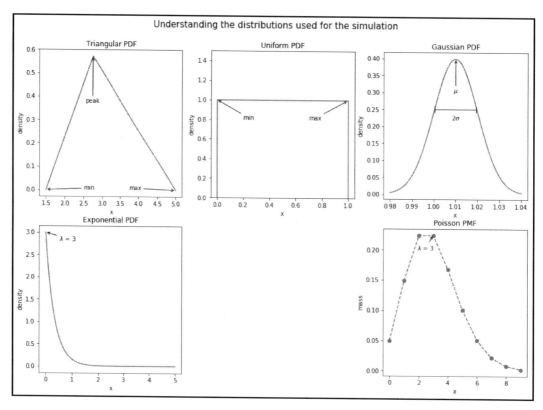

The _hack() method generates a random IP address for the hacker and carries out a brute-force attack on a given user list:

```
def _hack(self, when, user_list, vary_ips):
    """Simulate an attack by a random hacker.

    Parameters:
        - when: The datetime to start the attack.
        - user_list: The list of users to try to hack.
        - vary_ips: Whether or not to vary the IP address.
```

```
Returns:
    The hacker's IP address and the end time for recording.
"""
hacker_ip = random_ip_generator()
random.shuffle(user_list)
for user in user_list:
    when = self._hacker_attempts_login(
        when=when, username=user,
        source_ip=random_ip_generator() if vary_ips \
            else hacker_ip
    )
return hacker_ip, when
```

Now that we have the functionality to carry out the main parts of the simulation, we write the `simulate()` method to put it all together:

```
def simulate(self, *, attack_prob, try_all_users_prob, vary_ips):
    """
    Simulate login attempts.

    Parameters:
        - attack_probs: Probability a hacker attacks in a given
          hour.
        - try_all_users_prob: Probability the hacker will try to
          guess the credentials for all users vs a random subset
          of it.
        - vary_ips: Boolean indicating whether or not to vary the
          IP address.
    """
    hours_in_date_range = math.floor(
        (self.end - self.start).total_seconds() / 60 / 60
    )
    for offset in range(hours_in_date_range + 1):
        current = self.start + dt.timedelta(hours=offset)

        # simulate hacker
        if random.random() < attack_prob:
            attack_start = current \
                + dt.timedelta(hours=random.random())
            source_ip, end_time = self._hack(
                when=attack_start,
                user_list=self.users if random.random()\
                                        < try_all_users_prob \
                else random.sample(
                    self.users, random.randint(0, len(self.users))
                ),
                vary_ips=vary_ips
            )
```

```
        self.hack_log = self.hack_log.append(
            dict(
                start=attack_start, end=end_time,
                source_ip=source_ip
            ), ignore_index=True
        )

    # simulate valid users
    hourly_arrivals, interarrival_times = \
        self._valid_user_arrivals(current)
    random_user = random.choice(self.users)
    random_ip = random.choice(self.userbase[random_user])
    for i in range(hourly_arrivals):
        current += dt.timedelta(hours=interarrival_times[i])
        current = self._valid_user_attempts_login(
            current, random_user
        )
```

We want to save the logs, so we add the `_save()` method as a static method to allow for less repetition in the code for the two save methods (`save_log()` and `save_hack_log()`):

```
@staticmethod
def _save(data, filename, sort_column):
    """Sort dataframe by the datetime and save to a CSV file."""
    data.sort_values(sort_column).to_csv(filename, index=False)

def save_log(self, filename):
    """Save the login attempts log to a CSV file."""
    self._save(self.log, filename, 'datetime')

def save_hack_log(self, filename):
    """Save the record of the attacks to a CSV file."""
    self._save(self.hack_log, filename, 'start')
```

Notice that there were many private methods in this class; this is because users of this class only need to be able to create an instance of this class (`__init__()`), run a simulation by hour (`simulate()`), and save the output (`save_log()` and `save_hack_log()`)—all other methods are for internal use by objects of this class. The methods behind the scenes will handle the bulk of the work.

Lastly, we have the `__init__.py` file, which makes this a package, but also provides us with an easier way to import the main class:

```
"""Package for simulating login data."""

from .login_attempt_simulator import LoginAttemptSimulator
```

Simulating from the command line

Rather than writing the code to simulate the login attempts every time, we can package this up in a script that we can easily run from the command line. The Python standard library has the `argparse` module (`https://docs.python.org/3/library/argparse.html`), which allows us to specify arguments to our script that can be supplied from the command line. Let's take a look at the `simulate.py` file to see how to do this.

We start with our imports:

```
import argparse
import datetime as dt
import os
import logging
import random

import login_attempt_simulator as sim
```

In order to provide status updates when using this from the command line, we are going to set up logging messages using the standard library's `logging` module (`https://docs.python.org/3/library/logging.html`):

```
# Logging configuration
FORMAT = '[%(levelname)s] [ %(name)s ] %(message)s'
logging.basicConfig(level=logging.INFO, format=FORMAT)
logger = logging.getLogger(os.path.basename(__file__))
```

Next, we define some utility functions for generating file paths that we will need for reading and writing data during the simulation:

```
def get_simulation_file_path(path_provided, directory, default_file):
    """Get the path to the file creating the directory and using the
       default if necessary."""
    if path_provided:
        file = path_provided
    else:
        if not os.path.exists(directory):
            os.mkdir(directory)
        file = os.path.join(directory, default_file)
    return file

def get_user_base_file_path(path_provided, default_file):
    """Get the path for a user_data directory file."""
    return get_simulation_file_path(
        path_provided, 'user_data', default_file
    )
```

```
def get_log_file_path(path_provided, default_file):
    """Get the path for a logs directory file."""
    return get_simulation_file_path(
        path_provided, 'logs', default_file
    )
```

The largest part of this script defines which command-line parameters can be passed—we will allow the user to specify if they want to create a new user base, set a seed, when to start the simulation, how long to simulate, and where to save all the files. The actual simulation is taken care of in a few lines thanks to the package we built. This section will only run when this module is run, rather than imported:

```
if __name__ == '__main__':
    # command-line argument parsing
    parser = argparse.ArgumentParser()
    parser.add_argument(
        "days", type=float,
        help="number of days to simulate from start"
    )
    parser.add_argument(
        "start_date", type=str,
        help="datetime to start in the form 'YYYY-MM-DD(...)'"
    )
    parser.add_argument(
        "-m", "--make", action='store_true', help="make userbase"
    )
    parser.add_argument(
        "-s", "--seed", type=int,
        help="set a seed for reproducibility"
    )
    parser.add_argument(
        "-u", "--userbase", help="file to write the userbase to"
    )
    parser.add_argument(
        "-i", "--ip", help="file to write the user-ip map to"
    )
    parser.add_argument(
        "-l", "--log", help="file to write the attempt log to"
    )
    parser.add_argument(
        "-hl", "--hacklog", help="file to write the hack log to"
    )
```

After defining the arguments, we need to parse them in order to use them:

```
args = parser.parse_args()
```

Once we have the command-line arguments parsed, we check to see if we need to generate the user base or read it in:

```
user_ip_mapping_file = get_user_base_file_path(
    args.ip, 'user_ips.json'
)

if args.make:
    logger.warning(
        'Creating new user base and mapping IP addresses to them.'
    )
    user_base_file = get_user_base_file_path(
        args.userbase, 'user_base.txt'
    )

    # seed the creation of userbase
    random.seed(args.seed)

    # create usernames and write to file
    sim.utils.make_userbase(user_base_file)

    # create 1 or more IP addresses per user, save mapping to file
    valid_users = sim.utils.get_valid_users(user_base_file)
    sim.utils.save_user_ips(
        sim.utils.assign_ip_addresses(valid_users),
        user_ip_mapping_file
    )
```

Afterward, we parse the start date from the command-line arguments, and determine the end date by adding the duration from the command-line arguments to the start date:

```
try:
    start = dt.datetime(*map(int, args.start_date.split('-')))
except TypeError:
    logger.error('Start date must be in the format "YYYY-MM-DD"')
    raise
except ValueError:
    logger.warning(
        f'Could not interpret {args.start_date}, '
        'using January 1, 2019 at 12AM as start instead'
    )
    start = dt.datetime(2019, 1, 1)
end = start + dt.timedelta(days=args.days)
```

Check out the `try...except` in the previous code block. We have a single `try` block and multiple `except` blocks. We can specify how to handle specific errors by stating which error belongs to a given `except` block. In this case, we have the `logger` print a more helpful message for the user, and then re-raise the same error to end the program, by simply writing `raise`. Try triggering this error to see how much more useful this is. One thing to keep in mind, though, is that order matters—be sure to `except` the specific errors before having a general `except`; otherwise, the code specific to each error will never trigger. Also, note that using `except` without providing a specific error will catch everything, even errors not meant to be caught.

Finally, we run the actual simulation and write our results to the files specified (or the default paths). We set the probability of attack in a given hour to 5% (`attack_prob`), the probability the hacker will attempt to guess all usernames at 50% (`try_all_users_prob`), and have the hackers use the same IP address for all of their attempts (`vary_ips`):

```
try:
    logger.info(f'Simulating {args.days} days...')
    simulator = sim.LoginAttemptSimulator(
        user_ip_mapping_file, start, end, seed=args.seed
    )
    simulator.simulate(
        attack_prob=0.05, try_all_users_prob=0.5, vary_ips=False
    )

    # save logs
    logger.info('Saving logs')
    simulator.save_hack_log(
        get_log_file_path(args.hacklog, 'attacks.csv')
    )
    simulator.save_log(get_log_file_path(args.log, 'log.csv'))

    logger.info('All done!')
except:
    logger.error('Oops! Something went wrong...')
```

Notice that we used the `logger` object to print helpful messages to the screen throughout the script; this will help the users of this script know how far along in the process it is. These messages come in different levels of severity (we are using INFO, WARNING, and ERROR here), allowing them to be placed for debugging (the DEBUG level), and left there once the code goes into production, since the minimum level for printing can be raised to INFO, so that no DEBUG messages are printed. This is leaps and bounds above simple `print()` statements, since we don't have to worry about removing them as we move to production or adding back these messages as development continues.

Let's take a look at how we can run this script. We know that `simulate.py` can be run on the command line, but how can we see what arguments we need to pass? Simple—we add the help flag (-h or --help) to the call:

```
$ python simulate.py -h
usage: simulate.py [-h] [-m] [-s SEED] [-u USERBASE] [-i IP] [-l LOG]
                   [-hl HACKLOG]
                   days start_date

positional arguments:
  days                  number of days to simulate from start
  start_date            datetime to start in the form 'YYYY-MM-DD' or
                        'YYYY-MM-DD-HH'

optional arguments:
  -h, --help            show this help message and exit
  -m, --make            make userbase
  -s SEED, --seed SEED  set a seed for reproducibility
  -u USERBASE, --userbase USERBASE
                        file to write the userbase to
  -i IP, --ip IP        file to write the user-ip address map to
  -l LOG, --log LOG     file to write the attempt log to
  -hl HACKLOG, --hacklog HACKLOG
                        file to write the hack log to
```

Note that we didn't specify the `help` argument when we added the other arguments with `argparse`—it was automatically created by `argparse`.

Once we know which arguments we can pass, and have decided which of these we want to provide, we can run the simulation. Let's simulate 30 days, starting from 12 AM on November 1, 2018, while having the script create the user base and IP address mappings needed:

```
(book_env) $ python simulate.py -ms 0 30 '2018-11-01'
[WARNING] [ simulate.py ] Creating new user base and mapping IP
addresses to them.
[INFO] [ simulate.py ] Simulating 30.0 days...
[INFO] [ simulate.py ] Saving logs
[INFO] [ simulate.py ] All done!
```

 Since we set a seed (`-s 0`), the output of this simulation is reproducible. Simply remove the seed or change it and you'll get a different result.

Python modules can also be run as scripts. This is what we use `if __name__ == '__main__'` for; anything we put underneath will only be run when the module is run as a script (but not when importing the module), meaning we don't always need to write a separate script. Most of the modules we have built, defined functions and classes, so running them as scripts wouldn't do anything; however, the way we created our virtual environment with venv back in Chapter 1, *Introduction to Data Analysis*, was an example of this. The previous code block is therefore equivalent to the following command:

```
# leave off the .py
(book_env) $ python -m simulate -ms 0 30 "2018-11-01"
```

Now that we have our simulated data, let's begin our analysis.

Exploratory data analysis

In this scenario, we have the benefit of access to labeled data (`logs/attacks.csv`) and will use it to investigate how to distinguish between valid users and attackers. However, this is a luxury that we often don't have, especially once we leave the research phase and enter the application phase. In Chapter 11, *Machine Learning Anomaly Detection*, we will revisit this data, but begin without the labeled data for more of a challenge. As usual, we start with our imports and reading in the data:

```
>>> %matplotlib inline
>>> import matplotlib.pyplot as plt
>>> import numpy as np
```

```
>>> import pandas as pd
>>> import seaborn as sns

>>> log = pd.read_csv(
...     'logs/log.csv', index_col='datetime', parse_dates=True
... )
```

The login attempts dataframe (`log`) contains the date and time of each attempt in the `datetime` column, the IP address it came from (`source_ip`), the username that was used (`username`), whether the attempt was successful (`success`), and the reason for failure if it wasn't (`failure_reason`):

	source_ip	username	success	failure_reason
datetime				
2018-11-01 00:10:24.868560	142.89.86.32	vkim	True	NaN
2018-11-01 00:50:36.191231	142.89.86.32	vkim	True	NaN
2018-11-01 01:01:42.607900	53.218.180.231	ysmith	True	NaN
2018-11-01 01:02:06.374218	53.218.180.231	ysmith	True	NaN
2018-11-01 01:35:19.704392	53.218.180.231	ysmith	True	NaN

When approaching this data, we need to think about what normal activity and hacker activity would look like. Any big differences between the groups could potentially be leveraged to identify the hackers. We would expect valid users to have high success rates, with the most common reason for failure being an incorrect password. We would expect users to log in from a few different IP addresses (phone, home computer, work computer, and any other device they may have), and it is possible that people share devices. Without knowing the nature of this web application, we can't say anything about whether it is normal to log in many times throughout the day. We also don't know what time zone this data is in, so we can't make any inferences about the login times. Potentially, we could look at which countries these IP addresses are from, but there are ways of masking IP addresses, so we won't go down that path. This leaves us with a few viable options, given our available data:

- Investigate any spikes in attempts and failures (both overall, and per IP address)
- Examine cases where the failure reason was an incorrect username

- Look at the failure rate per IP address
- Find IP addresses trying to log in with many distinct usernames

One other thing to note is that we would want to flag anomalous behavior sooner rather than later. Waiting a month to flag something is less valuable (the value drops quickly over time), so we need to find a way to flag much sooner; say, using an hourly frequency. Since we are in the research phase, we have some labeled data to work with:

```
>>> attacks = pd.read_csv(
...     'logs/attacks.csv',
...     converters={'start' : np.datetime64, 'end': np.datetime64}
... ) # make start and end columns datetimes but not the index
```

This data is the record of attacks on the web application (`attacks`). It contains the date and time of the start of the attack (`start`), the date and time of the end of the attack (`end`), and the IP address associated with the attack (`source_ip`):

	start	end	source_ip
0	2018-11-01 10:44:29.667759	2018-11-01 10:48:37.667759	23.143.69.122
1	2018-11-02 03:27:23.313068	2018-11-02 03:31:37.313068	205.134.14.49
2	2018-11-03 08:13:58.834778	2018-11-03 08:18:13.834778	193.208.35.108
3	2018-11-04 14:57:08.609577	2018-11-04 14:58:36.609577	76.190.0.171
4	2018-11-04 23:06:30.356411	2018-11-04 23:09:05.356411	88.183.150.135

Using the `shape` property, we can see that we had 39 attacks and 9,338 login attempts from valid and nefarious users, and with `nunique()`, we see that 13% of the IP addresses that made login attempts were from attackers:

```
>>> attacks.shape, log.shape
((39, 3), (9338, 4))
>>> attacks.source_ip.nunique() / log.source_ip.nunique()
0.13220338983050847
```

 Normally, it wouldn't be this trivial to know when the hackers attacked. These attacks can go a long time without detection, and, even then, it's not so simple to isolate the attacker's actions from those of normal users.

Our data is pretty clean (we designed it just for this purpose, after all), so let's see if we can find anything interesting with some **exploratory data analysis (EDA)**. First, let's look to see how many attempts are coming through on an hourly basis:

```
>>> log.assign(attempts=1).attempts.resample('1H').sum().plot(
...     figsize=(15, 5), title='hourly attempts'
... )
>>> plt.xlabel('datetime')
>>> plt.ylabel('attempts')
```

Several hours had very large peaks, which could possibly be when attacks occurred. Using this plot, we could report on hours that had a high level of login attempt activity, but nothing beyond that:

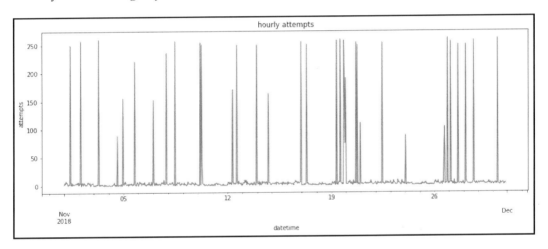

Another interesting avenue of exploration would be to see how many attempts came from each IP address. We can achieve this by running the following command:

```
>>> log.source_ip.value_counts().describe()
count    295.000000
mean      31.654237
std       70.843718
min        1.000000
25%        3.000000
50%        6.000000
75%       11.000000
max      258.000000
Name: source_ip, dtype: float64
```

This data definitely appears to have some outliers, which pull the number of attempts per IP address up quite high. Let's create some plots to better assess this:

```
>>> fig, axes = plt.subplots(1, 2, figsize=(15, 5))
>>> log.source_ip.value_counts().plot(
....      kind='box', ax=axes[0]
... ).set_ylabel('attempts')
>>> log.source_ip.value_counts().plot(
....      kind='hist', bins=50, ax=axes[1]
... ).set_xlabel('attempts')
>>> fig.suptitle('Attempts per IP Address')
```

The distribution of attempts per IP address is the sum of the distributions for both the valid users and the attackers. The histogram indicates that this distribution is bimodal, but we can't determine if all of those IP addresses with high attempts are actually the hackers by just looking at the plot:

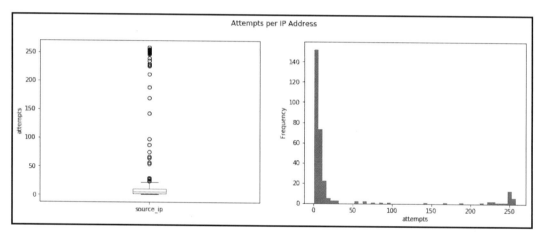

Since we have access to the details of each attack, we can check if the right part of the histogram is the distribution for the hackers. Their IP addresses make up 97% of the top IP addresses ranked by number of attempts:

```
>>> num_hackers = attacks.source_ip.shape[0]
>>> log.source_ip.value_counts().index[:num_hackers]\
...      .isin(attacks.source_ip).sum() / num_hackers
0.9743589743589743
```

We could simply stop here and flag any IP address that shows up in a list of IP addresses with most attempts per month, but we most likely want a more robust solution, since the hackers could simply change their IP address each time and avoid detection. Ideally, we would also be able to detect the attacks without waiting for a full month of data. Looking at the hourly attempts made by each IP address unfortunately doesn't give us much information, though:

```
>>> log.assign(attempts=1).groupby('source_ip').attempts\
...     .resample('1H').sum().unstack().mean()\
...     .plot(
...         figsize=(15, 5),
...         title='average hourly attempts per IP address'
...     ).set_ylabel('average hourly attempts per IP address')
```

Remember from Chapter 1, *Introduction to Data Analysis*, that the mean is not robust to outliers. If the attackers make many attempts, they will bring the average hourly attempts per IP address higher. We can see several large peaks in this line plot, but notice many of them only go up to two. Can we really expect only one user to access the web application from a single IP address? This is probably not a realistic assumption:

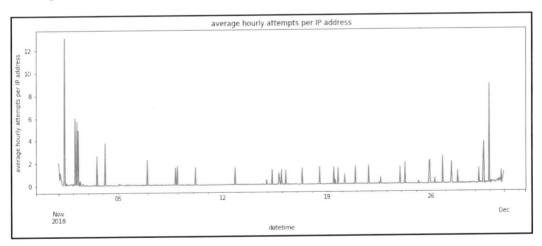

So if we can't rely on the IP address (after all, the hacker could be smart enough to spread the attack over many different addresses), what else can we try? Perhaps the hackers have more trouble logging in successfully:

```
>>> log[log.source_ip.isin(attacks.source_ip)]\
...     .success.value_counts(normalize=True)
False    0.830297
True     0.169703
Name: success, dtype: float64
```

The hackers are only successful 17% of the time, but how often are the valid users successful? This information is important for determining a baseline of what normal behavior looks like for the website. As we would expect, the valid users have much higher success rates:

```
>>> log[~log.source_ip.isin(attacks.source_ip)]\
...     .success.value_counts(normalize=True)
True     0.987304
False    0.012696
Name: success, dtype: float64
```

Since the logs come with the reason that a login attempt failed, we can use a crosstab to see why hackers and valid users fail to log in successfully. Any differences here may help us separate the two groups:

```
>>> pd.crosstab(
...     index=pd.Series(
...         log.source_ip.isin(attacks.source_ip), name='is_hacker'
...     ), columns=log.failure_reason
... )
```

Valid users sometimes enter their passwords or usernames wrong, but the hacker has way more issues getting both the username and password correct:

failure_reason	error_wrong_password	error_wrong_username
is_hacker		
False	20	1
True	2491	3889

The valid users don't make many mistakes with their credentials, so if the hackers make many attempts with many users, we can flag it. To confirm, we can look at average hourly attempts per user:

```
>>> log.assign(attempts=1).groupby('username').attempts\
...     .resample('1H').sum().unstack().mean().plot(
...         figsize=(15, 5), title='average hourly attempts per user'
...     )
```

For the most part, less than one attempt per hour is made per username. There's also no guarantee that spikes in this metric are indications of an attack. Perhaps, the website is having a flash sale; in that case, we would likely see a spike in this metric caused by valid users:

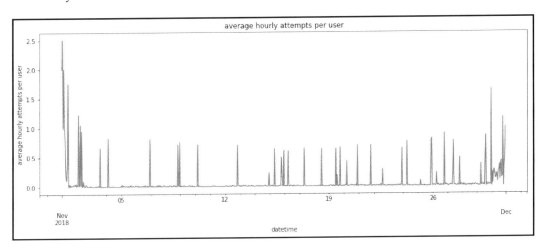

Based on our findings, error rates seem to be the most fruitful metric for detecting attacks, so we will look into IP addresses that have high error rates. To do so, we can create a pivot table to calculate some helpful metrics:

```
>>> pivot = pd.pivot_table(
...     log, values='success', index=log.source_ip,
...     columns=log.failure_reason.fillna('success'),
...     aggfunc='count', fill_value=0
... )
>>> pivot.insert(0, 'attempts', pivot.sum(axis=1))
>>> pivot = pivot.sort_values('attempts', ascending=False).assign(
...     success_rate=lambda x: x.success / x.attempts,
...     error_rate=lambda x: 1 - x.success_rate
... )
>>> pivot.head()
```

The `insert()` method allows us to create the `attempts` column as the sum of the errors and successes (we fill in `NaN`s on `failure_reason` as a success to count it here), by summing with `axis=1` and placing it in a specific position of the current dataframe in place.

This yields the following pivot table sorted by attempts (from most to fewest):

failure_reason source_ip	attempts	error_wrong_password	error_wrong_username	success	success_rate	error_rate
135.158.66.165	258	79	146	33	0.127907	0.872093
44.123.120.49	255	83	139	33	0.129412	0.870588
146.116.200.234	255	75	142	38	0.149020	0.850980
200.115.24.107	254	70	145	39	0.153543	0.846457
121.25.210.210	253	76	143	34	0.134387	0.865613

We know that certain IP addresses are making many attempts, so it's worth looking into how many usernames are attempting to log in per IP address; we would expect valid users to only log in from a few IP addresses and not to share their IP address with many others. This can be determined with a group by and an aggregation in `pandas`:

```
>>> log.groupby('source_ip').agg(
...        dict(username='nunique')
... ).username.value_counts().describe()
count      27.000000
mean       10.925926
std        48.783608
min         1.000000
25%         1.000000
50%         1.000000
75%         2.000000
max       255.000000
Name: username, dtype: float64
```

This definitely appears to be a good strategy for isolating the nefarious users; the majority of the IP addresses are used by two or fewer users, but the max is at 255. While this criteria could help us identify some of the attackers, it won't help if the hackers are clever enough to vary their IP addresses throughout their attack.

Before we move on to anomaly detection methods, let's see if we can visually identify the hackers. Let's create a scatter plot for the successes and attempts for each IP address:

```
>>> pivot.plot(
...     kind='scatter', x='attempts', y='success',
...     title='successes vs. attempts by IP address', alpha=0.25
... )
```

There appear to be a few distinct clusters. In the bottom-left corner of the plot, we see points forming a line with a one-to-one relationship of successes to attempts. The upper-right portion of the plot contains a less dense cluster with a high number of attempts and moderate successes. Since we used the `alpha` parameter to control transparency, we can see that the trail of points that seem to connect the two clusters is not highly populated. Even without the axis scales, we would predict the bottom-left cluster to be regular users and the top-right to be hackers (since we imagine there are more regular users than hackers, and regular users have higher success rates). The points in the middle are more difficult to judge, however:

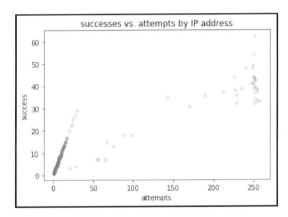

Without making any assumptions, we can draw a boundary line grouping the middle points with their nearest cluster:

```
>>> ax = pivot.plot(
...     kind='scatter', x='attempts', y='success',
...     title='successes vs. attempts by IP address', alpha=0.25
... )
>>> plt.axvline(
...     125, label='sample boundary', color='red', linestyle='--'
... )
>>> plt.legend(loc='lower right')
```

Of course, when lacking labeled data, it is impossible to evaluate the effectiveness of this decision boundary:

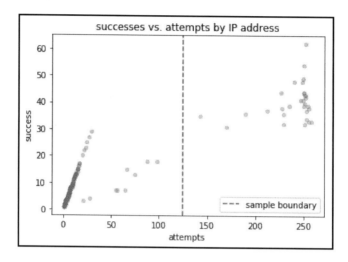

Luckily for us, we have data on which IP addresses the hackers used because we have been given labeled data to conduct our research, so we can use `seaborn` to actually see the separation:

```
>>> fig, axes = plt.subplots(1, 2, figsize=(15, 5))
>>> for ax in axes:
...     sns.scatterplot(
...         y=pivot.success, x=pivot.attempts,
...         hue=pivot.assign(
...             is_hacker=lambda x: x.index.isin(attacks.source_ip)
...         ).is_hacker,
...         ax=ax, alpha=0.5
...     )
>>> axes[1].set_xscale('log')
>>> plt.suptitle('successes vs. attempts by IP address')
```

Our intuition about there being two distinct clusters was dead-on. The middle area, however, was much trickier to determine. The blue points on the left do appear to be following a line upward, while the orange points on the left are following a line to the orange cluster. By plotting the log of the attempts instead, our orange cluster turns into a vertical line, and we get a little more separation between our orange middle points and the blue points:

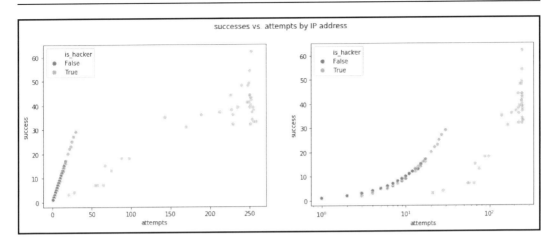

Remember, we can also use a box plot to check for possible outliers, which will be shown as points. Let's see what successes and attempts look like per IP address:

```
>>> pivot[['attempts', 'success']].plot(
...     kind='box',
...     subplots=True,
...     figsize=(10, 3),
...     title='stats per IP address'
... )
```

The points marked as outliers coincide with the points in the upper-right corner of the scatter plots we made:

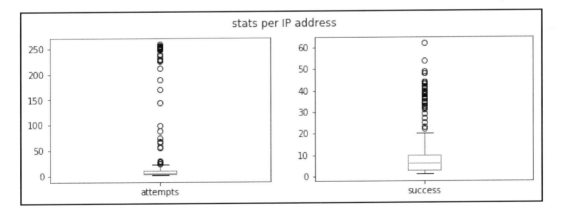

Rule-based anomaly detection

It's time to catch those hackers. After the EDA in the previous section, we have an idea of how we might go about this. In practice, this is much more difficult to do, as it involves many more dimensions, but we have simplified it here. **We want to find the IP addresses with excessive amounts of attempts accompanied by low success rates, and those attempting to log in with more unique usernames than we would deem normal (anomalies).** To do this, we will employ threshold-based rules as our first foray into anomaly detection; then, in Chapter 11, *Machine Learning Anomaly Detection*, we will explore a few machine learning techniques as we revisit this data.

Since we are interested in flagging IP addresses that are suspicious, we are going to arrange the data so that we have hourly aggregated data per IP address (if there was activity for that hour):

```
>>> hourly_ip_logs = log.assign(
...     failures=lambda x: np.invert(x.success)
... ).groupby('source_ip').resample('1H').agg(
...     {'username': 'nunique', 'success': 'sum', 'failures': 'sum'}
... ).assign(
...     attempts=lambda x: x.success + x.failures,
...     success_rate=lambda x: x.success / x.attempts,
...     failure_rate=lambda x: 1 - x.success_rate
... ).dropna().reset_index()
```

 The np.invert() function is an easy way to flip Boolean values. It turns True to False and False to True along a NumPy array-like structure.

The aggregated data looks like this:

	source_ip	datetime	username	success	failures	attempts	success_rate	failure_rate
0	1.138.149.116	2018-11-01 04:00:00	1	4.0	1.0	5.0	0.8	0.2
1	1.138.149.116	2018-11-01 05:00:00	1	1.0	0.0	1.0	1.0	0.0
2	1.138.149.116	2018-11-07 03:00:00	1	1.0	0.0	1.0	1.0	0.0
3	1.138.149.116	2018-11-29 T8:00:00	1	2.0	0.0	2.0	1.0	0.0
4	1.138.149.116	2018-11-29 19:00:00	1	2.0	0.0	2.0	1.0	0.0

The simplest form of rule-based anomaly detection involves calculating a threshold value and checking to see if the data is beyond the threshold. This could mean values falling below some lower bound threshold, or values exceeding some upper bound threshold. Since we are looking at login attempts, we are interested in values that are greater than normal; therefore, we will be calculating the threshold for our upper bounds and comparing that to our data.

Percent difference

Provided that we have an idea of what normal login attempt activity (minus the hackers) looks like on the site, we can flag values that deviate from this by a certain percentage. In order to calculate this baseline, we could take a few IP addresses at random with replacement for each hour, and average the number of login attempts they made; we are bootstrapping since we don't have much data (about 40 unique IP addresses to pick from for each of the 24 hours).

To do this, we could write a function that takes in the aggregated dataframe we just made, along with the name of a statistic to calculate per column of the data to use as the starting point for the threshold:

```
def get_baselines(hourly_ip_logs, func, *args, **kwargs):
    """
    Calculate hourly bootstrapped statistic per column.

    Parameters:
        - hourly_ip_logs: Data to sample from.
        - func: Statistic to calculate.
        - args: Additional positional arguments for `func`
        - kwargs: Additional keyword arguments for `func`

    Returns: A pandas DataFrame of hourly bootstrapped statistics
    """
    if isinstance(func, str):
        func = getattr(pd.DataFrame, func)

    return hourly_ip_logs.assign(
        hour=lambda x: x.datetime.dt.hour
    ).groupby('hour').apply(
        lambda x: x.sample(
            10, random_state=0, replace=True
        ).pipe(func, *args, **kwargs)
    )
```

In the previous code snippet, `random_state` is used with `sample()` for reproducibility; however, in practice we will probably not want to always pick the same rows.

Notice that we can get equally-sized samples for all groups (hours, here) if we use `sample()` inside `apply()` after grouping by the column we want to sample with. This means that we are selecting 10 rows with replacement per hour for each column. We have to sample by hour here because, if we do simple random sampling, there is a good chance we won't have a statistic for every hour. Let's use `get_baselines()` to calculate the column baselines using the mean:

```
>>> averages = get_baselines(hourly_ip_logs, 'mean')
>>> averages.shape
(24, 7)
```

 If, instead, we wanted to perform stratified random sampling, we could replace `10` in the `get_baselines()` function with `x.shape[0] * pct` where `pct` is the percentage we want to sample from each group.

Each column has the mean per hour for the 10 IP addresses chosen randomly to estimate normal behavior. This technique, however, doesn't guarantee that we won't mix any of the hacker activity into our baseline calculations. For instance, we might find it difficult to flag any activity at 4 AM with this method. Our valid users may well be asleep, but we won't notice the attack with this baseline:

hour	username	success	failures	attempts	success_rate	failure_rate	hour
0	1.0	1.3	0.0	1.3	1.000000	0.000000	0.0
1	1.0	1.0	0.0	1.0	1.000000	0.000000	1.0
2	1.0	1.8	0.0	1.8	1.000000	0.000000	2.0
3	1.0	1.5	0.0	1.5	1.000000	0.000000	3.0
4	14.9	4.9	22.0	26.9	0.893439	0.106561	4.0

To combat this issue, we could trim our summary statistics by making the top $x\%$ ineligible for use in our baseline calculation. Let's remove values greater than the 95th percentile of data from each hour. First, we will write a function to trim rows from a given hour that have data above a given quantile:

```
def trim(x, quantile):
    """
    Remove rows with entries for the username, attempts,
    or failure_rate columns above a given quantile.
    """
    mask = ((x.username <= x.username.quantile(quantile))\
        & (x.attempts <= x.attempts.quantile(quantile))\
        & (x.failure_rate <= x.failure_rate.quantile(quantile)))
    return x[mask]
```

Next, we will group the IP address data by hour and apply our trimming function. Since we will be using our bootstrapping function, we need to clean up some of the extra columns that will result from this operation, so we drop the hour column, reset the index, and then remove the group column and the old index:

```
>>> trimmed_hourly_logs = hourly_ip_logs.assign(
...     hour=lambda x: x.datetime.dt.hour
... ).groupby('hour').apply(
...     lambda x: trim(x, 0.95)
... ).drop(columns='hour').reset_index().iloc[:,2:]
```

Now, we can use the `get_baselines()` function to grab our baseline using the average with the trimmed data:

```
>>> averages = get_baselines(trimmed_hourly_logs, 'mean')
>>> averages.head()
```

Notice that the baseline for 4 AM is now different:

	username	success	failures	attempts	success_rate	failure_rate	hour
hour							
0	1.0	1.2	0.0	1.2	1.0	0.0	0.0
1	1.0	1.0	0.0	1.0	1.0	0.0	1.0
2	1.0	1.7	0.0	1.7	1.0	0.0	2.0
3	1.0	1.6	0.0	1.6	1.0	0.0	3.0
4	1.0	1.3	0.0	1.3	1.0	0.0	4.0

Now that we have our baseline, let's write a function that will do the heavy lifting of calculating the threshold from our baseline and the percentage difference per column, returning the IP addresses that have been flagged as hackers:

```
def pct_change_threshold(hourly_ip_logs, baselines, pcts=None):
    """
    Return flagged IP addresses based on thresholds.

    Parameters:
        - hourly_ip_logs: Aggregated hourly data per IP.
        - baselines: Hourly baselines per column in data.
        - pcts: Dictionary of custom percentages per column for
                calculating upper bound thresholds (baseline * pct).
                If not provided, pct will be 1

    Returns: Pandas series containing the IP addresses flagged.
    """
    pcts = {} if not pcts else pcts

    return hourly_ip_logs.assign(
        hour=lambda x: x.datetime.dt.hour
    ).join(
        baselines, on='hour', rsuffix='_baseline'
    ).assign(
        too_many_users=lambda x: x.username_baseline \
        * pcts.get('username', 1) <= x.username,
        too_many_attempts=lambda x: x.attempts_baseline \
        * pcts.get('attempts', 1) <= x.attempts,
        high_failure_rate=lambda x: x.failure_rate_baseline \
        * pcts.get('failure_rate', 1) <= x.failure_rate
    ).query(
        'too_many_users and too_many_attempts and high_failure_rate'
    ).source_ip.drop_duplicates()
```

This function joins the baseline dataframe to the hourly IP address logs on the hour column; since all the baseline columns have the same names as the hourly IP address logs, and we don't want to join on them, we suffix their names with '_baseline'. After that, all the data we need to check if the thresholds were exceeded is in the same dataframe; we use assign() to make three new Boolean columns indicating if each of our conditions (too many users, too many attempts, and high failure rate) has been violated. Then, we chain a call to query(), which lets us easily select rows where all of these Boolean columns are True (notice we don't need to explicitly say column == True). Lastly, we make sure to return just the IP addresses and to deduplicate them, in case the same IP address was flagged for multiple hours.

In order to use this function, we need to pick a percentage difference from each of our baselines. By default, that will be 100% of the baseline, which, since it is the average, will flag way too many IP addresses. Instead, let's get the IP addresses this flags with values 25% higher than the baseline for each criterion:

```
>>> pct_from_mean_ips = pct_change_threshold(
...     hourly_ip_logs, averages,
...     {key: 1.25 for key in [
...         'username', 'attempts', 'failure_rate'
...     ]}
... )
```

The percentages we use are in a dictionary, with the key being the column they are for and the value being the percentage itself. If the caller of the function doesn't provide these, we have default values of 100%, since we are using `get()` to select from the dictionary.

These rules flagged 40 IP addresses:

```
>>> pct_from_mean_ips.nunique()
40
```

In practice, we probably wouldn't run this rule on the entries used to calculate the baselines because they influence the definition of the baseline with their behavior.

Tukey fence

As we discussed in `Chapter 1`, *Introduction to Data Analysis*, the mean is not robust to outliers. If we feel there are many outliers influencing our baselines, we could go back to the percent difference and try out the median, or look into using a **Tukey fence**. Remember from previous chapters that the Tukey fence gets its bounds from the first and third quartiles, and the **interquartile range (IQR)**. Since we only care about exceeding the upper bound, this solves the issue with the mean, provided that outliers compose less than 25% of our data. We can use the following to calculate the upper bound:

$$Upper\ Bound = Q_3 + k \times IQR$$

Our `get_baselines()` function will still help us, but we need to do some additional processing. We will write a function that will calculate the upper bound of the Tukey fence and let us test out various values for the multiplier (k). Notice that we also have the option to use percentages with the Tukey fence here:

```
def tukey_fence_test(trimmed_data, logs, k, pct=None):
    """
    See which IP addresses get flagged with a Tukey Fence with
    multiplier k and optional percent differences.

    Parameters:
        - trimmed_data: The data to use to calculate the baselines
        - logs: The data to test
        - k: The Tukey fence multiplier
        - pct: Dictionary of percentages per column for use with
                `pct_change_threshold()`

    Returns: A pandas Series of flagged IP addresses
    """
    q3 = get_baselines(
        trimmed_data, 'quantile', .75
    ).drop(columns=['hour'])

    q1 = get_baselines(
        trimmed_data, 'quantile', .25
    ).drop(columns=['hour'])

    iqr = q3 - q1
    upper_bound = (q3 + k*iqr).reset_index()

    return pct_change_threshold(logs, upper_bound, pct)
```

Our function also lets us pass the percentages to be used with the `pct_change_threshold()` function that we defined earlier, so let's grab the IP addresses that exceed the upper bound of the Tukey fence with a multiplier of 3 by 5%:

```
>>> tukey_fence_flags = tukey_fence_test(
...     trimmed_hourly_logs, hourly_ip_logs, k=3,
...     pct={key: 1.05 for key in [
...         'username', 'attempts', 'failure_rate'
...     ]}
... )
```

We used a multiplier of 3 here, however, depending on the application, we may see 1.5 used to be less restrictive. In reality, we can use any number; finding the best one may require some trial and error.

We flag 39 IP addresses with this method:

```
>>> tukey_fence_flags.nunique()
39
```

Note that if we don't use the percentages, we flag 225 IP addresses. This huge difference in results is because the baselines are very low, making the IQR insignificant, or even zero in some cases, meaning no matter how high we raise the multiplier, it has no additional effect. For this reason, without the percentage, the upper bound flags some valid users that are simply more active.

Z-score

Remember, from `Chapter 1`, *Introduction to Data Analysis*, that we can also calculate Z-scores and flag IP addresses a given number of standard deviations from the mean. The `pct_change_threshold()` function we wrote earlier won't help us as is, since we aren't just comparing to the baseline; instead, we need to subtract the baseline for the mean from all the values and divide by the baseline for the standard deviation, so we must rework our approach.

Let's write a new function, `z_score_test()`, to perform our Z-score tests using any number of standard deviations above the mean as a cutoff. First, we will use the `get_baselines()` function to calculate the baseline standard deviations by hour with the trimmed data. Then, we join the standard deviations and means together, adding the suffixes; this allows us to adapt the logic of `pct_change_threshold()` for this task:

```
def z_score_test(trimmed_data, logs, cutoff):
    """
    See which IP addresses get flagged with a Z-score greater than
    or equal to a cutoff value.

    Parameters:
        - trimmed_data: The data to use to calculate the baselines
        - logs: The data to test
        - cutoff: Flag row when z_score >= cutoff
```

```
Returns: A pandas Series of flagged IP addresses
"""
std_dev = get_baselines(trimmed_data, 'std') \
    .drop(columns=['hour'])
averages = get_baselines(trimmed_data, 'mean') \
    .drop(columns=['hour'])

return logs.assign(hour=lambda x: x.datetime.dt.hour).join(
    std_dev.join(averages, lsuffix='_std', rsuffix='_mean'),
    on='hour'
).assign(
    too_many_users=lambda x: (
        x.username - x.username_mean
    )/x.username_std >= cutoff,
    too_many_attempts=lambda x: (
        x.attempts - x.attempts_mean
    )/x.attempts_std >= cutoff,
    high_failure_rate=lambda x: (
        x.failure_rate - x.failure_rate_mean
    )/x.failure_rate_std >= cutoff
).query(
    'too_many_users and too_many_attempts and high_failure_rate'
).source_ip.drop_duplicates()
```

Let's call our function with a cutoff of three or more standard deviations from the mean (in practice, we can use any number we wish):

```
>>> z_score_ips = z_score_test(trimmed_hourly_logs, hourly_ip_logs, 3)
```

With this method, we flag 32 IP addresses:

```
>>> z_score_ips.nunique()
32
```

Evaluating performance

So, we now have a series of IP addresses for each set of rules, but we would like to know how well each method did (assuming we can actually check). In this case, we have the attacker IP addresses for our research, so we can see how many each method got right—this is not so trivial in practice; instead, we could mark things that we have discovered to be malicious in the past and look out for similar behavior in the future.

This is a classification problem with two classes; we want to classify each IP address as either a valid user or a nefarious one. This leaves us with four possible outcomes that we can visualize using a **confusion matrix**:

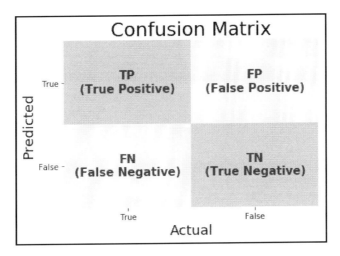

In this application, these outcomes mean the following:

- **True Positive (TP)**: Our method flagged it as malicious, and it was
- **True Negative (TN)**: Our method didn't flag it, and it wasn't malicious
- **False Positive (FP)**: Our method flagged it, but it wasn't malicious
- **False Negative (FN)**: Our method didn't flag it, but it was malicious

True positives and true negatives mean our method did well, but false positives and false negatives are possible areas for improvement (bear in mind that this will never be perfect). Let's write a function that will determine where each method stands:

```
def evaluate(alerted_ips, attack_ips, log_ips):
    """
    Calculate true positives (TP), false positives (FP),
    true negatives (TN), and false negatives (FN) for
    IP addresses flagged as suspicious.

    Parameters:
        - alerted_ips: Pandas series of flagged IP addresses
        - attack_ips: Pandas series of attacker IP addresses
        - log_ips: Pandas series of all IP addresses seen

    Returns: Tuple of form (TP, FP, TN, FN)
    """
```

```
tp = alerted_ips.isin(attack_ips).sum()
tn = log_ips[log_ips.isin(alerted_ips)].isin(attack_ips).sum()
fp = np.invert(
    log_ips[log_ips.isin(alerted_ips)].isin(attack_ips)
).sum()
fn = np.invert(
    log_ips[log_ips.isin(attack_ips)].isin(alerted_ips)
).sum()
return tp, fp, tn, fn
```

Before we begin calculating metrics, let's make a partial function so we don't have to keep passing the series of attacker IP addresses (`attacks.source_ip`) and IP addresses in the logs (`pivot.index`). Remember, a partial function allows us to fix the values for certain arguments and call them later:

```
>>> from functools import partial
>>> scores = partial(
...     evaluate,
...     attack_ips=attacks.source_ip,
...     log_ips=pivot.index
... )
```

Now, let's use this to calculate some metrics to measure our performance. One common metric is **accuracy**, which tells us the percentage we got correct:

$$accuracy = \frac{TP + TN}{TP + FP + TN + FN}$$

Unfortunately, there is a big drawback to using this metric in a classification problem such as this, because we have a **class imbalance**; the two classes in the data are not roughly equal in size—there is a huge disparity. As mentioned earlier, the percentage of IP addresses that were hackers was about 13%, meaning we could classify all of the IP addresses as valid users and still perform reasonably well with accuracy (87%). This problem becomes increasingly severe the more imbalanced the classes are—with only 1% of the IP addresses being hackers, if we say none of the activity was caused by a hacker, our accuracy will be 99%, but that is useless if we never catch anything. This problem stems from the fact that true negatives will be very large, and being in the numerator (in addition to the denominator), they will make the results look better than they are.

Precision and recall are often used to address this issue with accuracy when evaluating the performance of a classification task, especially when there is a class imbalance. **Precision** is the fraction of items flagged positive that are actually positive; in our case, this is the fraction of IP addresses flagged that are indeed malicious:

$$precision = \frac{TP}{TP + FP}$$

As it turns out, we don't even need our function to calculate this—we can do it with `value_counts()` by taking the percentage of flagged IP addresses that are in the hacker IP addresses, which will be assigned to `True`. This is because the values marked as `False` are the values flagged that weren't attacks (false positives), and those marked as `True` were attacks (true positives). Let's calculate the precision using the percentage difference from the mean results:

```
>>> pct_from_mean_ips.isin(attacks.source_ip) \
...     .value_counts(normalize=True)
True     0.975
False    0.025
Name: source_ip, dtype: float64
```

Recall is the percentage of hacker IP addresses we correctly flag, or the **true positive rate**. We calculate recall by dividing the true positive count by everything that should have been positive (true positives and false negatives):

$$recall = \frac{TP}{TP + FN}$$

Our precision was 97.5%; let's see how recall fared:

```
>>> tp, fp, tn, fn = scores(pct_from_mean_ips)
>>> tp / (tp + fn)
1.0
```

There is typically a trade-off here—do we want to catch as many hackers as possible, and risk flagging valid users (by focusing on recall), or do we want to keep from inconveniencing our valid users and risk missing hacker activity (by maximizing precision)? These questions are tough to answer and will depend on the domain, as the cost of false positives is not necessarily equal to (or even close in scale to) the cost of false negatives.

When the cost is somewhat similar, one common strategy is to balance precision and recall using a metric called **F_1 score**, which is the harmonic mean of precision and recall:

$$F_1 = 2 \times \frac{precision \times recall}{precision + recall}$$

This is a special case of the F_β score, which we will discuss in `Chapter 9`, *Getting Started with Machine Learning in Python*, that allows us to put more emphasis on precision or recall by varying β as we deem fit.

> The harmonic mean is the reciprocal of the arithmetic mean, and is used with rates to get a more accurate average (compared to the arithmetic mean of the rates).

Let's write a function to handle all these calculations for us:

```python
def classification_stats(tp, fp, tn, fn):
    """Calculate accuracy, precision, recall, and F1-score"""
    recall = tp / (tp + fn)
    precision = tp / (tp + fp)
    f1_score = 2 * precision * recall / (precision + recall)

    return {
        'accuracy' : (tp + tn) / (tp + fp + tn + fn),
        'precision' : precision,
        'recall' : recall,
        'F1-score' : f1_score
    }
```

We can use the results from the `evaluate()` function to calculate our metrics now. For percentage difference from the mean, we get the following output:

```python
>>> classification_stats(tp, fp, tn, fn)
{'accuracy': 0.9873417721518988,
 'precision': 0.975,
 'recall': 1.0,
 'F1-score': 0.9873417721518987}
```

When working with thresholds, we can plot precision-recall curves to show the precision and recall obtained at various thresholds. We can use this to pick a threshold that gives us satisfactory precision and recall. In Chapter 9, *Getting Started with Machine Learning in Python*, we will see how to make this plot, and in Chapter 11, *Machine Learning Anomaly Detection*, we will work through an example of finding a threshold that satisfies our criteria.

It looks like our trio of criteria did quite well. If we were concerned with the hacker IP addresses being chosen when we calculated the baselines, but didn't want to trim, we could have run this with the median instead of the mean:

```
>>> medians = get_baselines(hourly_ip_logs, 'median')
>>> pct_from_median_ips = pct_change_threshold(
...     hourly_ip_logs, medians,
...     {key: 1.25 for key in [
...         'username', 'attempts', 'failure_rate'
...     ]}
... )
>>> tp, fp, tn, fn = scores(pct_from_median_ips)
>>> classification_stats(tp, fp, tn, fn)
{'accuracy': 0.9873417721518988,
 'precision': 0.975,
 'recall': 1.0,
 'F1-score': 0.9873417721518987}
```

Using the median, we achieve identical performance to the mean in this case; however, we didn't need to trim the data beforehand. This is because the median is robust to outliers, meaning that picking a single hacker IP address in a given hour doesn't affect that hour's baseline as it would the mean. We can compare everything using dictionary comprehensions and a DataFrame:

```
>>> pd.DataFrame({
...     method : classification_stats(*scores(ips)) \
...     for method, ips in {
...         'means' : pct_from_mean_ips,
...         'medians' : pct_from_median_ips,
...         'tukey fence' : tukey_fence_flags,
...         'z-scores' : z_score_ips
...     }.items()
... })
```

The `scores()` function returns a tuple of (`tp`, `fp`, `tn`, `fn`), but the `classification_stats()` function expects four arguments. However, since `scores()` returns them in the same order that `classification_stats()` expects them, we can use `*` to unpack the tuple and send the values as four positional arguments.

The mean is affected by outliers, but once we trimmed the data, it became a viable method. We didn't need to trim the data to work with the median; the usefulness of the median hinges on the data containing less than 50% outliers. The Tukey fence takes this a step further by using the third quartile and assuming less than 25% of the data points are outliers. Since most of the data we are working with has the same value for the first and third quartiles, our IQR ends up being zero—meaning the upper bound is just the third quartile, and our multiplier can't raise the upper bound. For this reason, we had to use percent difference along with the upper bound. The Z-score method is also affected by outliers because it uses the mean; however, with the trimmed data, we were able to get good performance with a modest cutoff of three:

	means	medians	tukey_fence	z-scores
F1-score	0.987342	0.987342	1.0	0.901408
accuracy	0.987342	0.987342	1.0	0.901408
precision	0.975000	0.975000	1.0	1.000000
recall	1.000000	1.000000	1.0	0.820513

All the methods we tried performed well. Ultimately, which method we use in practice will depend on how costly it is to have a false positive versus a false negative—is it worse to raise the alarm when nothing is wrong, or to be silent when something is?

Another common use case for anomaly detection is in quality or process control in industrial settings, such as monitoring factory equipment performance and output. Process control uses threshold-based and pattern-based rules to determine if systems are out of control. These can be used for things like finding when the distribution of the underlying data has changed, which could be a precursor for later problems. **Western Electric rules** and **Nelson rules** are common ones. Links to both are in the *Further reading* section at the end of this chapter.

Summary

In our second application chapter, we learned how to simulate events in Python and got additional exposure to writing packages. We also saw how to write Python scripts that can be run from the command line, which we used to run our simulation of the login attempt data. Then, we performed some exploratory data analysis on the simulated data to see if we could figure out what would make hacker activity easy to spot.

This led us to zero in on the number of distinct usernames attempting to authenticate per IP address per hour, as well as the number of attempts and failure rates. Using these metrics, we were able to create a scatter plot, which appeared to show two distinct groups of points, along with some other points connecting the two groups; naturally, these represented the groups of valid users and the nefarious ones, with some of the hackers not being as obvious as others.

Finally, we set about creating rules that would flag the hacker IP addresses for their suspicious activity. First, we used `pandas` to reshape our data into hourly aggregates per IP address. Then, we wrote functions to trim values greater than the 95th percentile and calculate baselines for a given statistic per hour, which we used to create our rules based on percentage differences from the mean and median, exceeding the upper bound of a Tukey fence, and using Z-scores. We saw that building good rules depended on carefully tuning our parameters: the percentages for the difference from the mean and median, the multiplier for the Tukey fence, and the threshold for the Z-score. Being a classification task with class imbalance, we looked at precision, recall, and F_1 score to determine which of the rules was performing the best.

In the next two chapters, we will introduce machine learning in Python using `scikit-learn`, and in Chapter 11, *Machine Learning Anomaly Detection*, we will revisit this data for anomaly detection using machine learning.

Exercises

Complete the following exercises to practice the concepts covered in this chapter:

1. Run the simulation for December 2018 into new log files without making the user base again. Be sure to run `python simulate.py -h` to review the command-line arguments. Set the seed to `27`. This data will be used for the remaining exercises.

2. Find the number of unique usernames, attempts, successes, failures, and the success/failure rates per IP address, using the data simulated in exercise *#1*.

3. Create two subplots with failures versus attempts on the left, and failure rate versus distinct usernames on the right. Draw decision boundaries for the resulting plots. Be sure to color each data point by whether or not it is a hacker IP address.

4. Build a rule-based criteria using percentage difference from the median that flags an IP address if the failures and attempts are both five times their respective medians, or if the distinct usernames count is five times its median. Be sure to use a one-hour window. Remember to use the `get_baselines()` function to calculate the metrics needed for the baselines.

5. Calculate metrics to evaluate how well these rules performed using the `evaluate()` and `classification_stats()` functions from this chapter.

Further reading

Check out the following resources for more information on the topics covered this chapter:

- *A Gentle Introduction to the Bootstrap Method*: `https://machinelearningmastery.com/a-gentle-introduction-to-the-bootstrap-method/`
- *An Introduction to the Bootstrap Method*: `https://towardsdatascience.com/an-introduction-to-the-bootstrap-method-58bcb51b4d60`
- *Adding Salt to Hashing: A Better Way to Store Passwords*: `https://auth0.com/blog/adding-salt-to-hashing-a-better-way-to-store-passwords/`

- *Brute-force attack*: https://en.wikipedia.org/wiki/Brute-force_attack
- *Classification Accuracy is Not Enough: More Performance Measures You Can Use*: https://machinelearningmastery.com/classification-accuracy-is-not-enough-more-performance-measures-you-can-use/
- *Dictionary attack*: https://en.wikipedia.org/wiki/Dictionary_attack
- *Nelson rules*: https://en.wikipedia.org/wiki/Nelson_rules
- *Offline Password Cracking: The Attack and the Best Defense*: https://www.alpinesecurity.com/blog/offline-password-cracking-the-attack-and-the-best-defense-against-it
- *Poisson point process*: https://en.wikipedia.org/wiki/Poisson_point_process
- *Precision and recall*: https://en.wikipedia.org/wiki/Precision_and_recall
- *Probability Distributions in Python*: https://www.datacamp.com/community/tutorials/probability-distributions-python
- *Rainbow Tables: Your Password's Worst Nightmare*: https://www.lifewire.com/rainbow-tables-your-passwords-worst-nightmare-2487288
- *RFC 1597 (Address Allocation for Private Internets)*: http://www.faqs.org/rfcs/rfc1597.html
- *Sampling Techniques*: https://towardsdatascience.com/sampling-techniques-a4e34111d808
- *Trimmed Estimator*: https://en.wikipedia.org/wiki/Trimmed_estimator
- *Western Electric rules*: https://en.wikipedia.org/wiki/Western_Electric_rules

4

Section 4: Introduction to Machine Learning with Scikit-Learn

Up to this point in the book, we have focused on data analysis tasks using `pandas`, but there is so much more data science we can do with Python. These next three chapters will serve as an introduction to machine learning in Python with `scikit-learn`—that's not to say that we will be abandoning everything we have worked on so far, though. As we have seen, `pandas` is an essential tool for quickly exploring, cleaning, visualizing, and analyzing data—all of which still need to be done before attempting any machine learning. We won't go into any theory; instead, we will show how machine learning tasks, such as clustering, classification, and regression, can be easily implemented in Python.

The following chapters are included in this section:

- `Chapter 9`, *Getting Started with Machine Learning in Python*
- `Chapter 10`, *Making Better Predictions – Optimizing Models*
- `Chapter 11`, *Machine Learning Anomaly Detection*

Getting Started with Machine Learning in Python

9

This chapter will expose us to the vernacular of machine learning and common tasks that machine learning can be used to solve. Afterwards we will learn how we can prepare our data for use in machine learning models. We have discussed data cleaning already, but only for human consumption—machine learning models require different **preprocessing** (cleaning) techniques. There are quite a few nuances here, so we will take our time with this topic and discuss how we can use `scikit-learn` to build preprocessing pipelines that streamline this procedure, since our models will only be as good as the data they are trained on.

Next, we will walk through how we can use `scikit-learn` to build a model and evaluate its performance. Scikit-learn has a very user-friendly API, so once we know how to build one, we can build any number of them. We won't be going into any of the mathematics behind the models; there are entire books on this, and the goal of this chapter is to serve as an introduction to the topic. By the end of this chapter, we will be able to identify what type of problem we are looking to solve and some algorithms that can help us, as well as how to implement them.

The following topics will be covered in this chapter:

- Getting an overview of the machine learning landscape
- Performing exploratory data analysis using skills learned in previous chapters
- Preparing data for use in a machine learning model
- Clustering to help understand unlabeled data
- Learning when regression is appropriate and how to implement it with `scikit-learn`
- Understanding classification tasks and learning how to use logistic regression

Chapter materials

In this chapter, we will be working with three datasets. The first two come from data on wine quality that was donated to the UCI Machine Learning Data Repository (http://archive.ics.uci.edu/ml) by P. Cortez, A. Cerdeira, F. Almeida, T. Matos, and J. Reis, which contains information on the chemical properties of various wine samples, along with a rating of the quality from a blind tasting by a panel of wine experts. These files can be found in the data/ folder inside this chapter's folder in the GitHub repository (https://github.com/stefmolin/Hands-On-Data-Analysis-with-Pandas/tree/master/ch_09) as winequality-red.csv and winequality-white.csv for red and white wine, respectively.

Our third dataset was collected using the Open Exoplanet Catalogue database, which can be found at https://github.com/OpenExoplanetCatalogue/open_exoplanet_catalogue/. This database provides data in **eXtensible Markup Language** (XML) format, which is similar to HTML. The planet_data_collection.ipynb notebook on GitHub contains the code that was used to parse this information into the CSV files we will use in this chapter; while we won't be going over this explicitly, I encourage you to take a look at it. The data files can be found in the data/ folder, as well. We will use planets.csv for this chapter; however, the parsed data for the other hierarchies is provided for exercises and further exploration. These are binaries.csv, stars.csv, and systems.csv, which contain data on binaries (stars or binaries forming a group of two), data on a single star, and data on a planetary system, respectively.

We will be using the red_wine.ipynb notebook to predict red wine quality, the wine.ipynb notebook to classify wines as red or white based on their chemical properties, and the planets_ml.ipynb notebook to build a regression model to predict the year length of planets and perform clustering to find similar planet groups. We will use the preprocessing.ipynb notebook for the section on preprocessing.

Back in Chapter 1, *Introduction to Data Analysis*, when we set up our environment, we installed a package from GitHub called ml_utils. This package contains utility functions and classes that we will use for our three chapters on machine learning. Unlike the last two chapters, we won't be discussing how to make this package; however, those interested can look through the code at https://github.com/stefmolin/ml-utils/tree/pandas_book and follow the instructions from Chapter 7, *Financial Analysis – Bitcoin and the Stock Market*, to install it in editable mode.

The following are the reference links for the data sources:

- *Open Exoplanet Catalogue database,* available at `https://github.com/OpenExoplanetCatalogue/open_exoplanet_catalogue/#data-structure`.
- *P. Cortez, A. Cerdeira, F. Almeida, T. Matos and J. Reis. Modeling wine preferences by data mining from physicochemical properties. In Decision Support Systems, Elsevier, 47(4):547-553, 2009.* Available online at `http://archive.ics.uci.edu/ml/datasets/Wine+Quality`.
- *Dua, D. and Karra Taniskidou, E. (2017). UCI Machine Learning Repository* [`http://archive.ics.uci.edu/ml`]. *Irvine, CA: University of California, School of Information and Computer Science.*

Learning the lingo

Machine learning is a subset of **artificial intelligence (AI)** whereby an algorithm can learn to predict values from input data without explicitly being taught rules. These algorithms rely on statistics to make inferences as they learn; they then use what they learn to make predictions.

Machine learning can be found everywhere we look—applying for a loan, using a search engine, sending a robot vacuum to clean a specific room with a voice command—because it can be used for many purposes, for example, voice recognition by AI assistants such as Alexa, Siri, or Google Assistant, mapping floor plans by exploring surroundings, determining who will default on a loan, figuring out which search results are relevant, and even painting (`https://www.boredpanda.com/computer-deep-learning-algorithm-painting-masters/`).

There are three main types of machine learning: unsupervised, supervised, and reinforcement. We use **unsupervised learning** when we don't have labeled data telling us what our model should say for each data point. In many cases, gathering labeled data is costly or just not feasible, so unsupervised learning will be used. Note that it is more difficult to optimize the performance of these models because we don't know how well they are performing. If we do have access to the labels, we can use **supervised learning**; this makes it much easier for us to evaluate our models and look to improve them since we can calculate metrics on their performance compared to the true labels.

> **TIP** Since unsupervised learning looks to find meaning in the data without a correct answer, it can be used to learn more about the data as a part of the analysis or before moving on to supervised learning.

Reinforcement learning models learn to react to feedback from their environment; this is used for things like robots and AI in games. It is well beyond the scope of this book, but there are resources in the *Further reading* section for more information.

The most common machine learning tasks are clustering, classification, and regression. In **clustering**, we look to assign data into groups, with the goal being that the groups are well-defined, meaning that members of the group are close together and groups are separated from other groups. Clustering can be used in an unsupervised manner in an attempt to gain a better understanding of the data, or in a supervised manner to try to predict which cluster data belongs to (essentially classification). Note that clustering can be used for prediction in an unsupervised manner; however, we will need to decipher what each cluster means. Labels that are obtained from clustering can even be used as the input for a supervised learner to model how observations are mapped to each group; this is called **semi-supervised learning**.

Classification, as we discussed in the previous chapter, looks to assign a class label to the data, such as benign or malicious. This may sound like assigning it to a cluster, however we aren't worried about how similar the values that are assigned to benign are, just marking them as benign. Since we are assigning to a class or category, this class of models is used to predict a discrete label. **Regression**, on the other hand, is for predicting numeric values, like housing prices or gross domestic product (GDP); it models the strength and magnitude of the relationships between variables. Both can be performed as unsupervised or supervised learning; however, supervised models are more likely to perform better.

Machine learning models can be made to adapt to changes in the input over time and are a huge help in making decisions without the need for a human each time. Think about applying for a loan or a credit line increase on a credit card; the bank or credit card company will be relying on a machine learning algorithm to look up things from the applicant's credit score and history with them to determine whether the applicant should be approved. Most likely, they will only approve the applicant in that moment if the model predicts a strong chance he or she can be trusted with the loan or new credit limit. In the case where the model can't be so sure, they can send it over to a human to make the final decision. This reduces the amount of applications employees have to sift through to just the borderline cases, while also providing faster answers for those non-borderline cases (the process can be nearly instantaneous).

One important thing to call out here is that models that are used for tasks such as loan approvals, by law, have to be interpretable. There needs to be a way to explain to the applicant why they were rejected—saying *our model just said no* isn't going to cut it.

Nowadays, we hear a lot about **deep learning**, which aims to learn data representations using methods such as **neural networks**. Deep learning methods are often black boxes, so they can't be used for tasks such as predicting loan defaults, even if they would perform better, due to the aforementioned legal reasons. These are used for applications such as self-driving cars and image classification. They are also beyond the scope of this book, but it is good to be aware that these are also machine learning techniques.

Sometimes, reasons beyond technology can influence and limit what approaches or data we use.

Now that we know what machine learning is, we need to know how we can build our own models. Python offers many packages for building machine learning models; some libraries we should be aware of include the following:

- `scikit-learn`: Easy to use (and learn), it features a consistent API for machine learning in Python (`https://scikit-learn.org/stable/index.html`)
- `statsmodels`: A statistical modeling library that also provides statistical tests (`https://www.statsmodels.org/stable/index.html`)
- `tensorflow`: A machine learning library developed by Google that features faster calculations (`https://www.tensorflow.org/`)
- `keras`: A high-level API for running deep learning from libraries such as TensorFlow (`https://keras.io/`)
- `pytorch`: A deep learning library developed by Facebook (`https://pytorch.org`)

Most of these libraries use NumPy and SciPy, a library built on top of NumPy for statistics, mathematics, and engineering purposes. SciPy can be used to handle linear algebra, interpolation, integration, and clustering algorithms, among other things. More information on SciPy can be found at `https://docs.scipy.org/doc/scipy/reference/tutorial/general.html`.

In this book, we will be using `scikit-learn` for its user-friendly API. In `scikit-learn`, our base class is an **estimator** (not to be confused with a model when used in statistical terms), which is capable of learning from the data via its `fit()` method. We use **transformers** to prepare our data with their `transform()` method—transforming it into something **predictors** (classes for supervised or unsupervised learning) can use with their `predict()` method. The **model** classes are capable of calculating how well they perform using a `score()` method. Knowing just these four methods, we can easily build any machine learning model offered by `scikit-learn`. More information on this design pattern can be found at `https://scikit-learn.org/stable/developers/contributing.html#apis-of-scikit-learn-objects`.

Exploratory data analysis

As we have learned throughout this book, our first step should be to engage in some **exploratory data analysis** (EDA) to get familiar with our data. In the interest of brevity, this section will include a subset of the EDA that's available in each of the notebooks—be sure to check out the respective notebooks for the full version.

Let's start with our imports, which will be the same across the notebooks we will use in this chapter:

```
>>> %matplotlib inline
>>> import matplotlib.pyplot as plt
>>> import numpy as np
>>> import pandas as pd
>>> import seaborn as sns
```

Red wine quality data

Let's read in our red wine data and do some EDA using techniques we have learned throughout this book:

```
>>> red_wine = pd.read_csv('data/winequality-red.csv')
```

We have data on 11 different chemical properties of red wine, along with a column indicating the quality score from the wine experts that participated in the blind taste testing. We can try to predict the quality score by looking at the chemical properties:

	fixed acidity	volatile acidity	citric acid	residual sugar	chlorides	free sulfur dioxide	total sulfur dioxide	density	pH	sulphates	alcohol	quality
0	7.4	0.70	0.00	1.9	0.076	11.0	34.0	0.9978	3.51	0.56	9.4	5
1	7.8	0.88	0.00	2.6	0.098	25.0	67.0	0.9968	3.20	0.68	9.8	5
2	7.8	0.76	0.04	2.3	0.092	15.0	54.0	0.9970	3.26	0.65	9.8	5
3	11.2	0.28	0.56	1.9	0.075	17.0	60.0	0.9980	3.16	0.58	9.8	6
4	7.4	0.70	0.00	1.9	0.076	11.0	34.0	0.9978	3.51	0.56	9.4	5

Let's see what the distribution of the `quality` column looks like:

```
>>> ax = red_wine.quality.value_counts().sort_index(
...       ascending=False
... ).plot.barh(title='Red Wine Quality Scores', figsize=(12, 3))
>>> for bar in ax.patches:
...       ax.text(
...           bar.get_width(),
...           bar.get_y() + bar.get_height()/4,
...           f'{bar.get_width()/red_wine.shape[0]:.1%}'
...       )
>>> plt.xlabel('count of wines')
>>> plt.ylabel('quality score')
```

The information on the dataset says that `quality` varies from 0 (terrible) to 10 (excellent); however, we only have values in the middle of that range. An interesting task for this data could be to see if we can predict high-quality red wines (quality score of 7 or higher):

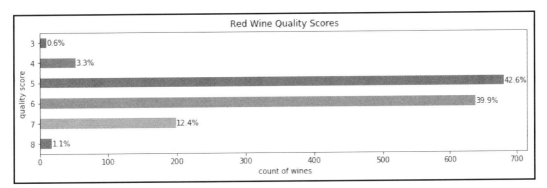

All of our data is numeric, so we don't have to worry about handling text values; we also don't have any missing values:

```
>>> red_wine.info()
<class 'pandas.core.frame.DataFrame'>
RangeIndex: 1599 entries, 0 to 1598
Data columns (total 12 columns):
fixed acidity           1599 non-null float64
volatile acidity        1599 non-null float64
citric acid             1599 non-null float64
residual sugar          1599 non-null float64
chlorides               1599 non-null float64
free sulfur dioxide     1599 non-null float64
total sulfur dioxide    1599 non-null float64
density                 1599 non-null float64
pH                      1599 non-null float64
sulphates               1599 non-null float64
alcohol                 1599 non-null float64
quality                 1599 non-null int64
dtypes: float64(11), int64(1)
memory usage: 149.9 KB
```

We can use `describe()` to get an idea of what scale each of the columns is on:

```
>>> red_wine.describe()
```

The result indicates that we will definitely have to do some scaling if our model uses distance metrics for anything because our columns aren't all on the same range:

	fixed acidity	volatile acidity	citric acid	residual sugar	chlorides	free sulfur dioxide	total sulfur dioxide	density	pH	sulphates	alcohol	quality
count	1599.000000	1599.000000	1599.000000	1599.000000	1599.000000	1599.000000	1599.000000	1599.000000	1599.000000	1599.000000	1599.000000	1599.000000
mean	8.319637	0.527821	0.270976	2.538806	0.087467	15.874922	46.467792	0.996747	3.311113	0.658149	10.422983	5.636023
std	1.741096	0.179060	0.194801	1.409928	0.047065	10.460157	32.895324	0.001887	0.154386	0.169507	1.065668	0.807569
min	4.600000	0.120000	0.000000	0.900000	0.012000	1.000000	6.000000	0.990070	2.740000	0.330000	8.400000	3.000000
25%	7.100000	0.390000	0.090000	1.900000	0.070000	7.000000	22.000000	0.995600	3.210000	0.550000	9.500000	5.000000
50%	7.900000	0.520000	0.260000	2.200000	0.079000	14.000000	38.000000	0.996750	3.310000	0.620000	10.200000	6.000000
75%	9.200000	0.640000	0.420000	2.600000	0.090000	21.000000	62.000000	0.997835	3.400000	0.730000	11.100000	6.000000
max	15.900000	1.580000	1.000000	15.500000	0.611000	72.000000	289.000000	1.003690	4.010000	2.000000	14.900000	8.000000

Lastly, let's use `cut()` to bin our high-quality red wines (roughly 14% of the data) for later:

```
>>> red_wine['high_quality'] = pd.cut(
...     red_wine.quality, bins=[0, 6, 10], labels=[0, 1]
... )
>>> red_wine.high_quality.value_counts(normalize=True)
0    0.86429
1    0.13571
Name: high_quality, dtype: float64
```

We are stopping our EDA here for brevity; however, we should make sure to fully explore our data and consult domain experts before attempting any modeling. One thing to pay particular attention to is correlations between variables and what we are trying to predict (high-quality red wine, in this case). Variables with strong correlations may be good features to include in a model. However, note that correlation does not imply causation. We already learned a few ways to use visualizations to look for correlations: the scatter matrix we discussed in Chapter 5, *Visualizing Data with Pandas and Matplotlib*, and the heatmap and pair plot from Chapter 6, *Plotting with Seaborn and Customization Techniques*. A pair plot is included in the red_wine.ipynb notebook.

Next, let's look at the red and white wine data together.

White and red wine chemical properties data

To do so, we read in both the red wine file we worked with previously and the white wine file. The white wine file is actually semi-colon (;) separated, so we must provide the sep argument to pd.read_csv():

```
>>> red_wine = pd.read_csv('data/winequality-red.csv')
>>> white_wine = pd.read_csv('data/winequality-white.csv', sep=';')
```

We can also look at the quality scores of the white wines, just as we did with the red ones, and we will find that the white wines tend to be rated higher overall. This might bring us to question whether the judges preferred white wine over red wine, thus creating a bias in their ratings. As it is, the rating system that was used seems to be pretty subjective:

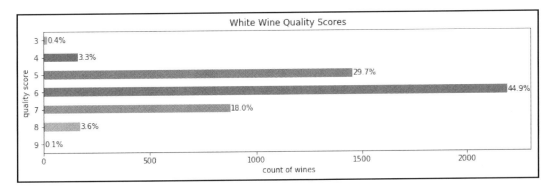

Both of these dataframes have the same columns, so we can combine them without further work. Here, we use `concat()` to stack the white wine data on top of the red wine data after adding a column to identify which wine type each observation belongs to:

```
>>> wine = pd.concat([
...     white_wine.assign(kind='white'), red_wine.assign(kind='red')
... ])
>>> wine.sample(5, random_state=10)
```

Like we did with the red wine, we can run `info()` to check if we need to perform type conversion or if we are missing any data; thankfully, we have no need here either. Our combined wine data looks like this:

	fixed acidity	volatile acidity	citric acid	residual sugar	chlorides	free sulfur dioxide	total sulfur dioxide	density	pH	sulphates	alcohol	quality	kind
848	6.4	0.64	0.21	1.8	0.081	14.0	31.0	0.99689	3.59	0.66	9.8	5	red
2529	6.6	0.42	0.13	12.8	0.044	26.0	158.0	0.99772	3.24	0.47	9.0	5	white
131	5.6	0.50	0.09	2.3	0.049	17.0	99.0	0.99370	3.63	0.63	13.0	5	red
244	15.0	0.21	0.44	2.2	0.075	10.0	24.0	1.00005	3.07	0.84	9.2	7	red
1551	6.6	0.19	0.99	1.2	0.122	45.0	129.0	0.99360	3.09	0.31	8.7	6	white

Using `value_counts()`, we can see that we have many more white wines than red wines in the data:

```
>>> wine.kind.value_counts()
white    4898
red      1599
Name: kind, dtype: int64
```

Lastly, let's examine box plots for each chemical property broken out by wine type using `seaborn`. This can help us identify **features** (model inputs) that will be helpful when building our model to distinguish between red and white wine:

```
>>> import math
>>> chemical_properties = [col for col in wine.columns \
...                        if col not in ['quality', 'kind']]
>>> melted = wine.drop(columns='quality').melt(id_vars=['kind'])
>>> fig, axes = plt.subplots(
...     math.ceil(len(chemical_properties) / 4), 4, figsize=(20, 10)
... )
>>> axes = axes.flatten()
>>> for prop, ax in zip(chemical_properties, axes):
...     sns.boxplot(
...         data=melted[melted.variable.isin([prop])],
...         x='variable', y='value', hue='kind', ax=ax
...     )
```

```
>>> for ax in axes[len(chemical_properties):]:
...     ax.remove()  # remove the extra subplots
>>> plt.suptitle(
...     'Comparing Chemical Properties of Red and White Wines'
... )
```

Given the following result, we might look to use fixed acidity, volatile acidity, total sulfur dioxide, and sulphates when building a model since they seem to be distributed differently for red and white wines:

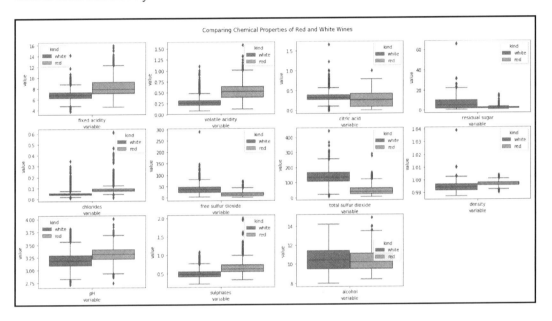

Comparing the distributions of variables across classes can help inform feature selection for our model. If we see that the distribution for a variable is very different between classes, that variable may be very useful to include in our model. It is essential that we perform an in-depth exploration of our data before moving on to modeling. Be sure to use the visualizations we covered in Chapter 5, *Visualizing Data with Pandas and Matplotlib*, and Chapter 6, *Plotting with Seaborn and Customization Techniques*, as they will prove invaluable for this process.

We will come back to this visualization in Chapter 10, *Making Better Predictions – Optimizing Models*, when we examine incorrect predictions made by our model. Now, let's take a look at the other dataset we will be working with.

Planets and exoplanets data

An **exoplanet** is simply a planet that orbits a star outside of our solar system, so from here on out we will refer to both collectively as planets. Let's read in our planets data now:

```
>>> planets = pd.read_csv('data/planets.csv')
```

Some interesting tasks we can do with this data would be to find clusters of similar planets based on their orbits and try to predict how long a year is on a planet, in Earth days. This is called the orbit period:

	period	name	eccentricity	description	discoverymethod	periastrontime	lastupdate	semimajoraxis	mass	periastron	list	discoveryyear
0	326.03	11 Com b	0.231	11 Com b is a brown dwarf-mass companion to th...	RV	2452899.60	15/09/20	1.290	19.400	94.800	Confirmed planets	2008.0
1	516.22	11 UMi b	0.080	11 Ursae Minoris is a star located in the cons...	RV	2452861.04	15/09/20	1.540	11.200	117.630	Confirmed planets	2009.0
2	185.84	14 And b	0.000	14 Andromedae is an evolved star in the conste...	RV	2452861.40	15/09/20	0.830	4.800	0.000	Confirmed planets	2008.0
3	1766.00	14 Her b	0.359	The star 14 Herculis is only 59 light years aw...	RV	NaN	15/09/21	2.864	4.975	22.230	Confirmed planets	2002.0
4	9886.00	14 Her c	0.184	14 Her c is the second companion in the system...	RV	NaN	15/09/21	9.037	7.679	189.076	Controversial	2006.0

We can build a correlation matrix heatmap to find the best features to use:

```
>>> fig = plt.figure(figsize=(7, 7))
>>> sns.heatmap(
...     planets.drop(columns='discoveryyear').corr(),
...     center=0, square=True, annot=True
... )
```

The heatmap shows us that the semi-major axis of a planet is highly positively correlated to the length of its year (`period`):

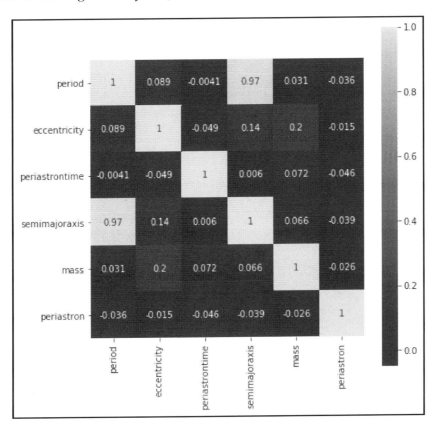

To predict `period`, we probably want to look at `semimajoraxis`, `mass`, and `eccentricity`. The orbit eccentricity quantifies how much the orbit differs from a perfect circle:

Eccentricity value	Orbit shape
0	Circular
(0, 1)	Elliptical
1	Parabolic
> 1	Hyperbolic

Let's see what shapes the orbits we have are:

```
>>> planets.eccentricity.min(), planets.eccentricity.max()
(0.0, 0.956) # circular and elliptical eccentricities
>>> planets.eccentricity.hist()
```

It looks like nearly everything is an ellipse, which we would expect since these are planets:

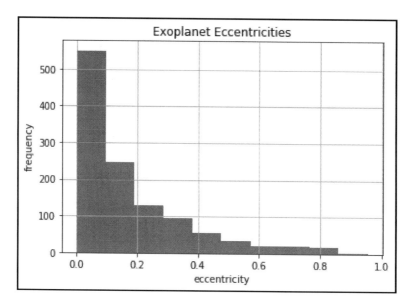

An ellipse, being an elongated circle, has two axes: *major* and *minor* for the longest and shortest ones, respectively. The semi-major axis is half the major axis. When compared to a circle, the axes are analogous to the diameter, crossing the entire shape, and the semi-axes are akin to the radius, being half the diameter. The following is how this would look in the case where the planet orbited a star that was exactly in the center of its elliptical orbit (due to gravity from other objects, in reality, the star can be anywhere inside the orbit path):

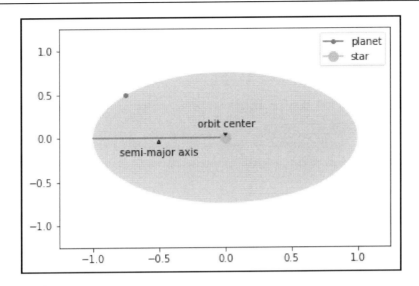

Now that we understand what these columns mean, let's do some EDA. This data isn't as clean as our red wine data was—it's certainly much easier to measure everything when we can reach out and touch it. It looks like we only have `eccentricity`, `semimajoraxis`, or `mass` data for a fraction of the planets, despite knowing most of the `periods`:

```
>>> planets[[
...     'period', 'eccentricity', 'semimajoraxis', 'mass'
... ]].info()
<class 'pandas.core.frame.DataFrame'>
RangeIndex: 3814 entries, 0 to 3813
Data columns (total 4 columns):
period          3684 non-null float64
eccentricity    1172 non-null float64
semimajoraxis   1456 non-null float64
mass            1417 non-null float64
dtypes: float64(4)
memory usage: 119.2 KB
```

If we were to drop data where any of these columns was null, we would be left with a third of it:

```
>>> planets[
...     ['period', 'eccentricity', 'semimajoraxis', 'mass']
...].dropna().shape
(1044, 4)
```

If we are simply looking for a way to predict the length of the year (when we have these values available) to learn more about their relationship, we wouldn't necessarily worry about throwing out the missing data. Imputing it here could be far worse for our model.

At least, everything is properly encoded as a float; however, let's check whether we need to do some scaling:

```
>>> planets[[
...     'period', 'eccentricity', 'semimajoraxis', 'mass'
... ]].describe()
```

This shows us that, depending on our model, we will definitely have to do some scaling because the `period` column is much larger than the others:

	period	eccentricity	semimajoraxis	mass
count	3684.000000	1172.000000	1456.000000	1417.000000
mean	517.715911	0.168518	1.610329	2.837145
std	7284.863699	0.190131	8.282760	9.043661
min	0.090706	0.000000	0.004420	0.000008
25%	4.725905	0.020000	0.052530	0.141600
50%	12.878744	0.109000	0.163518	0.914000
75%	48.350875	0.250000	1.250000	2.540000
max	320000.000000	0.956000	177.000000	263.000000

We could also look at some scatter plots. Note that there is a `list` column for the planet list the planet belongs to, like `Solar System` or `Controversial`. We might want to see if the period (and distance from the star) influences this:

```
>>> sns.scatterplot(
...     planets.semimajoraxis, planets.period,
...     hue=planets.list, alpha=0.5
... )
>>> plt.title('period vs. semimajoraxis')

# move legend to the right of the plot
>>> ax.legend(bbox_to_anchor=(1, 0.77))
```

The controversial planets appear to be spread throughout and have larger semi-major axes and periods. Perhaps they are controversial because they are very far from their star:

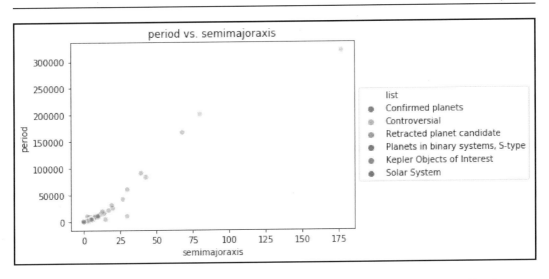

Unfortunately, we can see that the scale of period is making this pretty difficult to read, so we could try a log transformation on the *y*-axis to get more separation in the more dense section on the lower-left. Let's just point out the planets in our solar system this time:

```
>>> fig, axes = plt.subplots(1, 1, figsize=(10, 10))
>>> in_solar_system = (
...     planets.list == 'Solar System'
... ).rename('in solar system?')
>>> ax = sns.scatterplot(
...     planets.semimajoraxis,
...     planets.period,
...     hue=in_solar_system,
...     ax=axes
... )
>>> ax.set_yscale('log')
>>> solar_system = planets[planets.list == 'Solar System']
>>> for planet in solar_system.name:
...     data = solar_system.query(f'name == "{planet}"')
...     ax.annotate(
...         planet,
...         (data.semimajoraxis, data.period),
...         (7 + data.semimajoraxis, data.period),
...         arrowprops=dict(arrowstyle='->')
...     )
>>> ax.set_title('log(orbital period) vs. semi-major axis')
```

There were certainly a lot of planets hiding in that lower-left corner of the plot. We can see many planets with years shorter than Mercury's 88 Earth-day year, now:

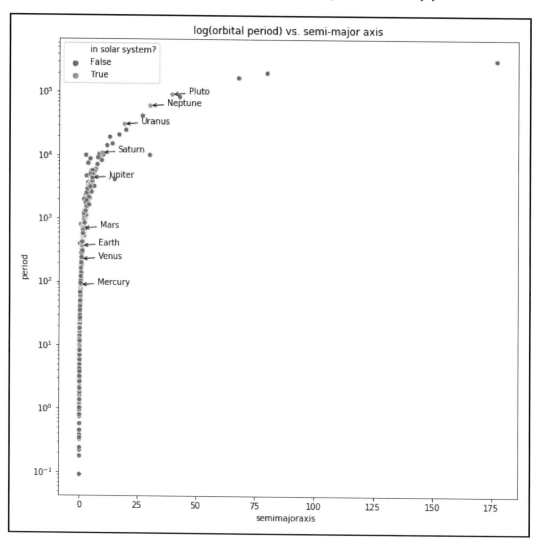

Now that we have a feel for the data we will be working with, let's learn how to prepare it for use in a machine learning model.

Preprocessing data

In this section, we will be working in the `preprocessing.ipynb` notebook, before we return to the notebooks we used for EDA. We will begin with our imports and read in the data:

```
>>> import numpy as np
>>> import pandas as pd

>>> planets = pd.read_csv('data/planets.csv')
>>> red_wine = pd.read_csv('data/winequality-red.csv')
>>> wine = pd.concat([
...     pd.read_csv(
...         'data/winequality-white.csv', sep=';'
...     ).assign(kind='white'),
...     red_wine.assign(kind='red')
... ])
```

Machine learning models follow the *garbage in, garbage out* principal. We have to make sure that we **train** our models (have them learn) on the best possible version of the data. What this means will depend on the model we choose. For instance, models that use a distance metric to calculate how similar observations are will easily be confused if our features are on wildly different scales. Unless we are working with a **natural language processing** (**NLP**) problem to try and understand the meaning of words, our model will have no use for—or worse, be unable to interpret—textual values. Missing or invalid data will also cause problems; we will have to decide whether to drop them or impute them. All of the adjustments we make to our data before giving it to our model to learn from are collectively called **preprocessing**.

Training and testing sets

So far, machine learning sounds pretty great, though—we can build a model that will learn how to perform a task for us. Therefore, we should give it all the data we have so that it learns well, right? Unfortunately, it's not that simple. If we give the model all of our data, we risk **overfitting** it, meaning that it won't be able to generalize well to new data points because it was fit to the sample rather than the population. On the other hand, if we don't give it enough data, it will **underfit** and be unable to capture the underlying information in the data.

When a model fits the randomness in the data, it is said to fit the **noise** in the data.

Another thing to consider is that, if we use all of our data to train the model, how can we evaluate its performance? If we test it on the data we used for training, we will be overestimating how good it is because our model will always perform better on the training data. For these reasons, it's important to split our data into a **training set** and **testing set**. To do so, we could shuffle our dataframe and select the top *x*% of the rows for training and leave the rest for testing:

```
shuffled = planets.reindex(np.random.permutation(planets.index))
train_end_index = int(np.ceil(shuffled.shape[0]*.75))
training = shuffled.iloc[:train_end_index,]
testing = shuffled.iloc[train_end_index:,]
```

This would work, but it's a lot to write every time. Thankfully, `scikit-learn` provides us with the `train_test_split()` function in the `model_selection` module, which is a more robust, easier to use solution. It requires us to separate our input data (X) from our output data (y) beforehand. Here, we will pick 75% of the data to be used for the training set (X_train, y_train) and 25% for the testing set (X_test, y_test). We will set a `random_state` so that the split is reproducible:

```
>>> from sklearn.model_selection import train_test_split

>>> X = planets[['eccentricity', 'semimajoraxis', 'mass']]
>>> y = planets.period

>>> X_train, X_test, y_train, y_test = train_test_split(
...     X, y, test_size=0.25, random_state=0
... )
```

The `train_test_split()` function supports stratified sampling. It does this by accepting the values to stratify on in the `stratify` argument, which we will need for our wine models.

While there are no specific criteria for what constitutes a good size for the test set, a rule of thumb is usually between 10% and 30% of the data. However, if we don't have much data, we will shift toward a 10% testing set to make sure that we have enough data to learn from. Conversely, if we have a lot of data, we may move toward 30% testing, since, not only do we not want to overfit, but we want to give our model a good amount of data to prove its worth. Note that there is a big caveat with this rule of thumb: there are diminishing returns on the amount of training data we use. If we have a ton of data, we will most likely use much less than 70% of it for training because our computational costs may rise significantly for possibly minuscule improvements and an increased risk of overfitting.

 When building models that require tuning, we split the data into training, validation, and testing sets. We will introduce validation sets in `Chapter 10`, *Making Better Predictions – Optimizing Models*.

Let's take a look at the dimensions of our training and testing sets now. Since we are using three features (`eccentricity`, `semimajoraxis`, and `mass`), `X_train` and `X_test` have three columns. The `y_train` and `y_test` sets will be a single column each. The number of observations in the `X` and `y` for training will be equal, as will be the case for the testing set:

```
>>> X.shape, y.shape # original data
((3814, 3), (3814,))
>>> X_train.shape, y_train.shape # training data
((2860, 3), (2860,))
>>> X_test.shape, y_test.shape # testing data
((954, 3), (954,))
```

`X_train` and `X_test` are returned to us as dataframes since that is the format we passed them in as. If we are working with data in `numpy` directly, we will get `numpy` arrays or `ndarrays` back instead. We are going to work with this data for other examples in the *Preprocessing data* section, so let's take a look at the first five rows of the `X_train` dataframe:

	eccentricity	semimajoraxis	mass
1846	NaN	NaN	NaN
1918	NaN	NaN	NaN
3261	NaN	0.074	NaN
3000	NaN	NaN	NaN
1094	0.073	2.600	1.6

y_train and y_test are both series since that is what we passed into the
train_test_split() function. If we had passed in a numpy array, that is what we
would have gotten back instead. The rows in y_train and y_test must line up with
the rows in X_train and X_test, respectively. Let's confirm this by looking at the
first five rows of y_train:

```
1846        52.661793
1918        23.622591
3261         7.008151
3000       226.890470
1094      1251.000000
Name: period, dtype: float64
```

Indeed, everything matches up, as expected. Now, let's move on to the rest of our
preprocessing.

Scaling and centering data

We've seen that our dataframes had columns with very different scales; if we want to
use any model that calculates a distance metric (such as k-means, which we will
discuss in this chapter, or **k-nearest neighbors (k-NN)**, which we will discuss briefly
in Chapter 10, *Making Better Predictions – Optimizing Models*), we will need to scale
these. As we discussed back in Chapter 1, *Introduction to Data Analysis*, we have quite
a few options for doing so. Scikit-learn provides options in the preprocessing
module for standardizing (scaling by calculating Z-scores) and min-max scaling (to
normalize data to be in [0, 1]), among others.

> We should check the requirements of the model we are building to
> see if the data needs to be scaled.

For standard scaling, we use the StandardScaler class. The fit_transform()
method combines fit(), which figures out the mean and standard deviation needed
to center and scale, and transform(), which applies the transformation to the data.
Note that, after this transformation, the planets data is mostly between -3 and 3
because everything is now a Z-score:

```
>>> from sklearn.preprocessing import StandardScaler

>>> standardized = StandardScaler().fit_transform(X_train)
```

```
# examine some of the non-NaN values
>>> standardized[~np.isnan(standardized)][:30]
array([-0.17649619, -0.5045706 ,  0.14712504, -0.12764807,
        1.09368797,  0.67240099, -0.01731216, -0.84296411,
       -0.18098025, -0.13758824, -0.00791305, -0.09869129,
       -0.26808282, -0.18032045, -0.15945662,  0.36484041,
       -0.15305095, -0.28352985, -0.17803358, -0.18017312,
       -0.238978  ,  0.05247717, -0.16875798, -0.26094578,
       -0.18022437, -0.22704979, -0.25988606, -0.17954522,
       -0.2851004 , -0.68678249])
```

When creating the `StandardScaler` object, we can have it not subtract the mean or not divide by the standard deviation by passing `False` to `with_mean` or `with_std`, respectively. Both are `True` by default. There are examples of this in the notebook.

Other scalers can be used with the same syntax. Let's try the `MinMaxScaler` on the planets data to get the data in the range of [0, 1]:

```
>>> from sklearn.preprocessing import MinMaxScaler

>>> MinMaxScaler().fit_transform(X_train)
```

```
# examine some of the non-NaN values
>>> normalized[~np.isnan(normalized)][:30]
array([3.93117161e-04, 7.63598326e-02, 1.46646600e-02, 6.08362087e-03,
       3.97489540e-01, 3.78290803e-02, 1.03041533e-02, 8.36820084e-03,
       1.95372110e-04, 5.70339272e-03, 1.76150628e-01, 3.82427629e-03,
       7.11757595e-04, 2.24468882e-04, 4.86689080e-03, 2.51046025e-01,
       1.42704129e-03, 1.20883052e-04, 3.25318858e-04, 2.30966220e-04,
       1.82506561e-03, 1.88284519e-01, 7.34368621e-04, 9.84761405e-04,
       2.28706276e-04, 2.28133939e-03, 1.25523013e-01, 2.58656177e-04,
       6.08070051e-05, 3.97489540e-02])
```

These values get returned to us in **scientific notation**. The `e` tells us where the decimal point got moved. In the case where the `e` is followed by a `+`, we move the decimal point to the right by the number of places indicated; we move to the left for `-`. Therefore, `1.00e+00` is equivalent to 1, `2.89e-02` is equivalent to `0.0289`, and `2.89e+02` is equivalent to 289.

There is also the `RobustScaler`, which uses the median and IQR for robust to outliers scaling. There are examples of this in the notebook. More preprocessing classes can be found at `https://scikit-learn.org/stable/modules/classes.html#module-sklearn.preprocessing`.

Encoding data

The scalers in the previous section address the preprocessing of our numeric data, but how can we deal with categorical data? We need to encode the categories into integer values. There are a few options here, depending on what the categories represent. If our category is binary (such as 0/1, True/False, or yes/no), then we will **encode** these as a single column for both options, where 0 is one option and 1 is the other. We can easily do this with the np.where() function. Let's encode the wine data's kind field as 1 for red and 0 for white:

```
>>> np.where(wine.kind == 'red', 1, 0)
array([0, 0, 0, ..., 1, 1, 1])
```

This is effectively a column that tells us whether or not the wine is red. Remember, we concatenated the red wines to the bottom of the white wines when we created our wine dataframe, so np.where() will return zeros for the top rows and ones for the bottom rows, just like we saw in the previous result.

 Note that we can also use the LabelBinarizer from scikit-learn. With numeric values, we can use the Binarizer and provide a threshold. There are examples of this in the notebook.

If our categories are ordered, we may want to use **ordinal encoding** on those columns; this will preserve the ordering of the categories. For instance, if we wanted to classify the red wines as 'low', 'med', or 'high' quality, we could encode this as 0, 1, and 2, respectively. The advantages of this are that we can use regression techniques to predict the quality, or we can use this as a feature in the model to predict something else; this model would be able to use the fact that high is better than medium, which is better than low quality. We can achieve this with the LabelEncoder if the order in which each category appears is the sorting order:

```
>>> from sklearn.preprocessing import LabelEncoder

>>> set(LabelEncoder().fit_transform(pd.cut(
...     red_wine.quality.sort_values(),
...     bins=[-1, 3, 6, 10],
...     labels=['low', 'med', 'high']
... )))
{0, 1, 2}
```

Note that `scikit-learn` provides the `OrdinalEncoder`, but our data is not in the correct format for it. This expects 2D data (such as a dataframe or `ndarray`), instead of the 1D series we are working with, here. We still need to ensure that the categories are in the proper order beforehand.

However, note that the ordinal encoding may create a potential data issue. In our example, if high-quality wines are now 2 and medium-quality wines are 1, the model may interpret that `2 * med = high`. This is implicitly creating an association between the levels of quality that we may not agree with.

Alternatively, a safer approach would be to perform **one-hot encoding** to create two new columns—`is_low` and `is_med`, which take only 0 or 1; using those two, we automatically know whether the wine quality was `'high'` (`is_low = is_med = 0`). These are called **dummy variables** or **indicator variables**; they numerically represent group membership for use in machine learning. If the indicator or dummy has a value of 1, that row is a member of that group; in our example of wine quality categories, if `is_low` is 1, then that row is a member of the low-quality group. This can be achieved with the `pd.get_dummies()` function and the `drop_first` argument, which will remove the redundant column.

Let's use one-hot encoding to encode the `list` column in the planets data, since the categories have no inherent order. Before we do any transformations, let's take a look at the lists we have in the data:

```
>>> planets.list.value_counts()
Confirmed planets                      3683
Controversial                           106
Retracted planet candidate               11
Solar System                              9
Kepler Objects of Interest                4
Planets in binary systems, S-type         1
Name: list, dtype: int64
```

We can use the `pd.get_dummies()` function to create dummy variables if we want to include the planet list in our models:

```
>>> pd.get_dummies(planets.list).head()
```

This turns our single series into the following dataframe, where the dummy variables were created in the order they appeared in the data:

	Confirmed planets	Controversial	Kepler Objects of Interest	Planets in binary systems, S-type	Retracted planet candidate	Solar System
0	1	0	0	0	0	0
1	1	0	0	0	0	0
2	1	0	0	0	0	0
3	1	0	0	0	0	0
4	0	1	0	0	0	0

 Note that `scikit-learn` provides the `OneHotEncoder`, but our data is not in the correct format for it. This is because the `OneHotEncoder` expects the data to come in a 2D array, and our series is just 1D.

As we discussed previously, one of these columns is redundant because the values in the remaining ones can be used to determine the value for the redundant one. Pandas allows us to remove one redundant column with `get_dummies()` by passing in the `drop_first` argument:

```
>>> pd.get_dummies(planets.list, drop_first=True).head()
```

Note that all the rows but the last one were in the `Confirmed Planets` list; observe that the first column from the previous result has been removed:

	Controversial	Kepler Objects of Interest	Planets in binary systems, S-type	Retracted planet candidate	Solar System
0	0	0	0	0	0
1	0	0	0	0	0
2	0	0	0	0	0
3	0	0	0	0	0
4	1	0	0	0	0

Note that we can obtain a similar result by using the `LabelBinarizer` from `scikit-learn` and its `fit_transform()` method on our planets list. This won't drop a redundant feature, so we once again have the first feature belonging to the confirmed planets list, which can be seen in bold in the following result:

```
>>> from sklearn.preprocessing import LabelBinarizer

>>> LabelBinarizer().fit_transform(planets.list)
array([[1, 0, 0, 0, 0, 0],
       [1, 0, 0, 0, 0, 0],
       ...,
       [1, 0, 0, 0, 0, 0],
       [1, 0, 0, 0, 0, 0]], dtype=int32)
```

If our data is actually continuous, but we want to treat it as a binary categorical value, we could use the `Binarizer` class or `pd.cut()`.

Imputing

We already know that we have some missing values in our planet data, so let's see what `scikit-learn` offers us for imputing. Currently, they only have two options in the `impute` module: imputing with a value (using constants or summary statistics) or indicating what is missing.

Back in the *Exploratory data analysis* section, we ran `dropna()` on the planet data we planned to model with. Let's say we don't want to get rid of it, and we want to try imputing it instead. The last few rows of our data have some missing values for `semimajoraxis`:

	semimajoraxis	mass	eccentricity
3809	0.0487	1.0770	0.00
3810	0.0815	1.9000	0.00
3811	NaN	0.3334	0.31
3812	NaN	0.4000	0.27
3813	NaN	0.4200	0.16

We can use the `SimpleImputer` to impute with a value, which will be the mean by default:

```
>>> from sklearn.impute import SimpleImputer
>>> SimpleImputer().fit_transform(
...     planets[['semimajoraxis', 'mass', 'eccentricity']]
... )
array([[ 1.29       , 19.4       , 0.231      ],
       [ 1.54       , 11.2       , 0.08       ],
       [ 0.83       ,  4.8       , 0.         ],
       ...,
       [ 1.61032944,  0.3334    , 0.31       ],
       [ 1.61032944,  0.4       , 0.27       ],
       [ 1.61032944,  0.42      , 0.16       ]])
```

The mean hardly seems like a good strategy here since the planets we know about may share something in common, and surely things like what system it is part of and its orbit can be good indicators of some of the missing data points. We have the option to provide the strategy parameter with a method other than the mean; currently, it can be `median`, `most_frequent`, or `constant` (specify the value with `fill_value`). None of these is really appropriate for us, so let's use the `MissingIndicator` to note where they don't have values; this could be a feature we use in our model:

```
>>> from sklearn.impute import MissingIndicator
>>> MissingIndicator().fit_transform(
...     planets[['semimajoraxis', 'mass', 'eccentricity']]
... )
array([[False, False, False],
       [False, False, False],
       [False, False, False],
       ...,
       [ True, False, False],
       [ True, False, False],
       [ True, False, False]])
```

All of these preprocessors have a `fit_transform()` method, along with `fit()` and `transform()` methods. This API design decision makes it very easy to figure out how to use new classes and is one of the reasons why `scikit-learn` is so easy to learn and use—it's very consistent.

Additional transformers

What if, rather than scaling our data or encoding it, we want to run a mathematical operation, like taking the square root or the logarithm? The `preprocessing` module also has some classes for this. While there are a few that do a specific transformation, like the `QuantileTransformer`, we will focus our attention on the `FunctionTransformer`, which lets us provide an arbitrary function to use:

```
>>> from sklearn.preprocessing import FunctionTransformer
>>> FunctionTransformer(
...     np.abs, validate=True
... ).fit_transform(X_train.dropna())
array([[0.073 , 2.6   , 1.6   ],
       ...,
       [0.249 , 4.62  , 2.99  ]])
```

Here, we took the absolute value of every number. Notice the `validate=True` argument; the `FunctionTransformer` knows that `scikit-learn` models won't accept `NaN` values, infinite values, or missing ones, so it will throw an error if we get those back. For this reason, we run `dropna()` here as well.

Notice that for scaling, encoding, imputing, and transforming data, everything we passed was transformed. What can we do if we have specific transformations for certain columns only? We can use the `ColumnTransformer` to map transformations to a column (or group of columns) in a single call:

```
>>> from sklearn.compose import ColumnTransformer
>>> from sklearn.impute import SimpleImputer
>>> from sklearn.preprocessing import MinMaxScaler, StandardScaler

>>> ColumnTransformer([
...     ('standard_scale', StandardScaler(), [0, 1]),
...     ('min_max', MinMaxScaler(), [2]),
...     ('impute', SimpleImputer(), [0, 2])
... ]).fit_transform(X_train)[15:20]
array([[           nan,            nan,            nan,
         1.69919971e-01,  2.88416362e+00],
       [-7.91305129e-03, -9.86912907e-02,  7.11757595e-04,
         1.68400000e-01,  1.87200000e-01],
       [           nan,            nan,            nan,
         1.69919971e-01,  2.88416362e+00],
       [           nan, -1.80320454e-01,  4.86689080e-03,
         1.69919971e-01,  1.28000000e+00],
       [ 3.64840414e-01, -1.53050946e-01,  1.20883052e-04,
         2.40000000e-01,  3.18000000e-02]])
```

There is also the `make_column_transformer()` function. Let's make one that will treat categorical data and numerical data differently:

```
>>> from sklearn.compose import make_column_transformer
>>> from sklearn.preprocessing import OneHotEncoder, StandardScaler

>>> categorical = [
...     col for col in planets.columns \
...     if col in [
...         'list', 'name', 'description',
...         'discoverymethod', 'lastupdate'
...     ]
... ]
>>> numeric = [
...     col for col in planets.columns if col not in categorical
... ]

>>> make_column_transformer(
...     (StandardScaler(), numeric),
...     (OneHotEncoder(sparse=False), categorical)
... ).fit_transform(planets.dropna())
array([[-0.49212919, -0.00209303, -0.22454741, ...,  1.          ,
         0.         ,  0.          ],
       ...,
       [-0.5785095 , -1.04338405, -0.20563417, ...,  1.          ,
         0.         ,  0.          ]])
```

We are passing `sparse=False` to the `OneHotEncoder` so that we can see our result. In practice, we don't need to do this since `scikit-learn` models know how to handle NumPy sparse matrices.

Pipelines

It sure seems like there are a lot of steps involved in preprocessing our data, and they need to be applied in the correct order for both training and testing data—quite tedious. Thankfully, `scikit-learn` offers the ability to create pipelines to streamline the preprocessing and ensure that the training and testing sets are treated the same. This prevents issues, such as calculating the mean using all the data in order to standardize it and then splitting it into training and testing sets, which will create a model that looks like it will perform better than it actually will.

When information from outside the training set (such as using the full dataset to calculate the mean for standardization) is used to train the model, it is referred to as **data leakage**.

We are learning about pipelines before we build our first models because they ensure that the models are built properly. Pipelines can contain all the preprocessing steps and the model itself. Making a pipeline is as simple as defining the steps and naming them:

```
>>> from sklearn.pipeline import Pipeline
>>> from sklearn.preprocessing import StandardScaler
>>> from sklearn.linear_model import LinearRegression

>>> Pipeline([(
...     'scale', StandardScaler()), ('lr', LinearRegression())
... ])
Pipeline(memory=None, steps=[
    ('scale', StandardScaler(
        copy=True, with_mean=True, with_std=True
    )),
    ('lr', LinearRegression(
        copy_X=True, fit_intercept=True, n_jobs=None, normalize=False
    ))])
```

Just like with the `ColumnTransformer`, we have a function that can make pipelines for us without having to name the steps. Let's make the same pipeline with `make_pipeline()`:

```
>>> from sklearn.pipeline import make_pipeline

>>> make_pipeline(StandardScaler(), LinearRegression())
Pipeline(memory=None, steps=[('standardscaler',
    StandardScaler(copy=True, with_mean=True, with_std=True)),
    ('linearregression', LinearRegression(
        copy_X=True, fit_intercept=True, n_jobs=None, normalize=False
    ))])
```

Note that the steps have been automatically named the lowercase version of the class name. As we will see in the next chapter, naming the steps will make it easier to optimize model parameters by name. The consistency of the `scikit-learn` API will also allow us to use this pipeline to fit our model and make predictions using the same object, which we will see in the next section.

Clustering

We use clustering to divide our data points into groups of similar points. The points in each group are more like their fellow group members than those of other groups. Clustering is commonly used for tasks such as recommendation systems (think of how Netflix recommends what to watch based on what other people who've watched similar things are watching) and market segmentation.

For example, say we work at an online retailer and want to segment our website users for more targeted marketing efforts; we can gather data on time spent on the site, page visits, products viewed, products purchased, and much more. Then, we can have an unsupervised clustering algorithm find groups of users with similar behavior; if we make three groups, we can come up with labels for each group according to its behavior:

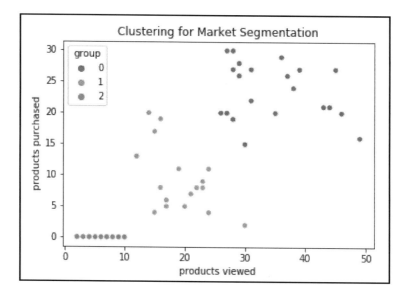

Since we can use clustering for unsupervised learning, we will need to interpret the groups that are created and then try to derive a meaningful name for each group. If our clustering algorithm identified the three clusters in the preceding scatter plot, we may be able to make the following behavioral observations:

- **Frequent customers (group 0)**: Purchase a lot and look at many products
- **Occasional customers (group 1)**: Have made some purchases, but less than the most frequent customers
- **Browsers (group 2)**: Visit the website, but haven't bought anything

Once these groups have been identified, the marketing team can focus on marketing to each of these groups differently; it's clear that the frequent customers will do more for the bottom line, but if they are already buying a lot, perhaps the marketing budget is better utilized trying to increase the purchases of the occasional customers or converting browsers into occasional customers.

 Deciding on the number of groups to create can clearly influence how the groups are later interpreted, meaning that this is not a trivial decision. We should at least visualize our data and obtain some subject matter knowledge on it before attempting to guess the number of groups to split it into.

Alternatively, clustering can be used in a supervised fashion if we know the group labels for some of the data for training purposes. Say we collected data on login activity, like in `Chapter 8`, *Rule-Based Anomaly Detection*, but we had some examples of what hacker activity looks like; we could gather those data points for all activity and then use a clustering algorithm to assign to the valid users group or to the hacker group. Since we have the labels, we can tweak our input variables and/or the clustering algorithm we use to best align these groups to their true group.

k-means

One common clustering algorithm is **k-means**, which iteratively assigns points to the nearest group using distance from the **centroid** of the group (center point), making k groups. Since this model uses distance calculations, it is imperative that we understand the effect scale will have on our results beforehand; we can then decide which columns, if any, to scale.

 There are many ways to measure distance between points in space. Often, Euclidean distance, or straight-line distance, is the default; however, another common one is Manhattan distance, which can be thought of as city-block distance.

Other clustering algorithms offered by `scikit-learn` can be found in the `cluster` module at `https://scikit-learn.org/stable/modules/classes.html#module-sklearn.cluster`.

Grouping planets by orbit characteristics

When we plotted out the period versus semi-major axis for all the planets using a log scale for the period, we saw a nice separation of the planets along an arc. We are going to use k-means to find groups of planets with similar orbits along that arc.

As we discussed in the *Preprocessing data* section, we can build a pipeline to isolate the scaling of our data, culminating with the KMeans object to make eight clusters (for the number of planets in our solar system):

```
>>> from sklearn.cluster import KMeans
>>> from sklearn.pipeline import Pipeline
>>> from sklearn.preprocessing import StandardScaler

>>> kmeans_pipeline = Pipeline([
...     ('scale', StandardScaler()),
...     ('kmeans', KMeans(8, random_state=0))
... ])
```

The random_state argument makes our model return the same cluster result each time. Since k-means randomly picks its starting centroids, it's possible we get different cluster results, unless we specify the random_state.

Once we have our pipeline, we fit on all the data since we aren't trying to predict anything (in this case)—we just want to find similar planets:

```
>>> kmeans_data = planets[['semimajoraxis', 'period']].dropna()
>>> kmeans_pipeline.fit(kmeans_data)
Pipeline(memory=None,
    steps=[('scale', StandardScaler(
        copy=True, with_mean=True, with_std=True)
    ), ('kmeans', KMeans(
        algorithm='auto', copy_x=True, init='k-means++',
        max_iter=300, n_clusters=8, n_init=10, n_jobs=None,
        precompute_distances='auto',random_state=0, tol=0.0001,
        verbose=0))])
```

Once the model is fit to our data, we can use the `predict()` method to get the cluster labels for each point (on the same data that we used previously). Let's show the clusters that k-means identified:

```
>>> fig, axes = plt.subplots(1, 1, figsize=(7, 7))
>>> ax = sns.scatterplot(
...     kmeans_data.semimajoraxis,
...     kmeans_data.period,
...     hue=kmeans_pipeline.predict(kmeans_data),
...     ax=axes, palette='Accent'
... )
>>> ax.set_yscale('log')
>>> solar_system = planets[planets.list == 'Solar System']
>>> for planet in solar_system.name:
...     data = solar_system.query(f'name == "{planet}"')
...     ax.annotate(
...         planet,
...         (data.semimajoraxis, data.period),
...         (7 + data.semimajoraxis, data.period),
...         arrowprops=dict(arrowstyle='->')
...     )
>>> ax.get_legend().remove()
>>> ax.set_title('KMeans Clusters')
```

Mercury, Venus, and Earth all landed in the same cluster; Jupiter and Saturn also share a cluster. Mars, Uranus, Neptune, and Pluto each belong to separate clusters:

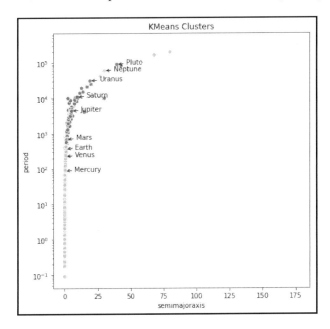

Elbow point method for determining k

We picked eight clusters arbitrarily here, since this is the number of planets in our solar system. Ideally, we would have some subject area knowledge about the true groupings, or need to pick a specific number. For example, say we want to fit wedding guests at five tables so that they all get along, then our *k* is 5; if we can run three marketing campaigns on user groups, we have a *k* of 3. If we have no intuition as to the number of groups there will be in the data, a rule of thumb is to try the square root of our observations, but this can yield an unmanageable amount of clusters. Therefore, if it doesn't take too long to create many k-means models on our data, we can use the **elbow point method**. This involves creating multiple models with many values of *k* and plotting each model's **inertia (within-cluster sum of squares)** versus the number of clusters. We want to minimize the sum of squared distances from points to their cluster's center while not creating too many clusters.

The `ml_utils.elbow_point` module contains our `elbow_point()` function, which has been reproduced here:

```python
import matplotlib.pyplot as plt

def elbow_point(data, pipeline, kmeans_step_name='kmeans',
                k_range=range(1, 11), ax=None):
    """
    Plot the elbow point to find an appropriate k for k-means
    clustering.

    Parameters:
        - data: The features to use
        - pipeline: The scikit-learn pipeline with KMeans
        - kmeans_step_name: The name of the KMeans step in the
                            pipeline
        - k_range: The values of `k` to try
        - ax: Matplotlib Axes to plot on.

    Returns: A matplotlib Axes object
    """
    scores = []
    for k in k_range:
        pipeline.named_steps[kmeans_step_name].n_clusters = k
        pipeline.fit(data)
        # score is -1 * inertia so we multiply by -1 for inertia
        scores.append(pipeline.score(data) * -1)
    if not ax:
        fig, ax = plt.subplots()
    ax.plot(k_range, scores, 'bo-')
    ax.set_xlabel('k')
```

```
        ax.set_ylabel('inertias')
        ax.set_title('Elbow Point Plot')
        return ax
```

Let's use the elbow point method to find an appropriate value for *k*:

```
>>> from ml_utils.elbow_point import elbow_point

>>> ax = elbow_point(
...         kmeans_data,
...         Pipeline([
...             ('scale', StandardScaler()),
...             ('kmeans', KMeans(random_state=0))
...         ])
... )
>>> ax.annotate(
...         'possible appropriate values for k', xy=(2, 730),
...         xytext=(2.5, 1500), arrowprops=dict(arrowstyle='->')
... )
>>> ax.annotate(
...         '', xy=(3, 350), xytext=(4.5, 1450),
...         arrowprops=dict(arrowstyle='->')
... )
```

The point at which we see diminishing returns is an appropriate *k*, which may be around two or three here:

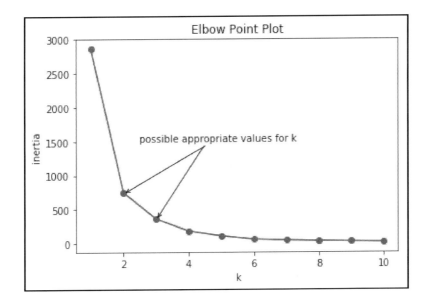

If we use k=2, we get the following clusters, which divide the planets into a group with most of the planets (green) and a second group with only a few (purple), which are likely to be outliers:

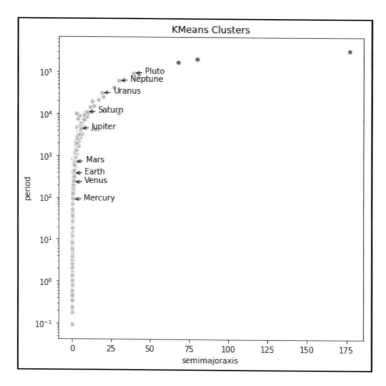

Note that while this may have been an appropriate amount of clusters, it doesn't tell us as much as the previous attempt. If we wanted to know about planets that are similar to each of the planets in our solar system, we would want to use a larger *k*.

Interpreting centroids and visualizing the cluster space

Since we standardized our data before clustering, we can look at the **centroids**, or cluster centers, to see the Z-score that the members are closest to. The centroids' location will be the average of each of the dimensions of the points in the cluster. We can grab this with the `cluster_centers_` attribute of the model. The centroid of the purple cluster is located at (17.8, 19.6), which is in the (semi-major axis, period) format; remember, these are Z-scores, so these are quite far from the rest of the data. The green cluster, on the other hand, is centered at (-0.038, -0.041).

Let's build a visualization that shows us the location of the centroids with the scaled input data and the cluster distance space (points are transformed into the distance to their cluster's centroid). First, we will set up our layout for a smaller plot inside of a larger one:

```
>>> fig = plt.figure(figsize=(8, 6))
>>> outside = fig.add_axes([0.1, 0.1, 0.9, 0.9])
>>> inside = fig.add_axes([0.7, 0.2, 0.25, 0.25])
```

Next, we grab the scaled version of the input data and the distances between those data points and the centroid of the cluster they belong to. We can use the `transform()` and `fit_transform()` (`fit()` followed by `transform()`) methods to convert the input data into cluster distance space. We get NumPy `ndarrays` back, where each value in the outer array represents the coordinates of a point:

```
>>> scaled = kmeans_pipeline_2.named_steps['scale'].fit_transform(
...     kmeans_data
... )
>>> cluster_distances = kmeans_pipeline_2.fit_transform(
...     kmeans_data
... )
```

Since we know that each array in the outer array will have the semi-major axis as the first entry and the period as the second, we use `[:,0]` to select all the semi-major axis values and `[:,1]` to select all the period values. These will be the x and y for our scatter plot. Note that we actually don't need to call `predict()` to get the cluster labels for the data because we want the labels for the data we trained the model on; this means that we can use the `labels_` attribute of the `KMeans` object:

```
>>> for ax, data, title, axes_labels in zip(
...     [outside, inside], [scaled, cluster_distances],
...     ['Visualizing Clusters', 'Cluster Distance Space'],
...     ['standardized', 'distance to centroid']
... ):
...     ax = sns.scatterplot(
...         data[:,0], data[:,1], ax=ax, palette='Accent', alpha=0.5,
...         hue=kmeans_pipeline_2.named_steps['kmeans'].labels_, s=100
...     )
...
...     ax.get_legend().remove()
...     ax.set_title(title)
...     ax.set_xlabel(f'semimajoraxis ({axes_labels})')
...     ax.set_ylabel(f'period ({axes_labels})')
...     ax.set_ylim(-1, None)
```

Lastly, we annotate the location of the centroids on the outer plot, which shows the scaled data:

```
>>> cluster_centers = kmeans_pipeline_2.named_steps['kmeans']\
...                    .cluster_centers_
>>> for color, centroid in zip(['green', 'purple'], cluster_centers):
...     outside.plot(*centroid, color=color, marker='x')
...     outside.annotate(
...         f'{color} center', xy=centroid, xytext=centroid + [0, 5],
...         arrowprops=dict(arrowstyle='->')
...     )
```

In the resulting plot, we can easily see that the three purple points are quite different from the rest, and that they are the only members of the second cluster:

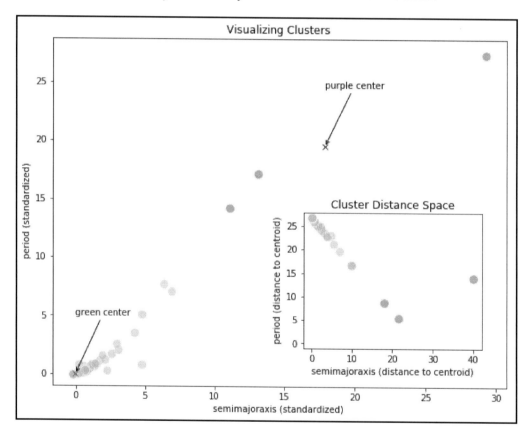

Not all models will support `transform()` or combination methods, like `fit_predict()` or `fit_transform()`. In general, most `scikit-learn` objects will support the following, based on what they are used for:

Method	Action	Used when...
`fit()`	Train the model or preprocessor	Modeling, preprocessing
`transform()`	Transform the data into the new space	Clustering, preprocessing
`fit_transform()`	Run `fit()`, followed by `transform()`	Clustering, preprocessing
`score()`	Evaluate the model using the default scoring method	Modeling
`predict()`	Use model to predict output values for given inputs	Modeling
`fit_predict()`	Run `fit()`, followed by `predict()`	Modeling
`predict_proba()`	Like `predict()`, but returns the probability of belonging to each class	Classification

Evaluating clustering results

The most important criterion for evaluating our clustering results is that they are useful for what we set out to do; we used the elbow point to pick an appropriate value for *k*, but that wasn't as useful to us as the eight clusters. That being said, when looking to quantify the performance, we need to pick metrics that match the type of learning we performed.

With the planets data, we performed unsupervised clustering because we don't have labels for what each cluster should be, and therefore we can't measure how well we did against those. This means that we have to use metrics that evaluate aspects of the clusters themselves, such as how far apart they are and how close the points in a cluster are together. We can compare multiple metrics to get a more well-rounded evaluation of the performance.

One such method is called the **silhouette coefficient**, which helps quantify cluster separation. It is calculated by subtracting the mean of distances between every two points in a cluster (*a*) from the mean of distances between points in a given cluster and the closest different cluster (*b*) and dividing by the maximum of the two:

$$\frac{b - a}{max(a, b)}$$

This metric returns values on [-1, 1], where –1 is the worst (clusters are wrongly assigned) and 1 is the best; values near 0 indicate overlapping clusters. The higher this number is, the better defined (more separated) the clusters are:

```
>>> from sklearn.metrics import silhouette_score
>>> silhouette_score(
...       kmeans_data, kmeans_pipeline.predict(kmeans_data)
... )
0.756431346264896
```

The metrics module in scikit-learn contains various metrics for evaluating model performance across clustering, regression, and classification tasks; the API lists the functions at https://scikit-learn.org/stable/modules/classes.html#module-sklearn.metrics.

Another score we could use to evaluate our k=8 clustering result is the ratio of **within-cluster distances** (distances between points in a cluster) to the **between-cluster distances** (distances between points in different clusters), called the **Davies-Bouldin score**. Values closer to zero indicate better partitions between clusters:

```
>>> from sklearn.metrics import davies_bouldin_score
>>> davies_bouldin_score(
...       kmeans_data, kmeans_pipeline.predict(kmeans_data)
... )
0.4432430729371101
```

One last metric for unsupervised clustering that we will discuss here is the **Calinski and Harabaz score**, or **Variance Ratio Criterion**, which is the ratio of dispersion within a cluster to dispersion between clusters. Higher values indicate better defined (more separated) clusters:

```
>>> from sklearn.metrics import calinski_harabaz_score
>>> calinski_harabaz_score(
...       kmeans_data, kmeans_pipeline.predict(kmeans_data)
... )
23153.731441632073
```

When we know the true clusters for our data, we can check that our clustering model places the points together in a cluster as they are in the true cluster. The cluster label given by our model can be different than the true one—all that matters is that the points in the same true cluster are also together in the predicted clusters. One such metric is the Fowlkes Mallows Index, which we will use in one of the exercises at the end of this chapter.

For a complete list of clustering evaluation metrics offered by `scikit-learn` (including supervised clustering) and when to use them, check out the *Clustering performance evaluation* section on their guide at `https://scikit-learn.org/stable/modules/clustering.html#clustering-evaluation`.

Regression

With our planet data, we want to predict the length of the year, which is a numeric value, so we turn to regression. As mentioned at the beginning of this chapter, regression is a technique for modeling the strength and magnitude of the relationship between independent variables (our X data)—often called regressors—and the dependent variable (our y) that we want to predict.

Linear regression

Scikit-learn provides many algorithms that can handle regression tasks, ranging from decision trees to linear regression, spread across modules according to the various algorithm classes. However, typically, the best starting point is a linear regression, which can be found in the `linear_model` module. In **simple linear regression**, we fit our data to a line of the following form:

$$y = \beta_0 + \beta_1 x + \epsilon$$

Here, epsilon (ε) is the error term and betas (β) are coefficients.

 The coefficients we get from our model are those that minimize the **cost function**, or error between the observed values (y) and those predicted ($\hat{y}$, pronounced y-hat) with the model. Our model gives us estimates of these coefficients, and we write them as $\hat{\beta}_i$ (pronounced beta-hat).

However, if we want to model additional relationships, we need to use **multiple linear regression**, which contains multiple regressors:

$$y = \beta_0 + \beta_1 x_1 + \beta_2 x_2 + \ldots + \beta_n x_n + \epsilon$$

Linear regression in `scikit-learn` uses **ordinary least squares (OLS)**, which yields the coefficients that minimize the sum of squared errors (measured as the distance between y and $\hat{y}$). The coefficients can be found using the closed-form solution, or estimated with optimization methods, such as **gradient descent**, which uses the negative gradient (direction of steepest ascent calculated with partial derivatives) to determine which coefficients to try next (see the link in the *Further reading* section for more information). We will use gradient descent in Chapter 11, *Machine Learning Anomaly Detection*.

Linear regression makes some assumptions of the data, which we must keep in mind when choosing to use this technique. It assumes that the residuals are normally distributed and homoskedastic and that there is no **multicollinearity** (high correlations between the regressors).

Predicting the length of a year on a planet

Before we can build our model, we must isolate the columns that are used to predict (`semimajoraxis`, `mass`, and `eccentricity`) from the column that will be predicted (`period`):

```
>>> data = planets[
...     ['semimajoraxis', 'period', 'mass', 'eccentricity']
... ].dropna()
>>> X = data[['semimajoraxis', 'mass', 'eccentricity']]
>>> y = data.period
```

This is a supervised task. We want to be able to predict the length of a year on a planet using its semi-major axis, mass, and eccentricity of orbit, and we have the period lengths for most of the planets in the data. Let's create a 75/25 split of training to testing data so that we can assess how well this model predicts year length:

```
>>> from sklearn.model_selection import train_test_split
>>> X_train, X_test, y_train, y_test = train_test_split(
...     X, y, test_size=0.25, random_state=0
... )
```

Once we have separated the data into the training and testing sets, we can create and fit the model:

```
>>> from sklearn.linear_model import LinearRegression
>>> lm = LinearRegression().fit(X_train, y_train)
```

Interpreting the linear regression equation

The equation derived from a linear regression model gives coefficients to quantify the relationships between the variables. Care must be exercised when attempting to interpret these coefficients if we are dealing with more than a single regressor. In the case of multicollinearity, we can't interpret them because we are unable to hold all other regressors constant to examine the effect of a single one.

Thankfully, the regressors we used for the planet data aren't correlated, as we saw from the correlation matrix heatmap we made in the *Exploratory data analysis* section. So, let's get the intercept and coefficients from the fitted linear model object:

```
# get intercept
>>> lm.intercept_
-1016.9414328876608

# get coefficients
>>> [(col, coef) for col, coef in zip(X_train.columns, lm.coef_)]
[('semimajoraxis', 2089.7990582230304),
 ('mass', -11.450731945992032),
 ('eccentricity', -4000.9101385815848)]
```

This yields the following equation for our linear regression model of planet year length:

$$period = -1017 + 2090 \times semimajoraxis - 11.5 \times mass - 4001 \times eccentricity$$

In order to interpret this more completely, we need to understand the units everything is in:

- period (length of year): Earth days
- semimajoraxis: **astronomical units (AUs)**
- mass: Jupiter masses (planet mass divided by Jupiter's mass)
- eccentricity: N/A

An astronomical unit is the average distance between the Earth and the Sun, which is equivalent to 149,597,870,700 meters.

The intercept in this particular model doesn't have any meaning: if the planet had a semi-major axis of zero, no mass, and a perfect circle eccentricity, its year would be -1,017 Earth days long. A planet must have non-negative, non-zero period, semi-major axis, and mass, so this clearly makes no sense. We can, however, interpret the other coefficients. The equation says that holding mass and eccentricity constant and adding one additional AU to the semi-major axis distance increases the year length by 2,090 Earth days. Holding the semi-major axis and eccentricity constant, each additional Jupiter mass decreases the year length by 11.5 Earth days.

Going from a perfect circular orbit (`eccentricity=0`) to a nearly parabolic escape orbit (`eccentricity=1`) will decrease the year length by almost 4,000 Earth days; these are approximate for this term because, at parabolic escape orbit, the planet will never return, and consequently, this equation wouldn't make sense. In fact, if we tried to use this equation for eccentricities greater than or equal to 1, we would be extrapolating because we have no such data in this dataset. This is a clear example of when extrapolation doesn't work. The equation tells us that the larger the eccentricity, the shorter the year, but once we get to eccentricities of one and beyond, the planets never come back (they have reached escape orbits), so the year is infinite.

 All the eccentricity values in the data are in [0, 1), so we are interpolating (predicting period values using data in the ranges we trained on) with this regressor.

Making predictions

Now that we have an idea of the effect each of our regressors has, let's use our model to make predictions of year length for the planets in the test set:

```
>>> preds = lm.predict(X_test)
```

Let's visualize how well we did by plotting the actual and predicted values:

```
>>> fig, axes = plt.subplots(1, 1, figsize=(5, 3))
>>> axes.plot(
...     X_test.semimajoraxis, y_test, 'bo', label='actuals',
...     alpha=0.5
... )
>>> axes.plot(
...     X_test.semimajoraxis, preds, 'ro', label='predictions',
...     alpha=0.5
... )
>>> plt.xlabel('semimajoraxis')
>>> plt.ylabel('period')
>>> plt.legend()
>>> plt.suptitle('Linear Regression')
```

The predicted values seem pretty close to the actual values and follow a similar pattern:

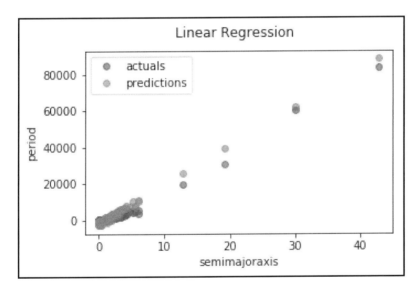

We can check their correlation to see how well our model tracks the true relationship:

```
>>> np.corrcoef(y_test, preds)[0][1]
0.9766538595075526
```

Our predictions are very strongly positively correlated with the actual values (0.98 correlation coefficient). Note that the correlation coefficient will tell us whether our model moves with the actual data; however, it will not tell us whether we are off magnitude-wise. For that, we will use the metrics discussed in the following section.

 Try running this regression with just the `semimajoraxis` regressor. Some reshaping of the data will be necessary, but this will show how much better this performs as we add in `eccentricity` and `mass`. In practice, we often have to build many versions of our model to find one we are happy with.

Evaluating regression results

When looking to evaluate a regression model, we are interested in how much of the variance in the data our model is able to capture, as well as how accurate the predictions are. We can use a combination of metrics and visuals to assess the model for each of these aspects.

Analyzing residuals

Whenever we work with linear regression, we should visualize our **residuals**, or the discrepancies between the actual values and the model's predictions; as we learned in Chapter 7, *Financial Analysis – Bitcoin and the Stock Market*, they should be centered around zero and homoskedastic (similar variance throughout). We can use a kernel density estimate to assess whether the residuals are centered around zero and a scatter plot to see if they are homoskedastic.

Let's look at the utility function in `ml_utils.regression`, which will create these subplots for checking the residuals:

```python
import matplotlib.pyplot as plt
import numpy as np

def plot_residuals(y_test, preds):
    """
    Plot residuals to evaluate regression.

    Parameters:
        - y_test: The true values for y
        - preds: The predicted values for y
```

```
Returns:
    Subplots of residual scatter plot and residual KDE plot.
"""
residuals = y_test - preds

fig, axes = plt.subplots(1, 2, figsize=(15, 3))

axes[0].scatter(np.arange(residuals.shape[0]), residuals)
axes[0].set_xlabel('Observation')
axes[0].set_ylabel('Residual')

residuals.plot(kind='kde', ax=axes[1])
axes[1].set_xlabel('Residual')

plt.suptitle('Residuals')
return axes
```

Now, let's look at the residuals for this linear regression:

```
>>> from ml_utils.regression import plot_residuals
>>> plot_residuals(y_test, preds)
```

It looks like our predictions don't have a pattern (left subplot), which is good; however, they aren't quite centered around zero and tend to have a long tail of negative residuals (right subplot), meaning that the predicted year was longer than the actual year:

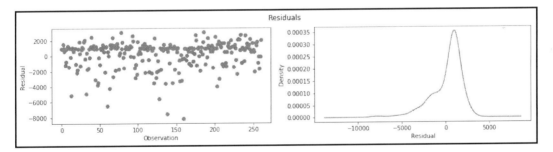

 If we find patterns in the residuals, our data isn't linear and chances are visualizing the residuals can help us plan our next move. This may mean employing strategies, such as polynomial regression or log transformations of the data.

Metrics

In addition to examining the residuals, we should calculate metrics to evaluate our regression model. Perhaps the most common is **R²** (pronounced R-squared), or the **coefficient of determination**, which quantifies the proportion of variance in the dependent variable that we can predict from our independent variables. It is calculated by subtracting the ratio of the sum of squared residuals to the total sum of squares from one:

$$R^2 = 1 - \frac{SS_{residual}}{SS_{total}} = 1 - \frac{\sum_i (y_i - \hat{y}_i)^2}{\sum_i (y_i - \bar{y})^2}$$

Sigma (Σ) represents the sum. The average of the y values is denoted as $\bar{y}$ (pronounced y-bar). The predictions are denoted with $\hat{y}$ (pronounced y-hat).

This value will be in [0, 1], where higher values are better. Objects of the `LinearRegression` class in `scikit-learn` use R^2 as their scoring method. Therefore, we can simply use the `score()` method to calculate it for us:

```
>>> lm.score(X_test, y_test)
0.9297571053513579
```

We can also get R^2 from the `metrics` module:

```
>>> from sklearn.metrics import r2_score
>>> r2_score(y_test, preds)
0.9297571053513579
```

This model has a very good R^2; however, keep in mind that there are many factors that affect the period, like the stars and other planets, which exert a gravitational force on the planet in question. Despite this abstraction, our simplification does pretty well because how long a year is on a planet is determined in large part by the distance that must be traveled, which we account for by using the `semimajoraxis` data.

There is a problem with R^2, though; we can keep adding regressors, which would make our model more and more complex while at the same time increasing R^2. We need a metric that penalizes model complexity. For that, we have **adjusted R^2**, which will only increase if the added regressor improves the model more than what would be expected by chance:

$$Adjusted\ R^2 = 1 - (1 - R^2) \times \frac{n\_obs - 1}{n\_obs - n\_regressors - 1}$$

Unfortunately, `scikit-learn` doesn't offer this metric; however, it is very easy to implement ourselves. The `ml_utils.regression` module contains a function for calculating the adjusted R^2 for us. Let's take a look at it:

```
from sklearn.metrics import r2_score

def adjusted_r2(model, X, y):
    """
    Calculate the adjusted R^2.

    Parameters:
        - model: Estimator object with a `predict()` method
        - X: The values to use for prediction.
        - y: The true values for scoring.

    Returns: The adjusted R^2 score.
    """
    r2 = r2_score(y, model.predict(X))
    n_obs, n_regressors = X.shape
    adj_r2 = 1 - (1 - r2) * (n_obs - 1)/(n_obs - n_regressors - 1)
    return adj_r2
```

Adjusted R^2 will always be lower than R^2. By using the `adjusted_r2()` function, we can see that our adjusted R^2 is slightly lower than the R^2 value:

```
>>> from ml_utils.regression import adjusted_r2
>>> adjusted_r2(lm, X_test, y_test)
0.9289371493826968
```

Unfortunately, R^2 (and adjusted R^2) values don't tell us anything about our prediction error or even if we specified our model correctly. Think back to when we discussed Anscombe's quartet in `Chapter 1`, *Introduction to Data Analysis*. These four different datasets have the same summary statistics. They also have the same R^2 when fit with a linear regression line (0.67), despite some of them not indicating a linear relationship:

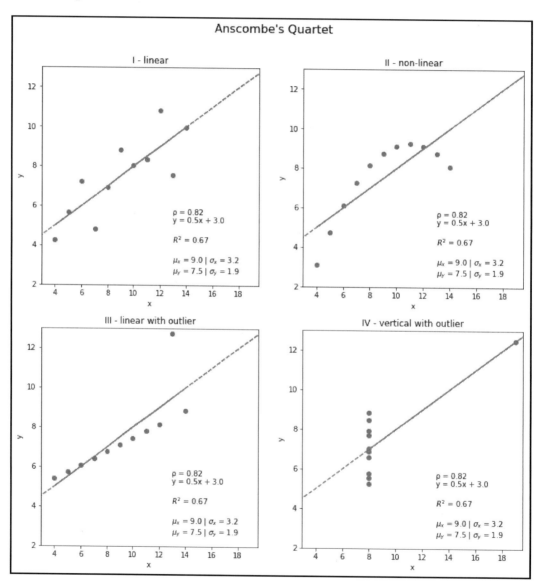

Another metric offered by `scikit-learn` is the **explained variance score**, which tells us the percentage of the variance that is explained by our model. We want this as close to one as possible:

$$explained\ variance = 1 - \frac{var(residuals)}{var(actuals)} = 1 - \frac{var(y - \hat{y})}{var(y)}$$

We can see that our model explains 93% of the variance:

```
>>> from sklearn.metrics import explained_variance_score
>>> explained_variance_score(y_test, preds)
0.9304626837290992
```

We aren't limited to looking at variance when evaluating our regression models; we can also look at the magnitude of the errors themselves. **Mean absolute error** (**MAE**) tells us the average error our model made in either direction. Values range from 0 to ∞ (infinity), with smaller values being better:

$$MAE = \frac{\sum_i |y_i - \hat{y}_i|}{n}$$

By using the `scikit-learn` function, we can see that our MAE was 1,396 Earth days:

```
>>> from sklearn.metrics import mean_absolute_error
>>> mean_absolute_error(y_test, preds)
1396.4042083885029
```

Root mean squared error (**RMSE**) allows for further penalization of poor predictions:

$$RMSE = \sqrt{\frac{\sum_i (y_i - \hat{y}_i)^2}{n}}$$

Scikit-learn provides a function for the **mean squared error** (**MSE**), which is the portion of the preceding equation inside the square root; therefore, we simply have to take the square root of the result. We would use this metric when large errors are undesirable:

```
>>> from sklearn.metrics import mean_squared_error
>>> np.sqrt(mean_squared_error(y_test, preds))
1777.2717945732813
```

An alternative to all these mean-based measures is the **median absolute error**, which is the median of the residuals. This can be used in cases where we have a few outliers in our residuals, and we want a more accurate description of the bulk of the errors. Note that this is smaller than the mean absolute error for our data:

```
>>> from sklearn.metrics import median_absolute_error
>>> median_absolute_error(y_test, preds)
1080.3627726120685
```

Scikit-learn also provides additional metrics to evaluate regression models at `https://scikit-learn.org/stable/modules/classes.html#regression-metrics`. Note that there is also a `mean_squared_log_error()` function, which can only be used for non-negative values. Some of the predictions are negative, which prevents us from using this. Negative predictions happen when the semi-major axis is very small (less than one) since that is the only portion of the regression equation with a positive coefficient. If the semi-major axis isn't large enough to balance out the rest of our equation, the prediction will be negative and, thus, automatically incorrect.

Classification

The goal of classification is to determine how to label data using a set of discrete labels. This probably sounds similar to supervised clustering; however, in this case, we don't care how close members of the groups are spatially. Instead, we concern ourselves with classifying them with the correct class label. Remember, in `Chapter 8`, *Rule-Based Anomaly Detection*, when we classified the IP addresses as hacker or not hacker? We didn't care how well-defined clusters of IP addresses were—we just wanted to find the hackers.

Just as with regression, `scikit-learn` provides many algorithms for classification tasks. These are spread across modules, but will usually say **Classifier** at the end for classification tasks, as opposed to **Regressor** for regression tasks. Some common methods are logistic regression, **support vector machines** (**SVMs**), k-NN, decision trees, and random forests; here, we will discuss logistic regression.

Logistic regression

Logistic regression is a way to use linear regression to solve classification tasks. However, it uses the logistic sigmoid function to return probabilities in [0, 1] that can be mapped to class labels:

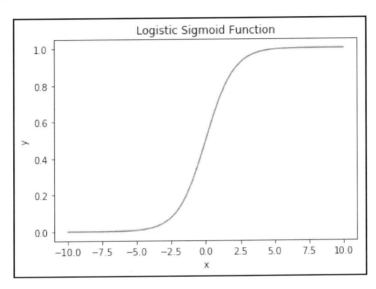

Let's use logistic regression to classify red wines as high or low quality and to classify wines as red or white based on their chemical properties. We can treat logistic regression as we did the linear regression in the previous section, using the `linear_model` module in `scikit-learn`. Just like the linear regression problem, we will be using a supervised method, so we have to split our data into testing and training sets.

While the examples discussed in this section are both binary classification problems (two classes), `scikit-learn` provides support for multiclass problems as well. The process of building multiclass models will be nearly identical to the binary case, but we may need to pass an additional parameter to let the model know that we have more than two classes. You will have a chance to build a multiclass classification model in the exercises at the end of this chapter.

Predicting red wine quality

We made the `high_quality` column back at the beginning of this chapter, but remember that there was a large imbalance in the amount of red wines that were `high_quality`. So, when we split our data, we will stratify by that column for a stratified random sample to make sure that both the training and testing sets preserve the ratio of high-quality to low-quality wines in the data (roughly 14% are high quality):

```
>>> from sklearn.model_selection import train_test_split

>>> red_y = red_wine.pop('high_quality')
>>> red_X = red_wine.drop(columns='quality')

>>> r_X_train, r_X_test, r_y_train, r_y_test = train_test_split(
...     red_X, red_y, test_size=0.1, random_state=0, stratify=red_y
... )
```

Let's make a pipeline that will first standardize all of our data and then build a logistic regression. We will provide the `random_state` for reproducibility and a `class_weight` of `'balanced'` to have `scikit-learn` compute the weights of the classes, since we have an imbalance:

```
>>> from sklearn.preprocessing import StandardScaler
>>> from sklearn.pipeline import Pipeline
>>> from sklearn.linear_model import LogisticRegression

>>> red_quality_lr = Pipeline([
...     ('scale', StandardScaler()),
...     ('lr', LogisticRegression(
...         solver='lbfgs', class_weight='balanced', random_state=0
...     ))
... ])
```

The class weights determine how much the model will be penalized for wrong predictions for each class. By selecting balanced weights, wrong predictions on smaller classes will carry more weight, where the weight will be inversely proportional to the frequency of the class in the data. These weights are used with the regularization parameter of the logistic regression (`C` with `scikit-learn`), which we will discuss more in Chapter 10, *Making Better Predictions – Optimizing Models*.

We are passing the `solver` here to silence the warning message indicating that a future change will alter the default for this parameter; typically, the default values are quite sensible, so don't worry about changing these.

Once we have our pipeline, we can fit it to the data with the `fit()` method:

```
>>> red_quality_lr.fit(r_X_train, r_y_train)
Pipeline(memory=None,
      steps=[('scale', StandardScaler(
                copy=True, with_mean=True, with_std=True)
          ), ('lr', LogisticRegression(
              C=1.0, class_weight='balanced', dual=False,
              fit_intercept=True, intercept_scaling=1,
              max_iter=100, multi_class='warn', n_jobs=None,
              penalty='l2', random_state=0, solver='lbfgs',
              tol=0.0001, verbose=0, warm_start=False))])
```

Lastly, we can use our model fit on the training data to predict the red wine quality for the test data:

```
>>> quality_preds = red_quality_lr.predict(r_X_test)
```

Scikit-learn makes it easy to switch between models because we can count on them to have the same methods, like `score()`, `fit()`, and `predict()`. In some cases, we also can use `predict_proba()` for probabilities or `decision_function()` to evaluate a point with the equation derived by the model instead of `predict()`.

Determining wine type by chemical properties

We want to know whether it is possible to tell red and white wine apart based solely on their chemical properties. To test this, we will build a second logistic regression which will predict whether a wine is red or white. First, let's split our data into testing and training sets:

```
>>> from sklearn.linear_model import LogisticRegression
>>> from sklearn.model_selection import train_test_split
>>> from sklearn.pipeline import Pipeline
>>> from sklearn.preprocessing import StandardScaler

>>> wine_y = np.where(wine.kind == 'red', 1, 0)
>>> wine_X = wine.drop(columns=['quality', 'kind'])

>>> w_X_train, w_X_test, w_y_train, w_y_test = train_test_split(
...     wine_X, wine_y, test_size=0.25,
...     random_state=0, stratify=wine_y
... )
```

We will once again use logistic regression in a pipeline:

```
>>> white_or_red = Pipeline([
...     ('scale', StandardScaler()),
...     ('lr', LogisticRegression(solver='lbfgs', random_state=0))
... ]).fit(w_X_train, w_y_train)
```

Finally, we will save our predictions of which kind of wine each observation in the test set was:

```
>>> kind_preds = white_or_red.predict(w_X_test)
```

Evaluating classification results

We evaluate the performance of classification models by looking at how well each class in the data was predicted by the model. The **positive class** is the class of interest to us; all other classes are considered **negative classes**. In our red wine classification, the positive class is high quality, while the negative class is low quality. Despite our problem only being a binary classification problem, the metrics that are discussed in this section extend to multiclass classification problems.

Confusion matrix

As we discussed in Chapter 8, *Rule-Based Anomaly Detection*, a classification problem can be evaluated by comparing the predicted labels to the actual labels using a **confusion matrix**:

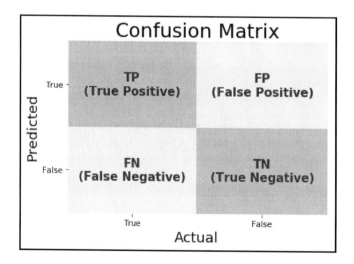

Each prediction can be one of four outcomes, based on how it matches up to the actual value:

- **True Positive (TP)**: Correctly predicted to be the positive class
- **False Positive (FP)**: Incorrectly predicted to be the positive class
- **True Negative (TN)**: Correctly predicted to not be the positive class
- **False Negative (FN)**: Incorrectly predicted to not be the positive class

 False positives are also referred to as **type I errors**, while false negatives are **type II errors**. Given a certain classifier, an effort to reduce one will cause an increase in the other.

Scikit-learn provides the `confusion_matrix()` function, which we can pair with the `heatmap()` function from `seaborn` to visualize our confusion matrix. In the `ml_utils.classification` module, the `confusion_matrix_visual()` function handles this for us:

```
import matplotlib.pyplot as plt
import numpy as np
import seaborn as sns
from sklearn.metrics import confusion_matrix

def confusion_matrix_visual(y_true, y_pred, class_labels, ax=None,
                            title=None, **kwargs):
    """
    Create a confusion matrix heatmap to evaluate classification.

    Parameters:
        - y_test: The true values for y
        - preds: The predicted values for y
        - class_labels: What to label the classes.
        - ax: The matplotlib Axes object to plot on.
        - title: The title for the confusion matrix
        - kwargs: Additional keyword arguments for `seaborn.heatmap()`

    Returns: A confusion matrix heatmap.
    """
    mat = confusion_matrix(y_true, y_pred)
    axes = sns.heatmap(
        mat.T, square=True, annot=True, fmt='d',
        cbar=True, cmap=plt.cm.Blues, ax=ax, **kwargs
    )
    axes.set_xlabel('Actual')
    axes.set_ylabel('Model Prediction')
```

```
tick_marks = np.arange(len(class_labels)) + 0.5
axes.set_xticks(tick_marks)
axes.set_xticklabels(class_labels)
axes.set_yticks(tick_marks)
axes.set_yticklabels(class_labels, rotation=0)
axes.set_title(title or 'Confusion Matrix')
return axes
```

Let's call our confusion matrix visualization function to see how we did for each of our classification models. First, let's see how well the model identified high-quality red wines:

```
>>> from ml_utils.classification import confusion_matrix_visual
>>> confusion_matrix_visual(r_y_test, quality_preds, ['low', 'high'])
```

Using the confusion matrix, we can see that the model had trouble finding the high-quality red wines consistently (bottom row):

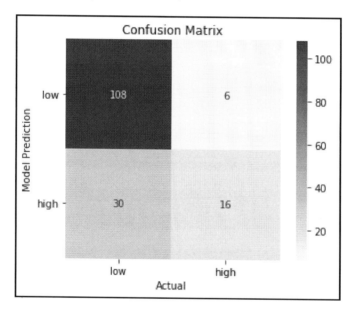

Now, let's look at how well the `white_or_red` model predicted the wine type:

```
>>> from ml_utils.classification import confusion_matrix_visual
>>> confusion_matrix_visual(w_y_test, kind_preds, ['white', 'red'])
```

It looks like this model had a much easier time, with very few incorrect predictions:

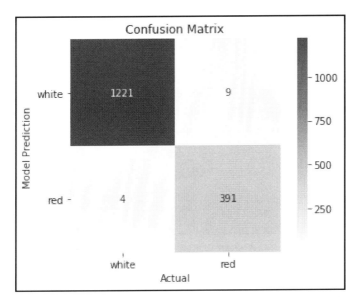

Classification metrics

Using the values in the confusion matrix, we can calculate metrics to help evaluate the performance of a classifier. The best metrics will depend on the goal for which we are building the model and whether our classes are balanced. The formulas in this section are derived from the data we get from the confusion matrix, where TP is the number of true positives, TN is the number of true negatives, and so on.

Accuracy and error rate

When our classes are roughly equal in size, we can use **accuracy**, which will give us the percentage of correctly classified values:

$$accuracy = \frac{TP + TN}{TP + FP + TN + FN}$$

The `accuracy_score()` function in `sklearn.metrics` will calculate the accuracy as per the formula; however, the `score()` method of our model will also give us the accuracy (this isn't always the case, as we will see with grid search in `Chapter 10`, *Making Better Predictions – Optimizing Models*):

```
>>> red_quality_lr.score(r_X_test, r_y_test)
0.775
```

Since accuracy is the percent we correctly classified (our **success rate**), it follows that our **error rate** (the percent we got wrong) can be calculated as follows:

$$error\ rate = 1 - accuracy = \frac{FP + FN}{TP + FP + TN + FN}$$

Our accuracy score tells us that we got 77.5% of the red wines correctly classified according to their quality. Conversely, the `zero_one_loss()` function from `scikit-learn` gives us the percent of values that were misclassified, which is 22.5% for the red wine quality model:

```
>>> from sklearn.metrics import zero_one_loss
>>> zero_one_loss(r_y_test, quality_preds)
0.2249999999999998
```

Note that while both of these are easy to compute and understand, they require a threshold. By default, this is 50%, but we can use any probability we wish as a cutoff when predicting the class using the `predict_proba()` method in `scikit-learn`. In addition, they can be misleading in cases of class imbalance.

Precision and recall

When we have a class imbalance, accuracy can become an unreliable metric for measuring our performance. For instance, if we had a 99/1 split between two classes, A and B, where the rare event, B, is our positive class, we could build a model that was 99% accurate by just saying everything belonged to class A. Clearly, we shouldn't bother building a model if it doesn't do anything to identify class B; thus, we need different metrics that will discourage this behavior. For this, we use precision and recall instead of accuracy. **Precision** tells us about the ratio of true positives to everything flagged positive:

$$precision = \frac{TP}{TP + FP}$$

Recall gives us the **true positive rate** (TPR), which is the ratio of true positives to everything that was actually positive:

$$recall = \frac{TP}{TP + FN}$$

In the case of the 99/1 split between classes A and B, the model that classifies everything as A would have a recall of 0% for the positive class, B (precision would be undefined—0/0). Precision and recall provide a better way of evaluating model performance in the face of a class imbalance. They will correctly tell us that the model has little value for our use case.

Scikit-learn provides a `classification_report()` function, which will calculate precision and recall for us. In addition to calculating these metrics per class label, it also calculates the **micro** average (metric calculated overall), **macro** average (unweighted average between classes), and **weighted** average (average between classes weighted by the amount of observations in each class). The **support** column indicates the count of observations that belong to each class using the labeled data.

The classification report indicates that our model does well at finding the low-quality red wines, but not so great with the high-quality red wines:

```
>>> from sklearn.metrics import classification_report
>>> print(classification_report(r_y_test, quality_preds))
              precision    recall  f1-score   support

           0       0.95      0.78      0.86       138
           1       0.35      0.73      0.47        22

   micro avg       0.78      0.78      0.78       160
   macro avg       0.65      0.75      0.66       160
weighted avg       0.86      0.78      0.80       160
```

Given that the quality scores are very subjective and not necessarily related to the chemical properties, it is no surprise that this simple model doesn't perform too well. On the other hand, chemical properties are different between red and white wines, so this information is more useful for the `white_or_red` model.

As we can imagine, based on the confusion matrix for the `white_or_red` model, the metrics are good:

```
>>> from sklearn.metrics import classification_report
>>> print(classification_report(w_y_test, kind_preds))
```

	precision	recall	f1-score	support
0	0.99	1.00	0.99	1225
1	0.99	0.98	0.98	400
micro avg	0.99	0.99	0.99	1625
macro avg	0.99	0.99	0.99	1625
weighted avg	0.99	0.99	0.99	1625

Just like accuracy, both precision and recall are easy to compute and understand, but require thresholds. In addition, precision and recall only consider half of the confusion matrix:

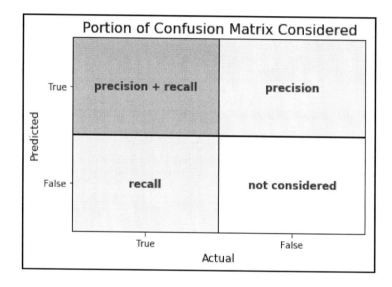

F score

The classification report also includes the **F₁ score**, which helps us balance precision and recall using the **harmonic mean** of the two:

$$F_1 = 2 \times \frac{precision \times recall}{precision + recall} = \frac{2 \times TP}{2 \times TP + FP + FN}$$

The harmonic mean is used for averaging rates. Both precision and recall are proportions on [0, 1], which we can treat as rates.

The **F$_\beta$ score**, pronounced F-beta, is the more general formulation for the F score. By varying β, we can put more weight on precision (β between 0 and 1) or on recall (β greater than 1), where β is how many more times recall is valued over precision:

$$F_\beta = (1 + \beta^2) \times \frac{precision \times recall}{\beta^2 \times precision + recall}$$

Some commonly used values for β are as follows:

β	Metric	Meaning
0.5	F0.5	Precision twice as important as recall
1	F1	Harmonic mean (equal importance)
2	F2	Recall twice as important as precision

Functions for accuracy, precision, recall, F$_1$ score, and F$_\beta$ score can be found in the `sklearn.metrics` module.

The F score is also easy to compute and relies on thresholds. However, it doesn't consider true negatives and is hard to optimize due to the trade-offs between precision and recall. Note that when working with large class imbalances, we are typically more concerned with predicting the positive class correctly, meaning that we may be less interested in true negatives, so using a metric that ignores them isn't necessarily an issue.

Sensitivity and specificity

Along the lines of the precision and recall trade-off, we have another pair of metrics that can be used to illustrate the delicate balance we strive to achieve with classification problems: sensitivity and specificity.

Sensitivity is the true positive rate, or recall, which we saw previously. **Specificity**, however, is the **true negative rate**, or the proportion of true negatives to everything that should have been classified as negative:

$$specificity = \frac{TN}{TN + FP}$$

Note that, together, specificity and sensitivity consider the full confusion matrix:

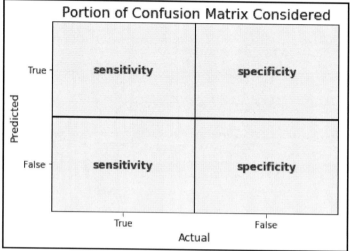

We would like to maximize both sensitivity and specificity; however, we could easily maximize specificity by decreasing the number of times we classify something as the positive class, which would decrease sensitivity. Scikit-learn doesn't offer specificity as a metric—preferring precision and recall—however, we can easily make our own by writing a function or using the `make_scorer()` function from `scikit-learn`. We are discussing them here because they form the basis of the sensitivity-specificity plot, or ROC curve, which is the topic of the following section.

ROC curve

In addition to using metrics to evaluate classification problems, we can turn to visualizations. By plotting the true positive rate (`sensitivity`) versus the false positive rate (`1 - specificity`), we get the **Receiver Operating Characteristic (ROC) curve**. This curve allows us to visualize the trade-off between the true positive rate and the false positive rate. We can identify a false positive rate that we are willing to accept and use that to find the threshold to use as a cutoff when predicting the class with probabilities using the `predict_proba()` method in `scikit-learn`. Say that we find the threshold to be 60%—we would require `predict_proba()` to return a value greater than or equal to 0.6 to predict the positive class (`predict()` uses 0.5 as the cutoff).

The `roc_curve()` function from `scikit-learn` calculates the false and true positive rates at thresholds from 0 to 100% using the probabilities of an observation belonging to a given class, as determined by the model. We can then plot this, with the goal being to maximize the **area under the curve** (**AUC**), which is in [0, 1]; values below 0.5 are worse than guessing and good scores are above 0.8. Note that when referring to the area under a ROC curve, the AUC may also be written as **AUROC**. The AUROC summarizes the model's performance across thresholds.

The following are examples of good ROC curves. The dashed line would be random guessing (no predictive value) and is used as a baseline; anything below that is considered worse than guessing. We want to be toward the top-left corner:

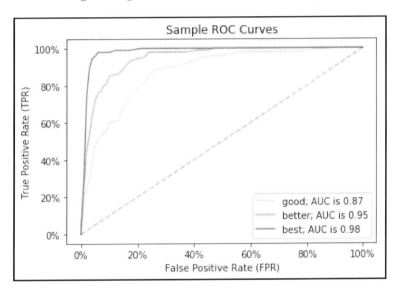

The `ml_utils.classification` module contains a function for plotting our ROC curve. Let's take a look at it:

```
import matplotlib.pyplot as plt
from sklearn.metrics import auc, roc_curve

def plot_roc(y_test, preds, ax=None):
    """
    Plot ROC curve to evaluate classification.

    Parameters:
        - y_test: The true values for y
        - preds: The predicted values for y as probabilities
        - ax: The Axes to plot on
```

```
Returns: Plotted ROC curve.
"""
if not ax:
    fig, ax = plt.subplots(1, 1)

fpr, tpr, thresholds = roc_curve(y_test, preds)

ax.plot(
    [0, 1], [0, 1], color='navy', lw=2,
    linestyle='--', label='baseline'
)
ax.plot(fpr, tpr, color='red', lw=2, label='model')

ax.legend(loc='lower right')
ax.set_title('ROC curve')
ax.set_xlabel('False Positive Rate (FPR)')
ax.set_ylabel('True Positive Rate (TPR)')

ax.annotate(f'AUC: {auc(fpr, tpr):.2}', xy=(.43, .025))

return ax
```

As we can imagine, our `white_or_red` model will have a very good ROC curve. Let's see what that looks like by calling the `plot_roc()` function from the `ml_utils.classification` module. Since we need to pass the probabilities of each entry belonging to the positive class, we need to use `predict_proba()` instead of `predict()`. This gives us the probabilities that each observation belongs to each class.

Here, for every row in `w_X_test`, we will have a NumPy array of the form `[probability wine is white, probability wine is red]`. Therefore, we use slicing to select the probabilities that the wine is red for the ROC curve (`[:,1]`):

```
>>> from ml_utils.classification import plot_roc
>>> plot_roc(w_y_test, white_or_red.predict_proba(w_X_test)[:,1])
```

Just as we expected, the ROC curve for the `white_or_red` model is very good, with an AUC of nearly 1:

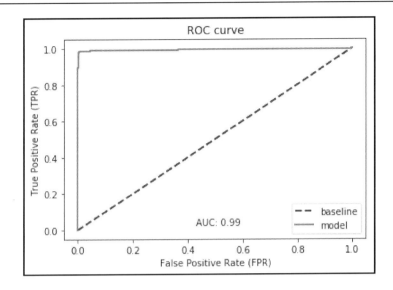

Given the other metrics we have looked at, we don't expect the red wine quality prediction model to have a great ROC curve. Let's call our function to see what the ROC curve for the red wine quality model looks like:

```
>>> from ml_utils.classification import plot_roc
>>> plot_roc(r_y_test, red_quality_lr.predict_proba(r_X_test)[:,1])
```

Our AUROC is 0.85; however, note that the AUROC provides optimistic estimates under class imbalance (since it considers true negatives):

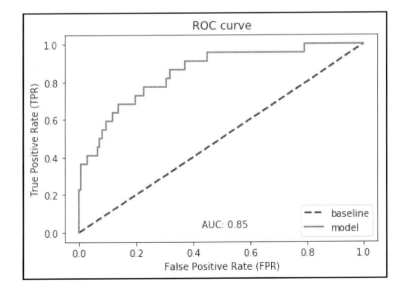

Precision-recall curve

When faced with a class imbalance, we use precision-recall curves instead of ROC curves. This curve shows precision versus recall at various probability thresholds that can be used when making predictions. The baseline is a horizontal line at the percentage of the data that belongs to the positive class. We want our curve above this line, with an **area under the precision-recall curve (AUPR)** greater than that percentage (the higher the better). The `ml_utils.classification` module contains the function for drawing precision-recall curves and providing the AUPR:

```
import matplotlib.pyplot as plt
from sklearn.metrics import (
    auc, average_precision_score, precision_recall_curve
)

def plot_pr_curve(y_test, preds, positive_class=1, ax=None):
    """
    Plot precision-recall curve to evaluate classification.

    Parameters:
        - y_test: The true values for y
        - preds: The predicted values for y as probabilities
        - positive_class: The label for the positive class in the data
        - ax: The matplotlib Axes object to plot on

    Returns: Plotted precision-recall curve.
    """
    precision, recall, thresholds = precision_recall_curve(
        y_test, preds
    )

    if not ax:
        fig, ax = plt.subplots()

    ax.axhline(
        sum(y_test == positive_class)/len(y_test), color='navy',
        lw=2, linestyle='--', label='baseline'
    )
    ax.plot(recall, precision, color='red', lw=2, label='model')
    ax.legend()
    ax.set_title(
        'Precision-recall curve\n'
        f""" AP: {average_precision_score(
            y_test, preds, pos_label=positive_class
        ):.2} | """
        f'AUC: {auc(recall, precision):.2}'
    )
```

```
ax.set_xlabel('Recall')
ax.set_ylabel('Precision')
ax.set_xlim(-0.05, 1.05)
ax.set_ylim(-0.05, 1.05)

return ax
```

Since the implementation of the AUC calculation in `scikit-learn` uses interpolation, it may give an optimistic result, so our function also calculates **average precision (AP)**, which summarizes the precision-recall curve as the weighted mean of the precision scores (P_n) achieved at various thresholds. The weights are derived from the change in recall (R_n) between one threshold and the next. Values are between zero and one, with higher values being better:

$$AP = \sum_n (R_n - R_{n-1}) \times P_n$$

Let's take a look at the precision-recall curve for the red wine quality model:

```
>>> from ml_utils.classification import plot_pr_curve
>>> plot_pr_curve(
...     r_y_test, red_quality_lr.predict_proba(r_X_test)[:,1]
... )
```

This still shows that our model is better than the baseline of random guessing; however, the performance reading we get here seems more in line with the lackluster performance we saw in the classification report. We can also see that the model loses lots of precision when going from a recall of `0.2` to `0.4`. Here, the trade-off between precision and recall is evident, and we will likely choose to optimize one:

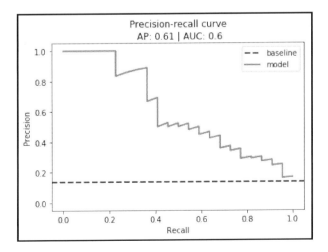

Since we have a class imbalance between the high-quality and low-quality red wines (less than 14% are high quality), we must make a choice as to whether we optimize precision or recall. Our choice would depend on who we work for in the wine industry. If we are renowned for producing high-quality wine, and we are choosing which wines to provide to critics for reviews, we want to make sure we pick the best ones and would rather miss out on good ones (false negatives) than tarnish our names with low quality ones that the model classifies as high quality (false positives). However, if we are trying to make the best profit from selling the wines, we wouldn't want to sell such a high-quality wine for the same price as a low-quality wine (false negative), so we would rather overprice some low-quality wines (false positives).

Note that we could easily have classified everything as low quality to never disappoint or as high quality to maximize our profit selling them; however, this isn't too practical. It's clear that we need to strike an acceptable balance between false positives and false negatives. To do so, we need to quantify this trade-off between the two extremes in terms of what matters to us more. Then, we can use the precision-recall curve to find a threshold that meets our precision and recall targets.

Now, let's take a look at the precision-recall curve for our red or white wine classifier:

```
>>> from ml_utils.classification import plot_pr_curve
>>> plot_pr_curve(w_y_test, white_or_red.predict_proba(w_X_test)[:,1])
```

Note that this curve is in the upper right-hand corner. With this model, we can achieve high precision and high recall:

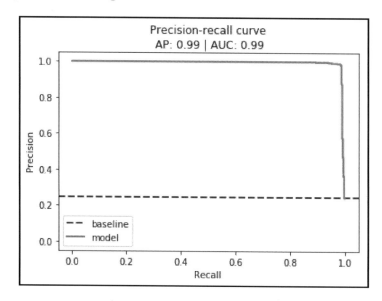

AUPR works very well with class imbalance, as we saw with the red wine quality model. However, it can't be compared across datasets, is expensive to compute, and is hard to optimize.

> This was a subset of metrics we can use to evaluate classification problems. All the classification metrics offered by `scikit-learn` can be found at `https://scikit-learn.org/stable/modules/classes.html#classification-metrics`.

Summary

This chapter served as an introduction to machine learning in Python. We discussed the terminology that's commonly used to describe learning types and tasks. Then, we practiced EDA using the skills we learned throughout this book to get a feel for the wine and planet datasets. This gave us some ideas for what kinds of models we would want to build. A thorough exploration of the data is essential before attempting to build a model.

Next, we learned how to prepare our data for use in machine learning models and the importance of splitting the data into training and testing sets before modeling. In order to prepare our data efficiently, we used pipelines in `scikit-learn` to package up everything from our preprocessing through our model.

We used unsupervised k-means to cluster the planets using their semi-major axis and period; we also discussed how to use the elbow point method to find a good value for *k*. Then, we moved on to supervised learning and made a linear regression model to predict the period of a planet using its semi-major axis, eccentricity of orbit, and mass. We learned how to interpret the model coefficients and how to evaluate the model's predictions. Finally, we turned to classification to identify high-quality red wines (which had a class imbalance) and distinguish between red and white wine by their chemical properties. Using precision, recall, F_1 score, confusion matrices, ROC curves, and precision-recall curves, we discussed how to evaluate classification models.

It's important to remember that machine learning models make assumptions of the underlying data, and while this wasn't a chapter on the mathematics of machine learning, we should make sure that we understand that there are consequences for violating these assumptions. In practice, when looking to build models, it's crucial that we have a solid understanding of statistics and domain-level expertise. We saw that there is a multitude of metrics for evaluating our models. Each metric has its strengths and weaknesses, and some are better than others; we must take care to choose the appropriate metrics for the task at hand.

In the next chapter, we will learn how to tune our models to improve their performance, so make sure to complete the exercises to practice this chapter's material before moving on.

Exercises

Practice building and evaluating machine learning models in `scikit-learn` with the following exercises:

1. Build a clustering model to distinguish between red and white wine by their chemical properties:
    1. Combine the red and white wine datasets (`data/winequality-red.csv` and `data/winequality-white.csv`, respectively) and add a column for the kind of wine (red or white).
    2. Perform some initial EDA.
    3. Build and fit a pipeline that scales the data and then uses k-means clustering to make two clusters. Be sure not to use the `quality` column.
    4. Use the Fowlkes Mallows Index (the `fowlkes_mallows_score()` function is in `sklearn.metrics`) to evaluate how well k-means is able to make the distinction between red and white wine.
    5. Find the center of each cluster.

2. Predict star temperature:
    1. Using the `data/stars.csv` file, build a linear regression model of all the numeric columns to predict the temperature of the star.
    2. Train the model on 75% of the initial data.
    3. Calculate the R^2 and MSE (mean squared error) of the model.
    4. Find the coefficients for each regressor and the intercept of the linear regression equation.
    5. Plot the residuals using the `plot_residuals()` function from `ml_utils.regression`.

3. Classify planets that have shorter years than Earth:
    1. Using the `data/planets.csv` file, build a logistic regression model with the `eccentricity`, `semimajoraxis`, and `mass` columns as regressors. You will need to make a new column to use for the y (year shorter than Earth).
    2. Find the accuracy score.
    3. Use the `classification_report()` function from scikit-learn to see the precision, recall, and F_1 score for each class.
    4. Plot the ROC curve using the `plot_roc()` function from `ml_utils.classification`.
    5. Create a confusion matrix using `confusion_matrix_visual()` from `ml_utils.classification`.

4. Multiclass classification of white wine quality:
    1. Using the `data/winequality-white.csv` file, perform some initial EDA on the white wine data. Be sure to look at how many wines had a given quality score.
    2. Build a pipeline to standardize the data and fit a multiclass logistic regression model. Pass `multi_class='multinomial'` to the logistic regression constructor.
    3. Look at the classification report for your model.
    4. Create a confusion matrix using `confusion_matrix_visual()` from `ml_utils.classification`. This will work as is for multiclass classification problems.
    5. Extend the `plot_roc()` function to work for multiple class labels. To do so, you will need to create a ROC curve for each class label (which are quality scores here), where a true positive is correctly predicting that quality score and a false positive is predicting any other quality score. Note that `ml_utils` has a function for this, but try to build your own implementation.
    6. Extend the `plot_pr_curve()` function to work for multiple class labels by following a similar method. However, give each class its own subplot. Note that `ml_utils` has a function for this, but try to build your own implementation.

5. We have seen how easy the `scikit-learn` API is to navigate, making it a cinch to change which algorithm we are using for our model. Rebuild the red wine quality model that we built in this chapter using an SVM instead of a logistic regression. We haven't discussed this model, but you should still be able to use it in `scikit-learn`. Check out the link in the *Further reading* section to learn more about the algorithm. Some guidance for this exercise is as follows:

- You will need to use the SVC (support vector classifier) class from `scikit-learn`, which can be found at `https://scikit-learn.org/stable/modules/generated/sklearn.svm.SVC.html`.
- Use `C=5` as a parameter to SVC.
- Pass `probability=True` to the SVC constructor to be able to use the `predict_proba()` method.
- Build a pipeline first using the `StandardScaler` and then the SVC.
- Be sure to look at the classification report, precision-recall curve, and confusion matrix for the model.

Further reading

Check out the following resources for more information on the topics that were covered in this chapter:

- *A Beginner's Guide to Deep Reinforcement Learning*: `https://skymind.ai/wiki/deep-reinforcement-learning`
- *An Introduction to Gradient Descent and Linear Regression*: `https://spin.atomicobject.com/2014/06/24/gradient-descent-linear-regression/`
- *Assumptions of Multiple Linear Regression*: `https://www.statisticssolutions.com/assumptions-of-multiple-linear-regression/`
- *Clustering*: `https://scikit-learn.org/stable/modules/clustering.html`
- *Generalized Linear Models*: `https://scikit-learn.org/stable/modules/linear_model.html`
- *In Depth: k-Means*: `https://jakevdp.github.io/PythonDataScienceHandbook/05.11-k-means.html`
- *MAE and RMSE – Which Metric is Better?*: `https://medium.com/human-in-a-machine-world/mae-and-rmse-which-metric-is-better-e60ac3bde13d`

- *Model evaluation: quantifying the quality of predictions*: https://scikit-learn.org/stable/modules/model_evaluation.html
- *Preprocessing data*: https://scikit-learn.org/stable/modules/preprocessing.html
- *Reinforcement Learning with Python*: https://towardsdatascience.com/reinforcement-learning-with-python-8ef0242a2fa2
- *Scikit-learn Glossary of Common Terms and API Elements*: https://scikit-learn.org/stable/glossary.html#glossary
- *Scikit-learn User Guide*: https://scikit-learn.org/stable/user_guide.html
- *Seeing Theory Chapter 6: Regression Analysis*: https://seeing-theory.brown.edu/index.html#secondPage/chapter6
- *Support Vector Machine – Introduction to Machine Learning Algorithms*: https://towardsdatascience.com/support-vector-machine-introduction-to-machine-learning-algorithms-934a444fca47
- *The 5 Clustering Algorithms Data Scientists Need to Know*: https://towardsdatascience.com/the-5-clustering-algorithms-data-scientists-need-to-know-a36d136ef68

10
Making Better Predictions - Optimizing Models

In the previous chapter, we learned how to build and evaluate our machine learning models. However, we didn't touch upon what we can do if we want to improve their performance. Of course, we could try out a different model and see if it performs better—unless there are requirements that we use a specific method for legal reasons or in order to be able to explain how it works. We want to make sure we use the best version of the model that we can, and for that, we need to discuss how to tune our models.

This chapter will introduce techniques for optimization of machine learning model performance using `scikit-learn`, as a continuation of the content in `Chapter 9`, *Getting Started with Machine Learning in Python*. Nonetheless, it should be noted that there is no panacea. It is entirely possible we try everything we can think of and still have a model with little predictive value; such is the nature of modeling.

Don't be discouraged though—if the model doesn't work, consider whether the data collected suffices to answer the question, and whether the algorithm chosen is appropriate for the task at hand. Often, subject matter expertise will prove crucial when building machine learning models, because it helps us determine which data points will be relevant, as well as take advantage of known interactions between the variables collected.

In particular, the following topics will be covered:

- Using grid search to find the best model hyperparameters in a given search space
- Getting an introduction to feature engineering
- Building ensemble models combining many estimators
- Interpreting a model's confidence in its classification predictions

- Utilizing the `imblearn` package to handle class imbalance
- Penalizing high regression coefficients with regularization

Chapter materials

In this chapter, we will be working with three datasets. The first two come from data on wine quality donated to the UCI Machine Learning Data Repository (`http://archive.ics.uci.edu/ml`) by P. Cortez, A. Cerdeira, F. Almeida, T. Matos, and J. Reis, and contain information on the chemical properties of various wine samples along with a rating of the quality from a blind tasting session by a panel of wine experts. These files can be found in the `data/` folder inside this chapter's folder in the GitHub repository (`https://github.com/stefmolin/Hands-On-Data-Analysis-with-Pandas/tree/master/ch_10`) as `winequality-red.csv` and `winequality-white.csv` for red and white wine, respectively.

Our third dataset was collected using the Open Exoplanet Catalogue database, at `https://github.com/OpenExoplanetCatalogue/open_exoplanet_catalogue/`, which provides data in XML format. The parsed planet data can be found in `data/planets.csv`. For the exercises, we will also be working with the star temperature data from *Chapter 9*, *Getting Started with Machine Learning in Python*, which can be found in the `data/stars.csv` file.

For reference, the following data sources were used:

- *Open Exoplanet Catalogue database*, available at `https://github.com/OpenExoplanetCatalogue/open_exoplanet_catalogue/#data-structure`.
- *P. Cortez, A. Cerdeira, F. Almeida, T. Matos and J. Reis. Modeling wine preferences by data mining from physicochemical properties. In Decision Support Systems, Elsevier, 47(4):547-553, 2009.* Available online at `http://archive.ics.uci.edu/ml/datasets/Wine+Quality`.
- *Dua, D. and Karra Taniskidou, E. (2017). UCI Machine Learning Repository* [`http://archive.ics.uci.edu/ml`]. *Irvine, CA: University of California, School of Information and Computer Science.*

We will be using the `red_wine.ipynb` notebook to predict red wine quality, `wine.ipynb` to distinguish between red and white wine based on their chemical properties, and the `planets_ml.ipynb` notebook to build a regression model to predict the year length of planets in Earth days.

Before we get started, let's handle our imports and read in our data:

```
>>> %matplotlib inline
>>> import matplotlib.pyplot as plt
>>> import numpy as np
>>> import pandas as pd
>>> import seaborn as sns

>>> planets = pd.read_csv('data/planets.csv')
>>> white_wine = pd.read_csv('data/winequality-white.csv', sep=';')
>>> red_wine = pd.read_csv('data/winequality-red.csv')
>>> red_wine['high_quality'] = pd.cut(
...     red_wine.quality, bins=[0, 6, 10], labels=[0, 1]
... )
>>> wine = pd.concat([
...     white_wine.assign(kind='white'), red_wine.assign(kind='red')
... ])
```

Let's also create our training and testing sets for the red wine quality, wine type by chemical properties, and planets models:

```
>>> from sklearn.model_selection import train_test_split

>>> red_y = red_wine.pop('high_quality')
>>> red_X = red_wine.drop(columns='quality')
>>> r_X_train, r_X_test, r_y_train, r_y_test = train_test_split(
...     red_X, red_y, test_size=0.1, random_state=0, stratify=red_y
... )

>>> wine_y = np.where(wine.kind == 'red', 1, 0)
>>> wine_X = wine.drop(columns=['quality', 'kind'])
>>> w_X_train, w_X_test, w_y_train, w_y_test = train_test_split(
...     wine_X, wine_y, test_size=0.25,
...     random_state=0, stratify=wine_y
... )

>>> data = planets[
...     ['semimajoraxis', 'period', 'mass', 'eccentricity']
... ].dropna()
>>> planets_X = data[['semimajoraxis', 'mass', 'eccentricity']]
>>> planets_y = data.period
>>> pl_X_train, pl_X_test, pl_y_train, pl_y_test = train_test_split(
...     planets_X, planets_y, test_size=0.25, random_state=0
... )
```

Hyperparameter tuning with grid search

No doubt you have noticed that we can provide various parameters to the model classes when we instantiate them. These model parameters are not derived from the data itself, and are referred to as **hyperparameters**. Some examples of these are regularization terms, which we will discuss later in this chapter, and weights. Through the process of **model tuning**, we seek to optimize our model's performance by tuning these hyperparameters.

How can we know we are picking the best values to optimize our model's performance? Well, we can use a technique called **grid search** to tune these hyperparameters. Grid search allows us to define a search space and test all combinations of hyperparameters in that space, keeping the ones that result in the best model. The scoring criterion we define will determine the best model.

Remember the elbow point method we discussed in Chapter 9, *Getting Started with Machine Learning in Python*, for finding a good value for *k* in k-means clustering? We can employ a similar visual method to find the best value for our hyperparameters. This will involve splitting our training data into **training** and **validation sets**. We need to save the test set for the final evaluation of the model, so we use the validation set to test each of our models when searching for the best values of the hyperparameters. To reiterate, the validation set and the test set are not the same—they must be disjoint. This split can be done with `train_test_split()`:

```
>>> from sklearn.model_selection import train_test_split

>>> r_X_train_new, r_X_validate,\
... r_y_train_new, r_y_validate = train_test_split(
...     r_X_train, r_y_train, test_size=0.3, random_state=0,
...     stratify=r_y_train
... )
```

Then, we can build the model multiple times for all the values of the hyperparameters we want to test, and score them based on the metric that matters most to us. Let's try to find a good value for C, the regularization strength, which determines the weight of the penalty term for the logistic regression (which is discussed more in-depth in the *Regularization* section toward the end of this chapter):

```
>>> import numpy as np
>>> from sklearn.linear_model import LogisticRegression
>>> from sklearn.metrics import f1_score
>>> from sklearn.pipeline import Pipeline
>>> from sklearn.preprocessing import MinMaxScaler
```

```
# we will try 10 values from 10^-1 to 10^1 for C
>>> regularization_strengths = np.logspace(-1, 1, num=10)
>>> scores = []

>>> for regularization_strength in regularization_strengths:
...     pipeline = Pipeline([
...         ('scale', MinMaxScaler()),
...         ('lr', LogisticRegression(
...             solver='lbfgs', class_weight='balanced',
...             random_state=0, C=regularization_strength
...         ))
...     ]).fit(r_X_train_new, r_y_train_new)
...     scores.append(
...         f1_score(pipeline.predict(r_X_validate), r_y_validate)
...     )
```

Here, we are using `np.logspace()` to get our range of values to try for C. To use this function, we supply starting and stopping exponents to use with a base number (10, by default). So `np.logspace(-1, 1, num=10)` gives us 10 evenly-spaced numbers between 10^{-1} and 10^{1}.

This is then plotted as follows:

```
>>> plt.plot(regularization_strengths, scores,'o-')
>>> plt.xlabel('regularization strength (C)')
>>> plt.ylabel('F1 score')
>>> plt.title('F1 score vs. Regularization Strength')
```

Using the resulting plot, we can pick the value that maximizes our performance:

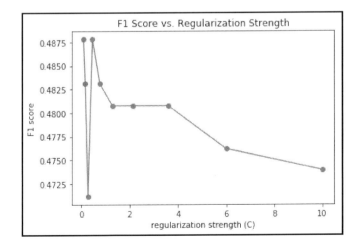

Scikit-learn provides the `GridSearchCV` class in the `model_selection` module for carrying out this exhaustive search much more easily. Notice the `CV` at the end of the class name; classes that end with `CV` utilize **cross-validation**, meaning they divide up the training data into subsets, some of which will be the validation set for scoring the model (without needing the testing data until after the model is fit).

One common method of cross-validation is **k-fold cross-validation**, which splits the training data into *k* subsets and will train the model *k* times, each time leaving one subset out to use as the validation set. The score for the model will be the average across the *k* validation sets. Our initial attempt was 1-fold cross-validation. When *k*=3, this process looks like the following diagram:

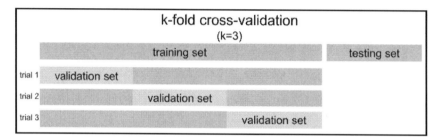

When working with classification problems, `scikit-learn` will implement stratified k-fold cross-validation. This ensures that the percentage of samples belonging to each class will be preserved across folds. Without stratification, it's possible some validation sets see a disproportionately low (or high) amount of a given class, which can distort the results.

`GridSearchCV` uses this to find the best hyperparameters in the search space, without the need to use the testing data. Remember, test data should not influence the training process in any way—neither when training the model nor when tuning parameters. If this is violated, the model will have issues generalizing. This happens because we would be picking the hyperparameters that give the best performance on the test set, thus leaving no way to test on unseen data, and overestimating our performance.

In order to use `GridSearchCV`, we need to provide a model (or pipeline) and a search space, which will be a dictionary mapping the hyperparameter to tune (by name) to a list of values to try. Optionally, we can provide a scoring metric to use, as well as the number of folds to use with cross-validation. We can tune any step in the pipeline by prefixing the hyperparameter name with the name of that step, followed by two underscores. For instance, if we have a logistic regression step called `lr` and want to tune `C`, we use `lr__C` as the key in the search space dictionary. Note that if our model has any preprocessing steps, it's imperative that we use a pipeline.

Let's use `GridSearchCV` for the red wine quality logistic regression, searching for whether or not to fit our model with an intercept and the best regularization strength (the `C` parameter), which determines the weight on the penalty term (discussed in the *Regularization* section coming up). We will use the F_1 score macro average as the scoring metric:

```
>>> from sklearn.linear_model import LogisticRegression
>>> from sklearn.model_selection import GridSearchCV
>>> from sklearn.pipeline import Pipeline
>>> from sklearn.preprocessing import MinMaxScaler

>>> pipeline = Pipeline([
...     ('scale', MinMaxScaler()),
...     ('lr', LogisticRegression(
...         solver='lbfgs', class_weight='balanced', random_state=0
...     ))
... ])

>>> search_space = {
...     'lr__C': np.logspace(-1, 1, num=10), # regularization strength
...     'lr__fit_intercept' : [True, False]
... }

>>> lr_grid = GridSearchCV(
...     pipeline, search_space, scoring='f1_macro', cv=5
... ).fit(r_X_train, r_y_train)
```

GridSearchCV is capable of performing multiple searches in parallel, greatly speeding up this process. We can set the `n_jobs` parameter to −1 to use all processors on the machine. Note that by default, this process will run in series.

From here, we can isolate the best hyperparameters from the search space with the
`best_params_` attribute of our grid. Notice that this result is different from our
1-fold cross-validation attempt because each of the folds has been averaged together
to find the best hyperparameters overall, not just for the first fold:

```
# best value of C in search space
>>> lr_grid.best_params_
{'lr__C': 3.593813663804626, 'lr__fit_intercept': True}
```

 We can also retrieve the best version of the pipeline we passed to
GridSearchCV through the `best_estimator_` attribute. If we
want to see the score the best estimator (model) had, we can grab it
from the `best_score_` attribute; note that this will be the score
defined with the `scoring` argument.

Our F_1 score macro average is now higher than what we achieved in Chapter 9,
Getting Started with Machine Learning in Python:

```
>>> from sklearn.metrics import classification_report
>>> print(classification_report(r_y_test, lr_grid.predict(r_X_test)))
              precision    recall  f1-score   support

           0       0.94      0.80      0.87       138
           1       0.36      0.68      0.47        22

   micro avg       0.79      0.79      0.79       160
   macro avg       0.65      0.74      0.67       160
weighted avg       0.86      0.79      0.81       160
```

The `cv` argument doesn't have to be an integer—we can provide one of the splitter
classes mentioned at `https://scikit-learn.org/stable/modules/classes.`
`html#splitter-classes` if we want to use a method other than the default of k-fold
for regression or stratified k-fold for classification. For example, let's use
`RepeatedStratifiedKFold` on the red wine quality score model instead of the
default `StratifiedKFold`, which will repeat the `StratifiedKFold` 10 times by
default. All we have to do is change what we pass to the `cv` parameter in the first
`GridSearchCV` example to be a `RepeatedStratifiedKFold` object:

```
>>> from sklearn.model_selection import RepeatedStratifiedKFold

>>> lr_grid = GridSearchCV(
...     pipeline, search_space, scoring='f1_macro',
...     cv=RepeatedStratifiedKFold(random_state=0)
... ).fit(r_X_train, r_y_train)
```

```
>>> print('Best parameters (CV score=%.2f): %s' % (
...      lr_grid.best_score_, lr_grid.best_params_
... )) # f1 macro score
Best parameters (CV score=0.69): {'lr__C': 5.994842503189409,
'lr__fit_intercept': True}
```

When working with time series, we can use `TimeSeriesSplit` as the cross-validation object to work with successive samples and avoid shuffling. Scikit-learn shows how the cross-validation classes compare at `https://scikit-learn.org/stable/auto_examples/model_selection/plot_cv_indices.html`.

Note that—despite using the same pipeline, search space, and scoring metric—we have different values for `best_params_` because our cross-validation process has changed.

Due to the consistency of the API, `GridSearchCV` can be used to score, fit, and predict with the same methods as the underlying models.

In addition to cross-validation, `GridSearchCV` allows us to specify the metric we want to optimize with the `scoring` parameter. This can be a string for the name of the score (as in the previous code blocks), provided that it is in the list at `https://scikit-learn.org/stable/modules/model_evaluation.html#common-cases-predefined-values`; otherwise, we can either pass the function itself, or make our own using the `make_scorer()` function from `sklearn.metrics`. We can even provide a dictionary of scorers (in the form of `{name: func}`) for grid search, provided that we specify which one we want to use for optimization by passing its name to the `refit` parameter. Therefore, we can use grid search to find the hyperparameters that help us maximize our performance on the metrics we discussed in the previous chapter.

The time it takes to train our model should also be something we evaluate and look to optimize. If it takes us double the training time to get one more correct classification, it's probably not worth it. If we use grid search, we will be able to see the average fit time by accessing the following on the grid search object: `cv_results_['mean_fit_time']`. Otherwise, we can use the `%%timeit` magic in our Jupyter Notebook to see how long a cell will take on average to complete. It must be in the cell we want to time; note that any variables created there won't exist outside that cell.

We can use `GridSearchCV` to search for the best parameters for any step in our pipeline. For example, let's use grid search with a pipeline of preprocessing and linear regression on the planets data (similar to when we modeled planet year length in the Chapter 9, *Getting Started with Machine Learning in Python*) while minimizing **mean absolute error (MAE)** instead of the default R^2:

```
>>> from sklearn.linear_model import LinearRegression
>>> from sklearn.metrics import make_scorer, mean_squared_error
>>> from sklearn.model_selection import GridSearchCV
>>> from sklearn.pipeline import Pipeline
>>> from sklearn.preprocessing import StandardScaler

>>> model_pipeline = Pipeline([
...     ('scale', StandardScaler()), ('lr', LinearRegression())
... ])

>>> search_space = {
...     'scale__with_mean' : [True, False],
...     'scale__with_std' : [True, False],
...     'lr__fit_intercept': [True, False],
...     'lr__normalize' : [True, False]
... }
>>> grid = GridSearchCV(
...     model_pipeline, search_space, cv=5,
...     scoring={
...         'r_squared': 'r2',
...         'mse' : 'neg_mean_squared_error',
...         'mae' : 'neg_mean_absolute_error',
...         'rmse' : make_scorer(
...             lambda x, y: np.sqrt(mean_squared_error(x, y))
...         )
...     }, refit='mae', iid=False
... ).fit(pl_X_train, pl_y_train)
```

In the previous code block, we passed `iid=False` to silence a warning that this parameter will be deprecated in future versions.

Let's check the best parameters for the scaling and linear regression in this grid:

```
>>> print('Best parameters (CV score=%.2f):\n%s' % (
...     grid.best_score_, grid.best_params_
... )) # MAE score
Best parameters (CV score=-1605.54):
{'lr__fit_intercept': False, 'lr__normalize': True,
 'scale__with_mean': False, 'scale__with_std': True}
```

The tuned model's MAE is more than 150 Earth days smaller than the MAE we got in `Chapter 9`, *Getting Started with Machine Learning in Python*:

```
>>> from sklearn.metrics import mean_absolute_error
>>> mean_absolute_error(pl_y_test, grid.predict(pl_X_test))
1235.4924651855556
```

The larger the search space, the longer it will take to find the optimal hyperparameters. When there is a large parameter grid to cover, consider using `RandomizedSearchCV` instead. It won't try out every combination, but it will try 10 random combinations (by default) and give the best estimator (model). We can change this number with the `n_iter` argument.

It's important to note that while a model may be fast to train, we shouldn't create a large, granular search space; in practice, it's better to start with a few different spread-out values, and then examine the results to see which areas warrant a more in-depth search. For instance, say we are looking to tune the `C` parameter. On our first pass, we may look in the result of `np.logspace(-1, 1)`. If we see that the best value for `C` is at either end of the spectrum, we can then look at values below/above the value. If the best value is in the range, we may look at a few values around it. This process can be performed iteratively, until we don't see additional improvement.

Since the process of tuning hyperparameters requires us to train our model multiple times, we must consider the time complexity of our models. Models that take a long time to train will be very costly to use with cross-validation. This will likely cause us to shrink our search space.

Feature engineering

When trying to improve performance, we may also consider ways to provide the best **features** (model inputs) to our model through the process of **feature engineering**. The *Preprocessing data* section in `Chapter 9`, *Getting Started with Machine Learning in Python*, introduced us to **feature transformation** when we scaled, encoded, and imputed our data. Unfortunately, feature transformation may mute some elements of our data that we want to use in our model, such as the unscaled value of the mean of a specific feature. For this situation, we can create a new feature with this value; this and other new features are added during **feature construction** (sometimes called **feature creation**).

Feature selection is the process of determining which features to train the model on. This can be done manually or through another process, such as machine learning. When looking to choose features for our model, we want features that have an impact on our dependent variable without unnecessarily increasing the complexity of our problem. Models built with many features increase in complexity, but also, unfortunately, have a higher tendency to fit noise, because our data is sparse in such a high-dimensional space. This is referred to as the **curse of dimensionality**. When a model has learned the noise in the training data, it will have a hard time generalizing to unseen data; this is called **overfitting**. By restricting the number of features the model uses, feature selection can help address overfitting.

Feature extraction is another way we can address the curse of dimensionality. During feature extraction, we reduce the dimensionality of our data by constructing combinations of features through a transformation. These new features can be used in place of the originals, thereby reducing the dimensionality of the problem. This process, called dimensionality reduction, also includes techniques where we find a certain number of components (less than the original) that explain most of the variance in the data. Feature extraction is often used in image recognition problems, since the dimensionality of the task is the total number of pixels in the image. For instance, the square ads on websites are 350x350 pixels (this is one of the most common sizes), so an image recognition task using images that size has 122,500 dimensions!

Feature engineering is the subject of entire books; however, as it is a more advanced topic, we will go over just a few techniques in this section. There is a good book on the subject in the *Further reading* section, which also touches upon using machine learning for feature learning.

Interaction terms and polynomial features

We discussed the use of dummy variables back in the *Preprocessing data* section of `Chapter 9`, *Getting Started with Machine Learning in Python*; however, we merely considered the effect of that variable on its own. In our model that tries to predict red wine quality by chemical properties, we are considering each property separately. However, it is important to consider if the interaction between these properties has an effect. Perhaps when the levels of citric acid and fixed acidity are both high or both low, the wine quality is different than if one is high and one is low. In order to capture the effect of this, we need to add an **interaction term**, which will be the product of the features.

We may also be interested in increasing the effect of a feature in the model through feature construction; we can achieve this by adding **polynomial features** made from this feature. This involves adding higher degrees of the original feature, so we could have `citric acid`, `citric acid`^{2}, `citric acid`^{3}, and so on in the model.

> We can generalize linear models by using interaction terms and polynomial features because they allow us to model the linear relationship of non-linear terms. Since linear models tend to underperform in the presence of multiple or non-linear decision boundaries (the surface or hypersurface that separates the classes), this can improve performance.

Scikit-learn provides the `PolynomialFeatures` class in the `preprocessing` module for easily creating interaction terms and polynomial features. This comes in handy when building models with categorical and continuous features. By specifying just the degree, we can get every combination of the features less than or equal to the degree. High degrees will increase model complexity greatly and may lead to overfitting.

If we use the default `degree` of two, we can turn `citric acid` and `fixed acidity` into `1 + citric acid + fixed acidity + citric acid`^{2} `+ citric acid * fixed acidity + fixed acidity`^{2}, where 1 is the bias term that can be used in a model as an intercept term:

```
>>> from sklearn.preprocessing import PolynomialFeatures
>>> PolynomialFeatures().fit_transform(
...     r_X_train[['citric acid', 'fixed acidity']]
... )
```

```
array([[1.000e+00, 5.500e-01, 9.900e+00, 3.025e-01, 5.445e+00,
        9.801e+01],
       [1.000e+00, 4.600e-01, 7.400e+00, 2.116e-01, 3.404e+00,
        5.476e+01],
       [1.000e+00, 4.100e-01, 8.900e+00, 1.681e-01, 3.649e+00,
        7.921e+01],
       ...,
       [1.000e+00, 1.200e-01, 7.000e+00, 1.440e-02, 8.400e-01,
        4.900e+01],
       [1.000e+00, 3.100e-01, 7.600e+00, 9.610e-02, 2.356e+00,
        5.776e+01],
       [1.000e+00, 2.600e-01, 7.700e+00, 6.760e-02, 2.002e+00,
        5.929e+01]])
```

Let's dissect the first row of our array in the previous code block (highlighted in bold) to understand how we got each of these values:

term	bias	citric acid	fixed acidity	citric acid^2	citric acid * fixed acidity	fixed acidity^2
value	1.000e+00	5.500e-01	9.900e+00	3.025e-01	5.445e+00	9.801e+01

If we are only interested in the interaction variables (citric acid * fixed acidity in this case), we can pass interaction_only=True to the PolynomialFeatures constructor instead. In this case, we also don't want the bias term, so we can pass include_bias=False as well. This will give us the original variables along with their interaction terms:

```
>>> PolynomialFeatures(
...     include_bias=False, interaction_only=True
... ).fit_transform(
...     r_X_train[['citric acid', 'fixed acidity']]
... )
array([[0.55 , 9.9  , 5.445],
       [0.46 , 7.4  , 3.404],
       [0.41 , 8.9  , 3.649],
       ...,
       [0.12 , 7.   , 0.84 ],
       [0.31 , 7.6  , 2.356],
       [0.26 , 7.7  , 2.002]])
```

We can add these polynomial features to our pipeline:

```
>>> from sklearn.linear_model import LogisticRegression
>>> from sklearn.model_selection import GridSearchCV
>>> from sklearn.pipeline import Pipeline
>>> from sklearn.preprocessing import MinMaxScaler, PolynomialFeatures

>>> pipeline = Pipeline([
...     ('poly', PolynomialFeatures()),
...     ('scale', MinMaxScaler()),
...     ('lr', LogisticRegression(
...         solver='lbfgs', class_weight='balanced', random_state=0
...     ))
... ]).fit(r_X_train, r_y_train)
```

Note that this model is slightly better than before we added these additional terms, which was the model used in `Chapter 9`, *Getting Started with Machine Learning in Python*:

```
>>> from sklearn.metrics import classification_report

>>> preds = pipeline.predict(r_X_test)
>>> print(classification_report(r_y_test, preds))
              precision    recall  f1-score   support
           0       0.95      0.79      0.86       138
           1       0.36      0.73      0.48        22

   micro avg       0.78      0.78      0.78       160
   macro avg       0.65      0.76      0.67       160
weighted avg       0.87      0.78      0.81       160
```

Dimensionality reduction

Sometimes, rather than looking to create more features, we look for ways to consolidate them and reduce the dimensionality of our data. **Dimensionality reduction** shrinks the number of features we train our model on. This is done to reduce the computational complexity of training the model without sacrificing much performance. We could just choose to train on a subset of the features (feature selection); however, if we think there is value in those features, albeit small, we may look for ways to extract the information we need from them.

One common strategy is to discard features with low variance. These features aren't very informative since they are mostly the same value throughout the data. Scikit-learn provides the `VarianceThreshold` class for carrying out feature selection according to a minimum variance threshold. By default, it will discard any features that have zero variance; however, we can provide our own threshold. Let's perform feature selection on our model that predicts if a wine is red or white based on its chemical composition. Since we have no features with zero variance, we will choose to keep features whose variance is greater than `0.01`:

```
>>> from sklearn.feature_selection import VarianceThreshold
>>> from sklearn.linear_model import LogisticRegression
>>> from sklearn.pipeline import Pipeline
>>> from sklearn.preprocessing import StandardScaler

>>> white_or_red_min_var = Pipeline([
...     ('feature_selection', VarianceThreshold(0.01)),
...     ('scale', StandardScaler()),
...     ('lr', LogisticRegression(solver='lbfgs', random_state=0))
... ]).fit(w_X_train, w_y_train)
```

This removed two features with low variance. We can get their names with the Boolean mask returned by the `get_support()` method of the `VarianceThreshold` class, which indicates the features that were kept:

```
>>> w_X_train.columns[
...     ~white_or_red_min_var.named_steps[
...         'feature_selection'
...     ].get_support()
... ]
Index(['chlorides', 'density'], dtype='object')
```

Using only 9 of the 11 features, our performance hasn't been affected much:

```
>>> from sklearn.metrics import classification_report
>>> print(classification_report(
...     w_y_test, white_or_red_min_var.predict(w_X_test)
... ))
```

	precision	recall	f1-score	support
0	0.98	0.99	0.99	1225
1	0.98	0.95	0.96	400
micro avg	0.98	0.98	0.98	1625
macro avg	**0.98**	**0.97**	**0.97**	**1625**
weighted avg	0.98	0.98	0.98	1625

Check out the other feature selection options in the `feature_selection` module at https://scikit-learn.org/ stable/modules/classes.html#module-sklearn.feature_ selection.

If we believe there is value in all the features, we may decide to use feature extraction rather than discarding them entirely. **Principal components analysis (PCA)** performs feature extraction by projecting high-dimensional data into lower dimensions, thereby reducing the dimensionality. In return, we get the *n* components that maximize explained variance. This will be sensitive to the scale of the data, so we need to do some preprocessing beforehand.

Let's take a look at the `pca_scatter()` function in `ml_utils.pca`, which will help us visualize our data when reduced to two dimensions:

```
import matplotlib.pyplot as plt
from sklearn.decomposition import PCA
from sklearn.pipeline import Pipeline
from sklearn.preprocessing import MinMaxScaler

def pca_scatter(X, labels, cbar_label, color_map='brg'):
    """Create a 2D scatter plot from 2 PCA components of X"""
    pca = Pipeline([
        ('scale', MinMaxScaler()), ('pca', PCA(2, random_state=0))
    ]).fit(X)
    data = pca.transform(X)
    ax = plt.scatter(
        data[:, 0], data[:, 1],
        c=labels, edgecolor='none', alpha=0.5,
        cmap=plt.cm.get_cmap(color_map, 2)
    )

    plt.xlabel('component 1')
    plt.ylabel('component 2')

    cbar = plt.colorbar()
    cbar.set_label(cbar_label)

    cbar.set_ticks([0, 1])
    plt.legend(
        ['explained variance\n'
        'comp. 1: {:.3}\ncomp. 2: {:.3}'.format(
            *pca.named_steps['pca'].explained_variance_ratio_
        )]
    )
    return ax
```

Let's visualize the wine data with two PCA components to see if there is a way to separate red from white:

```
>>> from ml_utils.pca import pca_scatter
>>> pca_scatter(wine_X, wine_y, 'wine is red?')
>>> plt.title('Wine Kind PCA (2 components)')
```

Most of the red wines are in the bright green mass of points at the top, and the white wines are in the blue point mass at the bottom. Visually, we can see how to separate them, but there is still some overlap:

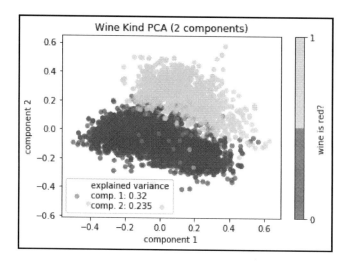

 PCA components will be linearly uncorrelated, since they were obtained through an orthogonal transformation (perpendicularity extended to higher dimensions). Linear regression assumes the regressors (input data) are not correlated, so this can help address multicolinearity.

Note the explained variances of each component from the previous plot's legend—the components explain over 50% of the variance in the wine data. Let's see if three dimensions improves the separation. The `pca_scatter_3d()` function in `ml_utils.pca` uses `mpl_toolkits`, which comes with `matplotlib` for 3D visualizations:

```
import matplotlib.pyplot as plt
from mpl_toolkits.mplot3d import Axes3D
from sklearn.decomposition import PCA
from sklearn.pipeline import Pipeline
from sklearn.preprocessing import MinMaxScaler
```

```
def pca_scatter_3d(X, labels, cbar_label, color_map='brg', elev=10,
                   azim=15
    ):
    """Create a 3D scatter plot from 3 PCA components of X"""
    pca = Pipeline([
        ('scale', MinMaxScaler()), ('pca', PCA(3, random_state=0))
    ]).fit(X)
    data = pca.transform(X)

    fig = plt.figure()
    ax = fig.add_subplot(111, projection='3d')

    p = ax.scatter3D(
        data[:, 0], data[:, 1], data[:, 2], alpha=0.5,
        c=labels, cmap=plt.cm.get_cmap(color_map, 2)
    )

    ax.view_init(elev=elev, azim=azim)

    ax.set_xlabel('component 1')
    ax.set_ylabel('component 2')
    ax.set_zlabel('component 3')

    cbar = fig.colorbar(p)
    cbar.set_ticks([0, 1])
    cbar.set_label(cbar_label)

    plt.legend(
        ['explained variance\n'
         'comp. 1: {:.3}\ncomp. 2: {:.3}\ncomp. 3: {:.3}'.format(
             *pca.named_steps['pca'].explained_variance_ratio_
         )]
    )

    return ax
```

Let's use our 3D visualization function on the wine data again to see if white and red are easier to separate with three PCA components:

```
>>> from ml_utils.pca import pca_scatter_3d
>>> pca_scatter_3d(wine_X, wine_y, 'wine is red?', elev=20, azim=-10)
>>> plt.suptitle('Wine Type PCA (3 components)')
```

It seems like we could slice off the green point mass from this angle, although we still have a few points in the wrong section:

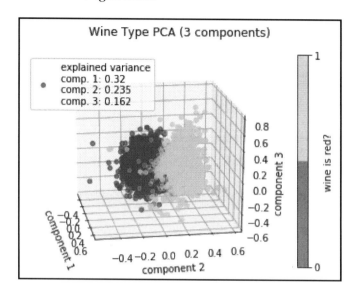

 PCA performs linear dimensionality reduction. Check out t-SNE and Isomap for manifold learning for non-linear dimensionality reduction.

We can use the `pca_explained_variance_plot()` function in the `ml_utils.pca` module to visualize the amount of explained variance covered by a given number of PCA components:

```
import matplotlib.pyplot as plt
import numpy as np

def pca_explained_variance_plot(pca_model, ax=None):
    """
    Plot the cumulative explained variance of PCA components.

    Parameters:
        - pca_model: The PCA model that has been fit already
        - ax: Matplotlib Axes to plot on.

    Returns:
        A matplotlib Axes objects
    """
```

```
if not ax:
    fig, ax = plt.subplots()
ax.plot(
    np.append(0, pca_model.explained_variance_ratio_.cumsum()),
    'o-'
)
ax.set_title('Total Explained Variance Ratio for PCA Components')
ax.set_xlabel('PCA components used')
ax.set_ylabel('cumulative explained variance ratio')

return ax
```

We can pass the PCA part of our pipeline to this function in order to see the cumulative explained variance:

```
>>> from sklearn.decomposition import PCA
>>> from sklearn.pipeline import Pipeline
>>> from sklearn.preprocessing import MinMaxScaler
>>> from ml_utils.pca import pca_explained_variance_plot

>>> pipeline = Pipeline([
...     ('normalize', MinMaxScaler()), ('pca', PCA(8, random_state=0))
... ]).fit(w_X_train, w_y_train)

>>> pca_explained_variance_plot(pipeline.named_steps['pca'])
```

The first four PCA components explain about 80% of the variance:

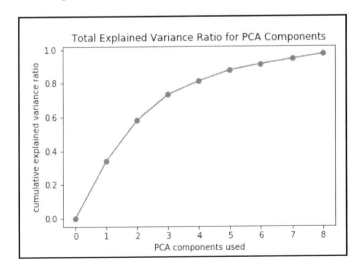

We can also use the elbow point method to find a good value for the number of PCA components to use, just as we did with k-means in Chapter 9, *Getting Started with Machine Learning in Python*. For this, we need to make a **scree plot**, which shows the explained variance versus the number of components used. The ml_utils.pca module has the pca_scree_plot() function for creating this visualization:

```python
import matplotlib.pyplot as plt
import numpy as np

def pca_scree_plot(pca_model, ax=None):
    """
    Plot the explained variance of each consecutive PCA component.

    Parameters:
        - pca_model: The PCA model that has been fit already
        - ax: Matplotlib Axes to plot on.

    Returns:
        A matplotlib Axes objects
    """
    if not ax:
        fig, ax = plt.subplots()

    ax.plot(np.arange(1, 9), pca_model.explained_variance_, 'o-')
    ax.set_title('Scree Plot for PCA Components')
    ax.set_xlabel('PCA components used')
    ax.set_ylabel('explained variance')

    return ax
```

We can pass the PCA part of our pipeline to this function in order to see the variance by each PCA component:

```python
>>> from sklearn.decomposition import PCA
>>> from sklearn.pipeline import Pipeline
>>> from sklearn.preprocessing import MinMaxScaler
>>> from ml_utils.pca import pca_scree_plot

>>> pipeline = Pipeline([
...     ('normalize', MinMaxScaler()), ('pca', PCA(8, random_state=0))
... ]).fit(w_X_train, w_y_train)

>>> pca_scree_plot(pipeline.named_steps['pca'])
```

The scree plot tells us we should try 4 PCA components because there are diminishing returns after that component:

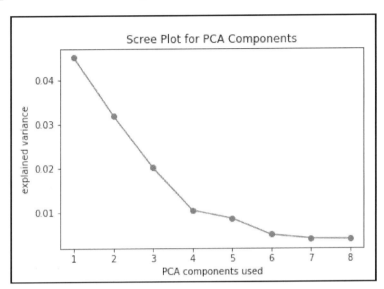

We can build a model on top of these four PCA features in a process called **meta-learning**, where the last model in the pipeline is trained on the output from a different model, not the original data itself:

```
>>> from sklearn.decomposition import PCA
>>> from sklearn.pipeline import Pipeline
>>> from sklearn.preprocessing import MinMaxScaler
>>> from sklearn.linear_model import LogisticRegression

>>> pipeline = Pipeline([
...     ('normalize', MinMaxScaler()),
...     ('pca', PCA(4, random_state=0)),
...     ('lr', LogisticRegression(
...         solver='lbfgs', class_weight='balanced', random_state=0
...     ))
... ]).fit(w_X_train, w_y_train)
```

Our new model performs nearly as well as the original logistic regression that used 11 features, with just 4 features made with PCA:

```
>>> preds = pipeline.predict(w_X_test)
>>> print(classification_report(w_y_test, preds))
```

	precision	recall	f1-score	support
0	0.99	0.99	0.99	1225
1	0.96	0.96	0.96	400
micro avg	0.98	0.98	0.98	1625
macro avg	0.98	0.98	0.98	1625
weighted avg	0.98	0.98	0.98	1625

Feature unions

We may want to build a model on features from a variety of sources, such as PCA, as we saw in the preceding section, in addition to selecting a subset of the features. For these purposes, `scikit-learn` provides the `FeatureUnion` class in the `pipeline` module. This also allows us to perform multiple feature engineering techniques at once, such as feature extraction followed by feature transformation, when we combine this with a pipeline.

Creating a `FeatureUnion` is just like creating a pipeline, but rather than passing the steps in order, we pass the transformations we want to make. These will be stacked side by side in the result. Let's use a `FeatureUnion` of interaction terms and select the features with a variance above `0.01` to predict red wine quality:

```
>>> from sklearn.feature_selection import VarianceThreshold
>>> from sklearn.pipeline import FeatureUnion, Pipeline
>>> from sklearn.preprocessing import MinMaxScaler, PolynomialFeatures
>>> from sklearn.linear_model import LogisticRegression

>>> combined_features = FeatureUnion([
...     ('variance', VarianceThreshold(0.01)),
...     ('poly', PolynomialFeatures(
...         include_bias=False, interaction_only=True
...     ))
... ])

>>> pipeline = Pipeline([
...     ('normalize', MinMaxScaler()),
...     ('feature_union', combined_features),
...     ('lr', LogisticRegression(
...         solver='lbfgs', class_weight='balanced', random_state=0
...     ))
... ]).fit(r_X_train, r_y_train)
```

To illustrate the transformation that took place, let's examine the first row from the training set for the red wine quality data after the `FeatureUnion` transforms it. Since we saw that our variance threshold results in nine features, we know they are the first nine entries in the resulting NumPy array, and the rest are the interaction terms:

```
>>> pipeline.named_steps['feature_union'].transform(r_X_train)[0]
array([9.900000e+00, 3.500000e-01, 5.500000e-01, 5.000000e+00,
       1.400000e+01, 9.971000e-01, 3.260000e+00, 1.060000e+01,
       9.900000e+00, 3.500000e-01, 5.500000e-01, 2.100000e+00,
       6.200000e-02, 5.000000e+00, 1.400000e+01, 9.971000e-01,
       ..., 3.455600e+01, 8.374000e+00])
```

We can also look at the classification report to see that we got a marginal improvement in F$_1$ score:

```
>>> from sklearn.metrics import classification_report

>>> preds = pipeline.predict(r_X_test)
>>> print(classification_report(r_y_test, preds))
              precision    recall  f1-score   support

           0       0.94      0.80      0.87       138
           1       0.36      0.68      0.47        22

   micro avg       0.79      0.79      0.79       160
   macro avg       0.65      0.74      0.67       160
weighted avg       0.86      0.79      0.81       160
```

Feature importances

Decision trees recursively split the data, making decisions on which features to use for each split. They are **greedy learners**, meaning they look for the largest split they can make each time; this isn't necessarily the optimal split when looking at the output of the tree. We can use a decision tree to gauge **feature importances**, which determine how the tree splits the data at the decision nodes. These feature importances can help inform feature selection. Note that feature importances will sum to 1, and higher values are better. Let's use a decision tree to see how red and white wine can be separated on a chemical level:

```
>>> from sklearn.tree import DecisionTreeClassifier

>>> dt = DecisionTreeClassifier(random_state=0).fit(
...     w_X_train, w_y_train
... )
```

```
>>> pd.DataFrame([(col, coef) for col, coef in zip(
...     w_X_train.columns, dt.feature_importances_
... )], columns=['feature', 'importance']
... ).set_index('feature').sort_values(
...     'importance', ascending=False
... ).T
```

This shows us that the most important chemical properties in distinguishing between red and white wine are total sulfur dioxide and chlorides:

feature	total sulfur dioxide	chlorides	density	volatile acidity	sulphates	pH	residual sugar	alcohol	fixed acidity	citric acid	free sulfur dioxide
importance	0.687236	0.210241	0.050201	0.016196	0.012143	0.01143	0.005513	0.005074	0.001811	0.000113	0.000042

 Using the top features, as indicated by the feature importances, we can try to build a simpler model (by using fewer features). If possible, we want to simplify our models without sacrificing much performance. See the `wine.ipynb` notebook for an example.

If we train another decision tree (with the same `random_state`) with a max depth of two, we can visualize the top of the tree (it is too large to visualize if we don't limit the depth):

```
>>> from sklearn.tree import export_graphviz
>>> import graphviz

>>> graphviz.Source(export_graphviz(
...     DecisionTreeClassifier(
...         max_depth=2, random_state=0
...     ).fit(w_X_train, w_y_train),
...     feature_names=w_X_train.columns
... ))
```

 Decision trees can be **pruned** after being grown to maximum depth, or provided with a max depth before training, to limit growth and thus avoid overfitting. The `scikit-learn` documentation provides tips to address overfitting and other potential issues when using decision trees at https://scikit-learn.org/stable/modules/tree.html#tips-on-practical-use.

This results in the following tree, which first splits on total sulfur dioxide (which has the highest feature importance), followed by chlorides on the second level. The information at each node tells us the criterion for the split (the top line), the value of the cost function (`gini`), the number of samples at that node (`samples`), and the number of samples in each class at that node (`values`):

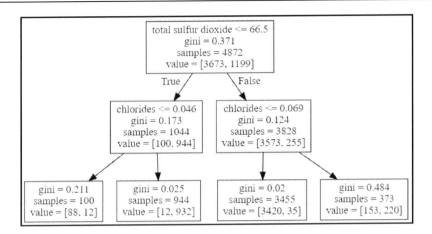

 Graphviz software will need to be installed (if it isn't already) in order to visualize the tree. It can be downloaded at `https://graphviz.gitlab.io/download/`, with the installation guide at `https://graphviz.readthedocs.io/en/stable/manual.html#installation`. Note that the kernel will need to be restarted after installing. Otherwise, we can pass `out_file='tree.dot'` to `export_graphviz()` and then generate a PNG file by running `dot -T png tree.dot -o tree.png` from the command line.

We can also apply decision trees to regression problems. Let's use the `DecisionTreeRegressor` to find the feature importances for the planet data:

```
>>> from sklearn.tree import DecisionTreeRegressor

>>> dt = DecisionTreeRegressor(random_state=0).fit(
...     pl_X_train, pl_y_train
... )
>>> [(col, coef) for col, coef in zip(
...     pl_X_train.columns, dt.feature_importances_
... )]
[('semimajoraxis', 0.9909470467126007),
 ('mass', 0.008457963837110774),
 ('eccentricity', 0.0005949894502886271)]
```

Basically, the semi-major axis is the main determinant in the period length, which we already knew, but if we visualize a tree of `max_depth=4`, we can see why. Any splits at nodes with many planets are split using the semi-major axis; mass and eccentricity seem to only be used to separate smaller groups:

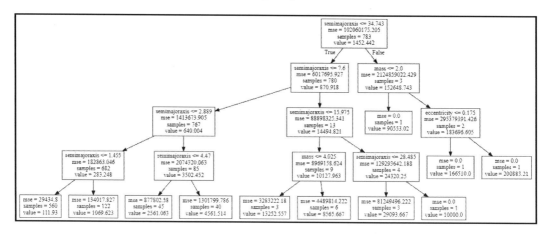

Ensemble methods

Ensemble methods combine many models (often weak ones) to create a stronger one that will either minimize average error between observed and predicted values (the **bias**), or improve how well it generalizes to unseen data (minimize the **variance**). We have to strike a balance between complex models that may increase variance, as they tend to overfit, and simple models that may have high bias, as these tend to underfit. This is called the **bias-variance trade-off**, which is illustrated in the following subplots:

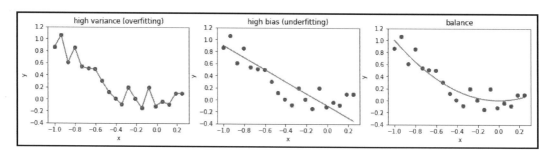

Ensemble methods can be broken down into three categories: boosting, bagging, and stacking. **Boosting** trains many weak learners, which learn from each other's mistakes to reduce bias, making a stronger learner. **Bagging**, on the other hand, uses **bootstrap aggregation** to train many models on bootstrap samples of the data and aggregate the results together (using voting for classification, and the average for regression) to reduce variance. We can also combine many different model types together with voting. **Stacking** is an ensemble technique where we combine many different model types using the outputs of some as the inputs to others; this is done to improve predictions. We saw an example of stacking when we combined PCA and logistic regression in the *Dimensionality reduction* section earlier in this chapter.

> In the `ensemble` module, `scikit-learn` provides classes for making our own bagging models: `BaggingClassifier` and `BaggingRegressor`. All we have to do is specify the base estimator, which defaults to a decision tree.

Random forest

The decision tree we trained in the previous section performed pretty well; however, decision trees have a tendency to overfit, especially if we don't set limits on how far they can grow (with the `max_depth` and `min_samples_leaf` parameters). We can address this overfitting issue with a **random forest**, which is a bagging algorithm where we train many decision trees in parallel using bootstrap samples of our data and aggregate the output. In addition, we have the option of scoring each tree on the data in the training set that it didn't receive in its bootstrap sample, called **out-of-bag samples**, with the `oob_score` parameter.

> The `min_samples_leaf` parameter requires a minimum number of samples to be on the final nodes in the tree (or leaves); this prevents the trees from being fit until they only have a single observation at each leaf.

Each of the trees also gets a subset of the features (random feature selection), which defaults to the square root of the number of features (the `max_features` parameter). This can help address the curse of dimensionality. As a consequence, however, the random forest can't be as easily interpreted as the decision trees that make it up. We can, however, extract feature importances from the random forest, just as we did with the decision tree.

We can use the `RandomForestClassifier` from the `ensemble` module to build a random forest (with `n_estimators` trees in it) for the classification of high-quality red wines:

```
>>> from sklearn.ensemble import RandomForestClassifier
>>> from sklearn.model_selection import GridSearchCV

>>> rf = RandomForestClassifier(n_estimators=100, random_state=0)

>>> search_space = {
...     'max_depth' : [4, 8], # keep trees small to avoid overfitting
...     'min_samples_leaf' : [4, 6]
... }

>>> rf_grid = GridSearchCV(
...     rf, search_space, cv=5, scoring='precision'
... ).fit(r_X_train, r_y_train)
```

Our precision with the random forest is already much better than the 0.35 we got in `Chapter 9`, *Getting Started with Machine Learning in Python*. The random forest is robust to outliers and able to model non-linear decision boundaries to separate the classes, which may explain part of this dramatic improvement:

```
# this is precision to match `scoring` from the grid search
>>> rf_grid.score(r_X_test, r_y_test)
0.6
```

Gradient boosting

Boosting looks to improve upon the mistakes of previous models. One way of doing this is to move in the direction of the steepest reduction in the loss function for the model. Since the **gradient** (the multi-variable generalization of the derivative) is the direction of steepest ascent, this can be done by calculating the negative gradient, which yields the direction of steepest descent, meaning the best improvement in the loss function from the current result. This technique is called **gradient descent**.

 Although gradient descent sounds great, there are some potential issues with it. It is possible that we end up in a local minimum (a minimum in a certain region of the cost function) and the algorithm stops, thinking that we have the optimal solution, when in fact we don't, because we would like the global minimum (the minimum over the whole region).

Scikit-learn's `ensemble` module provides the `GradientBoostingClassifier` and `GradientBoostingRegressor` classes for gradient boosting using decision trees. These trees will boost their performance through gradient descent. For example, let's use grid search and gradient boosting to train another model for classifying the red wine quality data. In addition to searching for the best values for the `max_depth` and `min_samples_leaf` parameters, we will search for a good value for `learning_rate`, which determines the contribution each tree will have in the final estimator:

```
>>> from sklearn.ensemble import GradientBoostingClassifier
>>> from sklearn.model_selection import GridSearchCV

>>> gb = GradientBoostingClassifier(n_estimators=100, random_state=0)

>>> search_space = {
...     'max_depth' : [4, 8], # keep trees small to avoid overfitting
...     'min_samples_leaf' : [4, 6],
...     'learning_rate' : [0.1, 0.5, 1]
... }

>>> gb_grid = GridSearchCV(
...     gb, search_space, cv=5, scoring='f1_macro'
... ).fit(r_X_train, r_y_train)
```

The F_1 macro score we achieve with gradient boosting is better than the 0.66 we got with logistic regression in Chapter 9, *Getting Started with Machine Learning in Python*:

```
# this is F1-score to match `scoring` from the grid search
>>> gb_grid.score(r_X_test, r_y_test)
0.7226024272287617
```

Note that gradient boosted trees are more sensitive to noisy training data than the random forest. In addition, we must consider the additional time required to build all the trees in series, unlike the parallel training we can benefit from with the random forest.

Voting

When trying out different models for classification, it may be interesting to measure their agreement using Cohen's kappa score. We can determine the agreement between models with the `cohen_kappa_score()` function in the `metrics` module. The score ranges from complete disagreement (–1) to complete agreement (1). Our boosting and bagging predictions agree nearly 72% of the time:

```
>>> from sklearn.metrics import cohen_kappa_score
>>> cohen_kappa_score(
...     rf_grid.predict(r_X_test), gb_grid.predict(r_X_test)
... )
0.7185929648241206
```

Sometimes, we can't find a single classification model that works well for all of our data, so we may want to find a way to combine the opinions of various models to make the final decision. Scikit-learn provides the `VotingClassifier` class for aggregating model opinions on classification tasks. We have the option of specifying the voting type, where `hard` results in majority rules and `soft` will predict the class with the highest sum of probabilities across the models. As an example, let's create a classifier for each voting type using the three estimators (models) from this chapter—logistic regression, random forest, and gradient boosting:

```
>>> from sklearn.ensemble import VotingClassifier

>>> majority_rules = VotingClassifier(
...     [('lr', lr_grid.best_estimator_),
...      ('rf', rf_grid.best_estimator_),
...      ('gb', gb_grid.best_estimator_)],
...     voting='hard'
... ).fit(r_X_train, r_y_train)

>>> max_probabilities = VotingClassifier(
...     [('lr', lr_grid.best_estimator_),
...      ('rf', rf_grid.best_estimator_),
...      ('gb', gb_grid.best_estimator_)],
...     voting='soft'
... ).fit(r_X_train, r_y_train)
```

Since the `VotingClassifier` will run `fit()`, we pass in the `best_estimator_` from each of our grid searches. This avoids running each grid search again unnecessarily, which will also give us our `VotingClassifier` faster.

Our `majority_rules` classifier required two of the three models to agree, while `max_probabilities` had each model vote with its predicted probabilities. We can measure how well they did with the `classification_report()` function, which tells us that `majority_rules` is a little better than `max_probabilities` in terms of precision. Both are better than the other models we have tried:

```
>>> from sklearn.metrics import classification_report
>>> print(classification_report(
...       r_y_test, majority_rules.predict(r_X_test)
... ))
```

	precision	recall	f1-score	support
0	0.92	0.95	0.93	138
1	0.59	0.45	0.51	22
micro avg	0.88	0.88	0.88	160
macro avg	**0.75**	**0.70**	**0.72**	160
weighted avg	0.87	0.88	0.87	160

```
>>> print(classification_report(
...       r_y_test, max_probabilities.predict(r_X_test)
... ))
```

	precision	recall	f1-score	support
0	0.92	0.93	0.92	138
1	0.52	0.50	0.51	22
micro avg	0.87	0.87	0.87	160
macro avg	**0.72**	**0.71**	**0.72**	160
weighted avg	0.87	0.87	0.87	160

> The `weights` parameter lets us place more or less emphasis on certain estimators when voting. For example, if we pass `weights=[1, 2, 2]` to `majority_rules`, we are giving extra weight to the predictions made by the random forest and gradient boosting estimators.

Inspecting classification prediction confidence

As we saw with ensemble methods, when we know the strengths and weaknesses of our model, we can employ strategies to attempt to improve performance. We may have two models to classify something, but they most likely won't agree on everything. However, say that we know that one does better on edge cases, while the other is better on the more common ones. In that case, we would likely want to investigate a voting classifier to improve our performance. How can we know how the models perform in different situations, though?

We can take a look at the probabilities the model predicts that an observation belongs to a given class. This can give us insight into how confident our model is when it is correct and when it errs. We can use our `pandas` data wrangling skills to make quick work of this. Let's see how confident our original `white_or_red` model from Chapter 9, *Getting Started with Machine Learning in Python*, was in its predictions:

```
>>> prediction_probabilities = pd.DataFrame(
...     white_or_red.predict_proba(w_X_test),
...     columns=['prob_white', 'prob_red']
... ).assign(
...     is_red=w_y_test == 1,
...     pred_white=lambda x: x.prob_white >= 0.5,
...     pred_red=lambda x: np.invert(x.pred_white),
...     correct=lambda x: (np.invert(x.is_red) & x.pred_white)\
...                       | (x.is_red & x.pred_red)
... )
```

We can tweak the probability threshold for our model's predictions by using `predict_proba()` to predict, instead of `predict()`. This will give us the probabilities that the observation belongs to each class. We can then compare that to our custom threshold. For example, we could use a 75% threshold: `white_or_red.predict_proba(w_X_test)[:,1] >= .75`. One way to identify this threshold is to determine the false positive rate we are comfortable with, and then use the data from the `roc_curve()` function in the `sklearn.metrics` module to find the threshold that results in that false positive rate. Another way is to find a satisfactory spot on the precision-recall curve and get the threshold from the `precision_recall_curve()` function. We will work through an example in Chapter 11, *Machine Learning Anomaly Detection*.

Let's use `seaborn` to make a plot showing the distribution of the prediction probabilities for red wine when the model was correct versus when it was wrong. The `distplot()` function makes it easy to plot the **kernel density estimate (KDE)** superimposed on a histogram. Here, we will also add a **rug plot**, which shows where each of our predictions ended up:

```
>>> fig, axes = plt.subplots(1, 2, figsize=(15, 5))
>>> for ax, state, color in zip(
...     axes, ['correct', 'not correct'], ['purple', 'orange']
... ):
...     sns.distplot(
...         prediction_probabilities.query(state).prob_red,
...         ax=ax, rug=True, bins=20, color=color
...     )
...     ax.set_xlabel('probability wine is red')
...     ax.set_ylabel('density')
...     ax.set_title(f'prediction was {state}')
>>> plt.suptitle('Prediction Confidence')
```

The KDE for correct predictions is bimodal, with modes near 0 and near 1, meaning the model is very confident when it is correct, which, since it is correct most of the time, means it is very confident in general. The peak of the correct predictions KDE at 0 is much higher than the one at 1 because we have many more whites than reds in the data. Note that the KDE shows probabilities of less than zero and greater than one as possible. For this reason, we add the histogram to confirm that the shape we are seeing is meaningful. The histogram for correct predictions doesn't have much in the middle of the distribution, so we include the rug plot to better see which probabilities were predicted. The incorrect predictions don't have many data points, but it appears to be all over the place, because when the model got it wrong, it got fooled pretty badly:

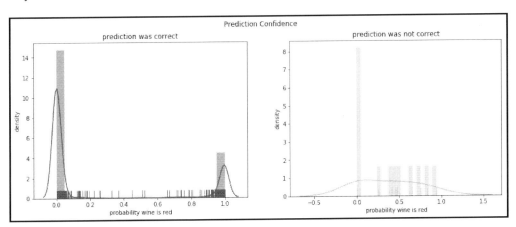

This outcome tells us we may want to look into the chemical properties of the wines that were incorrectly classified. It's possible they were outliers and that is why they fooled the model. We can modify the box plots by wine type from the *Exploratory data analysis* section in `Chapter 9`, *Getting Started with Machine Learning in Python*, to see if anything stands out.

First, we isolate the chemical properties for the incorrectly classified wines:

```
>>> incorrect = w_X_test.assign(
...        is_red=w_y_test
... ).iloc[prediction_probabilities.query('not correct').index, :]
```

Then, we add some calls to `scatter()` on the `Axes` object to mark these wines on the box plots from before:

```
>>> import math
>>> chemical_properties = [col for col in wine.columns \
...        if col not in ['quality', 'kind']
... ]
>>> melted = wine.drop(columns='quality').melt(id_vars=['kind'])

>>> fig, axes = plt.subplots(
...        math.ceil(len(chemical_properties) / 4), 4, figsize=(20, 10)
... )
>>> axes = axes.flatten()

>>> for prop, ax in zip(chemical_properties, axes):
...        sns.boxplot(
...            data=melted[melted.variable.isin([prop])],
...            x='variable', y='value', hue='kind', ax=ax,
...            palette='RdBu_r', saturation=0.5, fliersize=2
...        )
...        for _, wrong in incorrect.iterrows():
...            # _ is convention for collecting information we won't use
...            x_coord = -0.2 if not wrong['is_red'] else 0.2
...            ax.scatter(
...                x_coord, wrong[prop], marker='x', color='red', s=50
...            )

>>> for ax in axes[len(chemical_properties):]:
...        ax.remove()

>>> plt.suptitle(
...        'Comparing Chemical Properties of Red and White Wines'
...        '\n(classification errors are red x\'s)'
... )
```

This results in each of the incorrectly classified wines being marked with a red X. In each subplot, the points on the left box plot are white wines and those on the right box plot are red wines. It appears that some of them may have been outliers for a few characteristics—such as red wines with high residual sugar or sulfur dioxide, and whites with high volatile acidity:

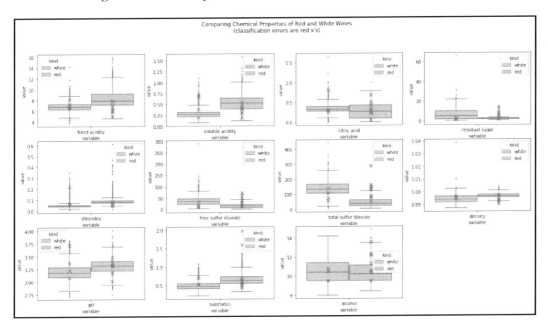

Addressing class imbalance

When faced with a class imbalance in our data, we may want to try to balance the training data before we build a model around it. In order to do this, we can use one of the following imbalanced sampling techniques:

- Over-sample the minority class
- Under-sample the majority class

In the case of **over-sampling**, we pick a larger proportion from the class with fewer values in order to come closer to the amount of the majority class; this may involve a technique such as bootstrapping, or generating new data similar to the values in the existing data (using machine learning algorithms such as nearest neighbors). **Under-sampling**, on the other hand, will take less data overall by reducing the amount taken from the majority class. The decision to use over-sampling or under-sampling will depend on the amount of data we started with, and in some cases, computational costs. In practice, we wouldn't try either of these without first trying to build the model with the class imbalance. It's important not to try to optimize things prematurely; not to mention that by building the model first, we have a baseline to compare our imbalanced sampling attempts against.

 Huge performance issues can arise if the minority class that we have in the data isn't truly representative of the full spectrum present in the population. For this reason, our method of collecting the data in the first place should be both known to us and carefully evaluated before proceeding to modeling. If we aren't careful, we can easily build a model that can't generalize to new data, regardless of how we handle the class imbalance.

The `scikit-learn` community also provides a package for making imbalanced learning tasks easier, called `imblearn`. The documentation can be found at `https://imbalanced-learn.readthedocs.io/en/stable/api.html`. This package provides implementations for over- and under-sampling using various methods, and it is just as easy to use as `scikit-learn`, since they both follow the same API conventions.

Before we explore `imblearn`, let's create a baseline model using **k-nearest neighbors (k-NN)** classification, which will classify observations according to the class of the k-nearest observations to it in the n-dimensional space of the data (our red wine quality data is 11-dimensional). For comparison purposes, we will use the same *k* for all the models in this section; however, it is certainly possible that the sampling techniques result in a different value of *k* performing better. We will use `k=5`:

```
>>> from sklearn.neighbors import KNeighborsClassifier

>>> knn = KNeighborsClassifier(n_neighbors=5).fit(
...     r_X_train, r_y_train
... )
>>> knn_preds = knn.predict(r_X_test)
```

Notice how fast k-NN was trained; this is because it is a **lazy learner**—calculations are made at classification time. It is important to keep in mind the time our models take to train and make predictions, as this can dictate which models we can use in practice. A model that performs marginally better but takes twice as long to train or predict may not be worth it. As the dimensionality of our data increases, the k-NN model will become less and less feasible. We can use the `%%timeit` magic to get an estimate of how long this process takes on average. Note that this will train the model multiple times, so it might not be the best strategy to time a computationally intense model:

```
>>> %%timeit
>>> from sklearn.neighbors import KNeighborsClassifier
>>> knn = KNeighborsClassifier(n_neighbors=5).fit(
...     r_X_train, r_y_train
... )
3.24 ms ± 599 µs per loop (mean ± std. dev. of 7 runs, 100 loops each)
```

Let's use the `%%timeit` magic to compare how fast k-NN is trained with a **support vector machine** (**SVM**), which projects the data into a higher dimension to find the **hyperplane** that separates the classes. A hyperplane is the n-dimensional equivalent of a plane, just like a plane is the two-dimensional equivalent of a line. SVMs are typically robust to outliers and can model non-linear decision boundaries; however, SVMs get slow very quickly, so it will be a good comparison:

```
>>> %%timeit
>>> from sklearn.svm import SVC
>>> svc = SVC(gamma='auto').fit(r_X_train, r_y_train)
153 ms ± 6.7 ms per loop (mean ± std. dev. of 7 runs, 1 loop each)
```

Now that we have our baseline model and an idea of how it works, let's see how the baseline k-NN model performs:

```
>>> from sklearn.metrics import classification_report
>>> print(classification_report(r_y_test, knn_preds))
              precision    recall  f1-score   support

           0       0.91      0.93      0.92       138
           1       0.50      0.41      0.45        22

   micro avg       0.86      0.86      0.86       160
   macro avg       0.70      0.67      0.69       160
weighted avg       0.85      0.86      0.86       160
```

Under-sampling

As we hinted at earlier, under-sampling will reduce the amount of data available to train our model on. This means we should only attempt this if we have enough data that we can accept eliminating some of it. Let's see what happens with the red wine quality data, since we don't have much data to begin with. We will use the `RandomUnderSampler` from `imblearn` to randomly under-sample the low-quality red wines in the training set:

```
>>> from imblearn.under_sampling import RandomUnderSampler
>>> X_train_undersampled, y_train_undersampled = RandomUnderSampler(
...     random_state=0
... ).fit_resample(r_X_train, r_y_train)
```

We went from almost 14% of the training data being high-quality red wine to 50% of it; however, notice that this came at the price of 1,049 training samples (more than half of our training data!):

```
# before
>>> r_y_train.value_counts()
0    1244
1     195
Name: high_quality, dtype: int64

# after
>>> pd.Series(y_train_undersampled).value_counts().sort_index()
0    195
1    195
dtype: int64
```

Fitting our model with the under-sampled data is no different from before:

```
>>> from sklearn.neighbors import KNeighborsClassifier
>>> knn_undersampled = KNeighborsClassifier(
...     n_neighbors=5
... ).fit(X_train_undersampled, y_train_undersampled)
>>> knn_undersampled_preds = knn_undersampled.predict(r_X_test)
```

Using the classification report, we see that under-sampling is definitely not an improvement—we hardly had any data for this model:

```
>>> from sklearn.metrics import classification_report
>>> print(classification_report(r_y_test, knn_undersampled_preds))
              precision    recall  f1-score   support

           0       0.93      0.65      0.77       138
           1       0.24      0.68      0.35        22

   micro avg       0.66      0.66      0.66       160
   macro avg       0.58      0.67      0.56       160
weighted avg       0.83      0.66      0.71       160
```

In situations where we have limited data to start with, under-sampling is simply not feasible. With the red wine, we lost over half of the already small amount of data we had. Models need a good amount of data to learn from.

Over-sampling

It's clear that with smaller datasets, it won't be beneficial to under-sample. Instead, we can try over-sampling the minority class (the high-quality red wines, in this case). Rather than doing random over-sampling with the `RandomOverSampler`, we are going to use the **Synthetic Minority Over-sampling Technique** (**SMOTE**) to create *new* (synthetic) red wines similar to the high-quality ones using the k-nearest neighbors algorithm. By doing this, we are making a big assumption that the data we have collected about the chemical properties of the red wine does influence the quality rating of the wine.

The SMOTE technique in `imblearn` comes from this paper:

N. V. Chawla, K. W. Bowyer, L. O.Hall, W. P. Kegelmeyer, SMOTE: synthetic minority over-sampling technique, Journal of Artificial Intelligence Research, 321-357, 2002, available at `https://arxiv.org/pdf/1106.1813.pdf`.

Let's use SMOTE with the five nearest neighbors (the default value for the k_neighbors parameter) to over-sample the high-quality red wines in our training data:

```
>>> from imblearn.over_sampling import SMOTE

>>> X_train_oversampled, y_train_oversampled = SMOTE(
...     random_state=0
... ).fit_resample(r_X_train, r_y_train)
```

Since we over-sampled, we will have more data than we did before, gaining an extra 1,049 high-quality red wine samples:

```
>>> r_y_train.value_counts() # before
0    1244
1     195
Name: high_quality, dtype: int64
>>> pd.Series(y_train_oversampled).value_counts().sort_index() # after
0    1244
1    1244
dtype: int64
```

Once again, we will fit a k-NN model with k=5, using the over-sampled data this time:

```
>>> from sklearn.neighbors import KNeighborsClassifier

>>> knn_oversampled = KNeighborsClassifier(
...     n_neighbors=5
... ).fit(X_train_oversampled, y_train_oversampled)

>>> knn_oversampled_preds = knn_oversampled.predict(r_X_test)
```

Over-sampling performed much better than under-sampling, but unless we were looking to maximize recall, we are better off sticking with our original strategy for k-NN:

```
>>> from sklearn.metrics import classification_report
>>> print(classification_report(r_y_test, knn_oversampled_preds))
              precision    recall  f1-score   support

           0       0.96      0.78      0.86       138
           1       0.37      0.82      0.51        22

   micro avg       0.78      0.78      0.78       160
   macro avg       0.67      0.80      0.68       160
weighted avg       0.88      0.78      0.81       160
```

Note that since SMOTE is creating synthetic data, we must carefully consider the side effects this may have on our model. If we can't make the assumption that all the values of a given class are representative of the full spectrum of the population and that this won't change over time, we cannot expect SMOTE to work well.

Regularization

When working with regressions, we may look to add a penalty term to our regression equation to reduce overfitting by punishing certain decisions for coefficients made by the model; this is called **regularization**. We are looking for the coefficients that will minimize this penalty term. The idea is to shrink the coefficients toward zero for features that don't contribute much to reducing the error of the model. Some common techniques are ridge regression, LASSO (short for *Least Absolute Shrinkage and Selection Operator*) regression, and elastic net regression, which combines the LASSO and ridge penalty terms.

Ridge regression, also called **L2 regularization**, punishes high coefficients ($\hat{\beta}$) by adding the sum of the squares of the coefficients to the cost function (which regression looks to minimize when fitting), as per the following penalty term:

$$L2\ penalty = \lambda \sum_j \hat{\beta_j}^2$$

This penalty term is also weighted by λ (lambda), which indicates how large the penalty will be. When this is zero, we have ordinary least squares regression, as before.

> Remember the C parameter from logistic regression? By default, the `LogisticRegression` class in `scikit-learn` will use the L2 penalty term, where C is the weight of this term (λ). `LogisticRegression` also supports L1, but only with certain solvers.

LASSO regression, also called **L1 regularization**, drives coefficients to zero by adding the sum of the absolute values of the coefficients to the cost function. This is more robust than L2 because it is less sensitive to extreme values:

$$L1\ penalty = \lambda \sum_j \left| \hat{\beta_j} \right|$$

Since LASSO drives coefficients of certain features in the regression to zero (where they won't contribute to the model), it is said to perform feature selection.

Both the L1 and L2 penalties are also referred to as **L1 and L2 norms** (a mathematical transformation on a vector to be in $[0, \infty)$) and written as $\|\hat{\beta}\|_1$ and $\|\hat{\beta}\|_1^2$, respectively.

Elastic net regression combines both LASSO and ridge penalty terms into the following penalty term, where we can tune both the strength of the penalty (λ), and the percentage of the penalty that is L1 (and consequently, the percentage that is L2) with α (alpha):

$$elastic\ net\ penalty = \lambda\left(\frac{1-\alpha}{2}\sum_{j}\hat{\beta}_j^2 + \alpha\sum_{j}|\hat{\beta}_j|\right)$$

Since these techniques rely on the magnitude of the coefficients, the data should be scaled beforehand.

Scikit-learn implements ridge, LASSO, and elastic net regressions with the `Ridge`, `Lasso`, and `ElasticNet` classes, respectively. There is also a CV version of each of these (`RidgeCV`, `LassoCV`, and `ElasticNetCV`), which features built-in cross-validation. These can be used in the same way as the `LinearRegression` class. Using all the defaults for these models, we find that elastic net performs the best at predicting the length of the year in Earth days on the planet data:

```
>>> from sklearn.linear_model import Ridge, Lasso, ElasticNet

>>> ridge, lasso, elastic = Ridge(), Lasso(), ElasticNet()

>>> for model in [ridge, lasso, elastic]:
...     model.fit(pl_X_train, pl_y_train)
...     print(
...         f'{model.__class__.__name__}: ' # get model name
...         f'{model.score(pl_X_test, pl_y_test):.4}' # get score
...     )
Ridge: 0.9302
Lasso: 0.9298
ElasticNet: 0.9375
```

These `scikit-learn` classes have an `alpha` parameter, which lines up with λ in our previous equations (not α). For `ElasticNet`, the α in our equations lines up with the `l1_ratio` parameter, which defaults to 50% LASSO. Note that, in practice, both of these hyperparameters are determined with cross-validation.

Summary

In this chapter, we reviewed various techniques we can employ to improve the performance of our models. We learned how to use grid search to find the best hyperparameters in a search space, and how to tune our model using the scoring metric of our choosing with `GridSearchCV`. This means we don't have to accept the default in the `score()` method of our model and can customize it to our needs.

In our discussion of feature engineering, we learned how to reduce the dimensionality of our data using techniques such as PCA and feature selection. We saw how to use `PolynomialFeatures` to add interaction terms to models with categorical and numerical features. Next, we learned how to use a `FeatureUnion` to augment our training data with transformed features. In addition, we saw how decision trees can help us understand which features in the data contribute most to the classification or regression task at hand, using feature importances. This helped us see the importance of sulfur dioxide and chlorides in distinguishing between red and white wine on a chemical level, as well as the importance of a planet's semi-major axis in determining the length of its period.

Afterward, we took a look at the random forest, gradient boosting, and voting classifiers to discuss ensemble methods and how they seek to address the bias-variance trade-off through bagging, boosting, and voting strategies. We also saw how to measure agreement between classifiers with Cohen's kappa score. This led us to examine our `white_or_red` wine classifier's confidence in its correct and incorrect predictions. Once we know the ins and outs of our model's performance, we can try to improve upon it through the appropriate ensemble method to capitalize on its strengths and mitigate its weaknesses.

Next, we learned how to use the `imblearn` package to implement over- and under-sampling strategies when faced with a class imbalance. We tried to use this to improve our ability to predict red wine quality scores. In this example, we got exposure to the k-NN algorithm and the issues with modeling small datasets. Finally, we learned how we can use regularization to penalize high coefficients and reduce overfitting with regression, using ridge (L2 norm), LASSO (L1 norm), and elastic net penalties; remember, LASSO is often used as a method of feature selection since it drives coefficients to zero.

In the next chapter, we will revisit the simulated login attempt data and use machine learning to detect anomalies. We will also see how we can apply both unsupervised and supervised learning in practice.

Exercises

Complete the following exercises to practice the skills covered in this chapter. Be sure to consult the *Machine learning workflow* section in the appendix as a refresher for the process of building models:

1. Predict star temperature with elastic net linear regression as follows:
    1. Using the `data/stars.csv` file, build a pipeline to normalize the data with the `MinMaxScaler` and then run elastic net linear regression using all the numeric columns to predict the temperature of the star.
    2. Run grid search on the pipeline to find the best values for `alpha`, `l1_ratio`, and `fit_intercept` for the elastic net in the search space of your choice.
    3. Train the model on 75% of the initial data.
    4. Calculate the R^2 of your model.
    5. Find the coefficients for each regressor and the intercept.
    6. Plot the residuals using the `plot_residuals()` function from the `ml_utils.regression` module.

2. Perform multiclass classification of white wine quality using a support vector machine and feature union as follows:

   1. Using the `data/winequality-white.csv` file, build a pipeline to standardize data, then create a `FeatureUnion` between interaction terms and a feature selection method of your choice from `sklearn.feature_selection`, followed by an SVM (use the `SVC` class).

   2. Run grid search on your pipeline with 85% of the data to find the best values for `include_bias` with `PolynomialFeatures` and the `C` parameter of `SVC` in the search space of your choosing with `scoring='f1_macro'`.

   3. Look at the classification report for your model.

   4. Use the `confusion_matrix_visual()` function from the `ml_utils.classification` module to create a confusion matrix.

   5. Plot a precision-recall curve for multiclass data using the `plot_multi_class_pr_curve()` function from `ml_utils.classification`.

3. Perform multiclass classification of white wine quality using k-NN and over-sampling as follows:

   1. Using the `data/winequality-white.csv` file, create a test and training set with 85% of the data in the training set. Stratify on `quality`.

   2. With `imblearn`, use the `RandomOverSampler` to over-sample the minority quality scores.

   3. Build a pipeline to standardize data and run k-NN.

   4. Run grid search on your pipeline with the over-sampled data on the search space of your choosing to find the best value for k-NN's `n_neighbors` with `scoring='f1_macro'`.

   5. Look at the classification report for your model.

   6. Use the `confusion_matrix_visual()` function from the `ml_utils.classification` module to create a confusion matrix.

   7. Plot a precision-recall curve for multiclass data using the `plot_multi_class_pr_curve()` function from `ml_utils.classification`.

4. Can wine type (red or white) help determine the quality score?
    1. Using the `data/winequality-white.csv` and `data/winequality-red.csv` files, create a `DataFrame` with the concatenated data and a column indicating which wine type the data belongs to (red or white).
    2. Create a test and training set with 75% of the data in the training set. Stratify on `quality`.
    3. Build a pipeline using a `ColumnTransformer` to standardize the numeric data while one-hot encoding the wine type column (something like `is_red` and `is_white`, each with binary values), and then build a random forest.
    4. Run grid search on your pipeline with the search space of your choosing to find the best value for the random forest's `max_depth` parameter with `scoring='f1_macro'`.
    5. Take a look at the feature importances from the random forest.
    6. Look at the classification report for your model.
    7. Using the `plot_multi_class_roc()` function from the `ml_utils.classification` module, plot a ROC curve for multiclass data.
    8. Use the `confusion_matrix_visual()` function from the `ml_utils.classification` module to create a confusion matrix.

5. Make a multiclass voting classifier to predict wine quality with majority rules by performing the following steps:
    1. Using the `data/winequality-white.csv` and `data/winequality-red.csv` files, create a `DataFrame` with concatenated data and a column indicating which wine type the data belongs to (red or white).
    2. Create a test and training set with 75% of the data in the training set. Stratify on `quality`.
    3. Build a pipeline for each of the following models: random forest, gradient boosting, k-NN, logistic regression, and Naive Bayes (GaussianNB). The pipeline should use a `ColumnTransformer` to standardize the numeric data while one-hot encoding the wine type column (something like `is_red` and `is_white`, each with binary values), and then build the model. We will discuss Naive Bayes in Chapter 11, *Machine Learning Anomaly Detection*.

4. Run grid search on each pipeline except Naive Bayes (just run `fit()` on it) with `scoring='f1_macro'` on the search space of your choosing to find the best values for the following:

  - **Random forest**: `max_depth`
  - **Gradient boosting**: `max_depth`
  - **k-NN**: `n_neighbors`
  - **Logistic regression**: `C`

5. Find the level of agreement between each pair of two models using the `cohen_kappa_score()` function from the `metrics` module in `scikit-learn`. Note that you can get all the combinations of the two easily using the `combinations()` function from `itertools` in the Python standard library.

6. Build a `VotingClassifier` with the five models built using majority rules (`voting='hard'`) and weighting the Naive Bayes model half as much as the others.

7. Look at the classification report for your model.

8. Use the `confusion_matrix_visual()` function from the `ml_utils.classification` module to create a confusion matrix.

Further reading

Check out the following resources for more information on the topics covered in this chapter:

- *A Gentle Introduction to the Gradient Boosting Algorithm for Machine Learning*: `https://machinelearningmastery.com/gentle-introduction-gradient-boosting-algorithm-machine-learning/`
- *A Kaggler's Guide to Model Stacking in Practice*: `http://blog.kaggle.com/2016/12/27/a-kagglers-guide-to-model-stacking-in-practice/`
- *Cross-validation: evaluating estimator performance*: `https://scikit-learn.org/stable/modules/cross_validation.html`
- *Decision Trees in Machine Learning*: `https://towardsdatascience.com/decision-trees-in-machine-learning-641b9c4e8052`
- *Ensemble Learning to Improve Machine Learning Results*: `https://blog.statsbot.co/ensemble-learning-d1dcd548e936`

- *Ensemble Methods*: `https://scikit-learn.org/stable/modules/ensemble.html`
- *Feature Engineering Made Easy by Divya Susarla and Sinan Ozdemir*: `https://www.packtpub.com/big-data-and-business-intelligence/feature-engineering-made-easy`
- *Feature Selection*: `https://scikit-learn.org/stable/modules/feature_selection.html#feature-selection`
- *Gradient Boosting vs Random Forest*: `https://medium.com/@aravanshad/gradient-boosting-versus-random-forest-cfa3fa8f0d80`
- *Hyperparameter Optimization in Machine Learning*: `https://www.datacamp.com/community/tutorials/parameter-optimization-machine-learning-models`
- *L1 Norms versus L2 Norms*: `https://www.kaggle.com/residentmario/l1-norms-versus-l2-norms`
- *Modern Machine Learning Algorithms: Strengths and Weaknesses*: `https://elitedatascience.com/machine-learning-algorithms`
- *Principal component analysis*: `https://en.wikipedia.org/wiki/Principal_component_analysis`
- *Regularization in Machine Learning*: `https://towardsdatascience.com/regularization-in-machine-learning-76441ddcf99a`

11
Machine Learning Anomaly Detection

For our final application chapter, we will be revisiting **anomaly detection** on login attempts. Let's imagine we work for a company that launched its web application in the beginning of 2018. This web application has been collecting log events for all login attempts since it launched. We know the IP address that the attempt was made from, the result of the attempt, when it was made, and which username was entered. What we don't know is whether the attempt was made by one of our valid users or a nefarious party.

Our company has been expanding and, since data breaches seem to be in the news every day, has created an information security department to monitor the traffic. The CEO saw our rule-based approach to identifying hackers from `Chapter 8`, *Rule-Based Anomaly Detection*, and was intrigued by our initiative, but wants us to move beyond using rules and thresholds for such a vital task. We have been tasked with developing a machine learning model for anomaly detection of the login attempts on the web application.

Since this will require a good amount of data, we have been given access to all the logs from January 1, 2018 through December 31, 2018. In addition, the newly formed **security operations center (SOC)** will be auditing all this traffic now and will indicate which time frames contain nefarious users based on their investigations. Since the SOC members are subject matter experts, this data will be exceptionally valuable to us. We will be able to use the labeled data they provide to build a supervised learning model for future use; however, it will take them some time to sift through all the traffic, so we should get started with some unsupervised learning until they have that ready for us.

In this chapter, we will cover the following topics:

- Exploring the data of simulated login attempts
- Testing out unsupervised anomaly detection methods on login attempts
- Implementing supervised anomaly detection
- Incorporating a feedback loop with online learning

Chapter materials

The materials for this chapter can be found at `https://github.com/stefmolin/Hands-On-Data-Analysis-with-Pandas/tree/master/ch_11`. In this chapter, we will be revisiting attempted login data; however, the `simulate.py` script has been updated to allow for additional command-line arguments. We won't be running the simulations, but be sure to take a look at the script and to check out the `0-simulating_the_data.ipynb` notebook for the process that was followed to generate the data files and create the database for this chapter. The `user_data/` directory contains files used for this simulation, but we won't be using them directly in this chapter.

The `merge_logs.py` file contains the Python code to merge the logs from each of the individual simulations, and `run_simulations.sh` contains a Bash script for running the entire process; these are provided for completeness, but we don't need to use them (or worry about Bash).

The log data we will be using for this chapter can be found in the `logs/` directory. The `logs_2018.csv` and `hackers_2018.csv` files are logs of login attempts and a record of hacker activity from all 2018 simulations, respectively. Files with the `hackers` prefix are treated as the labeled data we will receive from the SOC, so we will pretend we don't have them initially. The files with `2019` instead of `2018` in the name are the data from simulating the first quarter of 2019, rather than the full year. The simulations used the following parameters per month:

Month	Probability of attack in a given hour	Probability of trying entire userbase	Vary IP addresses?
Jan 2018	1.00%	50%	Yes
Feb 2018	0.50%	25%	Yes
Mar 2018	0.10%	10%	Yes

Month	Probability of attack in a given hour	Probability of trying entire userbase	Vary IP addresses?
Apr 2018	1.00%	65%	Yes
May 2018	0.01%	5%	Yes
Jun 2018	0.05%	5%	Yes
Jul 2018	1.00%	15%	Yes
Aug 2018	0.50%	10%	Yes
Sep 2018	0.50%	10%	No
Oct 2018	0.20%	12%	No
Nov 2018	0.70%	17%	Yes
Dec 2018	8.00%	88%	Yes
Jan 2019	0.80%	8%	Yes
Feb 2019	0.10%	18%	Yes
Mar 2019	0.10%	18%	Yes

Notice that the parameters of the simulation vary across the months, and that in most months, the hackers are varying their IP addresses for each username they attempt to log in with. This will make our method from `Chapter 8`, *Rule-Based Anomaly Detection*, useless because we were looking for IP addresses with many attempts and high failure rates. If the hackers now vary their IP addresses, we won't have many attempts associated with them. Therefore, we won't be able to flag them with that strategy, so we will have to find another way around this.

The CSV files in the `logs/` directory have been written to the `logs.db` SQLite database. The `logs` table contains the data from `logs_2018.csv` and `logs_2019.csv`; the `attacks` table contains the data from `hackers_2018.csv` and `hackers_2019.csv`.

Our workflow for this chapter has been split across several notebooks, which are all preceded by a number indicating their order. Before we have the labeled data, we will conduct some **exploratory data analysis** (**EDA**) in `1-EDA_unlabeled_data.ipynb`, and then move to the `2-unsupervised_anomaly_detection.ipynb` notebook to try out some unsupervised anomaly detection methods. Once we have the labeled data, we will perform some additional EDA in the `3-EDA_labeled_data.ipynb` notebook, and then move to `4-supervised_anomaly_detection.ipynb` for supervised methods. Finally, we will use `5-online_learning.ipynb` for our discussion of online learning. As usual, the text will indicate when it is time to switch between notebooks.

Exploring the data

We don't have labeled data yet, but we can still examine the data to see whether there is something that stands out. This data is different from the data in Chapter 8, *Rule-Based Anomaly Detection*. The hackers are smarter in this simulation—they don't always try as many users or stick with the same IP address every time. Let's see whether we can come up with some features that will help with anomaly detection by performing some EDA in the 1-EDA_unlabeled_data.ipynb notebook.

As usual, we begin with our imports. These will be the same for all notebooks, so it will be reproduced in this section only:

```
>>> %matplotlib inline
>>> import matplotlib.pyplot as plt
>>> import numpy as np
>>> import pandas as pd
>>> import seaborn as sns
```

Next, we read in the 2018 logs from the logs table in the SQLite database:

```
>>> import sqlite3

>>> with sqlite3.connect('logs/logs.db') as conn:
...     logs_2018 = pd.read_sql(
...         """SELECT *
...         FROM logs
...         WHERE datetime BETWEEN "2018-01-01" AND "2019-01-01";""",
...         conn, parse_dates=['datetime'], index_col='datetime'
...     )
```

The with statement in the previous code block is a more concise way of writing a try...except...finally block. We are already familiar with try...except blocks. The finally block comes last and will always be run; for this reason, we put our cleanup code there. This means that we can try to do something with our database connection and, whether or not it works, we will close the connection when we are finished.

The previous code block is therefore equivalent to the following code block:

```
>>> import sqlite3
>>> conn = sqlite3.connect('logs/logs.db')
>>> try:
...     logs_2018 = pd.read_sql(
...         """SELECT *
...         FROM logs
...         WHERE datetime BETWEEN "2018-01-01" AND "2019-01-01";""",
...         conn, parse_dates=['datetime'], index_col='datetime'
...     )
... except: # something went wrong
...     pass # add a contingency plan
... finally: # clean up
...     conn.close()
```

In order to be able to use the `with` statement instead of a `try...except...finally` block, we need to use a **context manager**. It is good practice to use a context manager when working with resources such as files or connections to a database, in order to make sure they are properly closed when no longer needed—after all, it's pretty easy to forget to close a connection.

Classes that can be used as context managers define two additional **dunder methods** (double-underscore methods for the inner workings of a Python class): `__enter__()` and `__exit__()`. These are used by the `with` statement. The database connection we are creating is a context manager. It gives us an open connection to the database (in the `conn` variable); once we finish with the work we need the open connection for, it closes the connection for us.

 Be sure to check out `contextlib` from the standard library for utilities using the `with` statement and context managers. The documentation is at https://docs.python.org/3/library/contextlib.html.

If the SQLAlchemy package (`https://www.sqlalchemy.org/`) is installed in the environment we are working with (as is the case for us), we have the option of providing the database **uniform resource identifier** (**URI**) for the connection. In our case, this would be `'sqlite:///logs/logs.db'`, where `sqlite` is the dialect and `logs/logs.db` is the path to the file. Note there are three `/` characters in a row:

```
>>> logs_2018 = pd.read_sql(
...     """
...     SELECT *
...     FROM logs
...     WHERE datetime BETWEEN "2018-01-01" AND "2019-01-01";
...     """,
...     'sqlite:///logs/logs.db',
...     parse_dates=['datetime'], index_col='datetime'
... )
```

Note that we are using a SQLite database here because the Python standard library provides the means to make the connection already (`sqlite3`); if we want to use another type of database, such as MySQL or PostgreSQL, we will need to install SQLAlchemy (and possibly additional packages, depending on the database dialect). More information can be found at `https://pandas.pydata.org/pandas-docs/stable/user_guide/io.html#sql-queries`. Check the *Further reading* section at the end of this chapter for a SQLAlchemy tutorial.

Our data looks like this:

datetime	source_ip	username	success	failure_reason
2018-01-01 00:06:19.353126	223.178.55.3	djones	1	None
2018-01-01 00:09:07.147971	223.178.55.3	djones	1	None
2018-01-01 01:08:08.610041	6.252.142.27	asmith	1	None
2018-01-01 02:37:50.329298	124.178.25.98	akim	1	None
2018-01-01 02:45:20.382080	98.43.141.103	akim	1	None

Our data types will be the same as in Chapter 8, *Rule-Based Anomaly Detection*, with the exception of the success column. SQLite doesn't support Boolean values, so this column was converted to the binary representation of its original form (stored as an integer) upon writing the data to the database:

```
>>> logs_2018.dtypes
source_ip         object
username          object
success            int64
failure_reason    object
dtype: object
```

Using the info() method, we see that failure_reason is the only column with nulls. It is null when the attempt was successful. When looking to build a model, we should also pay attention to the memory usage of our data. Some models will require increasing the dimension of our data, which can quickly get too large to hold in memory:

```
>>> logs_2018.info()
<class 'pandas.core.frame.DataFrame'>
DatetimeIndex: 43283 entries, 2018-01-01 ... to 2018-12-31
23:24:52.807237
Data columns (total 4 columns):
source_ip         43283 non-null object
username          43283 non-null object
success           43283 non-null int64
failure_reason    19127 non-null object
dtypes: int64(1), object(3)
memory usage: 1.2+ MB
```

Running the describe() method tells us that the most common reason for failure is providing the wrong username, which suggests that the majority of the failed attempts are from hackers. We can also see that the unique usernames tried (3,351) is well over the number of users in our user base (133), indicating some suspicious activity.

The most frequent IP address made 248 attempts, but since that isn't even one per day (remember we are looking at the full year of 2018), we can't make any assumptions:

```
>>> logs_2018.describe(include='all')
           source_ip username       success         failure_reason
count          43283    43283  43283.000000                  19127
unique         11559     3351           NaN                      2
top    78.174.30.56      kim           NaN   error_wrong_username
freq             248      352           NaN                  11815
mean             NaN      NaN      0.558094                    NaN
std              NaN      NaN      0.496619                    NaN
min              NaN      NaN      0.000000                    NaN
25%              NaN      NaN      0.000000                    NaN
50%              NaN      NaN      1.000000                    NaN
75%              NaN      NaN      1.000000                    NaN
max              NaN      NaN      1.000000                    NaN
```

We can look at the unique usernames with attempted logins per IP address, as in Chapter 8, *Rule-Based Anomaly Detection*, which shows us most of the IP addresses have a few usernames, but there is at least one with many:

```
>>> logs_2018.groupby('source_ip').agg(
...     dict(username='nunique')
... ).username.describe()
count    11559.000000
mean         1.175275
std          2.726389
min          1.000000
25%          1.000000
50%          1.000000
75%          1.000000
max        135.000000
Name: username, dtype: float64
```

Let's calculate the metrics per IP address:

```
>>> pivot = pd.pivot_table(
...     logs_2018, values='success', index=logs_2018.source_ip,
...     columns=logs_2018.failure_reason.fillna('success'),
...     aggfunc='count', fill_value=0
... )
>>> pivot.insert(0, 'attempts', pivot.sum(axis=1))
>>> pivot = pivot.sort_values('attempts', ascending=False).assign(
...     success_rate=lambda x: x.success / x.attempts,
...     error_rate=lambda x: 1 - x.success_rate
... )
```

The three IP addresses with the most attempts have many failures; however, the fourth and fifth appear to be valid users:

failure_reason source_ip	attempts	error_wrong_password	error_wrong_username	success	success_rate	error_rate
78.174.30.56	248	67	141	40	0.161290	0.838710
228.144.254.255	243	71	130	42	0.172840	0.827160
215.189.60.53	211	75	106	30	0.142180	0.857820
158.11.94.79	210	2	0	208	0.990476	0.009524
226.227.77.216	193	1	0	192	0.994819	0.005181

Let's use this dataframe to plot successes versus attempts per IP address to see whether there is a pattern we can exploit to separate valid activity from malicious activity:

```
>>> pivot.plot(
...        kind='scatter', x='attempts', y='success',
...        title='successes vs. attempts by IP address', alpha=0.25
... )
```

There appear to be two distinct groups in the shape of diagonal lines of varying density:

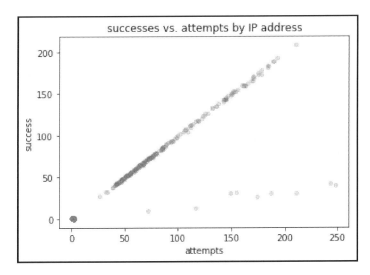

Remember, this is a binary classification problem where we want to find a way to distinguish between valid user and attacker login activity. We want to build a model that will learn some decision boundary that separates the valid users from the attackers. By quickly eyeballing this, we may imagine the separation boundary looking something like this:

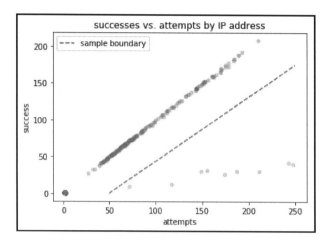

Now, the question is, which of those two groups are the hackers? Well, if more of the IP addresses are the hackers (since they use different IP addresses for each username they attempt), then the valid users would be considered outliers, and the hackers would be considered "inliers" with a box plot:

```
>>> pivot[['attempts', 'success']].plot(
...     kind='box', subplots=True, figsize=(10, 3),
...     title='stats per IP address'
... )
```

Indeed, this appears to be what is happening. Our valid users have more successes than the hackers because they only use 1-3 different IP addresses:

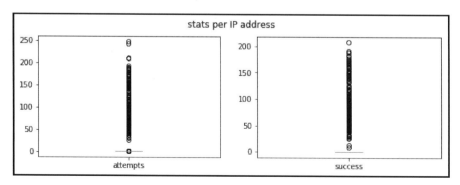

Clearly, looking at the data like this isn't helping too much, so let's see whether a smaller granularity can help us. Let's visualize the distributions of attempts, the number of usernames, and the number of failures per IP address on a minute-by-minute resolution for January 2018:

```
>>> from matplotlib.ticker import MultipleLocator
>>> ax = logs_2018['2018-01'].assign(
...         failures=lambda x: 1 - x.success
... ).groupby('source_ip').resample('1min').agg(
...         {'username': 'nunique', 'success': 'sum', 'failures': 'sum'}
... ).assign(
...         attempts=lambda x: x.success + x.failures
... ).dropna().query('attempts > 0').reset_index().plot(
...         y=['attempts', 'username', 'failures'], kind='hist',
...         subplots=True, layout=(1, 3), figsize=(20, 3),
...         title='January 2018 distributions of minutely stats' \
...              'by IP address'
... )

>>> for axes in ax.flatten():
...         axes.xaxis.set_major_locator(MultipleLocator(1))
```

It looks like most of the IP addresses have just a single username associated with them; however, some IP addresses also have multiple failures for their attempts:

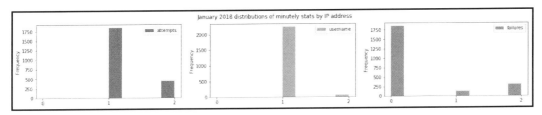

Perhaps a combination of unique usernames and failures will give us something that doesn't rely on the IP address being constant. Let's visualize the number of usernames with failures per minute over 2018:

```
>>> logs_2018['2018'].assign(
...         failures=lambda x: 1 - x.success
... ).query('failures > 0').resample('1min').agg(
...         {'username':'nunique', 'failures': 'sum'}
... ).dropna().rename(
...         columns={'username':'usernames_with_failures'}
... ).usernames_with_failures.plot(
...         title='usernames with failures per minute in 2018',
...         figsize=(15, 3)
... )
```

This looks promising; we should definitely be looking into spikes in usernames with failures. It could be an issue with our website, or something malicious:

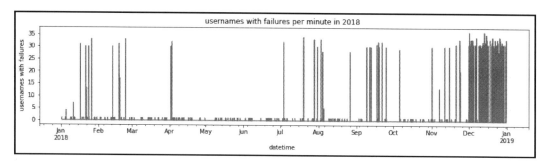

Unsupervised methods

While we wait for our labeled data, let's work on some unsupervised methods for anomaly detection. If the hackers are conspicuous and distinct from our valid users, unsupervised methods may prove pretty effective. This is a good place to start before we have labeled data, or if the labeled data is difficult to gather or not guaranteed to be representative of the full spectrum we are looking to flag. Note that, in most cases, we won't have labeled data, so it is crucial that we are familiar with some unsupervised methods.

In our initial EDA, we identified the number of usernames with a failed login attempt in a given minute as a feature for anomaly detection. We will now pursue some unsupervised anomaly detection, using this feature as the jumping-off point. Scikit-learn provides a few algorithms for unsupervised anomaly detection. In the `2-unsupervised_anomaly_detection.ipynb` notebook, we will look at the isolation forest and local outlier factor algorithms; a third method, using a one-class **support vector machine (SVM)**, is in the exercises.

Before we can try out these methods, we need to prepare our training data. We will be using the minute-by-minute data for January 2018 for our unsupervised models. Our features will be the day of the week (one-hot encoded), the hour of the day (one-hot encoded), and the number of usernames with failures. See the *Encoding data* section in `Chapter 9`, *Getting Started with Machine Learning in Python,* for a refresher on one-hot encoding, if needed.

Let's write a utility function to grab this data easily:

```
def get_X(log, day):
    """
    Get data we can use for the X

    Parameters:
        - log: The logs dataframe
        - day: A day or single value we can use as a datetime index
                slice

    Returns: A pandas DataFrame
    """
    return pd.get_dummies(log[day].assign(
        failures=lambda x: 1 - x.success
    ).query('failures > 0').resample('1min').agg(
        {'username':'nunique', 'failures': 'sum'}
    ).dropna().rename(
        columns={'username':'usernames_with_failures'}
    ).assign(
        day_of_week=lambda x: x.index.dayofweek,
        hour=lambda x: x.index.hour
    ).drop(columns=['failures']), columns=['day_of_week', 'hour'])
```

Now we can grab January and store it in X:

```
>>> X = get_X(logs_2018, '2018-01')
>>> X.columns
Index(['usernames_with_failures', 'day_of_week_0', 'day_of_week_1',
       'day_of_week_2', 'day_of_week_3', 'day_of_week_4',
       'day_of_week_5', 'day_of_week_6', 'hour_0',
       'hour_1', ..., 'hour_22', 'hour_23'],
      dtype='object')
```

Isolation forest

The **isolation forest** algorithm is a random forest where the splits are made on randomly chosen features. A random value of that feature between its maximum and its minimum is selected to split on. Note this range is from the range of the feature at that node in the tree, not the starting data.

A single tree in the forest will look something like the following:

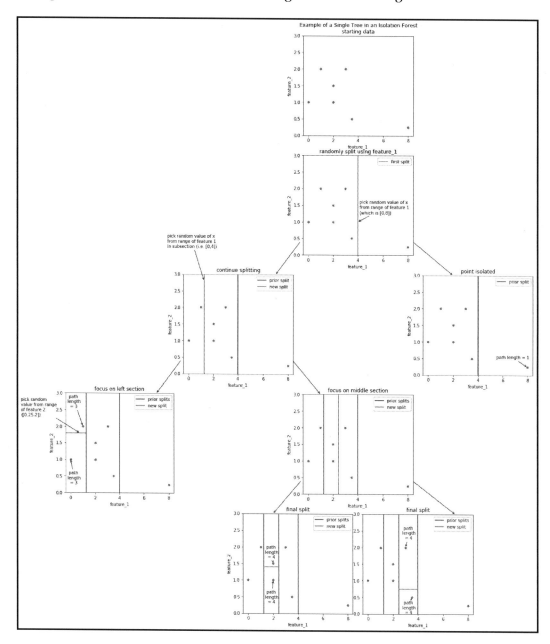

The average length of the path that must be traveled from the top of each tree in the forest to the leaf containing a given point is used to score a point as an outlier or inlier. The outliers have much shorter paths, since they will be one of the few on a given side of a split and have less in common with other points. Conversely, points with many dimensions in common will take more splits to separate.

 More information on this algorithm can be found at `https://scikit-learn.org/stable/modules/outlier_detection.html#isolation-forest`.

Let's implement an isolation forest with a pipeline that first standardizes our data:

```
>>> from sklearn.ensemble import IsolationForest
>>> from sklearn.pipeline import Pipeline
>>> from sklearn.preprocessing import StandardScaler

>>> iso_forest_pipeline = Pipeline([
...     ('scale', StandardScaler()),
...     ('iforest', IsolationForest(
...         random_state=0, contamination=0.05, behaviour='new'
...     ))
... ]).fit(X)
```

We pass `behaviour='new'` here to align the isolation forest's behavior with that of other anomaly detection algorithms implemented in `scikit-learn` that return 1 or −1 if the point is an inlier or outlier, respectively. In addition, we had to specify how much of the data was expected to be outliers (`contamination`), which we estimated to be 5%; this will be difficult to choose, since we don't have labeled data. There is an `auto` option that will determine a value for us but, in this case, it gives us no outliers, so it's clear that value isn't the one we want.

The `predict()` method can be used to tell us whether each data point was an outlier:

```
>>> isolation_forest_preds = iso_forest_pipeline.predict(X)
>>> pd.Series(np.where(
...     isolation_forest_preds == -1, 'outlier', 'inlier'
... )).value_counts()
inlier     39624
outlier     1993
dtype: int64
```

Since we don't have the labeled data yet, we will come back to evaluate this later.

Local outlier factor

The **local outlier factor (LOF)** algorithm scores all points based on the ratio of the density around each point to that of its nearest neighbors. Points that are considered normal will have similar densities to their neighbors; those with few others nearby will be considered abnormal.

 More information on this algorithm can be found at `https://scikit-learn.org/stable/modules/outlier_detection.html#local-outlier-factor`.

Let's build another pipeline, but swap out the isolation forest for LOF:

```
>>> from sklearn.neighbors import LocalOutlierFactor
>>> from sklearn.pipeline import Pipeline
>>> from sklearn.preprocessing import StandardScaler

>>> lof_pipeline = Pipeline([
...     ('scale', StandardScaler()),
...     ('lof', LocalOutlierFactor())
... ]).fit(X)
```

Note that we have to guess the best value for n_neighbors here, because GridSearchCV has nothing to score models on if we don't have labeled data. We are using the default for this parameter, which is 20.

Now, let's see how many outliers we have this time. LOF doesn't have a predict() method, so we have to check the negative_outlier_factor_ attribute of the LOF object to see the scores of each of the data points we fit it with:

```
>>> lof_preds = lof_pipeline.named_steps['lof'] \
...             .negative_outlier_factor_
>>> lof_preds
array([-1.91486343e+10, -1.00000000e+00, -1.00000000e+00, ...,
       -1.00000000e+00, -1.00000000e+00, -1.91486343e+10])
```

There is another difference between LOF and isolation forests: the values for the `negative_outlier_factor_` aren't strictly –1 or 1. In fact, they can be any number—take a look at the first and last values in the previous result, and you'll see that they are way less than –1. This means we can't use the method we used with the isolation forest to count the inliers and outliers. Instead, we need to compare the `negative_outlier_factor_` to the `offset_` of the LOF model, which tells us the cutoff value as determined by the LOF model during training (using the `contamination` parameter):

```
>>> pd.Series(np.where(
...     lof_preds < lof_pipeline.named_steps['lof'].offset_,
...     'outlier', 'inlier'
... )).value_counts()
inlier     41577
outlier       40
dtype: int64
```

Comparing models

LOF indicates fewer outliers than the isolation forest, but perhaps they don't even agree with each other. As we learned in `Chapter 10`, *Making Better Predictions – Optimizing Models*, we can use the `cohen_kappa_score()` function from `sklearn.metrics` to check their level of agreement:

```
>>> from sklearn.metrics import cohen_kappa_score

>>> is_lof_outlier = np.where(
...     lof_preds < lof_pipeline.named_steps['lof'].offset_,
...     'outlier', 'inlier'
... )
>>> is_iso_outlier = np.where(
...     isolation_forest_preds == -1, 'outlier', 'inlier'
... )

>>> cohen_kappa_score(is_lof_outlier, is_iso_outlier)
0.012896350639585386
```

They agree only on 1.3% of the data points, indicating it's not so obvious which data points are anomalies. Without labeled data, however, it really is impossible for us to tell which one is better. We would have to work with the consumers of the results to determine which model gives them the most useful data.

Thankfully, the SOC has just sent over some labeled data, so we can determine which of our models is better and let them start using it until we get a supervised model ready. They have sent us all of the labeled 2018 data, but since our models were only trained on January 2018, let's see how these models handle that data (remember that we can't predict with LOF).

First, we will read in the labeled data they wrote to the database in the `attacks` table and add some columns indicating the minute the attack started, the duration, and when it ended:

```
>>> with sqlite3.connect('logs/logs.db') as conn:
...     hackers_2018 = pd.read_sql(
...         """
...         SELECT *
...         FROM attacks
...         WHERE start BETWEEN "2018-01-01" AND "2019-01-01";
...         """, conn, parse_dates=['start', 'end']
...     ).assign(
...         duration=lambda x: x.end - x.start,
...         start_floor=lambda x: x.start.dt.floor('min'),
...         end_ceil=lambda x: x.end.dt.ceil('min')
...     )
>>> hackers_2018.shape
(111, 6)
```

Note that the SOC only has a single IP address for the ones involved in each attack, so it's a good thing we aren't relying on that anymore. Instead, the SOC wants us to tell them in which minute there was suspicious activity so that they can investigate further. Also note that, while the attacks are quick in duration, our minute-by-minute data means we will trigger many alerts per attack:

	start	end	source_ip	duration	start_floor	end_ceil
0	2018-01-05 06:03:42.470259	2018-01-05 06:03:51.470259	170.9.4.108	00:00:09	2018-01-05 06:03:00	2018-01-05 06:04:00
1	2018-01-11 03:08:43.284085	2018-01-11 03:09:14.284085	27.255.30.3	00:00:31	2018-01-11 03:08:00	2018-01-11 03:10:00
2	2018-01-17 00:41:43.985324	2018-01-17 00:45:56.985324	226.98.192.152	00:04:13	2018-01-17 00:41:00	2018-01-17 00:46:00
3	2018-01-21 10:34:57.842776	2018-01-21 10:38:01.842776	102.178.107.171	00:03:04	2018-01-21 10:34:00	2018-01-21 10:39:00
4	2018-01-21 23:12:10.852725	2018-01-21 23:12:38.852725	48.172.61.152	00:00:28	2018-01-21 23:12:00	2018-01-21 23:13:00

Using the `start_floor` and `end_ceil` columns, we can create a range of datetimes and can check whether the data we marked as outliers falls within that range. For this, we will use the following function:

```
def get_y(datetimes, hackers, resolution='1min'):
    """
    Get data we can use for the y
    (whether or not a hacker attempted a log in during that time).

    Parameters:
        - datetimes: The datetimes to check for hackers
        - hackers: The dataframe indicating when the
                   attacks started and stopped
        - resolution: The granularity of the datetime.
                      Default is 1 minute.

    Returns:
        A pandas Series of booleans.
    """
    date_ranges = hackers.apply(
        lambda x: pd.date_range(
            x.start_floor, x.end_ceil, freq=resolution
        ),
        axis=1
    )
    dates = pd.Series()
    for date_range in date_ranges:
        dates = pd.concat([dates, date_range.to_series()])
    return datetimes.isin(dates)
```

Now, let's find the datetimes in our X data that had hacker activity:

```
>>> is_hacker = get_y(X.reset_index().datetime, hackers_2018)
```

We now have everything we need to make a classification report and a confusion matrix. Since we will be passing the `is_hacker` column a lot, we will make some partials to reduce our typing a bit:

```
>>> from functools import partial
>>> from sklearn.metrics import classification_report
>>> from ml_utils.classification import confusion_matrix_visual

>>> report = partial(classification_report, is_hacker)
>>> conf_matrix = partial(
...     confusion_matrix_visual, is_hacker, class_labels=[False, True]
... )
```

Let's start with the classification reports, which indicate LOF is much better:

```
>>> iso_forest_predicts_hacker = isolation_forest_preds == - 1
>>> print(report(iso_forest_predicts_hacker)) # isolation forest
              precision   recall   f1-score    support

       False       1.00     0.95       0.98      41588
        True       0.00     0.31       0.01         29

   micro avg       0.95     0.95       0.95      41617
   macro avg       0.50     0.63       0.49      41617
weighted avg       1.00     0.95       0.97      41617

>>> lof_predicts_hacker = lof_preds \
...       < lof_pipeline.named_steps['lof'].offset_
>>> print(report(lof_predicts_hacker)) # LOF
              precision   recall   f1-score    support

       False       1.00     1.00       1.00      41588
        True       0.55     0.76       0.64         29

   micro avg       1.00     1.00       1.00      41617
   macro avg       0.77     0.88       0.82      41617
weighted avg       1.00     1.00       1.00      41617
```

Let's create confusion matrices for our unsupervised methods side by side:

```
>>> fig, axes = plt.subplots(1, 2, figsize=(15, 5))
>>> conf_matrix(
...       iso_forest_predicts_hacker,
...       ax=axes[0],
...       title='Isolation Forest'
... )
>>> conf_matrix(
...       lof_predicts_hacker,
...       ax=axes[1],
...       title='Local Outlier Factor'
... )
```

This results in the following plots, confirming that LOF is better. The isolation forest has fewer true positives and a greater number of both false positives and false negatives:

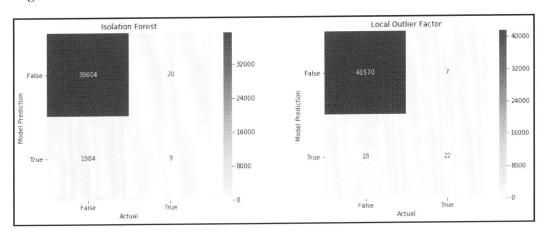

The SOC has informed us that false negatives are much more costly than false positives. However, they would like us to keep false positives in check to avoid bogging down the team with an excessive number of false alarms. This tells us that recall (the **true positive rate (TPR)**) is more valuable than precision as a performance metric. The SOC wants us to target a **recall of at least 75%**. Since we have a very large class imbalance, the **false positive rate (FPR)** won't be too informative for us. Remember, FPR is the ratio of false positives to the sum of false positives and true negatives (everything belonging to the negative class). Due to the nature of the attacks being rare, we will have a very large number of true negatives and, therefore, our FPR will remain very low. Consequently, the secondary metric determined by the SOC is to attain a **precision of 95% or greater**.

The LOF model exceeds our target recall, but the precision is too low. Since we were able to obtain some labeled data, we can now use supervised learning to find the minutes with suspicious activity (note this won't always be the case). Let's see whether we can use this extra information to find the minutes of interest more precisely.

Supervised methods

With our additional data, we should revisit our EDA to make sure our plan of looking at the number of usernames with failures on a minute resolution does separate the data. After some data wrangling in the `3-EDA_labeled_data.ipynb` notebook, we are able to create the following scatter plot, which shows that this strategy does indeed appear to separate the suspicious activity:

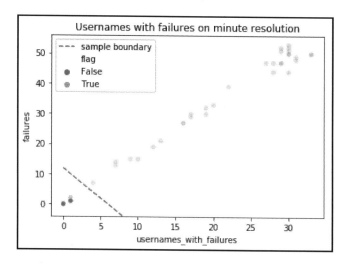

In the `4-supervised_anomaly_detection.ipynb` notebook, we will create some supervised models. Before we build our models, however, let's create a new function that will create both X and y at the same time. The `get_X_y()` function will use the `get_X()` and `get_y()` functions we made earlier, returning both X and y:

```
def get_X_y(log, day, hackers):
    """
    Get the X, y data to build a model with.

    Parameters:
        - log: The logs dataframe
        - day: A day or single value we can use as a datetime index
                slice
        - hackers: The dataframe indicating when the attacks
                    started and stopped
    Returns:
        X, y tuple where X is a pandas DataFrame and y is a pandas
        Series
    """
```

```
    X = get_X(log, day)
    y = get_y(X.reset_index().datetime, hackers)
    return X, y
```

Now, let's make a training set with January 2018 data and a testing set with February 2018 data, using our new function:

```
>>> X_train, y_train = get_X_y(logs_2018, '2018-01', hackers_2018)
>>> X_test, y_test = get_X_y(logs_2018, '2018-02', hackers_2018)
```

 Note that while we have a very large class imbalance, we don't jump right to imbalanced training sets. It's crucial to try out the model without premature optimization. If we build our model and see that it is being affected by the class imbalance, then we can try those techniques. Remember to be very cautious with over-/under-sampling techniques, as some make assumptions of the data that aren't always applicable or realistic. Think about SMOTE—would we really expect all future attackers to be similar to the ones we have in the data?

Baselining

Our first step will be to build some baseline models, so we know that our machine learning algorithms are performing better than some simpler models and have predictive value. We will build two such models:

- A dummy classifier that will predict labels based on the stratification in the data
- A Naive Bayes model that will predict the labels using Naive Bayes

Dummy classifier

This classifier will give us a model that is equivalent to the baseline we have been drawing on our ROC curves. The results will be poor on purpose. We will never use this classifier to actually make predictions; rather, we can use it to see whether the models we are building are better than random guessing strategies. In the dummy module, scikit-learn provides the DummyClassifier class precisely for this purpose.

Some interesting options for the `strategy` parameter of the `DummyClassifier` class are as follows:

- `uniform`: The classifier will guess each time whether or not the observation belongs to a hacking attempt.
- `most_frequent`: The classifier will always predict the most frequent label, which, in our case, will result in never marking anything as nefarious. This will achieve high accuracy, but be useless.
- `stratified`: The classifier will use the class distribution from the training data and maintain that ratio with its guesses.

Let's build a dummy model with the `stratified` strategy:

```
>>> from sklearn.dummy import DummyClassifier

>>> dummy_model = DummyClassifier(
...     strategy='stratified', random_state=0
... ).fit(X_train, y_train)
>>> dummy_preds = dummy_model.predict(X_test)
```

Now that we have our first baseline model, let's measure its performance for comparisons. We will be using both the ROC curve and precision-recall curve to show how the class imbalance can make the ROC curve optimistic of performance. To reduce typing, we will once again make some partials:

```
>>> from functools import partial
>>> from sklearn.metrics import classification_report
>>> from ml_utils.classification import (
...     confusion_matrix_visual, plot_pr_curve, plot_roc
... )

>>> report = partial(classification_report, y_test)
>>> roc = partial(plot_roc, y_test)
>>> pr_curve = partial(plot_pr_curve, y_test)
>>> conf_matrix = partial(
...     confusion_matrix_visual, y_test, class_labels=[False, True]
... )
```

Recall from our initial discussion of ROC curves in `Chapter 9`, *Getting Started with Machine Learning in Python*, that the diagonal line was random guessing of a dummy model. If our performance isn't better than this line, our model has no predictive value. The dummy model we just created is equivalent to this line. Let's visualize the baseline ROC curve, precision-recall curve, and confusion matrix using subplots:

```
>>> fig, axes = plt.subplots(1, 3, figsize=(20, 5))
>>> roc(dummy_model.predict_proba(X_test)[:,1], ax=axes[0])
>>> conf_matrix(dummy_preds, ax=axes[1])
>>> pr_curve(dummy_model.predict_proba(X_test)[:,1], ax=axes[2])
>>> plt.suptitle('Dummy Classifier with Stratified Strategy')
```

The dummy classifier wasn't able to flag any of the attackers. The ROC curve (TPR versus FPR) indicates that the dummy model has no predictive value, with an **area under the curve** (**AUC**) of 0.5. Note that the area under the precision-recall curve is nearly zero:

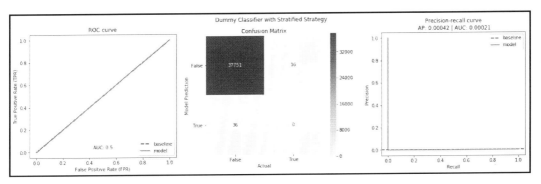

Since we have a very large class imbalance, the stratified random guessing strategy should perform horrendously on the minority class, and very well on the majority class. We can observe this by examining the classification report:

```
>>> print(report(dummy_preds))
              precision    recall  f1-score   support

       False       1.00      1.00      1.00     37787
        True       0.00      0.00      0.00        16

   micro avg       1.00      1.00      1.00     37803
   macro avg       0.50      0.50      0.50     37803
weighted avg       1.00      1.00      1.00     37803
```

Naive Bayes

Our last baseline model will be a Naive Bayes classifier. Before we discuss this model, we need to review a few concepts of probability. The first is conditional probability. When dealing with two events, *A* and *B*, the probability of event *A* happening, *given* that event *B* happened, is the **conditional probability** and is written as *P(A|B)*. When events *A* and *B* are independent, meaning *B* happening doesn't tell us anything about *A* happening and vice versa, *P(A|B)* is *P(A)*.

The conditional probability is defined as the **joint probability** of both *A* and *B* occurring (which is the intersection of these events), written as *P(A ∩ B)*, divided by the probability of *B* occurring (provided this is not zero):

$$P(A|B) = \frac{P(A \cap B)}{P(B)}, \ if \ P(B) \neq 0$$

This equation can be rearranged as follows:

$$P(A \cap B) = P(A|B) \times P(B)$$

The joint probability of *A ∩ B* is equivalent to *B ∩ A*, therefore, we get the following equation:

$$P(A \cap B) = P(B \cap A) = P(B|A) \times P(A)$$

It then follows that we can change the first equation to use conditional probabilities instead of the joint probability. This gives us **Bayes' theorem**:

$$P(A|B) = \frac{P(B|A) \times P(A)}{P(B)}$$

When working with the previous equation, *P(A)* is referred to as the **prior probability**, or initial degree of belief that event *A* will happen. After accounting for event *B* occurring, this initial belief gets updated; this is represented as *P(A|B)* and is called the **posterior probability**. The **likelihood** of event *B* given event *A* is *P(B|A)*. The support that event *B* occurring gives to our belief of observing event *A* is the following:

$$\frac{P(B|A)}{P(B)}$$

Let's take a look at an example—say we are building a spam filter, and we find that 10% of emails are spam. This 10% is our prior, or *P(spam)*. We want to know the probability an email we just received is spam given that it contains the word *free*—we want to find *P(spam|free)*. In order to find this, we need the probability that the word *free* is in an email given that it is spam, or *P(free|spam)*, and the probability of the word *free* being in an email.

Let's say we learned that 12% of emails contained the word *free* and 20% of the emails that were determined to be spam contained the word *free*. Plugging all this into the equation from before, we see that once we know an email contains the word *free*, our belief of whether or not it is spam increases from 10% to 16.7%, which is our posterior probability:

$$P(spam|free) = \frac{P(free|spam) \times P(spam)}{P(free)} = \frac{0.20 \times 0.10}{0.12} \approx 16.7\%$$

Bayes' theorem can be leveraged in a type of classifier called **Naive Bayes (NB)**. Depending on the assumptions we make of the data, we get a different member of the Naive Bayes family of classifiers. These models are very fast to train because they make a simplifying assumption of conditional independence of each pair of the X features, given the y variable (meaning $P(x_i|y, x_1...x_n)$ is equivalent to $P(x_i|y)$). They are called **naive** because this assumption is often incorrect; however, these classifiers have worked well in building spam filters.

Let's say we also find multiple dollar signs in the email and the word *prescription*, and we want to know the probability of it being spam. While some of these features may depend on each other, the Naive Bayes model will treat them as conditionally independent. This means our equation for the posterior probability is now the following:

$$P(spam|free, \$\$\$, prescription) = \frac{P(free|spam) \times P(\$\$\$|spam) \times P(prescription|spam) \times P(spam)}{P(free) \times P(\$\$\$) \times P(prescription)}$$

Suppose we find out that 5% of spam emails contain multiple dollar signs, 55% of spam emails contain the word *prescription*, 25% of emails contain multiple dollar signs, and the word *prescription* is found in 2% of emails overall. This means that our belief of the email being spam, given that it has the words *free* and *prescription* and multiple dollar signs, increases from 10% to 91.7%:

$$P(spam|free, \$\$\$, prescription) = \frac{0.20 \times 0.05 \times 0.55 \times 0.10}{0.12 \times 0.25 \times 0.02} \approx 91.7\%$$

Now that we understand the basics of the algorithm, let's build a Naive Bayes classifier. Note that `scikit-learn` provides many different Naive Bayes classifiers that differ by the assumed distributions of the likelihoods of the features, which we defined as $P(x_i|y,x_1...x_n)$. We will use the version that assumes they are normally distributed, `GaussianNB`:

```
>>> from sklearn.naive_bayes import GaussianNB
>>> from sklearn.pipeline import Pipeline
>>> from sklearn.preprocessing import StandardScaler

>>> nb_pipeline = Pipeline([
...     ('scale', StandardScaler()), ('nb', GaussianNB())
... ]).fit(X_train, y_train)
>>> nb_preds = nb_pipeline.predict(X_test)
```

We can retrieve the class priors from the model, which, in this case, tells us that the prior for a minute containing normal activity is 99.93% versus 0.07% for abnormal activity:

```
>>> nb_pipeline.named_steps['nb'].class_prior_
array([9.99303169e-01, 6.96830622e-04])
```

Naive Bayes makes a nice baseline model because we don't have to tune any hyperparameters, and it is quick to train. Let's see how it is performing:

```
>>> fig, axes = plt.subplots(1, 3, figsize=(20, 5))
>>> roc(nb_pipeline.predict_proba(X_test)[:,1], ax=axes[0])
>>> conf_matrix(nb_preds, ax=axes[1])
>>> pr_curve(nb_pipeline.predict_proba(X_test)[:,1], ax=axes[2])
>>> plt.suptitle('Naive Bayes Classifier')
```

The Naive Bayes classifier finds 6 out of the 16 attackers and is above the baseline (the dashed line) in both the ROC curve and precision-recall curve, meaning this model has some predictive value. However, the performance is very weak and won't be acceptable to the SOC:

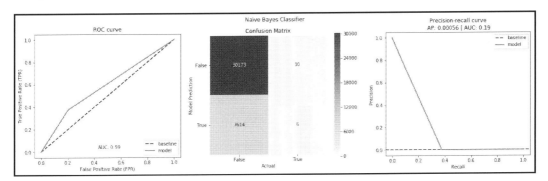

Unfortunately, we are triggering an enormous quantity of false positives (7,614). For the month of February, only 1 out of every 1,270 attack classifications was indeed an attack. This has the effect of desensitizing the users of these classifications. They may choose to always ignore our classifications because they are too noisy, and, consequently, miss a real issue.

This trade-off can be captured in the metrics of the classification report:

```
>>> print(report(nb_preds))
              precision    recall  f1-score   support

       False       1.00      0.80      0.89     37787
        True       0.00      0.38      0.00        16

   micro avg       0.80      0.80      0.80     37803
   macro avg       0.50      0.59      0.44     37803
weighted avg       1.00      0.80      0.89     37803
```

Precision rounds to zero for the target class because we have lots of false positives. Recall is higher than precision because the model is better with false negatives than false positives (since it isn't very discerning). This leaves the F_1 score at zero. Now, let's try to beat these baseline models.

Logistic regression

Since logistic regression is another simple model, let's try it out next. We used logistic regression in Chapter 9, *Getting Started with Machine Learning in Python*, for classification problems, so we already know how it works. As we learned in Chapter 10, *Making Better Predictions – Optimizing Models*, we will use a grid search to find a good value for the regularization parameter in our desired search space, using recall_macro for scoring. Remember there is a large cost associated with false negatives, so we are focusing on recall. The _macro suffix indicates that we want to average the recall between the positive and negative classes, instead of looking at it overall (due to the class imbalance).

 If we know exactly how much more valuable recall is to us over precision, we can replace this with a custom scorer made using the make_scorer() function in sklearn.metrics. The notebook we are working in has an example.

When using grid search, warnings from scikit-learn may be printed at each iteration. Therefore, to avoid having to scroll through all that, we will use the %%capture magic command to capture everything that would have been printed, keeping our notebook clean:

```
>>> %%capture
>>> from sklearn.linear_model import LogisticRegression
>>> from sklearn.model_selection import GridSearchCV
>>> from sklearn.pipeline import Pipeline
>>> from sklearn.preprocessing import StandardScaler

>>> lr_pipeline = Pipeline([
...     ('scale', StandardScaler()),
...     ('lr', LogisticRegression(solver='lbfgs', random_state=0))
... ])

>>> search_space = {'lr__C' : [0.1, 0.5, 1, 2]}

>>> lr_grid = GridSearchCV(
...     lr_pipeline, search_space, scoring='recall_macro', cv=5
... ).fit(X_train, y_train)

>>> lr_preds = lr_grid.predict(X_test)
```

With `%%capture`, all errors and output will be captured by default. We have the option of writing `--no-stderr` to hide errors only and `--no-stdout` to hide output only. These go after `%%capture`—for example, `%%capture --no-stderr`. If we want to hide specific errors, we can use the `warnings` module, instead. For example, after running `from warnings import filterwarnings`, we can run the following to ignore warnings of future deprecations: `filterwarnings('ignore', category=DeprecationWarning)`

Now that we have our logistic regression model trained, let's check on the performance:

```
>>> fig, axes = plt.subplots(1, 3, figsize=(20, 5))
>>> roc(lr_grid.predict_proba(X_test)[:,1], ax=axes[0])
>>> conf_matrix(lr_preds, ax=axes[1])
>>> pr_curve(lr_grid.predict_proba(X_test)[:,1], ax=axes[2])
>>> plt.suptitle('Logistic Regression Classifier')
```

This model has no false positives and is much better than the baselines. The ROC curve is significantly closer to the top-left corner, as is the precision-recall curve to the top-right corner. Notice that the ROC curve is a bit more optimistic of the performance:

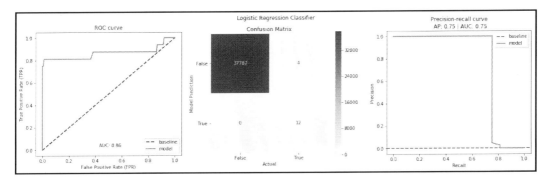

This model meets the requirements of the SOC. Our recall is at least 75% and our precision is at least 95%:

```
>>> print(report(lr_preds))
              precision   recall  f1-score   support

      False      1.00       1.00     1.00       37787
       True      1.00       0.75     0.86          16

  micro avg      1.00       1.00     1.00       37803
  macro avg      1.00       0.88     0.93       37803
weighted avg     1.00       1.00     1.00       37803
```

The SOC has given us data for January and February 2019, and they want us to update our model. Unfortunately, our model has already been trained, so we have the choice of rebuilding from scratch or ignoring this new data. Ideally, we would build a model with a feedback loop to incorporate this (and future) new data. In the next section, we will discuss how to do this.

Online learning

There are some big issues with the models we have built so far. Unlike the data we worked with in Chapter 9, *Getting Started with Machine Learning in Python*, and Chapter 10, *Making Better Predictions – Optimizing Models*, we wouldn't expect the hacker behavior to be static over time. There is also a limit to how much data we can hold in memory, which limits how much data we can train our model on. Therefore, we will now build an online learning model to flag anomalies in usernames with failures per minute. An **online learning** model is constantly getting updated (in near real time via streaming, or in batches). This allows us to learn from new data as it comes and then get rid of it (to keep space in memory).

In addition, the model can evolve over time and adapt to changes in the underlying distribution of the data. We will also be providing our model feedback as it learns, so that we are able to make sure it stays robust to changes in the hacker behavior over time. This is called **active learning**. Not all models in scikit-learn support this kind of behavior; so we are limited to the models that offer a partial_fit() method (models without this need to be trained from scratch with new data).

Scikit-learn refers to models implementing the partial_fit() method as **incremental learners**. More information, including which models support this, can be found at https://scikit-learn.org/0. 17/modules/scaling_strategies.html#incremental-learning.

Our data is currently being rolled up to the minute and then passed to the model, so this will be batch learning, not streaming; however, note that if we were to put this into production, we could update our model each minute, if desired.

Creating the PartialFitPipeline subclass

We saw in Chapter 9, *Getting Started with Machine Learning in Python*, that the Pipeline class made streamlining our machine learning processes a cinch, but unfortunately, we can't use it with the partial_fit() method. To get around this, we can create our own PartialFitPipeline class, which is a subclass of the Pipeline class, but supports calling partial_fit(). The PartialFitPipeline class is in the ml_utils.partial_fit_pipeline module.

We simply inherit from sklearn.pipeline.Pipeline and define a single new method—partial_fit()—that will call fit_transform() on all the steps except the last one, and partial_fit() on the last step:

```
from sklearn.pipeline import Pipeline

class PartialFitPipeline(Pipeline):
    """
    Subclass of sklearn.pipeline.Pipeline that supports the
    `partial_fit()` method.
    """

    def partial_fit(self, X, y):
        """
        Run `partial_fit()` for online learning estimators
        when used in a pipeline.
        """
        # for all but last step
        for _, step in self.steps[:-1]: # tuples of (name, object)
            X = step.fit_transform(X)

        # grab object from tuple position 1 for partial_fit()
        self.steps[-1][1].partial_fit(X, y)

        return self
```

Stochastic gradient descent classifier

Now that we have the `PartialFitPipeline` class, the last piece that remains is to select a model capable of online learning. Our logistic regression model performed well—it met the requirements for recall and precision. However, the `LogisticRegression` class does not support online learning because the method it uses to calculate the coefficients is a closed-form solution. We have the option of using an optimization algorithm, such as gradient descent, to determine the coefficients instead; this will be capable of online learning.

Rather than use a different incremental learner, we can train a new logistic regression model with the `SGDClassifier` class. It uses **stochastic gradient descent (SGD)** to optimize the loss function of our choice. For this example, we will be using log loss, which gives us a logistic regression where the coefficients are found using SGD.

Whereas standard gradient descent optimization looks at all the samples or batches to estimate the gradient, SGD reduces computational cost by selecting samples at random (stochastically). How much the model learns from each sample is determined by the **learning rate**, with earlier updates having more effect than later ones. A single iteration of SGD is carried out as follows:

1. Shuffle the training data
2. For each sample in the training data, estimate the gradient and update the model with decreasing strength as determined by the learning rate
3. Repeat *step 2* until all samples have been used

In machine learning, we use **epochs** to refer to the number of times the full training set is used. The process of SGD we just outlined is for a single epoch. When we train for multiple epochs, we repeat the preceding steps for the desired number of epochs, continuing each time from where we left off.

Now that we understand how SGD works, let's get an overview of the process we will follow to build our model for showcasing to the SOC:

Building our initial model

Let's build our online learning model in the `5-online_learning.ipynb` notebook.
First, we will use the `get_X_y()` function to get our `X` and `y` training data using the
full year of 2018:

```
>>> X_2018, y_2018 = get_X_y(logs_2018, '2018', hackers_2018)
```

Since we will be updating this model in batches, our test set will always be the data
we are using for our current predictions. After we do so, it will become the training
set and be used to update the model. Let's build our initial model trained on the 2018
labeled data:

```
>>> from sklearn.linear_model import SGDClassifier
>>> from sklearn.preprocessing import StandardScaler
>>> from ml_utils.partial_fit_pipeline import PartialFitPipeline

>>> model = PartialFitPipeline([
...     ('scale', StandardScaler()),
...     ('sgd', SGDClassifier(
...         random_state=0, max_iter=1000, tol=1e-3, loss='log'
...         average=1000, learning_rate='adaptive', eta0=0.01
...     )
... ]).fit(X_2018, y_2018)
```

The `PartialFitPipeline` object is created in the same way we create a `Pipeline`.
First, we standardize our data, and then we use the `SGDClassifier`. We start
building our model using the `fit()` method so that we have a good starting point for
our updates with `partial_fit()` later. The `max_iter` parameter defines the
number of epochs for the training. The `tol` parameter (tolerance) specifies when to
stop iterating, which occurs when the loss from the current iteration is greater than
the previous loss minus the tolerance (or we have reached `max_iter` iterations). We
are using the value that will be set as the default for future versions of `scikit-
learn`. We specified `loss='log'` to use logistic regression; however, there are many
other options for the loss functions, including the default value of `'hinge'` for a
linear SVM.

Here, we also passed in a value for the `average` parameter, telling the
`SGDClassifier` to store the coefficients as averages of the results once 1,000 samples
have been seen; note that this parameter is optional and, by default, this won't be
calculated. Examining these coefficients can be achieved as follows:

```
>>> [(col, coef) for col, coef in zip(
...     X_2018.columns, model.named_steps['sgd'].coef_[0]
... )]
```

```
[('usernames_with_failures', 1.5344651587934435),
 ('day_of_week_0', 0.06164314245322163),
 ...,
 ('hour_23', -0.0425106195612339)]
```

Lastly, we passed in `eta0=0.01` for our starting learning rate and specified to only adjust the learning rate when we have failed to improve our loss by the tolerance defined for a given number of consecutive epochs (`learning_rate='adaptive'`). This number of epochs is defined by the `n_iter_no_change` parameter, which will be 5 (the default), since we aren't setting it explicitly.

Evaluating the model

Since we now have labeled data for January and February 2019, we can evaluate how the model performs each month. First, we read in the 2019 data from the database:

```
>>> with sqlite3.connect('logs/logs.db') as conn:
...     logs_2019 = pd.read_sql(
...         """
...         SELECT *
...         FROM logs
...         WHERE datetime BETWEEN "2019-01-01" AND "2020-01-01";
...         """, conn, parse_dates=['datetime'], index_col='datetime'
...     )
>>>     hackers_2019 = pd.read_sql(
...         """
...         SELECT *
...         FROM attacks
...         WHERE start BETWEEN "2019-01-01" AND "2020-01-01";
...         """, conn, parse_dates=['start', 'end']
...     ).assign(
...         start_floor=lambda x: x.start.dt.floor('min'),
...         end_ceil=lambda x: x.end.dt.ceil('min')
...     )
```

Next, we isolate the January 2019 data:

```
>>> X_jan, y_jan = get_X_y(logs_2019, '2019-01', hackers_2019)
```

The classification report indicates this model performs pretty well, but our recall for the positive class is lower than our target:

```
>>> from sklearn.metrics import classification_report
>>> print(classification_report(y_jan, model.predict(X_jan)))
              precision    recall  f1-score   support

       False       1.00      1.00      1.00     42549
        True       1.00      0.70      0.82        30

   micro avg       1.00      1.00      1.00     42579
   macro avg       1.00      0.85      0.91     42579
weighted avg       1.00      1.00      1.00     42579
```

Remember, our stakeholders have specified we must achieve a recall (TPR) of at least 75% and a precision of at least 95%. Let's write a function that will show us the ROC curve, confusion matrix, precision-recall curve, and indicate the region we need to be in:

```
>>> from ml_utils.classification import (
...     confusion_matrix_visual, plot_pr_curve, plot_roc
... )

>>> def plot_performance(model, X, y, threshold=None, title=None,
...                      show_target=True):
...     """
...     Plot the ROC, confusion matrix, and precision-recall curve.
...
...     Parameters:
...         - model: The model object to use for prediction.
...         - X: The training set features to pass in for prediction.
...         - y: The actuals to evaluate the prediction.
...         - threshold: Value to use as when predicting
...                      probabilities.
...         - title: A title for the subplots.
...         - show_target: Whether to show the target regions.
...
...     Returns: Matplotlib Axes.
...     """
...     fig, axes = plt.subplots(1, 3, figsize=(20, 5))
...
...     # plot each visualization
...     plot_roc(y, model.predict_proba(X)[:,1], ax=axes[0])
...     confusion_matrix_visual(
...         y, model.predict_proba(X)[:,1] >= (threshold or 0.5),
...         class_labels=[False, True], ax=axes[1]
...     )
...     plot_pr_curve(y, model.predict_proba(X)[:,1], ax=axes[2])
```

```
...        if show_target: # show the target regions, if desired
...            axes[0].axvspan(0, 0.05, color='palegreen', alpha=0.5)
...            axes[0].axhspan(0.75, 1, color='paleturquoise', alpha=0.5)
...            axes[0].annotate(
...                'region with acceptable FPR and TPR', xy=(0.05, 0.75),
...                xytext=(0.07, 0.69), arrowprops=dict(arrowstyle='->')
...            )
...
...            axes[2].axvspan(0.75, 1, color='palegreen', alpha=0.5)
...            axes[2].axhspan(0.95, 1, color='paleturquoise', alpha=0.5)
...            axes[2].annotate(
...                'region with acceptable\nprecision and recall',
...                xy=(0.75, 0.95), xytext=(0.3, 0.6),
...                arrowprops=dict(arrowstyle='->')
...            )
...
...        if title: # show the title if specified
...            plt.suptitle(title)
...
...        return axes
```

Now, let's call the function to see how we are doing:

```
>>> axes = plot_performance(
...     model, X_jan, y_jan,
...     title='Stochastic Gradient Descent Classifier '\
...         '(Tested on January 2019 Data)'
... )
>>> axes[0].annotate(
...     'current performance\n- FPR = 0%\n- TPR = 70%',
...     xy=(0, .7), xytext=(0.05, 0.5),
...     arrowprops=dict(arrowstyle='->')
... )
>>> axes[2].annotate(
...     'current performance\n- precision = 100%\n- recall = 70%',
...     xy=(.7, 1), xytext=(0.3, 0.8),
...     arrowprops=dict(arrowstyle='->')
... )
```

Notice we are not currently meeting the specifications of our stakeholders; our performance is not in the target region:

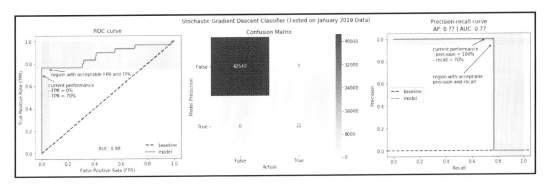

Our resulting recall (TPR) is 70%, which doesn't meet the goal of 75% or better. By default, when we use the `predict()` method, our probability threshold is 50%. If we are targeting a specific precision/recall or TPR/FPR region, we may have to change the threshold and use `predict_proba()` to get the desired performance.

The `ml_utils.classification` module contains the `find_threshold_roc()` and `find_threshold_pr()` functions, which will help us pick a threshold along the ROC curve or precision-recall curve, respectively. Since we are targeting a specific precision/recall region, we will use the latter. This function uses the `precision_recall_curve()` function from `scikit-learn` also, but instead of plotting the resulting precision and recall data, we use it to select the thresholds that meet our criteria:

```
from sklearn.metrics import precision_recall_curve

def find_threshold_pr(y_test, y_preds, *, min_precision, min_recall):
    """
    Find the threshold to use with `predict_proba()` for
    classification based on the minimum acceptable precision
    and the minimum acceptable recall.

    Parameters:
        - y_test: The actual labels.
        - y_preds: The predicted labels.
        - min_precision: The minimum acceptable precision.
        - min_recall: The minimum acceptable recall.
    Returns:
        The thresholds that produce a classification meeting the
        criteria.
    """
```

```
precision, recall, thresholds = precision_recall_curve(
    y_test, y_preds
)
# precision and recall have one extra value at the end for
# plotting this needs to be removed to make a mask
# with the thresholds
return thresholds[
    (precision[:-1] >= min_precision) &
    (recall[:-1] >= min_recall)
]
```

 The notebook also shows an example of finding a threshold for a TPR/FPR goal. Our current target precision/recall happens to give the same threshold as targeting a TPR (recall) of at least 75% and a FPR of at most 5%.

Let's use this function to find a threshold that meets our stakeholders' specifications. We take the max of the probabilities that fall in the desired region to pick the least sensitive of the candidate thresholds:

```
>>> from ml_utils.classification import find_threshold_pr

>>> threshold = find_threshold_pr(
...     y_jan, model.predict_proba(X_jan)[:,1],
...     min_precision=0.95, min_recall=0.75
... ).max()
>>> threshold
0.011191747078992526
```

This result tells us we can reach the desired precision and recall if we flag results that have 1.12% chance of being in the positive class. No doubt this seems like a very low probability, or that the model isn't sure of itself, but we can think about it this way: if the model thinks there is even a slight chance that the login activity is suspicious, we want to know.

Let's see how our performance looks, using this threshold. First, we grab the TPR, FPR, precision, and recall at this threshold:

```
>>> from sklearn.metrics import precision_recall_curve, roc_curve

>>> fpr, tpr, thresholds = roc_curve(
...     y_jan, model.predict_proba(X_jan)[:,1]
... )
>>> mask = thresholds == threshold
>>> fpr_at_threshold, tpr_at_threshold = fpr[mask], tpr[mask]

>>> precision, recall, thresholds = precision_recall_curve(
...     y_jan, model.predict_proba(X_jan)[:,1]
... )
>>> mask = thresholds == threshold
# precision and recall have one extra value added at the end for
# plotting, so we have to remove to use the mask
>>> p_at_threshold, r_at_threshold = \
...     precision[:-1][mask], recall[:-1][mask]
```

Then, we create a ROC curve and precision-recall curve, indicating where we are on each and the confusion matrix for that threshold:

```
>>> axes = plot_performance(
...     model, X_jan, y_jan, threshold=threshold,
...     title='Stochastic Gradient Descent Classifier '\
...         '(Tested on January 2019 Data)'
... )

>>> axes[0].annotate(
...     f'chosen threshold = {threshold:.2%}\n'
...     f'- FPR={fpr_at_threshold[0]:.2%}\n'
...     f'- TPR={tpr_at_threshold[0]:.2%}',
...     xy=(fpr_at_threshold, tpr_at_threshold), xytext=(0.05, 0.42),
...     arrowprops=dict(arrowstyle='->')
... )

>>> axes[2].annotate(
...     f'chosen threshold = {threshold:.2%}\n'
...     f'- precision={p_at_threshold[0]:.2%}\n'
...     f'- recall={r_at_threshold[0]:.2%}',
...     xy=(r_at_threshold, p_at_threshold), xytext=(0.1, 0.75),
...     arrowprops=dict(arrowstyle='->')
... )
```

This threshold gives us a recall of 76.67%, satisfying our stakeholders. Our precision is in the acceptable range, as well:

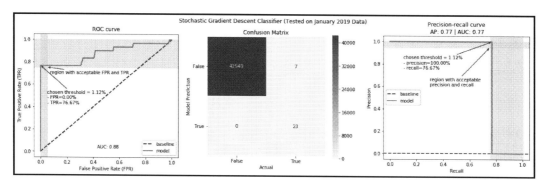

Using the custom threshold, we have correctly identified another two cases, reducing our false negatives, which are very costly for the SOC. Here, this improvement didn't come at the cost of additional false positives, but, remember, there is often a trade-off between reducing false negatives (**type II error**) and reducing false positives (**type I error**). In some cases, we have very low tolerance for type I errors (the FPR must be very small), whereas in others, we are more concerned with finding all the positive cases (the TPR must be high). In information security, we have a low tolerance for false negatives because they are very costly; therefore, we will move forward with the custom threshold.

 Sometimes, requirements of a model's performance aren't feasible. It's important to maintain an open line of communication with stakeholders to explain the issues and discuss relaxing criteria when necessary.

Updating the model

Continuous updating will help the model adapt to changes in hacker behavior over time. Now that we have evaluated our January predictions, we can use them to update the model. To do so, we use the `partial_fit()` method and the labeled data for January, which will run a single epoch on the January data:

```
>>> model.partial_fit(X_jan, y_jan)
```

Our model has now been updated, so we can test its performance on the February data now. Let's grab the February data, first:

```
>>> X_feb, y_feb = get_X_y(logs_2019, '2019-02', hackers_2019)
```

February had fewer attacks, but we caught a higher percentage of them (79%):

```
>>> from sklearn.metrics import classification_report
>>> print(classification_report(
...       y_feb, model.predict_proba(X_feb)[:,1] >= threshold
... ))
              precision    recall  f1-score   support

       False       1.00      1.00      1.00     39373
        True       1.00      0.79      0.88        28

   micro avg       1.00      1.00      1.00     39401
   macro avg       1.00      0.89      0.94     39401
weighted avg       1.00      1.00      1.00     39401
```

Let's look at the performance plots for February to see how they changed:

```
>>> plot_performance(
...       model, X_feb, y_feb, threshold=threshold,
...       title='Stochastic Gradient Descent Classifier '\
...             '(Tested on February 2019 Data)'
... )
```

Notice the area under both curves has increased and more of each curve is in the target region:

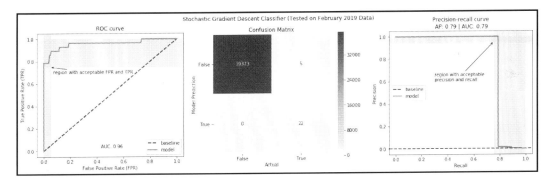

Presenting our results

The SOC has finished up the March data. They want us to implement into our model the feedback they gave on our February predictions, and then make predictions for the March data for them to review. They will be evaluating our performance on each minute in March, using the classification report, ROC curve, confusion matrix, and precision-recall curve. It's time to put our model to the test.

First, we need to update our model for the February data:

```
>>> model.partial_fit(X_feb, y_feb)
```

Next, we grab the March data and make our predictions, using the threshold of 1.12%:

```
>>> X_march, y_march = get_X_y(logs_2019, '2019-03', hackers_2019)
>>> march_2019_preds = model.predict_proba(X_march)[:,1] >= threshold
```

Our classification report looks good. We have a recall of 77%, perfect precision, and a solid F_1 score:

```
>>> from sklearn.metrics import classification_report
>>> print(classification_report(y_march, march_2019_preds))
              precision    recall  f1-score   support

       False       1.00      1.00      1.00     41494
        True       1.00      0.77      0.87        30

   micro avg       1.00      1.00      1.00     41524
   macro avg       1.00      0.88      0.93     41524
weighted avg       1.00      1.00      1.00     41524
```

Now, let's see how the plots look:

```
>>> axes = plot_performance(
...     model, X_march, y_march, threshold=threshold,
...     title='Stochastic Gradient Descent Classifier '\
...         '(Tested on March 2019 Data)'
... )

>>> axes[0].annotate(
...     'current performance\n- FPR=0%\n- TPR=77%',
...     xy=(0, 23/30), xytext=(0.05, 0.45),
...     arrowprops=dict(arrowstyle='->')
... )

>>> axes[2].annotate(
...     'current performance\n- precision=100%\n- recall=77%',
...     xy=(23/30, 1), xytext=(0.2, 0.75),
...     arrowprops=dict(arrowstyle='->')
... )
```

Our AUC for the precision-recall curve is slightly higher now, while it dropped for the ROC curve:

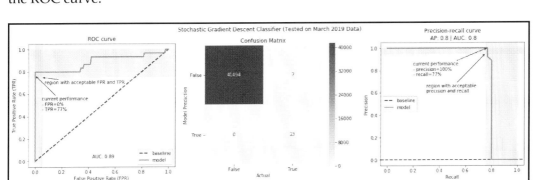

Further improvements

They are happy with our results, and now want us to provide them with predictions each minute. They have also promised to provide feedback within an hour. We won't implement this request here, but we will briefly discuss how we could go about this.

We have been using batch processing to update the model each month; however, in order to provide our stakeholders with what they want, we will need to shorten our feedback loop by performing the following actions:

- Running `predict()` on our model every single minute and having the predictions sent to our stakeholders. This will require setting up a process to pass the logs one minute at a time to a preprocessing function, and then to the model itself.
- Delivering the results to our stakeholders via an agreed upon medium.
- Updating the model with `partial_fit()` every hour using the feedback we receive from the stakeholders (once we have determined how to have them share this information with us).

Summary

In practice, this isn't easy. Real-life hackers are much more savvy than the ones in this simulation. Attacks are also much less frequent, creating a huge class imbalance. Building machine learning models that will catch everything just isn't possible. That is why it is so vital we work with those who have subject area knowledge; they can help us squeeze some extra performance out of our models by really understanding the data and its peculiarities. No matter how experienced we become with machine learning, we should never turn down help from someone who often works with the data in question.

Our initial attempts at anomaly detection were unsupervised while we waited for the labeled data from our subject matter experts. We tried LOF and isolation forest using `scikit-learn`. Once we received the labeled data, we determined that LOF was better for our data.

However, we didn't stop there. Since we had just been given the labeled data, we tried our hand at supervised methods. We learned how to build baseline models using dummy classifiers and Naive Bayes. Then, we revisited logistic regression to see whether it could help us. Our logistic regression model performed well; however, since it used a closed-form solution to find the coefficients, we were unable to incorporate a feedback loop without retraining the model from scratch.

This limitation led us to build an online learning model, which is constantly updated. First, we had to make a subclass to allow pipelines to use the `partial_fit()` method. Then, we tried SGD classification with log loss. We were able to train on an entire year of data at once, and then update our model when we received new labeled data. This was the best performer and allows the model to adjust to changes in the distributions of the features over time. Our stakeholders were very pleased with this model. Now, all that remains is for us to put the model into production and determine the update and prediction frequencies everyone will be accountable for meeting.

Exercises

Complete the following exercises for some practice with the machine learning workflow and exposure to some additional anomaly detection strategies:

1. A one-class SVM is another model that can be used for unsupervised outlier detection. Build a one-class SVM model with the default parameters, using a pipeline with the `StandardScaler` and the `OneClassSVM`. Train the model on January 2018 data, just as we did for the isolation forest. Make predictions on that same data. Count the number of inliers and outliers this model identifies.

2. Using the 2018 minutely data, build a k-means model with two clusters after standardizing the data with the `StandardScaler`. With the labeled data in the `attacks` table in the SQLite database (`logs/logs.db`), see whether this model gets a good Fowlkes-Mallows score (use the `fowlkes_mallows_score()` function in `sklearn.metrics`).

3. Evaluate the performance of a random forest classifier for supervised anomaly detection. Set `n_estimators` to 100 and use the remaining defaults, including the prediction threshold. Train on January 2018 and test on February 2018.

4. The `partial_fit()` method isn't available with the `GridSearchCV` object. Instead, we can use its `fit()` method with a model that has a `partial_fit()` method (or the `PartialFitPipeline`) to find the best hyperparameters in our search space. Then, we can grab the `best_estimator_` from the grid search and use `partial_fit()` on it. Try this with the `PassiveAggressiveClassifier` from the `sklearn.linear_model` module and the `PartialFitPipeline`. This online learning classifier is passive when it makes a correct prediction, but aggressive in correcting itself when it makes an incorrect prediction. Don't worry about selecting a custom threshold. Be sure to follow these steps:

   1. Run a grid search using the January 2018 data for the initial training.
   2. Grab the tuned model with the `best_estimator_` attribute.
   3. Evaluate the best estimator with the February 2018 data.
   4. Make updates with the February 2018 data.
   5. Evaluate the final model on March through June 2018 data.

Further reading

Check out the following resources for more information on the topics covered in this chapter:

- *Deploying scikit-learn Models at Scale*: https://towardsdatascience.com/deploying-scikit-learn-models-at-scale-f632f86477b8
- *Local Outlier Factor for Anomaly Detection*: https://towardsdatascience.com/local-outlier-factor-for-anomaly-detection-cc0c770d2ebe
- *Model Persistence (from the scikit-learn user guide)*: https://scikit-learn.org/stable/modules/model_persistence.html
- *Novelty and Outlier Detection (from the scikit-learn user guide)*: https://scikit-learn.org/stable/modules/outlier_detection.html
- *Naive Bayes (from the scikit-learn user guide)*: https://scikit-learn.org/stable/modules/naive_bayes.html
- *Outlier Detection with Isolation Forest*: https://towardsdatascience.com/outlier-detection-with-isolation-forest-3d190448d45e
- *Passive Aggressive Algorithm (video explanation)*: https://www.youtube.com/watch?v=uxGDwyPWNkU
- *Python Context Managers and the "with" Statement*: https://medium.com/@ramojol/python-context-managers-and-the-with-statement-8f53d4d9f87
- *Seeing Theory - Chapter 5 Bayesian Inference*: https://seeing-theory.brown.edu/index.html#secondPage/chapter5
- *SQLAlchemy — Python Tutorial*: https://towardsdatascience.com/sqlalchemy-python-tutorial-79a577141a91
- *Stochastic Gradient Descent (from the scikit-learn user guide)*: https://scikit-learn.org/stable/modules/sgd.html
- *Strategies to scale computationally: bigger data (from the scikit-learn user guide)*: https://scikit-learn.org/0.17/modules/scaling_strategies.html#incremental-learning
- *Unfair Coin Bayesian Simulation*: https://github.com/xofbd/unfair-coin-bayes

Section 5: Additional Resources 5

In this concluding section, we will recap everything we have covered in the book and provide you with some additional books, web resources, and documentation that you can use to dive further into various data science topics and practice your skills.

The following chapter comprises this section:

- Chapter 12, *The Road Ahead*

12
The Road Ahead

Throughout this book, we have covered a lot of material, and you are now capable of performing data analysis and machine learning tasks entirely in Python. We began our journey by learning about some introductory statistics and how to set up our environment for data science in Python. Then, we learned about the basics of using `pandas` and how to bring data into Python. With this knowledge, we were able to work with APIs, read from files, and query databases to grab data for our analyses.

After we collected our data, we learned how to perform data wrangling in order to clean up our data and get it into a usable format. Next, we learned how to work with time series and combine data from different sources, as well as aggregate it. Once we had a good handle on data wrangling, we moved on to visualizations and used `pandas`, `matplotlib`, and `seaborn` to create a variety of plot types, and also learned how to customize them.

Armed with this knowledge, we were able to tackle some real-world analyses by looking at the financial data for bitcoin and the **Facebook, Apple, Amazon, Netflix, and Google (FAANG)** stocks, and trying to detect hackers attempting to authenticate to a web application. In addition, we learned how to build our own Python packages, write our own classes, and simulate data.

Finally, we got an introduction to machine learning using `scikit-learn`. We discussed how to build model pipelines, taking us from preprocessing the data through model fitting. Afterwards we discussed how we can evaluate the performance of our models and how we can try to improve their performance. Our discussion of machine learning culminated in using machine learning models to detect hackers attempting to gain access to a web application through a brute-force attack.

Now that you have obtained all this knowledge, it is important to nurture it so that you retain it. This means that you must practice every chance you get. This chapter provides the following resources for continuing your data science journey:

- Resources for finding data on a variety of topics
- Websites and services to practice working with data
- Coding challenges and educational content to improve your Python skills

Data resources

As with any skill, to get better we need to practice, which, for us, means we need to find data to practice on. There is no best dataset to practice with; rather, each person should find data they are interested in exploring. While this section is by no means comprehensive, it contains resources for data from various topics in the hopes that everyone can find something they want to use.

Unsure of what kind of data to look for? What are some of the things you have wondered about, relating to a topic you find interesting? Has data been collected on this topic, and can you access it? Let your curiosity guide you!

Python packages

Both `seaborn` and `scikit-learn` provide built-in sample datasets that you can experiment with in order to get more practice with the material we've covered in the book and to try out new techniques. These datasets are often very clean, and thus easy to work with. Once you're comfortable with the techniques, you can move on to finding data using the other resources that are mentioned in the following sections, which will be more representative of real-world data.

Seaborn

Seaborn provides the `load_dataset()` function, which reads the data from a CSV file in a small GitHub repository for `seaborn` data. These datasets are the ones that are used in the `seaborn` documentation, so it is important to keep in mind that they may change. The data can be obtained from the repository directly at `https://github.com/mwaskom/seaborn-data`.

Scikit-learn

Scikit-learn includes a `datasets` module, which can be used to generate random datasets to test algorithms or to import certain datasets that are popular in the machine learning community. Be sure to check out the documentation for more information:

- **Generating random datasets for machine learning tasks**: `https://scikit-learn.org/stable/modules/classes.html#samples-generator`
- **Loading supported datasets**: `https://scikit-learn.org/stable/modules/classes.html#loaders`

There is also the `fetch_openml()` function in the `sklearn.datasets` module that will fetch datasets by name from OpenML (`https://www.openml.org/`), which contains many free datasets for machine learning.

Searching for data

The following are a few places you can use to search for data on a variety of topics:

- **DataHub**: `https://datahub.io/search`
- **Google Dataset Search**: `https://toolbox.google.com/datasetsearch`
- **Open Data on Amazon Web Services**: `https://registry.opendata.aws/`
- **OpenML**: `https://www.openml.org`
- **SNAP library of datasets collected by Stanford University**: `https://snap.stanford.edu/data/index.html`
- **UCI Machine Learning Repository**: `http://archive.ics.uci.edu/ml/index.php`

APIs

We saw how great working with APIs can be for gathering data; the following are some APIs for gathering data that may be of interest to you:

- **Facebook API**: `https://developers.facebook.com/docs/graph-api`
- **NOAA Climate data API**: `https://www.ncdc.noaa.gov/cdo-web/webservices/v2`
- **NYTimes API**: `https://developer.nytimes.com/`

- **OpenWeatherMapAPI**: `https://openweathermap.org/api`
- **Twitter API**: `https://developer.twitter.com/en/docs.html`
- **USGS Earthquake API**: `https://earthquake.usgs.gov/fdsnws/event/1/`

Websites

This section contains selected data resources across various topics that can be accessed through a website. Obtaining the data for an analysis may be as simple as downloading a CSV file or may require parsing HTML with `pandas`. If you must resort to scraping the page (make sure you have tried the ways we discussed in this book first), be sure that you aren't violating the terms of use of the website.

Finance

We worked with finance data several times throughout this book. If you are interested in further financial analysis, in addition to the `pandas_datareader` package we discussed in `Chapter 7`, *Financial Analysis – Bitcoin and the Stock Market*, consult the following resources:

- **Google Finance**: `https://www.google.com/finance`
- **NASDAQ historical stock prices**: `https://www.nasdaq.com/quotes/historical-quotes.aspx`
- **Quandl**: `https://www.quandl.com`
- **Yahoo! Finance**: `https://finance.yahoo.com`

Government data

Government data is often open to the public. The following resources contain data provided by some governments:

- **European Union open data**: `http://data.europa.eu/euodp/en/data`
- **NASA**: `https://data.nasa.gov/`
- **NYC data**: `https://opendata.cityofnewyork.us/data/`
- **UK government data**: `https://data.gov.uk/`
- **UN data**: `http://data.un.org/`
- **US census data**: `https://census.gov/data.html`
- **US government data**: `https://www.data.gov/`

Health and economy

Economic, medical, and social data from around the world is available at the following websites:

- **Gapminder**: `https://www.gapminder.org/data/`
- **Health Data**: `https://healthdata.gov/search/type/dataset`
- **World Health Organization**: `https://www.who.int/gho/en/`

Social networks

For those interested in text-based data or graph data, check out the following resources on social networks:

- **List of Twitter data resources**: `https://github.com/shaypal5/awesome-twitter-data`
- **Social network data**: `https://snap.stanford.edu/data/ego-Facebook.html`

Sports

For the sports-lover, check out the following websites, which provide databases and web pages for statistics on all your favorite players:

- **Baseball database (practice working with a DB)**: `http://www.seanlahman.com/baseball-archive/statistics/`
- **Baseball player statistics**: `https://www.baseball-reference.com/players/`
- **Basketball player statistics**: `https://www.basketball-reference.com/players/`
- **Football (American) player statistics**: `https://www.pro-football-reference.com/players/`
- **Football (soccer) statistics**: `https://www.whoscored.com/Statistics`
- **Hockey player statistics**: `https://www.hockey-reference.com/players/`

Miscellaneous

The following resources vary in topic, but be sure to check these out if nothing has piqued your interest so far:

- **Amazon reviews data**: https://snap.stanford.edu/data/web-Amazon.html
- **Data extracted from Wikipedia**: https://wiki.dbpedia.org/develop/datasets
- **Google Trends**: https://trends.google.com/trends/
- **Movies from MovieLens**: https://grouplens.org/datasets/movielens/
- **Yahoo Webscope (reference library of datasets)**: https://webscope.sandbox.yahoo.com/

Practicing working with data

Throughout this book, we have worked with various datasets from different sources with guided instructions. It doesn't have to stop here, though. This section is dedicated to some resources that can be used to continue with guided instruction and, eventually, work toward building a model for a predefined problem.

DataCamp (https://www.datacamp.com/), while not entirely free, provides various data science courses in Python. They include instructional videos and fill-in-the-blank coding practice problems so that you can build up your understanding of the topics.

Kaggle (https://www.kaggle.com/) offers content for learning data science, datasets for exploration that are shared by members of the community, and competitions that have been posted by companies—perhaps the Netflix recommendation contest sounds familiar (https://www.kaggle.com/netflix-inc/netflix-prize-data)? These contests are a great way for you to practice your machine learning skills and to become more visible in the community (especially for potential employers).

 Kaggle isn't the only place you can participate in data science competitions. Some additional ones are listed at https://towardsdatascience.com/top-competitive-data-science-platforms-other-than-kaggle-2995e9dad93c.

Python practice

We have seen, throughout this book, that working with data in Python isn't just `pandas`, `matplotlib`, and `numpy`; there are many ways our workflow can benefit from us being strong Python programmers in general. With strong Python skills, we can build web applications with Flask, make requests of an API, efficiently iterate over combinations or permutations, and find ways to speed up our code. While this book didn't focus on honing these skills directly, here are some free resources for practicing with Python and thinking like a programmer:

- **HackerRank**: `https://www.hackerrank.com`
- **CodeWars**: `https://www.codewars.com`
- **LeetCode**: `https://www.leetcode.com`
- **CodinGame**: `https://www.codingame.com`

While not free, **Python Morsels** (`https://www.pythonmorsels.com/`) provides weekly Python exercises that will help you learn to write more Pythonic code and get more familiar with the Python standard library. Exercises vary in difficulty, but can be set to a higher or lower difficulty as needed.

Another great resource is **Pramp** (`https://www.pramp.com`), which lets you practice for a programming interview with a peer. Your peer will interview you with a random question and evaluate how you approach the interview, your code, and how well you explain yourself. After 30 minutes, it's your turn to interview your peer. The peers are randomly assigned.

Khan Academy (`https://www.khanacademy.org/`) can be a great resource for learning more about a subject. If you want a primer on computer science algorithms, or some of the mathematics behind machine learning algorithms (such as linear algebra and calculus), then this is a great place to start.

Lastly, **LinkedIn Learning** (`https://www.linkedin.com/learning/`) has many video courses on a wide range of topics, including Python, data science, and machine learning. New users get a free month-long trial. Consider taking the *Learning the Python 3 Standard Library* course (`https://www.linkedin.com/learning/learning-the-python-3-standard-library`) to level up your Python skills; as we saw throughout this book, a solid command of the standard library helps us write more concise and efficient code.

Summary

This chapter provided many places where you can find datasets across myriad topics. In addition, you also learned about various websites where you can take courses and tutorials, practice machine learning, and improve your Python skills.

It's important to keep your skills sharp and stay curious, so, for whatever interests you, look for data and perform your own analyses. These are things you can put on your GitHub account as your data portfolio.

Thank you for reading this book! I hope you got just as much out of it as these two data analyzing pandas.

Exercises

The exercises in this chapter are open-ended—no solutions are provided. They are meant to give you some ideas so that you can get started on your own:

1. Practice machine learning classification by participating in the Titanic challenge on Kaggle at `https://www.kaggle.com/c/titanic`.

2. Practice machine learning regression techniques by participating in the housing prices challenge on Kaggle at `https://www.kaggle.com/c/house-prices-advanced-regression-techniques`.

3. Perform an analysis on something that interests you. Some interesting ideas include:

    - *Predicting likes on Instagram*: `https://towardsdatascience.com/predict-the-number-of-likes-on-instagram-a7ec5c020203`

    - *Analyzing delays of NJ transit trains*: `https://medium.com/@pranavbadami/how-data-can-help-fix-nj-transit-c0d15c0660fe`

    - *Using visualizations to solve data science problems*: `https://towardsdatascience.com/solving-a-data-science-challenge-the-visual-way-355cfabcb1c5`

4. Complete five challenges across any one of the sites in the *Python practice* section of this chapter. For example, you can try the following challenges:

    - *Finding two numbers that add to a specific sum exactly*: `https://leetcode.com/problems/two-sum/`

    - *Validating credit card numbers*: `https://www.hackerrank.com/challenges/validating-credit-card-number/problem`

Further reading

You can consult the following blogs and articles to stay up to date with Python and data science:

- *Armin Ronacher's Blog (Author of Flask)*: `http://lucumr.pocoo.org/`
- *Data Science Central*: `http://www.datasciencecentral.com/`
- *Data Science Topic on Medium*: `https://medium.com/topic/data-science`
- *Kaggle Blog*: `http://blog.kaggle.com/`
- *KD Nuggets*: `http://www.kdnuggets.com/websites/blogs.html`

- *Machine Learning Topic on Medium*: `https://medium.com/topic/machine-learning`
- *Planet Python*: `https://planetpython.org/`
- *Programming Topic on Medium*: `https://medium.com/topic/programming`
- *Python Tips*: `http://book.pythontips.com/en/latest/index.html`
- *Python 3 Module of the Week*: `https://pymotw.com/3/`
- *Towards Data Science*: `https://towardsdatascience.com/`
- *Trey Hunner's Blog (Creator of Python Morsels)*: `https://treyhunner.com/blog/archives/`

The following resources contain information for learning how to build custom `scikit-learn` classes:

- *Building Scikit-Learn Compatible Transformers*: `https://dreisbach.us/articles/building-scikit-learn-compatible-transformers/`
- *Creating your own estimator in scikit-learn*: `http://danielhnyk.cz/creating-your-own-estimator-scikit-learn/`
- *Scikit-Learn BaseEstimator*: `https://scikit-learn.org/stable/modules/generated/sklearn.base.BaseEstimator.html`
- *Scikit-Learn Rolling Your Own Estimator*: `https://scikit-learn.org/stable/developers/contributing.html#rolling-your-own-estimator`
- *Scikit-Learn TransformerMixin*: `https://scikit-learn.org/stable/modules/generated/sklearn.base.TransformerMixin.html#sklearn.base.TransformerMixin`

Cheat sheets for coding with Python's data science stack can be found here:

- *Jupyter Notebook Cheat Sheet*: `https://s3.amazonaws.com/assets.datacamp.com/blog_assets/Jupyter_Notebook_Cheat_Sheet.pdf`
- *Jupyter Notebook Keyboard Shortcuts*: `https://www.cheatography.com/weidadeyue/cheat-sheets/jupyter-notebook/pdf_bw/`
- *Matplotlib Cheat Sheet*: `https://s3.amazonaws.com/assets.datacamp.com/blog_assets/Python_Matplotlib_Cheat_Sheet.pdf`
- *Numpy Cheat Sheet*: `https://s3.amazonaws.com/assets.datacamp.com/blog_assets/Numpy_Python_Cheat_Sheet.pdf`
- *Pandas Cheat Sheet*: `http://pandas.pydata.org/Pandas_Cheat_Sheet.pdf`
- *Scikit-learn Cheat Sheet*: `https://s3.amazonaws.com/assets.datacamp.com/blog_assets/Scikit_Learn_Cheat_Sheet_Python.pdf`

Cheat sheets for machine learning algorithms, mathematics, probability, and statistics can be found here:

- *Calculus Cheat Sheet*: `https://ml-cheatsheet.readthedocs.io/en/latest/calculus.html`
- *Linear Algebra in 4 Pages*: `https://minireference.com/static/tutorials/linear_algebra_in_4_pages.pdf`
- *Probability and Statistics Cheat Sheet*: `http://web.mit.edu/~csvoss/Public/usabo/stats_handout.pdf`
- *15 Statistical Hypothesis Tests in Python (Cheat Sheet)*: `https://machinelearningmastery.com/statistical-hypothesis-tests-in-python-cheat-sheet/`

For additional resources on machine learning algorithms, linear algebra, calculus, probability, and statistics, you can refer to the following:

- *An Interactive Guide to the Fourier Transform*: `https://betterexplained.com/articles/an-interactive-guide-to-the-fourier-transform/`
- *Introduction to Probability by Joseph Blitzstein and Jessica Hwang*: `https://www.amazon.com/Introduction-Probability-Chapman-Statistical-Science/dp/1138369918`
- *An Introduction to Statistical Learning by Gareth James, Daniela Witten, Trevor Hastie and Robert Tibshirani*: `https://www-bcf.usc.edu/~gareth/ISL/`
- *Fourier Transforms (scipy)*: `https://docs.scipy.org/doc/scipy/reference/tutorial/fftpack.html`
- *Find likeliest periodicity for time series with numpy's Fourier Transform? (StackOverflow question)*: `https://stackoverflow.com/questions/44803225/find-likeliest-periodicity-for-time-series-with-numpys-fourier-transform`
- *Numerical Computing is Fun (GitHub)*: `https://github.com/eka-foundation/numerical-computing-is-fun`
- *Probabilistic Programming and Bayesian Methods for Hackers (GitHub)*: `https://github.com/CamDavidsonPilon/Probabilistic-Programming-and-Bayesian-Methods-for-Hackers`
- *Seeing Theory (A visual introduction to probability and statistics)*: `https://seeing-theory.brown.edu/index.html`
- *Think Stats: Exploratory Data Analysis in Python*: `http://greenteapress.com/thinkstats2/html/index.html`

Miscellaneous reading on Python and programming in general can be found here:

- *Defining Custom Magics (IPython):* `https://ipython.org/ipython-doc/3/config/custommagics.html`
- *Flask Tutorial (Build Web Applications in Python):* `http://flask.pocoo.org/docs/1.0/tutorial/`
- *IPython Tutorial:* `https://ipython.readthedocs.io/en/stable/interactive/`
- *Programming Best Practices:* `https://thefullstack.xyz/dry-yagni-kiss-tdd-soc-bdfu`

Relevant MOOCs and videos can be found here:

- *Advanced Optimization (Harvard):* `https://online-learning.harvard.edu/course/advanced-optimization`
- *Linear Algebra – Foundations to Frontiers (edX):* `https://www.edx.org/course/linear-algebra-foundations-to-frontiers-0`
- *Machine Learning (Coursera with Andrew Ng):* `https://www.coursera.org/learn/machine-learning`
- *Mathematics for Machine Learning (Coursera):* `https://www.coursera.org/specializations/mathematics-machine-learning`
- *Statistics 110 (Harvard) on YouTube:* `https://www.youtube.com/playlist?list=PL2SOU6wwxB0uwwH80KTQ6ht66KWxbzTIo`
- *Statistical Learning (Stanford):* `https://lagunita.stanford.edu/courses/HumanitiesSciences/StatLearning/Winter2016/about`

The following books are helpful for getting experience with many different facets of the Python language:

- *Automate the Boring Stuff with Python by Al Sweigart:* `https://automatetheboringstuff.com/`
- *Learn Python 3 the Hard Way by Zed A. Shaw:* `https://learnpythonthehardway.org/python3/preface.html`

Python machine learning books and training resources can be found here:

- *Hands-on Machine Learning with Scikit-Learn and TensorFlow Jupyter Notebooks*: `https://github.com/ageron/handson-ml`
- *Introduction to Machine Learning with Python: A Guide for Data Scientists by Andreas C. Müller and Sarah Guido*: `https://www.amazon.com/Introduction-Machine-Learning-Python-Scientists/dp/1449369413`
- *ML training repositories from scikit-learn core developer Andreas Müller (training given at conferences)*: `https://github.com/amueller?utf8=%E2%9C%93amp;tab=repositoriesamp;q=ml-trainingamp;type=amp;language=`
- *Python Machine Learning - Second Edition by Sebastian Raschka, and Vahid Mirjalili*: `https://www.packtpub.com/big-data-and-business-intelligence/python-machine-learning-second-edition`

Visualization resources can be found here:

- *How to Create Animated Graphs in Python*: `https://towardsdatascience.com/how-to-create-animated-graphs-in-python-bb619cc2dec1`
- *Interactive Data Visualization in Python with Bokeh*: `https://realpython.com/python-data-visualization-bokeh/`
- *PyViz Tutorial*: `https://pyviz.org/tutorial/index`

Solutions

Solutions for each chapter's exercises can be found at `https://github.com/stefmolin/Hands-On-Data-Analysis-with-Pandas/tree/master/solutions` in their respective folders.

Appendix

Data analysis workflow

The following diagram depicts a generalized data analysis workflow from data collection and processing through drawing conclusions and deciding next steps:

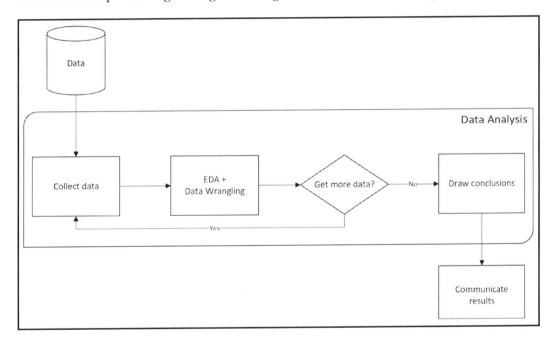

Choosing the appropriate visualization

When creating a data visualization, it is paramount that we select an appropriate plot type; the following diagram can be used to help select the proper visualization:

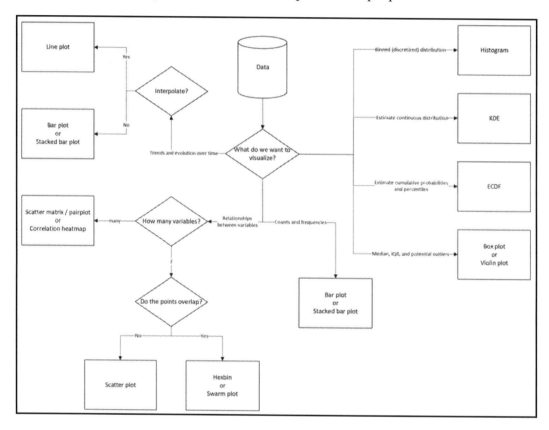

Machine learning workflow

The following diagram summarizes the workflow for building machine learning models from data collection and data analysis through training and evaluating the model:

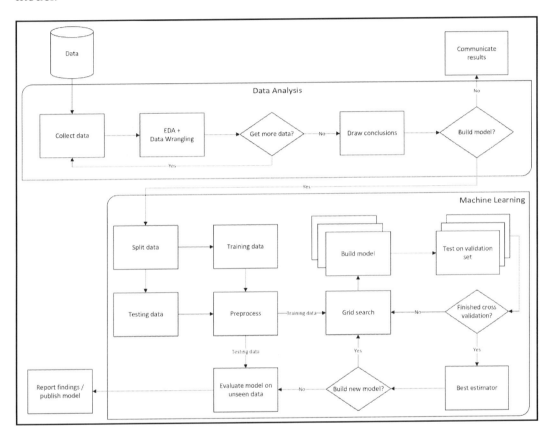

Other Books You May Enjoy

If you enjoyed this book, you may be interested in these other books by Packt:

Data Analysis with Python
David Taieb

ISBN: 9781789950069

- A new toolset that has been carefully crafted to meet for your data analysis challenges
- Full and detailed case studies of the toolset across several of today's key industry contexts
- Become super productive with a new toolset across Python and Jupyter Notebook
- Look into the future of data science and which directions to develop your skills next

Hands-On Data Analysis with NumPy and Pandas
Curtis Miller

ISBN: 9781789530797

- Understand how to install and manage Anaconda
- Read, sort, and map data using NumPy and pandas
- Find out how to create and slice data arrays using NumPy
- Discover how to subset your DataFrames using pandas
- Handle missing data in a pandas DataFrame
- Explore hierarchical indexing and plotting with pandas

Leave a review - let other readers know what you think

Please share your thoughts on this book with others by leaving a review on the site that you bought it from. If you purchased the book from Amazon, please leave us an honest review on this book's Amazon page. This is vital so that other potential readers can see and use your unbiased opinion to make purchasing decisions, we can understand what our customers think about our products, and our authors can see your feedback on the title that they have worked with Packt to create. It will only take a few minutes of your time, but is valuable to other potential customers, our authors, and Packt. Thank you!

Index

5

5-number summary 24

A

absolute path 74
abstract method 393, 401
abstraction 45
accuracy 571
active learning 670
alpha 432, 437
Anaconda installation
  references 43
anomaly detection 457, 639
Anscombe's quartet
  about 32
  reference link 33
Application Programming Interface (API)
  about 13
  data, importing into pandas DataFrame 76,
    78, 79
area under the curve (AUC) 577, 663
area under the precision-recall curve (AUPR)
  580
argparse module
  reference link 473
ARIMA 446
AssetGroupAnalyzer class 433, 435
assets
  comparing 435, 438
astronomical units (AUs) 555
attributes 55
AUROC 577
autocorrelation plot 309
average precision (AP) 581

B

baselining
  about 661
  dummy classifier 661, 663
  Naive Bayes (NB) 664, 665, 667
Bayes' theorem 664
bear market 432, 437
Bernoulli trial 29
Bessel's correction
  reference link 22
beta 416, 431, 437
bias-variance trade-off 616
binning 214
Bitcoin historical data
  from HTML 390
bootstrap plot 310
bootstrap sample 18
bootstrapping 18, 310
box plot 25
brute-force attack 457
bull market 432

C

Calinski and Harabaz score 552
categorical data 15, 317, 318, 319
central tendency 19
centroid 543, 548
chaining 91
class imbalance
  about 500
  addressing 625, 627
  addressing, with over-sampling 629, 631
  addressing, with under-sampling 628
class method 385
classes 55
classification metrics

weighted average 573
Western Electric rules 504
wide data format 125, 127
Windows
   virtual environment, creating with venv 41, 42

wrappers 45

Z

Z-scores 497, 498
Zen of Python 369